FIRST PEOPLES

A Documentary Survey of American Indian History

Fifth Edition

Colin G. Calloway
DARTMOUTH COLLEGE

Bedford/St. Martin's
A Macmillan Education Imprint

Boston • New York

For Marcia, Graeme, and Megan, as usual.

For Bedford/St. Martin's

Vice President, Editorial, Macmillan Higher Education Humanities: Edwin Hill
Publisher for History: Michael Rosenberg
Senior Executive Editor for History and Technology: William J. Lombardo
Director of Development for History: Jane Knetzger
Developmental Editor: Jennifer Jovin
Production Editors: Annette Pagliaro Sweeney; Louis C. Bruno, Jr.
Publishing Services Manager: Andrea Cava
Senior Production Supervisor: Lisa McDowell
Executive Marketing Manager: Sandra McGuire
Project Management: MPS North America LLC
Cartography: Mapping Specialists, Ltd.
Director of Rights and Permissions: Hilary Newman
Permissions Manager: Kalina Ingham
Permissions Researcher: Eve Lehmann
Photo Researcher: Naomi Kornhauser
Photo Editor: Robin Fadool
Senior Art Director: Anna Palchik
Text Design: MPS North America LLC
Cover Design: John Callahan
Composition: MPS North America LLC
Printing and Binding: RR Donnelley

Manufactured in the United States of America.

0 9 8 7 6 5
f   e   d   c   b   a

For information, write: Bedford/St. Martin's, 75 Arlington Street, Boston, MA 02116   (617-399-4000)

ISBN 978-1-4576-9624-4

Acknowledgments

PREFACE

Many people for many years considered Native American history to have little or no relevance to the history of the United States. The first peoples to inhabit this continent were routinely ignored, dismissed, or relegated to the sidelines in history texts. If Native people appeared at all in American history books, it was at first contact with the English (Pocahontas) or during the "Indian Wars" in the West (Sitting Bull and Geronimo). Today, scholars increasingly recognize that one cannot understand the relatively short history of this nation without acknowledging the very long history, cultural diversity, and enduring presence of America's indigenous peoples, who first shaped this continent and then shaped the histories of European colonists and their descendants on this continent. In short, American history must include American Indians.

First Peoples provides both an overview of Native American history and an opportunity for students to tackle historical evidence firsthand. The narrative and the documents together tell a more complete and more richly textured story of Indian peoples and their place in United States history than is usually presented in history books. Consequently, this fifth edition follows the same approach and pursues the same goals as the previous editions. Each chapter includes a narrative section, followed by primary documents and then a picture essay. By combining historical background with textual and visual evidence, the book provides students with enough context to begin asking questions of the documents and pictures. The structure of the book enables instructors to go beyond giving an outline of events, laws, leaders, and battles and provides them with materials for exploring other issues and examining how Indian history has been written and remembered. The documents give students the opportunity to try to reconstruct the past through the words of people — Indians and non-Indians — who lived in a different time, saw the world in different ways, and had their own reasons for acting as they did.

FEATURES OF THIS EDITION

The text for the fifth edition has been thoroughly reviewed and, where necessary, revised or updated to take account of developments in Indian country and recent scholarship in Indian history. Nine new documents are featured, four of them from a Native perspective, and in each chapter documents have been paired to help provide different perspectives on particular events and issues. In Chapter 1, a version of the Iroquois creation story given by an adopted Mohawk complements the account of the creation of the Iroquois League and also offers a comparison with the Navajo creation story. The extracts from William Bradford's *History of Plymouth Plantation* in Chapter 2 enable students to compare early English contacts with the Indians with early French contacts with the Indians and also to compare first encounters between Indian peoples and the English in New England with the bloody conflicts of King Philip's War more than fifty years later. Two new documents in Chapter 3 offer students the rare opportunity to read a colonial treaty alongside a critique of that treaty by an Indian who was present at the negotiations but remembered things rather differently than how they were recorded. A third document, extracted from the journal of a Moravian missionary who went as a peace emissary to the Delawares, coupled with an Abenaki chief's defiant speech to the English, conveys the enduring power and influence of Indian peoples during the French and Indian War. In Chapter 4, the declaration of neutrality by Oneida Indians at the start of the American Revolution, like the British account of the Cherokee decision to go to war, documents the divisive and destructive repercussions of the Revolution in Indian country. In Chapter 5, I have followed a recommendation made to me by students that including a petition against Indian Removal submitted to Congress by white women from Steubenville in Ohio would nicely complement the anti-Removal petitions of Cherokee women. And finally, with the long debate over Indian mascots still going on, Chapter 10 now includes opposing viewpoints on the controversial case of the Washington Redskins.

As with the previous editions, the book is generously illustrated to provide copious visual evidence and add another dimension to the narrative. Over 140 images appear throughout the text, 20 percent of them new to this edition. The picture essays in Chapters 9 and 10 include new images as well. Bedford/St. Martin's has made all of the images and the text's map program available for download, in full color where available, from the online catalog at **macmillanhighered .com/calloway/catalog**.

In addition to the timelines that appear at the beginning of each chapter for students' quick reference, this edition continues to feature Focus Questions to encourage active reading and critical analysis. The discussion-provoking Questions for Consideration appear at the end of each set of documents and follow each picture essay. The Suggested Readings at the end of each chapter have been updated to include the latest scholarly works.

New to the fifth edition, students have the option to purchase a low-cost PDF e-book of *First Peoples*. For a list of our publishing partners' sites, see **macmillanhighered.com/ebookpartners**. As with previous editions, instructors can choose to package *First Peoples* with titles from the Bedford Series in History and Culture and with trade books from other Macmillan imprints. For a complete list of titles, visit **bedfordstmartins.com/history/series** and **macmillanhighered.com/tradeup**. Instructors looking for digital packaging options can package *First Peoples* with the Bedford Digital Collections for Native American History, a source collection that provides a flexible and affordable online repository of discovery-oriented primary-source projects that you can easily customize and link to from your course management system or Web site. Native American history projects include "Pontiac's War" by Eric Hinderaker,

"Building a Creek Nation: Reading the Letters of Alexander McGillivray" by Kathleen DuVal, "Debating Federal Indian Removal Policy in the 1830s" by John P. Bowes, "Sand Creek: Battle or Massacre?" by Elliott West, and "The Laguna Pueblo Baseball Game Controversy of the 1920s" by Flannery Burke. For more information, visit **macmillanhighered.com/bdcnativeamerican/catalog**.

ACKNOWLEDGMENTS

I am indebted to the following readers who reviewed the fourth edition with an eye to preparation of the fifth: Douglas Firth Anderson, Northwestern College (IA); JoEllen Anderson, Stanford University; Lisa M. Bunkowski, Texas A&M University–Central Texas; John R. Burch Jr., Campbellsville University; Louise Edwards-Simpson, St. Catherine University; Jeffrey Gordon, Bowling Green State University; Gabriel Loiacono, University of Wisconsin–Oshkosh; Vin Lyon-Callo, Western Michigan University; Daniel Mandell, Truman State University; Charlie Presti, Portland Community College; Emily Rader, El Camino College; John Shaw, Portland Community College; Steven E. Silvern, Salem State University; John Howard Smith, Texas A&M University–Commerce; Tamara Shircliff Spike, University of North Georgia; Diane Wenger, Wilkes University; and Rick L. Woten, Simpson College. Their comments were invariably helpful, even if they did not always agree with one another!

As always, I have benefited from daily interactions with Native students at Dartmouth and with my colleagues in Native American studies: Melanie Benson-Taylor, N. Bruce Duthu, Sergei Kan, Vera B. Palmer, Nicholas Reo, and Dale Turner. As in previous editions, Bruce Duthu reviewed and helped tweak my chapters dealing with contemporary issues. Theresa Smith, then an undergraduate student and Dartmouth presidential scholar, also lent valuable assistance in updating the final chapters. In addition, I am fortunate at Dartmouth to have fine colleagues in the Department of History, the Baker and Rauner libraries, and the Hood Museum of Art.

The staff at Bedford/St. Martin's maintained their usual exemplary standards with this publication. The efforts of Michael Rosenberg, publisher; William Lombardo, senior executive editor; Jane Knetzger, director of development; Jen Jovin, developmental editor; Annette Pagliaro Sweeney and Louis Bruno, production editors; and Dawn Adams, copyeditor, were integral to the completion of this edition, and Naomi Kornhauser's and Robin Fadool's visual research yielded excellent new images.

I am grateful to all of the above for their help with this new and expanded edition of *First Peoples*. There have been many changes over five editions, but the dedication never changes: to Marcia, Graeme, and Meg, with love and thanks.

BRIEF CONTENTS

CONTENTS

CHAPTER 3
Indians in Colonial Worlds,
1680–1763
138

CHAPTER **4**
Revolutions East and West, 1763–1800
200

CHAPTER **5**
American Indians and the New Nation, 1800–1840
254

MAPS, TABLES, AND CHARTS

Introduction:
American Indians
in American History

PERSPECTIVES ON THE PAST

IN 1870 CHARLES WINDOLPH emigrated from Prussia to the United States to avoid being drafted into the Franco-Prussian War. But for Windolph America did not live up to its promise as a land of opportunity. Unable to find work in New York, Windolph joined the army—the very fate he had left home to avoid. Six years later, on the night of June 25, 1876, he found himself pinned down with other survivors of Major Marcus Reno's battalion of the Seventh Cavalry, on a hill overlooking the Little Bighorn River. That day, Windolph and his comrades had attacked the south end of the great Lakota (western Sioux) and Cheyenne village that had assembled in the valley of the Little Bighorn under the leadership of Sitting Bull. Rallying to defend their homes and families, Indian warriors had swept out of the village, routed Reno's command, and sent the survivors scrambling back up the ridge where they dug in for a siege. Only the assault by George Armstrong Custer at the other end of the village saved Windolph and his comrades from being overwhelmed; most of the Indian warriors had hurried off to the north to attack Custer.

That night, as Charles Windolph looked down into the valley, his mind plagued with terrible scenes from the day's disaster and agonizing questions about what had happened to Custer's men, he heard the Indians drumming and singing in what he imagined were "wild victory dances." "We felt terribly alone on that dangerous hilltop," Windolph recalled later. "We were a million miles from nowhere. And death was all around us." He expected to be killed come morning.

But Windolph's peril was more imagined than real. The "wild victory dances" he thought he was hearing were in fact the mourning songs of Lakota and Cheyenne women who had lost husbands, brothers, and sons in the fighting. A Cheyenne warrior named Wooden Leg also recalled that night in his later years. "There was no dancing or celebrating in any of the camps," he said. "Too many people were in mourning. Too many Cheyenne and Sioux women had gashed their arms and legs to show their grief."

Late the next day, the Indians dismantled their lodges and moved off toward the Big Horn Mountains. On the morning of the 27th, an army relief column arrived. Charles Windolph did not die on Reno Hill. He died in 1950, at the age of ninety-eight, the last American soldier to survive the Battle of the Little Bighorn.[1]

Windolph's experience vividly illustrates some important points about living through and reconstructing historical events, and about the need to use a variety of sources in retelling the past. Windolph's understanding of what was going on down in the Indian village was dead wrong, and any historian who repeated it without question would be equally wrong. Only the Indian people in the village knew what was really happening there and only by hearing from them can we know whether Windolph was really in any danger. But Windolph's terror was also real, and we need his testimony to help us appreciate the depth of his feelings and to remind us that fear, prejudice, and ignorance often shape one group's perceptions of another. Windolph and Wooden Leg remember the same night, and the same events, very differently. Each one gives a vivid account of his own experience, but we need them both to get the full story. In short, Indian sources are vital to understanding Indian history, but they can also foster a fuller understanding of non-Indians' history; non-Indian sources, used carefully, can be important for understanding Native American relations with non-Indians and throw light on Indian experiences.

AMERICA'S MASTER NARRATIVE

History is not, as someone once said, "just one damn thing after another." Unless it is badly taught or written, it is not a dry record of events; it is about how people experience, study, and interpret the past. Each generation reviews and rewrites history in the light of its own experiences and understandings, aspirations, and anxieties. Different societies, different groups within society, and even different individuals will often disagree about the meaning of events, the ways in which events happened, and even, sometimes, whether events happened at all. There is no single history that tells the whole story; there can be many different *histories,* telling many different stories, and many different ways of remembering, recording, and recounting the past.[2]

American history, however, was for a long time written and taught as a single story, a narrative of nation building and unending progress that united the diverse participants in the country's past in a single American "experience." It was a national success story, celebrating the human triumphs made possible in a society based on the principles of liberty and equality. American historians tended to ignore or dismiss people whose experiences and interpretations of the past did not conform to the master narrative. The experiences of American Indians during the years of nation building seemed to tell a story of decline and suffering rather than of "progress" and "the pursuit of happiness." As a result, notes historian Frederick E. Hoxie, the authors of United States history textbooks had "great difficulty shaping the Native American experience to fit the upbeat format of their books."[3] The Indians' story was not the American story; best to leave it out.

When the Indians' story was told at all, it was usually portrayed as one of futile resistance to the march of civilization. As in the movies, "Indian history" was little more than a chronicle of hostility to Euro-American settlers. The image of savage warriors attacking hardy pioneers became firmly fixed in popular conceptions of the past: in the *New York Times Magazine* as recently as 1996, journalist Melissa Bloch said that when she learned she was about to lose a breast to cancer, "The first thing I thought of was ambushed wagon trains, debreasted pioneer women lying in their dying campfires."[4] When Indians were not killing settlers, their "history" was usually a narrative of the federal government's efforts to solve the "Indian problem." In many classrooms and in most history books, Indian people were either conspicuous by their absence or treated in such stereotypical and distorted terms so as to rob them of their humanity.

Times change and history — the stories we tell about the past and how we understand them — changes too. Fifty years ago, few colleges or universities offered courses in American Indian history or Native American studies. But in the late 1960s and early 1970s, unrest at home and anxiety about America's war in Vietnam caused many people to question long-accepted views about American society and its relation to Native peoples. Political pressure from students and community activists resulted in new college courses, and scholars began to reexamine the Native American past. For a long time, books about Native American history dealt mainly with "Indian wars," and Indian people figured variously as savage, heroic, or tragic enemies. Even when scholars began to look in more depth at American Indian history, they tended to focus on "Indian policies" adopted by colonial governments and the United States. Indian history was written from non-Indian sources and perspectives. Although such studies of military encounters and government policies contained important information and often provided a foundation for future studies, they did not include Indian people as full participants in their own histories, or accord them much of a role in shaping the history of America. Eventually scholars, both Native and non-Native, began to write histories that tried to do both. It was not easy, and historians who had been trained to rely on written documentation found they had to consider other sources of information and other ways of understanding the past. These *ethnohistorians* endeavored to combine historical research with an understanding of anthropological principles, asking new questions of their sources and incorporating oral history into their research to gain a better sense of how Indian people perceived, experienced, and shaped their own histories. In doing so, they began to change how historians looked at American history.

History books, films, and television today are likely to portray Indians in a much more positive and romantic light: they might depict Indian people living in harmony with nature and with each other before Europeans arrive, and then fighting courageously to defend their lands and way of life against racist and aggressive invaders. No longer seen as savage foes of civilization, Indians are often portrayed as tragic victims of Euro-American expansion. Unfortunately, their basic role in American history has changed little. They continue to be depicted in one-dimensional terms and enter the mainstream narrative of American history only to fight and be defeated.

INDIAN HISTORY: A SHARED PAST

Renditions of United States history that portray Indian people only as warriors or victims may serve to justify past actions or present agendas, but they do not tell a story that includes all participants as real people with human qualities and failings. They either assign blame for or excuse the past, allowing us to feel good or guilty about what happened, but they do little to help us understand *how* it happened. Understanding the past involves looking at history from the viewpoints of the many people who made it over several centuries rather than from a single modern stance seeking to celebrate or condemn the actions of people who lived in very different times. Indians must be included as a central strand in the history of the United States — after all, the nation was built on Indian land — and their historical experiences require looking beyond stereotypes, old and new, and rethinking some basic assumptions.

The history of the millions of Indian people who have inhabited North America, and of the several million who still do, is important in itself, but it also provides alternative perspectives on the history of the United States. It reminds us that America has an ancient history that stretches back millennia before the United States was born; that one people's triumph often means another's tragedy; that building a new nation often entails destruction or displacement of other, older nations; and that the expansion of one civilization often brings chaos and suffering to another. It demands that we recognize invasion, racism, and acts of genocide, along with pioneering, liberty, and equality, as part of America's history, and that Native struggles to protect their resources and rights continue today. It is a story of conquest and colonization, but it is also a story of resilience, innovation, and survival.

Native American history is more than a mirror image of United States history; it is also part of a shared past. Including Indian people as participants in that history requires us to acknowledge that American history began long *before* Columbus reached the continent in 1492 and that Indian history did not end when Indians stopped fighting. Instead of viewing American history as the story of a westward-moving frontier — a line with Indians on one side, Europeans or Americans on the other — it might be more appropriate to think of it as a kaleidoscope, in which numerous Europeans, Africans, and Indians were continually shifting positions. European invasions changed forever the world Indian peoples inhabited (Map I.1). The biological disasters that befell Indian America after 1492 had tremendous repercussions in Indian communities, as well as creating the notion that America was vacant land awaiting European settlement. The policies of European powers and the United States affected Indian lives and limited Indian options. But Indian people also made their own histories and helped shape the story of this country. They responded to invasion in a variety of ways and coexisted with the newcomers as often as they fought against them. They fought to survive as Indians long after the so-called Indian wars were over and continue to exert influence on the legal, political, economic, cultural, and spiritual climate of the United States. They also — from first contact to the present — married Europeans and later Africans, producing families and populations of mixed ancestry and multiple heritages.

◆ **Map I.1 Approximate Tribal Locations at First Sustained Contact with Europeans**
Many maps that purport to show America in 1492 place Indian tribes in their modern
locations, conveying the impression that these communities have remained unchanged
in composition and place. In reality, groups formed, separated, amalgamated, and moved
throughout history. Many so-called tribes did not exist in 1492; others were evolving, and
many communities that did exist subsequently disappeared as their members died or joined
other groups. By the time they came into contact with Europeans, many tribes had incorporated other peoples, and Indian villages commonly included visitors, traders, spouses,
refugees, and others from different tribes. European contact produced additional disruption,
dislocation, and social reorganization.

WORKING WITH SOURCES

The shared past is a complicated place. Whether we study American history, Native American history, or any other area or era, we need to draw on multiple perspectives and listen to many voices to get a well-rounded and richly textured picture. I grew up hearing about the Second World War. My parents met while serving in the British Royal Air Force, aunts and uncles served in various capacities across the globe, and everyone remembered the impact of the war on their lives. There were many stories, and I learned things I never could have read in books. But only when I began to read written accounts and histories of the war did I get a sense of the conflict as a whole, and its different meanings for the different countries involved, even as I read things that were contradicted by what I had heard as a child. My understanding of that enormous event was enriched by both sets of sources; it would have been incomplete without either of them.

Scholars working to reconstruct American Indian history cannot just rely on "American" sources. Information on Indian peoples in colonial America is often found in Dutch, French, and Spanish, as well as English, records. In addition, students of Indian history must also consider sources other than the written word, sources they are not accustomed to "reading," and which they are often ill equipped to understand. Native American pictographs, winter counts or calendars recorded on buffalo robes, events depicted on pages torn from account books and known as ledger art, and oral traditions that rely on stories recounted to an audience may strike us as strange, lacking in "hard evidence," or "inaccessible." As with any other historical sources, including written documents, we need to learn how to "read" these texts, to understand their purposes and conventions, and to interpret them. Archaeologists working in the Southwest have found that Native teachings and oral traditions can help them to understand the hard physical evidence they recover from the earth, and that so-called myth and science can be complementary rather than competing sources of knowledge.[5] Likewise, we as historians must become "literate" in reading these sources so that we can better appreciate them as repositories of knowledge and history and begin to incorporate them into a more fully grounded reconstruction of the past.

Most historians are trained to trust the printed word and many distrust oral sources of history as "unreliable." Samuel Purchas, writing in the early seventeenth century, said that literacy made history possible. "By speech we utter our minds once, at the present, to the present, as present occasions move . . . us: but by writing Man seems immortall." French commandant Nicolas Perrot spent much of his life among the Indians of the Great Lakes, but his faith in the authority of the printed word prevented him from appreciating Native ways of recounting and of preserving their histories. "Among them there is no knowledge of letters or the art of writing," he wrote, "and all their history of ancient times proves to be only confused and fabulous notions, which are so simple, so gross, and so ridiculous, that they only deserve to be brought to light in order to show the ignorance and rudeness of these people."[6] Even Lewis and Clark, who depended on Indian information for guidance and survival during their epic journey to the Pacific and back in 1804–6, shared similar prejudices. In October 1804, William Clark noted in his journal that an Indian chief on the upper Missouri told him "a number of their Traditions about Turtles, Snakes, &c and the power of a perticular rock or Cave on the next river which informs of everr[y] thing," but Clark paid little attention: "none of those I think worth while mentioning," he wrote.[7]

Indians in colonial America were not so slow to recognize the power of European ways of recording the past, especially the printed words employed in treaties. Nevertheless, Native peoples continued to attribute great power to spoken words. Living in an oral tradition, they stood in what Kiowa writer N. Scott Momaday describes as "a different relation to language." Momaday, himself a master of the written as well as the spoken word, suspects that writing, because it allows us to store vast quantities of words indefinitely, "encourages us to take words for granted." But in an oral tradition, words "are rare and therefore dear. They are jealously preserved in the ear and in the mind. . . . They matter, and they must not be taken for granted; they must be taken seriously and they must be remembered." In Native cultures, ritually uttered words possessed magical powers. "By means of words can one quiet the raging weather, bring forth the harvest, ward off evil, rid the body of sickness and pain, subdue an enemy, capture the heart of a lover, live in the proper way, and venture beyond death." For Momaday there is "nothing more powerful" than words, but he has "come to know that much of the power and magic and beauty of words consist not in meaning but in sound," an element that is preserved in an oral tradition and deemphasized in a written one.[8] Other Indian writers echo his sentiments. "Where I come from," says Laguna writer Leslie Marmon Silko, "the words most highly valued are those spoken from the heart, unpremeditated and unrehearsed. Among the Pueblo people, a written speech or statement is highly suspect because the true feelings of the speaker remain hidden as she reads words that are detached from the occasion and the audience."[9]

Writing can be as fallible as oral history as a way of remembering the past. Written documents are valuable but they are not always to be trusted. They do not convey the "truth" of what happened; they convey only what their authors thought, wanted to think, or wanted others to think happened. The repercussions of colonialism were felt far beyond zones of direct contact, with the result that by the time Europeans turned up and wrote "firsthand" accounts of Native people, they often described societies that had already experienced change and disruption. Like the oral traditions of Native peoples, their accounts were created by individuals and influenced by the times and culture that produced them. The documents that historians use may be simply the ones that survived by chance: how many hundreds more, telling perhaps a different story, have been destroyed by fire, flood, malice, or mice?

Daniel Richter, who spent years working in colonial records to reconstruct a history of the Iroquois, acknowledges and explains the limitations and frustrations of trying to recapture the lives of people long since dead:

> As a Euro-American of the late twentieth century, I do not pretend to have plumbed the mind of seventeenth-century native Americans, for most

of the mental world of the men and women who populate these pages is irrevocably lost. Neither historians who study documents produced by the colonizers, nor anthropologists who make inferences from their knowledge of later culture patterns, nor contemporary Iroquois who are heirs to a rich oral tradition but who live in profoundly changed material circumstances can do more than partially recover it. . . . In more ways than one, we must all remain outsiders to a long-gone Iroquois world because of the inadequacies of the source material available.[10]

As Richter recognizes, the views of a seventeenth-century Jesuit priest about Iroquoian people were shaped by his own experiences, values, and prejudices as a Frenchman in a world that was alien to him. The views of a twentieth-century Iroquois about seventeenth-century missionaries and Indians must surely be shaped by his or her sense of history, views of Native and non-Native society, and experiences in the modern world. But the views of both — the seventeenth-century priest and the contemporary Iroquois — are valuable, even essential, in attempting to reconstruct as complete a picture as possible of the Native American past.

The distinctions between oral and written cultures can be exaggerated. One of the obstacles faced by historians of Native America is dispelling the myth that Indians were "people without history" because they produced no written records or histories of their own. Of course, Indian people have as much history as anyone else. They had their own ways of recording it, and oral cultures typically preserve memories of the past in traditions, songs, and stories passed from generation to generation instead of in newspapers, letters, and journals. Nevertheless, a dearth of documents written by Native people does constitute one of the challenges in doing Indian history. Some Indians did read and write, though, and literacy assumed a significant if limited role in Native societies alongside other European imports. Indians who were educated at colonial colleges or American boarding schools wrote, sometimes well, and some wrote often. For example, Mohegan preacher Samson Occom (see "Atlantic Travelers: Indians in Eighteenth-Century London," pages 188–93) studied Hebrew, Greek, and Latin as well as English and wrote what is generally believed to be the first autobiography by a Native American. He also wrote diaries, letters, ethnographies, sermons and hymns, and petitions to colonial assemblies. "Mastering the dominant voice," notes Bernd Peyer, "enabled him to defend himself against colonial repression."[11] Indians often used literacy as a means of resistance. As with all historical documents, one must consider the circumstances, motivations, and restrictions of the writer. Some letters conceal more than they reveal; for example, Indian students were expected to adopt a subordinate tone in their writing and to express appropriate gratitude for their education, and they often shielded their individual humanity and their quiet resistance behind the veil of their writing. Dakota physician and author Ohiyesa, better known as Charles Eastman, was often extremely deferential to his white teachers and benefactors; nonetheless, like Luther Standing Bear (see "What a School Could Have Been Established," pages 424–8), Eastman used his pen to defend Indian rights and values and to critique the non-Indian society that presumed to call Native people savage (see also "The Two Worlds of Ohiyesa and Charles Eastman," pages 400–2).

Not all educated Indians attained the degree of literacy shown by Occom, Eastman, and Standing Bear, but many acquired an appreciation of the "power of print" and understood that literacy could serve Indian people as a weapon in the war for cultural and political survival. After the Cherokees acquired a written language in the 1820s, written Cherokee spread quickly; according to a census in 1835, 18 percent of Cherokees could read English and 43 percent could read Cherokee. As assaults on their land and sovereignty increased, the Cherokees used writing, printed documents, and their newspaper, *The Cherokee Phoenix*, in a campaign to publicize their civilization, rights, and sufferings, and Cherokee women resorted to written petitions to register their opposition to removal (see "Cherokee and White Women Oppose Removal," pages 286–91). Pequot writer William Apess (see pages 279–81), Paiute activist Sarah Winnemucca (see pages 383–84), Yavapai Apache physician Carlos Montezuma ("What Indians Must Do," pages 420–22), and others were not afraid to use their pens to "talk back" to colonizers, oppressors, and bureaucrats who stifled Indian life.[12]

Contrary to commonly held opinion, Indian people are not mute in the written records of the past. They spoke often and at length in meetings with Europeans, and Europeans recorded their words. But the fact that Indian words made it into print should not give those words instant authority or authenticity, any more than the writings of European people should enjoy such status without question. The Iroquois were master diplomats in colonial America, and the treaty councils in which they spoke are rich and essential sources for understanding Iroquois history and colonial Indian relations. Those speeches also have serious limitations: "all were recorded by Europeans rather than Iroquois," notes Richter; "all were translated by amateur linguists who lost volumes of the meaning conveyed in the original, a few were deliberately altered to further colonizers' designs, and none preserves the body language and social context that were central to the native orators' messages." Indian speeches that made it into Europeans' records were often imperfectly translated, hurriedly transcribed, and then rewritten, edited, and editorialized.[13] At the same time, many European records of Indian speeches are fairly accurate — after all, as historian Nancy Shoemaker reminds us, they contain some pretty forthright denunciations of European behavior: "assuming the unauthenticity of Indian speeches simply because they appear in European records relegates to the shadows the grievances that Indian speakers so persistently tried to bring to light."[14]

Just as some historians insist that Native oral traditions are unreliable, so some Native Americans insist that only Indian people grounded in their tribal culture and oral traditions can understand or attempt to tell Indian history. They argue that historical records are inevitably biased and inaccurate and that Western concepts of history and time are irrelevant to understanding Native American experiences and worldviews. Certainly many non-Indian observers, like Charles Windolph on his hill, totally misunderstood what they saw, and non-Indian writers have often misrepresented Native American life. But although the documents written by observers and the histories written by Euro-American academics may be flawed, they are not always worthless. As Canadian historians Jennifer S. H. Brown and Elizabeth Vibert note in their anthology, *Reading Beyond Words,* "the encounter between Native and non-Native people has been a long and complex engagement of mutual dialogue, communication, and miscommunication. Given the intensity of the engagement, even the most confidently Eurocentric of texts cannot help but provide glimpses of Native actions, traces of Native voices."[15] A Jesuit priest may not have understood, or even liked, the people among whom he lived, but he was there, sometimes for most of his life. He was able to recount things that happened and affected people's lives even if he was unable to understand how those people thought or felt about those events.

Documents are invaluable to historians, but they must be used carefully, scrutinized, examined for bias, and checked against other sources. The fact that they are in print does not guarantee their reliability. After all, most documents were produced for particular purposes, not to add to the historical record; if they were produced specifically to inform historians they are probably even more suspect. "There is no such thing as an objective, innocent, primary document," wrote the French historiographer Jacques le Goff. "In the end, there is no documentary truth. Every document is a lie. It is up to historians not to feign innocence."[16] But as anthropologist Marshall Sahlins warns, neither can they adopt cynicism and assume "that an author who may be suspected of lying on the grounds of interest or ideology therefore *is* lying — not even a Christian missionary."[17] Scholars may dream of a "historian's heaven" where, wrote the late Michael Dorris, "if we have been good little historians," we will finally learn what really happened. In reality, the biases, gaps, and *possible* distortions in the sources, combined with the historian's own subjectivity, sympathies, and biases, mean that anyone attempting to write Indian history had better "admit in advance to fallibility."[18] The sources historians use "present us with complex subjectivities, multiple ways of knowing the world." The different voices in the sources "can be listened for, articulated, balanced with one another; but only through silencing or suppression can they be melded into a single voice or unquestioned truth."[19]

Rather than chase the illusory historian's heaven or attempt to provide a single voice, this book offers a historical overview, in this case written from the perspective of a European student of American Indian history living in the United States, and a selection of documents that present multiple perspectives on the past. The documents have been chosen and edited to illustrate key themes, highlight significant events, and provide broad coverage, but they represent only a small sampling of the many different sources available to scholars and students of Indian history. (Likewise, the references and suggested readings located at the end of each chapter offer a plethora of resources, but again, they represent a fraction of the historical material available.) The documents in this text should not be read just to gather information, find "the facts," or learn "what really happened." They represent different experiences, perspectives, and agendas. Often, one can learn more by reading critically between the lines than by accepting documents at face value.

The book also includes historic images in a series of picture essays and in-text illustrations. Pictures, like written documents, can help us to understand the past, but they too must be used critically and carefully. They illustrate history and help bring it to life, but they also interpret the past, often in subtle ways that might escape those not accustomed to reading and analyzing images. What was the artist's purpose in creating the picture? Where was the picture displayed and for what audience? Is the painting based on firsthand observation, accurate information, pure imagination, or a mixture of all three? Is the photograph a candid shot or is it staged? Are the images most valuable for what they tell us about the subjects and the events they portray, or for what they reveal about the assumptions, aspirations, and agenda of the artists who created them and their intended audiences? As with written documents, each picture "must be evaluated on its own merits," with knowledge acquired from other sources. The late John Ewers, a scholar of Plains Indian history and culture and art of the West, warned that it "is dangerous to appraise the individual works on the basis of the general reputation of the artist who created them."[20] What's more, warns another writer, sometimes each element in a picture must be evaluated separately, since pictures often contain "a mixture of observed facts, added fiction, and borrowed material." It is often said that a picture is worth a thousand words, but if it is to be used as a historical source, "it may require a thousand words of documentary evidence to show that it is based on actual observation by a credible witness, that it is accurately drawn . . . and that no well-meaning person has tried to 'improve' it."[21] "Works of art are, of course, historical documents," notes Plains art scholar Janet Berlo, "but . . . they are not *merely* historical documents."[22]

The past is a complex story, made up of many interwoven lives and experiences. American history without Indians is mythology — it never happened. The last 500 years of American Indian history likewise include increasing numbers of non-Indian participants in a range of roles. As with the different views of the Battle of the Little Bighorn, we need to take into account many stories and sources if we are to have a history that includes all people and if we are to understand the past not as *his*tory but as a **shared** story.

A NOTE ON NAME USAGE AND GEOGRAPHIC FOCUS

Neither *Indian* nor *Native American* is entirely satisfactory as a description of the indigenous peoples — the first peoples — of North America. The very term *Indian* is a European conception, or rather misconception, about the first Americans. When Columbus landed in the Caribbean he mistakenly believed he had found a westward route around the world to the East Indies. He called the people he met "los Indios," and the name stuck. Many people today prefer *Native American,* but that term can mean anyone born in America and can cause confusion if used in references to American *Indian* policy. Both *Indian* and *Native American* serve as collective terms in the absence of any more suitable designation that does not require explanation or create confusion. I use the terms interchangeably, giving preference to *Indian* as stylistically less problematic and because most of the Indian people I have met, especially in the West, employ the term. My preference is to use the term *Indian people,* with *Indian* as an adjective for *people,* rather than on its own as a category.

The names that Indian groups applied to themselves usually translate into "the people," "the real people," or something similar. However, many of the names that have been used historically and that continue to be used to designate Indian tribes — *Iroquois, Huron, Sioux* — are names that were applied to them by enemies and carry pejorative connotations. Sioux, for example, is a French corruption of an Algonquian word meaning "snakes" or "adders," that is, "enemies." Some Native people find these terms offensive; others continue to use them. I use the tribal names that seem to be most easily recognizable to readers, and do so in recognition, and with apologies, that some of these terms are inappropriate. I use the term *Lakota* when referring only to the western branch of the Sioux people; I use *Sioux* when referring to that nation in general or to several groups of the nation. The names *Chippewa* and *Ojibwa* are used historically to refer to groups of essentially the same people; this is still often the case. To use both, or to use one and exclude the other, is confusing, however, and I employ the name that most of these people use to refer to themselves: *Anishinaabeg* (noun) and *Anishinaabe* (adjective), meaning "original people," except in cases where individuals or communities self-describe as Chippewa or Ojibwa. I use *Pueblos* when referring to the Indian groups living along the Rio Grande and *pueblos* (lowercase) when referring to the towns they inhabited.

Before contact and colonialism, Native America was the entire continent. As competing European and later American powers divided up the continent, separate settler nations emerged: Canada, the United States, and Mexico. This book focuses on the historical experiences of the Indian peoples in what is now the United States. Native lives and experiences were not confined or defined within the relatively recent borders of the United States and understanding their histories requires attention to French colonial activities to the north and Spanish colonial activities to the south, but limitations of space preclude sustained attention to the histories of Native peoples and the Indian policies of Canada and Mexico. As you read this study of Native America, be mindful always of the myriad untold stories the continent holds as well as the many recorded stories that are not included here — you will be a better historian for it.

REFERENCES

1. The information on Charles Windolph is from James Welch, with Paul Stekler, *Killing Custer: The Battle of the Little Bighorn and the Fate of the Plains Indians* (New York: W. W. Norton, 1994).
2. Peter Nabokov, *A Forest of Time: American Indian Ways of History* (Cambridge: Cambridge University Press, 2002), explores these issues in greater depth.
3. Frederick E. Hoxie, "The Indians versus the Textbooks: Is There Any Way Out?" *Perspectives* 23 (April 1985), 18.
4. *New York Times Magazine,* October 6, 1996, 6.
5. Robert S. McPherson, *Viewing the Ancestors: Perceptions of the Anaasázi, Mokwič, and Hisatsinom* (Norman:

University of Oklahoma Press, 2014); Peter M. Whiteley, "Archaeology and Oral Tradition: The Scientific Importance of Dialogue," *American Antiquity* 67 (July 2002), 405–15.
6. Purchas quoted in Jill Lepore, *The Name of War: King Philip's War and the Origins of American Identity* (New York: Alfred A. Knopf, 1998), 26; Emma Helen Blair, ed., *The Indian Tribes of the Upper Mississippi Valley and Region of the Great Lakes* (1911; repr., Lincoln: University of Nebraska Press, 1996), 2:31.
7. Gary E. Moulton, ed., *The Journals of the Lewis and Clark Expedition* (Lincoln: University of Nebraska Press, 1987), 3:180.

8. James Axtell, "The Power of Print in the Eastern Woodlands," *After Columbus: Essays in the Ethnohistory of Colonial North America* (New York: Oxford University Press, 1988), chap. 6; N. Scott Momaday, *The Man Made of Words: Essays, Stories, Passages* (New York: St. Martin's Press, 1997), 15–16.

9. Leslie Marmon Silko, *Yellow Woman and a Beauty of the Spirit: Essays on Native American Life Today* (New York: Simon and Schuster, 1996), 48.

10. Daniel K. Richter, *The Ordeal of the Longhouse: The Peoples of the Iroquois League in the Era of European Colonization* (Chapel Hill: University of North Carolina Press, 1992), 4–5.

11. Bernd C. Peyer, *The Tutor'd Mind: Indian Missionary-Writers in Antebellum America* (Amherst: University of Massachusetts Press, 1997), 101.

12. On early Indian writers and Indian literacy, see James Dow McCallum, ed., *The Letters of Eleazar Wheelock's Indians* (Hanover, N.H.: Dartmouth College Publications, 1932); Charles A. Eastman, *From the Deep Woods to Civilization: Chapters in the Autobiography of an Indian* (1916; repr., Lincoln: University of Nebraska Press, 1977); Axtell, "Power of Print"; Peyer, *Tutor'd Mind*; Hilary E. Wyss, *Writing Indians: Literacy, Christianity, and Native Community in Early America* (Amherst: University of Massachusetts Press, 2000); Wyss, *English Letters and Indian Literacies: Reading, Writing, and New England Missionary Schools, 1750–1830* (Philadelphia: University of Pennsylvania Press, 2013); Karen L. Kilcup, ed., *Native American Women's Writing, 1800–1924* (Malden, Mass.: Blackwell, 2000); Frederick E. Hoxie, ed., *Talking Back to Civilization: Indian Voices from the Progressive Era* (Boston: Bedford/St. Martin's, 2001); Maureen Konkle, *Writing Indian Nations: Native Intellectuals and the Politics of Historiography, 1827–1863* (Chapel Hill: University of North Carolina Press, 2004); Joanna Brooks, ed., *The Collected Writings of Samson Occom, Mohegan: Leadership and Literacy in Eighteenth-Century Native America* (New York: Oxford University Press, 2006); Lisa Brooks, *The Common Pot: The*

Recovery of Native Space in the Northeast (Minneapolis: University of Minnesota Press, 2008); Phillip H. Round, *Removable Type: Histories of the Book in Indian Country, 1663–1880* (Chapel Hill: University of North Carolina Press, 2010); and Drew Lopenzina, *Red Ink: Native Americans Picking Up the Pen in the Colonial Period* (Albany: State University of New York Press, 2012).

13. Richter, *Ordeal of the Longhouse*, 6; James H. Merrell, "'I Desire All That I Have Said . . . May Be Taken Down Aright': Revisiting Teedyuscung's 1756 Treaty Council Speeches," *William and Mary Quarterly* 63 (October 2006), 777–826.

14. Nancy Shoemaker, *A Strange Likeness: Becoming Red and White in Eighteenth-Century North America* (New York: Oxford University Press, 2004), 10.

15. Jennifer S. H. Brown and Elizabeth Vibert, eds., *Reading beyond Words: Contexts for Native History* (Peterboro, Ont.: Broadview Press, 1996), xiv.

16. Jacques Le Goff, "Documento/Monumento," *Enciclopedia Einaudi* (Turin: Einaudi, 1978), 5:44–45.

17. Marshall Sahlins, *How "Natives" Think: About Captain Cook, for Example* (Chicago: University of Chicago Press, 1995), 42.

18. Michael Dorris, "Indians on the Shelf," in *The American Indian and the Problem of History*, ed. Calvin Martin (New York: Oxford University Press, 1987), 104.

19. Brown and Vibert, *Reading beyond Words*, x–xi.

20. John C. Ewers, "Fact and Fiction in the Documentary Art of the American West," in *The Frontier Re-examined*, ed. John Francis McDermott (Urbana: University of Illinois Press, 1967), 94.

21. Ingeborg Marshall quoted in Arthur Einhorn and Thomas S. Abler, "Bonnets, Plumes, and Headbands in West's Painting of Penn's Treaty," *American Indian Art Magazine* 21 (Summer 1996), 46.

22. Janet Catherine Berlo, ed., *Plains Indian Drawings, 1865–1935: Pages from a Visual History* (New York: Harry Abrams, 1996), 10.

14

1

⟫⟪⟫⟪⟫⟪⟫⟪⟫⟪⟫⟪⟫⟪⟫

American History before Columbus

FOCUS QUESTIONS

1. What are some of the proposed theories about how Native people populated the North American continent?

2. Before the arrival of European explorers and settlers, what sorts of Native American societies existed from coast to coast? How did their diverse environments influence their social structures?

3. Most of North America's history happened long before Columbus's arrival in 1492. How did early American societies change in the centuries before Columbus?

DETERMINING WHAT CAME BEFORE

FOR INDIAN PEOPLE, history did not begin when Christopher Columbus landed in San Salvador in October 1492; it began when their ancestors fell from the sky (Iroquois), emerged from under the earth (Pueblo, Navajo, Mandan), were transformed from ash trees into people (New England Algonquian), entered the world through a hollow log (Kiowa) — or entered North America via the Bering Strait from Siberia (archaeologists). (See "A Navajo Emergence Story and an Iroquois Creation Story," pages 40–52.) Countless generations of Indian people settled the land and developed ways of living on it, built communities, and maintained relationships with their spirit world. What Columbus "discovered" was not a "new world" but another old world, rich in diverse peoples, histories, communities, and cultures.

As recently as thirty years ago, a widely used U.S. history textbook, written by a team of eminent historians, declared that while human beings elsewhere in the world were developing civilizations over thousands of centuries, "the continents we now know as the Americas stood empty of mankind and its works." The story of America, in the minds of these historians, was "the story of the creation of a civilization where none existed." (Subsequent editions of the textbook acknowledged that there was "as much variety among the civilizations of the Americas as among the civilizations of Europe, Asia and Africa.")[1] Still today, most U.S. textbooks are hundreds of pages long but devote only a few pages to "America before Columbus." Far from being "empty," the pre-Columbian Americas were teeming with people — as many as lived in Europe at the time, if not more — who spoke hundreds of different languages, shaped their environments and organized their societies in a variety of ways, lived in huge cities as well as small villages, developed local economies and long-distance exchange networks, and already had "American histories" dating back thousands of years.[2]

Without written documents to guide them, historians face a daunting challenge in trying to understand the thousands of years of history that predate Columbus. They have to turn to other people and sources and rely on oral traditions and on evidence extracted from the ground rather than from the archives. But knowledge of America's ancient past is growing all the time, as archaeologists employ more sophisticated and more culturally sensitive methods of research such as federal- and state-mandated cultural resource management (CRM) projects, new scientific tools and laboratory testing, a better understanding of past climate change and its impact on human societies, and greater collaborative efforts between research institutions and Indian tribes. These tools and methods—combined with a growing number of Native archaeologists and better, if belated, appreciation by non-Indian scholars of how indigenous oral traditions can inform and enrich academic scholarship—all mean that our knowledge of ancient North America "becomes more detailed and more nuanced every year."[3]

c. 850–1150
Rise and Fall of Pueblo Bonito

c. 1000
Corn emerges as the major food crop in the Eastern Woodlands

Bows and arrows in use throughout the Great Plains

Drought in the American Southwest

c.1064
Sunset Crater volcano erupts in the Southwest, affecting climate and settlement patterns

c. 1070
Great Serpent Mound in Ohio built

c. 1100
Chaco Canyon in northwest New Mexico at height

Mesa Verde built in southern Colorado

c. 1100–1300
Ancestral Pueblo culture at its peak in the Four Corners region of Utah, Colorado, Arizona, and New Mexico

c. 1200–1400
Ancestors of Navajos and Apaches separate from northern Athabascans and migrate to the Southwest

1276–1299
Drought in the Southwest

c. 1300
Floods, an earthquake, and increasing social unrest send Mississippian culture at Cahokia into decline

Droughts and enemy raids prompt abandonment of Ancestral Pueblo towns in the Southwest

Pre-1400
Iroquois Great League of Peace formed

Precontact Population

Basing their estimates on numbers recorded by explorers, traders, and colonists who often arrived after diseases had hit Indian America, scholars used to believe that the Native population of North America numbered no more than 1 million in 1492. Modern scholars employing more sophisticated techniques of demographic calculation have dramatically increased their estimates of pre-Columbian populations. Their figures still vary widely, from as low as 2 million to as many as 18 million people for the area north of Mexico. Most estimates fall between these extremes. The total population of North and South America may have constituted as much as one-fifth of the population of the world at that time. Whatever the actual figures, much of America was well populated by 1492.

Revisions of Native American population sizes explode many stereotypes about the nature of Indian society on the eve of European invasion. They also discredit old theories that rationalized dispossession and conquest on the premise that America was virgin wilderness and that the few Indians living there "wandered" the land but made no good use of it. Heavier concentrations of population suggest more sophisticated social structures, political systems, and economic activities than most Europeans imagined; they also mean that the idea of America as a pristine landscape before 1492 is a European fiction. In different times and places, Indian peoples had modified the extent and composition of forests, created and expanded grasslands, built towns and earthworks, trails and roads, irrigation canals and ditches. They sometimes placed pressure on food sources and occasionally degraded the environment. The notion of America as an untouched land may stem from the observations of seventeenth-century Europeans, made at a time when the Indian presence had largely disappeared after epidemics caused massive declines in Native populations and before European immigrant populations increased significantly.[4]

Creation Stories and Migration Theories

Estimates of how long Indians have lived in America also vary. There is firm archaeological evidence of human presence in North America more than 12,000 years ago, and some estimates push habitation back as far as 40,000 years. The creation stories and oral traditions of most Indian tribes tell how their people had always lived in the land that Europeans called America but that they knew as Ndakinna (Abenaki), Anishinaabewaki (Anishinaabe), or Dinétah (Navajo). European theories have suggested that American Indians were one of the lost tribes of Israel; that they were descendants of a legendary Welsh prince named Madoc and his followers who arrived in the twelfth century; or that they are descended from early voyagers from Polynesia, Phoenicia, the Middle East, or Japan.

Most non-Indian historians and archaeologists believe that Indian peoples migrated to America from Asia via the Bering Strait, and they cite genetic, dental, and even linguistic evidence linking Native populations of the Americas to the peoples of Asia. The theory holds that the Ice Age of c. 75,000–8000 B.C. lowered ocean levels worldwide and exposed a land bridge of perhaps a thousand miles across what is now the Bering Strait between Siberia and Alaska. Nomadic hunters made their way across this land bridge over hundreds, perhaps thousands, of years, following migrating game. Finding rich hunting territories and more hospitable climates, they edged their way onward along corridors that opened up as the ice shield receded. The newcomers continued to arrive and scatter as some groups pushed on south to the tip of South America. During the Archaic period (c. 8000–1000 b.c.), small bands moved into almost every area of the continent. But migration via land from Asia offers only one explanation of the peopling of America: maritime people would have been more likely to make the trip by sea, expanding back the time when migration may have taken place. Native traditions say the ancestors have always been here.

Key archaeological evidence of early settlement has been found at many North American sites (Map 1.1). In 1925, at Folsom, New Mexico, archaeologists found worked flint alongside the bones of a bison species that had been extinct for about 8,000 years. Seven years later, at Clovis, New Mexico, archaeologists discovered weapon points that were even older than the Folsom artifacts. Since then, similar Clovis points, as this type of stone weapon is known, have been found from Mexico to Nova Scotia. The oldest Clovis spear points — about 11,500 years old — were for a long time considered the benchmark for the beginning of human habitation in the Americas. But the Meadowcroft Rock Shelter in Pennsylvania may have been occupied as long as 20,000 years ago, and some archaeologists say humans could have lived in North America much earlier. The evidence is inconclusive, and many scholars remain skeptical. The most widely accepted estimates for the earliest human occupation of America range between 12,000 and 14,000 years ago, but new evidence and clues emerge each year.

Archaeologists working in Daisy Cave on San Miguel Island off the coast of California uncovered stone cutting tools used about 10,500 years ago, and researchers have dated skeletal remains from the area to be about 11,000 years old. After long debate, many archaeologists reached consensus that humans inhabited southern Chile 12,500 years ago. Bone and stone tools found at the Monte Verde site in southern Chile have been dated as more than a thousand years older than the oldest Clovis points in North America. "Nothing at Monte Verde was more evocative of its former inhabitants than a single footprint beside a hearth," reported the *New York Times*. "A child had stood there by the fire 12,500 years ago and left a lasting impression in the soft clay."[5] If the people living in Chile migrated south via ice-free corridors through the glaciers that engulfed North America between 13,000 and 20,000 years ago, they must have spread with remarkable speed to the southern end of America. If they did not travel south overland, as previously supposed, they must have come by a different route, perhaps by sea along the western coast. "This is not to say that none came by land," writes archaeologist Stephen Lekson; "of course they did. But others came by sea, faster and farther."[6] Or they entered the Americas more than 20,000 years ago; as Native traditions assert, they may have been here from the beginning.

◆ **Map 1.1 Native North America before Columbus: Selected Peoples and Key Sites**
Indian peoples sometimes shifted location over time, and different societies developed,
changed, and disappeared, but environmental conditions determined broad areas of cultural
similarity in Native North America. People exchanged foods, materials, influences, and ideas
within and across regions.

In 2008, scientists using radiocarbon dating and DNA analysis concluded that fossilized feces found in a cave in Oregon are one thousand years older than any previously discovered human remains, indicating human habitation of North America more than 14,000 years ago. Then archaeologists working at the Buttermilk Creek site in Texas found flint knife blades, chisels, and other artifacts lying in a soil layer almost 16,000 years old. Archaeologists working at Serra Da Capivra National Park in northeastern Brazil, the site of ancient rock paintings, believe that they have found stone tools used by humans who were living there as long as 22,000 years ago. Some scholars argue that Ice Age mariners from areas of France and Spain also made it to America more than 20,000 years ago, bringing their stone tool technology.[7] All of these discoveries have made us even less certain than before about how and when humans first settled America. Perhaps, as Native traditions assert, they must have already been there. At any rate such new evidence and interpretations suggest that "people were thriving from Alaska to Chile" when the Ice Age still rendered large parts of Europe uninhabitable[8]—quite the reverse of an "empty" North American continent.

Debates over Native Origins

Many Native people refute the idea that their ancestors came to America via the Bering Strait and insist that they are truly indigenous people, not just the first immigrants to America. The Miami chief Little Turtle (c. 1752–1812) offered a different interpretation of the Bering Strait theory. On a visit to the East, Little Turtle is reported to have met Thomas Jefferson and a group of French scientists who were debating the origins of the American Indians. They pointed out the similarities between American Indians and people from Siberia, which they believed proved that Indians came from Asia. Little Turtle considered the evidence but came to a different conclusion: the Asian people must have migrated from *America*.[9] The late Lakota writer and scholar Vine Deloria Jr. took a more militant position. He dismissed the idea that Indians came to America via the Bering Strait as something that "exists and existed only in the minds of scientists," and asserted that "immense political implications" make it difficult for people to let go of this theory. Portraying Indians as "latecomers who had barely unpacked before Columbus came knocking on the door" allowed Europeans to brush aside Indian claims to aboriginal occupancy based on having "always been here." Lakota writer Joseph Marshall III offers another perspective that might help readers to reconcile opposing beliefs about the peopling of America and to understand Native peoples' insistence that they have always been here, in the face of what may seem to be weighty evidence pointing to Asian origins and Bering Strait migration. The original stories among many Native peoples in North America "do not bother with when," Marshall explains.

> Instead, many such stories deal with the obvious fact that we are here and have always been here. When a moment or an event happened so long ago that it has ceased to exist in collective memory, it then begins to exist — as my grandfather liked to say — on the other side of memory. In such an

instance, *always* becomes a relative factor. And what emerges as a far more important factor is *first*.[10]

However, as scientists continue to assemble their own versions of the Native origin story, questions of who was where when spark heated debate among the interested communities. In 1996 the skeleton of an adult male aged between forty and fifty-five years was discovered on the banks of the Columbia River near Kennewick, Washington. The skeleton showed evidence of violence, including a stone projectile point lodged in the left hip, and was dated as between eight and nine thousand years old. When physical archaeologists reported that the skeleton exhibited Caucasoid features, suggesting that the man was European rather than Native American, "Kennewick Man" became the center of a storm of controversy. Five tribes — the Yakama, Colville, Nez Perce, Wanapum, and Umatilla — demanded that the remains be returned to them for reburial, but in August 2002 a United States District Court found that scientists must be allowed access to the skeletal remains.[11] In 2006 *Time* magazine ran an article reporting that Kennewick Man was likely younger than scientists first thought and suggested that "the bones have more secrets to reveal," such as what he ate and where he came from. "If scientists treat those bones with respect and Native American groups acknowledge the importance of unlocking their secrets, the mystery of how and when the New World was populated may finally be laid to rest," the article concluded.[12]

For many Native people, however, how the "New World" was populated is no mystery, and the new "findings" do not justify the continued abuse of human remains. "After the scientists probed and prodded this individual, we thought they would return the remains to us so we could have a burial for the bones," said Yakama Tribal Council member LaRena Sohappy. Instead, it seemed the bones would be subjected to more investigation. She called it "disgraceful." Suzan Shown Harjo, a Cheyenne and Muscogee activist and president of the Morning Star Institute in Washington, D.C., accused the scientists and *Time* magazine of turning "the Ancient One" into a freak show: "The Greatest Show Unearthed." Federal legislation passed in 1990 was supposed to prevent such human rights abuses; instead scientists seemed intent on proving that the first Americans came from Asia or Europe and that scientists and museums somehow "owned" the human remains of Native people.[13] The five Northwest tribes continued to fight in court for reburial and the debate over the origins and the remains of America's first peoples continues.

GLIMPSES OF PRECONTACT SOCIETIES

It is too easy to dismiss scholars' skepticism and insistence on meeting scientific criteria as stemming from political or racist motivations. And few scholars today would argue that precontact (the time before interaction with Europeans) America was "empty" before the Europeans arrived. America was "a pre-European cultural landscape, one that represented the trial and error as well as the achievement of countless human generations."[14] Indian peoples in different times and regions pursued varied activities. They built irrigation systems that allowed them to farm in the deserts. They cultivated new strains of crops and built settled and populous communities based on corn, beans, and squash. They improved hunting and fishing techniques and crafted more efficient weapons and tools. They exchanged commodities and ideas across far-reaching trade networks. They fought wars, established protocols of diplomacy and peace making, and learned to communicate with speakers of many different languages. They developed various forms of architecture suited to particular environments, different seasons, and shifting social, political, and economic purposes. While medieval Christians were erecting Gothic cathedrals in Europe, Indians in the Mississippi basin were constructing temple mounds around open plazas, creating ritual spaces, and demonstrating the power of their chiefdoms. Throughout America, people built societies held together by kin, clan, and tradition. They created rich forms of art, music, dance, and oral literature and developed ceremonies and religious rituals that helped keep their world in balance.

West Coast Affluence

People were harvesting the rich marine resources of the California coast ten thousand years ago. As the climate stabilized and came to resemble that of today, the coastal regions of California supported large populations of hunter-gatherers who lived in permanent communities (Map 1.2). The inhabitants cultivated only one crop—tobacco—but harvested an abundant variety of natural foods. Women gathered acorns and ground them into bread meal; men fished the rivers and ocean shores and hunted deer and smaller mammals. The Chumash Indians of the Santa Barbara region lived well from the ocean and the land, following an annual cycle of subsistence that allowed them to harvest and store marine mammals, fish, shellfish, acorns, pine nuts, and other wild plants. Chumash traders were part of an extensive regional exchange network, and Chumash villages sometimes housed a thousand people. The sophisticated and diversified hunter-gatherer lifestyle in California supported a population of 300,000 people, speaking perhaps as many as one hundred languages, before Europeans arrived. California was a land of cultural diversity. Population was least dense and most mobile in the Mojave Desert, while being much more heavily concentrated and more sedentary in fertile coastal valleys, on the banks of the San Joaquin River, and along the shores of Tulure Lake. Networks of alliance and exchange linked peoples across different regions. In many areas, acorns were the staff of life. Fifteen different types of oak trees grow in California, and it is estimated that Native Californians harvested as many as 600,000 tons of acorns a year at the time Europeans first arrived. Gathering, pounding, and processing acorns was labor intensive but produced plentiful supplies of nutritious food, which could be stored. Everyone assisted with the harvesting, but the women did the processing while men returned to hunting and fishing. Bountiful acorn harvests supported large populations. By the time Spanish explorer Juan Rodríguez Cabrillo reached present-day Santa Barbara in 1542, some 15,000 Chumash people inhabited the coast and islands of the region, many in permanent villages of several hundred people. They developed hunting and gathering to a high level and paddled the sea in canoes (first constructed from bundles

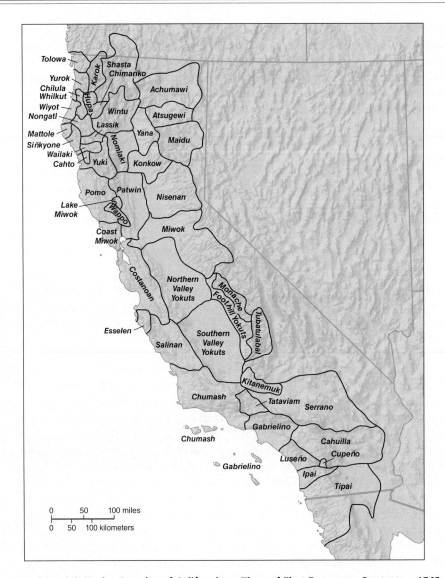

◆ **Map 1.2 Native Peoples of California at Time of First European Contact, c. 1542**
Then, as now, California was a region of tremendous cultural and linguistic diversity.
SOURCE: Adapted from Robert F. Heizer, ed., *Handbook of North American Indians. Vol. 8: California*
(Washington, D.C.: Smithsonian Institute Press, 1978), ix. Reprinted by permission.

of tule reeds for inshore fishing) and later in more substantial and maneuverable
planked vessels known as *tomols*. When Spanish missionaries and explorers arrived in the coastal region of southern California in 1769, Chumash chiefs received
them with lavish feasts.[15]

On the Northwest Pacific Coast, from northern California to Alaska, seagoing peoples were harvesting rich marine resources five thousand years ago.

Men fished with harpoons and nets from canoes, and villages accumulated reserves of dried fish and sea-mammal meat. Large villages of communal rectangular plank houses were built in sheltered coves. In time, these peoples created prosperous and stratified societies. Craftsmen developed specialized woodworking tools and skills, producing seagoing canoes and ceremonial carvings. At Ozette on the Olympic Peninsula of present-day Washington State, Makah Indians occupied an ideal site for sea-mammal hunting. The village was inhabited for at least two thousand years before a massive springtime mudslide engulfed it — probably around 1700 — preserving its contents like a North American Pompeii.

Columbia Plateau Fishers

On the Columbia Plateau, between the Cascade Mountains on the west and the Rocky Mountains on the east, salmon were central to Indian life and culture. Huge and fast-flowing rivers like the Fraser, the Columbia, and the Snake

◆ Kettle Falls, Fort Colville

Paul Kane's 1847 painting shows Indians fishing salmon at Kettle Falls on the upper Columbia River, near present-day Spokane, Washington, as they had done for centuries. Men used harpoons, traps, and dip nets to catch the fish; women dried and stored the catch. Fishing sites often became centers of social and ceremonial activity when the salmon were running.

Paul Kane (1810–71), Kettle Falls, 1847, oil on paper, 8.125 × 13.375 inches, Stark Museum of Art, Orange, Texas, 31.78.216.

provided a regular harvest for people inhabiting their banks. At The Dalles, a site at the upstream end of the Long Narrows where the Columbia River rushed for miles through a rocky channel, Indian people harvested salmon runs more than seven thousand years ago. Men caught the salmon with harpoons, dip nets, weirs, and traps; women butchered, dried, and stored the catch. Fish were dried or smoked on racks and packed in baskets for eating or for trading, and fishing stations became sites of social and ceremonial activity. Described as "the finest salmon fishery in the world" and located where Chinookan-speaking peoples from downriver met Sahaptian-speakers from upstream, The Dalles became one of the largest trade fairs in western North America, linked to trade routes that extended south to California, east to Yellowstone, and, ultimately, all the way across the continent.[16]

Rituals accompanied the start of the spring salmon runs, and only after the ceremonies were completed was the fishing season open. People threw salmon bones back into the water to allow the spirit of the salmon to return to the sea, thus ensuring that the cycle of abundance would continue. Taboos limited women's contact with salmon and water, especially during menstruation when their blood had the power to offend the salmon and jeopardize the run.[17] Earthquakes and landslides occasionally blocked salmon runs on the Columbia River, and changes in water temperature and mineral content could discourage the fish from returning to their spawning grounds—events explained and retold in Native stories handed down across generations.

Great Basin Foragers

In 2013 archaeologists studying rock art at the dried-up Winnemucca Lake in the Nevada desert determined that the art was between 10,500 and 14,800 years old—the oldest rock art in North America by several thousand years. This art was found within the region known as the Great Basin, an area of some 400,000 square miles between the Rocky Mountains and the Sierra Nevada that embraces tremendous environmental and topographical diversity, and where ancient inhabitants exploited a broad range of food sources to survive. They knew how to live in a hard land: between ten and twelve thousand years ago, lakes in the region shrank, rivers dried up, and the lusher vegetation retreated to higher elevations and to the north. Temperatures rose until about 4000 or 3000 B.C., and hot, arid conditions continued to characterize the region into historic times. Then, between about A.D. 900 and 1400, a series of droughts struck the American West. The diverse environments of the Great Basin underwent constant change, and populations moved regularly to take advantage of unevenly distributed and often precarious resources. For instance, on the shores of Pyramid Lake and Walker River in Nevada, people lived in sedentary communities for most of the year, supplementing a staple diet of fish with game and plants. In other areas, people harvested wild plants and small game, a subsistence strategy that required intimate knowledge of the land and its animals, regular movement to take advantage of seasonal diversity and changing conditions, and careful exploitation of the environment. Amid these adaptations, however, hunting and gathering endured for ten thousand years.[18]

Trade, too, was a part of Great Basin life: shells from the Pacific coast and obsidian — volcanic glass — from southern Idaho, which may have been present in the Great Basin as early as seven thousand years ago, were traded over vast areas along with food, hides, and other perishable items. Surviving and subsisting in this harsh and changing environment demanded innovation, adaptation, and advance planning. Successful hunter-gatherers did not live hand-to-mouth or move aimlessly across the landscape, as many people assume. "Ancient residents of the Great Basin were travelers in an endless cycle, always thinking about their next move to another spot, where they would find the things they needed to survive."[19] In summer, they prepared for winter; they stored caches of food in anticipation of future need, and they cached hunting gear, duck decoys, traps for snaring rodents, baskets and basket-making tools, fishing gear, and other equipment in places they knew they would return to. Rediscovered, such caches have given archaeologists glimpses into seasonally mobile hunting-and-gathering lifestyles that persisted for more than eight thousand years until Euro-Americans arrived.

About two thousand years ago, horticultural communities began to emerge in Utah, eastern Nevada, western Colorado, and southern Idaho, growing corn, making pottery, and living relatively sedentary lives. Called "Fremont Culture" by archaeologists and anthropologists, this way of life proved short-lived in Great Basin terms — a mere 1,300 years.

First Buffalo Hunters of the Plains

Life in ancient America was varied and changing, but nowhere did Indians wearing feather headdresses hunt buffalo from horseback; the horse-and-buffalo culture of the Plains Indians developed much later, a byproduct of contact with Europeans. The way of life that popular stereotypes depict as typical of all Indians at all times never existed in most of North America and was not even typical of the Great Plains until the eighteenth and nineteenth centuries.

Between about 12,000 and 8000 B.C., Native American peoples of the Great Plains hunted on foot for big game — mammoths, mastodons, and bison. Over time, these people, known as Paleo-Indians, worked increasingly lethal projectiles, such as Clovis points flaked on both sides, to produce stone spear points bound into split wooden shafts. Experiments by archaeologist George Frison demonstrated that hunters using Clovis point spears could inflict mortal wounds on animals as large as African elephants.[20] As Paleo-Indians refined their hunting toolkits, they also developed more effective methods of hunting large game, such as buffalo drives and corrals. These communal hunting techniques required greater degrees of social organization. At Head-Smashed-In buffalo jump in Alberta — the largest, oldest, and best-preserved buffalo drive site in the western Plains — Indians hunted and slaughtered buffalo for more than seven thousand years. Many species of large animals became extinct — mastodons, mammoths, giant beaver and bear, saber-toothed cats, and American lions, camels, and horses—but the demise of the large Ice Age mammals was a worldwide phenomenon and was most likely the result of climatic change rather than relentless human predators. By 8500 B.C. most Paleo-Indians were hunting bison. Bows and arrows—a major innovation in hunting and warfare—spread south from the Arctic and were in use throughout the Plains by A.D. 1000.

When the first Spaniards ventured onto the "vast and beautiful" southern Plains in the 1520s, they saw huge herds of buffalo. They noted that the Indians of the region "live upon them and distribute an incredible number of hides into the interior."[21] Nomadic hunters traded with farming groups on the edges of the Great Plains, but they did not yet travel by horseback. The Plains hunters had improvised other ways to transport their belongings and goods. In 1541, Spaniards on the

◆ **Pecos Pueblo around 1500**
One of the easternmost Pueblo communities, Pecos functioned as a trade center and rendezvous point between the farming peoples of the Rio Grande valley and the hunting peoples of the Great Plains long before the Spanish arrived. This 1973 painting by Tom Lovell depicts a harvest-time trade fair at Pecos. The inhabitants of the pueblo trade corn, squash, pottery, and other items to visiting Plains Apaches, who have transported the products of their buffalo hunt on dogsleds. Later, Spanish seizures of Pueblo food surpluses disrupted these long-standing trade relationships, while access to Spanish horses increased the Apaches' mobility and military power. Horses also enabled the Indians to transport larger tipis. Dogs would have been hard pressed to transport tipis of the size depicted in this picture. Pecos Pueblo, *by Tom Lovell. Courtesy of Abell-Hanger Foundation and of the Permian Basin Petroleum Museum, Library, and Hall of Fame in Midland, Texas, where this painting is on display.*

southern Plains encountered peoples who traded each winter with the Pueblos° in the Rio Grande valley and who "go about like nomads with their tents and with packs of dogs harnessed with little pads, pack-saddles and girths."[22]

First Farmers of the Southwest

For virtually the entire span of human life on Earth, people have survived as hunters and gatherers, living on wild plants and animals. Then, beginning about ten thousand years ago, many hunters became farmers at various places around the world. Within the relatively short period of about five thousand years, people began cultivating domesticated plants in Southeast and Southwest Asia, China, South America, Mesoamerica, and parts of North America. As long as seven thousand years ago, Indian farmers in Mesoamerica crossbred wild grasses and created maize, or corn, which has become a staple food throughout much of the world; over time, corn cultivation spread north into what is now the United States. The transition to agriculture involved more than simply developing a new food source; it entailed a changed relationship with the environment. Ultimately it produced new social structures and organizations,° as people cleared lands, cultivated and stored foods, adopted new technologies for farming, and lived in more populous and sedentary communities.[23]

The ancient inhabitants of the southwestern United States developed agriculturally based societies approximately three thousand years ago. About two thousand years ago in the highlands of the Arizona–New Mexico border and in northwest Mexico, Mogollon people grew corn and squash. They first lived in pit house villages but later built multi-apartment structures above ground. Southwestern peoples began making clay pots by about A.D. 200, and pottery was widespread by A.D. 500, improving methods for preparing and storing food. Mogollon potters were making distinctive black-on-white Mimbres-style pottery more than a thousand years ago, although their culture went into decline after about 1100.

For a thousand years, from about 450 to 1450, the people archaeologists call the Hohokam lived in the Sonoran Desert in southern Arizona. Ancestors of the Akimel O'odham, or Pimas, and the Tohono O'odham, or Papagos, the Hohokam not only subsisted in a harsh environment but also made the desert agriculturally productive. They built sophisticated irrigation systems to tap sources of precious

---

° The name *Pueblo* comes from the Spanish term for a town and was applied by early Spaniards to the people they met living in multistory adobe towns in New Mexico and Arizona. At the time of first contacts with Europeans, the Pueblo Indians lived in many communities and belonged to eight different language groups. Then, as now, most Pueblo communities — Taos, San Juan, Cochiti, Ácoma — nestled in the Rio Grande valley, but the Zunis of western New Mexico and the Hopis of Arizona are also regarded as Pueblo Indians.

° Contrary to assumptions that a transition from hunting to farming constituted "progress," there is evidence that hunting-and-gathering lifestyles in areas of abundant resources provided a more nutritious diet with less work than did agriculture. In rich and temperate areas like California and the Eastern Woodlands, plant, animal, and fish resources were so abundant that people were able to live in sedentary communities before agriculture became important. For many Indian peoples, the transition to agriculture was an option, not a necessity.

water and created a network of canals that transported water hundreds of miles, engineering feats that required expending huge amounts of coordinated labor. Freed from dependence on the unpredictable Gila River, the Hohokam people grew corn, beans, squash, and cotton. They were able to store crops and traded extensively across the Southwest, and they developed larger and more permanent communities. They built villages of adobe houses, earthen platform mounds, and ball courts. Snaketown, near present-day Phoenix, had three to six hundred inhabitants and was continuously occupied for twelve hundred years. Droughts, floods, and increased soil salinity may explain the decline of Hohokam culture by the 1400s.[24]

In the Four Corners region of the Southwest where the present states of Utah, Colorado, Arizona, and New Mexico meet, Ancestral Pueblo culture emerged around A.D. 900 and reached its height between 1100 and 1300, about the time of the Crusades in Europe (Map 1.3). The Ancestral Pueblos—often called Anasazi,

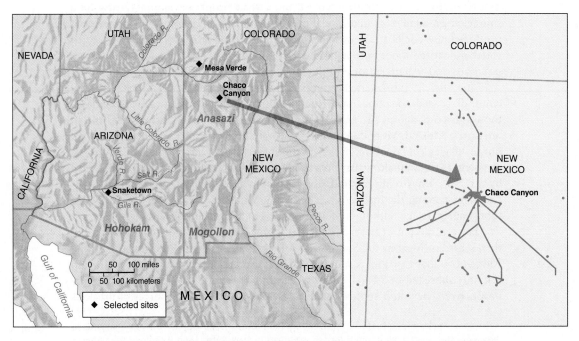

◆ **Map 1.3 Southwest Civilizations and Chaco Canyon as Trade Center, c. 900–1200**
Structures like the cliff dwellings at the town of Pueblo Bonito and Mesa Verde (see pages 63 and 64) show that the ancient Southwest was a region of remarkable activity and lasting achievement. Pueblo Bonito sat in Chaco Canyon, itself the center of a series of communities in the San Juan River basin and a focus of trade in which turquoise was exchanged for goods from as far away as Mexico, California, and the Rocky Mountains. The dots on the detail map (right) locate some of the outlying settlements. The lines show straight ancient roads, some stretching four hundred miles, that have been documented by either ground or aerial surveys. *Source:* After Tracy Wellman in Brian M. Fagan, *Ancient North America* (New York: Thames and Hudson, Inc.). Reprinted by permission.

although the name is not preferred by modern Pueblos—grew and stored corn, wove and decorated baskets, made pottery, studied the stars, and were master architects. In Chaco Canyon, in New Mexico's San Juan River basin, they constructed a dozen towns and perhaps two hundred outlying villages. D-shaped Pueblo Bonito, one of many such structures in the canyon, contained hundreds of rooms and could have housed hundreds of people;° it has been described as "the largest apartment building in North America until New York City surpassed it in the nineteenth century." But it also contained thirty-six kivas (underground ceremonial chambers) and many scholars now believe that it functioned as a ritual center rather than a population center, with relatively few permanent residents. Chacoan farmers inhabited a world where rain was scarce, where their "lives revolved around agriculture and religion, where the performance of ritual, of dance and chant, was as important as tilling the soil."[25]

With more than four hundred miles of straight roads spoking out from it, it appears that Chaco Canyon was a center of trade linked to many outlying settlements in the San Juan Basin. But the purpose of the roads remains something of a mystery. Many of them seem to lead nowhere and they may have had symbolic meaning, connecting Chaco to other communities or to sacred places, rather than facilitating the movement of people and goods.[26] The people of Chaco Canyon imported corn and exchanged turquoise with distant peoples, obtaining seashells from the Gulf of California, exotic birds and feathers from Central America, and minerals and ores from the Rocky Mountains. Recent chemical analyses of organic residues in fragments of pottery from Pueblo Bonito reveal theobromine, a biomarker for cacao. This earliest evidence of cacao drinking in North America—possibly for ritual purposes—indicates that Chacoan people were exchanging with cacao cultivators in Mesoamerica between A.D. 1000 and 1125; people may have been drinking chocolate in North America for a thousand years.[27]

Most Ancestral Pueblo villages housed a few families and were located on mesa tops, but people also built impressive cliff dwellings, especially in times of drought and competition for resources. At Mesa Verde in southwestern Colorado, people occupied more than two hundred rooms in a multitiered fortresslike cliff dwelling that provided defense against enemies. (See Pueblo Bonito and Mesa Verde images, pages 63–64.)[28] The lifestyle of the Ancestral Pueblos began to change in the mid-eleventh century, however, when natural disaster and climatic change altered their lives and locations. In 1064 or spring 1065, Sunset Crater volcano, near present-day Flagstaff, Arizona, erupted, filling the sky with fire and smoke and causing dramatic shifts in patterns of settlement. Beginning in the twelfth century, a severe and prolonged cycle of droughts hit the American Southwest. A major drought that began around 1139 and lasted fifty years seems to have caused many people to abandon Chaco Canyon, and there appears to have been another huge drought between 1276 and 1299 that further damaged

---

° Chaco Canyon's population may have exceeded ten thousand, but such estimates have to be revised downward if, as some scholars have asserted, Pueblo Bonito and other "great houses" were monumental ritual centers or elite residences rather than the homes of Chacoan people.

the settlement. Soil erosion, crop failure, and increased competition for farming lands intensified social tensions and generated new levels of violence.[29] Ancestral Pueblo people began to disperse into smaller, less stable settlements. Many people migrated south from the Mesa Verde region. Some joined the Zunis and Hopis in western New Mexico and eastern Arizona. The rest moved east and mingled with Pueblo communities that had developed in the Rio Grande valley, causing a dramatic population upsurge in that area. Some scholars believe that a new religion — what they call the Kachina phenomenon — drew people eastward to the Rio Grande. In a period of drought, southwestern farming peoples may well have placed more faith in kachinas, the spirits that brought rain.

According to one account, Pueblo people had a rather different explanation. They said that the Ancient Pueblo people "kept a great black snake in the kiva,° who had power over their life." They fed him the fruits of the hunt — deer, rabbits, antelope, bison, and birds — and he gave them corn, squash, berries, yucca, cactus, and all they needed to wear. Then one night he left them. They followed his track until it disappeared in the water of a big river, the Rio Grande. So they gathered up their things and moved to the river, "where they found another town already living. There they took up their lives again amidst the gods of that place."[30] Some Navajo and Hopi teachings attribute the decline of the Ancestral Pueblos and the drought that drove them away to societal decay, even to hubris that angered the gods, and they see the rise and fall of these ancient societies as a warning for the future.[31] The depopulation of the Ancestral Pueblos' settlements is one of the great mysteries of American archaeology, and scholars continue to debate its causes and timing, finding new evidence and attaching varying weight to climate change, environmental degradation, social problems, and conflict.[32]

Whatever the causes, over the next 150 years, a period known as the Great Migration, Ancestral Pueblo people abandoned their sophisticated towns and moved away to be amalgamated with other established peoples. No new Chacoan buildings were constructed after 1150, and by 1300 the canyon was abandoned. Great cliff dwellings that had once echoed with human activity became empty and silent. At about the same time other movements of peoples altered the human landscape. Nomadic Athapaskan peoples, ancestors of the Apaches and Navajos, who had migrated from far northwestern Canada, began to arrive in the Southwest.[33] Looking back over the centuries, the abandonments and migrations may appear sudden and suggest dramatic and catastrophic causes, but relocating to more hospitable environments in response to changing climate conditions was also a regular part of life in the Southwest.[34]

Long before Europeans arrived in America, Ancestral Pueblo civilization had emerged in the Southwest, flourished for centuries, and declined. The Pueblo cultures and communities the Spanish invaders encountered in the Southwest in the sixteenth century were descendants of ancient civilizations that stretched back thousands of years. People had migrated, scattered, and regrouped and

---

° A kiva is an underground ceremonial chamber.

were able to survive and often flourish in a challenging and sometimes harsh environment. The Hopis, for example, succeeded in growing crops on the arid lands of northern Arizona by farming near major rivers and streams or through the use of canal irrigation; in archaeologist Stephen Lekson's words, the Hopis "wrote the book" on desert agriculture.[35] When a Spanish expedition reached the Hopi town of Walpi in 1582:

> More than one thousand souls came, laden with very fine earthen jars containing water, and with rabbits, cooked venison, tortillas, atole (corn flour gruel), and beans, cooked calabashes, and quantities of corn and pinole, so that, although our friends were many and we insisted our friends should not bring so much, heaps of food were left over.[36]

Farmers and Mound Builders of the Eastern Woodlands

Indian women may have begun domesticating indigenous seed plants such as sunflowers, squash, and marsh elder that thrived in the floodplains of the eastern United States as many as four thousand years ago.[37] Some Indians in present-day Illinois were growing squash by 5000 B.C. Corn was present in Tennessee about 350 B.C., in the Ohio valley by 300 B.C., and in the Illinois valley by A.D. 650.

Corn does not grow without human care and cultivation; Indian farmers selected the seeds of plants that did best in their environments and developed new strains for particular soils, climates, and growing seasons. Corn provided people with food they could store. By about A.D. 1000 corn had become the major field crop in the Eastern Woodlands and the core of society and economy. It was a staple of life that also reflected the rhythmic cycle of life. Indian peoples developed a system of agriculture based on corn, beans, and squash—the "sacred three sisters" of the Iroquois—supplemented with a variety of other crops.[38]

◆ **Indian Woman of Florida**
John White (c. 1540–c. 1593), who made the voyage to the Roanoke Island settlement off Virginia in 1585, was the first Englishman to paint Indian people in North America. His watercolors, now in the British Museum, provide a valuable record of the people and plant life of early America. This tattooed Timucuan woman from northeastern Florida offers corn, testifying to the importance of the crop in southeastern Indian culture and to the role of women in producing it. *Snark/Art Resource, NY.*

"The only reason we have corn today is that for thousands of years humans have selected seeds and planted them," says Jane Mt. Pleasant, an Iroquois agronomist who studies Native methods of cultivation and crop yields.[39] When Frenchman Jacques Cartier visited the Iroquoian town of Hochelaga (modern Montreal) in 1536, he found it inhabited by several thousand people and surrounded by extensive cornfields. The Hochelagans brought the French fish and loaves of corn bread, "throwing so much of it into our longboats that it seemed to rain bread."[40] Huron Indians north of Lake Ontario tried to grow enough corn each year so that they had a two- or three-year surplus to guard against crop failure and enough left over to trade to other tribes. Huron cornfields were so large that a visiting Frenchman got lost in them.[41]

More stable food sources and growing populations produced changes in living patterns and made possible the construction of large towns and impressive structures. Over a period of about 4,000 years, Indian peoples in the Eastern Woodlands constructed tens of thousands of large earthen mounds. They built mounds for burials, mounds for ceremonial and ritual events, flat-topped pyramid-shaped mounds on which sat temples and other important buildings, and effigy mounds in the shape of birds, reptiles, and animals. Archaeologists have discovered a complex of eleven mounds near the town of Watson Brake in northeast Louisiana that was built between 5,000 and 5,400 years ago. It is the earliest mound-building complex yet found in America, predating other known sites by almost 2,000 years.[42] More than three thousand years ago at Poverty Point in the Mississippi valley in Louisiana, between two and five thousand people inhabited or assembled periodically at a town of elaborate earthworks constructed in a semicircle surrounding an open plaza, with a huge ceremonial mound (640 by 710 feet) in the shape of a falcon. The earthworks contained "nearly 1 million cubic yards of dirt and required perhaps 5 million man-hours of sustained, coordinated effort" by people who dug with stone tools and transported the earth in woven baskets. The site received its name in the nineteenth century because it was considered a poor location for a modern plantation, but in its heyday around 1500 B.C. it was "the largest, most prosperous locality in North America," standing at a crossroads of commerce for the whole lower Mississippi valley.[43] It is now listed by UNESCO as a World Heritage site. (See Map 1.1, "Native North America before Columbus: Selected Peoples and Key Sites," page 18.)

Trade for raw materials for ceremonial use, burial goods, and personal adornment connected peoples as distant as Florida and the Missouri valley. The Poverty Point people seem to have exported stone and clay items and transported heavy, bulky goods by dugout canoe; their imports ranged from copper from the Great Lakes, flint from the Ohio valley, and chert (flaked stone) from the Tennessee valley and the Ozarks to steatite (soapstone) from the Appalachians and galena (a lead sulphide ore usually ground into a powder and used to make white body paint) from the upper Mississippi valley and southern Missouri.

More than two thousand years ago in the Ohio valley, people of the Adena culture built mounds that held their honored dead. The Hopewellian culture that emerged from the Adena around the first century flourished for some four hundred years. Hopewellian people built more elaborate burial mounds and earthen architecture and developed greater ceremonial complexity than the Adena. Their culture spread through extensive exchange networks, and they obtained valuable raw materials from vast distances: grizzly bears' teeth from the Rockies, obsidian for spear points and blades from Yellowstone, silver from Ontario, copper from the Great Lakes, mica and copper from the southern Appalachians, galena from the upper Mississippi, quartz from Arkansas, and pottery, marine shells, turtle shells, and shark and alligator teeth from the Gulf of Mexico (Map 1.4). Hopewellian craftsmen and artists fashioned the raw materials into tools and intricate ornaments. Many of the items were deposited with the dead in mortuary mounds; others were traded to outside communities.

The Hopewellian culture went into decline around A.D. 300 and seems to have disappeared by about 550. But the spread of corn agriculture throughout eastern North America between 500 and 800 brought population increases and the emergence of more complex societies. For example, the Great Serpent Mound, a one-quarter mile long, three-foot high serpentine effigy in southwestern Ohio (and the largest serpentine effigy in the world) was once thought to have been built by Adena or Hopewellian people, but many archaeologists now believe that most of the mound was constructed by people descended from Hopewell called the Fort Ancient culture (c. 1000–1650). Some of the work has been dated to around 1070.

Beginning in the lower Mississippi valley around 700 and displaying evidence of Mesoamerican influences, Mississippian cultures spread north to the Great Lakes and east to Florida and the Carolinas, reaching their height between 1100 and 1300. Mississippian societies were typically stable, agriculturally based settlements, close to floodplains, with relatively large populations and complex ceremonial and political structures. Powerful chiefs from elite families collected tribute, mobilized labor, distributed food among their followers, waged war against neighboring chiefdoms, were buried with large quantities of elaborate goods, and appear to have been worshipped as deities. Mississippian towns contained temples, public buildings, and elite residences built atop earthen mounds that surrounded open plazas where ceremonies were conducted and ballgames were played.

The Mississippian town of Cahokia was a thriving urban market center. Founded around A.D. 700 near the confluence of the Missouri, Mississippi, and Illinois rivers and occupied for about seven hundred years, Cahokia at its height was the contemporary of Chaco and had a population of between 10,000 and 30,000, or about the population of medieval London.[44] (See Cahokia Mounds image, page 65.) Looming large over the Illinois prairie, Cahokia was the largest settlement to have existed north of the Rio Grande before the end of the eighteenth century, when it was surpassed by New York and Philadelphia. Trade routes linked Cahokia to distant regions of the continent, bringing shells from the Atlantic coast, copper from Lake Superior, obsidian from the Rocky Mountains, and mica from the southern Appalachians.

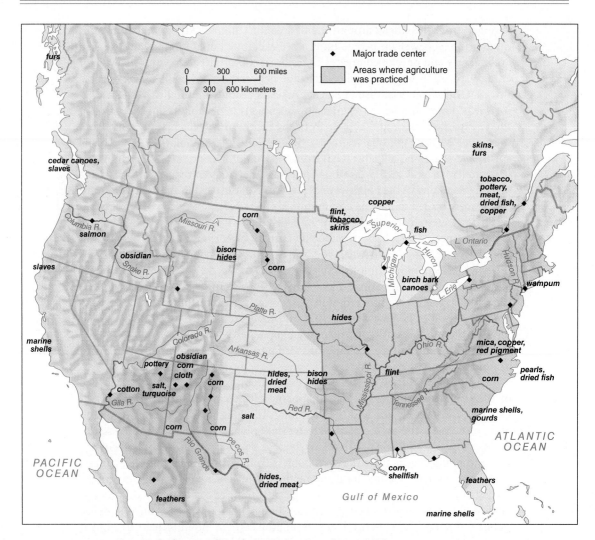

◆ **Map 1.4 Agriculture and Trade in Native America, c. 1450**

Europeans often pictured Indians as nomadic hunters living in isolation. In reality, long before European contact, much of Indian America was farming country crisscrossed by well-traveled networks of trade and communication. For centuries, Indian people had been developing and farming corn. Hunting people regularly developed reciprocal economic relations with farming people. Prized items were traded over vast distances, usually along river systems, from community to community or by wide-ranging individual traders.

SOURCE: Adapted from *The Settling of North America: The Atlas of the Great Migrations into North America from the Ice Age to Ellis Island and Beyond,* by Helen Hornbeck Tanner, Janice Reiff, and John H. Long, eds. Copyright © 1995 by Swanston Publishing Ltd.

◆ **Great Serpent Mound, Adams County, Ohio**
Aerial view of the Great Serpent Mound, crawling along a bluff in Adams County, Ohio. The world's largest serpent effigy, the mound is 1,254 feet long. The oval at top right may represent the snake's head or eye, or an egg it is about to swallow. © *Georg Gerster/Science Source.*

Archaeologists excavating the Cahokia site in the late twentieth century found a planned city that included pyramid mounds of packed earth arranged around huge open plazas, temples and astronomical observatories, and thousands of thatched-roof houses. They also uncovered evidence of a society in which elite rulers claiming divine descent controlled the distribution of food and were buried with shell beads, copper, and the bodies of sacrificial victims. In one mound, the archaeologists unearthed two corpses, one lying below the other on top of a two-inch-thick layer of twenty thousand beads, the remains of a beaded cloak or cape in the shape of a falcon or thunderbird. Around the two bodies lay the remains of fifty-three mostly young women, likely slaves who had been taken in raids and ritually sacrificed. Nowhere else in North America has such stunning evidence been found of mass human sacrifice and mortuary practices honoring dead rulers. The monumental architecture and the public killing of slaves demonstrate "the paramount importance of human labor" at Cahokia and the chiefs' ability "to coordinate, control, and sacrifice it."[45]

Floods caused by upriver deforestation, an earthquake in the thirteenth century, and increasing social unrest sent Cahokia into decline by the fourteenth century. Most likely, the growing population of the town had exhausted the resources needed to support it in a period of climatic change; archaeological

◆ **Two Faces of Cahokia**

Sculptured figurines and effigy pots in human shape may have had both religious significance and trade value in Mississippian culture, symbolizing life, fertility, power, and people's
place in the universe. These two effigies reveal different, and yet complementary, aspects of
Cahokian life. One, a bottle effigy from Cahokia, depicts a mother nursing a child. The other,
a pipe carved from soapstone and discovered at Spiro in Oklahoma, although thought by
scholars to have been traded from Cahokia, depicts a warrior beheading a crouching victim
or with a bound captive at his feet. *Nursing-mother-effigy bottle: St. Louis Museum of Science &*
Natural History, Missouri, U.S./Photo © The Detroit Institute of Arts/Bridgeman Images. Caddoan
Mississippian pipe: © Werner Forman/Werner Forman/Corbis.

evidence suggests there also may have been increasing pressure from enemies.
The once-thriving metropolis lay abandoned half a century before Columbus, but
the remains of Cahokia's spectacular mounds can still be seen after five hundred
years of erosion — "[t]he great pyramid at Cahokia is greater in extent than that at
Gizeh, in Egypt."[46] The Cahokia mounds offer impressive testimony to a civilization that developed before Europe entered its Middle Ages, flourished longer than
the United States has existed as a nation, and declined before Europeans set foot
in America.[47]

Peoples living on the eastern edges of the Plains also began cultivating corn
and beans, as warmer climatic conditions between about A.D. 700 and 1100
fostered westward expansion of the tall-grass prairie. By the end of the first

millennium, eastern Plains peoples were living in earth-lodge villages, growing corn and beans as well as hunting and gathering. In the twelfth century, other farming peoples moved into the middle Missouri valley, although agriculture on the Plains became more precarious by the mid-thirteenth century as the climate grew colder and drier.

Not everyone in the East became farmers. Many of Florida's first peoples never adopted agriculture. As did Indians in California, they inhabited an environment rich in natural resources and sustained their lifeways by hunting, fishing, and gathering — subsistence strategies that amply satisfied their needs and required less time, labor, and organization than farming. About 350,000 people lived in Florida at the time of European contact.[48]

Emerging Tribes and Confederacies

The influences of the Mississippian cultures were still very visible when the Spaniards invaded the Southeast in the sixteenth century. Chiefdoms and temple mound towns were common. Moundville in Alabama, Etowah in Georgia, and Spiro in the Arkansas valley of eastern Oklahoma were mound centers of population, trade, and artistic and ceremonial life. At the time of the Spaniards' arrival in northern Florida, the Apalachee and Timucua Indians lived in permanent settlements, planted two crops annually, and rotated their fields to keep the soil fertile; the Spaniards sustained their campaigns by seizing the Natives' corn supplies.[49] But following contact with the Spaniards in the sixteenth century, the great Mississippian chiefdoms that ruled in the South collapsed in the wake of escalating warfare, epidemics, and slave raiding. The Natchez in the lower Mississippi valley continued to display significant elements of Mississippian culture until they were effectively destroyed by the French in 1731, but elsewhere the historic peoples of the Southeast — Caddos, Choctaws, Chickasaws, Cherokees, and various tribes of Creeks — emerged from the ruins of Mississippian societies. Cherokee traditions tell that their ancestors originated in the southern Appalachians, in what is today the western Carolinas and eastern Georgia and Tennessee, and that from time immemorial Cherokee men hunted and Cherokees women farmed, planting and harvesting corn, beans, and squash in the fertile valleys of the Appalachians. The Cherokees called themselves *Ani-Yun Wiya*, the Real People.

In the North, over the course of several centuries, the Iroquoian-speaking Hurons, Petuns, and Neutrals moved from scattered settlements to fortified villages. Eventually, they formed loose confederacies numbering thousands of people. Sometime before direct contact with Europeans, the Iroquoian-speaking peoples of upstate New York ended intertribal conflict and organized a Great League of Peace (see "The Iroquois Great League of Peace," pages 52–61). The league, composed of Mohawks, Oneidas, Onondagas, Cayugas, and Senecas, met in council and reached decisions by consensus, pursuing common policies on issues of mutual concern. But the individual tribes retained autonomy over questions of more local interest, and daily life revolved around the village and the longhouse. Iroquoian villages consisted of elm and bark longhouses, sometimes exceeding a hundred feet, that

◆ **Indian Sugar Camp**

This nineteenth-century painting by Seth Eastman (1808–75) depicts Great Lakes Indian women collecting sap from maple trees and boiling it to produce sugar. Sugar making was a female activity, and the sugar camp was primarily a female space. *Newberry Library, Chicago, Illinois, USA/Bridgeman Images.*

sheltered families related by clan through the female line. Iroquoian women tended the homes; cultivated and harvested the extensive cornfields that surrounded their villages; gathered berries, fruits, and nuts; made clothing and pottery; and cared for children. Iroquoian men prepared the fields for planting, but the main foci of their activities — war, trade, and diplomacy — lay outside the villages.

The Iroquois fought, traded, and communicated with Algonquian-speaking peoples who surrounded the Iroquoian homeland in New York and Ontario: Ottawas, Algonquins, and Montagnais to the north; Mahicans, Abenakis, and Wampanoags to the east in New England; Delawares and Nanticokes to the south; and Shawnees, Potawatomis, Anishinaabeg,° Illinois, and Foxes to the west. Algonquians lived in semipermanent villages of wigwams and longhouses

---

° The names *Anishinaabeg* (noun) and *Anishinaabe* (adjective) refer to the peoples variously termed *Ojibwas* or *Chippewas*.

and followed a mobile lifestyle, "commuting" from one resource locale to another and practicing varying methods of farming, hunting, fishing, and gathering and harvesting food according to the seasons.

SEABORNE STRANGERS

The first Europeans who came to America did not enter a void; they entered a Native American world where alliances, rivalries, commerce, and artistic and cultural exchanges had been going on for centuries, where civilizations had risen and fallen. Great centers had reached their height in the Mississippi valley and the Southwest around A.D. 1100, and populations in the Southwest seem to have peaked around 1300. Then drought, floods, internal rifts, and escalating conflicts took their toll.[50] Chaco and Cahokia were already ancient history by the time Europeans arrived. In a sense, Europeans entered Indian America "through the back door" and arrived late. They saw only the edges of that world and only hints of its past. Before Europeans, Indian populations and activities had tended to focus on the great river and exchange systems in the heart of the continent. After Europeans arrived, Indian peoples "did an about-face toward the new oceanic powers" and were forced to confront the seaborne strangers.[51]

Native traditions from throughout North America tell of ancient prophecies predicting the coming of Europeans. We may suspect these as the products of hindsight or of rumors running along trade networks, but they became an important part of historical memory. Some tribes said that the arrival of Europeans was foretold in dreams; in many East Coast traditions, the strangers arrived on what appeared to be floating islands or giant white seabirds. The prophecies generally carried a sense of foreboding and omens of hard times. Later, other dreams prophesied disaster in the West. "There is a time coming," the Cheyenne prophet Sweet Medicine warned his people, "when many things will change. Strangers called Earth Men will appear among you. Their skins are light-colored and their ways are powerful." Sweet Medicine urged the Cheyennes to keep their own ways, but he predicted that "at last you will not remember. . . . You will take after the Earth Men's ways and forget good things by which you have lived and in the end become worse than crazy."[52] Another prophecy, said to have been made by a Spokane Indian just before American missionaries penetrated the Columbia Plateau region of present-day Idaho, Oregon, and Washington, warned the people that "soon there will come from the rising sun a different kind of man from any you have yet seen, who will bring with them a book and will teach you everything." After that, said the prophet, "the world will fall to pieces."[53]

The history of Indian peoples in North America stretches back thousands of years, but the last five hundred have been the story of how their world fell to pieces, and of how those who survived tried to rebuild it.

DOCUMENTS

A Navajo Emergence Story and an Iroquois Creation Story

❖❖❖❖❖❖◆❖❖❖❖❖❖

Historians often do not know quite what to make of stories and consequently dismiss them as myths, not appropriate or useful as historical evidence. But oral transmission of stories is common to all human societies and is "probably the oldest form of history making." They may not always provide an accurate record of what happened, but stories do offer insights into the lives of the people who told and heard them, and into how they recalled the past and understood change. They interweave dramatic events with practical human experience and are often moral tales, containing and preserving the values of the society. Anthropologist Julie Cruikshank, who worked for years with tribal elders in Yukon Territory, learned that "narratives about a boy who went to live in the world of salmon, about a girl who married a bear, . . . or about women who went to live with stars provided pivotal philosophical, literary, and social frameworks essential for guiding young and not-so-young people, framing ways of thinking about how to live life appropriately." These narratives "erased any distinction between 'story' and 'history.'" Although often told to children, such narratives are not just for children. They frequently contain a society's deepest-held values and core beliefs.[54]

That is particularly true of stories that tell how a people came into being. The late Lakota scholar Vine Deloria Jr. explained that the idea of the people usually began "somewhere in the primordial mists," at a time when the people were gathered together "but did not yet see themselves as a distinct people." Then, "a holy man had a dream or a vision; quasi-mythological figures of cosmic importance revealed themselves, or in some other manner the people were instructed. They were given ceremonies and rituals that enabled them to find their place on the continent."[55] "Through the stories we hear who we are," writes Laguna Pueblo author Leslie Marmon Silko. But, she adds, origin stories "are not to be taken as literally as the anthropologists might wish." Rather, the journey into the world was "an interior process of the imagination," a growing awareness that human beings were different from other forms of life and yet inseparable from them.[56] Like the legends of any people, Native American origin stories embody communal experience, communal wisdom, and guides for proper conduct. They explain how the world came to be and why things are the way they are. They define people's place in the world and tie them to the landscape and history of their homeland, whose lessons they must not forget. On the basis of his experiences among the Western Apaches, the late anthropologist Keith Basso explained:

> For Indian men and women, the past lies embedded in features of the earth—in canyons and lakes, mountains and arroyos, rocks and vacant fields—which together endow their lands with multiple forms of significance that reach into their lives and shape the ways they think. Knowledge of places is therefore closely linked to knowledge of the self, to grasping one's position in the larger scheme of things, including one's own community, and to securing a confident sense of who one is as a person.[57]

The Navajo Indians, one of the largest Indian tribes in North America with more than 300,000 people today, emerged into written history in the 1620s when Spaniards began to distinguish from the Apaches a people whom they called "Apaches del Navajo." Long before that—some scholars say as many as five hundred years earlier, others no more than a hundred—the ancestors of the historic Apaches and Navajos migrated from northern Canada and traveled south. The people who became the Navajos (or the Diné, in their own language) settled in the Colorado Plateau country of what is now northeastern Arizona, northwestern New Mexico, and southeastern Utah (Map 1.5). There they raided and traded with Pueblos and Spaniards and adopted cultural elements from both of them. In time, they evolved from a nomadic hunting people into a more settled farming and herding society.

Sifting through early documents, scholars can piece together increasing "sightings" of the Navajos as they emerge from the distant past into "recorded history," where sources are richer and easier to analyze. Still, many Indian peoples have a much clearer sense of their ancient past than recorded history captures for scholars.

Navajo origin stories also tell how people emerged into this world from several lower worlds. There are many versions of these creation and emergence stories, but they share common themes and messages. In some versions, the first world was black, the second blue, the third yellow, and the fourth or present world bright or glittering. First Man and First Woman exist alongside, and talk with, insects and animals—"people" of nonhuman form. But in each of the worlds they fight, squabble, and behave badly. Each time, the people flee to a higher world, where they meet new people. In one version, the fourth world is covered with water, but eventually the waters recede. Finally, the people emerge into the present world.

Dinétah, the Navajo homeland, takes shape, bounded by four sacred mountains: Abalone Shell Mountain (San Francisco Peaks) in the west, Dawn or White Shell Mountain (Blanca Peak) in the east, Blue Bead or Turquoise Mountain (Mount Taylor) in the south, and Obsidian Mountain (Hesperus Peak) to the north (see Map 1.5, "The Navajo World," page 42). About the time Dinétah takes form, the sun, the moon and stars, night and day, and the four seasons of the year appear. With the four sacred mountains in each of the four directions, the four seasons, men and women living in harmony, and humans living together with the animals and plants, the Navajos had moved from lower worlds of chaos and strife

◆ Map 1.5 **The Navajo World**
Whether they migrated from the far north of Canada or emerged from lower worlds,
the Navajos made their home in the Southwest, in an area bordered by sacred mountain
ranges representing the four directions, recognized as sources of knowledge and named for
their minerals or the colors they represent: Sisnaajiní (shell white; Blanca Peak); Tsoodził
(turquoise; blue; Mount Taylor); Dook'oosłiid (abalone; yellow; San Francisco Peaks); and
Dibé nitsaa (black jet or obsidian; Hesperus Peak). It was also a world surrounded by other
peoples with whom, over time, the Navajos experienced both contact and conflict.

into a higher world of beauty and harmony. The stories establish proper relations
with other peoples and with other living things. Antisocial behavior and conflict
produce misfortune. Aberrant sexual behavior is destructive; good relationships
between the sexes, between First Man and First Woman, are crucial to creation
and to social harmony. The stories of recurrent movement emphasize the need to
restore balance to produce healing; they make clear the Navajos' responsibility for
maintaining order and harmony through good living and ritual.

The creation story is part of a dynamic Navajo oral tradition. One scholar
who studied it in depth found it to be not a single story so much as a "boundless,
sprawling narrative with a life of its own." It could change from telling to telling, "depending upon the singer, the audience, the particular storytelling event, and a very
complicated set of ceremonial conditions having to do with illness, departure, return,
celebration, or any one of a number of other social occasions."[58] Any written text
can do only partial justice to the poetic and social richness of the storytelling event.

The version of the Navajo creation story reprinted here was told to Aileen
O'Bryan in November 1928 at Mesa Verde National Park. The storyteller was
a Navajo chief named Sandoval or Hastin Tlo'tsi hee (Old Man Buffalo Grass)

whose words were translated by his nephew Sam Ahkeah. "You look at me and you see only an ugly old man," Sandoval told O'Bryan, "but within I am filled with great beauty. I sit as on a mountaintop and I look into the future. I see my people and your people living together. In time to come my people will have forgotten their early way of life unless they learn it from white men's books. So you must write down what I tell you; and you must have it made into a book that coming generations may know this truth." O'Bryan recorded the story "without inter-polation, and presented it, in so far as is possible, in the old man's words."[59] It is reprinted together with the notes Sandoval provided.

When the French, Dutch, and English began to penetrate present-day upstate New York in the early seventeenth century, they encountered the Hodenosaunee or "People of the Longhouse." Five Iroquoian nations — the Mohawks, Oneidas, Onondagas, Cayugas, and Senecas — occupied the region from the Hudson valley in the east to Lake Erie in the west and cooperated in a league that preserved peace among its members and exerted tremendous influence upon its neighbors (Map 1.6). Iroquois traditions recall how this remarkable political system was formed in the mythic past (see pages 52–61), but, like the Navajos in the Southwest, the Iroquois in the Northeast also have a rich tradition of stories recounting the creation of the world and their place in it. Many indigenous peoples share a tradition that they entered this world from a lower world, but the Iroquois and many other peoples in the Northeast share a tradition that the world was created on the back of a giant sea turtle (many still refer to North America as Turtle Island) and that their ancestors fell from the sky. The Iroquois origin story was passed from generation to generation by word of mouth and there are now more than forty recorded versions, the first taken down as early as 1632.[60] The versions vary in detail and emphasis but they share the central story line and essential themes, convey-ing the importance of women in Iroquois society, the du-ality of good and evil, and the need for balance in the world, in society, and in in-dividual lives. Most accounts of the creation story were re-corded by anthropologists in

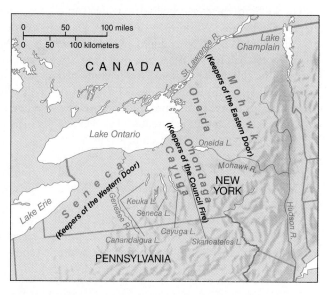

◆ **Map 1.6 The Five Nations of the Iroquois**
The Iroquois saw their league as an extended longhouse, stretch-ing from the Mohawk Valley to Lake Erie. Each member tribe occupied a position and performed a role, and the longhouse could be extended to include other people who sought its shelter. The Tuscaroras joined the league as the sixth nation around 1722 after moving north from the Carolinas.

the nineteenth and twentieth centuries and those are the ones most commonly related, but the account reprinted here is one of the earliest to be written down, recorded by John Norton around 1816.

John Norton (Teyoninhokarawen) was the son of Scottish and Cherokee parents and an adopted Mohawk. He played a prominent role in his people's affairs in the early nineteenth century, traveled widely among the Indian nations of the eastern woodlands, and also visited England. He had a special interest in the mythology of the Iroquois, and he gave a condensed version of the story recounted here to an audience at Trinity College, Cambridge, in 1805.

HASTIN TLO'TSI HEE
The Beginning

THE FIRST WORLD

These stories were told to Sandoval, Hastin Tlo'tsi hee, by his grandmother, Esdzan Hosh kige. Her ancestor was Esdzan at a', the medicine woman who had the Calendar Stone in her keeping. Here are the stories of the Four Worlds that had no sun, and of the Fifth, the world we live in, which some call the Changeable World.

The First World, Ni'hodilqil,° was black as black wool. It had four corners, and over these appeared four clouds. These four clouds contained within themselves the elements of the First World. They were in color, black, white, blue, and yellow.

The Black Cloud represented the Female Being or Substance. For as a child sleeps when being nursed, so life slept in the darkness of the Female Being. The White Cloud represented the Male Being or Substance. He was the Dawn, the Light-Which-Awakens, of the First World.

In the East, at the place where the Black Cloud and the White Cloud met, First Man, Atse'hastqin, was formed; and with him was formed the white corn, perfect in shape, with kernels covering the whole ear. Dohonot i'ni is the name of this first seed corn,° and it is also the name of the place where the Black Cloud and the White Cloud met.

The First World was small in size, a floating island in mist or water. On it there grew one tree, a pine tree, which was later brought to the present world for firewood.

Man was not, however, in his present form. The conception was of a male and a female being who were to become man and woman. The creatures of the First World are thought of as the Mist People; they had no definite form, but were to change to men, beasts, birds, and reptiles of this world.°

Now on the western side of the First World, in a place that later was to become the Land of Sunset, there appeared the Blue Cloud, and opposite it there appeared the Yellow Cloud. Where they came together First Woman was formed, and with her the yellow corn. This ear of corn was also perfect. With First Woman there came the white shell and the turquoise and the yucca.°

° Five names were given to this First World in its relation to First Man. It was called Dark Earth, Ni'hodilqil; Red Earth, Ni'halchi; One Speech, Sada hat lai; Floating Land, Ni'ta na elth; and One Tree, De east'da eith.

SOURCE: Aileen O'Bryan, *The Diné: Origin Myths of the Navaho Indians*, Bureau of American Ethnology, Bulletin 163 (Washington, D.C.: U.S. Government Printing Office, 1956), 1–13.

° Where much corn is raised one or two ears are found perfect. These are always kept for seed corn.

° The Navaho people have always believed in evolution.

° Five names were given also the First World in its relation to First Woman: White Bead Standing, Yolgai'na ziha; Turquoise Standing, Dolt i'zhi na ziha; White Bead Floating Place, Yolgai'dana elth gai; Turquoise Floating Place, Dolt 'izhi na elth gai; and Yucca Standing, Tasas y ah gai. Yucca represents cleanliness and things ceremonial.

First Man stood on the eastern side of the First World. He represented the Dawn and was the Life Giver. First Woman stood opposite in the West. She represented Darkness and Death.

First Man burned a crystal for a fire. The crystal belonged to the male and was the symbol of the mind and of clear seeing. When First Man burned it, it was the mind's awakening. First Woman burned her turquoise for a fire. They saw each other's lights in the distance. When the Black Cloud and the White Cloud rose higher in the sky First Man set out to find the turquoise light. He went twice without success, and again a third time; then he broke a forked branch from his tree, and, looking through the fork, he marked the place where the light burned. And the fourth time he walked to it and found smoke coming from a home.

"Here is the home I could not find," First Man said.

First Woman answered: "Oh, it is you. I saw you walking around and I wondered why you did not come."

Again the same thing happened when the Blue Cloud and the Yellow Cloud rose higher in the sky. First Woman saw a light and she went out to find it. Three times she was unsuccessful, but the fourth time she saw the smoke and she found the home of First Man.

"I wondered what this thing could be," she said.

"I saw you walking and I wondered why you did not come to me," First Man answered.

First Woman saw that First Man had a crystal for a fire, and she saw that it was stronger than her turquoise fire. And as she was thinking, First Man spoke to her. "Why do you not come with your fire and we will live together." The woman agreed to this. So instead of the man going to the woman, as is the custom now, the woman went to the man.

About this time there came another person, the Great-Coyote-Who-Was-Formed-in-the-Water,° and he was in the form of a male being. He told the two that he had been hatched from an egg.

He knew all that was under the water and all that was in the skies. First Man placed this person ahead of himself in all things. The three began to plan what was to come to pass; and while they were thus occupied another being came to them. He also had the form of a man, but he wore a hairy coat, lined with white fur, that fell to his knees and was belted in at the waist. His name was Atse'hashke', First Angry or Coyote.° He said to the three: "You believe that you were the first persons. You are mistaken. I was living when you were formed."

Then four beings came together. They were yellow in color and were called the tsts'na or wasp people. They knew the secret of shooting evil and could harm others. They were very powerful.

This made eight people.

Four more beings came. They were small in size and wore red shirts and had little black eyes. They were the naazo'zi or spider ants. They knew how to sting, and were a great people.

After these came a whole crowd of beings. Dark colored they were, with thick lips and dark, protruding eyes. They were the wolazhi'ni, the black ants. They also knew the secret of shooting evil and were powerful; but they killed each other steadily.

By this time there were many people. Then came a multitude of little creatures. They were peaceful and harmless, but the odor from them was unpleasant. They were called the wolazhi'ni nlchu nigi, meaning that which emits an odor.°

And after the wasps and the different ant people there came the beetles, dragonflies, bat people, the Spider Man and Woman, and the Salt Man and Woman,° and others that rightfully had no definite form but were among those people who peopled the First World. And this world, being

---

° The Great Coyote who was formed in the water, Mai tqo y elth chili.

° Some medicine men claim that witchcraft came with First Man and First Woman; others insist that devil conception or witchcraft originated with the Coyote called First Angry.
° No English name is given this insect. Ants cause trouble, as also do wasps and other insects, if their homes are harmed.
° Beetle, ntlsa'go; Dragonfly, tqanil ai'; Bat people, ja aba'ni; Spider Man, nashjei hastqin; Spider Woman, nashjei esdza; Salt Man, ashi hastqin; Salt Woman, ashi esdza.

small in size, became crowded, and the people quarreled and fought among themselves, and in all ways made living very unhappy.

THE SECOND WORLD

Because of the strife in the First World, First Man, First Woman, the Great-Coyote-Who-Was-Formed-in-the-Water, and the Coyote called First Angry, followed by all the others, climbed up from the world of Darkness and Dampness to the Second or Blue World.°

They found a number of people already living there: blue birds, blue hawks, blue jays, blue herons, and all the blue-feathered beings.° The powerful swallow people° lived there also, and these people made the Second World unpleasant for those who had come from the First World. There was fighting and killing.

The First Four found an opening in the World of Blue Haze; and they climbed through this and led the people up into the Third or Yellow World.

THE THIRD WORLD

The bluebird was the first to reach the Third or Yellow World. After him came the First Four and all the others.

A great river crossed this land from north to south. It was the Female River. There was another river crossing it from east to west, it was the Male River. This Male River flowed through the Female River and on;° and the name of this place is tqo alna'osdli, the Crossing of the Waters.

There were six mountains in the Third World.° In the East was Sis na'jin, the Standing

Black Sash. Its ceremonial name is Yol gai'dzil, the Dawn or White Shell Mountain. In the South stood Tso'dzil, the Great Mountain, also called Mountain Tongue. Its ceremonial name is Yodolt i'zhi dzil, the Blue Bead or Turquoise Mountain. In the West stood Dook'oslid, and the meaning of this name is forgotten. Its ceremonial name is Dichi'li dzil, the Abalone Shell Mountain. In the North stood Debe'ntsa, Many Sheep Mountain. Its ceremonial name is Bash'zhini dzil, Obsidian Mountain. Then there was Dzil na'odili, the Upper Mountain. It was very sacred; and its name means also the Center Place, and the people moved around it. Its ceremonial name is Ntl'is dzil, Precious Stone or Banded Rock Mountain. There was still another mountain called Chol'i'i or Dzil na'odili choli, and it was also a sacred mountain.

There was no sun in this land, only the two rivers and the six mountains. And these rivers and mountains were not in their present form, but rather the substance of mountains and rivers as were First Man, First Woman, and the others. . . .

Within this land there lived the Kisa'ni, the ancients of the Pueblo People. On the six mountains there lived the Cave Dwellers or Great Swallow People.° On the mountains lived also the light and dark squirrels, chipmunks, mice, rats, the turkey people, the deer and cat people, the spider people, and the lizards and snakes. The beaver people lived along the rivers, and the frogs and turtles and all the underwater people in the water. So far all the people were similar. They had no

---

° The Second World was the Blue World, Ni'hodotl'ish.
° The names of the blue birds are bluebird, do'le; blue hawk, gi'ni tso dolt ish; blue jay, jozh ghae'gi; and blue heron, tqualtl a'gaale.
° The swallow is called tqash ji'zhi.
° The introduction of generation.
° Sis na'jin, Mount Baldy near Alamosa, Colo.; Tso'dzil, Mount Taylor, N. Mex.; Dook'oslid, San Francisco Mountain, Ariz.; Debe'ntsa, San Juan Mountains, Colo.; Dzil na'odili, El Huerfano Peak, N. Mex.; and Choli, also given

as El Huerfano or El Huerfanito Peak, N. Mex. These mountains of the Third World were not in their true form, but rather the substance of the mountains.

Recorder's note: Although both Matthews and the Franciscan Fathers give Sis na'jin as Pelado Peak, Sam Ahkeah, the interpreter, after checking, identified it as Mount Baldy near Alamosa, Colo. Also, although the Franciscan Fathers give Dzil na odili choli as Huerfanito Peak [sic], Sam Ahkeah says that it is the Mother Mountain near Taos.
° The Great Swallow People, Tqashji'zhi ndilk'si, lived in rough houses of mud and sticks. They entered them from holes in the roof.

definite form, but they had been given different names because of different characteristics.

Now the plan was to plant.

First Man called the people together. He brought forth the white corn which had been formed with him. First Woman brought the yellow corn. They laid the perfect ears side by side; then they asked one person from among the many to come and help them. The Turkey stepped forward. They asked him where he had come from, and he said that he had come from the Gray Mountain.° He danced back and forth four times, then he shook his feather coat and there dropped from his clothing four kernels of corn, one gray, one blue, one black, and one red. Another person was asked to help in the plan of the planting. The Big Snake came forward. He likewise brought forth four seeds, the pumpkin, the watermelon, the cantaloup, and the muskmelon. His plants all crawl on the ground.

They planted the seeds, and their harvest was great. . . .

At this time the Great-Coyote-Who-Was-Formed-in-the-Water came to First Man and told him to cross the river. They made a big raft and crossed at the place where the Male River followed through the Female River. And all the male beings left the female beings on the river bank; and as they rowed across the river they looked back and saw that First Woman and the female beings were laughing. They were also behaving very wickedly.

In the beginning the women did not mind being alone. They cleared and planted a small field. On the other side of the river First Man and the chiefs hunted and planted their seeds. They had a good harvest. Nadle° ground the corn and cooked the food. Four seasons passed. The men continued to have plenty and were happy; but the women became lazy, and only weeds grew on their land. The women wanted fresh meat. Some of them tried to join the men and were drowned in the river.

First Woman made a plan. As the women had no way to satisfy their passions, some fashioned long narrow rocks, some used the feathers of the turkey, and some used strange plants (cactus). First Woman told them to use these things. One woman brought forth a big stone. This stone-child was later the Great Stone that rolled over the earth killing men. Another woman brought forth the Big Birds of Tsa bida'hi; and others gave birth to the giants and monsters who later destroyed many people.

On the opposite side of the river the same condition existed. The men, wishing to satisfy their passions, killed the females of mountain sheep, lion, and antelope. Lightning struck these men. When First Man learned of this he warned his men that they would all be killed. He told them that they were indulging in a dangerous practice. Then the second chief spoke: he said that life was hard and that it was a pity to see women drowned. He asked why they should not bring the women across the river and all live together again.

"Now we can see for ourselves what comes from our wrong doing," he said. "We will know how to act in the future." The three other chiefs of the animals agreed with him, so First Man told them to go and bring the women.

After the women had been brought over the river First Man spoke: "We must be purified," he said. "Everyone must bathe. The men must dry themselves with white corn meal, and the women, with yellow."

This they did, living apart for 4 days. After the fourth day First Woman came and threw her right arm around her husband. She spoke to the others and said that she could see her mistakes, but with her husband's help she would henceforth lead a good life. Then all the male and female beings came and lived with each other again.

° The Gray Mountain is the home of the Gray Yei, Hasch el'ba'i, whose other name is Water Sprinkler. The turkey is connected with water and rain.

Interpreter's note: Gray Mountain is San Francisco Mountain, Ariz. Tqo'neinili, the Water Sprinkler, whose color is gray, lives there. He is also called the Gray God, Hasch e'lbai, and the Clown whose call is "do do," and whose name is Hasch e'dodi.

° Nadle means that which changes.

The people moved to different parts of the land. Some time passed; then First Woman became troubled by the monotony of life. She made a plan. She went to Atse'hashke, the Coyote called First Angry, and giving him the rainbow she said: "I have suffered greatly in the past. I have suffered from want of meat and corn and clothing. Many of my maidens have died. I have suffered many things. Take the rainbow and go to the place where the rivers cross. Bring me the two pretty children of Tqo holt sodi, the Water Buffalo, a boy and a girl."

The Coyote agreed to do this. He walked over the rainbow. He entered the home of the Water Buffalo and stole the two children; and these he hid in his big skin coat with the white fur lining. And when he returned he refused to take off his coat, but pulled it around himself and looked very wise.

After this happened the people saw white light in the East and in the South and West and North. One of the deer people ran to the East, and returning, said that the white light was a great sheet of water. The sparrow hawk flew to the South, the great hawk to the West, and the kingfisher to the North. They returned and said that a flood was coming. The kingfisher said that the water was greater in the North, and that it was near.

The flood was coming and the Earth was sinking. And all this happened because the Coyote had stolen the two children of the Water Buffalo, and only First Woman and the Coyote knew the truth.

When First Man learned of the coming of the water he sent word to all the people, and he told them to come to the mountain called Sis na'jin. He told them to bring with them all of the seeds of the plants used for food. All living beings were to gather on the top of Sis na'jin. First Man traveled to the six sacred mountains, and, gathering earth from them, he put it in his medicine bag.

The water rose steadily.

When all the people were halfway up Sis na'jin, First Man discovered that he had forgotten his medicine bag. Now this bag contained not only the earth from the six sacred mountains, but

his magic, the medicine he used to call the rain down upon the earth and to make things grow. He could not live without his medicine bag, and he wished to jump into the rising water; but the others begged him not to do this. They went to the kingfisher and asked him to dive into the water and recover the bag. This the bird did. When First Man had his medicine bag again in his possession he breathed on it four times and thanked his people. . . .

First Man had with him his spruce tree° which he planted on the top of Sis na'jin. He used his fox medicine° to make it grow; but the spruce tree began to send out branches and to taper at the top, so First Man planted the big Male Reed.° All the people blew on it, and it grew and grew until it reached the canopy of the sky. They tried to blow inside the reed, but it was solid. They asked the woodpecker to drill out the hard heart. Soon they were able to peek through the opening, but they had to blow and blow before it was large enough to climb through. They climbed up inside the big male reed, and after them the water continued to rise.

THE FOURTH WORLD

When the people reached the Fourth World they saw that it was not a very large place. Some say that it was called the White World; but not all medicine men agree that this is so.°. . .

° Recorder's note: That the tree is here called a spruce and earlier a pine is not explained.

° First Man's name, Aste'hastqin, corresponds to the sacred name of the kit fox.

° The big Male Reed is called luka'tso. It grows near Santo Domingo Pueblo, not far from the home of the Turquoise Boy, the little turquoise mountain south of Santa Fe, N. Mex.

° The Four Worlds were really twelve worlds, or stages of development, but different medicine men divide them differently according to the ceremony held. For the narrative they call them the Four Dark Worlds, and the Fifth World, the one we live in. An old medicine man explained that the Sixth World would be that of the spirit; and that the one above that would be "cosmic," melting into one.

THE FIFTH WORLD

First Man was not satisfied with the Fourth World. It was a small, barren land; and the great water had soaked the earth and made the sowing of seeds impossible. He planted the big Female Reed° and it grew up to the vaulted roof of this Fourth World. First Man sent the newcomer, the badger, up inside the reed, but before he reached the upper world water began to drip, so he returned and said that he was frightened. . . .

Now two dark clouds and two white clouds rose, and this meant that two nights and two days had passed, for there was still no sun. First Man again sent the badger to the upper world, and he returned covered with mud, terrible mud. First Man gathered chips of turquoise which he offered to the five Chiefs of the Winds° who lived in the uppermost world of all. They were pleased with the gift, and they sent down the winds and dried the Fifth World.

First Man and his people saw four dark clouds and four white clouds pass, and then they sent the badger up the reed. This time when the badger returned he said that he had come out on solid earth. So First Man and First Woman led the people to the Fifth World, which some call the Many Colored Earth and some the Changeable Earth. They emerged through a lake surrounded by four mountains. The water bubbles in this lake when anyone goes near.°

Now after all the people had emerged from the lower worlds First Man and First Woman dressed the Mountain Lion with yellow, black, white, and grayish corn and placed him on one side. They dressed the Wolf with white tail feathers and placed him on the other side. They divided the people into two groups. The first group was told to choose whichever chief they wished. They made their choice, and, although they thought they had chosen the Mountain Lion, they found that they had taken the Wolf for their chief. The Mountain Lion was the chief for the other side. And these people who had the Mountain Lion for their chief turned out to be the people of the Earth. They were to plant seeds and harvest corn. The followers of the Wolf chief became the animals and birds; they turned into all the creatures that fly and crawl and run and swim.

And after all the beings were divided, and each had his own form, they went their ways.

This is the story of the Four Dark Worlds and the Fifth, the World we live in. Some medicine men tell us that there are two worlds above us, the first is the World of the Spirits of Living Things, the second is the Place of Melting into One.

° The big Female Reed is thought to be the joint cane which grows along the Colorado River.
° The First Chief, Nlchi ntla'ie, the Left Course Wind; the Second Chief, Nlchi lichi, the Red Wind; the Third Chief, Nlchi shada ji na'laghali, the Wind Turning from the Sun; the Fourth Chief, Nlchi qa'hashchi, the Wind with Many Points; the Fifth Chief, Nlchi che do et siedee, the Wind with the Fiery Temper.

° The place of emergence is said to be near Pagosa Springs, Colo. The white people have put a wire fence around our Sacred Lake.

JOHN NORTON
Iroquois Creation Story
c. 1816

The tradition of the Nottowegui or Five Nations says, "that in the beginning before the formation of the earth; the country above the sky was inhabited by Superior Beings, over whom the Great Spirit presided. His daughter having become pregnant by an illicit connection, he pulled up a great tree by the roots, and threw her through the cavity thereby formed; but, to prevent her utter destruction, he previously ordered the Great Turtle, to get from the bottom of the waters, some slime on its back, and to wait on the surface of the water to receive her on it. When she had fallen on the back of the Turtle, with the mud she found there, she began to form the earth, and by the time of her delivery had encreased it to the extent of a little island. Her child was a daughter, and as she grew up the earth extended under their hands. When the young woman had arrived at the age of discretion, the Spirits who roved about, in human forms, made proposals of marriage for the young woman: the mother always rejected their offers, until a middle aged man, of a dignified appearance, his bow in his hand, and his quiver on his back, paid his addresses. On being accepted, he entered the house, and seated himself on the birth of his intended spouse; the mother was in a birth on the other side of the fire. She observed that her son-in-law did not lie down all night; but taking two arrows out of his quiver, he put them by the side of his bride: at the dawn of day he took them up, and having replaced them in his quiver, he went out.

"After some time, the old woman perceived her daughter to be pregnant, but could not discover where the father had gone, or who he was. At the time of delivery, the twins disputed which way they should go out of the womb; the wicked one said, let us go out of the side; but the other said, not so, lest we kill our mother; then the wicked one pretending to acquiesce, desired his brother to go out first: but as soon as he was delivered, the wicked one, in attempting to go out at her side, caused the death of his mother.

"The twin brothers were nurtured and raised by their Grandmother; the eldest was named Teharonghyawago, or the Holder of Heaven; the youngest was called Tawiskaron, or Flinty rock, from his body being entirely covered with such a substance. They grew up, and with their bows and arrows, amused themselves throughout the island, which encreased in extent, and they were favoured with various animals of Chace. Tawiskaron was the most fortunate hunter, and enjoyed the favour of his Grandmother. Teharonghyawago was not so successful in the Chace, and suffered from their unkindness. When he was a youth, and roaming alone, in melancholy mood, through the island, a human figure, of noble aspect, appearing to him, addressed him thus. 'My son, I have seen your distress, and heard your solitary lamentations; you are unhappy in the loss of a mother, in the unkindness of your Grandmother and brother. I now come to comfort you, I am your father, and will be your Protector; therefore take courage, and suffer not your spirit to sink. Take this (giving him an ear of *maize*) plant it, and attend it in the manner, I shall direct; it will yield you a certain support, independent of the Chace, at the same time that it will render more palatable the viands, which you may thereby obtain. I am the Great Turtle which supports the earth, on which you move. Your brother's ill treatment will increase with his years; bear it with patience till the time appointed, before which you shall hear further.'

"After saying this, and directing him how to plant the corn, he disappeared. Teharonghyawago planted the corn, and returned home. When its verdant sprouts began to flourish above the ground, he spent his time in clearing from it all growth of grass and weeds, which might smother it or retard its advancement while yet in its tender state, before it had acquired sufficient grandeur to shade the ground. He now discovered that his wicked brother caught the timid deer, the stately elk with branching horns, and all the harmless inhabitants of the Forest; and imprisoned them in an extensive cave, for his own particular use, depriving mortals from having the benefit of them that was originally intended by the Great Spirit. Teharonghyawago discovered the direction his brother took in conducting these animals captive to the Cave; but never could trace him quite to the spot, as he eluded his sight with more than common dexterity!

SOURCE: From Colin G. Calloway, *The World Turned Upside Down: Indian Voices from Early America*. Boston: Bedford/ St. Martin's, 1994, pages 23–26.

"Teharonghyawago endeavoured to conceal himself on the path that led to the cave, so that he might follow him imperceptibly; but he found it impossible to hide himself from the penetrating Tawiskaron. At length he observed, that altho' his brother saw, with extraordinary acuteness, every surrounding object, yet he never raised his eyes to look above: Teharonghyawago then climbed a lofty tree, which grew near to where he thought the place of confinement was situated: in the meantime, his brother passed, searching with his eyes the thickest recesses of the Forest, but never casting a glance above. He then saw his brother take a straight course, and when he was out of sight, Teharonghyawago descended, and came to the Cave, a short time after he had deposited his charge; and finding there an innumerable number of animals confined, he set them free, and returned home.

"It was not long before Tawiskaron, visiting the Cave, discovered that all his captives, which he had taken so much pains to deprive of their liberty, had been liberated: he knew this to be an act of his brother, but dissembling his anger, he mediated revenge, at some future period.

"Teharonghyawago laboured to people the earth with inhabitants, and to found Villages in happy situations, extending the comforts of men. Tawiskaron was equally active in destroying the works his brother had done; and in accumulating every evil in his power on the heads of ill fated mortals. Teharonghyawago saw, with regret, his brother persevere in every wickedness; but waited with patience the result of what his father had told him.

"At one time, being in conversation with his brother, Tawiskaron said 'Brother, what do you think there is on earth, with which you might be killed?' Teharonghyawago replied, 'I know of nothing that could affect my life, unless it be the foam of the billows of the Lake or the downy topped*

reed.' 'What do you think would take your life?' Tawiskaron answered, 'Nothing except horn or flint.' Here their discourse ended.

"Teharonghyawago returning from hunting, heard a voice singing a plaintive air: he listened and heard it name his Mother, who was killed by Tawiskaron; he immediately hastened towards the spot from whence the voice proceeded, crying, 'Who is that, who dares to name my deceased mother in my hearing?' When he came there, he saw the track of a fawn, which he pursued, without overtaking it, till the autumn, when it dropped its first horns; these he took up, and fixed upon the forked branches of a tree.

"He continued the pursuit seven years; and every autumn, when its horns fell, he picked them up, and placed them as he had done the first. At last, he overtook the deer, now grown to be a stately buck: it begged its life, and said, 'Spare me, and I will give you information that may be great service to you.' When he had promised it its life, it spoke as follows, 'It was to give you the necessary information that I have been subjected to your pursuit, and that which I shall now tell you was the intended reward of your perseverance and clemency. Your brother, in coming into the world, caused the death of your Mother; if he was then wicked in his infancy, his malice has grown with his stature; he now premeditates evil against you; be therefore on your guard: as soon as he assaults you, exert yourself, and you will overcome him.'

"He returned home; and not long after this adventure, was attacked by his brother. They fought; the one made use of the horn and flint stone which he had provided: the other sought for froth and the reed, which made little impression on the body of Teharonghyawago. They fought a long time, over the whole of the island, until at last Tawiskaron fell under the conquering hand of his brother. According to the varied tones of their voices in the different places through which they passed during the contest, the people, who afterwards sprung up there, spoke different languages."

*It is called Fox-tail, in America; from the resemblance it bears to it. It is a reed or strong grass that grows in wild, low meadows, . . . the top containing a down, almost like cotton.

QUESTIONS FOR CONSIDERATION

The Navajos' and the Iroquois' stories of their origins can be read literally or understood metaphorically.

1. What do these stories convey about the Navajos' and Iroquois' view of their place in the world and their relations with animals?

2. In what ways do the stories define identity? What do they say about what it means to be Navajo and Iroquois? What do they suggest about gender roles in Navajo and Iroquois society?

3. What do the stories convey about Navajo and Iroquois ideals and morality; of their beliefs about the consequences of wrongdoing; of their responsibilities?

4. In what ways are the stories in conflict or consonance with historical explanations of tribal migrations from other places to their homelands?

The Iroquois Great League of Peace

T HE LEAGUE OF THE IROQUOIS, as the Europeans called it, played a dominant role in the history of northeastern North America before the American Revolution, and Iroquois power and foreign policies shaped colonial, intertribal, and international relations. Despite the devastating impact of the colonial and revolutionary wars, the league continues to function to this day and is one of the oldest political bodies in North America.

No one knows exactly when the league was formed. In 1900 a committee of Six Nations chiefs estimated that it "took place about the year 1390," and some Iroquois assert that it was even earlier. One more recent article argues that the league was founded on the afternoon of August 31, 1142! Archaeologist and anthropologist Dean Snow, on the other hand, maintains that "Iroquois oral tradition and archaeological evidence for endemic warfare suggest that the League could not have formed prior to around 1450," and suggests that the confederation "was probably complete by around 1525."[61] Whatever the date, Iroquois people already referred to their league as ancient by the time they first met Europeans. "We, the five Iroquois Nations, compose but one cabin," a Mohawk envoy declared in 1654. "We maintain but one fire; and we have, from time immemorial, dwelt under one and the same roof."[62]

The league that united the Iroquois in peace was forged in a time of violence. Before its formation, the traditions say, Iroquois people lived in a state of constant warfare: "Everywhere there was peril and everywhere mourning. . . . Feuds with outer nations, feuds with brother nations, feuds of sister towns and feuds of families and of clans made every warrior a stealthy man who liked to kill. . . . A man's life was valued as nothing."[63] Warriors fought to avenge the deaths of relatives in an endless cycle of killing and retribution.

An Onondaga chieftain, who became known to posterity as Hayenwatha or Hiawatha, lost three daughters. Some traditions attributed their deaths to the evil powers of Atotarho or Tadodaho, an Onondaga shaman twisted in body and mind, with snakes twined in his hair. The "mourning war" culture of the Iroquois demanded that Hiawatha assuage his grief and appease the spirits of his loved ones by taking the life of an enemy; instead, he chose to break the cycle of vengeance and violence and create a new world order for the Iroquois. The stories tell how, wandering the forests in his grief, Hiawatha met a Huron called Deganawidah (sometimes Dekanahwideh) who came from north of Lake Ontario. In some versions of the tradition, Deganawidah was a Huron; in others he was an adopted Mohawk; in others he was a healing spirit who had assumed human form. Whatever his identity, he became known as the Peacemaker. He eased Hiawatha's grief with words of condolence and beads of wampum, symbolically wiping his tears and restoring his reason. The rituals became part of the protocol of the Iroquois League and of their diplomatic dealings with outsiders: healing words, not bloody deeds, assuaged grief and redressed wrongs. Deganawidah and Hiawatha composed the laws of a great peace that would restore order and preserve harmony in Iroquois country. Recording each law on a string of wampum so that future generations would remember and observe them, the two set out to carry their message to the warring tribes.

They traveled from village to village, teaching the laws of peace and persuading people to replace war and weapons with words and wampum. The Mohawks agreed, then the Oneidas, Cayugas, and Senecas. The fierce Tadodaho resisted, but Hiawatha is said to have combed the snakes from his hair to ease his torment. Finally Tadodaho accepted the pact. Onondaga became the site of the league's central council fire and Tadodaho the fire's guardian. Deganawidah placed deer antlers on the heads of the chiefs of the Five Nations as symbols of their authority.

The Five Nations agreed to stop fighting among themselves and unite in common defense. The individual tribes retained control of their own affairs at the local level but acted through the Grand Council at Onondaga in matters of common concern. The league reflected the traditional Iroquois longhouse, sheltering many families, each with their own fire but who from time to time gathered around a central fire and functioned as one family. Like a longhouse, the league could be expanded to incorporate new members, as occurred early in the eighteenth century when the Tuscaroras migrated from the South and joined the league as a junior, sixth nation. The Mohawks, who defended the eastern borders of the Iroquois homeland, were designated the Keepers of the Eastern Door; the Senecas were Keepers of the Western Door; the Onondagas were Keepers of the Council Fire. Iroquois people likened their league to a bundle of arrows, symbolizing the strength they achieved in unity: single arrows could be snapped easily but a bundle was difficult to break. The Five Nations saw their league as a great tree providing shelter to other peoples who would follow its roots of peace and take their place in its shade. They adopted so many captives and took in so many refugees that by the seventeenth century French observers estimated there were more non-Iroquois than Iroquois in Iroquois country.

Fifty council chiefs or sachems (called "lords" in the document reprinted here) were chosen by clan mothers from the member tribes. The names of the original chiefs passed as titles from generation to generation, as new chiefs succeeded the older ones in the council. (The Mohawks had/have nine sachems, the Oneidas nine, the Onondagas fourteen, the Cayugas ten, and the Senecas eight.) League sachems had to be thick-skinned — "seven thumbs thick," said Deganawidah — and above criticism and petty jealousies. "Tadodaho represents the mind which promotes peace and the welfare of all people," said Chief Leon Shenandoah, who held the title of Tadodaho from 1967 until his death in 1996. "He must be kind to the people and express love for their welfare, and he must never hurt anybody."[64] The league sachems met, and still meet, at Onondaga, near Syracuse, New York. "They hold every year a general assembly," wrote a Jesuit observer in 1668. "There all the Deputies from the different Nations are present, to make their complaints and receive the necessary satisfaction in mutual gifts, — by means of which they maintain a good understanding with one another."[65] The sachems were divided into two moieties or "sides" — the elder moiety included the Mohawks, Onondagas, and Senecas; the younger, the Oneidas and Cayugas. The two moieties exchanged the ceremonial words of condolence prescribed by Deganawidah to wipe away the grief of those who had lost chiefs and to renew the league. The Mohawks and the Senecas passed matters for discussion back and forth to the Oneidas and the Cayugas, with the Onondagas and Tadodaho, the Firekeeper, presiding and mediating, until consensus was reached or the matter was dropped. The sachems possessed no power of coercion: the chiefs had to be "of one mind." People who could not abide by the general consensus were free to go their own way so long as their actions did not threaten the league as a whole.

Though the league functioned to make and preserve peace, it also freed Iroquois warriors from internal conflict, and with new strength in unity they were able to turn their attentions to outside enemies. "By 1600," says historian Daniel Richter, "the cultural ideal of peace and the everyday reality of war had long been intertwined."[66] European invasion unleashed new forces that threw Indian peoples into increasing competition and conflict with rival colonial powers and with other Indian tribes. Formed to end war, the League of Peace found itself participating in wars on a scale previously unknown to Native North America. Iroquois power made the Six Nations key players in the contests for North America. "The firmness of this league, the great extent of land it claims, the number of great warriors it produces, and the undaunted courage and skill which distinguish the members of it," wrote English trader John Long, "all conspire to prove the good policy of an alliance with them."[67] The league was able to negotiate from a position of strength and to pursue a path of formal neutrality in the wars of the eighteenth century. The American Revolution imposed strains the confederacy could not withstand and produced civil war in Iroquois country, but the ideas and ideals of the league survived.

Many Iroquois people and some non-Iroquois scholars believe that the League of the Iroquois served as a model for the Constitution of the United States. In 1987 the United States Senate passed a resolution acknowledging "the historical debt" that the United States owed to the Iroquois "for their demonstration of enlightened, democratic principles of government and their example of a free association of independent Indian nations." The Iroquois model was there for the colonists to emulate — in 1744 the Onondaga orator Canasatego urged them to follow the model of "union and amity" established by "our wise Forefathers," and Benjamin Franklin asked why, if the Six Nations could create "such a Union," could not a dozen or so colonies do likewise?[68] But whether or not the founding fathers looked to the Iroquois League in creating their constitution remains a hotly contested debate.

The Great Law of the League that Deganawidah gave to the Iroquois was preserved for generations through oral tradition before it was written in the nineteenth century, most notably by Lewis Henry Morgan in his *League of the Hodenosaunee,* published in 1851. Several versions now exist. In 1900, the Six Nations Council of Grand River in Ontario appointed a committee of ten chiefs to prepare an "official version" of the code of Deganawidah and the tradition of the formation of the league. The chiefs noted that "books have been written by white men in the past, but these have been found to be too voluminous and inaccurate in some cases." They offered instead a record compiled "by the elder ceremonial chiefs" who perpetuated "that system of government by hereditary succession as it was constituted by Deganawidah." They acknowledged that some of the ancient traditions had been modified or lost, but noted that the traditions relating to the formation of the league and the procedures for installing chiefs that Deganawidah established had been handed down from father to son for centuries and were "still strictly observed and adhered to by the chiefs of the Six Nations and their people." They produced their history "so that the future generations of the people of the Six Nations may have preserved to them the traditions of their forefathers which otherwise in time would become lost."[69] The laws of the confederacy reprinted here are taken from this "chiefs' version."

CHIEFS OF THE SIX NATIONS
The Laws of the Confederacy (1900)

Then Dekanahwideh again said: "We have completed the Confederation of the Five Nations, now therefore it shall be that hereafter the lords who shall be appointed in the future to fill vacancies caused by death or removals shall be appointed from the same families and clans from which the first lords were created, and from which families the hereditary title of lordships shall descend."

Then Dekanahwideh further said: "I now transfer and set over to the women who have the lordships' title vested in them, that they shall in the future have the power to appoint the successors from time to time to fill vacancies caused by death or removals from whatever cause."

SOURCE: Arthur C. Parker, *The Constitution of the Five Nations of the Iroquois Book of the Great Law* (Albany: New York State Museum Bulletin, No. 184, 1916), 97–113.

Then Dekanahwideh continued and said: "We shall now build a confederate council fire from which the smoke shall arise and pierce the skies and all nations and people shall see this smoke. And now to you, Thadodahho, your brother and cousin colleagues shall be left the care and protection of the confederate council fire, by the Confederate Nations."

Then Dekanahwideh further said: "The lords have unanimously decided to spread before you on the ground this great white wampum belt Ska-no-dah-ken-rah-ko-wah and Ka-yah-ne-renh-kowah, which respectfully signify purity and great peace, and the lords have also laid before you this great wing, Ska-weh-yeh-seh-ko-wah, and whenever any dust or stain of any description falls upon the great belt of white wampum, then you shall take this great wing and sweep it clean." (Dust or stain means evil of any description which might have a tendency to cause trouble in the Confederate Council.)

Then Dekanahwideh said: "The lords of this confederacy have unanimously decided to lay by you this rod (Ska-nah-ka-res) and whenever you see any creeping thing which might have a tendency to harm our grandchildren or see a thing creeping toward the great white wampum belt (meaning the Great Peace), then you shall take this rod and pry it away with it, and if you and your colleagues fail to pry the creeping, evil thing out, you shall then call out loudly that all the Confederate Nations may hear and they will come immediately to your assistance."

Then Dekanahwideh said: "Now you, the lords of the several Confederate Nations, shall divide yourselves and sit on opposite sides of the council fire as follows: You and your brother colleagues shall sit on one side of the council fire (this was said to the Mohawks and the Senecas), and your sons, the Oneidas and Cayugas, shall sit on the opposite side of the council fire. Thus you will begin to work and carry out the principles of the Great Peace (Ka-yah-ne-renh-ko-wah) and you will be guided in this by the great white wampum belt (Ska-no-dah-ke-rah-ko-wah) which signifies Great Peace."

Then Dekanahwideh said: "You, Thadodahho, shall be the fire keeper, and your duty shall be to open the Confederate Council with praise and thanksgiving to the Great Ruler and close the same."

Then Dekanahwideh also said: "When the council is opened, Hahyonhwatha and his colleagues shall be the first to consider and give their opinion upon any subject which may come before the council for consideration, and when they have arrived at a decision, then shall they transfer the matter to their brethren, the Senecas, for their consideration, and when they, the Senecas, shall have arrived at a decision on the matter then they shall refer it back to Hahyonhwatha and his colleagues. Then Hahyonhwatha will announce the decision to the opposite side of the council fire.

"Then Ohdahtshedeh and his colleagues will consider the matter in question and when they have arrived at a decision they will refer the matter to their brethren, the Cayugas, for their consideration and after they have arrived at a decision, they will refer the matter back to Ohdahtshedeh and his colleagues. Then Ohdahtshedeh will announce their decision to the opposite side of the council fire. Then Hahyonhwatha will refer the matter to Thadodahho and his colleagues for their careful consideration and opinion of the matter in question and if Thadodahho and his colleagues find that the matter has not been well considered or decided, then they shall refer the matter back again to the two sides of the council fire, and they shall point out where, in their estimation, the decision was faulty and the question not fully considered, and then the two sides of the council will take up the question again and reconsider the matter, and after the two sides of the council have fully reconsidered the question, then Hahyonhwatha will again refer it to Thadodahho and his colleagues, then they will again consider the matter and if they see that the decision of the two sides of the council is correct, then Thadodahho and his colleagues will confirm the decision."

Then Dekanahwideh further said: "If the brethren of the Mohawks and the Senecas are divided in their opinion and can not agree on any matter which they may have for their consideration, then Hahyonhwatha shall announce the two decisions to the opposite of the council fire. Then Ohdahtshedeh and his brother colleagues, after they have considered the matter, and if they also are divided in their decision, shall so report, but if the divided factions each agree with the decision announced from the opposite side of the council, then Ohdahtshedeh shall also announce their two decisions to the other side of the council fire; then Hahyonhwatha shall refer the matter to Thadodahho and his colleagues who are the fire keepers. They will fully consider the matter and whichever decision they consider correct they will confirm."

Then Dekanahwideh said: "If it should so happen that the lords of the Mohawks and the lords of the Senecas disagree on any matter and also on the opposite side of the council fire, the lords of the Oneidas and the lords of the Cayugas disagree among themselves and do not agree with either of the two decisions of the opposite side of the council fire but of themselves give two decisions which are diverse from each other, then Hahyonhwatha shall refer the four decisions to Thadodahho and his colleagues who shall consider the matter and give their decision and their decision shall be final."

Then Dekanahwideh said: "We have now completed the system for our Confederate Council."

Then Dekanahwideh further said: "We now, each nation, shall adopt all the rules and regulations governing the Confederate Council which we have here made and we shall apply them to all our respective settlements and thereby we shall carry out the principles set forth in the message of Good Tidings of Peace and Power, and in dealing with the affairs of our people of the various dominions, thus we shall secure to them contentment and happiness."

Then he, Dekanahwideh, said: "You, Kanyen-ke-ha-ka (Mohawk), you, Dekarihoken, Hahyonhwatha and Sadekarihwadeh, you shall sit in the middle between your brother lords of the Mohawks, and your cousin lords of the Mohawks, and all matters under discussion shall be referred to you by your brother lords and your cousin lords for your approval or disapproval.

"You, O-nen-do-wa-ka (Senecas), you, Skanyhadahriyoh and Sadeh-ka-ronh-yes, you shall sit in the middle or between your brother lords and your cousin lords of the Senecas and all matters under discussion shall be referred to you by them for your approval or disapproval.

"You, Ohnenyohdehaka (Oneidas), you, Ohdahtshedeh, Kanonkweyoudoh and Deyouhahkwedeh, you shall sit in the middle between your brother lords and your cousin lords of the Oneidas and all matters under discussion shall be referred to you by them for your approval or disapproval.

"You, the Que-yenh-kwe-ha-ka (Cayugas), you, Dekaehyonh and Jinondahwehonh, you shall sit in the middle between your lords and your cousin lords of the Cayugas and all matters under discussion shall be referred to you by them for your approval or disapproval."

Then Dekanahwideh said: "We have now completed arranging the system of our local councils and we shall hold our annual Confederate Council at the settlement of Thadodahho, the capitol or seat of government of the Five Nations' Confederacy."

Dekanahwideh said: "Now I and you lords of the Confederate Nations shall plant a tree Ska-renj-heh-se-go-wah (meaning a tall and mighty tree) and we shall call it Jo-ne-rak-deh-ke-wah (the tree of the great long leaves).

"Now this tree which we have planted shall shoot forth four great, long, white roots (Jo-dohra-ken-rah-ko-wah). These great, long, white roots shall shoot forth one to the north and one to the south and one to the east and one to the west, and we shall place on the top of it Oh-donyonh (an eagle) which has great power of long vision, and we shall transact all our business beneath the shade of this great tree. The meaning of planting this great tree, Skarehhehsegowah, is to symbolize

Ka-yah-ne-renh-ko-wa, which means Great Peace, and Jo-deh-ra-ken-rah-ke-wah, meaning Good Tidings of Peace and Power. The nations of the earth shall see it and shall accept and follow the roots and shall follow them to the tree and when they arrive here you shall receive them and shall seat them in the midst of your confederacy. The object of placing an eagle, Skadjíenă', on the top of the great, tall tree is that it may watch the roots which extend to the north and to the south and to the east and to the west, and whose duty shall be to discover if any evil is approaching your confederacy, and he shall scream loudly and give the alarm and all the nations of the confederacy at once shall heed the alarm and come to the rescue."

Then Dekanahwideh again said: "We shall now combine our individual power into one great power which is this confederacy and we shall therefore symbolize the union of these powers by each nation contributing one arrow, which we shall tie up together in a bundle which, when it is made and completely tied together, no one can bend or break."

Then Dekanahwideh further said: "We have now completed this union by securing one arrow from each nation. It is not good that one should be lacking or taken from the bundle, for it would weaken our power and it would be still worse if two arrows were taken from the bundle. And if three arrows were taken any one could break the remaining arrows in the bundle."

Then Dekanahwideh continued his address and said: "We shall tie this bundle of arrows together with deer sinew which is strong, durable and lasting and then also this institution shall be strong and unchangeable. This bundle of arrows signifies that all the lords and all the warriors and all the women of the Confederacy have become united as one person."

Then Dekanahwideh again said: "We have now completed binding this bundle of arrows and we shall leave it beside the great tree (Skareh-hehsegowah) and beside the Confederate Council fire of Thadodahho."

Then Dekanahwideh said: "We have now completed our power so that we the Five Nations' Confederacy shall in the future have one body, one head and one heart."

Then he (Dekanahwideh) further said: "If any evil should befall us in the future, we shall stand or fall united as one man."

Then Dekanahwideh said: "You lords shall be symbolized as trees of the Five Confederate Nations. We therefore bind ourselves together by taking hold of each other's hands firmly and forming a circle so strong that if a tree shall fall prostrate upon it, it could neither shake nor break it, and thus our people and our grandchildren shall remain in the circle in security, peace and happiness. And if any lord who is crowned with the emblem of deer's horns shall break through this circle of unity, his horns shall become fastened in the circle, and if he persists after warning from the chief matron, he shall go through it without his horns and the horns shall remain in the circle, and when he has passed through the circle, he shall no longer be lord, but shall be as an ordinary warrior and shall not be further qualified to fill any office."

Then Dekanahwideh further said: "We have now completed everything in connection with the matter of Peace and Power, and it remains only for us to consider and adopt some measure as to what we shall do with reference to the disposal of the weapons of war which we have taken from our people."

Then the lords considered the latter and decided that the best way which they could adopt with reference to the disposal of the weapons would be to uproot the great tall tree which they had planted and in uprooting the tree a chasm would form so deep that it would come or reach the swift current of the waters under it, into which the weapons of war would be thrown, and they would be borne and swept away forever by the current so that their grandchildren would never see them again. And they then uprooted the great tree and they cast into the chasm all manner of weapons of war which their people had been in the custom of using, and they then replaced the tree in its original position.

Then Dekanahwideh further continued and said: "We have completed clearing away all manner of weapons from the paths of our people."

Then Dekanahwideh continued and said: "We have still one matter left to be considered and that is with reference to the hunting grounds of our people from which they derive their living."

They, the lords, said with reference to this matter: "We shall now do this: We shall only have one dish (or bowl) in which will be placed one beaver's tail and we shall all have coequal right to it, and there shall be no knife in it, for if there be a knife in it, there would be danger that it might cut some one and blood would thereby be shed." (This one dish or bowl signifies that they will make their hunting grounds one common tract and all have a coequal right to hunt within it. The knife being prohibited from being placed into the dish or bowl signifies that all danger would be removed from shedding blood by the people of these different nations of the confederacy caused by differences of the right of the hunting grounds.)

Then Dekanahwideh continued and said: "We have now accomplished and completed forming the great Confederacy of the Five Nations together with adopting rules and regulations in connection therewith."

Then he, Dekanahwideh, continued and said: "I will now leave all matters in the hands of your lords and you are to work and carry out the principles of all that I have just laid before you for the welfare of your people and others, and I now place the power in your hands and to add to the rules and regulations whenever necessary and I now charge each of you lords that you must never seriously disagree among yourselves. You are all of equal standing and of equal power, and if you seriously disagree the consequences will be most serious and this disagreement will cause you to disregard each other, and while you are quarreling with each other, the white panther (the fire dragon of discord) will come

and take your rights and privileges away. Then your grandchildren will suffer and be reduced to poverty and disgrace.". . .

Then Dekanahwideh said: "I shall now therefore charge each of your lords, that your skin be of the thickness of seven spreads of the hands (from end of thumb to the end of the great finger) so that no matter how sharp a cutting instrument may be used it will not penetrate the thickness of your skin. (The meaning of the great thickness of your skins is patience and forbearance, so that no matter what nature of question or business may come before you, no matter how sharp or aggravating it may be, it will not penetrate to your skins, but you will forbear with great patience and good will in all your deliberations and never disgrace yourselves by becoming angry.) You lords shall always be guided in all your councils and deliberations by the Good Tidings of Peace and Power."

Then Dekanahwideh said: "Now, you lords of the different nations of the confederacy, I charge you to cultivate the good feeling of friendship, love and honor amongst yourselves. I have now fulfilled my duty in assisting you in the establishment and organization of this great confederacy, and if this confederation is carefully guarded it shall continue and endure from generation to generation and as long as the sun shines. I shall now, therefore, go home, conceal and cover myself with bark and there shall none other be called by my name."

Then Dekanahwideh further continued and said: "If at any time through the negligence and carelessness of the lords, they fail to carry out the principles of the Good Tidings of Peace and Power and the rules and regulations of the confederacy and the people are reduced to poverty and great suffering, I will return."

Then Dekanahwideh said: "And it shall so happen that when you hear my name mentioned disrespectfully without reason or just cause, but spoken in levity, you shall then know that you are on the verge of trouble and sorrow. And it shall be that the only time when it shall be proper for my name to be mentioned is when the condolence ceremonies are being performed or when the Good Tidings of Peace and Power which I have established and organized are being discussed or rehearsed."

Then the lords (Ro-de-ya-ner-shoh) said: "We shall begin to work and carry out the instructions which you, Dekanahwideh, have laid before us."

Then they said: "We shall therefore begin first with the Confederate Council of the Five Nations and other nations who shall accept and come under the Great Law of the confederacy will become as props, supports of the long house.

"The pure white wampum strings shall be the token or emblem of the council fire, and it shall be that when the fire keepers shall open the council, he shall pick up this string of wampum and hold it on his hand while he is offering thanksgiving to the Great Ruler and opening the council." And then they also said: "That while the council is in session the strings of the white wampum should be placed conspicuously in their midst and when they should adjourn then, the fire keepers should pick up these strings of wampum again, offer thanksgiving, close the council and all business in connection with the council should then be adjourned."

Then they said: "We shall now establish as a custom that when our annual Confederate Council shall meet we shall smoke the pipe of peace."

And they, the lords, then said: "We shall now proceed to define the obligations and position of the lords of the Confederacy as follows:

"If a lord is found guilty of wilful murder, he shall be deposed without the warning (as shall be provided for later on) by the lords of the confederacy, and his horns (emblem of power) shall be handed back to the chief matron of his family and clan.

"If a lord is guilty of rape he shall be deposed without the usual warning by the lords of the confederacy, and his horns (the emblem of power) shall be handed back to the chief matron of his family and clan.

"If a lord is found guilty of theft, he shall be deposed without the usual warning by the lords of the confederacy and his horns . . . shall be handed back to the chief matron of his family and clan.

"If a lord is guilty of unwarrantably opposing the object of decisions of the council and in that his own erroneous will in these matters be carried out, he shall be approached and admonished by the chief matron of his family and clan to desist from such evil practices and she shall urge him to come back and act in harmony with his brother lords.

"If the lord refuses to comply with the request of the chief matron of his family and clan and still persists in his evil practices of unwarrantably opposing his brother lords, then a warrior of his family and clan will also approach him and admonish him to desist from pursuing his evil course.

"If the lord still refuses to listen and obey, then the chief matron and warrior shall go together to the warrior and they shall inform him that they have admonished their lord and he refused to obey. Then the chief warrior will arise and go there to the lord and will say to him: 'Your nephew and niece have admonished you to desist from your evil course, and you have refused to obey.' Then the chief warrior will say: 'I will now admonish you for the last time and if you continue to resist, refuse to accede and disobey this request, then your duties as lord of our family and clan will cease, and I shall take the deer's horns from off your head, and with a broad edged stone axe I shall cut down the tree' (meaning that he shall be deposed from his position as lord or chief of the confederacy). Then, if the lord merits dismissal, the chief warrior shall hand back the deer's horns . . . of the deposed lord to the chief matron of the family or clan."

Whenever it occurs that a lord is thus deposed, then the chief matron shall select and appoint another warrior of her family or clan and crown him with the deer's horns and thus a new lord shall be created in the place of the one deposed.

The lords of each of the confederate nations shall have one assistant and their duty, each of them, shall be to carry messages through the forests between our settlements and also in the absence of the lord through illness or any other impediment he shall be deputed by him (his lord) to act in his place in council.

The lords then said: "We have now completed defining the obligations and positions of a lord (Royaner) and therefore in accordance with the custom which we now have established, it shall be that when a lord is deposed and the deer's horns . . . are taken from him, he shall no longer be allowed to sit in council or even hold an office again."

Then the lords continued and said: "What shall we do in case some of us lords are removed by sudden death and in whom so much dependence is placed?"

"In such case . . . the chief matron and the warriors of the family and clan of the deceased lord, shall nominate another lord from the warriors of the family and clan of the dead lord to succeed him, then the matter will be submitted to the brother lords and if they (the brother lords) confirm the nomination, then the matter will be further submitted to their cousin lords and if they also confirm the nomination, then the candidate shall be qualified to be raised by the condolence ceremony (Honda nas)."

Then the lords continued and said: "In case the family and clan in which a lordship title is vested shall become extinct, this shall be done: It shall then be transferred and vested in the hands of the confederate lords and they will consider the matter and nominate and appoint a successor from any family of the brother lords of the deceased lord, and the lords may in their discretion vest the said lordship title in some family, and such title will remain in that family so long as the lords are satisfied.

"If ever it should occur that the chief matron in a family or clan in which a lordship title is vested should be removed by death and leave female infants who, owing to their infancy can not nominate a candidate to bear their lordship title, then the lords (of the same nation) at their pleasure may appoint an adult female of a sister family who shall make a temporary appointment, shall come before the lords and request that the lordship title be restored to them, then the lords must obtain the title and restore it accordingly."

Then the lords continued and said: "We now have completed laying the foundation of our rules and methods (Kayanehrenokowa) and we will now proceed to follow and carry out the working of these rules and methods of the confederacy, and the local affairs of our respective settlements, and whenever we discover a warrior who is wise and trustworthy and who will render his services for the benefit of the people and thus aid the lords of the confederacy, we will claim him into our midst and confer upon him the title of 'He has sprung up as a Pine Tree' (Eh-ka-neh-do-deh) and his title shall only last during his lifetime and shall not be hereditary and at his death it shall die with him." . . .

QUESTIONS FOR CONSIDERATION

1. What are the rights and duties of the chiefs as described in the laws of the confederacy?

2. What are the meanings and purposes of the emblems, metaphors, and rituals conveyed in the laws of the confederacy?

3. Compare the Constitution of the United States with that of the Iroquois reprinted here. Evaluate the evidence suggesting that the former was modeled on the latter.

PICTURE ESSAY

Early American Cities, Settlements, and Centers

EUROPEAN COLONISTS OFTEN DEPICTED the Indians they encountered in North America as "wandering savages," hunting people who lacked permanent settlements. Americans inherited this view, and the U.S. government incorporated it into its Indian policies, which, throughout the nineteenth century, operated on the conviction that Indians must be taught to farm and live in one place if they were ever to become "civilized." The notion that Indians were nomads who lived in small hunting bands with no fixed homes helped justify their dispossession; Euro-Americans needed the land for agriculture and they had every right to take it because the Indians were not making good use of it anyway.

Throughout North America, Indian people lived in small villages *and* hunted. In some areas, Indians were nomadic and followed game in small hunting bands. But centuries before Europeans arrived, most Indians were farmers, and some inhabited towns and structures that were as large as those of contemporary Europeans and colonists. Southwestern Indian peoples constructed multistory apartment buildings; Mississippian societies erected towns and temples on earthen mounds; Iroquoian people lived in towns of multifamily longhouses surrounded by palisades and cornfields. Arriving in the wake of Indian losses to epidemic diseases only recently introduced by explorers and colonists, Europeans often saw mere traces of the civilizations that had existed in North America. On the basis of these impressions, history books portrayed Indian people only as hunters and village dwellers, rarely as farmers and city dwellers.

As the illustrations here indicate, there was an "urban America" long before Europeans arrived—not the kind of crowded metropolitan sprawl we associate with cities today, but important centers of population, ritual, and exchange nonetheless. Archaeologist Stephen Lekson describes North America in the eleventh century as "a continent of cities, big and small."[70] The ruins and remains of some of these places provide clues to American Indian worlds and experiences that must have been very different from those described by most European observers and most American historians.

Pueblo Bonito ("Beautiful Town"; Figure 1.1) was the largest of the "great houses" built in Chaco Canyon. A planned, multistoried structure, it was laid out as a giant D-shaped amphitheater around a central plaza covering three acres and linked to numerous outlying settlements. At its height it contained four stories, and between 650 and 800 rooms, although not all or even most of these were residences. It also contained three great kivas, and thirty-three smaller kivas, and

◆ **Figure 1.1 The Ruins of Pueblo Bonito**
Chris Selby/age fotostock/SuperStock.

its main importance may have been as a ceremonial center. The walls were constructed of stones and filled with rubble; thousands of wooden roof beams were made from logs carried from almost fifty miles away. Ring-dated beams indicate that Pueblo Bonito was built between about A.D. 900 and 1085. Pueblo Bonito has intrigued archaeologists for years and scholars still try to understand its economic and spiritual significance in the Ancestral Pueblo world.

At Mesa Verde in southeastern Colorado, people were living in many small villages on top of the mesa as early as A.D. 700. As the villages increased in size, the inhabitants developed more sophisticated structures and building techniques. The largest Mesa Verde town was at Yellow Jacket in southwestern Colorado: twelve hundred rooms, twenty towers, and two hundred kivas, and it may have housed 2,500 people.[71] By 1150, most of the inhabitants of Mesa Verde were living in large cliff houses constructed within the huge caves in the canyon walls, which provided security against attack. Cliff Palace (Figure 1.2) was the largest cliff dwelling in the area, with more than two hundred rooms and twenty-three kivas, but there may have been between five hundred and one thousand cliff houses and as many as seven thousand people at Mesa Verde during its peak in the mid-thirteenth century.[72]

◆ Figure 1.2 **Cliff Palace at Mesa Verde**
George H.H. Huey/age fotostock/SuperStock.

At its height between A.D. 1050 and 1250, Cahokia (as rendered in Figure 1.3, a later painter's depiction of the city) covered two thousand acres and was the largest city north of Mexico, with a population numbering at least 10,000 and perhaps as many as 30,000 residents. (By contrast, Philadelphia, the largest city in colonial North America, had a population of only 23,000 as late as 1763.) Cahokia was a city of ceremonial pyramids, open plazas, extensive cornfields, satellite villages, and suburbs. The rectangular field with two poles in the middle of the plaza was a ball court. The circle of posts at the far left — known as "Woodhenge" to archaeologists — seems to have been a calendric device that allowed priests to predict the coming of the solstices and equinoxes and to predict the correct timing for planting and ceremonies. The Cahokia site has been eroded over the years by farming, highways, and building developments, but impressive mounds remain at Cahokia State Park as testimony to the metropolis that once thrived there.

When English colonists first set foot in North America, they saw little sign of the great mound-building cultures that had flourished before contact, but they did see organized Native communities. John White's 1585 painting of the Algonquian

◆ **Figure 1.3 Cahokia Mounds, c. A.D. 1150–1200**
Cahokia Mounds State Historic Site. Painting of imagined reconstruction by William R. Iseminger.

village of Secoton in Virginia (Figure 1.4) is in the form of a town plan, showing the various purposes and functions of the buildings and spaces and leading the viewer up the "main street" from foreground to background. The multifamily houses are constructed of saplings bent over and covered with bark and woven mats that could be removed to let in air and light. The inhabitants depended on corn and practiced field rotation (note the three fields of corn at different stages of growth at the right of the picture — "rype corne," "greene corne," and "corne newly sprung") but supplemented their diet with hunting. A fire burns at "the place of solemne prayer" while, across the main street, a ritual is in progress. White's English viewers would have recognized many similarities with English towns and fields. It is possible that White's *Indian Village* was a composite painting, depicting various aspects of Indian life.

The Iroquois or Hodenosaunee — the "People of the Longhouse" — tended to build their villages on high ground in forest clearings, with fields surrounding the village. Some settlements were quite small, no more than hamlets with several houses, but others were large towns with a hundred or more houses. The village

◆ Figure 1.4 **John White,** *Indian Village of Secoton* **(1585)**
© The Trustees of the British Museum/Art Resource, NY.

◆ Figure 1.5 **Iroquois Longhouse**
Stock Montage/Getty Images.

might contain smaller houses for one or two families but the characteristic structure was a multifamily longhouse, a log structure with elm wood poles covered with elm bark (Figure 1.5). Longhouses stood 15 to 20 feet high, about 20 feet wide, and generally between 50 and 150 feet long, although sometimes much longer. Smoke holes along the center of the roof provided light and ventilation for hearth fires; compartments with raised platforms along the inside walls provided sleeping space for individual families. Members of a single matrilineal clan inhabited the longhouse, along with the women's husbands, who belonged to different clans. The Iroquois moved their villages every ten or twenty years because of soil and resources depletion.

In 1664 when the Dutch surrendered New Netherland (New York) to the English, the population of the Dutch colony was fewer than 10,000 people. With as many as fifty people inhabiting a single longhouse, an Iroquois town with many longhouses was a substantial settlement by the standards of the time.

QUESTIONS FOR CONSIDERATION

1. What do these images of Indian towns and sites reveal about how the inhabitants lived in relation to their environment? About how they organized their space and their societies? About their religious obligations, economic activities, and needs for defense?

2. Why, and with what effects, did white Americans tend to refer to all Indian settlements, regardless of their size, as villages? What are the differences between a village, a town, and a city?

REFERENCES

1. Richard N. Current, T. Harry Williams, and Alan Brinkley, *American History: A Survey,* quoted in Alvin M. Josephy Jr., ed., *America in 1492: The World of the Indian Peoples before the Arrival of Columbus* (New York: Alfred A. Knopf, 1992), 6, and (from the 1983 edition) Frederick E. Hoxie, "The Indians versus the Textbooks: Is There Any Way Out?" *Perspectives* 23 (April 1985), 19; Alan Brinkley, *American History: A Survey,* 9th ed. (New York: McGraw-Hill, 1995), 1–5.

2. Charles C. Mann, *1491: New Revelations of the Americas before Columbus* (New York: Alfred A. Knopf, 2005).

3. Brian Fagan, *The First North Americans: An Archaeological Journey* (London: Thames and Hudson, 2011), 7; Robert S. McPherson, *Viewing the Ancestors: Perceptions of the Anaasázi, Mokwič, and Hisatsinom* (Norman: University of Oklahoma Press, 2014).

4. William M. Denevan, "The Pristine Myth: The Landscape of the Americas in 1492," *Annals of the Association of American Geographers* 82 (September 1992), 369–85.

5. John Noble Wilford, "Human Presence in Americas Is Pushed Back a Millennium," *New York Times,* February 11, 1997.

6. Stephen Lekson, *A History of the Ancient Southwest* (Santa Fe: School for Advanced Research Press, 2008), 28.

7. Dennis J. Stanford and Bruce A. Bradley, *Across Atlantic Ice: The Origins of America's Clovis Culture* (Berkeley: University of California Press, 2012).

8. Marc Kaufman, "Human Traces Found to Be Oldest in N. America," *Washington Post,* April 4, 2008; Michael R. Waters, et al., "The Buttermilk Creek Complex and the Origins of Clovis," *Science* 331 (March 25, 2011), 1599–1603. Mann, *1491,* 173.

9. Raymond D. Fogelson, "A Final Look and Glance at the Bearing of Bering Straits on Native American History," D'Arcy McNickle Center for the History of the American Indian, *Occasional Papers in Curriculum Series,* no. 5 (1987), 247.

10. Vine Deloria Jr., *Red Earth, White Lies: Native Americans and the Myth of Scientific Fact* (New York: Scribner, 1995), chap. 4; Joseph Marshall III, *On Behalf of the Wolf and the First Peoples* (Santa Fe: Red Crane Books, 1995), 207.

11. David Hurst Thomas, *Skull Wars: Kennewick Man, Archaeology, and the Battle for Native American Identity* (New York: Basic Books, 2000); James C. Chatters, *Ancient Encounters: Kennewick Man and the First Americans* (New York: Simon and Schuster, 2001).

12. Michael D. Lemonick and Andrea Dorfman, "Who Were the First Americans?" *Time,* March 13, 2006.

13. Suzan Shown Harjo, "Kennewick Man: The Greatest Show Unearthed," *Indian Country Today,* March 17, 2006.

14. Karl Butzer, "The Indian Legacy in the American Landscape," in Michael P. Conzen, ed., *The Making of the American Landscape* (Boston: Unwin Hyman, 1990), 27–28.

15. Brian Fagan, *Before California* (Walnut Creek, Calif.: AltaMira Press, 2003); Robert F. Heizer, ed., *California,* vol. 8 of *Handbook of North American Indians,* ed. William Sturtevant (Washington, D.C.: Smithsonian Institution Press, 1978); Lynn Gamble, *The Chumash World at European*

Contact: Power, Trade, and Feasting among Complex Hunter-Gatherers (Berkeley: University of California Press, 2008).

16. Richard D. Daugherty, "People of the Salmon," in Josephy, *America in 1492,* 54–55; Brian M. Fagan, *Ancient North America: The Archaeology of a Continent,* 3rd ed. (London: Thames and Hudson, 2000), 232–34; Kenneth M. Ames and Herbert D. G. Maschner, *Peoples of the Northwest Coast: Their Archaeology and Prehistory* (London: Thames and Hudson, 1999), 23, 83, 115, 127, 171.

17. Judith Roche and Meg McHutchinson, eds., *First Fish, First People: Salmon Tales of the North Pacific Rim* (Seattle: University of Washington Press, 1998); Robert Bringhurst, *A Story as Sharp as a Knife: The Classical Haida Mythtellers and Their World* (Vancouver: Douglas and McIntyre, 1999), 65, 120, 155, 288–89.

18. Fagan, *Ancient North America,* chap. 12.

19. Catherine S. Fowler and Don D. Fowler, eds., *The Great Basin: People and Places in Ancient Times* (Santa Fe: School for Advanced Research Press, 2008), 27.

20. George Frison, "Experimental Use of Clovis Weaponry and Tools on African Elephants," *American Antiquity* 54, no. 4 (1989), 766–84.

21. Cyclone Covey, trans. and ed., *Cabeza de Vaca's Adventures in the Unknown Interior of America* (Albuquerque: University of New Mexico Press, 1983), 81.

22. Quoted in James P. Ronda, ed., *Revealing America: Image and Imagination in the Exploration of North America* (New York: Simon and Schuster, 1996), 63.

23. T. Douglas Price and Anne Birgitte Gebauer, eds., *Last Hunters—First Farmers: New Perspectives on the Prehistoric Transition to Agriculture* (Santa Fe: School of American Research Press, 1995), 3, 6.

24. Suzanne K. Fish and Paul R. Fish, eds., *The Hohokam Millennium* (Santa Fe: School for Advanced Research Press, 2008).

25. David Grant Noble, ed., *In Search of Chaco: New Approaches to an Archaeological Enigma* (Santa Fe: School of American Research Press, 2004), 4, 23–31; Francis Jennings, *The Founders of America* (New York: W. W. Norton, 1993), 54 ("apartment building"); Brian Fagan, *Chaco Canyon: Archaeologists Explore the Lives of an Ancient Society* (New York: Oxford University Press, 2005), xi ("dance and chant"); Ruth M. Van Dyke, *The Chaco Experience: Landscape and Ideology at the Center Place* (Santa Fe: School for Advanced Research Press, 2007), 21.

26. Fagan, *Chaco Canyon,* chaps. 10–11.

27. Patricia L. Crown and W. Jeffrey Hurst, "Evidence of Cacao Use in the Prehispanic American Southwest," *PNAS (Proceedings of the National Academy of Sciences)* 106 (February 2009), 2110–13.

28. Francis Jennings, *The Founders of America* (New York: W. W. Norton, 1993), 54; David Grant Noble, ed., *The Mesa Verde World: Explorations in Ancestral Pueblo Archaeology* (Santa Fe: School of American Research Press, 2006).

29. Deborah L. Nichols and Patricia L. Crown, eds., *Social Violence in the Prehispanic American Southwest* (Tucson: University

of Arizona Press, 2008); McPherson, *Viewing the Ancestors,* 35–41.

30. Paul Horgan, *Great River: The Rio Grande in North American History* (Hanover, N.H.: University Press of New England, 1984), 22.

31. McPherson, *Viewing the Ancestors,* chap. 3.

32. Timothy A. Kohler, Mark D. Varien, and Aaron M. Wright, eds., *Leaving Mesa Verde: Peril and Change in the Thirteenth-Century Southwest* (Tucson: University of Arizona Press, 2010).

33. Deni J. Seymour, ed., *From the Land of Ever Winter to the American Southwest: Athapaskan Migrations, Mobility, and Ethnogenesis* (Salt Lake City: University of Utah Press, 2012), provides a variety of up-to-date essays in a variety of disciplines about how, when, and where the Navajos and Apaches arrived in the Southwest.

34. Fagan, *Chaco Canyon,* 99–100, 198–99.

35. Lekson, *History of the Ancient Southwest,* 20.

36. Quoted in Stephen Plog, *Ancient Peoples of the American Southwest* (London: Thames and Hudson, 1997), 170–71.

37. Bruce D. Smith, *Rivers of Change: Essays on Early Agriculture in Eastern North America* (Washington, D.C.: Smithsonian Institution Press, 1992); Smith, "Seed Plant Domestication in Eastern North America," in Price and Gebauer, eds., *Last Hunters—First Farmers,* 193–213.

38. R. Douglas Hurt, *Indian Agriculture in America: Prehistory to the Present* (Lawrence: University Press of Kansas, 1987), 11.

39. Quoted in Richard Wolkomir, "Bringing Ancient Ways to Our Farmers' Fields," *Winds of Change,* Summer 1996, 30.

40. Quoted in Ronda, *Revealing America,* 36.

41. Hurt, *Indian Agriculture in America,* 34.

42. Joe W. Saunders et al., "A Mound Complex in Louisiana at 5400–5000 Years before the Present," *Science* 277 (September 1997), 1796–99.

43. *Through Indian Eyes* (New York: Reader's Digest, 1995), 31.

44. Lekson, *History of the Ancient Southwest,* 114.

45. Timothy R. Pauketat, *Ancient Cahokia and the Mississippians* (Cambridge: Cambridge University Press, 2004), 92–93.

46. Roger G. Kennedy, *Hidden Cities: The Discovery and Loss of Ancient North American Civilization* (New York: Penguin, 1994), 12.

47. Timothy R. Pauketat, *Cahokia: Ancient America's Great City on the Mississippi* (New York: Viking Penguin, 2009).

48. Jerald T. Milanich, *Florida's Indians from Ancient Times to the Present* (Gainesville: University Press of Florida, 1998), 74.

49. Hurt, *Indian Agriculture in America,* 27.

50. Lekson, *History of the Ancient Southwest,* 189.

51. Lynda Norene Shaffer, *Native Americans before 1492: The Moundbuilding Centers of the Eastern Woodlands* (Armonk, N.Y.: M. E. Sharpe, 1992), 95.

52. John Stands In Timber and Margot Liberty, *Cheyenne Memories* (Lincoln: University of Nebraska Press, 1972), 40.

53. Quoted in Christopher L. Miller, *Prophetic Worlds: Indians and Whites on the Columbia Plateau* (New Brunswick, N.J.: Rutgers University Press, 1985), title page.

54. Julie Cruikshank, "Oral History, Narrative Strategies, and Native American Historiography: Perspectives from the Yukon Territory, Canada," in Nancy Shoemaker, ed., *Clearing a Path: Theorizing the Past in Native American Studies* (New York: Routledge, 2002), 3–27, 13.

55. Vine Deloria Jr. and Clifford Lytle, *The Nations Within: The Past and Future of American Indian Sovereignty* (New York: Pantheon, 1984), 8.

56. Leslie Marmon Silko, *Yellow Woman and a Beauty of the Spirit: Essays on Native American Life Today* (New York: Simon and Schuster, 1996), 30–37.

57. Keith H. Basso, *Wisdom Sits in Places: Landscape and Language among the Western Apache* (Albuquerque: University of New Mexico Press, 1996), 34.

58. Paul G. Zolbrod, *Diné bahane´: The Navajo Creation Story* (Albuquerque: University of New Mexico Press, 1984), 19.

59. Aileen O'Bryan, *The Diné: Origin Myths of the Navaho Indians,* Bureau of American Ethnology, Bulletin 163 (Washington, D.C.: U.S. Government Printing Office, 1956), vii.

60. Dean R. Snow, *The Iroquois* (Cambridge, Mass.: Blackwell, 1994), 4.

61. Arthur C. Parker, *The Constitution of the Five Nations or the Iroquois Book of the Great Law* (Albany: New York State Museum Bulletin, No. 184, 1916), 61; Barbara A. Mann and Jerry L. Fields, "A Sign in the Sky: Dating the League of the Haudenosaunee," *American Indian Culture and Research Journal* 21, no. 2 (1997), 105–63; Snow, *The Iroquois,* 60.

62. Quoted in Matthew Dennis, *Cultivating a Landscape of Peace: Iroquois-European Encounters in Seventeenth-Century America* (Ithaca, N.Y.: Cornell University Press, 1993), 76.

63. Parker, *Constitution of the Five Nations,* 17.

64. Leon Shenandoah, foreword to *White Roots of Peace: The Iroquois Book of Life,* by Paul Wallace (Santa Fe: Clear Light Publishers, 1994), 13.

65. Quoted in Daniel K. Richter, *The Ordeal of the Longhouse: The Peoples of the Iroquois League in the Era of European Colonization* (Chapel Hill: University of North Carolina Press, 1992), 39.

66. Richter, *Ordeal of the Longhouse,* 31.

67. Milo M. Quaife, ed., *John Long's Voyages and Travels in the Years 1768–1788* (Chicago: R. R. Donnelley, 1922), 18.

68. Canasatego's speech is reprinted in Colin G. Calloway, ed., *The World Turned Upside Down: Indian Voices from Early America* (Boston: Bedford Books, 1994), 104; Franklin's opinion is quoted in Bruce E. Johansen, *Forgotten Founders: Benjamin Franklin, the Iroquois, and the Rationale for the American Revolution* (Ipswich, Mass.: Gambit, 1982), 66.

69. Parker, *Constitution of the Five Nations,* 61–63.

70. Lekson, *History of the Ancient Southwest,* 125.

71. Lekson, *History of the Ancient Southwest,* 160–61, 166; Fagan, *The First North Americans,* 196.

72. Stuart J. Fiedel, *Prehistory of the Americas* (Cambridge: Cambridge University Press, 1987), 219.

SUGGESTED READINGS

Ames, Kenneth M., and Herbert D. G. Maschner. *Peoples of the Northwest Coast: Their Archaeology and Prehistory.* London: Thames and Hudson, 1999.

Brose, David S. *Ancient Art of the American Woodland Indians.* New York: Abrams, 1985.

Coe, Michael, Dean Snow, and Elizabeth Benson. *Atlas of Ancient America.* New York: Facts on File, 1986.

Cordell, Linda S. *Ancient Pueblo Peoples.* Washington, D.C.: Smithsonian, 1994.

Dillehay, Thomas D. *The Settlement of the Americas: A New Prehistory.* New York: Basic Books, 2000.

Fagan, Brian M. *Ancient North America: The Archaeology of a Continent.* 4th ed. London: Thames and Hudson, 2005.

———. *Chaco Canyon: Archaeologists Explore the Lives of an Ancient Society.* New York: Oxford University Press, 2005.

———. *The First North Americans: An Archaeological Journey.* London: Thames and Hudson, 2011.

Fenton, William N. *The Great Law and the Longhouse: A Political History of the Iroquois Confederacy.* Norman: University of Oklahoma Press, 1998.

———, ed. *Parker on the Iroquois: Iroquois Uses of Maize and Other Food Plants, the Code of Handsome Lake, the Seneca Prophet, the Constitution of the Five Nations, by Arthur C. Parker.* Syracuse: Syracuse University Press, 1968.

Fiedel, Stuart. *Prehistory of the Americas.* Cambridge: Cambridge University Press, 1987.

Fish, Suzanne K., and Paul R. Fish, eds. *The Hohokam Millennium.* Santa Fe: School for Advanced Research Press, 2008.

Fowler, Catherine S., and Don D. Fowler, eds. *The Great Basin: People and Places in Ancient Times.* Santa Fe: School for Advanced Research Press, 2008.

Goodman, James M. *The Navajo Atlas: Environments, Resources, People, and History of the Diné Bikeyah.* Norman: University of Oklahoma Press, 1982.

Grinde, Donald A., Jr., and Bruce E. Johansen, eds. *Exemplar of Liberty: Native America and the Evolution of Democracy.* Los Angeles: UCLA American Indian Studies Center, 1991.

Haynes, Gary. *The Early Settlement of North America: The Clovis Era.* Cambridge: Cambridge University Press, 2002.

Iverson, Peter. *The Navajos.* New York: Chelsea House, 1990.

Jennings, Jesse D. *Prehistory of North America.* Mountain View, Calif.: Mayfield, 1989.

Josephy, Alvin M., Jr., ed. *America in 1492: The World of the Indian Peoples before the Arrival of Columbus.* New York: Alfred A. Knopf, 1992.

Kennedy, Roger G. *Hidden Cities: The Discovery and Loss of Ancient North American Civilization.* New York: Penguin, 1994.

Kohler, Timothy A., Mark D. Varien, and Aaron M. Wright, eds., *Leaving Mesa Verde: Peril and Change in the Thirteenth-Century Southwest.* Tucson: University of Arizona Press, 2010.

Kopper, Philip. *The Smithsonian Book of North American Indians: Before the Coming of the Europeans.* Washington, D.C.: Smithsonian, 1986.

Lekson, Stephen. *A History of the Ancient Southwest.* Santa Fe: School for Advanced Research Press, 2008.

Lyons, Oren, et al. *Exiled in the Land of the Free: Democracy, Indian Nations, and the U.S. Constitution.* Santa Fe: Clear Light Publishers, 1992.

Mann, Charles C. *1491: New Revelations of the Americas before Columbus.* New York: Alfred A. Knopf, 2005.

Matthews, Washington, comp. and trans. *Navaho Legends.* 1897. Reprint, Salt Lake City: University of Utah Press, 1994.

McPherson, Robert S. *Viewing the Ancestors: Perceptions of the Anaasázi, Mokwič, and Hisatsinom.* Norman: University of Oklahoma Press, 2014.

Milner, George R. *The Moundbuilders: Ancient Peoples of Eastern North America.* London: Thames and Hudson, 2004.

Morgan, Lewis Henry. *League of the Hodenosaunee, or Iroquois.* Rochester, N.Y.: Sage and Brother, 1851.

Nabokov, Peter. *Where the Lightning Strikes: The Lives of American Indian Sacred Places.* New York: Viking, 2006.

Noble, David Grant, ed. *In Search of Chaco: New Approaches to an Archaeological Enigma.* Santa Fe: School of American Research Press, 2004.

———, ed. *The Mesa Verde World: Explorations in Ancestral Pueblo Archaeology.* Santa Fe: School of American Research Press, 2006.

Pauketat, Timothy R. *Cahokia: Ancient America's Great City on the Mississippi.* New York: Viking Penguin, 2009.

Plog, Stephen. *Ancient Peoples of the American Southwest.* London: Thames and Hudson, 1997.

Shaffer, Lynda Norene. *Native Americans before 1492: The Moundbuilding Centers of the Eastern Woodlands.* Armonk, N.Y.: M. E. Sharpe, 1992.

Silko, Leslie Marmon. *Yellow Woman and a Beauty of the Spirit: Essays on Native American Life Today.* New York: Simon and Schuster, 1996.

Snow, Dean R. *The Iroquois.* Oxford: Blackwell, 1994.

Stuart, David E. *Anasazi America.* Albuquerque: University of New Mexico Press, 2000.

Thomas, David Hurst. *Exploring Native North America.* New York: Oxford University Press, 2000.

Van Dyke, Ruth M. *The Chaco Experience: Landscape and Ideology at the Center Place.* Santa Fe: School for Advanced Research Press, 2007.

Wallace, Paul. *White Roots of Peace: The Iroquois Book of Life.* Santa Fe: Clear Light Publishers, 1994.

Young, Biloine Whiting, and Melvin L. Fowler. *Cahokia: The Great Native American Metropolis.* Urbana: University of Illinois Press, 2000.

Zolbrod, Paul G. *Diné bahané: The Navajo Creation Story.* Albuquerque: University of New Mexico Press, 1984.

2

The Invasions of America

1492–1680

FOCUS QUESTIONS

1. Why did Europeans travel to North America?

2. In what ways, if any, did the Spanish, French, and English differ in their dealings with Indian peoples?

3. What effects did European diseases have on Indian communities and on the history of the continent?

FIRST CONTACTS AND MUTUAL APPRAISALS

SOME PEOPLE ARGUE THAT AFRICANS from the Nile Delta, Buddhist monks from Japan, European mariners, Celtic priests, or even visitors from outer space got to America long before Columbus. Viking sagas and archaeological evidence confirm that Scandinavian seafarers made contact with Native people — Skraelings, the Vikings called them — in Greenland, Newfoundland, and Labrador around A.D. 1000. Relations with the Natives broke down in violence, and the Viking colonies were short-lived. But at the end of the fifteenth century, Europe broke its bounds and embarked on a program of expansion overseas that reached into America, Asia, Africa, and Australia. In America, this expansion entailed the defeat and dispossession of the Native inhabitants over almost four centuries of coercion and conflict. It also witnessed widespread and sometimes violent competition between rival European powers.

In the seventeenth century, Spanish, French, Dutch, Swedish, and English colonizers all contended for a foothold on the American continent. European immigrants who encroached on Indian country in the seventeenth and eighteenth centuries included Finns, Germans, Scots, Irish, and many others; and Russian expansion eastward, which began in Siberia in the sixteenth and seventeenth centuries, brought traders and missionaries to Alaska and northern California in the eighteenth and nineteenth centuries (Map 2.1). But Spain, France, and Britain came to dominate the struggle for hegemony and had the most enduring effects on Indian America.

European colonists endeavored to create societies that mirrored those they had left behind, giving them names that evoked home — New Spain, New Mexico, New France, New England, Nova Scotia, New Netherlands — but the communities that emerged were quite different from their European counterparts. At the same time, the invasion of European peoples, plants, products, and plagues transformed America, creating what historian James Merrell aptly described as "a new world" for Indian peoples.[1]

Native America through the European Lens

The first Europeans to arrive in America brought germs, animals, plants, technologies, and concepts of land use and ownership that would forever change the face of America. They also brought attitudes and opinions about "primitive" people that would govern their relations with the Native peoples they encountered and established images of Indians that endured for centuries.

Because the recent development of the printing press had greatly increased the circulation of news and literature by the time of the first contacts between Indian and European people, Europeans soon had access to a variety of descriptions of the "New World" and the people who lived here. Some of these were favorable: Christopher Columbus described the first Indians he met as simple children of nature, timid, generous, and guileless. They were "very well formed, with handsome bodies and good faces" and went "as naked as their mothers bore them." They accepted whatever they were offered in trade and "gave of what they had very willingly." With an eye to what he saw in store for these people, the admiral reckoned they would make "good

1614	Dutch establish trading post on Hudson River near Albany, New York
1616–1619	Major epidemic among New England Indians
1620	Pilgrims establish Plymouth Colony
1622	Powhatan Indians go to war against English in Virginia
1625	The Dutch purchase Manhattan Island
1629	England charters the Massachusetts Bay Colony
1630s	20,000 English Puritans migrate to New England
1634–1649	Jesuit missionaries active in Huronia in present-day Ontario
1633–1634	Smallpox epidemic throughout the Northeast
1636–1637	Puritan war against the Pequots
1638	English terminate Pequot sovereignty in Treaty of Hartford
1640s	Mayhew family missionaries active on Martha's Vineyard
1644	Second Powhatan war against the English
1646–1675	John Eliot's missionary work in New England
1649	Iroquois destroy Huron villages in Beaver Wars
1670	Charlestown, South Carolina, founded
1671	Sieur de Saint Lusson and Claude Allouez lay claim to the whole interior of North America for France
1675–1676	King Philip's War in New England
1676	Bacon's Rebellion targets Indians in Virginia
1680	Pueblo War of Independence drives Spaniards from New Mexico
1681–1682	René-Robert Cavelier, Sieur de La Salle, travels down the Mississippi and claims the Mississippi valley for Louis XIV (Louisiana)

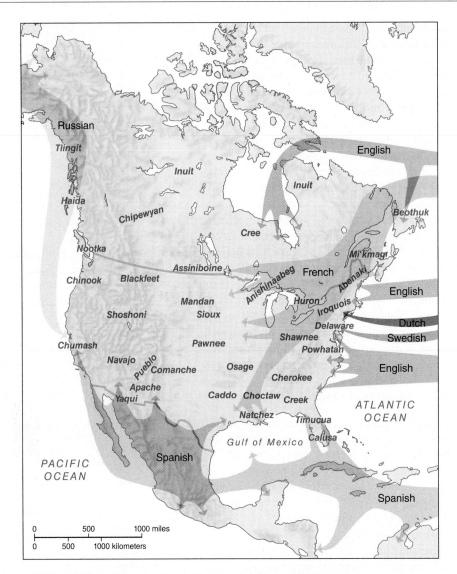

◆ **Map 2.1 European Invasions of Indian America, c. 1500–1800**
At different times in the course of the sixteenth, seventeenth, and eighteenth centuries, various major European nations penetrated North America. Other peoples—Finns, Scotch-Irish, Germans, African slaves—also pushed into the continent. Their intrusion set off ripple effects throughout Indian country, often affecting the lives of people who had never laid eyes on a European and generating migrations by Indian groups.

and intelligent servants" and "would become Christians very easily, for it seemed to me that they had no religion." The Indians were "very gentle and do not know what evil is."² Other observers spoke of the Indians' agility, health, dignity, and bravery. The image of Indians as "noble savages" and "simple children of nature" took a firm hold in the imagination of Europeans. At the same time, however, Columbus and others also reported stories of fierce cannibals, and the idea of Indians as "treacherous savages" and "dirty savages" became another common image. The very diversity in Native American life that the label "Indian" ignored presented Europeans with contradictions in what they found and thus produced conflicting sets of beliefs about Indians.

Inevitably, Europeans judged Indians by European values, social orders, and gender assumptions. They assessed them in terms of Western views of civilization, noting what Indians lacked rather than what they had achieved. By "civilization" Europeans usually meant social standards such as wearing "proper" clothing, speaking a language intelligible to their ears, living in "orderly" social and political structures, practicing a sedentary agricultural economy in which men, not women, did the farming, dwelling in permanent housing, and observing some form of Christianity. They saw that Indians had no sailing ships, printing presses, wheeled vehicles, stone arches, churches, iron tools, steel weapons, or guns, and they assumed that Indian men were lazy and Indian women were "drudges" because the women cultivated and harvested the crops. Based on their observations, most Europeans did not think they were displacing existing civilizations when they came to America.

For the most part, Indian people greeted the newcomers with cautious hospitality and goodwill. They seem to have been impressed by the Europeans' technology, particularly their ships, guns, and metal tools, but shocked by their appearance, language, and behavior. Europeans frequently claimed that Indians regarded them with awe, as godlike, but Indians regularly dismissed European pretensions to superiority and sometimes poked fun at Europeans' ineptitude in coping with their new environment. (See "A Mi'kmaq Questions French Civilization," pages 119–20.)

Even as European numbers increased, Natives and newcomers often found ways of coexisting and cooperating, adapting to each other's presence, and borrowing from what the other had to offer. Colonists learned to plant corn and adopted Native hunting and fishing techniques; Indians wrapped themselves in woolen blankets and cooked in metal pots. As each society labored for subsistence, they made use of the knowledge and goods of the other.

Enduring Images

Hospitality turned to hostility, however, when understanding failed to bridge the cultural gulf and Indians began to experience mistreatment at the hands of Europeans. As early as 1524, sailing from North Carolina to Newfoundland, the Florentine explorer Giovanni da Verrazzano found that Indians on the coast of Maine would not allow his crew ashore to trade; the Natives had already had unpleasant dealings with Europeans, perhaps Basque or Breton sailors and fishermen or a Portuguese expedition that had passed through the area the year before. It was not long before Indians and Europeans clashed. To Europeans, the Indians' hostility was proof of their savagery. Like later Americans, they invoked that savagery to justify their actions and continued assaults on Indian cultures.

Still, the notion of Indians as "noble savages" endured. From the journals of Columbus in 1492, through the writings of eighteenth-century philosophers like Jean-Jacques Rousseau, to modern movies, many non-Indians have portrayed Indians living lives of simplicity and purity as a contrast to their own societies, which they depict as aggressive and materialistic. The habit of viewing the diverse Native inhabitants of North America as a single collective category in mirror image of Western society has roots in the first contacts between Indian and European people and has persisted for more than five hundred years. Non-Indian images of Indians usually reveal more about how the image makers feel about themselves and their own society than they do about real Indian people.

COLUMBIAN EXCHANGES

In 1493 Columbus made his second voyage to Hispaniola (an island now divided between Haiti and the Dominican Republic). This time his purpose was colonization of the lands he had "discovered." He took with him seventeen ships, more than a thousand settlers, and a cargo that included horses, pigs, cattle, sheep, goats, chickens, dogs, seeds, and cuttings for fruit trees, wheat, and sugarcane. Columbus's cargo illustrated the many levels on which the European invasion of America occurred as animals, plants, insects, germs, and new technologies accompanied European peoples into Indian country. Even though this invasion was one-way, from Europe to America, an exchange was in fact taking shape. In time, American people, foods, and ideas spread across the Atlantic to permanently change the Old World, and Native American ways of life subtly influenced the European colonists. Contact between Europe and America initiated what historian Alfred Crosby termed "the Columbian exchange" between two worlds. The economic, environmental, and cultural reverberations of the exchange affected the subsequent histories of Europe, Africa, and Asia as well as America. New foods and plants, new sources of wealth, and new resources produced more trade networks and more activity along existing trade networks, which brought people, plants, and animals into contact. Europeans tasted chocolate and tobacco for the first time. Slave and trade routes brought America into contact with Africa. Areas of the world that were previously ecologically distinct became more alike; in place of separate worlds, a single new world emerged. This marked the beginning of globalization and shaped the world we know today.[3] Finally, interaction with Indian people contributed to transforming European colonists into Americans.

Changing New World Landscapes

Europeans entered a continent that bore the marks of thousands of years of human habitation and activity. As they moved inland, they continued to encounter settled or recently abandoned agricultural landscapes. Assisted by Indian guides and subsisting on Native food, "the pioneers at the head of the Euro-American advance followed the signposts of cleared fields and orchards that recorded the long experience of Native Americans in selecting good soils and managing local ecologies."[4] But Europeans began to alter the landscape in ways Native Americans never had. They brought new plants and crops — rice, wheat, barley, oats — and new grasses and weeds, along with fruits such as peaches and oranges. They introduced domesticated animals such as horses, sheep, goats, and pigs, which trod down grasses unaccustomed to pastoralism, trampled Indian cornfields, and drove away wild game. Their world, quite literally, changed before Indians' eyes as European colonists transformed the forest into farmland: "these English have gotten our land," declared a Narragansett chief only twenty years after the Pilgrims arrived in New England. "They with scythes cut down the grass, and with axes fell the trees; their cows and horses eat the grass, and their hogs spoil our clam banks."[5] In the Southeast, hogs ran wild. Sheep and goats became permanent parts of the economy and culture of Pueblo and Navajo peoples in the Southwest. Horses transformed the lives and cultures of Indian peoples on the Plains. Europeans also brought honeybees, black rats, cats, and cockroaches to America.

Some Indians crossed the Atlantic eastward to Europe, as kidnap victims, slaves, and diplomats (see Picture Essay, "Atlantic Travelers: Indians in Eighteenth-Century London," pages 188–93), but most American exports were the foods that Native peoples had developed and cultivated. Potatoes transformed the diets of ordinary people in northern Europe, for example, and tomatoes became incorporated into Italian cooking. Meanwhile, Europeans in America quickly incorporated Indian foods into their diets: corn, for example, fed European soldiers and became a staple of life for European pioneers on the frontier.

Biological Catastrophes

Europe's deadliest export was invisible. Nothing hit Indian societies harder or did more to shape the subsequent course of American history than Old World diseases. The inhabitants of both North America and Europe suffered from ailments and injuries and had a life expectancy that most twenty-first-century Westerners would find shocking. But until 1492 Indians were isolated from the massive, deadly epidemics that ravaged Europe and Asia in medieval times. When Europeans arrived on the continent they carried germs and viruses that devastated indigenous populations that had no exposure to these new diseases.[6]

Epidemics of smallpox, measles, bubonic plague, influenza, cholera, and other killer diseases spread like wildfire through Indian societies. Different diseases struck different regions at different times, but sooner or later imported diseases struck all Native populations, which varied in their responses. In some cases entire populations perished; 90 percent mortality rates were common. It's impossible to say exactly how much the effects of European colonialism contributed to population decline and prevented population recovery.[7] Estimates of precontact Indian populations in North America must always be tentative since so many people died

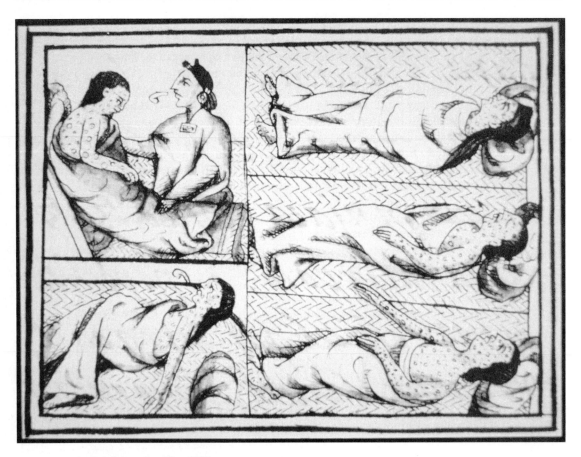

◆ **Smallpox, the Silent Killer**
This sixteenth-century portrayal of smallpox records the effects of a disease that would strike Native peoples repeatedly from first contacts to the twentieth century. *Private Collection/Peter Newark American Pictures/Bridgeman Images.*

before Europeans conducted head-counts of survivors. In some areas, populations increased as refugees sought shelter from war and disease elsewhere.

Some scholars may have produced inflated estimates of population size and decline, but their work points to one of the greatest demographic disasters in history. The population of Hispaniola was estimated at some 8 million in 1492, but by 1535 the original inhabitants were all but extinct; the Native population of Mexico dropped from an estimated 25 million in 1519 to perhaps 1.3 million by the end of the century; Peru's population dwindled from as high as 9 million to a half million in 1600. Indians and Europeans struggled to comprehend and explain the huge mortalities caused by disease, and the pattern of epidemic disease and depopulation in North America is still not fully understood. Combined with the impacts of increased warfare, slave raiding, famine, and other traumas of colonization, recurrent epidemics and chronic diseases caused continual attrition of Indian numbers from

the fifteenth to the twentieth centuries and steadily eroded Indian capacity for dealing with the invaders. One estimate suggests that the Native population of North
America fell by 74 percent between 1492 and 1800, while that of the American
hemisphere as a whole plummeted by 89 percent between 1492 and 1650.[8]

The Indians whom European invaders encountered were often the survivors
of shattered societies; abandoned villages and smallpox-scarred faces testified to
the suffering that had preceded the colonists. The natural environments Europeans encountered were also in part the products of demographic disaster: in some
areas plummeting human populations allowed animal populations and vegetation
to increase unchecked, producing dense forests and vast herds that European colonists assumed were "virgin wilderness." A "hunters' paradise" was often testimony
to an absence of Indian hunters rather than to untouched natural bounty.[9]

INDIANS CONFRONT THE SPANISH

In the late fall of 1528, Indians in eastern Texas came upon a group of bearded and
bedraggled men who had washed up on the Gulf Coast. The Indian men, probably
Karankawas, were astonished and brought their women and children to look at
the strangers. The Indians took pity on them, fed them roots and fish, and gave
them shelter in their village. Eventually "half the natives died from a disease of the
bowels."[10] The strange men were Spanish soldiers, would-be conquistadors and
survivors of an ill-fated expedition that had landed in Florida. Four of them —
including the royal treasurer of the expedition, Álvar Núñez Cabeza de Vaca — later
lived for years among the Indians. It was the first of many encounters in North
America, and not the last in which Spaniards and Indians would live in close contact. But the power dynamics in subsequent years would very often be reversed.

A Mission for Gold and God

Spanish soldiers, priests, and colonizers in the South and Southwest preceded English colonists on the Atlantic coast by almost a century. Christopher Columbus had
sailed west in 1492 in the employ of the Spanish monarchs Ferdinand and Isabella.
The marriage of Ferdinand of Aragon and Isabella of Castile in 1469 joined their
crowns into the kingdom of Spain and turned Spain from a power in the Mediter-
ranean to one spanning the Atlantic Ocean.[11] In 1492 the two monarchs completed
the liberation of their kingdom from Muslim power that had both limited Spain's
expansion and influenced its development throughout the Middle Ages. Spaniards
now looked to the New World as an area for empire building. Seven centuries of
warfare to drive the "infidels" out of the Iberian Peninsula left an indelible mark on
the militant Christian warrior culture of Spain: young noblemen now looked elsewhere for infidels to fight. In the next hundred years or so, Spaniards came into contact with Indian peoples from Florida to California, from Peru to the Great Plains.

The Spanish believed they had a divine and royal mandate to reduce Indian
peoples to submission. Spanish law required the conquistadors to read the
Requerimiento to the Indians they encountered. The *Requerimiento*, worked out

by theologians in 1513 at the request of the king of Spain, required Indians to "acknowledge the Church as the Ruler and Superior of the whole world," the pope as high priest, and the king and queen of Spain as lords of their lands. If they did so, the Spaniards would "receive you in all love and charity, . . . leave you, your wives, and your children, and your lands, free without servitude, . . . and . . . not compel you to turn Christians." But, the document continued,

> if you do not do this, and wickedly and intentionally delay to do so, I certify to you that, with the help of God, we shall forcibly enter into your country and shall make war against you in all ways and manners that we can, and shall subject you to the yoke and obedience of the Church and of their High-nesses; we shall take you and your wives and your children, and shall make slaves of them, and as such shall sell and dispose of them as their Highnesses may command; and we shall take away your goods, and shall do all the harm and damage that we can, as to vassals who do not obey, and refuse to receive their lord, and resist and contradict him; and we protest that the deaths and losses which shall accrue from this are your fault, and not that of their High-nesses, or ours, nor of these gentlemen who come with us.

Read in Spanish to Indian people who understood neither its language nor its concepts, the *Requerimiento* became little more than a "ceremony of possession," allowing the Spaniards to justify conquest — and any accompanying atrocities.[12]

The Spaniards also had settlements in the Caribbean, especially on Cuba and Hispaniola, before 1520. Despite mass enslavements of the Native populations, these colonies did not produce the wealth the colonizers had hoped for. Legends and reports of great riches on the mainland attracted Spanish attention and ambitions, and in the next thirty years Spanish forces penetrated as far as Mexico and the central plateau of the Andes. There they found the gold and silver they sought. They plundered and destroyed the civilizations they encountered and forced Indian slaves to work in silver mines. Driven by militant Christianity and a relentless search for precious metals, the Spanish invaders took possession of the most densely populated areas of the Americas, thereby establishing the first European land empire overseas.

Conquest of the Aztecs

In 1519 the Aztecs of central Mexico began to hear reports of strange white men wearing armor and riding animals. The news followed a series of bad omens and portents of disaster. Aztec life revolved around cyclical rituals based on a solar year of eighteen months. The end of a cycle was regarded as a time of great peril. Around 1507, a major cycle of the Aztec calendar had come to an end. Fifteen years later the Aztec Empire lay in ruins. The conqueror was Hernán Cortés, who landed near Vera Cruz in 1519 with a force of only 508 men, burned his ships to demonstrate there was no turning back, and marched inland.

The Spaniards were entering a complex and highly structured civilization whose impressive cities left the invaders in wonderment. The Mexica and other tribes whom the Spaniards designated the Aztecs were only the most recent in a *series* of ruling peoples in the area. Invading from the north, they had achieved ascendancy relatively recently, in the fifteenth century, and exacted tribute and labor from subject peoples over a wide area. The Aztec emperor headed a society rigidly divided by castes, attuned to the predictions of priests, and dependent on human sacrifice as the key to ensuring agricultural fertility and the daily return of the sun. Efficiently irrigated fields produced crops of maize, tobacco, and tomatoes—all unknown in Europe at that time—and pyramid-shaped temples dominated the large plazas of Aztec towns. The capital, Tenochtitlán, on the site of present-day Mexico City, housed more than 200,000 people, making it several times the size of most European capitals at the time. Then, as now, Mexico City was one of the largest cities in the world.

◆ **A Tlaxcalan Depiction of Nuño Beltrán de Guzmán's Conquest of Northwestern Mexico, c. 1530**
In 1529–31 Spaniard Nuño Beltrán de Guzmán led expeditions of Spanish soldiers and Mexican Indian allies into northwestern Mexico. He looted and burned his way up the West Coast, enslaving thousands of people and committing so many atrocities that he was recalled by administrators of the Spanish crown. His Tlaxcalan Indian allies, who assisted in his conquests, left a depiction of the invasion in which Spaniards used horses to their advantage, unleashed dogs trained for war, and hanged those who resisted. *Private Collection/Archives Charmet/Bridgeman Images.*

Boldly marching through jungle to the high plateau of central Mexico, the Spaniards won over the outlying towns as tribes eager to throw off Aztec rule joined them. It was a pattern repeated throughout Mesoamerica as Native allies participated in conquests that would not have been possible without them.[13] Communication with the Indians was aided by an Aztec woman who could speak both Mayan and Nahuatl, the language of the Aztecs, and whom the Spaniards called Doña Marina; she served as Cortés's mistress and interpreter — one of the first of many people to serve as a culture broker between Indians and Europeans.° Hearing advance warning of their arrival, the Aztec emperor Moctezuma sent gifts to the invaders and allowed them to enter Tenochtitlán; in return, Cortés seized Moctezuma and held him hostage in his own palace.

In 1520, after a tenuous peace, Spanish cruelties and desecration of temples finally produced a furious Aztec counterassault. Moctezuma was killed by disaffected Aztecs, and Cortés had to fight his way out of the city. The Spaniards lost a third of their men but regrouped for another attack. Meanwhile, a massive smallpox epidemic broke out in Tenochtitlán. It lasted for seventy days, according to a Native text, "striking every where in the city and killing a vast number of our people."[15] The epidemic killed Moctezuma's brother, Cuitláhuac, who had spearheaded the Aztec resistance. Strengthened by allies from the coastal tribes and by Spanish reinforcements from Cuba, Cortés's troops looted and destroyed Tenochtitlán in 1521. A year later, Cortés was appointed "Captain General of New Spain." Bernal Díaz, a young foot soldier in the invasion, wrote a lengthy account of the conquest in his old age. He recalled the march inland, the awe with which the Spaniards viewed island cities built in the water, the long causeway leading straight for Tenochtitlán, rich orchards, and rose gardens. "Some of our soldiers even asked whether the things that we saw were not a dream," he said. "Seeing things as we did that had never been heard of or seen before, not even dreamed about." But he was imagining a paradise before the fall: "Of all these wonders that I then beheld today all is overthrown and lost, nothing [is] left standing."[16]

Contemporaries and many later historians saw the rapid and total collapse of the Aztec Empire as evidence of European superiority over Native people. The Spaniards fought with courage, discipline, and ruthless brutality and had the advantages of horses, firearms, and metal armor. The Aztecs were unable to sustain — or even, perhaps, to understand — the kind of prolonged campaign mounted by Spaniards who, driven by a single-minded faith in their mission and a lust for gold, laid siege to cities and starved and killed whole populations. But there were major internal reasons for the collapse of the highly structured Aztec Empire. Rebellious subject peoples sided with the invaders, and Indian defenders died from disease faster than Spaniards could kill them.[17]

° Doña Marina, or Malinche, had apparently been stolen in childhood by traders and sold to the Tabascans. The Tabascans gave her to Cortés. Her native language was Nahuatl, but in Tabascó she had learned the Maya language. She spoke in Mayan to Jéronimo de Aguilar, a shipwrecked Spaniard who lived among Mayan-speaking Indians, who then translated from Mayan to Spanish for Cortés.[14]

Searching for Other Empires

In the wake of Cortés's stunning conquest, the Spaniards sent expeditions into other areas of America. In 1532 Francisco Pizarro invaded Peru with 168 men and 67 horses. The people of the Inca Empire were learned in mathematics and astronomy, irrigated their fields, built huge temples and palaces, and constructed a network of paved roads linking major towns with the capital city, Cuzco. But smallpox preceded Pizarro to Peru, and the Spaniards caught the Incas in the midst of a civil upheaval with a usurper named Atahualpa on the throne. Pizarro captured Atahualpa by treachery, held him hostage until his people filled a storeroom with a ransom of treasure, and then had him strangled. The Spanish suppressed resistance to their conquest with bloody reprisals, and Incan civilization was soon reduced to ruins, although Indian resistance to Spanish colonial rule continued for generations.

Indian peoples in the area of the present-day United States encountered Spanish soldiers and missionaries as other expeditions pushed north. New Spain's northern frontier ultimately stretched from California to Florida. In 1513 Juan Ponce de León sailed along the coast of Florida. Calusa Indians traded and skirmished with his party. Eight years later Ponce died after a pitched battle with the Indians. Other Spaniards explored the Florida coastline, some of them looking for slaves. Lucas Vásquez de Ayllón attempted to establish a colony in 1526, but disease, hunger, and Indian resistance defeated his efforts.

In 1528 Pánfilo de Narváez landed on the west coast of Florida and divided his force, marching inland with his troops while his ships paralleled their route up the coast carrying supplies. After an arduous trek, the Spaniards reached the Indian town of Apalachee in northern Florida, but the Indians harassed them with guerilla tactics. The Spaniards headed for the coast, but when they arrived there, their ships were nowhere to be seen. In desperation, the Spaniards built makeshift barges and set sail. Narváez and most of his followers were never seen again. Cabeza de Vaca and other survivors made it to an island off the coast of eastern Texas where local Indians took them in. After six years living among the coastal Indians, often as slaves, Cabeza de Vaca and three companions escaped. As Cabeza de Vaca later recorded, they spent two more years wandering across the Southwest, "through so many different villages of such diverse tongues that my memory gets confused." They earned a reputation as healers, and "the Indians treated us kindly . . . deprived themselves of food to give to us, and presented us skins and other tokens of gratitude." After passing through Pima country in present-day Sonora, they saw signs they were nearing their objective: Spanish slavers had been at work, carrying off women and children. "With heavy hearts we looked out over the lavishly watered, fertile, and beautiful land," wrote Cabeza de Vaca, "now abandoned and burned and the people thin and weak, scattered or hiding in fright." The Indians could not believe that the sun-darkened Cabeza de Vaca and his companions were the same people as the Christians who raided them for slaves: "We had come from the sunrise, they from the sunset; we healed the sick, they killed the sound; we came naked and barefoot, they clothed, horsed, and lanced; we coveted nothing but gave whatever we were given, while they robbed whomever they found and bestowed nothing on anyone."[18]

Cabeza de Vaca and his companions made their way to Mexico City. The stories they told of finding emerald arrowheads and of wealthy Indian nations to the north convinced some that Spain was on the brink of locating the famed Seven Cities of Cíbola, which, legend had it, had been founded centuries before somewhere in the West by seven fugitive bishops.

Between 1539 and 1543, in what is now the southeastern United States, Indian peoples faced a brutal invasion by Hernando de Soto and an army of more than six hundred men, with two hundred horses, herds of pigs, and dogs trained for war. De Soto had come to New Spain as a teenager, won his spurs in the bloody Spanish conquest of Panama between 1517 and 1523, and participated in the invasion of Nicaragua in 1523–27. He earned a reputation even among fellow conquistadors as an accomplished Indian-killer. His expedition sailed from Cuba and landed at Tampa Bay on the west coast of Florida in May 1539. For four years, his army blundered and plundered its way through present-day Florida, Georgia, Alabama, North and South Carolina, Tennessee, Mississippi, Louisiana, Arkansas, and Texas, searching for riches to match those won by Cortés in Mexico and Pizarro in Peru (Map 2.2). They occupied Indian towns,

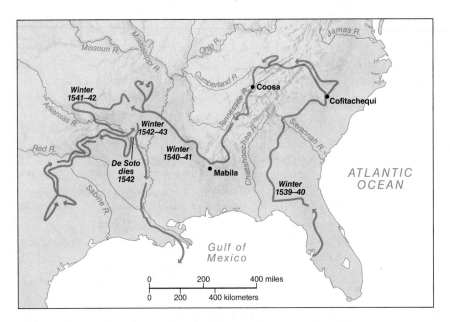

◆ Map 2.2 **Probable Route of the de Soto Expedition, 1539–1542**
The conquistadors' hopes of finding great wealth and emulating the successes of Cortés and Pizarro drew them across vast expanses of the American South, disrupting Indian lives and destabilizing relations between chiefdoms.
SOURCE: Based on Charles Hudson and Carmen C. Tesser, eds., *The Forgotten Centuries: Indians and Europeans in the American South, 1521–1704* (Athens: University of Georgia Press, 1994). Copyright © 1994 by the University of Georgia Press.

commandeered food supplies and guides, and pressed on in a relentless search for gold. They killed, kidnapped, raped, and enslaved hundreds of people. Spanish terror tactics, firearms, and war dogs — large hounds and mastiffs trained to kill — left a trail of devastation from Florida to Texas. Indian people tried to deal with the strangers by employing methods of diplomacy and gift giving, fleeing from their approach, harassing them with hit-and-run guerilla tactics, and fighting desperate battles. After crossing almost four thousand miles of Indian country, the conquistadors had found no great riches. Almost half of them died in the attempt.[19]

If the expedition was a failure from the Spanish point of view, it was a disaster for the Indians. Disease and famine killed thousands more in the wake of the expedition.[20] The human landscape of the South changed forever after de Soto's men cut their bloody trail across it. De Soto's men had entered a world full of Indians, passed through some densely settled regions, and dealt with powerful chiefs. When Europeans returned to the interior of the Southeast in the next century, many of the towns had disappeared and the people they met were fewer in number, poorer, and more scattered. Most of the powerful and populous Mississippian chiefdoms that dotted the region in 1540 had collapsed in a world of escalating violence, slave raiding, and epidemics. Their descendants rebuilt smaller communities, regrouped, and transformed their cultures and ways of life to become the peoples Europeans encountered as Creeks, Choctaws, Chickasaws, and others.[21]

As de Soto's men pushed west toward and then beyond the Mississippi, another Spanish expedition approached the great river from the west. From 1540 to 1542, Francisco Vásquez de Coronado led an expedition of Spanish soldiers and Indian allies north from New Spain in search of treasures. A Franciscan friar named Marcos de Niza had reported seeing the cities of Cíbola in 1539 when he looked from a distance on the Zuni pueblos in western New Mexico, and there were other stories of great cities in the North. There had indeed been cities in the North — in Chaco Canyon, the Phoenix basin, and elsewhere — but they were long gone before the Spaniards arrived.[22]

Coronado reached the Zuni towns, but the inhabitants of Hawikuh resisted in a desperate battle in 1540. As the Spaniards commandeered food, most Pueblo peoples adopted a strategy of urging the invaders north in the hope they would get lost in the Great Plains. An Indian guide whom the Spaniards acquired at the pueblo of Pecos spoke of his native country to the east as a land of great riches. The Spaniards called this place Quivira and wandered on to the Great Plains looking for it. When they reached the villages they called Quivira, probably those of the Wichitas in Kansas, they realized there were no cities of gold and strangled their guide. Meanwhile, in 1542, Juan Rodríguez Cabrillo sailed up the coast of California.

In 1550 the impact of the Spanish invasions on Indian peoples gave rise to a formal debate about the moral basis of Spanish treatment of those peoples. According to a priest named Bartolomé de Las Casas, "What we committed in the Indies stands out among the most unpardonable offenses committed against God and mankind."[23] Las Casas's opponent, Juan de Sepulveda, declared that Indians were naturally inferior and therefore were meant to be slaves; if the Indians refused to submit, the Spanish were justified in using force against them. Indians were like children and would benefit from subordination to "civilized" Christians. Sepulveda would not be the last person to justify taking Indian lands and destroying Indian culture on the assumption that "it was good for them" or that assimilation was their only alternative to destruction.

North American Attempts to Colonize and Christianize

Spaniards established permanent colonies along with conducting expeditions through Indian country. They established missions among the Florida tribes and founded St. Augustine in 1565. In 1598 Juan de Oñate led a colonizing expedition into New Mexico. As elsewhere, the Spaniards aimed to transform Indian peoples into Christians and laborers. In the wake of their conquests to the south, Spaniards established the *encomienda* system, whereby the authorities assigned Indian workers to mines and to plantation owners on the understanding that the recipients would defend the colony and teach the workers Christianity. After 1550, however, that system was largely replaced by the *repartimento*, which required Indian towns to supply a pool of labor. Indians resisted the systems, and Spanish missionaries often played a leading role in extracting labor as well as confessions of faith from Indian people. The Spaniards founded Santa Fe in 1610, though Indian laborers built most of the city.

Indian people who survived the demographic disasters unleashed by the diseases the Spaniards brought responded to invasion and colonization in a variety of ways. Many fled from the invaders, generating a "domino effect" of population pressures and group migrations over thousands of miles. In Florida, some Indians saw the Spanish missions as a source of stability in a chaotic world. Some became practicing Catholics, while others sought to incorporate the Spaniards' spiritual power into their own. Some Indians resisted violently. Guale Indians in Florida killed missionaries in 1597. A year later and more than two thousand miles to the west, during Juan de Oñate's conquest of New Mexico, the people of Ácoma Pueblo attacked a party of Spanish soldiers. Oñate retaliated by dispatching troops who climbed to the top of the mesa where Ácoma sat, turned cannons on the inhabitants, and killed as many as eight hundred people. The Spaniards put the survivors on trial and "made an example" of them: males over the age of twenty-five were sentenced to have one foot cut off; women over twelve years of age were sentenced to twenty years of servitude; children under twelve were placed in the care of missionaries to be raised as Christians and as servants.

Franciscan friars among the Pueblos forbade dancing and ceremonies and even raided kivas to confiscate religious objects. They also demanded that Pueblo people change their attitudes toward sex: what Pueblo men and women regarded as a natural, life-affirming, and perhaps even sacred act that united male and female, missionaries taught was a "sin of the flesh." Pueblo women traditionally enjoyed considerable influence as a result of their control of the household, their production of corn, and their fertility. The patriarchal Catholic church sought to undermine female influence and rights in Pueblo communities.[24] Pueblo people resisted in subtle ways. They accommodated the Spanish presence and adopted some of the outward forms of Catholicism but kept Spanish missionaries at arm's length, preserving their religion underground in the kivas. Missionaries were unable to stamp out traditional beliefs and rituals even among Pueblos who participated in Catholic services. Friars did not supplant local religious leaders and medicine men. "Kivas and village plazas, not churches and mission compounds, remained the focus of village life," wrote Pueblo anthropologist Alfonso Ortiz. "The Christian faith was, if accepted to any degree, regarded as a supplement, not an alternative, to a religion that had served the Pueblos and their ancestors well."[25]

The Pueblo War of Independence

In 1680, after years of economic and religious oppression, the Rio Grande Pueblos rose in synchronized revolt against the Spaniards (Map 2.3). The Pueblo Revolt was one of the most effective Indian resistance movements in

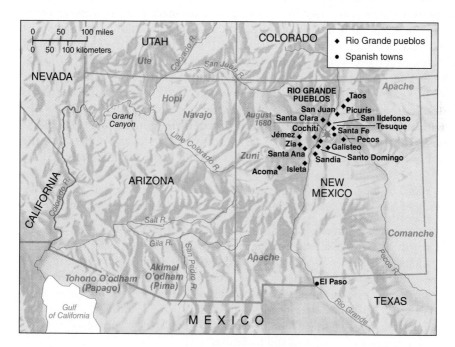

◆ Map 2.3 **The Pueblos and Their Neighbors, c. 1680**
The Pueblo War of Independence brought together most of the Pueblo communities of the Rio Grande valley in unprecedented united action, culminating in the siege of the Spaniards at Santa Fe in August 1680 and securing a twelve-year liberation from Spanish rule.

American history, what Pueblo historian Joe S. Sando calls "the first American revolution."[26] For more than eighty years, Pueblo peoples had endured Spanish persecution of their religious practices, Spanish demands for corn and labor, and Spanish abuses of their women. New diseases as well as famines resulting from the disruption of their traditional economies had scythed their numbers, from as many as 100,000 in the late sixteenth century to a mere 17,000 by 1680.[27] Many Pueblos blamed their misfortunes on Spanish assaults on the religious ceremonies that kept their world in balance, and there was a resurgence of the ancient rituals. Spanish officials responded with intensified oppression: in 1675 they hanged three Pueblo religious leaders and whipped many others. Meanwhile, drought produced food scarcities among Plains nomads to the east, and the Apaches stepped up their raids on Pueblo farming communities: "the whole land is at war with the widespread heathen nation of the Apache Indians, who kill all the Christian Indians they can find," wrote a Franciscan friar in 1669.[28] By 1680, the Pueblos were facing crisis. They could no longer save themselves by coexistence and accommodation.

The move to open confrontation came initially from northern Pueblo leaders. The Spaniards credited Popé, a medicine man from San Juan Pueblo who had been publicly flogged and fled, with masterminding the revolt. But Luis Tupàtü, governor of Picuris Pueblo and "an Indian respected among all the nations,"[29] and other leaders also played important roles. They made plans to strike at a time when the Spaniards would be low on supplies — just before the arrival of a Spanish supply caravan from the south. Their goals were to cut off the Spanish capital at Santa Fe and overwhelm Spanish settlements in the outlying areas. As historian David Weber noted, it required careful planning to coordinate "an offensive involving some 17,000 Pueblos living in more than two dozen independent towns spread out over several hundred miles and further separated by at least six different languages and countless dialects, many of them mutually unintelligible."[30] Runners carrying knotted strings that indicated the number of days until the revolt went from pueblo to pueblo, "under penalty of death if they revealed the secret."[31]

Word of the planned revolt leaked but Popé advanced the date, and, as the viceroy of New Spain reported to the king the following February, the Indians

> fell upon all the pueblos and farms at the same time with such vigor and cruelty that they killed twenty-one missionary religious — nineteen priests and two lay brothers — and more than three hundred and eighty Spaniards, not sparing the defenselessness of the women and children. They set fire to the temples, seizing the images of the saints and profaning the holy vessels with such shocking desecrations and insolences that it is indecent to mention them. They left thirty-four pueblos totally desolated and destroyed, not counting many other farms and haciendas. . . .[32]

Some Indians plunged into rivers to scrub themselves and their clothing, believing that in this way they would be cleansed of "the character of the holy sacraments."[33]

The Indians laid siege to Santa Fe for nine days and cut off the town's water supply. Rather than face the prospect of dying from starvation and thirst, Governor Don Antonio de Otermín fought his way through the Pueblo cordon and led about one thousand Spanish soldiers, "their families and servants . . . Mexican natives, and all classes of people" in retreat south to El Paso.[34] Bewildered by the scale and success of the uprising, Spaniards interrogated captured Indians to understand how it happened (see "Declaration of the Indian Juan," pages 125–26).

The coalition that Popé and others had woven together began to unravel soon after the Pueblos had liberated their land. Beginning in 1692, Diego de Vargas reconquered New Mexico for the Spanish. Pueblos revolted again in 1696 but resistance was promptly crushed. Some Pueblos moved beyond the Spaniards' reach, joining Hopis or Navajos in what is now Arizona. Most opted for more subtle forms of resistance, quietly maintaining their cultures and communities, preserving a Pueblo world within a Spanish colony. The Spaniards for their part learned to govern with less of an iron hand. They reduced demands for labor and tribute, and the *encomienda* system was never reestablished after 1680. They assigned land grants to individual Pueblos, giving them clear European title to their own lands. And they adopted a more tolerant approach to the traditional religion of the Pueblos. Spanish New Mexico in the eighteenth century became more concerned with defending its northern borders against Apache, Navajo, Ute, and Comanche attacks than it was with subjugating and converting its Pueblo populations. Change occurred at a slower rate and in both directions as Hispanic and Pueblo people interacted and intermarried. The Spanish colony was restored and survived in New Mexico, but not entirely on Spanish terms. Pueblo people had to make adjustments and accommodations in order to survive, but their resistance and resilience also reshaped Spanish New Mexico.

The New Mexican borderlands remained volatile and violent places as the repercussions of Spanish colonialism reverberated far beyond the Rio Grande valley. Many Pueblos fought alongside Spaniards in conflicts against Indian peoples to the east, north, and west of New Mexico. Utes and Comanches raided Spaniards and Pueblos and Apaches and Navajos. Spanish slave-raiding expeditions continued to strike deep into Indian country, and some Indian people raided more distant neighbors to feed the Spanish demand for slaves. In the recurrent raiding between Apaches, Navajos, Utes, Comanches, Kiowas, and Hispanos, many people were taken captive, and patterns of captive taking and captive exchange generated cross-cultural kinship connections within and among competing societies.[35]

By the time Mexico surrendered California, Arizona, New Mexico, and parts of Utah and Colorado to the United States in 1848, Indian peoples living in those regions had been in contact with Spanish-speaking peoples for almost three hundred years. Many of them displayed the marks of that contact: they rode horses, tended sheep and goats, carried crucifixes, spoke Spanish, and wore Spanish-style clothing. Indians and Hispanos had intermarried extensively. Despite population collapse and the surface addition of new elements and practices, Indian people also had long experience of preserving their identity and culture in the face of tremendous pressures. The United States stepped up the pressures, but it was dealing with veterans in a long war for cultural survival.

INDIANS CONFRONT THE FRENCH

While Indian peoples were encountering, accommodating, and resisting Spanish soldiers and priests in the Southeast and Southwest, Indians in the Northeast faced French explorers, traders, and priests. Indians on the Atlantic coast probably made contact with French fishermen in the fifteenth century. When the Montagnais Indians on the banks of the St. Lawrence River saw their first French ship, they thought it was a floating island; when French sailors then offered them biscuits and wine, the Indians remarked that "the Frenchmen drank blood and ate wood," and threw the biscuits overboard. Mi'kmaq people likewise saw an island float close to shore: "there were trees on it, and branches to the trees, on which a number of bears, as they supposed, were crawling about." They soon found that these were not bears, but men with hairy faces. One was a priest "who came towards them making signs of friendship, raising his hands towards heaven, and addressing them in an earnest manner, but in a language which they could not understand."[36] These tribal traditions recall the opening contacts in a relationship in which Frenchmen and Indians met, traded, lived together, and fought over huge areas of North America.

Commerce and Conflict

In 1534 Jacques Cartier sailed up the St. Lawrence River. He visited populous Indian towns at Stadacona (near present-day Quebec) and Hochelaga (present-day Montreal) and reported extensive crops and orchards covering the banks of the river. Seventy years later, when Samuel de Champlain traveled the same route in 1603, everything had changed. Deadly diseases and intertribal warfare generated by competition for European trade had raged through the valley. The villages were gone and the riverbanks were overgrown.

Champlain founded Quebec City in 1608, explored the lake that bears his name, and helped put France on the path that led to an empire built on the fur trade. But Indians played crucial roles in establishing the patterns and terms of that empire. Champlain began a policy of sending young traders into Indian villages to learn Native languages and ways of living. He reportedly told a gathering of Indians that "our young men will marry your daughters, and we shall be one people."[37] He made alliances with the Algonquins, Montagnais, and Hurons (Wendats) to gain access to rich fur territories farther west; the Indians pursued alliances with the French as a means of securing European trade goods.

However, this cooperation threatened the powerful Iroquois of upstate New York. In 1609 a group of Algonquins and Hurons with whom Champlain was

◆ **Champlain's Fight with the Iroquois**

This engraving from *The Voyages of Samuel de Champlain* (1613) is often attributed to
Champlain himself, but the inaccuracies in the picture suggest that the artist was not present
at the battle. The depiction of this fight in 1609 between Mohawks (right) and Champlain
and his Indian allies (left) contains many errors: there are no palm trees on the shores of
Lake Champlain, the Indians did not use hammocks, and the boats at the water's edge do
not resemble canoes. Nevertheless, the picture does convey the deadly impact of firearms
on warriors accustomed to fighting in ranks, using bows and arrows, and protecting themselves with wooden or wicker shields. *Library and Archives Canada.*

traveling encountered an Iroquois war party at the southern end of Lake Champlain. The two groups of Indians engaged in a ritual exchange of insults, paddled
their canoes to the shore, and lined up in preparation for battle. Traditionally, such
a conflict would have involved firing arrows and hurling spears, with relatively few
casualties. Champlain and his French companions, however, introduced a deadly
new element into American Indian warfare. Stepping forward with their guns
loaded, they opened fire on the Iroquois, killing several of the startled Indians
outright and putting the rest to flight.

Indians quickly developed new ways of fighting to adapt to the new equipment. When Indian warriors obtained guns they adopted guerilla tactics that

allowed them to employ the new weapons with deadly effect. Indian people traded for a wide range of European manufactured goods, but firearms and metal weapons were among the most sought after. In the hands of skilled archers who could fire arrows accurately and in rapid succession, bows and arrows possessed some notable advantages over seventeenth-century firearms, which were heavy, unreliable, and inaccurate and required constant maintenance. Many ethnohistorians question the degree to which Indian people became immediately dependent on European firearms and have reassessed the long-held belief that Iroquois warfare in this period became driven by the pelts-for-guns trade. The Iroquois continued to wage wars for traditional reasons — to secure honor, revenge, and captives — even as they fought in a world of new economic threats and opportunities.[38] Nevertheless, guns brought supremacy over unarmed neighbors, and a tribe needed guns to survive. Guns could be acquired only by trade with Europeans, and Europeans wanted only one thing: beaver pelts. Indian hunters frequently "trapped out" beaver territories in an effort to supply an endless demand, and competition between Indian bands for trade and furs became intense at the same time that guns made intertribal conflict more lethal. The Iroquois turned to Dutch traders, who established a trading post on the Hudson River near Albany in 1614, to supply them with guns. They fought and defeated the local Mahican Indians in the 1620s to secure easier access to the Dutch trade. In the so-called Beaver Wars of the mid-seventeenth century, Iroquois attacked the Huron people and their neighbors who lived in the Great Lakes region and raided as far afield as Quebec, New England, and the Carolinas. The Hurons were still reeling from the impact of a series of epidemic diseases, and the Iroquois assault in 1649 dispersed and destroyed their confederacy. Survivors dispersed to build new communities in Quebec and Ohio.[39] Other tribes in the Ohio valley and Great Lakes area waged recurrent warfare in contests for guns, goods, and furs.

Pelts and Priests

France's empire, based on the fur trade, needed Indian alliances to sustain it. The French offered their religion and metal goods in the hope of winning Indian converts, customers, and allies. Over the course of the seventeenth century, French explorers, missionaries, and traders made contact with Indian peoples deep in the heart of the continent. In 1671 at Sault Sainte Marie in present-day Michigan, Simon François Daumont, Sieur de Saint Lusson, and Jesuit missionary Claude Allouez laid formal claim to the whole interior of North America for the crown. The target audience for this event was rival European nations. The Indians who were assembled for the purpose of bearing witness to the pageant were probably bemused by it: French rituals of possession and rhetoric of empire had little meaning to them, and French efforts to designate them as allied nations made little sense to Algonquian peoples who lived in fluid and mobile bands.[40] Louis Joliet and Jacques Marquette reached Green Bay and explored the Mississippi River in 1673; René-Robert Cavelier, Sieur de La Salle, followed the Mississippi to the Gulf of Mexico in 1682 and claimed the region — Louisiana — for his king, Louis XIV. French traders and explorers pushed out on to the Great Plains in the eighteenth century. French traders lived with Indian tribes, and people of French descent continued to be active in the fur trade long after the collapse of the French empire in North America. Many modern North American cities, including Detroit, St. Louis, and Montreal, began life as French trading posts, and many families in the Great Lakes region descended from French and Indian marriages.

Black-robed Jesuit priests worked diligently among northern tribes like the Abenakis, Hurons, and Algonquins and reached down the Mississippi to the Illinois, Quapaw, and other tribes. Indian peoples adopted elements of the Catholic religion, sometimes praying and singing hymns in their Native languages; Jesuit missionaries learned Indian languages, adapted some Native rituals, and spent much of their lives in Indian country.[41] Often the missionaries brought their message of salvation at a time when the Indians saw their world falling apart under the impact of new diseases. Father Jean de Brébeuf led the Jesuits to Huron country, north of Lake Ontario, in 1634, but the missionaries encountered considerable resistance (see "A Jesuit Assesses the Hurons and a Mi'kmaq Assesses the French," pages 110–20). Growing dependence on French trade, increasing assaults from the Iroquois, and devastating smallpox epidemics brought turmoil to Huron villages, however, and hundreds of Hurons turned from the ensuing chaos to the Jesuits.

Throughout New France, many Indians converted to the Catholic faith, settled in French mission villages, attended Mass, and wore crucifixes. Kateri Tekakwitha, a Mohawk-Algonquin girl who lost her family to smallpox when she was a child and was herself disfigured by the disease, converted to Christianity and found meaning and hope in the church. She fled to the Jesuit mission at Kahnawake or Caughnawaga near Montreal and modeled her life on that of the local nuns. She so devoted herself to a life of chastity, prayer, and

◆ **Kateri Tekakwitha**
Scarred by smallpox and family tragedy in her youth, Kateri Tekakwitha (1656–80) embraced Catholicism and an ascetic way of life at the mission village of Kahnawake. In 2012 she became the first Native American to be made a saint. © *Alessandra Tarantino/AP Photo.*

penitence that when she died at the age of twenty-four in 1680, pilgrims began to visit her shrine. The Catholic Church conferred sainthood on her in 2012.[42] Other Indians, however, continued to practice their traditional religion or to observe a mixture of the two, and the French did not resort to forced conversions as the Spaniards did.

Writing in the seventeenth century, Nicholas Perrot complained that the Indians of the Great Lakes had the "arrogant notion that the French cannot get along without them, and that we could not maintain ourselves in the Colony without the assistance that they give us."[43] His complaint may have stemmed in part from a realization that the Indians were right. Recognizing that their empire depended on maintaining a network of Indian alliances, French officials, traders, and officers in Indian country tried to employ diplomacy, tact, and respect for Native culture. In the Great Lakes region, French leaders and Indian chiefs worked tirelessly to create order out of the chaos that followed the Beaver Wars. Each group adjusted to the presence and the cultural expectations of the other and shared a common interest in maintaining peace and trade. As historian Richard White observed, French and Indians negotiated "a middle ground" of coexistence that could only be maintained by constant mediation and compromise. Employing the kinship language of forest diplomacy, the French claimed to be "fathers" to the Indians, and Indians often addressed them as such; but fulfilling that role in Indian country meant giving gifts, not giving orders; observing rituals, not expecting obedience; and bestowing protection, not invoking paternal authority.[44] Indian peoples in the Great Lakes and Mississippi valley regions often incorporated Frenchmen into their societies through marriage and the ritual of the calumet, the ceremonial pipe, which brought peace and order to relationships and turned strangers into kinfolk.

Franco-Indian relations were not always smooth. Some Mohawks embraced French Catholicism, but most Iroquois resisted French expansion into their homelands, compelling the French to focus their energies to the west and build a trade empire along the Great Lakes and the area north of the Ohio River. French armies invaded Iroquois country several times in the late seventeenth century. The fur trade that lay at the heart of Franco-Indian relations also produced chaos in Indian country as it facilitated the spread of guns, contagious diseases, and alcohol. French demand for Indian slaves generated Indian–Indian raids deep into the interior of the continent (see Chapter 3, "Indian Slavery," pages 145–49). Jesuit missionaries who worked to save souls also generated social and political divisions in Indian communities.

Religious and commercial ties bound many tribes to the French, however. Confronted with a powerful rival in the form of English colonies to the south, the French in Canada needed Indian allies to provide assistance in the event of war. The French were relatively few in number, wanted Indian furs rather than land, and carefully cultivated Indian alliances. Confronted with the threat of English settlers encroaching on their lands, many Indians saw the French as their best hope for protection and military support. Thus, the stage was set for Indian involvement in over a half century of bitter conflict between France and England in eighteenth-century North America.

◆ **Frederic Remington, *Radisson and Groseilliers* (1905)**
Remington depicts a typical scene in the French penetration of North America, where
French explorers, traders, and missionaries relied on canoes, Indian paddlers, and Indian
guides. Pierre Esprit Radisson (1636–1710) was captured by the Iroquois, lived as an adopted
Mohawk, and then worked as an interpreter. His brother-in-law, Médard Chouart, Sieur des
Groseilliers (c. 1618–c. 1697), worked with Jesuit missionaries in Huronia from 1641 to 1646
(see pages 110–19) and became a *coureur de bois* or Indian trader after the Iroquois-Huron
wars. Radisson and Groseilliers journeyed west to Lake Superior and Lake Michigan in
1659–60, making contact with Anishinaabeg, Ottawas, Potawatomis, and perhaps Sioux.
Buffalo Bill Center of the West, Cody, Wyoming. Gift of Mrs. Karl Frank; 14.86.

INDIANS CONFRONT THE ENGLISH

The English were relative latecomers in the invasion and colonization of North
America. John Cabot, an Italian sailing for the king of England, explored the
coasts of Maine and Nova Scotia in 1497 and 1498, but not until 1607 was the first
permanent English settlement founded at Jamestown, Virginia. The English were
not new to colonization, however; from the Middle Ages, England had extended
dominion north into Scotland, west to Wales, and across the Irish Sea. Many of
the attitudes and ways of treating "heathen people" that the English developed
in Ireland carried over into their dealings with Indians in America. Also, Indian
policies that the various English colonies and the British government developed
over a century and a half of Indian relations established important precedents

for later U.S. government policies. English and Indians on the East Coast in the seventeenth century negotiated agreements and alliances, and the treaty-making practices they worked out became fundamental in later British and U.S. relations with Indian nations.[45] Treaties were easily broken, however, and Indian relations with the English took place in a context of increasing warfare, as initially amicable relations broke down under intensifying pressure for Indian lands and gave way to open conflict.

Securing a Beachhead in Virginia

One of the first English settlements in North America—at Roanoke Island off North Carolina in 1585–88—seems to have been destroyed after the settlers alienated the local Indians, although what exactly became of the settlers has remained a mystery; some of them may have been absorbed into Indian communities.[46] Anglo-Indian relations in Virginia followed a similar course after the establishment of Jamestown. Many of the settlers at Jamestown were soldiers of fortune expecting to win great riches in their enterprise, not farmers who knew how to extract a modest living from the land. Half of them died in the first year and recent archaeological excavations have revealed evidence of cannibalism. Modern findings from analyses of cypress tree growth rings indicate that English attempts to establish colonies at Roanoke and Jamestown occurred during one of the worst droughts ever to affect that area.[47]

English colonists had to contend with Native power before they could finally establish a foothold and exploit the rich resources of the Potomac River system. The clash of Indian and European is often depicted as one between hunters and farmers, but in the Potomac valley, as in many other places, the contest between European *and* Indian farmers made the competition for the best lands deadly and the outcome catastrophic for Native peoples.[48]

Few in number at first, and evidently inept in their new environment, the English settlers cannot have seemed much of a threat to the local Indians, members of the powerful Powhatan chiefdom that embraced some thirty tribes and extended across most of eastern Virginia. The Indians had been growing corn since the fourteenth century, and they supplied corn to the colonists. The paramount chief, Powhatan, seems to have tried to incorporate the English into his domain. John Smith, the leader of the colonists, recalled several years later how he was captured by the Indians in December 1607 and saved from execution by Powhatan's daughter, Pocahontas, "a childe of twelve or thirteene years of age." Pocahontas threw her body across his "at the minute of my execution." Smith's account has become legendary, perpetuated in history books and Disney movies for its romantic impact rather than its accuracy. In fact, if the events occurred as Smith described them, Pocahontas was most likely performing a prescribed role in a standard ritual by which Powhatan could adopt Smith and make him a *werowance,* or subordinate chieftain.[49]

But Smith was not interested in becoming a secondary leader. Rather, he looked to Spanish experiences in Mexico as his guide to dealing with Indians.

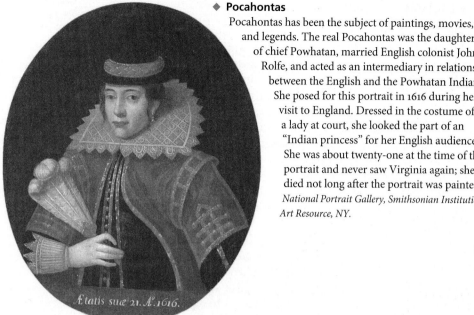

♦ **Pocahontas**

Pocahontas has been the subject of paintings, movies, and legends. The real Pocahontas was the daughter of chief Powhatan, married English colonist John Rolfe, and acted as an intermediary in relations between the English and the Powhatan Indians. She posed for this portrait in 1616 during her visit to England. Dressed in the costume of a lady at court, she looked the part of an "Indian princess" for her English audience. She was about twenty-one at the time of the portrait and never saw Virginia again; she died not long after the portrait was painted. *National Portrait Gallery, Smithsonian Institution/ Art Resource, NY.*

The English began to demand and seize corn. "What will it availe you to take that by force you may quickly have by love, or destroy them that provide you food?" asked Powhatan in bewilderment.[50] Tensions increased as the English expanded up the James River. After Smith left the colony in 1609, fighting broke out between the Indians and the English. Pocahontas seems to have played an intermediary role between Indians and colonists, and her marriage in 1614 to John Rolfe, one of the colonists, helped restore peace. She traveled to England with him, only to die there in 1617 as her ship was about to leave for America. In 1622 Powhatan's brother Opechancanough led Indians in what the English called "the Virginia massacre"; four hundred colonists died. But the Indians were unable to drive the English away. The colonists retaliated and kept up pressure on Indian lands. War broke out again in 1644, and the English captured and killed the aged and now blind Opechancanough.[51]

In 1676, denouncing the governor's Indian policies as too lenient, Nathaniel Bacon, an English aristocrat who had come to America three years earlier, led Virginians in a series of attacks on Indians in the backcountry of the colony. Bacon coerced the Virginia House of Burgesses into appointing him commander-in-chief in the Indian war and demanded that the governor grant approval for the expedition. When the governor refused and declared Bacon a rebel, Bacon led his men against Jamestown. Bacon died soon after, in October 1676, and "Bacon's Rebellion" collapsed.[52] As a result of the rebellion, several small reservations — the first in the present United States — were established for the survivors of the tribes that had once composed the powerful Powhatan chiefdom.

Making a *New* England

In New England, the English adventurer Sir Humphrey Gilbert dreamed of establishing a colony in the region of Maine, which he called Norumbega, in the 1580s, but Gilbert died at sea before any of his ambitions could be realized. Several English expeditions skirted the coast of Maine in the first decade of the seventeenth century, trading with the Indians and, on occasion, kidnapping and fighting with them. In 1607 the English established a short-lived colony at Sagadahoc at the mouth of the Kennebec River in Maine. In 1614 John Smith voyaged to the region, produced a detailed map of it, and renamed the area: from Norumbega (or North Virginia, as some called it), it became New England.

Permanent English settlement in New England began when the Pilgrims settled north of Cape Cod in 1620 and established Plymouth Colony. They found the coast of Massachusetts depopulated by an epidemic that had ravaged the area between 1616 and 1619. God, so the Pilgrims believed, had prepared the way for their coming by sending a plague among the Indians. Fewer than half the Pilgrims survived their first winter in America, but God seemed to offer help again when, early in the spring, they met an Abenaki Indian named Samoset, who had been brought to Cape Cod from Maine on an English ship and learned the language from the sailors. Samoset introduced the Pilgrims to Squanto, a local Patuxet Indian who had been captured and taken to Spain before traveling to England and then back home, only to find his people wiped out by disease. Squanto helped the Pilgrims adjust to their new world; he showed them how to plant corn and where to fish, and he functioned as interpreter and intermediary in their dealings with the local Indians. (See "Of Plymouth Plantation," pages 106–9.) He was, said Governor William Bradford of Plymouth, "a spetiall instrument sent of God."[53] In 1621 Massasoit, chief of the Wampanoags of southern Massachusetts and Rhode Island, made a treaty of peace and friendship with the Pilgrims. The English presence in New England grew when the crown chartered the Massachusetts Bay Colony in 1629. More than twenty thousand English colonists arrived over the next fourteen years. Boston was founded in 1630 and was soon ringed by English towns inland.

As English settlers arrived at an increasing rate, Indian people found themselves pushed off their lands, deprived of game, and cheated in trade. Smallpox struck the Indians of New England in 1633–34 and Governor William Bradford of Plymouth Plantation reported a mortality rate of 95 percent among Indians on the Connecticut River. (See "Of Plymouth Plantation," pages 106–9.) The Pequot Indians of southern Connecticut suffered appalling losses in the epidemic. The Pequots were a once-powerful people whose location at the mouth of the Connecticut River allowed them to control the region's trade in wampum — strings of shells used in intertribal trade and diplomacy. Two years after the smallpox epidemic, the English went to war against the Pequots.

The Pequot War has been a source of controversy among historians: some blame the Pequots; others see it as an act of genocide on the part of the English. A scholar of the conflict concludes that it was "the messy outgrowth of petty squabbles over trade, tribute, and land" among various Indian tribes, Dutch traders, and

◆ The English Attack on the Pequots at Their Mystic River Village in 1637
This stylized engraving of the massacre, from John Underhill's *Newes from America* (1638),
shows English soldiers armed with muskets and backed by a ring of Narragansett Indian
allies armed with bows and arrows. They surround the palisaded Pequot village and shoot
down the inhabitants as they attempt to escape. *Library of Congress.*

English Puritans. The Puritans, however, transformed it into a mythic struggle
between savagery and civilization.[54] A Puritan army broke Pequot resistance in
a surprise attack on their main village in 1637. Surrounding the palisaded village,
the soldiers put the Pequots' lodges to the torch, and shot or cut down the people
who tried to escape. Hundreds died in the ensuing slaughter. (See "Of Plymouth
Plantation," pages 106–9). The English hunted down the survivors, executing
some, selling women and children into slavery, and handing over others to the
Mohegans and Narragansetts who had assisted the English in the war. At the
Treaty of Hartford in 1638, the English terminated Pequot sovereignty and outlawed the use of the tribal name.

Similar events occurred in New York. The Dutch came to America as traders,
but like the English they acquired Indian land (famously purchasing Manhattan
Island in 1625), undermined Native cultures, and transformed initially peaceful
encounters into open conflict. In 1643–45 — just a few years after the Puritans had
defeated the Pequots in Connecticut and at the same time as the Virginia colonists

were defeating the Powhatans — the Dutch in New York inflicted crushing defeats on the Indians of the lower Hudson valley and Long Island.[55]

In Massachusetts, meanwhile, Puritan missionaries worked to convert the Native peoples to Christianity. Thomas Mayhew and his son began missionary work among the Wampanoags on Martha's Vineyard in the 1640s. On the mainland, John Eliot, minister of the English church at Roxbury, gathered Indian converts into "praying towns" like Natick where they were expected to give up Indian ways and live like their Christian English neighbors. Working with an Indian interpreter and an Indian printer, Eliot even translated the Bible into the Massachusett dialect of the Algonquian language for his Indian congregations. Indian people embraced Christianity in varying degrees and for a variety of reasons. Some found it offered hope and strength in a world that seemed to be unraveling under the impact of disease, alcohol, and escalating violence. For some, Christian services and prayers replaced or supplemented traditional rituals that provided no protection against diseases new to them. Some found in a Christian community, even in Eliot's rigidly regulated praying towns, a refuge from English racism and the turmoil in their own villages. In the praying town of Natick, Massachusetts, for example, individuals and families from several different tribal groups rebuilt a community within their southeastern New England homeland.[56] Algonquian women sometimes found that Christianity honored their traditional roles and gave them an opportunity to learn to read and write. Many people blended elements of old and new religions, invested Christian messages and rituals with Native meanings, and made Christianity an Indian religion. Christianity, for some, was a strategy of survival. On Martha's Vineyard, Wampanoag people constructed a Christian community that helped them carve out their own space and keep their colonial neighbors at arm's length — even during the catastrophe of King Philip's War.[57]

King Philip's War

After Massasoit made peace with the English in 1621, he worked to preserve it. Colonists and Indians became, to a degree, economically interdependent. Even the Puritan war against the Pequots of Connecticut in 1636–37 did not spill over into conflict with the Wampanoags. Ongoing rivalries divided the Mohegans, Narragansetts, and other tribes and Native leaders like Ninigret, sachem (chief) of the Narragansetts and Niantics from the mid-1630s through the mid-1670s, worked to maintain the balance of power in both Indian–colonial and intertribal relations.[58] Indians and English settlers managed for a time to share the same world. But Puritans held to the belief that Indians were heathen savages and continued to trespass on Indian lands. Relations rapidly deteriorated after Massasoit's death in 1661. His son Wamsutta, whom the English called Alexander, continued his father's policy of selling lands to the English, but in 1662, fearing they could not control the young sachem, the Plymouth colonists brought Wamsutta to Plymouth at gunpoint for questioning. Wamsutta was ill, and the colonists released him but kept his two sons as hostages. The ordeal proved too much for the leader, and he died on the way home. Many Wampanoags believed the Puritans had poisoned their sachem.

♦ A Seventeenth-Century New England Sachem
Contemporary depictions of Metacom were vicious caricatures; later pictures were imaginative recreations. This painting by an unidentified artist around 1681 is generally regarded as the only accurate portrait of a seventeenth-century southern New England Indian. The subject is usually identified as Ninigret II, son of the Niantic-Narragansett sachem of the same name, but some scholars now believe he may be a Pequot sachem named Robin Cassinamon. *Artist unknown, Native American Sachem, ca. 1700. Photography by Erik Gould, courtesy of the Museum of Art, Rhode Island School of Design, Providence.*

Wamsutta's younger brother, Metacomet (called King Philip by the English), now became the leader of his people at a critical juncture. The Puritans continued to encroach on Wampanoag land and to assert their judicial authority over Indian actions. Indian hunters found themselves being arrested and jailed for "trespassing" on lands the English now claimed as their own. As the Indians displayed growing resentment, the colonists in 1671 demanded that Metacomet surrender the Wampanoags' weapons. Metacomet was backed into a corner: "I am determined not to live until I have no country," he said.[59] The Plymouth colonists and the Wampanoags squared off for a fight. Rumors of impending war flew through the settlements.

In December 1674, John Sassamon, a Christian Indian, reported to Plymouth governor John Winslow that Metacomet was preparing for war. The next month, Sassamon was found under the ice of a pond with a broken neck. In June, the Puritans seized three Wampanoags and charged them with Sassamon's murder. The evidence was flimsy, but a Plymouth jury found the men guilty and executed them. (Indians sat on the jury but they had no vote.) It was the first time the English had executed an Indian for a crime committed against another Indian.[60]

Faced with escalating assaults on their sovereignty, the Indian tribes had to succumb or resist.[61] Metacomet began to forge a multitribal coalition, and Indians and colonists steeled themselves for war. An Indian was shot as he ransacked a colonist's house; a party of Indians retaliated by killing a colonist and his son. Metacomet withdrew from his home in present-day Rhode Island at Montaup, or Mount Hope to the English, and took refuge with Wetamoo, the "squaw sachem" (female chief) of the Pocassets and widow of Wamsutta. Some Indian people faced difficult decisions and divided loyalties as the impending war threatened to sever ties they had built with English neighbors over the previous generation.[62]

Wetamoo seems to have been reluctant to commit to war, but many of her warriors rallied to Metacomet, as did most Nipmucks in central Massachusetts.

Aligning with the English, Awashunkes, squaw sachem of the Sakonnets of Rhode Island, put her people under the protection of the Plymouth colony. The Mohegan sachem, Uncas, supported the English, as he had in the Pequot War, as a way of preserving Mohegan autonomy and enhancing his own position.[63] The powerful Narragansetts declared their intention to remain neutral, and many of Metacomet's followers sent their women and children to take refuge with them. Individuals from Natick and other praying towns had given the English warnings of the brewing crisis and assisted them during the war as scouts, informants, and soldiers.[64] But the English feared all Indians, and as the war spread they incarcerated more than five hundred Christian Indians from the praying towns on Deer Island in Boston Harbor. Without adequate food or shelter during the winter of 1675–76, many of them died.

Scattered acts of violence escalated into the brutal conflict known as King Philip's War (Map 2.4). Metacomet's warriors ambushed English militia companies and burned English towns. In November 1675 the English declared war against the Narragansetts, interpreting their offer of sanctuary to noncombatants from other tribes as an act of hostility. The next month, an English army of more than a thousand men marched through deep snow and attacked the main Narragansett stronghold near Kingston, Rhode Island. Hundreds of Narragansett men, women, and children died in what became known as the Great Swamp Fight. An Englishman, Joshua Tefft, who had an Indian wife and was in the Narragansett stronghold at the time of the attack, was captured, hanged, and quartered by the Puritans.[65] The surviving Narragansetts joined Metacomet's war of resistance.

Both sides suffered terribly that winter from cold and hunger. English homes lay in ruins and fields lay barren. Puritan ministers thundered from pulpits that the war was God's way of punishing his sinful people. Disease broke out in the Indian camps. Metacomet tried to broaden the conflict by bringing in the Mahicans and Abenakis; Governor Edmund Andros of New York prevailed upon the Mohawks to attack Metacomet's army in its winter camps, a devastating blow to the Wampanoag alliance, which now found itself fighting on two fronts.

In February 1676 English troops found a note nailed to a post outside Medfield, Massachusetts, that conveyed the Native point of view: "Know by this paper, that the Indians that thou has provoked to wrath and anger, will war this twenty-one years if you will; there are many Indians yet, we come three hundred at this time. You must consider the Indians lost nothing but their life; you must lose your fair houses and cattle."[66] That same month, the Indians attacked and burned Lancaster, Massachusetts. They took two dozen prisoners, including Mary Rowlandson, who later produced a narrative of her experience as a captive with Metacomet's army as the war was slipping away from the Indians.[67] The tribal coalition was falling apart and Indian resistance was faltering. In April, the colonists captured the Narragansett sachem Canonchet and handed him over to their Mohegan allies for execution. In May, Captain William Turner attacked an Indian encampment at Peskeompscut, now Turner's Falls, Massachusetts, where families had gathered

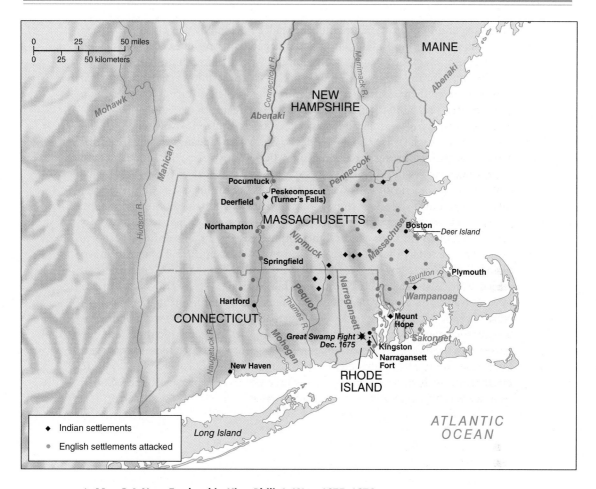

◆ Map 2.4 **New England in King Philip's War, 1675–1676**
In proportion to population, King Philip's War is reckoned to have been the bloodiest conflict in American history. English towns were attacked and burned. Unknown numbers of
Native people died, and many — even the Christian Indians from John Eliot's praying towns
west of Boston — were relocated to Deer Island in Boston Harbor and suffered terrible hardship during their confinement there.

for springtime fishing on the Connecticut River. Surprising the camp at dawn,
Turner's men killed hundreds of people. Captain Benjamin Church, effectively
applying Indian tactics of guerilla warfare, harried Metacomet's remaining followers. That summer, he captured Metacomet's wife, Wootonekanuska, and nine-
year-old son and sent them to Plymouth for trial; they were probably sold as slaves
in the West Indies. On the night of August 11, Church and his men, including
some Indian allies, caught up with Metacomet. Jolted from sleep, Metacomet ran
for safety but was shot and killed. Church ordered Metacomet's head cut off and

his body cut into quarters. Even after the leader's death, the war continued along the coast of Maine, but Indian power and independence in southern New England were broken. Many people fled north, joining Abenakis in Maine, Vermont, and New Hampshire and siding with the French in future conflicts against the English who had driven them from their homelands. The war left a searing impression on New England and a bitter legacy for Anglo-Indian relations.

Within the five-year period 1675–80, Indian peoples in New England and New Mexico fought wars of independence against Europeans who had invaded and had begun colonizing their homelands. In both instances, the Indians scored impressive victories but ultimately lost the wars. The defeat of those movements did not mean the end of Indian resistance, which continued in other ways and other places, but it did mark the end of a phase: on both sides of the continent, Europeans had weathered their most severe test and secured their beachheads. By the end of the seventeenth century, the outposts of New France dotted the shores of the St. Lawrence, the Great Lakes, and the Mississippi. New Spain included Florida and New Mexico. New Netherland had fallen. English colonists had settled from New England to South Carolina. African slaves were being shipped to American ports to provide labor for colonial agriculture. Throughout most of North America, Indian peoples followed their ancient cycles of life without disruption; participated in ceremonies to keep crops growing, game plentiful, and the universe in harmony; and lived, fought, and traded with other Indians, not with Europeans. But European people, European animals, and European diseases were infiltrating North America. Europeans were a permanent presence, and colonial America was being established in Indian America.

DOCUMENTS

Cooperation, Contagion, and Conflict

⁘⁘◆◆◆◆◆◆◆◆◆◆◆⁘⁘

L OOKING BACK ACROSS THE CENTURIES, and condensing multiple human experiences into simple stories represented by single events, we can easily assume that violence between Indian people and European invaders was immediate and incessant. To be sure, there was plenty of bloodshed. Yet almost everywhere Indians and Europeans met, there were instances of cooperation and periods of coexistence. Rather than instantly attacking the indigenous inhabitants, Europeans often depended on them for food, information, and assistance in finding their way, adjusting to a new environment, and in dealing with other Indian peoples. Lacking our knowledge that the trickle of European invaders would grow into a tsunami, Indian people at first saw few reasons to try and destroy the newcomers. Instead, often, they watched the Europeans with interest (and suspicion), incorporated them into their alliances, and traded with them for the new goods they brought. Patterns of coexistence and conflict varied from region to region, but the bloodshed that stained encounters between Native people and Europeans often occurred later, after the newcomers had weathered their early years, after the balance of power shifted dramatically in favor of the Europeans, and after relations of cautious coexistence and mutual dependence broke down amid escalating pressure on Native land and resources. As European populations grew through continuing immigration and natural increase, Native populations plummeted under the impact of the epidemic diseases the Europeans brought with them. Formerly powerful tribes that might easily have snuffed out infant European settlements were rendered vulnerable to the invaders' growing power, increasing demands, and lethal technology and tactics.

The following excerpts from William Bradford's history, *Of Plymouth Plantation*, illustrate these three aspects of encounter in the shifting relationship between the English and Native people in southern New England. Born in Yorkshire around 1590, William Bradford belonged to a group of religious dissenters who, despairing of ever being able to reform the Church of England, broke all ties with it. These Separatists, as they were called, suffered persecution. In 1608 some, Bradford among them, fled to Leiden in the Dutch Republic, where they were free to practice their religion. After nine years in Leiden, about fifty of the Separatists decided to migrate to the English colony of Virginia and joined other colonists departing from Plymouth, England, aboard the *Mayflower* in September 1620. The 102 passengers became known as "Pilgrims." They reached Cape Cod, in present-day Massachusetts, in November, but rough seas prevented them continuing south to Virginia, and they built their settlement at Plymouth Bay instead. It had been the site of an Indian village called Patuxet, but the Pilgrims found the village empty and its fields abandoned; a series of epidemics had swept the coast in 1616–19, killing or driving away the inhabitants. The Pilgrims saw God's hand at work, clearing the way for his chosen people, but almost half of the Pilgrims died over the course of their first New England winter. The assistance of a well-traveled Indian named Tisquantum or Squanto and peaceful relations with the local Wampanoag chief, Massasoit, who saw the newcomers as possible allies against the powerful Narragansetts to his west, helped the Pilgrims to make it through. In the fall of 1621 the Pilgrims held a feast to give thanks for their survival; Indians joined them and provided most of the food. Reimagined and remembered, it became an iconic moment in American history — the First Thanksgiving. The following winter, one of the colonists, Edward Winslow, hearing that Massasoit had fallen ill, traveled to the Wampanoag village at Sowams (near present-day Warren, Rhode Island), and helped nurse the chief back to health. For a time, "the Wampanoags and colonists recognized that their stories were connected and that they needed one another to survive."[68] The English peace with the Wampanoags lasted, despite growing tensions, until King Philip's War broke out in 1675; relations with some other tribes in New England turned violent much sooner.

William Bradford served multiple terms as governor of Plymouth Colony from 1621 to his death in 1657. Between 1630 to 1651 he wrote a journal setting down the story of the Pilgrims from their migration to Leiden until 1647, although his work was not published until 1856. Historians regard Bradford's history of Plymouth Plantation as a key source for early New England (one calls it "certainly the greatest book written in seventeenth-century America")[69] but they also bear in mind that Bradford wrote about many of the events long after they happened, and that he brought his particular worldview to his interpretation of those events and to his descriptions of Indian people. The following excerpts record the meeting with Samoset and Squanto and the terms of the peace treaty negotiated with Massasoit, reports of a smallpox epidemic that devastated the Pequots and other tribes in the Connecticut valley in 1633, and the English war against the Pequots in 1636–37.

WILLIAM BRADFORD (1590–1657)
Of Plymouth Plantation

[1620–21]

All this while the Indians came skulking about them, and would sometimes show them selves a loofe of, but when any aproached near them,

SOURCE: *Bradford's History of Plymouth Plantation, 1606–1646.* Edited by William T. Davis. New York: Charles Scribner's Sons, 1908, 110–112;312–13; 335; 338–40. Early Americas Digital Archive. http://mith.umd.edu/eada/html/display .php?docs=bradford_history.xml&action=show.

they would rune away. And once they stoale away their tools wher they had been at worke, and were gone to diner. But about the 16. of March a certaine Indian came bouldly amongst them, and spoke to them in broken English, which they could well understand, but marvelled at it. At length they understood by discourse with him, that he was not of these parts, but belonged to the eastrene parts, wher some English-ships came to fhish, with whom he was aquainted, and could name sundrie of them by their names, amongst whom he had gott his language. He became proftable to them in aquainting them with many things concerning the state of the cuntry in the east-parts wher he lived, which was afterwards profitable unto them; as also of the people hear, of their names, number, and strength; of their situation and distance from this place, and who was cheefe amongst them. His name was Samaset; he tould them also of another Indian whos name was Squanto, a native of this place, who had been in England and could speake better English then him selfe. Being, after some time of entertainmente and gifts, dismist, a while after he came againe, and 5. more with him, and they brought againe all the tooles that were stolen away before, and made way for the coming of their great Sachem, called Massasoyt; who, about 4. or 5. days after, came with the cheefe of his freinds and other attendance, with the aforesaid Squanto. With whom, after frendly entertainment, and some gifts given him, they made a peace with him (which hath now continued this 24 years) in these terms.

1. That neither he nor any of his, should injurie or doe hurte to any of their peopl.
2. That if any of his did any hurte to any of theirs, he should send the offender, that they might punish him.
3. That if any thing were taken away from any of theirs, he should cause it to be restored; and they should doe the like to his.
4. If any did unjustly warr against him, they would aide him; if any did warr against them, he should aide them.
5. He should send to his neighbours confederats, to certifie them of this, that they might not wrong them, but might be likewise comprised in the conditions of peace.
6. That when ther men came to them, they should leave their bows and arrows behind them.

After these things he returned to his place caled Sowams, some 40. mile from this place, but Squanto continued with them, and was their interpreter, and was a spetiall instrument sent of God for their good beyond their expectation. He directed them how to set their corne, wher to take fish, and to procure other comodities, and was also their pilott to bring them to unknowne places for their profitt, and never left them till he dyed. He was a native of this place, and scarce any left alive beside him selfe. He was caried away with diverce others by one Hunt,° a mr of a ship, who thought to sell them for slaves in Spaine; but he got away for England, and was entertained by a marchante in London, and imployed to New-foundland and other parts, and lastly brought hither into these parts by one Mr. Dermer, a gentle-man imployed by Sr. Ferdinando Gorges and others, for discovery, and other designes in these parts.

[1634]

I am now to relate some strang and remarkable passages. Ther was a company of people lived in the country, up above in the river of Conigtecut, a great way from their trading house ther, and were enimise to those Indeans which lived aboute them, and of whom they stood in some fear (being a stout people). About a thousand of them had inclosed them selves in a forte, which they had strongly palissadoed° about. 3. or 4. Dutch men went up in the begining of winter to live with them, to gett their trade, and prevente them for bringing it to the English, or to fall into amitie with them; but at spring to bring all downe to their place. But their enterprise failed, for it pleased God to visite these Indeans with a great sicknes, and such a mortalitie that of a 1000. above 900. and a halfe of them dyed, and many of them did rott above ground for want of buriall, and the Dutch men allmost starved before they could gett away, for ise and snow. But about Feb: they got with much difficultie to their trading house; whom they kindly releeved, being

---

° Thomas Hunt captained one of the ships in John Smith's voyage to New England in 1614.

° Palissadoed: palisaded; surrounded with a stockade.

allmost spente with hunger and could. Being thus refreshed by them diverce days, they got to their owne place, and the Dutch were very thankfull for this kindnes.

This spring, also, those Indeans that lived aboute their trading house there fell sick of the small poxe, and dyed most miserably; for a sorer disease cannot befall them; they fear it more then the plague; for usualy they that have this disease have them in abundance, and for wante of bedding and linning and other helps, they fall into a lamentable condition, as they lye on their hard matts, the poxe breaking and mattering, and runing one into another, their skin cleaving (by reason therof) to the matts they lye on; when they turne them, a whole side will flea of at once, (as it were,) and they will be all of a gore blood, most fearfull to behold; and then being very sore, what with could and other distempers, they dye like rotten sheep. The condition of this people was so lamentable, and they fell downe so generally of this diseas, as they were (in the end) not able to help on another; no, not to make a fire, nor to fetch a litle water to drinke, nor any to burie the dead; but would strivie as long as they could, and when they could procure no other means to make fire, they would burne the woden trayes and dishes they ate their meate in, and their very Bowes and arrowes; and some would crawle out on all foure to gett a litle water, and some times dye by the way, and not be able to gett in againe. But those of the English house, (though at first they were afraid of the infection,) yet seeing their woefull and sadd condition, and hearing their pitifull cries and lamentations, they had compassion of them, and dayly fetched them wood and water, and made them fires, gott them victualls whilst they lived, and buried them when they dyed. For very few of them escaped, notwithstanding they did what they could for them, to the haszard of them selvs. The cheefe Sachem him selfe now dyed, and allmost all his freinds and kinred. But by the marvelous goodnes and providens of God not one of the English was so much as sicke, or in the least measure tainted with this disease, though they dayly did these offices for them for many weeks togeather.

[**1637**]
In the fore parte of this year, the Pequents fell openly upon the English at Conightecute, in the lower parts of the river, and slew sundry of them, (as they were at work in the feilds,) both men and women, to the great terrour of the rest; and wente away in great prid and triumph, with many high threats. They allso assalted a fort at the rivers mouth, though strong and well defended; and though they did not their prevaile, yet it struk them with much fear and astonishmente to see their bould attempts in the face of danger; which made them in all places to stand upon their gard, and to prepare for resistance, and ernestly to solissite their freinds and confederate in the Bay of Massachusets to send them speedy aide, for they looked for more forcible assaults.

In the mean time, the Pequents, espetially in the winter before, sought to make peace with the Narigansets, and used very pernicious arguments to move them therunto: as that the English were strangers and begane to overspred their countrie, and would deprive them therof in time, if they were suffered to grow and increse; and if the Narigansets did assist the English to subdue them, they did but make way for their owne overthrow, for if they were rooted out, the English would soone take occasion to subjugate them; and if they would harken to them, they should not neede to fear the strength of the English; for they would not come to open battle with them, but fire their houses, kill their katle, and lye in ambush for them as they went abroad upon their occasions; and all this they might easily doe without any or litle danger to them selves. The which course being held, they well saw the English could not long subsiste, but they would either be starved with hunger, or be forced to forsake the countrie; with many the like things; insomuch that the Narigansets were once wavering, and were halfe minded to have made peace with them, and joyned against the English. But againe when they considered, how much wrong they had received from the Pequents, and what an oppertunitie they now had by the help of the English to right them selves, revenge was so sweete unto them, as it prevailed above all the rest; so as they resolved to joyne with the English against them, and did. The Court here agreed forwith to send 50. men at their owne charg; and with as much speed as posiblie they could, gott them armed, and had made them ready under sufficiente leaders, and provided a barke to carrie them provisions and tend upon them for all occasions; but when they were ready to march (with a supply from the Bay) they had word to stay, for the enimy was as good as vanquished, and their would be no neede.

I shall not take upon me exactly to describe their proceedings in these things, because I expecte it will be fully done by them selves, who best know the carrage and circumstances of things; I shall therfore but touch them in generall. From Connightecute (who were most sencible of the hurt sustained, and the present danger), they sett out a partie of men, and an other partie mett them from the Bay, at the Narigansets, who were to joyne with them. The Narigansets were ernest to be gone before the English were well rested and refreshte, espetially some of them which came last. It should seeme their desire was to come upon the enemie sudenly, and undiscovered. Ther was a barke of this place, newly put in ther, which was come from Conightecutte, who did

incourage them to lay hold of the Indeans forwardnes, and to shew as great forwardnes as they, for it would incorage them, and expedition might prove to their great advantage. So they went on, and so ordered their march, as the Indeans brought them to a forte of the enimies (in which most of their cheefe men were) before day. They approached the same with great silence, and surrounded it both with English and Indeans, that they might not breake out; and so assualted them with great courage, shooting amongst them, and entered the forte with all speed; and those that first entered found sharp resistance from the enimie, who both shott at and grapled with them; others rane into their houses, and brought out fire, and sett them on fire, which soone tooke in their matts, and, standing close togeather, with the wind, all was quickly on a flame, and therby more were burnte to death then was otherwise slain; it burnte their bowstrings, and made them unservisable. Those that scaped the fire were slaine with the sword; some hewed to peeces, others rune throw with their rapiers, so as they were quickly dispatchte, and very few escaped. It was conceived they thus destroyed about 400. at this time. It was a fearfull sight to see them thus frying in the fyer, and the streams of blood quenching the same, and horrible was the stinck and sente ther of; but the victory seemed a sweete sacrifice, and they gave the prays therof to God, who had wrought so wonderfuly for them, thus to inclose their enimise in their hands, and give them so speedy a victory over so proud and insulting an enimie.

QUESTIONS FOR CONSIDERATION

1. What do these excerpts from William Bradford's "Of Plymouth Plantation" suggest about the possibilities of cooperation and coexistence between Indian people and the English? Who facilitated this cooperative coexistence?

2. What do the excerpts tell us about the causes of conflict? Was conflict inevitable? How do the English understand and explain the events recorded here?

A Jesuit Assesses the Hurons and a Mi'kmaq Assesses the French

ALTHOUGH EUROPEANS THOUGHT AND WROTE as if they were "discovering" new peoples and new lands when they invaded America, in reality colonial encounters always involved *mutual* discoveries, as Indian people also observed, weighed up, and tried to understand the newcomers. Some Europeans, like the Jesuit missionaries who traveled throughout New France searching for souls to save, regularly kept detailed records of the Indian peoples they met and lived with. Indian attitudes and responses to the French are much more rare, although occasionally their sentiments, if not their actual words, made it into the records of encounter written down by Europeans.

The Huron or Wendat Indians were early and important allies of the French. Huronia, their homeland, was relatively small, no more than twenty miles north to south and thirty-five miles across, between Lake Simcoe and Georgian Bay in present-day Ontario. The area was densely settled, with between twenty and thirty thousand people living in villages. Lying at the northern limit of southern Ontario's rich farmland, it was also an important center of trade between hunters and farmers in the upper Great Lakes region. From the villages of the Hurons, French traders and missionaries could set forth north, west, and south into distant Indian regions (Map 2.5).

In 1609 Huron and Algonquin warriors arrived at Quebec to ask Samuel de Champlain for support in a raid against their Iroquois enemies. Champlain was anxious to establish commercial relations with the Hurons and Algonquins and agreed. He accompanied the Indians to Lake Champlain and participated in a skirmish with the Mohawks. (See page 91.) Three years later, Champlain dispatched a young man named Étienne Brulé to live among the Hurons and strengthen Franco-Huron trade connections. (Brulé "went Indian" and spent the rest of his life in Indian country.) In 1615 Champlain journeyed to Huronia himself and was compelled to join the Hurons in another battle against the Iroquois. The Iroquois became increasingly disturbed at the threat posed by this alliance between their old enemies and the French. Meanwhile, the French looked to Huronia as the potential center of a new Catholic and commercial empire. Father Gabriel Sagard, a Recollect° missionary who traveled to Huronia and lived there in the winter of 1623–24, found much in Huron life that was distasteful and reported many things he did not understand, but he acknowledged the love Hurons showed one another: "If they were Christians these would be families among whom God would take pleasure to dwell," he wrote.[70]

An English expedition captured Quebec in 1629 and Champlain returned to France. But this loss was reversed by a peace settlement in Europe and

---

° The Recollects were Franciscans and the first missionaries in Canada.

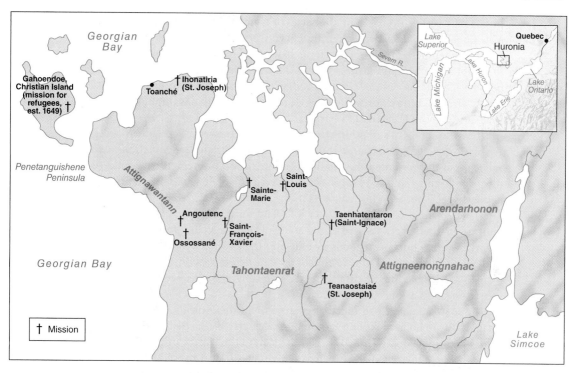

◆ **Map 2.5 Jesuits in Huronia, 1615–1650**
In the early seventeenth century, the Hurons—four major tribes living in eighteen to twenty-five villages—represented a rich field for Jesuit missionaries. This map shows the location of the major tribal groups, key Jesuit missions, and the village of Toanché, with which Brébeuf was associated.
SOURCE: Reprinted with permission of the publisher from *Bitter Feast: Amerindians and Europeans in Northeastern North America, 1600–64* by Denys Delâge. © University of British Columbia Press, 1993. All rights reserved by the publisher.

Champlain was back in 1633. Accompanying him was Father Jean de Brébeuf. Born to a noble family in Normandy in 1593, Brébeuf entered the Society of Jesus in 1617 and was sent to Canada in 1625 as one of the first Jesuit missionaries. After a year among the Montagnais on the north shore of the St. Lawrence, he went to Huronia in 1626, where he lived for three years in the village of Toanché and learned the Hurons' language. In 1634 he set out again for Huronia. With the exception of three years in Quebec, Brébeuf spent the rest of his life in Indian country.

The Jesuit order had a long record of missionary work, and their North American venture was launched with characteristic zeal. They learned Native languages, committed their lives to their work, and risked (some would say sought) martyrdom in their efforts to save people they regarded as heathen. At first, the

Jesuits, like earlier Recollect missionaries in New France and Puritan ministers in New England, tried to coerce their Indian converts to abandon traditional ways. In time, they tempered their approach, realizing that Indian people were more likely to accept a new religion if they did not have to give up being Indians in order to become Christians. Jesuits adopted Indian words and ways to get their message across: Brébeuf himself presented the Huron council with a wampum belt of 1,200 beads to "smooth their road to Paradise."[71]

Even so, Brébeuf's mission struggled in its early years. The Hurons tolerated the black-gowned Jesuits because they wanted to maintain trade relations with the French, but they resented the missionaries' intrusion in their rituals and ceremonies. The Jesuits criticized Huron sexual practices, gender relations, child rearing, and festivals. They won few converts in these early years.

Then disease began to take its toll. The location and participation of the Hurons in trade networks reaching to the Atlantic guaranteed that European germs as well as European goods would enter their villages. Smallpox struck in the mid-1630s. Influenza hit in 1636. Smallpox returned in 1639. At first, many Hurons blamed the Jesuits for the disaster and some sought vengeance, but soon Huron people began to ask for baptism.

By 1640 smallpox had killed as many as half the Hurons.[72] The disease devastated Huron society, killing children and elders. With their loved ones dying before their eyes, many Hurons began to listen to the words of Jesuit missionaries who, unaffected by the disease, were clearly men of great power. The Huron shamans had failed to forewarn or protect their people from the catastrophe; perhaps the Jesuit shamans had some answers — perhaps they were right that the Hurons were being punished for living in sin. At the same time, escalating raids by Iroquois war parties threatened the Hurons. By the mid-1640s, hundreds of Hurons were accepting baptism from the Jesuit fathers, although they may well have seen it as a curative ritual rather than a path to heaven.

Whether or not the Jesuits saved the Hurons from damnation, they were unable to save them from the Iroquois. In the spring of 1649, the Iroquois launched a massive assault on Huronia. They destroyed the mission villages at St. Ignace and St. Louis, captured Fathers Brébeuf and Gabriel Lalemant, and tortured them to death. Huronia was destroyed — its people killed, starved, and scattered; many of the survivors were adopted into Iroquois communities as was the tradition with captives. The missions lay in ruins and the Jesuits abandoned Huronia. Some Hurons eventually resettled at the mission village of Lorette near Quebec.

The Jesuits blamed the Iroquois for the destruction of Huronia and historians have generally followed their lead, but as the Huron scholar Georges Sioui reminds us, European microbes had already done their deadly work, leaving relatively little for the Iroquois to destroy. In Sioui's view, Hurons and Iroquois were both engaged in a desperate war for cultural survival in the wake of European invasion, and the Iroquois were less interested in destroying an economic rival than in adopting captives to offset their own losses.[73] The Jesuits themselves contributed to the collapse of Huronia by undermining the Hurons' stabilizing traditions, advocating social revolution, and promoting factionalism.

Brébeuf's account of his journey to Huronia and of his work there in 1635 gives a graphic portrayal of the hardships Jesuit missionaries faced as they trekked deep into Indian country and of the challenges they then faced in Huron villages. "Truly, to come here much strength and patience are needed," he wrote, "and he who thinks of coming here for any other than God, will have made a sad mistake."[74] Brébeuf also wrote an instruction manual for subsequent missionaries to the Hurons, telling them what to expect and how to behave. These instructions convey Jesuit strategy in dealing with the Indians and suggest some of the reasons why the Jesuits fared better than their English rivals in winning Indian converts. Jesuit missionaries went into Indian country and adapted to the way of life there. They did not die of smallpox, they did not seek Indian land, and they did not molest Indian women. Instead, they traveled with Indians by canoe and snowshoe, they shared Indian lodges and Indian food, they displayed impressive shamanistic powers, and they dedicated their lives to their calling. Brébeuf himself paid with his life and shared in the disaster that befell Huronia in 1649.

Brébeuf wrote based on his experience of daily life among the Hurons, but his relation allows us only a glimpse of Huronia filtered through the eyes of a seventeenth-century missionary. From 1611 to 1768, Jesuit missionaries in North America followed the practice of sending lengthy reports to their superiors in Quebec, who compiled them into *Relations* and sent them on to Paris. The Jesuit order published the reports from 1632 to 1673 to publicize its missionary work. The *Relations* were edited and translated by American historian Reuben Gold Thwaites and published in seventy-one volumes at the turn of the twentieth century; they are among the most comprehensive sources of Indian–European encounters in seventeenth-century North America. (English translations of the *Jesuit Relations* are available online at www.puffin.creighton.edu/jesuit/relations.) These reports contain information on everyday life, religious beliefs, and customs, but their main purpose was to record the progress of the missions rather than to document the life of the Indians. Jesuits went into Indian country to change the culture they saw, not to study it.

French missionaries like Brébeuf may have found traveling in Canadian forests hard going, living in Indian lodges miserable, and eating Indian food distasteful, but they found few Indians willing to exchange their way of life for that of the Europeans. Indians readily accepted some of the things that Europeans had to offer and tolerated others, but, as the Mi'kmaq document shows, they remained unconvinced, and sometimes openly amused, by European assumptions about the superiority of European civilization.

The Mi'kmaq Indians of present-day Nova Scotia and the Gaspé Peninsula were among the first people in North America to meet Europeans. According to their own traditions, they had foreknowledge of the encounter: one of their spiritual beings was said to have visited Europe and taught that blue-eyed people would come and disrupt their lives, and a young Mi'kmaq woman had a vision of a floating island that turned out to be a European sailing ship (see page 39). The first Europeans they met were probably French Breton fishermen who came to harvest the rich shoals of cod off the Newfoundland Banks. Other fishermen — Normans, Basques, English, and even Portuguese — followed. By the time the Mi'kmaqs met Jacques Cartier in the 1530s, they already had experience trading with Europeans: they held furs aloft on sticks for Cartier's men to see, indicating their willingness to trade. They soon assumed a middleman position in the fur trade. Some Mi'kmaqs traveled to Europe — a chief named Messamoet spent two years as a guest of the governor of Bayonne, a Basque seaport north of the Pyrenees, and several Mi'kmaqs visited Paris.[75]

Between trading with Frenchmen on their home shores and visiting France, Mi'kmaqs had plenty of firsthand experience of Europeans. Although they were impressed with aspects of European technology — sailing ships, guns, and metal tools and weapons — they were not overly impressed with Europeans. According to a Jesuit missionary writing in 1611, Mi'kmaqs believed themselves generally "superior to all Christians" and regarded themselves "as much richer than [the French], although they are poor and wretched in the extreme." They told him: "You are always fighting and quarreling among yourselves; we live peaceably. You are envious and are all the time slandering each other; you are thieves and deceivers; you are covetous, and are neither generous nor kind; as for us, if we have a morsel of bread we share it with our neighbor."[76]

The Mi'kmaqs suffered appalling losses from European diseases. In the eighteenth century, their homeland became contested ground in the imperial rivalry between France and England, changing hands many times, and British colonists took over their lands. But in the seventeenth century, the Mi'kmaqs still controlled their homeland and spoke with a confident voice.

Chrestien LeClerq, a Recollect missionary who composed a dictionary for future missionaries coming to the region, interpreted and recorded the speech by a Mi'kmaq elder to a group of French settlers reproduced in this chapter. The cultural relativism it displays is typical of many statements by Indian people when confronted by European demands or expectations that they embrace European "civilization." French pretensions carried little weight in Indian country, and by 1677 Mi'kmaqs were already accustomed to telling off the French.

JEAN DE BRÉBEUF
The Mission to the Hurons (1635–37)

RELATION OF WHAT OCCURRED AMONG THE HURONS IN THE YEAR 1635

It remains now to say something of the country, of the manners and customs of the Hurons, of the inclination they have to the Faith, and of our insignificant labors.

As to the first, the little paper and leisure we have compels me to say in a few words what might justly fill a volume. The Huron country is not large, its greatest extent can be traversed in three or four days. Its situation is fine, the greater part of it consisting of plains. It is surrounded and intersected by a number of very beautiful lakes or rather seas, whence it comes that the one to the North and to the Northwest is called "fresh-water sea."° We pass through it in coming from the Bissiriniens.° There are twenty Towns, which indicate about 30,000 souls speaking the same tongue, which is not difficult to one who has a master. It has distinctions of genders, number, tense, person, moods; and, in short, it is very complete and very regular, contrary to the opinion of many. . . .

It is so evident that there is a Divinity who has made Heaven and earth that our Hurons cannot entirely ignore it. But they misapprehend him grossly. For they have neither Temples, nor Priests, nor Feasts, nor any ceremonies.

They say that a certain woman called *Eataensic* is the one who made earth and man. They give her an assistant, one named *Jouskeha,* whom they declare to be her little son, with whom she governs the world. This *Jouskeha* has care of the living, and of the things that concern life, and consequently they say that he is good. *Eataensic* has care of souls; and, because they believe that she makes men die, they say that she is wicked. And there are among them mysteries so hidden that only the old men, who can speak with authority about them, are believed.

This God and Goddess live like themselves, but without famine; make feasts as they do, are lustful as they are; in short, they imagine them exactly like themselves. And still, though they make them human and corporeal, they seem nevertheless to attribute to them a certain immensity in all places.

They say that this *Eataensic* fell from the Sky, where there are inhabitants as on earth, and when she fell, she was with child. If you ask them who made the sky and its inhabitants, they have no

other reply than that they know nothing about it. And when we preach to them of one God, Creator of Heaven and earth, and of all things, and even when we talk to them of Hell and Paradise and of our other mysteries, the headstrong reply that this is good for our Country and not for theirs; that every Country has its own fashions. But having pointed out to them, by means of a little globe that we had brought, that there is only one world, they remain without reply.

I find in their marriage customs two things that greatly please me; the first, that they have only one wife; the second, that they do not marry their relatives in a direct or collateral line, however distant they may be. There is, on the other hand, sufficient to censure, were it only the frequent changes the men make of their wives, and the women of their husbands.

They believe in the immortality of the soul, which they believe to be corporeal. The greatest part of their Religion consists of this point. We have seen several stripped, or almost so, of all their goods, because several of their friends were dead, to whose souls they had made presents. Moreover, dogs, fish, deer, and other animals have, in their opinion, immortal and reasonable souls. In proof of this, the old men relate certain fables, which they represent as true; they make no mention either of punishment or reward, in the place to which souls go after death. And so they do not make any distinction between the good and the bad, the virtuous and the vicious; and they honor equally the interment of both, even as we have seen in the case of a young man who poisoned himself from the grief he felt because his wife had been taken away from him. Their superstitions are infinite, their feast, their medicines, their fishing, their hunting, their wars, — in short almost their whole life turns upon this pivot; dreams, above all have here great credit. . . .

As regards morals, the Hurons are lascivious, although in two leading points less so than many Christians, who will blush some day in their presence. You will see no kissing nor immodest caressing; and in marriage a man will remain two or

---

° Lake Huron.

° The Nipissing Indians, who lived north of the Hurons.

SOURCE: Reuben G. Thwaites, ed., *The Jesuit Relations and Allied Documents: Travels and Explorations of the Jesuit Missionaries in New France, 1610–1791,* 71 vols. (Cleveland: Burrows Brothers, 1896–1901), 8:113–53; 12:117–24.

three years apart from his wife, while she is nursing. They are gluttons, even to disgorging; it is true, that does not happen often, but only in some superstitious feasts,° — these, however, they do not attend willingly. Besides they endure hunger much better than we, — so well that after having fasted two or three entire days you will see them still paddling, carrying loads, singing, laughing, bantering, as if they had dined well. They are very lazy, are liars, thieves, pertinacious beggars. Some consider them vindictive; but, in my opinion, this vice is more noticeable elsewhere than here.

We see shining among them some rather noble moral virtues. You note, in the first place, a great love and union, which they are careful to cultivate by means of their marriages, of their presents, of their feasts, and of their frequent visits. On returning from their fishing, their hunting, and their trading, they exchange many gifts; if they have thus obtained something unusually good, even if they have bought it, or if it has been given to them, they make a feast to the whole village with it. Their hospitality towards all sorts of strangers is remarkable; they present to them, in their feasts, the best of what they have prepared, and, as I have already said, I do not know if anything similar, in this regard, is to be found anywhere. They never close the door upon a Stranger, and, once having received him into their houses, they share with him the best they have; they never send him away, and when he goes away of his own accord, he repays them by a simple "thank you."

What shall I say of their strange patience in poverty, famine, and sickness? We have seen this year whole villages prostrated, their food a little insipid sagamité;° and yet not a word of complaint, not a movement of impatience. They

receive indeed the news of death with more constancy than those Christian Gentlemen and Ladies to whom one would not dare to mention it. Our Savages hear of it not only without despair, but without troubling themselves, without the slightest pallor or change of countenance. We have especially admired the constancy of our new Christians. The next to the last one who died, named Joseph *Oatij,* lay on the bare ground during four or five months, not only before but after his Baptism, — so thin that he was nothing but bones; in a lodge so wretched that the winds blew in on all sides; covered during the cold of winter with a very light skin of some black animals, perhaps black squirrels, and very poorly nourished. He was never heard to make a complaint. . . .

About the month of December, the snow began to lie on the ground, and the savages settled down into the village. For, during the whole Summer and Autumn, they are for the most part either in their rural cabins, taking care of their crops, or on the lake fishing, or trading; which makes it not a little inconvenient to instruct them. Seeing them, therefore, thus gathered together at the beginning of this year, we resolved to preach publicly to all, and to acquaint them with the reason of our coming into their Country, which is not for their furs, but to declare to them the true God and his son, Jesus Christ, the universal Saviour of our souls.

The usual method that we follow is this: We call together the people by the help of the Captain of the village, who assembles them all in our house as in Council, or perhaps by the sound of the bell. I use the surplice° and the square cap, to give more majesty to my appearance. At the beginning we chant on our knees the *Pater noster,* translated into Huron verse. Father Daniel, as its author, chants a couplet alone, and then we all together chant it again; and those among the Hurons, principally the little ones, who already know it, take pleasure

---

° "Eat all feasts," where guests were expected to consume everything, even if they had to empty their stomachs by vomiting in order to do so, usually had a ritual purpose.

° Corn compounded into meal and boiled in water, sometimes with meat, fish, or vegetables added; called "samp" or hominy by the English.

° A white liturgical (or ecclesiastical) vestment, in the form of a tunic.

in chanting it with us. That done, when every one is seated, I rise and make the sign of the Cross for all; then, having recapitulated what I said last time, I explain something new. After that we question the young children and the girls, giving a little bead of glass or porcelain to those who deserve it. The parents are very glad to see their children answer well and carry off some little prize, of which they render themselves worthy by the care they take to come privately to get instruction. On our part, to arouse their emulation, we have each lesson re-traced by our two little French boys, who question each other,—which transports the Savages with admiration. Finally the whole is concluded by the talk of the Old Men, who propound their difficulties, and sometimes make me listen in my turn to the statement of their belief.

Two things among others have aided us very much in the little we have been able to do here, by the grace of our Lord; the first is, as I have already said, the good health that God has granted us in the midst of sickness so general and so widespread. The second is the temporal assistance we have rendered to the sick. Having brought for ourselves some few delicacies, we shared them with them, giving to one a few prunes, and to another a few raisins, to others something else. The poor people came from great distances to get their share.

Our French servants having succeeded very well in hunting, during the Autumn, we carried portions of game to all the sick. That chiefly won their hearts, as they were dying, having neither flesh nor fish to season their sagamité. . . .

YOUR REVERENCE'S:
From our little House of St. Joseph, in the village of Ihonatiria° in the Huron country, this 27th of May, 1635, the day on which the Holy Spirit descended visibly upon the Apostles.

Very humble and obedient
servant in our Lord,
JEAN DE BRÉBEUF.

° The most northerly Huron village, on the Penetanguish-ene Peninsula. (See Map 2.5.)

INSTRUCTIONS FOR THE FATHERS OF OUR SOCIETY WHO SHALL BE SENT TO THE HURONS, 1637

The Fathers and Brethren whom God shall call to the holy Mission of the Hurons ought to exercise careful foresight in regard to all the hardships, annoyances, and perils that must be encountered in making this journey, in order to be prepared betimes for all emergencies that may arise.

You must have sincere affection for the Savages,—looking upon them as ransomed by the blood of the son of God, and as our Brethren with whom we are to pass the rest of our lives.

To conciliate the Savages, you must be careful never to make them wait for you in embarking.

You must provide yourself with a tinder box or with a burning mirror, or with both, to furnish them fire in the daytime to light their pipes, and in the evening when they have to encamp; these little services win their hearts.

You should try to eat their sagamité or salma-gundi in the way they prepare it, although it may be dirty, half-cooked, and very tasteless. As to the other numerous things which may be unpleasant, they must be endured for the love of God, without saying anything or appearing to notice them.

It is well at first to take everything they offer, although you may not be able to eat it all; for, when one becomes somewhat accustomed to it, there is not too much.

You must try and eat at daybreak unless you can take your meal with you in the canoe; for the day is very long, if you have to pass it without eating. The Barbarians eat only at Sunrise and Sunset, when they are on their journeys.

You must be prompt in embarking and disembarking; and tuck up your gowns so that they will not get wet, and so that you will not carry either water or sand into the canoe. To be properly dressed, you must have your feet and legs bare; while crossing the rapids, you can wear your shoes, and, in the long portages, even your leggings.

You must so conduct yourself as not to be at all troublesome to even one of these Barbarians.

It is not well to ask many questions, nor should you yield to your desire to learn the language and to make observations on the way; this may be carried too far. You must relieve those in your canoe of this annoyance, especially as you cannot profit much by it during the work. Silence is a good equipment at such a time.

You must bear their imperfections without saying a word, yes, even without seeming to notice them. Even if it be necessary to criticise anything, it must be done modestly, and with words and signs which evince love and not aversion. In short, you must try to be, and to appear, always cheerful.

Each one should be provided with half a gross of awls, two or three dozen little knives called jambettes (pocket-knives), a hundred fish-hooks, with some beads of plain and colored glass, with which to buy fish or other articles when the tribes meet each other, so as to feast the Savages; and it would be well to say to them in the beginning, "Here is something with which to buy fish." Each one will try, at the portages, to carry some little thing, according to his strength; however little one carries, it greatly pleases the savages, if it be only a kettle.

You must not be ceremonious with the Savages, but accept the comforts they offer you, such as a good place in the cabin. The greatest conveniences are attended with very great inconvenience, and these ceremonies offend them.

Be careful not to annoy anyone in the canoe with your hat; it would be better to take your nightcap. There is no impropriety among the Savages.

Do not undertake anything unless you desire to continue it; for example, do not begin to paddle unless you are inclined to continue paddling. Take from the start the place in the canoe that you wish to keep; do not lend them your garments, unless you are willing to surrender them during the whole journey. It is easier to refuse at first than to ask them back, to change, or to desist afterwards.

Finally, understand that the Savages will retain the same opinion of you in their own country that they will have formed on the way; and one who has passed for an irritable and troublesome person will have considerable difficulty afterwards in removing this opinion. You have to do not only with those of your own canoe, but also (if it must be so stated) with all those of the country; you meet some today and others tomorrow, who do not fail to inquire, from those who brought you, what sort of man you are. It is almost incredible, how they observe and remember even the slightest fault. When you meet Savages on the way, as you cannot yet greet them with kind words, at least show them a cheerful face, and thus prove that you endure gayly the fatigues of the voyage. You will thus have put to good use the hardships on the way, and have already advanced considerably in gaining the affection of the Savages.

This is a lesson which is easy enough to learn, but very difficult to put into practice; for, leaving a highly civilized community, you fall into the hands of barbarous people who care but little for your Philosophy or your Theology. All the fine qualities which might make you loved and respected in France are like pearls trampled under the feet of swine, or rather mules, which utterly despise you when they see that you are not as good pack animals as they are. If you could go naked, and carry the load of a horse upon your back, as they do, then you would be wise according to their doctrine, and would be recognized as a great man, otherwise not. Jesus Christ is our true greatness;

it is He alone and His cross that should be sought in running after these people, for, if you strive for anything else, you will find naught but bodily and spiritual affliction. But having found Jesus Christ in His cross, you have found the roses in the thorns, sweetness in bitterness, all in nothing.

CHRESTIEN LECLERQ
A Mi'kmaq Questions French "Civilization" (1677)

I am greatly astonished that the French have so little cleverness, as they seem to exhibit in the matter of which thou hast just told me on their behalf, in the effort to persuade us to convert our poles, our barks, and our wigwams into those houses of stone and of wood which are tall and lofty, according to their account, as these trees. Very well! But why now, . . . do men of five to six feet in height need houses which are sixty to eighty? For, in fact, as thou knowest very well thyself, Patriarch — do we not find in our own all the conveniences and the advantages that you have with yours, such as reposing, drinking, sleeping, eating, and amusing ourselves with our friends when we wish? This is not all, . . . my brother, hast thou as much ingenuity and cleverness as the Indians, who carry their houses and their wigwams with them so that they may lodge wheresoever they please, independently of any seignior whatsoever? Thou art not as bold nor as stout as we, because when thou goest on a voyage thou canst not carry upon thy shoulders thy buildings and thy edifices. Therefore it is necessary that thou preparest as many lodgings as thou makest changes of residence, or else thou lodgest in a hired house which does not belong to thee. As for us, we find ourselves secure from all these inconveniences, and we can always say, more truly than thou, that we are at home everywhere, because we set up our wigwams with ease wheresoever we go, and without asking permission of anybody. Thou reproachest us, very inappropriately, that our country is a little hell in contrast with France, which thou comparest to a terrestrial paradise, inasmuch as it yields thee, so thou sayest, every kind of provision in abundance. Thou sayest of us also that we are the most miserable and most unhappy of all men, living without religion, without manners, without honour, without social order, and, in a word, without any rules, like the beasts in our woods and our forests, lacking bread, wine, and a thousand other comforts which thou hast in superfluity in Europe. Well, my brother, if thou dost not yet know the real feelings which our Indians have towards thy country and towards all thy nation, it is proper that I inform thee at once. I beg thee now to believe that, all miserable as we seem in thine eyes, we consider ourselves nevertheless much happier than thou in this, that we are very content with the little that we have; and believe also once for all, I pray, that thou deceivest thyself greatly if thou thinkest to persuade us that thy country is better than ours. For if France, as thou sayest, is a little terrestrial paradise, art thou sensible to leave it? And why abandon wives, children, relatives, and friends? Why risk thy life and thy property every year, and why venture thyself with such risk, in any season whatsoever, to the storms and tempests of the sea in order to come to a strange and barbarous country which thou considerest the poorest and least fortunate of the world? Besides, since we are wholly convinced of the contrary, we scarcely take the trouble to go to France, because we fear, with good reason, lest we find little satisfaction there, seeing, in our own

SOURCE: Chrestien LeClerq, *New Relation of Gaspesia, with the Customs and Religion of the Gaspesian Indians,* trans. and ed. William F. Ganong (Toronto: Champlain Society, 1910), 104–6. [10.3138/9781442618213] Reprinted with permission of the Champlain Society (www.utpjournals.com).

experience, that those who are natives thereof leave it every year in order to enrich themselves on our shores. We believe, further, that you are also incomparably poorer than we, and that you are only simple journeymen, valets, servants, and slaves, all masters and grand captains though you may appear, seeing that you glory in our old rags and in our miserable suits of beaver which can no longer be of use to us, and that you find among us, in the fishery for cod which you make in these parts, the wherewithal to comfort your misery and the poverty which oppresses you. As to us, we find all our riches and all our conveniences among ourselves, without trouble and without exposing our lives to the dangers in which you find yourselves constantly through your long voyages. And, whilst feeling compassion for you in the sweetness of our repose, we wonder at the anxieties and cares which you give yourselves night and day in order to load your ship. We see also that all your people live, as a rule, only upon cod which you catch among us. It is everlastingly nothing but cod — cod in the morning, cod at midday, cod at evening, and always cod, until things come to such a pass that if you wish some good morsels, it is at our expense; and you are obliged to have recourse to the Indians, whom you despise so much, and to beg them to go a-hunting that you may be regaled. Now tell me this one little thing, if thou hast any sense: Which of these two is the wisest and happiest — he who labours without ceasing and only obtains, and that with great trouble, enough to live on, or he who rests in comfort and finds all that he needs in the pleasure of hunting and fishing? It is true, . . . that we have not always had the use of bread and of wine which your France produces; but, in fact, before the arrival of the French in these parts, did not the Gaspesians° live much longer than now? And if we have not any longer among us any of those old men of a hundred and thirty to forty years, it is only because we are gradually adopting your manner of living, for experience is making it very plain that those of us live longest who, despising your bread, your wine, and your brandy, are content with their natural food of beaver, of moose, of waterfowl, and fish, in accord with the custom of our ancestors and of all the Gaspesian nation. Learn now, my brother, once for all, because I must open to thee my heart: there is no Indian who does not consider himself infinitely more happy and more powerful than the French.

° Indians of the Gaspé Peninsula in southeastern Quebec.

QUESTIONS FOR CONSIDERATION

1. What different kinds of information does Brébeuf include in his report, and what use could his superiors potentially make of it? How do Brébeuf's religion and missionary focus direct his relationship with the Hurons he lives among and studies and perhaps limit the usefulness of the information he provides?

2. What things do Brébeuf and the Mi'kmaq speaker criticize? What aspects of a different culture did they witness but not necessarily understand?

3. What examples of cultural adjustment do these documents provide? How do the Jesuits adjust? How do the Hurons and Mi'kmaqs adjust?

4. Does the Mi'kmaq speech appear to be a literal translation, or does it contain indications that the transcriber may have embellished it somewhat? If so, what might the transcriber's purpose have been?

Two Indian Wars of Independence

IN 1675 KING PHILIP'S WAR shattered two generations of coexistence between Indians and English in Massachusetts. Fifty-two English towns were attacked and a dozen were destroyed, and many Indian villages were burned. More than 2,500 colonists died, perhaps 30 percent of the English population of New England. At least twice as many Indians died in the fighting, and some estimates suggest that the combined effects of war, disease, and starvation killed half the Indian population of New England. The war was one of the bloodiest conflicts in American history. In terms of proportionate populations it was the bloodiest. It left an enduring legacy in its imprint on subsequent attitudes and policies toward Indian peoples in America.

In 1680, after generations of oppression but little outright conflict, Pueblo peoples rose up in an orchestrated assault that drove the Spaniards out of New Mexico. One of the most successful Indian wars in history, the Pueblo Revolt left an enduring legacy in its imprint on the society that Spaniards and Indians subsequently rebuilt in New Mexico.

These two revolts, more accurately termed wars of independence, occurred within a few years of one another, but they occurred more than two thousand miles apart, and they involved different Indian peoples and different European colonists. Were there any parallels or commonalities in causation and in the Indians' experiences of colonialism? The two documents reprinted here provide glimpses into Indian understandings and explanations of the causes of the war in testimonies recorded by European pens and filtered through the lens of European culture.

Not surprisingly, the interpretation of King Philip's War has generated extreme views, as participants and historians recount the catastrophe and evaluate its meaning. The English at the time saw the conflict as a civil rebellion[77] and laid the blame squarely on the shoulders of Metacomet, whom they called King Philip. Even as the English preached the war as divine punishment for their own erring ways, they regarded Metacomet as a fiend and traitor who deserved the traitor's death and dismemberment he received. Generations of American historians, accepting the Puritans' accounts of the conflict as fact, portrayed the war as a vital victory in securing the Anglo-Saxon beachhead in North America and saw it as forging a new American identity that forever excluded Indians. Indian people and most modern ethnohistorians blame Puritan land hunger, arrogance, and aggression for triggering the bloodshed. Historian Francis Jennings in 1975 renamed King Philip's War "The Second Puritan Conquest" (the first being the Pequot War) and denounced vicious and hypocritical colonists for fomenting war in a campaign to seize Indian lands.[78] More than three hundred years after the conflict, historians are still trying to achieve a balanced understanding of a racial war that shattered patterns of coexistence.[79]

Sometimes, how wars are remembered and written about can be as important as how they were fought, and a "contest of words" ensues over the memory and meaning of the conflict.[80] In this war, perhaps more than any other, the winners wrote the history books. The English, not the Wampanoags, recorded assessments of Metacomet, and their views were the primary ones available to later historians. Reverend Increase Mather, one of the leading scholars and theologians in Puritan New England, wrote two books about King Philip's War, one of them while the war was still in progress. For Mather, as for most Puritans, the war was both divine punishment and an ordeal that tested the colonists' virtue, courage, and devotion to God. In Mather's account, the Puritans brought the war on themselves by their sinful ways amongst each other, not by their treatment of the Indians. Despite this placement of blame, he named the Indians as the instigators of the conflict: "The Heathen people amongst whom we live, and whose Land the Lord God of our Fathers hath given to us for a rightfull Possession, have at sundry times been plotting mischievous devices," he wrote. Metacomet was the villain and had to be destroyed. Mather later recounted Metacomet's grisly end at the hands of the English and their Indian allies: "And in that very place where he first contrived and began his mischief, was he taken and destroyed, and there was he . . . was cut into four quarters, and is now hanged up as a monument of revenging Justice, his head being cut off and carried away to Plymouth, his Hands were brought to *Boston. So let all thine Enemies perish, O Lord!*"[81]

Although no Indian voices could challenge Mather's in the wake of the bloody war, Metacomet himself had already provided an Indian explanation of the causes of the conflict. In June 1675, just about a week before the war broke out, Rhode Island deputy governor John Easton and a delegation from his colony met with Metacomet in an effort to mediate the Indians' escalating dispute with the United Colonies of New England (Massachusetts Bay, Plymouth, and Connecticut). This effort to stop the drift to war failed, but the meeting did produce a record of the Indians' accumulating grievances against the colonists.

In 1681 Governor Otermín attempted to retake New Mexico from the Pueblos, who had defended their independence in the war of 1680 (see "The Pueblo War of Independence," pages 87–90). Divisions had quickly surfaced among the Pueblos, and the town of Isleta welcomed the returning Spaniards. But elsewhere Pueblo resistance remained strong, and Otermín was able to do little more than interrogate captured Indians as to their reasons "for rebelling, forsaking the law of God and obedience to his Majesty, and committing such grave and atrocious crimes." The Indians said "that the uprising had been deliberated upon for a long time." Some placed blame on Popé or the devil. Others cited continued Spanish oppression and said "they were tired of the work they had to do for the Spaniards . . . and that, being weary, they rebelled." One eighty-year-old man, whose life spanned the era of Spanish colonial rule, declared "that the resentment which all the Indians have in their hearts has been so strong, from the time this kingdom was discovered, because the religious and the Spaniards took away their idols and forbade their sorceries and idolatries." He had "heard this resentment spoken of since he was of an age to understand."[82]

A twenty-eight-year-old Indian named Juan, from the Pueblo of Tesuque, provided information about the rebellion after Spanish priests absolved him and had him swear an oath to tell the truth. They recorded his answers in the document that follows the account of King Philip's War.

JOHN EASTON
Metacomet Explains the Causes of "King Philip's War," from A Relacion of the Indyan Warre (1675)

For forty years' time reports and jealousies of war had been very frequent that we did not think that now a war was breaking forth, but about a week before it did we had cause to think it would. Then to endeavor to prevent it, we sent a man to Philip [Metacomet] that if he would come to the ferry we would come over to speak with him. About four mile we had to come thither. Our messenger come to them, they not aware of it behaved themselves as furious but suddenly appeased when they understood who he was and what he came for. He called his council and agreed to come to us came himself unarmed and about forty of his men armed. Then five of us went over. Three were magistrates. We sat very friendly together. We told him our business was to endeavor that they might not receive or do wrong. They said that was well they had done no wrong, the English wronged them, we said we knew the English said they [the Wampanoag] wronged them and the Indians said the English wronged them but our desire was the quarrel might rightly be decided in the best way, and not as dogs decided their quarrels. The Indians owned that fighting was the worst way then they propounded how right might take place, we said by arbitration.

They said all English agreed against them and so by arbitration they had had much wrong, many square miles of land so taken from them for English would have English Arbitrators, and once they were persuaded to give in their arms, that thereby jealousy might be removed and the English having their arms would not deliver them as they had promised, until they consented to pay 100 pounds, and now they had not so much land or money, that they were as good be killed as leave all their livelihood. We said they might choose a Indian king,° and the English might choose the governor of New York that neither had cause to say either were parties in the difference. They said they had not heard of that way and said we honestly spoke so we were persuaded if that way had been tendered they would have accepted. We did endeavor not to hear their complaints, said it was not convenient for us now to consider of, but to endeavor to prevent war, said to them when in war against English blood was spilled that engaged all Englishmen for we were to be all under one king.° We knew what their complaints would be, and in our colony had removed some of them in sending for Indian rulers in what the

---

SOURCE: John Easton, "A Relacion of the Indyan Warre," (1675; publ. 1858), as modernized and reprinted in *Narratives of the Indian Wars, 1675–1699*, ed. Charles H. Lincoln (New York: Charles Scribner's Sons, 1913), 8–12.

° The English often called Indian chiefs "kings," although the term creates a misleading impression of the power and position of Native leaders.

° *when in war . . . under one king:* Once war broke out, the English would be united against the Indians.

crime concerned Indians lives which they very lovingly accepted and agreed with us to their execution and said so they were able to satisfy their subjects when they knew an Indian suffered duly, but said in what was only between their Indians and not in townships that we had purchased, they would not have us prosecute and that they had a great fear to have any of their Indians should be called or forced to be Christian Indians. They said that such were in everything more mischievous, only dissemblers, and then the English made them not subject to their kings, and by their lying to wrong their kings. We knew it to be true, and we promising them that however in government to Indians all should be alike and that we knew it was our kings will it should be so, that although we were weaker than other colonies, they having submitted to our king to protect them others dared not otherwise to molest them. So they expressed they took that to be well, that we had little cause to doubt but that to us under the king they would have yielded to our determinations in what any should have complained to us against them, but Philip charged it to be dishonesty in us to put off the hearing the complaints; therefore we consented to hear them. They said they had been the first in doing good to the English, and the English the first in doing wrong, said when the English first came their king's father° was as a great man and the English as a little child, he constrained other Indians from wronging the English and gave them corn and showed them how to plant and was free to do them any good and had let them have a 100 times more land, then now the king had for his own people, but their king's brother when he was king came miserably to die by being forced to court as they judged poisoned,° and another grievance was if 20 of their honest Indians testified that a Englishman had done them wrong, it was as nothing, and if but one of their worst Indians testified against any Indian or their king when it pleased the English that

was sufficient. Another grievance was when their kings sold land the English would say it was more than they agreed to and a writing must be proof against all them, and sum of their kings had done wrong to sell so much. He left his people none and some being given to drunkeness the English made them drunk and then cheated them in bargains, but now their kings were forewarned not for to part with land for nothing in comparison to the value thereof. Now whom the English had owned for king or queen they [the English] would disinherit, and make another king that would give or sell them their land, that now they had no hopes left to keep any land. Another grievance the English cattle and horses still increased that when they removed 30 miles from where English had anything to do, they could not keep their corn from being spoiled, they never being used to fence, and thought when the English bought land of them that they would have kept their cattle upon their own land. Another grievance the English were so eager to sell the Indians liquors that most of the Indians spent all in drunkeness and then ravened upon [plundered] the sober Indians and they did believe often did hurt the English cattle, and their kings could not prevent it. We knew before these were their grand complaints, but then we only endeavored to persuade that all complaints might be righted without war, but could have no other answer but that they had not heard of that way for the Governor of York and an Indian king to have the hearing of it. We had cause to think if that had been tendered it would have been accepted. We endeavored that however they should lay down their arms for the English were too strong for them. They said then the English should do to them as they did when they were too strong for the English. So we departed without any discourteousness, and suddenly had letter from Plimouth Governor they intended in arms to conform [subjugate] Philip, but no information what that was they required or what terms he refused to have their quarrel decided, and in a weeks time after we had been with the Indians the war thus begun.

° Philip's father, Massasoit.

° Wamsutta (see pages 100–1).

Declaration of the Indian Juan (1681)

Having been questioned according to the tenor of the case, and asked for what reasons and causes all the Indians of the kingdom in general rebelled, returning to idolatry, forsaking the law of God and obedience to his Majesty, burning images and temples, and committing the other crimes which they did, he said that what he knows concerning this question is that not all of them joined the said rebellion willingly; that the chief mover of it is an Indian who is a native of the pueblo of San Juan, named El Popé, and that from fear of this Indian all of them joined in the plot that he made. Thus he replied.

Asked why they held the said Popé in such fear and obeyed him, and whether he was the chief man of the pueblo, or a good Christian, or a sorcerer, he said that the common report that circulated and still is current among all the natives is that the said Indian Popé talks with the devil, and for this reason all held him in terror, obeying his commands although they were contrary to the orders of the señores governors, the prelate and the religious, and the Spaniards, he giving them to understand that the word which he spoke was better than that of all the rest; and he states that it was a matter of common knowledge that the Indian Popé, talking with the devil, killed in his own house a son-in-law of his named Nicolás Bua, the governor of the pueblo of San Juan. On being asked why he killed him, he said that it was so that he might not warn the Spaniards of the rebellion, as he intended to do. And he said that after the rebellion was over, and the señor governor and captain-general had left, defeated, the said Indian Popé went in company with another native of the pueblo of Taos named Saca through all the pueblos

of the kingdom, being very well pleased, saying and giving the people to understand that he had carried out the said uprising, and that because of his wish and desire the things that had happened had been done, the religious and the people who died had been killed, and those who remained alive had been driven out. He [the deponent] said that the time when he learned of the rebellion was three days before it was carried out.

Asked how the said Indian, Popé, convoked all the people of the kingdom so that they obeyed him in the treason, he said that he took a cord made of maguey fiber and tied some knots in it which indicated the number of days until the perpetration of the treason. He sent it through all the pueblos as far as that of La Isleta, there remaining in the whole kingdom only the nation of the Piros who did not receive it; and the order which the said Popé gave when he sent the said cord was under strict charge of secrecy, commanding that the war captains take it from pueblo to pueblo. He [the deponent] learned of this circumstance after the kingdom was depopulated.

Asked to state and declare what things occurred after they found themselves without religious or Spaniards, he said that what he, the declarant, knows concerning this question is that following the departure of the señor governor and captain-general, the religious, and the Spaniards who were left alive, the said Indian, Popé, came down in person with all the war captains and many other Indians, proclaiming through the pueblos that the devil was very strong and much better than God, and that they should burn all the images and temples, rosaries and crosses, and that all the people should discard the names given them in holy baptism and call themselves whatever they liked. They should leave the wives whom they had taken in holy matrimony and take any one whom they might wish, and they were not to mention in any manner the name of God, of the most holy Virgin, or of the Saints,

Source: Declaration of the Indian Juan, December 18, 1681, in Charles Wilson Hackett, ed., *Revolt of the Pueblo Indians of New Mexico and Otermín's Attempted Reconquest, 1680–1682* 2 vols. (Albuquerque: University of New Mexico Press, 1942), vol. 2, 233–35. Reprinted by permission.

on pain of severe punishment, particularly that of lashing, saying that the commands of the devil were better than that which they taught them of the law of God. They were ordered likewise not to teach the Castilian language in any pueblo and to burn the seeds which the Spaniards sowed and to plant only maize and beans, which were the crops of their ancestors. And he said that all the nations obeyed in everything except in the command concerning Spanish seeds, which some of them sowed because of their fondness for the Spaniards. Thus he replied.

Asked whether they thought that perhaps the Spaniards would never return to this kingdom at any time, or that they would have to return as their ancestors did, and in this case what plans or dispositions they would make, and what else he knew about this matter, he said that they were of different minds regarding it, because some said that if the Spaniards should come they would have to fight to the death, and others said that in the end they must come and gain the kingdom because they were sons of the land and had grown up with the natives.

QUESTIONS FOR CONSIDERATION

1. What information do these documents convey about the causes of the revolts and the situation Indian peoples faced in New England and New Mexico?

2. What do the documents reveal about the Indian people's grievances, fears, and understanding of the colonists? What do they reveal about the colonists' understanding of Indian grievances and the causes of conflict?

3. What values and problems do the documents present as historical sources?

PICTURE ESSAY

Images of Invasion

T HE IDEA THAT AMERICA was ever invaded strikes many people as odd. The arrival of Europeans usually has been portrayed in terms of exploration, settlement, and building a new society and nation. But viewed from Indian country that same story was one of invasion, conquest, and devastating assault on their cultures and communities. Native American images of European invaders are rare, and they lack the detailed content common in lavish European paintings depicting similar events (such as Figure 2.1). Yet most of the images reproduced here offer insights into how Indian people have viewed the Europeans they encountered and provide evidence of the nature of those encounters.

As depicted in the rotunda of the U.S. Capitol (Figure 2.1), Hernando de Soto "discovers" the Mississippi in 1541. The Indians are awed and submissive

◆ **Figure 2.1 William Powell, *The Discovery of the Mississippi by De Soto in 1541* (1853)**
The Historic New Orleans Collection/The Bridgeman Art Library.

127

in the face of Spanish power and the coming of "civilization." The tribes of the area (about thirty miles south of modern Memphis) would in fact have inhabited Mississippian-style towns, not Plains-style tepees. The half-naked Indian women at the feet of de Soto's charger also satisfy nineteenth-century convention: like the land, the women are suggested to be vulnerable and available to European conquest. In reality, the Indians would have been more likely to hide their women, knowing in advance that de Soto's expedition had raped and abused hundreds of Indian women farther east. When de Soto's half-starved soldiers reached the Mississippi, they were more interested in seizing corn from the Indians than in impressing them with displays of European pageantry. By the time the Spaniards pushed north into what is now the southwestern United States, their reputation had preceded them. The pictograph of mounted Spaniards bearing lances etched into the wall of Cañon del Muerte in Arizona conveys some sense of the impression the arrival of militant strangers made on the Indian inhabitants (Figure 2.2).

◆ **Figure 2.2 Spaniards on Horseback**
© Danita Delimont/Alamy.

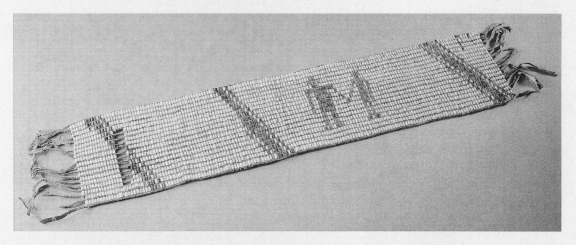

◆ Figure 2.3 **Wampum Belt, Made by Lenni Lenape (Delaware) Indian People, Pennsylvania**
© Philadelphia History Museum at the Atwater Kent/Courtesy of Historical Society of Pennsylvania Collection/The Bridgeman Art Library.

Early encounters were not always violent. The beaded wampum belt commemorating a verbal treaty of friendship between the Delaware Indians and William Penn, the founding governor of Pennsylvania, in 1682, depicts a much less threatening encounter: the Indian and the European in the broad-brimmed hat hold hands in token of friendship (Figure 2.3). The figures may well represent William Penn and Delaware Chief Tamanend. While the simple wampum belt was a Native record of the event, later European depictions of the same meeting were created as part of a political and social agenda (see Benjamin West's *Penn's Treaty with the Indians*, page 153).

Europeans arrived relatively late on the Pacific Northwest Coast, not until the mid-eighteenth century. But the repercussions of their arrival were much the same as in other areas of the country, and Indians formed clear impressions of the newcomers. An Indian who had been to the Pacific Ocean and seen European and American ships there told explorer Simon Fraser that the ship's captains "were well dressed and very proud, for, continued he, getting up and clapping his two hands upon his hips, then strutting about with an air of consequence, 'This the way they go.'"[83] In the mid-nineteenth century, Haida Indians in the region of Queen Charlotte Island likewise poked fun at those who tried to colonize and convert them, as in this miniature wood-and-bone sculpture of a pale-faced, humorless, and stiff missionary (Figure 2.4).

Despite the heavily patriotic thrust of U.S. history that depicts European invasion of America as relatively benign and the defeat of Indian resistance as a necessary prelude to nation building, many Native people remember that history

◆ Figure 2.4 **Haida Carving of a Missionary, c. 1820–60**
Miniature Portrait Figure of a Missionary. British Columbia. Materials: wood, bone, and black pigment (1820–60), Hood Museum of Art, Dartmouth College, Hanover, New Hampshire; gift of Margaret Barnhill Roosevelt Kimberly.

as a story of violence and aggression against the indigenous inhabitants of the country. In the twenty-first century, in the wake of terrorist attacks on the World Trade Center and elsewhere, this poster featuring a photograph of Geronimo and three Apache warriors became popular in Indian country; the image was also featured on T-shirts, bumper stickers, and tote bags. Humorous but hard hitting, the picture speaks to Native Americans' views of their history in conjunction with current events (Figure 2.5).

◆ Figure 2.5 **Homeland Security: Fighting Terrorism since 1492**
© Allan Cash Picture Library/Alamy.

QUESTIONS FOR CONSIDERATION

1. What do these different images suggest about how Native peoples experienced and remembered their early encounters with non-Indians?

2. What characteristics of the Europeans do the Native artists emphasize?

REFERENCES

1. James H. Merrell, *The Indians' New World: Catawbas and Their Neighbors from European Contact through the Era of Removal* (Chapel Hill: University of North Carolina Press, 1989).

2. Oliver Dunn and James E. Kelley Jr., trans. and eds., *The Diario of Christopher Columbus's First Voyage to America, 1492–1493* (Norman: University of Oklahoma Press, 1989), 65–69, 143.

3. Charles C. Mann, *1493: Uncovering the World Columbus Created* (New York: Alfred Knopf, 2011; Marcy Norton, *Sacred Gifts, Profane Pleasures: A History of Tobacco and Chocolate in the Atlantic World* (Ithaca, N.Y.: Cornell University Press, 2008).

4. Karl W. Butzer, ed., "The Americas before and after 1492: An Introduction to Current Geographical Research," *Annals of the Association of American Geographers* 82 (September 1992), 359.

5. Quoted in Colin G. Calloway, ed., *The World Turned Upside Down: Indian Voices from Early America* (Boston: Bedford Books, 1994), 80; Virginia DeJohn Anderson, *Creatures of Empire: How Domestic Animals Transformed Early America* (New York: Oxford University Press, 2004).

6. Alfred W. Crosby Jr., "Virgin Soil Epidemics as a Factor in the Aboriginal Depopulation in America," *William and Mary Quarterly*, 3rd ser., 33 (April 1976), 289–99. David S. Jones, "Virgin Soils Revisited," *William and Mary Quarterly*, 3rd ser., 60 (2003), 703–42, challenges the "virgin soil" interpretation of epidemic diseases and the assumption that Indians lacked immunity.

7. David S. Jones, *Rationalizing Epidemics: Meanings and Uses of American Indian Mortality since 1600* (Cambridge, Mass.: Harvard University Press, 2004); Suzanne Austin Alchon, *A Pest in the Land: New World Epidemics in a Global Perspective* (Albuquerque: University of New Mexico Press, 2003); Paul Kelton, *Epidemics and Enslavement: Biological Catastrophe in the Native Southeast, 1492–1715* (Lincoln: University of Nebraska Press, 2007); Paul Kelton, *Cherokee Medicine, Colonial Germs: An Indigenous Nation's Fight against Smallpox, 1518–1824* (Norman: University of Oklahoma Press, 2015).

8. Russell Thornton, *American Indian Holocaust and Survival: A Population History since 1492* (Norman: University of Oklahoma Press, 1987); Thornton, "Aboriginal North American Population and Rates of Decline, ca. A.D. 1500–1900," *Current Anthropology* 38 (April 1997), 310–15; Noble David Cook, *Born to Die: Disease and New World Conquest, 1492–1650* (Cambridge: Cambridge University Press, 1998). The depopulation estimates are by William M. Denevan, ed., *The Native Population of the Americas in 1492*, 2nd ed. (Madison: University of Wisconsin Press, 1992), xvii–xxix. David Henige, *Numbers from Nowhere: The American Indian Contact Population Debate* (Norman: University of Oklahoma Press, 1998), critiques the premises, methodology, and conclusions of scholars he calls "the High Counters."

9. Charles C. Mann, chap. 10 in *1491: New Revelations of the Americas before Columbus* (New York: Alfred A. Knopf, 2005).

10. Cyclone Covey, trans. and ed., *Cabeza de Vaca's Adventures in the Unknown Interior of America* (Albuquerque: University of New Mexico Press, 1983), 56–60.

11. John R. Chávez, *Beyond Nations: Evolving Homelands in the North Atlantic World, 1400–2000* (Cambridge: Cambridge University Press, 2009), 55; Kirstin Downey, *Isabella: The Warrior Queen* (New York: Nan A. Talese/Doubleday, 2014) recounts the role of the queen of Castile in Spain's transformation.

12. The *Requerimiento* is quoted in Albert L. Hurtado and Peter Iverson, eds., *Major Problems in American Indian History: Documents and Essays* (Lexington, Mass.: D. C. Heath, 1994), 83–84. Patricia Seed examines Spanish protocols of conquest in chap. 3 of *Ceremonies of Possession in Europe's Conquest of the New World, 1492–1640* (Cambridge: Cambridge University Press, 1995).

13. Laura E. Matthew and Michael R. Oudijk, eds., *Indian Conquistadors: Indigenous Allies in the Conquest of Mesoamerica* (Norman: University of Oklahoma Press, 2007).

14. Patricia de Fuentes, trans. and ed., *The Conquistadors: First-Person Accounts of the Conquest of Mexico* (Norman: University of Oklahoma Press, 1993), 21, 24, 215.

15. Quoted in W. George Lovell, "'Heavy Shadows and Black Night': Disease and Depopulation in Colonial Spanish America," *Annals of the Association of American Geographers* 82 (September 1992), 429.

16. Bernal Díaz del Castillo, *The Discovery and Conquest of Mexico, 1517–1521* (New York: Farrar, Straus, and Cudahy, 1956), 190–91. See also Stuart B. Schwartz, ed., *Victors and Vanquished: Spanish and Nahua Views of the Conquest of Mexico* (Boston: Bedford/St. Martin's, 2000).

17. Matthew and Oudijk, eds., *Indian Conquistadors*.

18. Covey, *Cabeza de Vaca's Adventures*, 56, 65, 106, 123, 128; Paul Schneider, *Brutal Journey: The Epic Story of the First Crossing of North America* (New York: Holt, 2006); Andrés Reséndez, *A Land So Strange: The Epic Journey of Cabeza de Vaca* (New York: Basic Books, 2007); Robin Varnum, *Álvar Nuñez Cabeza De Vaca: American Trailblazer* (Norman: University of Oklahoma Press, 2014).

19. The late Charles Hudson, a leading scholar of the de Soto expedition, provided a concise itinerary in *The Forgotten Centuries: Indians and Europeans in the American South, 1521–1704*, ed. Charles M. Hudson and Carmen Chaves Tesser (Athens: University of Georgia Press, 1994), 74–103, and in his *Knights of Spain, Warriors of the Sun: Hernando de Soto and the South's Ancient Chiefdoms* (Athens: University of Georgia Press, 1997).

20. Ann F. Ramenofsky and Patricia Galloway in "Disease and the Soto Entrada," in *The Hernando de Soto Expedition: History, Historiography, and "Discovery" in the Southeast*, ed. Patricia Galloway (Lincoln: University of Nebraska Press, 1997), 259–79, list nineteen diseases possibly brought by the Spanish and, despite slim evidence, identify ten diseases that were likely to have been transmitted to the Indians.

21. Robbie Ethridge and Sheri M. Shuck-Hall, eds., *Mapping the Mississippian Shatter Zone: The Colonial Indian Slave Trade and Regional Instability in the American South* (Lincoln: University of Nebraska Press, 2009); Robbie Ethridge, *From Chicaza to Chickasaw: The European Invasion and the Transformation of the Mississippian World, 1540–1715* (Chapel Hill: University of North Carolina Press, 2010). Paul Kelton, *Epidemics and Enslavement*, argues that the massive depopulations occurred after the advent of widespread slave raiding in the mid-seventeenth century.

22. Stephen Lekson, *A History of the Ancient Southwest* (Santa Fe: School for Advanced Research Press, 2008), 247.

23. Bartolomé de Las Casas, *History of the Indies*, trans. and ed. Andrée M. Collard (New York: Harper and Row, 1971), 289.

24. Ramón A. Gutiérrez, *When Jesus Came, the Corn Mothers Went Away: Marriage, Sexuality, and Power in New Mexico, 1500–1846* (Stanford: Stanford University Press, 1991).

25. Alfonso Ortiz, *The Pueblo* (New York: Chelsea House, 1994), 50.

26. Joe S. Sando, *Pueblo Nations: Eight Centuries of Pueblo Indian History* (Santa Fe: Clear Light Publishers, 1992), 63.

27. Daniel T. Reff, *Disease, Depopulation, and Culture Change in Northwestern New Spain, 1518–1764* (Salt Lake City: University of Utah Press, 1991), 229.

28. Quoted in Andrew L. Knaut, *The Pueblo Revolt of 1680: Conquest and Resistance in Seventeenth-Century New Mexico* (Norman: University of Oklahoma Press, 1995), 162.

29. Charles Wilson Hackett, ed., and Charmion Clair Shelby, trans., *Revolt of the Pueblo Indians of New Mexico and Otermín's Attempted Reconquest, 1680–1682* (Albuquerque: University of New Mexico Press, 1942), 2:237.

30. David J. Weber, *The Spanish Frontier in North America* (New Haven: Yale University Press, 1992), 134.

31. Hackett, *Revolt of the Pueblo Indians*, 2:246. Pueblo people still commemorate this event each year with foot races along the routes taken by the runners. Peter Nabokov, *Indian Running* (Santa Barbara: Capra Press, 1981).

32. Hackett, *Revolt of the Pueblo Indians*, 2:3.

33. Hackett, *Revolt of the Pueblo Indians*, 2:247.

34. Hackett, *Revolt of the Pueblo Indians*, 1:19.

35. Ned Blackhawk, *Violence over the Land: Indians and Empires in the Early American West* (Cambridge, Mass.: Harvard University Press, 2006); James F. Brooks, *Captives and Cousins: Slavery, Kinship, and Community in the Southwest Borderlands* (Chapel Hill: University of North Carolina Press, 2002).

36. Calloway, *World Turned Upside Down*, 33–34.

37. Quoted in Guillaume Aubert, "'The Blood of France': Race and Purity of Blood in the French Atlantic World," *William and Mary Quarterly*, 3rd ser., 61 (July 2004), 439–78, quote at 451.

38. Brian J. Given, *A Most Pernicious Thing: Gun Trading and Native Warfare in the Early Contact Period* (Ottawa: Carleton University Press, 1994). José António Brandão, "*Your Fyre Shall Burn No More*": *Iroquois Policy toward New France and Its Native Allies to 1701* (Lincoln: University of Nebraska Press, 1997), provides a thorough reassessment of the "Beaver Wars" thesis.

39. Kathryn Magee Labelle, *Dispersed But Not Destroyed: A History of the Seventeenth-Century Wendat People* (Vancouver: UBC Press, 2013).

40. Michael Witgen, "The Rituals of Possession: Native Identity and the Invention of Empire in Seventeenth-Century Western North America," *Ethnohistory* 54, no.4 (2007), 639–68.

41. Tracy Neal Leavelle, *The Catholic Calumet: Colonial Conversions in French and Indian North America* (Philadelphia: University of Pennsylvania Press, 2012).

42. Allan Greer, *Mohawk Saint: Catherine Tekakwitha and the Jesuits* (New York: Oxford University Press, 2005).

43. Emma Helen Blair, ed., *The Indian Tribes of the Upper Mississippi Valley and Region of the Great Lakes* (1911; repr., Lincoln: University of Nebraska Press, 1996), 1:262.

44. Richard White, *The Middle Ground: Indians, Empires, and Republics in the Great Lakes Region, 1650–1815* (Cambridge: Cambridge University Press, 1991).

45. Cynthia J. Van Zandt, *Brothers among Nations: The Pursuit of Intercultural Alliances in Early America, 1580–1660* (New York: Oxford University Press, 2008); Jeffrey Glover, *Paper Sovereigns: Anglo-Native Treaties and the Law of Nations, 1604–1664* (Philadelphia: University of Pennsylvania Press, 2014).

46. James Horn, *A Kingdom Strange: The Brief and Tragic History of the Lost Colony of Roanoke* (New York: Basic Books, 2010).

47. William K. Stevens, "Drought May Have Doomed the Lost Colony," *New York Times,* April 24, 1998, A1, A14.

48. James D. Rice, *Nature and History in the Potomac Country: From Hunter-Gatherers to the Age of Jefferson* (Baltimore: Johns Hopkins University Press, 2009).

49. Smith's account of his rescue, embellished in a letter to the queen of England at the time Pocahontas visited London, is reprinted in Karen Ordahl Kupperman, ed., *Captain John Smith: A Select Edition of His Writings* (Chapel Hill: University of North Carolina Press, 1988), 69. In Smith's writings of his life and his adventures, beautiful women save him from dire peril "not once but three times." Helen C. Rountree, *Pocahontas's People: The Powhatan Indians of Virginia through Four Centuries* (Norman: University of Oklahoma Press, 1990), 38. For a discussion of the rescue as ritual adoption, see chap. 4 in Frederic W. Gleach, *Powhatan's World and Colonial Virginia: A Conflict of Cultures* (Lincoln: University of Nebraska Press, 1997).

50. Quoted in Calloway, *World Turned Upside Down,* 39.

51. On Pocahontas's experiences, see Camilla Townsend, *Pocahontas and the Powhatan Dilemma* (New York: Hill and Wang, 2004), and Helen C. Rountree, *Pocahontas, Powhatan, Opechancanough: Three Indian Lives Changed by Jamestown* (Charlottesville: University of Virginia Press, 2005).

52. James D. Rice, *Tales from a Revolution: Bacon's Rebellion and the Transformation of Early America* (New York: Oxford University Press, 2012). Rice emphasizes the role of Native peoples in the rebellion in "Bacon's Rebellion in Indian Country," *Journal of American History* 101 (December 2014), 726–50.

53. William Bradford, *Of Plymouth Plantation*, ed. Harvey Wish (New York: Capricorn Books, 1962), 72.

54. Alfred A. Cave, *The Pequot War* (Amherst: University of Massachusetts Press, 1996), 178; Alden T. Vaughan, *New England Frontier: Puritans and Indians, 1620–1675,* 2nd ed. (New York: W. W. Norton, 1979), and Francis Jennings, *The Invasion of America: Indians, Colonialism, and the Cant of Conquest* (New York: W. W. Norton, 1976), represent the polar positions in the debate over the causes of the Pequot War.

55. Donna Merwick, *The Shame and the Sorrow: Dutch-Amerindian Encounters in New Netherland* (Philadelphia: University of Pennsylvania Press, 2006).

56. Jean M. O'Brien, *Dispossession by Degrees: Indian Land and Identity in Natick, Massachusetts, 1650–1790* (Cambridge: Cambridge University Press, 1997), 11.

57. David J. Silverman, *Faith and Boundaries: Colonists, Christianity, and Community among the Wampanoag Indians of Martha's Vineyard, 1600–1871* (Cambridge: Cambridge University Press, 2005); Julius H. Rubin, *Tears of Repentance: Christian Indian Identity and Community in Colonial Southern New England* (Lincoln: University of Nebraska Press, 2013).

58. Julie A. Fisher and David J. Silverman, *Ninigret, Sachem of the Niantics and Narragansetts* (Ithaca: Cornell University Press, 2014).

59. Quoted in Russell Bourne, *The Red King's Rebellion: Racial Politics in New England, 1675–1678* (New York: Oxford University Press, 1990), 107.

60. Yasuhide Kawashima, *Igniting King Philip's War: The John Sassamon Murder Trial* (Lawrence: University Press of Kansas, 2001).

61. Jenny Hale Pulsipher, *Subjects unto the Same King: Indians, English, and the Contest for Authority in Colonial New England* (Philadelphia: University of Pennsylvania Press, 2005).

62. James D. Drake, *King Philip's War: Civil War in New England, 1675–1676* (Amherst: University of Massachusetts Press, 1999).

63. On Uncas and Awashunkes, see Michael Leroy Oberg, *Uncas: First of the Mohegans* (Ithaca, N.Y.: Cornell University Press, 2003); Eric S. Johnson, "Uncas and the Politics of Contact," and Ann Marie Plane, "Putting a Face on Colonization: Factionalism and Gender Politics in the Life History of Awashunkes, the 'Squaw Sachem' of Saconet," in Robert S. Grumet, ed., *Northeastern Indian Lives, 1632–1816* (Amherst: University of Massachusetts Press, 1996), 39–47, 140–65.

64. O'Brien, *Dispossession by Degrees*, 61.

65. Colin G. Calloway, "Rhode Island Renegade: The Enigma of Joshua Tefft," *Rhode Island History* 43 (November 1984), 136–45.

66. Daniel Gookin, "An Historical Account of the Doings and Sufferings of the Christian Indians in New England in the Years 1675, 1676, 1677," *Transactions and Collections of the American Antiquarian Society* 2 (1836), 494, quoted in Neal Salisbury, "Embracing Ambiguity: Native Peoples and Christianity in Seventeenth-Century New England," *Ethnohistory* 50 (Spring 2003), 247.

67. Neal Salisbury, ed., *"The Sovereignty and Goodness of God" by Mary Rowlandson, with Related Documents* (Boston: Bedford Books, 1997).

68. Nathaniel Philbrick, *Mayflower* (New York: Viking/Penguin, 2006); Kelly Wisecup, ed., *"Good News from New England" by Edward Winslow* (Amherst: University of Massachusetts Press, 2014), 1–5, 16.

69. Philbrick, *Mayflower*, 7.

70. George M. Wrong, ed., *The Long Journey to the Country of the Hurons by Father Gabriel Sagard* (Toronto: The Champlain Society, 1939), 102.

71. Reuben Gold Thwaites, ed., *The Jesuit Relations and Allied Documents: Travels and Explorations of the Jesuit Missionaries in New France, 1610–1791*, vol. 10, *Hurons, 1636* (Cleveland: Burrows Brothers, 1898), 27–29.

72. Gary Warrick, *A Population History of the Huron-Petun, A.D. 500–1650* (Cambridge: Cambridge University Press, 2008), provides a thorough history of the Wendat-Tionontaté (Huron-Petun) population using archaeological, paleodemographic, historical, and epidemiological research.

73. Georges E. Sioui, "The Destruction of Huronia," chap. 4 in *For an Amerindian Autohistory*, trans. Sheila Fischman (Montreal: McGill-Queen's University Press, 1992).

74. Thwaites, *Jesuit Relations*, vol. 8, *Québec, Hurons, Cape Breton, 1634 to 1635* (1898), 99.

75. Harald E. L. Prins, *The Mi'kmaq: Resistance, Accommodation, and Cultural Survival* (Fort Worth: Harcourt Brace, 1996), 44–54; Frederick E. Hoxie, ed., *Encyclopedia of North American Indians: Native American History, Culture, and Life from Paleo-Indians to the Present* (Boston: Houghton Mifflin, 1996), 377.

76. Thwaites, *Jesuit Relations*, vol. 1, *Acadia, 1610–1613* (1898), 175.

77. Drake, *King Philip's War*.

78. Jennings, *Invasion of America*, 298.

79. For example, Bourne, *Red King's Rebellion*.

80. Jill Lepore, *The Name of War: King Philip's War and the Origins of American Identity* (New York: Alfred A. Knopf, 1998).

81. Richard Slotkin and James K. Folsom, eds., *So Dreadfull a Judgment: Puritan Responses to King Philip's War, 1676–1677* (Middletown, Conn.: Wesleyan University Press, 1978), 86, 138–39.

82. Hackett, *Revolt of the Pueblo Indians*, 1:24–25, 61; 2:232–49.

83. W. Kaye Lamb, ed., *The Letters and Journals of Simon Fraser, 1806–1808* (Toronto: Macmillan Co. of Canada, 1960), 79.

SUGGESTED READINGS

Alchon, Suzanne Austin. *A Pest in the Land: New World Epidemics in a Global Perspective.* Albuquerque: University of New Mexico Press, 2003.

Anderson, Virginia DeJohn. *Creatures of Empire: How Domestic Animals Transformed Early America.* New York: Oxford University Press, 2004.

Axtell, James. *The Invasion Within: The Contest of Cultures in Colonial North America.* New York: Oxford University Press, 1985.

Blackburn, Carole. *Harvest of Souls: The Jesuit Missions and Colonialism in North America, 1632–1650.* Montreal: McGill-Queens University Press, 2000.

Blackhawk, Ned, ed. *Ethnohistory* 54, no. 4, "Between Empires: Indians in the American West during the Age of Empire" (Fall 2007).

———. *Violence over the Land: Indians and Empires in the Early American West.* Cambridge, Mass.: Harvard University Press, 2006.

Bourne, Russell. *The Red King's Rebellion: Racial Politics in New England, 1675–1678.* New York: Oxford University Press, 1990.

Bowden, Henry Warner. *American Indians and Christian Missions: Studies in Cultural Conflict.* Chicago: University of Chicago Press, 1981.

Brooks, James F. *Captives and Cousins: Slavery, Kinship, and Community in the Southwest Borderlands.* Chapel Hill: University of North Carolina Press, 2002.

Cave, Alfred A. *Lethal Encounters: Englishmen and Indians in Colonial Virginia.* Paperback, Lincoln: University of Nebraska Press, 2013.

———. *The Pequot War.* Amherst: University of Massachusetts Press, 1996.

Clayton, Lawrence A., Vernon James Knight Jr., and Edward C. Moore, eds. *The De Soto Chronicles: The Expedition of Hernando de Soto to North America in 1539–1543.* 2 vols. Tuscaloosa: University of Alabama Press, 1993.

Cronon, William. *Changes in the Land: Indians, Colonists, and the Ecology of New England.* New York: Hill and Wang, 1983.

Crosby, Alfred W., Jr. *The Columbian Exchange: Biological and Cultural Consequences of 1492.* Westport, Conn.: Greenwood Press, 1972.

Cushner, Nicholas P. *Why Have You Come Here? The Jesuits and the First Evangelization of Native America.* New York: Oxford University Press, 2006.

Delâge, Denys. *Bitter Feast: Amerindians and Europeans in Northeastern North America, 1600–64.* Translated by Jane Brierley. Vancouver: University of British Columbia Press, 1993.

Drake, James D. *King Philip's War: Civil War in New England, 1675–1676.* Amherst: University of Massachusetts Press, 1999.

Duncan, David Ewing. *Hernando de Soto: A Savage Quest in the Americas.* New York: Crown Publishers, 1995.

Ethridge, Robbie. *From Chicaza to Chickasaw: The European Invasion and the Transformation of the Mississippian World,* 1540–1715. Chapel Hill: University of North Carolina Press, 2010.

Ethridge, Robbie, and Sheri M. Shuck-Hall, eds. *Mapping the Mississippian Shatter Zone: The Colonial Indian Slave Trade and Regional Instability in the American South.* Lincoln: University of Nebraska Press, 2009.

Fischer, David Hackett. *Champlain's Dream: The European Founding of North America.* New York: Simon & Schuster, 2008.

Fisher, Julie A., and David J. Silverman, *Ninigret, Sachem of the Niantics and Narragansetts.* Ithaca, N.Y.: Cornell University Press, 2014.

Flint, Richard. *No Settlement, No Conquest: A History of the Coronado Entrada.* Albuquerque: University of New Mexico Press, 2008.

Gallay, Alan. *The Indian Slave Trade: The Rise of the English Empire in the American South, 1670–1717.* New Haven: Yale University Press, 2002.

Galloway, Patricia, ed. *The Hernando de Soto Expedition: History, Historiography, and "Discovery" in the Southeast.* Lincoln: University of Nebraska Press, 1997.

Gleach, Frederic W. *Powhatan's World and Colonial Virginia: A Conflict of Cultures.* Lincoln: University of Nebraska Press, 1997.

Glover, Jeffrey. *Paper Sovereigns: Anglo-Native Treaties and the Law of Nations, 1604–1664.* Philadelphia: University of Pennsylvania Press, 2014.

Grant, John Webster. *The Moon of Wintertime: Missionaries and the Indians of Canada in Encounter since 1534.* Toronto: University of Toronto Press, 1984.

Greer, Allan. *Mohawk Saint: Catherine Tekakwitha and the Jesuits.* New York: Oxford University Press, 2005.

Grumet, Robert S. *First Manhattans: A History of the Indians of Greater New York.* Norman: University of Oklahoma Press, 2011.

———. *The Munsee Indians: A History.* Norman: University of Oklahoma Press, 2009.

Gutiérrez, Ramón A. *When Jesus Came, the Corn Mothers Went Away: Marriage, Sexuality, and Power in New Mexico, 1500–1846.* Stanford: Stanford University Press, 1991.

Hackett, Charles Wilson, ed., and Charmion Clair Shelby, trans. *Revolt of the Pueblo Indians of New Mexico and Otermín's Attempted Reconquest, 1680–1682.* 2 vols. Albuquerque: University of New Mexico Press, 1942.

Henige, David. *Numbers from Nowhere: The American Indian Contact Population Debate.* Norman: University of Oklahoma Press, 1998.

Hudson, Charles M. *Conversations with the High Priest of Coosa.* Chapel Hill: University of North Carolina Press, 2003.

———. *Knights of Spain, Warriors of the Sun: Hernando de Soto and the South's Ancient Chiefdoms.* Athens: University of Georgia Press, 1997.

Hudson, Charles M., and Carmen Chaves Tesser, eds. *The Forgotten Centuries: Indians and Europeans in the American South, 1521–1704.* Athens: University of Georgia Press, 1994.

Hudson, Charles M., and Jerald T. Milanich. *Hernando de Soto and the Indians of Florida.* Gainesville: University Press of Florida, 1993.

Jennings, Francis. *The Invasion of America: Indians, Colonialism, and the Cant of Conquest.* New York: W. W. Norton, 1976.

Kelton, Paul. *Cherokee Medicine, Colonial Germs: An Indigenous Nation's Fight against Smallpox, 1518–1824.* Norman: University of Oklahoma Press, 2015.

———. *Epidemics and Enslavement: Biological Catastrophe in the Native Southeast, 1492–1715.* Lincoln: University of Nebraska Press, 2007.

Kessell, John L. *Pueblos, Spaniards, and the Kingdom of New Mexico.* Norman: University of Oklahoma Press, 2008.

Knaut, Andrew. *The Pueblo Revolt of 1680: Conquest and Resistance in Seventeenth-Century New Mexico.* Norman: University of Oklahoma Press, 1995.

Kugel, Rebecca, and Lucy Eldersveld Murphy, eds. *Native Women's History in Eastern North America before 1900: A Guide to Research and Writing.* Lincoln: University of Nebraska Press, 2007.

Kupperman, Karen Ordahl. *Indians and English: Facing Off in Early America.* Ithaca, N.Y.: Cornell University Press, 2000.

Labelle, Kathryn Magee, *Dispersed But Not Destroyed: A History of the Seventeenth-Century Wendat People.* Vancouver: UBC Press, 2013.

Leavelle, Tracy Neal, *The Catholic Calumet: Colonial Conversions in French and Indian North America.* Philadelphia: University of Pennsylvania Press, 2012.

Lepore, Jill. *The Name of War: King Philip's War and the Origins of American Identity.* New York: Alfred A. Knopf, 1998.

Mancall, Peter C., and James H. Merrell, eds. *American Encounters: Natives and Newcomers from European Contact to Indian Removal, 1500–1850.* 2nd ed. New York: Routledge, 2007.

Mandell, Daniel R. *King Philip's War: Colonial Expansion, Native Resistance, and the End of Indian Sovereignty.* Baltimore: Johns Hopkins University Press, 2010.

Mann, Charles C., *1493: Uncovering the World Columbus Created.* New York: Alfred Knopf, 2011.

Merwick, Donna. *The Shame and the Sorrow: Dutch-Amerindian Encounters in New Netherland.* Philadelphia: University of Pennsylvania Press, 2006.

Midtrød, Tom Arne, *The Memory of All Ancient Customs: Native American Diplomacy in the Colonial Hudson Valley.* Ithaca, N.Y.: Cornell University Press, 2012.

Milanich, Jerald T. *Florida Indians and the Invasion from Europe.* Gainesville: University Press of Florida, 1995.

Parmenter, Jon. *The Edge of the Woods: Iroquoia, 1534–1701.* East Lansing: Michigan State University Press, 2010.

Pulsipher, Jenny Hale. *Subjects unto the Same King: Indians, English, and the Contest for Authority in Colonial New England.* Philadelphia: University of Pennsylvania Press, 2005.

Reséndez, André. *A Land So Strange: The Epic Journey of Cabeza de Vaca.* New York: Basic Books, 2007.

Rice, James D. *Nature and History in the Potomac Country: From Hunter-Gatherers to the Age of Jefferson.* Baltimore: Johns Hopkins University Press, 2009.

———. *Tales from a Revolution: Bacon's Rebellion and the Transformation of Early America.* New York: Oxford University Press, 2012.

Richter, Daniel K. *Before the Revolution: America's Ancient Pasts.* Cambridge, Mass.: Harvard University Press, 2011.

———. *Facing East from Indian Country: A Native History of Early America.* Cambridge, Mass.: Harvard University Press, 2001.

Riley, Carroll L. *The Kachina and the Cross: Indians and Spaniards in the Early Southwest.* Salt Lake City: University of Utah Press, 1999.

Rountree, Helen C. *Pocahontas, Powhatan, Opechancanough: Three Indian Lives Changed by Jamestown.* Charlottesville: University of Virginia Press, 2005.

———. *Pocahontas's People: The Powhatan Indians of Virginia through Four Centuries.* Norman: University of Oklahoma Press, 1990.

Rubin, Julius H. *Tears of Repentance: Christian Indian Identity and Community in Colonial Southern New England.* Lincoln: University of Nebraska Press, 2013.

Salisbury, Neal. *Manitou and Providence: Indians, Europeans, and the Making of New England, 1500–1643.* New York: Oxford University Press, 1982.

———, ed. *"The Sovereignty and Goodness of God" by Mary Rowlandson, with Related Documents.* Boston: Bedford Books, 1997.

Sando, Joe S. *Pueblo Nations: Eight Centuries of Pueblo Indian History.* Santa Fe: Clear Light Publishers, 1992.

Silverman, David J. *Faith and Boundaries: Colonists, Christianity, and Community among the Wampanoag Indians of Martha's Vineyard, 1600–1871.* Cambridge: Cambridge University Press, 2005.

Sioui, Georges E. *For an Amerindian Autohistory.* Translated by Sheila Fischman. Montreal: McGill-Queen's University Press, 1992.

———. *Huron-Wendat: The Heritage of the Circle.* Translated by Jane Brierley. Vancouver: University of British Columbia Press; East Lansing: Michigan State University Press, 1999.

Slotkin, Richard, and James K. Folsom, eds. *So Dreadfull a Judgment: Puritan Responses to King Philip's War, 1676–1677.* Middletown, Conn.: Wesleyan University Press, 1978.

Starna, William A. *From Homeland to New Land: A History of the Mahican Indians, 1600–1830.* Lincoln: University of Nebraska Press, 2013.

Steele, Ian K. *Warpaths: Invasions of North America.* New York: Oxford University Press, 1994.

Thornton, Russell. *American Indian Holocaust and Survival: A Population History since 1492.* Norman: University of Oklahoma Press, 1987.

Townsend, Camilla. *Pocahontas and the Powhatan Dilemma*. New York: Hill and Wang, 2004.

Trigger, Bruce G. *The Children of Aataentsic: A History of the Huron People to 1660*. 2 vols. Montreal: McGill-Queen's University Press, 1976.

———. *Natives and Newcomers: Canada's "Heroic Age" Reconsidered*. Montreal: McGill-Queen's University Press, 1985.

Van Zandt, Cynthia J. *Brothers among Nations: The Pursuit of Intercultural Alliances in Early America, 1580–1660*. New York: Oxford University Press, 2008.

Weber, David J. *The Spanish Frontier in North America*. New Haven: Yale University Press, 1992.

———, ed. *What Caused the Pueblo Revolt of 1680?* Boston: Bedford/St. Martin's, 1999.

White, Richard. *The Middle Ground: Indians, Empires, and Republics in the Great Lakes Region, 1650–1815*. Cambridge: Cambridge University Press, 1991.

Witgen, Michael J., *An Infinity of Nations: How the Native New World Shaped Modern America*. Philadelphia: University of Pennsylvania Press, 2012.

3

Indians in Colonial Worlds

1680–1763

FOCUS QUESTIONS

1. As Native peoples and Europeans encountered one another, what kinds of relationships did they establish? Who had the advantage?

2. Who established trade routes, and for what purposes?

3. What tools did Europeans and Native groups use to communicate, and were their efforts at communication successful?

4. What effect did long-standing rivalries between European nations have on Native and European communities in colonial America?

5. How did the introduction of horses change life on the Great Plains?

ECONOMIC AND CULTURAL EXCHANGES

COLONIAL AMERICA WAS A NEW WORLD for Europeans and Indians alike. Indian peoples on the East Coast confronted settler colonies that demanded their lands and eventually would demand their expulsion.[1] Indian peoples in the interior of the continent felt the repercussions of invasion and colonialism as horses, goods, diseases, and slave raiders penetrated their worlds. Europeans imposed laws, power structures, and ways of thinking that confirmed, perpetuated, and justified their invasion and occupation of America.[2] In the eighteenth century, however, Indians and Europeans together shaped the character and history of colonial America. Indigenous power limited European ambitions, and Europeans adapted to indigenous ways even as they tried to change them. Doing business in Indian country meant following Indian rules and practices, which often revolved around kinship ties and gift exchanges more than military and economic power.[3]

Despite the cartographic claims of rival European powers and the ravages of war and disease inflicted on Indian populations, at the beginning of the eighteenth century the European presence in North America existed only on the edges and along the arteries of the continent. Indian people still held sway over the interior. Indians resisted European intrusion but also sought out Europeans as sources of new commercial opportunities and political alliance. Indian people came to colonial settlements and cities to trade and otherwise participate in the economic life of the new communities. Indians lived near, and sometimes in, colonial societies. Indians and Europeans coexisted and adjusted to each other's presence, engaging in what historian James Axtell describes as a "contest of cultures"[4] — colonial governments, teachers, and missionaries endeavored to change Indians into "civilized Christians," but Indian captors often tried to convert their captives to Indian ways, with some successes. Indian ways of life also exerted subtle influence on many Europeans who experienced them firsthand. Indians and Europeans also killed each other in a world of escalating violence. While Indians participated in colonial wars, the ultimate outcome of those wars was the creation of a new nation committed to expansion onto Indian lands and the exclusion of Indians from that nation.

Indians in Colonial Societies

Indian people played important roles in helping Europeans establish their initial settlements in North America. They served as guides, sometimes willingly, sometimes under coercion; they acted as interpreters and intermediaries with more distant tribes; they provided food supplies and taught Europeans how to grow, hunt, and fish for their own food in unfamiliar environments.

Indians often constituted an integral part of the colonial societies and economies. In New Spain, Indian people

1754	Albany Congress: English colonies meet to discuss unified Indian policy
1755	French and Indians defeat British forces led by General Edward Braddock
1756–1763	Seven Years' (or French and Indian) War
1758	Treaty of Easton French abandon Fort Duquesne
1759–1761	War between the Cherokees and colonists
1763	Treaty of Paris ends Seven Years' War; France divides its North American empire between Britain and Spain
1763	British captives resist liberation from Delawares and Shawnees

were subjected to labor drafts; worked in Spanish mines, plantations, and households; and built Spanish missions and towns. Indian women cooked in Spanish kitchens; sold pottery and foodstuffs in markets at St. Augustine, New Orleans, and Santa Fe; and wove textiles in Santa Fe. Indian men worked on Spanish ranches and herded Spanish cattle. Franciscan priests established missions in Florida and New Mexico. They assaulted the Indians' traditional religions, insisted on baptism, and tried to transform them into communities of Christian peasants living within sound of the mission bells. Concentrating Indian populations into mission communities at a time when new epidemic diseases stalked the land often proved fatal. Nevertheless, thousands of Indians became at least nominal Catholics. Accepting certain tenets and symbols of Christianity to which they attached their own meanings, without abandoning their traditional beliefs and rituals, Indians created their own versions of Christianity. Indians and Spaniards intermarried and borrowed each other's foods, clothing, technologies, and words. The centuries-long influence of Spanish people and culture on Indians, and of Indian culture and peoples on Hispanos, is evident in areas of the Southwest today.

Between the 1560s and 1760s, Spain established more than 150 missions between present-day Miami and Chesapeake Bay, most in northern Florida and southern Georgia, among the Timucuas, Guales, and Apalachees. The missions aimed to save souls by converting Indians to Christianity, but at the same time they converted the Native population into a labor force. Working through local chiefs whom they baptized in elaborate ceremonies, the missionaries recruited laborers to plant, grow, harvest, and grind corn; to work as porters and household servants; and to carry out building projects. (Indian laborers built the fortress of Castillo de San Marcos in Saint Augustine that, renamed Fort Marion, later based Indian POWs [see pages 380–81].) Missionaries instilled in their converts the notion that it was their duty to labor for the Lord. The mission populations succumbed to the epidemic diseases that swept through Florida, and many of the missions themselves fell victim to attacks by the English and their Indian allies in the early eighteenth century.[5]

On the Atlantic seaboard, Indians mingled with Dutch, Swedes, Finns, Scots, Irish, Englishmen, Germans, and African slaves, although British population and power predominated by the eighteenth century. Despite intense pressures on their lands and periodic eruptions of hostilities, Indians lived in and around colonial settlements and took advantage of the new economic opportunities they afforded even as those same settlements curtailed their traditional mobile economy. They worked for wages in colonial towns, labored on colonial plantations alongside African slaves, served on colonial ships, and enlisted in colonial armies. Sometimes, Indians lived with the colonial families who employed them. Indian healers, many of them women, drew on their extensive knowledge of plant-derived medicines to cure European as well as Indian patients. Indian men traded the products of their hunting; Indian women traded the corn they grew and the baskets they made. In South Carolina, for instance, many Catawbas traveled the roads as peddlers, selling moccasins, baskets, mats, and pottery. Like basketmaking, pottery was an ancient skill, and Indians, recognizing the potential for profit, began manufacturing baskets and pots for sale.[6]

In the English colonies, as in the French and Spanish missions, Indian responses to Christianity were varied, involved complex cultural interactions, and changed over time. For some Native people, conversion to Christianity no doubt involved a complete and permanent personal and spiritual transformation. Others, however, adopted Christianity as a strategy for survival or saw it as a new source of Native identity rather than as a means of assimilating into colonial society. Confronted with colonialism, escalating violence, land loss, and cultural assault, Indian people affiliated with Christianity for a variety of reasons and in a variety of ways that often reflected social, political, economic, or simply pragmatic realities. Many Native people refused to convert and shared the sentiments of the Indians who told a Swedish missionary in 1704: "If the Christians lived better than we according to their religion, then we would become Christians. But we cannot find that they do, because we see and hear them drink, fight, whore, murder, steal, lie, cheat, etc. Such things we have never known. Thus we are better off as we are." Other Indians accepted Christianity. As had the inhabitants of John Eliot's praying towns in seventeenth-century Massachusetts, some Native people found a haven in mission communities from the turmoil around them, and women sometimes took on important roles in these communities. Many Indians worshipped, married, and were buried in colonial churches. They sometimes established and maintained their own Christian churches, with their own deacons and ministers. But they made Christianity an Indian religion.[7] Some also attended colonial schools, where they were taught to read and write, to study the Bible, and to dress and behave in English ways. A few colonial colleges, like Harvard, William and Mary, and later Dartmouth, had "Indian schools." Many Indian people recognized the new education as a useful tool, and after attending school they took up work as interpreters or assumed roles as culture brokers: Mohegan minister Samson Occom, for example, preached Christianity to Indian peoples and traveled to Britain to raise money for the Indian school at Dartmouth College (see pages 192–94).

Other Indians were more guarded in their responses. At the Treaty of Lancaster, Pennsylvania, in 1744, commissioners from Virginia invited the Iroquois delegates to send their children to William and Mary, where they would receive the benefits of an English education. The Onondaga orator Canasatego thanked them for their kind offer but politely declined. In the expanded version of his reply recorded by Benjamin Franklin (who printed many colonial Indian treaties), Canasatego went further. Young Indians who had gone to school in the colonies, he said, came home "good for nothing," unable to hunt a deer, paddle a canoe, or find their way in the woods. Tongue in cheek, he returned the compliment: if the Virginians would like to send some of their young men to the Iroquois, the Indians would teach them their ways and make real men of them![8]

Colonists in Indian Societies

As Indian societies reacted to foreign religious ideas, labor and economic systems, educational institutions, and trade currencies, colonists in turn observed and adopted certain Native ways of life. France's North American empire constituted a veneer of French population and culture spread thinly over an Indian world. Indian converts and customers were attracted to French missions and trading posts, and French traders, priests, soldiers, and agents ventured into Indian country to bolster Indian allegiance, but the French population remained relatively small and scattered in settlements from the mouth of the St. Lawrence to the mouth of the Mississippi. Nevertheless, in regions such as Louisiana, French settlers and Indians intermarried; exchanged foods, commodities, and knowledge; and, along with African slaves, built networks of cross-cultural exchange through individual, face-to-face interactions.[9]

Many Europeans who pushed into Indian country adopted Indian ways, which suited their new environment and eased their interactions with Native populations. They hunted using Indian techniques; dressed in Indian hunting shirts, leggings, and moccasins; wore their hair Indian-style; bore body paint and tattoos; spoke Indian languages; and smoked Indian pipes. One fur trader who lived and worked among the Chipewyan Indians in northwestern Canada recorded in his journal: "This night dreamed in the Chipewyan Language for the first time."[10] Colonial authorities sometimes became alarmed by the numbers of their citizens who "went Indian." Like Joshua Tefft (see page 102), some individuals chose to live with Indians and even fought beside them against Europeans. Indians also took hundreds of captives from European settlements during the colonial wars, adopting them into their societies and turning them from enemies into relatives. Some of these captives became so accustomed to life in Indian country and Indian communities that they stayed permanently, even refusing opportunities to return home (see pages 182–87). Benjamin Franklin said that Europeans who had lived in Indian societies and then returned to colonial society soon "become disgusted with our manner of life."[11]

For long periods over large areas of America, Indians and Europeans coexisted closely, interacting with and adjusting to each other's presence and culture and sometimes taking on aspects of one another's identity and way of life. The intimate familiarity that was characteristic of many frontier societies in eighteenth-century America made fighting all the more bitter when wars broke out between former neighbors.[12]

FUR TRADES AND SLAVE TRADES

Trade in animal hides was a major component of the economy of early America. Pelts from beavers trapped in Canada and the northern British colonies were extremely valuable in Europe, where wearing fur provided warmth and social prestige. Farther south, deerskins, originating in the interior and shipped out of Charleston to European tanners, were equally sought after. Metal tools, weapons, and utensils, woven cloth, and other European goods exchanged for furs were equally valuable to Indians. But Europeans and Indians in colonial America trafficked in human beings as well as in animal pelts. Some Indian societies kept slaves before European contact — usually captives taken in war — but with conflict escalating and demands for labor increasing, more and more Indian people raided for slaves, held slaves, or became slaves themselves.

The Impact of the Fur Trade

Swedes, Dutch, French, British, Spaniards, Russians, and Americans all participated in the pelt trade. In Alaska, Russian traders, *promyshleniki*, began to hunt for sea otter pelts after Vitus Bering, a Dane in the czar's service who gave his name to the straits, reached the Aleutian Islands in 1741. Before the end of the century, ships from several European nations and from New England were plying the coastline from Oregon to Alaska, trading for sea otter pelts that they then transported across the Pacific and sold at great profits in China.

Many cities, including Montreal, St. Louis, Detroit, Charleston, and Albany, New York, began as fur or deerskin trade markets, and many individual and family fortunes were built on the production and marketing of beaver and deerskins. Trading posts became centers of cultural as well as economic interaction. The search for new sources of furs and new customers fueled continued European exploration and penetration of Indian country. The fur trade was part of everyday life in early America, and it continued for centuries: the Hudson's Bay Company, established by British royal charter in 1670, joked that its initials stood for "Here Before Christ."

Europeans provided capital, organization, manufactured goods, and equipment for the trade. Indians provided much of the labor force: they hunted the animals, guided the fur traders, and paddled the canoes that carried pelts to market. Indian women prepared the skins. Various Indian groups acted as middlemen, securing lucrative roles by conveying pelts and manufactured goods between Europeans and more distant tribes. Indian women played a valuable role as cultural mediators. They lived with and frequently married European traders, translated for them, and provided them with access to the kinship networks of Indian societies.[13] The children of these unions often grew up to become influential leaders in Indian communities and skilled negotiators with colonial society.

In areas of Canada and around the Great Lakes, Indian women who married French traders played a central role in the fur trade, operating as brokers between Indian and European society and linking Indian country to an expanding transatlantic economy. They and their husbands produced a new population, known as Métis; built kinship networks that were Catholic as well as indigenous; and created communities that remained long after France officially withdrew from the area.[14] In tribes where clan descent followed the father's line, children of European traders might lack a place in their Indian mother's society. But in matrilineal societies, children of mixed ancestry inherited their mother's clan and community: by the eighteenth century, it was not uncommon to find Creek and Cherokee Indians in the Southeast who bore the Scottish surnames of the traders who fathered them — McIntosh, McGillivray, Ross, or McDonald, for example — and who inherited their clan and tribal identity intact from their mothers. Such individuals often acted as intermediaries between colonial and Indian societies, became influential in their tribes, and introduced European ways of thinking about land, trade, and property.[15]

In return for the pelts they supplied and the services they provided, Indians obtained steel knives and axes, firearms, metal cooking vessels, woolen blankets and clothing, glass beads, mirrors, scissors, awls, spoons, linen shirts, hats, buckles, and a

◆ **Fur Trading**

This detail from William Fadden's "A Map of the Inhabited Part of Canada . . . With the Frontiers of New York and New England," engraved in London in 1777, shows the commerce that became crucial to the economy of Indian and colonial America. Indian hunters traded beaver pelts and other skins for European merchandise. Scenes such as the one depicted here were part of a centuries-long exchange between Indian America and industrializing Europe, although the participants often attached very different values and meanings to the items being exchanged. *Library and Archives Canada.*

host of other goods. The new items sometimes replaced traditional ones: metal axes were better than stone ones. Sometimes they simply supplemented existing items: birchbark containers continued to be used for maple sugaring long after copper kettles were introduced (see "Indian Sugar Camp," page 38). Sometimes Indians refashioned the new items in traditional ways: metal pots might be cut up for jewelry. Some items cheaply produced in European factories and traded as trinkets and tools took on a social and spiritual significance once they entered Indian hands. For northeastern Algonquian peoples, glass beads and metal objects were often identified with native crystal and copper, both of which possessed special healthful properties.[16]

The Cost of the Fur Trade

All told, the costs of the fur trade to Indians were enormous. Contagious diseases spread from tribe to tribe as Indians traded with Europeans and then with other Indians. Overhunting depleted animal populations to the point of extinction in some regions and undermined traditional hunting rituals and reciprocal relationships in which hunters treated animal spirits with respect and animals allowed themselves to be hunted. New tools made life easier but traditional craft skills sometimes declined. Competition for new weapons made warfare more common; the new weapons themselves made warfare more lethal. Balanced and diversified patterns of subsistence were disrupted as communities focused their energies on hunting and trapping to meet the insatiable demands of European fur markets. Indian people in some areas traded for European goods but resisted being pulled into a dependent relationship on traders; others became heavily dependent on European goods: "Every necessary of life we must have from the white people," a Cherokee chief lamented in the 1750s. "We have been used so long to wrap up our Children as soon as they are born in Goods procured of the white People," said a Creek in the 1770s, "that we cannot do without it."[17] As Native environments became degraded, subsistence patterns changed and Indian people became increasingly dependent on Europeans for goods, clothing, and food. Europeans in turn sought to bring Native resources, land, and labor into the market.[18] Indians were becoming tied to developing European capitalism as both producers and consumers and being incorporated into a world market. They fell into debt to European traders who offered credit, then sometimes demanded land in payment for accumulated debts. And traders brought alcohol into Indian country.

Alcohol was a crucial commodity for European traders. It could be transported easily in concentrated form and diluted for sale at huge profits, and it was quickly consumed. Traders soon found that liquor was a good way of attracting Indians to trade and then getting them to make that trade on favorable terms. Not all Indians drank and not all who did suffered from it, but alcohol had disastrous effects in many Indian societies. John Lawson, an English botanist who traveled through the Carolinas in 1701 (and who was killed by Indians ten years later), reported the Indians were "much addicted to drunkenness, a Vice they never were acquainted with, till the Christians came amongst them." English traders plied them with rum "to buy Skins, Furs, Slaves and other of their Commodities."[19] Indian hunters who sold their catch for a bottle of rum often left their families in poverty. Drunken brawls disrupted social relations in communities that traditionally stressed harmony and help between individuals and families. "You Rot Your grain in Tubs, out of which you take and make Strong Spirits You sell it to our young men," said the Catawba chief Hagler to his English neighbors in South Carolina in the 1750s; "it Rots their guts and Causes our men to get very sick and many of our people has Lately Died by the Effects of that Strong Drink."[20]

Scholars and clinicians still do not fully understand the exact causes and nature of alcoholism. Like other people, Indians who drank to excess did so for a variety of social, cultural, genetic, and behavioral reasons. Some drank because they enjoyed the sensations alcohol produced; some sought solace in alcohol as they were forced to adjust to the radical changes to their ways of life. Indian leaders throughout colonial America complained about the rum trade and asked that it be halted, but colonial governments could not or would not stem the tide of alcohol into Indian villages.[21]

Indian Slavery

Slavery existed in North America long before the English shipped the first African slaves to Jamestown in 1619. Before contact with Europeans, Indian warriors often took their enemies captive rather than killing them. They carried off war captives as slaves, humiliated and held them in subordination as markers of prowess in battle, gave them as gifts while making alliances, and sometimes adopted them in place of deceased relatives. But European colonialism introduced different concepts of slavery, brought new slave peoples to America from Africa, and drove Indian–Indian slave raiding to unprecedented levels. Like the trade in furs, trade in Indian slaves became a routine feature of the developing Atlantic economy. Indian hunters of human flesh, like Indian hunters of animal pelts, ranged farther afield and increased their catch to meet new demands. All European colonies in America used Indian slaves. The Native tradition of taking war captives and the European tradition of purchasing humans as property came together to shape a new slave market.[22]

In the "shatter zone" generated by Spanish invasion in the colonial South, competition for trade, escalating warfare, slave raiding, and epidemic disease were all interconnected.[23] The English founded Charlestown (later Charleston), South Carolina, in 1670 and quickly began shipping in African slaves and shipping out Indian slaves to the Caribbean. Indians exchanged slaves for guns, which they then turned on Indian enemies to take more slaves. It was a perilous strategy, and one to which slave-raiding tribes themselves often fell victim. Westo Indians, originally a group of Eries who had fled Iroquois attacks in the north and moved to the James River, began slave raiding to supply English slave traders at Jamestown. By the 1660s they were raiding for slaves even farther south, in Georgia and Florida. Armed with English guns, the Westos preyed on bow-and-arrow tribes for slaves to sell in Charleston, until they themselves were destroyed in 1682 by Shawnee Indians in the pay of Carolina traders. The Westos in turn became victims of the Indian slave trade.[24]

By the end of the seventeenth century, French movement down the Mississippi and westward penetration of English traders from Charleston brought guns and

◆ **Iroquois Warriors and Captive, c. 1666**
This seventeenth-century French sketch shows Iroquois warriors returning from a raid with scalps and an Indian captive. *From Edmund B. O'Callaghan, ed.,* Documents Relative to the Colonial History of the State of New York, *15 volumes (Albany, 1853–87).*

slave raiding to the lower Mississippi valley. Newly armed bands of Indians raided villages on both sides of the Mississippi for slaves, whom they sold to English traders; the traders marched the slaves east, to be used in colonial households and on plantations or to be shipped to the Caribbean. The Chickasaws emerged as the dominant slave traders in the region. Pierre LeMoyne d'Iberville, the founder of France's Louisiana colony, reported in 1699 that the Chickasaws "were going among all the other nations to make war on them and to carry off as many slaves as they could, whom they buy and use in extensive trading, to the distress of all these Indian nations." Chickasaw raiding parties crossed the Mississippi and then herded their captives east to Charleston, causing reverberations throughout the lower Mississippi valley as other Indians fell victim, migrated, or sought refuge with other tribes.[25]

The Indian slave trade and the violence associated with it helped spread European diseases. Slave raiders who had come in contact with Europeans and their germs ranged far and wide through Indian country; refugees from their raids huddled together in communities, prime targets for lethal new epidemics. Disease hit populations already disrupted, displaced, weakened, and malnourished by the changes that followed in the wake of colonialism. The "Great Southeastern Smallpox Epidemic" of 1696–1700 broke out among English and African populations that were in frequent contact with Indians and spread via South Carolina's Indian trading allies to the Mississippi valley and the Gulf Coast. Some historians estimate that the deadly combination of smallpox and rum reduced the Indian population living within two hundred miles of the English settlements to less than one-sixth of its original size within fifty years. The population collapse led to war in 1715 between South Carolina and its former Yamasee allies, who were indebted to colonial traders but could no longer supply the number of slaves South Carolina demanded and who now adopted more captives to bolster their own declining population. Before 1715 English colonists had captured, sold, and enslaved an estimated thirty to fifty thousand Indians, but now the flow of Indian captives into Charleston slowed to a trickle, and South Carolina turned to imports of African slaves to supply its labor needs.[26] In some areas Africans came to outnumber Europeans, and the new people Indians encountered as a result of European colonialism were more likely to be black than white. Later in the eighteenth century, Indians, for whom the age and gender of captives had traditionally determined their suitability for seizure and treatment as slaves, began to target African Americans and to adopt racial attitudes toward slavery. By the turn of the century many Indians held African slaves, regarding them much as their white neighbors did.[27]

Indian slavery was widespread in Spanish colonies as well. As Cabeza de Vaca and his companions made their way south through Sonora in northwestern Mexico at the end of their eight-year odyssey, they met Spanish slave raids pushing north, searching for Indians to work the silver mines of central Mexico (see page 83). In later years, as Spain's mines gobbled up Indian labor, tribes like the Utes became slave traders. Mounted on horses they had acquired from Spaniards, they raided neighboring tribes to their north and west for slaves, whom they supplied to the Spanish, rather than fall victim themselves to Spanish slavery. The trade in Indian slaves reached far beyond the arena of

Spanish control, involving Ute Indians from the Rockies, Plains Apaches, and many other peoples. Indian slaves in colonial New Mexico came to compose a separate class, known as *genizaros,* and were looked down upon by Pueblo Indians and Hispanic settlers alike.[28]

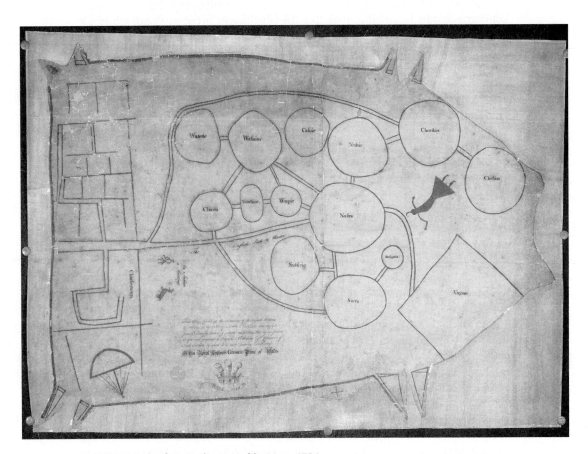

◆ **Photograph of Catawba Deerskin Map, 1721**

Although European cartographers often dispossessed Indian peoples of their land when depicting the new country, Indian people were themselves capable mapmakers who possessed extensive geographical knowledge and who often served as guides. Not all of the maps they created, however, were intended to convey geographical information. In this English copy of a Catawba map on deerskin that was presented to the governor of South Carolina around 1721, the circles and lines portray the disposition as well as the location of various tribes in the region and their trade relations with the English. The various tribes are connected to the English in Virginia and in Charleston by paths of trade and alliance. Although Charleston lay southeast of the Indians, it is portrayed on the left-hand side of the map (as a grid of streets with a boat in the harbor). The purpose of the map was to convey the social and political geography of the landscape and to depict a network of relationships in which the Nasaws (one of the groups who became known as Catawbas), not the English, occupied the central position. *British Library, London, UK/© British Library Board. All Rights Reserved/Bridgeman Images.*

In New France, Indian traders sold or gave captives to Frenchmen, sometimes as gifts to cement and maintain their commercial and military alliances with France. French and Indian traders sold many slaves to the English in Carolina and transferred others to Quebec and Montreal, where they might serve in French households or get shipped to the Caribbean. Illinois raiders ranged out across the prairies, taking captives as slaves and trading them to the Ottawas and other tribes for guns and metal weapons. So many Indians were captured from the eastern Plains that French slaveholders called almost all Indian slaves "panis," whether or not they were actually Pawnees. As Indian slaves passed from Indian to French hands, two forms of slavery overlapped and altered: the French adjusted to giving and receiving Indian slaves as a means of sustaining alliances and trade, and Indian slave raiders responded to the lure of French markets and money.[29]

DIPLOMACY IN COLONIAL AMERICA

History books have often portrayed a colonial America in which European settlers built new homes in a new world, wresting the land from Indians who emerged from the forests to burn cabins and lift scalps. In reality, the lines of conflict and competition were more complicated, and colonial America was often a more dangerous place for Indians than for Europeans. The invasion of America by European powers created a bewildering and volatile situation, involving many players in changing roles. European settlers competed with Indians for prime lands (Map 3.1). European powers competed for North American resources and dominance, as well as for Indian allies to help them secure that dominance. Indians resisted European intrusions and pretensions yet often forged alliances with the newcomers. Europeans competed for Indian trade; Indians competed with other Indians for European trade. Relations between different tribes sometimes altered dramatically; friends became enemies and vice versa. Indian nations developed their own foreign policies for dealing with the representatives of various European powers, colonial governments, and other tribes. Indian diplomats sometimes crossed the Atlantic to visit European capitals (see Picture Essay, "Atlantic Travelers: Indians in Eighteenth-Century London," pages 188–93). Europeans sought Indian allies and learned the customs of doing business in Indian country.

Relations often broke down in bloody conflict. As they had in King Philip's War (1675–76) and the Pueblo War of Independence (1680), Indian warriors fought for tribal lands and independence in recurrent conflicts against colonial expansion. Increasingly, wars between Indians and Europeans occurred in a larger context of wars between Europeans. The so-called French and Indian wars, which included King William's War, Queen Anne's War, and King George's War, as well as the Seven Years' War or French and Indian War proper (see Table 3.1, page 156), involved Indian warriors fighting on both sides *alongside* European armies, as well as fighting *against* European armies invading Indian country. But through it all, Europeans and Indians also reached across cultural

◆ **Map 3.1 Indian Nations and European Territorial Claims, c. 1750**
Eighteenth-century maps showed North America as a vast zone of competing and sometimes overlapping European claims. In most regions, the actual European presence was slight or nonexistent and Indian people and power predominated. Yet European ambitions generated repercussions that reached far into Indian country.

divides and engaged in negotiation to achieve what they wanted — peace, trade, land — through diplomacy rather than war.

The Language and Lessons of Diplomacy

When Europeans went into Indian country to conduct business, they entered a world crisscrossed by exchange networks between communities and between cultures, where the constant renewal of alliances and good relations was vital to avoiding violence. Gift exchanges lay at the heart of Indian relations with other

Indians, and they became equally important in Indian relations with the Spanish, French, and English. Different peoples attached different meanings to gifts, and Europeans had to learn that such exchanges were not conducted solely for profit but involved social, political, and even spiritual aspects as well as economic incentives.[30] Indians and Europeans who endeavored to deal with each other across cultural gulfs had to negotiate a collision and confluence of worldviews. In doing so they forged uniquely American forms of diplomacy.[31]

France's North American empire, huge in extent but sparsely populated, depended on maintaining the goodwill of an array of Indian peoples. Lacking the advantages in population and in the price and quality of trade goods enjoyed by their British rivals, the French developed diplomacy into a fine art. French officers and agents lived in Indian country, married Indian wives, learned Indian ways, and became adept at speaking Indian languages. They followed appropriate protocol, smoking the long-stemmed calumet or "peace pipe," presenting and receiving wampum belts, giving gifts, and making lengthy orations. Failure to do so was courting disaster: when Antoine de la Mothe Cadillac, founder of Detroit and governor of Louisiana, refused to stop and smoke the calumet with the Natchez Indians on a 1715 trip down the Mississippi, the Natchez interpreted the refusal as an act of war and killed four French traders in retaliation.[32] Preserving Indian alliances was expensive and time-consuming, but ultimately unavoidable: "one is a slave to Indians in this country," wrote one French officer.[33]

◆ **Huron Chief with Wampum Belt**
In 1825 Huron chief Nicholas Vincent Isawaholi and three other chiefs visited England and met King George IV. Indicative of the interplay of influences that characterized frontier diplomacy, Isawaholi is depicted wearing a European coat and medals, but he presents a wampum belt in the traditional manner. In the forest diplomacy of eighteenth-century northeastern North America, wampum belts — pieces of polished shell or beads roped together into strands — conveyed messages, initiated proceedings, recorded agreements, and guaranteed promises. Iroquois orators opened councils by offering wampum to produce a state of mind conducive to calm discussion. Speakers punctuated their talks by handing wampum belts to their listeners; refusing a wampum belt meant the listener rejected what was said. When talks were finished, the wampum belts became part of the tribal record and the collective memory. *Library and Archives Canada, Acc. No. R9266-3181, Peter Winkworth Collection of Canadiana.*

In the heart of the continent, Indians remained in control well into the eighteenth century. Some Indian people incorporated the outsiders into their kinship systems and exchange networks, but the onus was on the Europeans to adjust to Indian ways when they dealt with the powerful Osages between the Missouri and Red rivers, and with the Caddos, Comanches, Lipan Apaches, and Wichitas who held the upper hand in Texas. In the Southwest, after the Pueblo War of Independence (1680), Spaniards learned to temper force with diplomacy in their dealings with Indian peoples. In the eighteenth century, when mounted Ute, Comanche, and Apache nomads proved more than a match for heavily equipped Spanish soldiers in thinly spread garrisons, Spaniards came to rely on Pueblo and Pima allies and on diplomacy to defend their provinces.[34]

Despite a reputation for unrelenting land hunger that prevented anything but hostile and exploitive relations with Indians, the British, like the Spanish, also became skilled in the art of diplomacy and recognized the importance of Indians to their imperial ambitions. "The Importance of Indians is now generally known and understood," wrote South Carolina merchant and Superintendent of Indian Affairs Edmond Atkin in his report to the Board of Trade in England in 1755. "[A] Doubt remains not, that the prosperity of our Colonies on the Continent, will stand or fall with our Interest and favour among them. While they are our Friends, they are the Cheapest and strongest Barrier for the Protection of our Settlements; when Enemies, they are capable by ravaging in their method of War, in spite of all we can do, to render those Possessions almost useless."[35] Englishmen regarded treaties and property deeds as legitimate ways to acquire Indian lands, even though they sometimes practiced fraud and deception in securing these documents. They also used treaties as a forum in which to assert that Indians were subjects of the king, that they were subject to English laws, that they must provide assistance against the French and hostile Indian tribes, and that Indians bore responsibility for past conflicts. Indians regarded treaties and councils as an opportunity to make and cement alliances, air their grievances, secure goods and guarantees in return for land, and exercise a small measure of control over the diminution of their homelands. Indians also, on occasion, rejected English claims to sovereignty and jurisdiction and pointed out English breaches of former agreements. Indians who read the texts of treaties, or who had them read to them, sometimes complained that "these writings appear to contain things that are not," and cited English misinterpretations and misrepresentations of their words point by point. (See "An English Treaty and a Penobscot Response," pages 173–77.) Nevertheless, the English established the system of treaty making as the principal means by which to acquire and legitimize the acquisition of Indian land; inherited and continued by the United States government, this system was the vehicle through which much of America passed from Indian to non-Indian hands.

Anglo-Indian relations varied from colony to colony. Indian leaders often dealt with representatives of several colonies; they sometimes exploited the situation to their advantage and to preserve their independence. In Pennsylvania, William Penn and the Quakers earned a reputation in the late seventeenth

◆ Benjamin West, *Penn's Treaty with the Indians* (1771)

Benjamin West's famous painting of William Penn's *Treaty with the Indians When He Founded the Province of Pennsylvania in North America* (1771) shows Penn and his Quakers meeting with the Delawares at Shackamaxon in 1682. Penn stands with his arms outstretched in welcome in a scene of peaceful encounter and open exchange (bows and arrows laid on the ground, light gently diffused, Indian woman and baby in the foreground) while Philadelphia is being built on the banks of the Delaware River. The Indians exchange land for bales of cloth and other manufactured goods while "civilization" advances in the background, with ships in the harbor and houses under construction edging onto the forested area of Indian lodges. West includes some valuable ethnographic documentation in the picture, but the meeting never happened as he depicted it: the Indians wear clothing combining the styles of several tribes, and most scholars see the picture as an allegory of colonial America and a representation of a succession of Indian treaties. By the time West painted this picture in 1771, Pennsylvania had experienced bloody conflicts: colonists often killed Indians out of hand and seized their lands. Thomas Penn, the proprietor of Pennsylvania, commissioned the painting ostensibly as a tribute to his father, but probably to invoke an image of more peaceful times that would reinforce the Penn family claim to proprietorship of the colony during a time of political dissension. West's depiction of the Delawares as willing participants in the sale of their land permanently established the image of William Penn as a man of peace, but it also justified more recent and more blatant thefts of Indian land. *Pennsylvania Academy of the Fine Arts, Philadelphia, USA/Bridgeman Images.*

century for fair dealings with the Indians by obtaining their lands through negotiated treaties and deeds. But the Quakers lost control of the colonial legislature, and unfair trade practices, demands for Indian land, and the influx of land-hungry Scotch-Irish settlers turned Pennsylvania into a bloody battleground in the eighteenth century. The Delawares lost the last of their lands in the upper Delaware and Lehigh valleys in the infamous "Walking Purchase" of 1737, when Pennsylvanians produced a team of runners to measure out an old deed that supposedly granted William Penn and his heirs land "as far as a man can go in a day and a half."[36] In the second half of the century William Penn's "peaceable kingdom" became a zone of racial hatred and frontier conflict with no place for cultural mediators, a decline into violence that revealed "the final incompatibility of colonial and native dreams about the continent they shared."[37] The Delawares continued to retreat westward before the advancing edge of the colonial frontier.

Attempts at Diplomatic Balance

In New York, the Iroquois dealt with the Dutch until 1664. After the English takeover, they shifted their diplomatic attentions to the British crown and its representatives, building an alliance they likened to the links of a "Covenant Chain" and entering King William's War against the French (1689–97). But the war took a heavy toll. French campaigns struck Iroquois villages and starvation stalked the longhouses. By 1700 the Iroquois population had been cut in half. Iroquois diplomats traveled to Montreal, to Albany, and to the Great Lakes region to make peace with France, Britain, and their Indian allies. They charted a new course of neutrality between competing powers that allowed them to halt their losses, restore some power, and remain autonomous. The Iroquois combined statesmanship with a reputation for military prowess and held the balance of power in northeastern North America well into the eighteenth century. They compelled the British, like the French, to deal with them on Iroquois terms, paying constant attention to keeping strong the Covenant Chain that symbolically linked the Iroquois and their allies. Even the Albany Congress of 1754, an important step in forging unity among the British colonies, was a cultural encounter, where colonial officials met with Iroquois men who spoke on wampum belts and Indian women strung belts for use in council.[38]

The British superintendent of Indian affairs in the North during the mid-eighteenth century, Sir William Johnson, set the tone of the British Indian Department for more than a generation. A former trader, Irishman Johnson took a Mohawk wife, immersed himself in Mohawk culture, spoke Mohawk, and became an expert practitioner in the intricate world of Iroquois politics. Known to Mohawks as *Warraghiyagey,* "he who does much business," or "a man who undertakes great things," he cultivated good relations with important chiefs, gave generous gifts, and mastered the protocol of council-fire diplomacy.[39] Other agents of the British Indian Department married into Indian societies and functioned as intermediaries between crown and tribe.

European Indian agents learned to speak Indian languages, to understand the metaphors of Indian speeches, to smoke the calumet pipe, and to provide a steady flow of gifts that indicated they were men of their word and representatives of a powerful and generous king. In turn, Indians had to adjust and hone their diplomatic skills to survive and succeed in a dangerous new world where European powers and various colonies competed for their trade and allegiance and recorded agreements in writing rather than wampum. Powerful and strategically located tribes like the Iroquois in New York and the Choctaws in the lower Mississippi valley played one European power off another to secure trade while maintaining independence. The Creek Indians, a loose confederacy of some fifty autonomous towns in Georgia and Alabama, also attempted to pursue policies of neutrality as three European powers competed for dominance in the Southeast, even though individual towns cultivated their own relations with British colonies and British traders.[40] "To preserve the Ballance between us and the French," wrote one British colonial official, "is the great ruling Principle of the Modern Indian Politics."[41] Smaller tribes surrounded by European populations sometimes pursued similar strategies at a local level. The Catawbas of South Carolina, reduced to fewer than five hundred people by 1760 and dependent on Europeans for trade goods, admitted "we cannot live without the assistance of the English." But, as historian James Merrell observes, "they were not willing to become English themselves."[42] Indian leaders soon realized that Europeans who invited them to the treaty table generally wanted their land, resources, or young men as soldiers. They juggled competing demands, weighing what they gave against what they got, walking a fine line to preserve their independence in an environment of increasing dependency.

Indians and Europeans alike spent tremendous amounts of time and energy talking in an effort to maintain peace, establish and restore friendships, settle disputes, and transfer land. But as international, intercolonial, interethnic, and intertribal rivalries escalated in North America, diplomacy often unraveled, followed by a bloodbath.

WARS FOR AMERICA

King William's War, Queen Anne's War, King George's War, and the Seven Years' (or French and Indian) War all had origins in the old-world rivalry of England and France but also produced fighting in North America that involved Indian warriors as well as French and English soldiers and militia. French relations with Indians were not uniformly harmonious in the eighteenth century: the French waged genocidal wars against the Natchez in the lower Mississippi valley in 1729–31, against the Chickasaws in 1736, and against the Fox, or Mesquakie, Indians in Wisconsin in 1712–16 and again in 1730–33. Nevertheless in the wars between France and England, Abenakis, Ottawas, Shawnees, Delawares, and Potawatomis, and other Algonquian tribes tended to support their French allies. Mohegans and Mahicans (sometimes spelled Mohicans) often supplied scouts to the English; when the

◆ Table 3.1 **A Century of Conflict, 1689–1783**

Dates	American Conflict	European Conflict
1689–97	King William's War	War of the League of Augsburg
1702–13	Queen Anne's War	War of the Spanish Succession
1711–13	Tuscarora War in North Carolina	
1715–18	Yamasee War in South Carolina	
1712–16, 1730–33	Franco-Fox wars	
1723–27	Anglo-Abenaki wars in Maine and Vermont	
1736	Franco-Chickasaw War	
1744–48	King George's War	War of the Austrian Succession
1756–63	French and Indian War	Seven Years' War
1759–61	Anglo-Cherokee War	
1763–65	"Pontiac's War"	
1774	Lord Dunmore's War	
1775–83	American Revolution	

Iroquois abandoned their neutrality, the Mohawks tended to side with the British, although Senecas occasionally fought with the French.

The Abenakis of northern New England found themselves occupying a borderland between the two competing European powers. French and English agents, missionaries, and traders competed for Abenaki allegiance, and Abenakis sometimes kept their options open, praying with the French yet traveling south to get better prices and goods at English trading posts. As English pressure on Abenaki lands increased, however, most Abenakis made common cause with the French. For almost eighty years, Abenaki warriors launched lightning raids, stalling the northward advance of the English frontier. Abenakis earned a reputation as stalwart allies of the French and implacable enemies of New England. The nineteenth-century historian Francis Parkman, describing the Abenakis at the time of the Seven Years' War (1756–63), wrote:

> They were nominal Christians, and had been under the control of their missionaries for three generations; but though zealous and sometimes fanatical to the forms of Romanism [Catholicism], they remained thorough savages in dress, habits, and character. They were the scourge of the New England borders, where they surprised and burned farmhouses and small hamlets, killed men, women, and children without distinction, carried prisoners to their village, subjected them to the torture of "running the gauntlet," and compelled them to witness dances of triumph around the scalps of parents, children, and friends.[43]

In fact, like other Indians enmeshed in the French and Indian War, the Abenakis fought for their own reasons (see "Speech Defying the English," pages 179–80).

A World Transformed by War

At the same time, Indians often sought European allies in their struggles against other Indian tribes. As war became endemic in eighteenth-century North America, Indian villages and countryside bore the brunt of the fighting. War had always played an important but limited role in Indian societies; now it began to dominate Indian life. Communities found that they had to survive on a war footing. Traditional non-military activities were often disrupted as husbands, sons, and fathers — producers and protectors — spent more time at war away from the villages, placing greater burdens on the women. Ceremonial and social calendars were interrupted, and cycles of planting, harvesting, hunting, and fishing were subordinated to the demands of campaigns. Effectively, Indians became more dependent on European allies for goods and provisions. Destruction of crops by enemy forces resulted in hunger and rendered people more susceptible to disease.

Indians fled from regions that had been transformed into battlegrounds between French and English, European and Indian, Indian and Indian. Algonquian people driven from southern and central New England after King Philip's War (1675–76) took refuge to the north in Abenaki country; as English pressure increased along the southern edges of Abenaki territory, many Abenakis in turn withdrew farther north. Tuscarora war refugees migrated north from North Carolina in 1722 to the

◆ **Watercolor of an Abenaki Man and Woman from the Mission Village at Bécancoeur, Quebec**
By the eighteenth century, many Abenaki people from Maine, Vermont, and New Hampshire had moved north and built new communities at French mission villages like St. Francis (Odanak) and Bécancoeur on the St. Lawrence River. With assistance from their French allies, they raided English colonists on their former homelands during the French and Indian War. The conical peaked caps worn by these people were also common among the Penobscots, Passamaquoddies, and Mi´kmaqs; they may have been modeled and adapted from Basque caps worn by early French sailors in Canada. *Courtesy of the City of Montreal Archives.*

country of the Iroquois, where they were adopted as the sixth tribe of the Iroquois Confederacy.[44] (Thereafter, the English referred to the Iroquois as the Six Nations.) Coocoochee, a Mohawk woman born near Montreal around 1740, was forced to move five times during a quarter century of war and upheaval in the Northeast, and finally took up residence among the Shawnees in the Ohio country. The Shawnees had migrated from their Ohio homelands in the late seventeenth century in the wake of the Iroquois wars. Many of them relocated to the Southeast, where they developed close contacts with the Creeks and encountered the English. By the mid-eighteenth century most of them were back in Ohio, where they were joined by Mingoes (Iroquois people who had moved west), Delawares, and other displaced peoples in a zone of escalating imperial friction. For Shawnees, mobility and migration became a way to survive in a world of violence and turmoil.[45]

The French and English War

Escalating conflict between Britain and France came to a head in the Ohio valley and erupted into the Seven Years' War (Map 3.2). Though known in America as the French and Indian War, from a Native American perspective the conflict is better understood as a French and English war. "Why don't you & the French fight in the old country and on the sea?" Delawares asked Moravian missionary Christian Frederick Post. "Why do you come to fight on our land? This makes everybody believe you want only to take & settle the Land."[46] (See pages 180–82.)

In 1754 the French began building Fort Duquesne at the source of the Ohio River — the Forks — where the Allegheny and Monongahela rivers meet. George Washington, an officer in the Virginia militia who had gone to the Ohio country the year before to find out what the French were up to, now returned with a small force of soldiers and Indian warriors under a Seneca chief named Tanaghrisson. After ambushing a company of French soldiers, Tanaghrisson and his warriors killed the captured French officer and ten of his men, but Washington was compelled to surrender to a superior French and Indian force and signed capitulation terms that accepted responsibility for the officer's murder. Within two years France and Britain had issued formal declarations of war against each other, and what began as a backwoods skirmish between France and Britain spread into a global conflict that was fought in North America, the Caribbean Islands, West Africa, India, and continental Europe, as well as on the oceans, and that ultimately involved British and French, Americans and Canadians, American Indians, Prussians, Austrians, Russians, Spaniards, and even East Indian moguls.

The Native Americans who fought in the war, however, did so for Indian, not imperial, purposes, to keep their country free of foreign domination. "It is you who are the Disturbers in this Land, by coming and building your Towns, and taking it away unknown to us," Tanaghrisson told the French. "Both you and the English are white, we live in a Country between; therefore the Land belongs to neither one nor t' other: But the Great Being above allow'd it to be a Place of Residence for us; so Fathers, I desire you to withdraw, as I have done our Brothers the English."

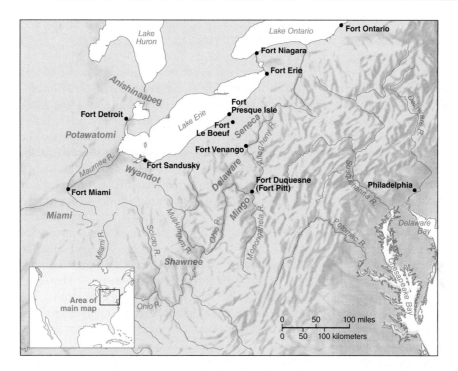

◆ **Map 3.2 The Ohio Country during the Seven Years' War**
By the mid-eighteenth century, the Ohio country was home to many Indian peoples, some of them pushed there by the pressure of European settlement in the east. The forks of the Ohio (where the French built Fort Duquesne and the British later built Fort Pitt) were regarded as the key to the West and became the focus of Anglo-French rivalry. When war broke out, the Ohio country became an international and intertribal battleground.

Indian country was off limits to the English and French alike, except for purposes of trade. "I am not afraid to discharge you off this Land," Tanaghrisson declared.[47]

In 1755 General Edward Braddock marched against Fort Duquesne at the head of more than two thousand troops, the largest army that had ever been assembled in North America. Braddock ignored Indian advice and refused to give assurances that Indian lands would be protected under a British regime. Instead, he told the Delaware war chief Shingas that "no Savage should inherit the Land." Most of Braddock's Indian allies promptly abandoned him.[48] After hacking a road through the wilderness, Braddock's army was almost in sight of Fort Duquesne when it clashed with a force of French and Indians sent to intercept it. In the ensuing battle in the forest the French-aligned Indians fired from cover into ranks of confused redcoats, routing the British soldiers. Braddock was killed; his aide, George Washington, escaped unwounded. The British suffered almost one thousand casualties. Ohio valley Indians who had hesitated now joined the French. As news of Braddock's defeat and Indian attacks spread along the frontiers, backcountry settlers fled east for safety. Years of vicious warfare followed on the frontiers of

Pennsylvania and Virginia, both of which offered bounties for Indian scalps, and Indians and colonists increasingly regarded each other as race enemies.[49]

By the summer of 1757 hundreds of Indians from the West had joined the French, drawn by ties of trade, alliance, and kinship, and by the promise of war honors. In 1757 the British garrison at Fort William Henry on Lake George surrendered to the army of French general Louis-Joseph de Montcalm. But Montcalm's victory turned into a disaster when his Indian allies, who felt betrayed by the terms of capitulation, attacked the surrendered garrison, grabbing scalps and captives. The slaughter—made famous by the James Fenimore Cooper book *The Last of the Mohicans* (and by subsequent movie versions of the novel)—forever stained Montcalm's honor.[50] The British, meanwhile, began to mount a joint national and colonial war effort that carried them from dark days of defeat to stunning victories all around the globe. William Pitt took over as British prime minister and pursued the war with new vigor and new strategies. He increased the subsidies that enabled German allies to keep French and Austrian armies bogged down in European bloodbaths, and he devoted attention and resources to the war in America. Despite a disastrous assault on Fort Ticonderoga in 1758, the British war effort gathered momentum. That same year, British forces captured Louisburg, a French fort overlooking the mouth of the St. Lawrence River, and Fort Frontenac on Lake Ontario. French supply lines to the West were severed. French–Indian relations began to unravel, and many Indians began to mend fences with the British. The Ohio Indians made peace, clearing the way for the British under General John Forbes to advance on Fort Duquesne. Unable to hold the fort without Indian support, the French blew it up and retreated. Then, despite British assurances that their lands would be protected, the Indians watched with apprehension as the redcoats built Fort Pitt on the ruins of Fort Duquesne.[51]

In July 1759 the British took Fort Niagara. In September the British general James Wolfe seized Quebec. Wolfe died in the battle; so did Montcalm. In October Robert Rogers and his New Hampshire Rangers attacked and burned the Abenaki town at Odanak.[52] In November Admiral Hawke destroyed the French Atlantic fleet at Quiberon Bay, and Britain won command of the seas. French forces in Canada could expect no reinforcements; France's Indian alliance in the West began to wither from lack of supplies, and France's remaining overseas empire could be picked apart. The next year, Montreal surrendered to British armies, further opening Indian land in the north to the British.

Meanwhile, the Cherokees and British went to war. Cherokee warriors had participated in Forbes's campaign against Fort Duquesne, but Virginian settlers killed some of them on their way home. Cherokee chiefs were unable to prevent retaliatory raids by their warriors, who were also frustrated by the colonists' constant encroachment on their hunting territories. Following a series of Cherokee attacks on white settlements on the South Carolina border, open war with the British broke out in 1759.

An incident at the beginning of the war, while the Cherokees laid siege to Fort Loudon, reveals much about the nature of relationships on the frontier, the influence of women in Cherokee society, and the workings of clan vengeance. Many British soldiers in the garrison had Cherokee wives, and during the siege these women brought their husbands daily supplies of food, undermining the efforts of Cherokee warriors to starve the garrison into surrender. The Cherokee chief Willinawaw threatened the women with death for assisting the enemy, "but they laughing at his threats, boldly told him, they would succour their husbands every day, and were sure, that, if he killed them, their relations would make his death atone for theirs." Willinawaw knew better than to act on his threats, and "the garrison subsisted a long time on the provisions brought to them in this manner."[53] Though Fort Loudon eventually fell, smallpox struck the Cherokee population, and through the spring and summer of 1761 Lieutenant Colonel James Grant's army of Scottish soldiers, South Carolina militia, and Indian allies burned many Cherokee towns, destroying the crops needed for winter food. Attakullakulla, the chief aptly known as Little Carpenter for his diplomatic ability to fashion agreements, made peace in the fall.[54]

In 1763 Britain and France signed the Treaty of Paris (also called the Peace of Paris), ending the Seven Years' War. Under the terms of the treaty, France handed over to Britain all of its North American territory east of the Mississippi, apart from New Orleans (which France had secretly ceded to Spain the previous year; Map 3.3). Indians were stunned to learn that France had given up Native lands without even

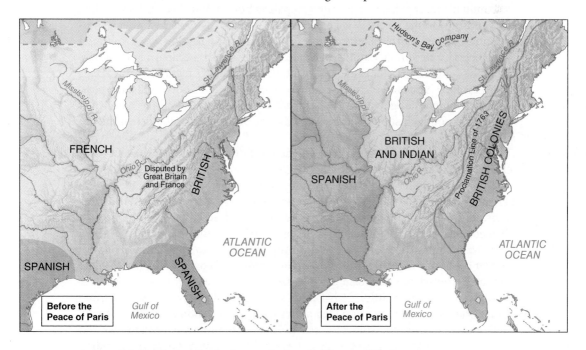

◆ Map 3.3 **North America before and after the Treaty of Paris**
The Treaty of Paris in 1763 redrew the political map of North America. France withdrew from North America, handing its territory east of the Mississippi to Britain and west of the Mississippi to Spain. Indian peoples in the heart of the continent, who had been accustomed to dealing with the French, now had to deal with the British or the Spanish, and in some cases both. By royal proclamation that same year, Britain attempted to regulate colonial expansion beyond the Appalachian Mountains and triggered events that contributed to the American Revolution.

consulting them: they were undefeated and the French had no right to give their country to anyone. Britain's long-sought victory was complete, but its attempts to regulate its newly acquired empire would generate resistance and wars of independence, in both Indian country and the American colonies.

Division within Tribal Communities

Some tribes split into factions over issues of peace, war, and alliance with competing European powers. Militants from different tribes joined forces in intertribal alliances, while at home they were increasingly divided from those who advocated a less militant stance.[55] New communities formed as refugees from different tribes fled to safer areas or congregated in armed camps to continue the fight.

Recurrent warfare produced repercussions for social and political structures. Most Indian societies in the Eastern Woodlands had two classes of chiefs. Older civil or village chiefs, often called sachems, guided the community in daily affairs and in reaching consensus on issues of importance. Younger chiefs with impressive military records led warriors on campaigns but relinquished authority when they returned to the village. Violent deeds had no place in kin-based Indian communities where, with no courts, police, or jails, social harmony was a common and necessary condition, not just an ideal. However, as war became a normal state of affairs and war parties came and went with increasing regularity, war chiefs exerted more influence in tribal councils. European allies bolstered their position with supplies of guns and gifts of medals and uniforms, and the number of contenders for such support increased. Civil or peace chiefs saw their influence decline.

The Iroquois who moved into Ohio acted with growing independence from the Iroquois League centered at Onondaga. Ten warriors who traveled from the Ohio to Philadelphia in 1747 explained to the colonists: "the old men at the Fire at Onondaga are unwilling to come into the War so the Young Indians, the Warriors, and the Captains consulted together and resolved to take up the English Hatchet against the will of their old People, and to lay their old People aside as of no value but in time of Peace."[56] A group of Seneca warriors in 1762 told Sir William Johnson that they, not the sachems, had "the power & Ability to settle Matters"; the sachems, they said, were "a parcell of Old People who say Much, but who Mean or Act very little."[57] Civil chiefs lost their ability to restrain headstrong young warriors, which had provided an important generational balance in many Indian societies, and the voices for war in Indian communities grew louder and less restrained. Generations of recurrent warfare left an indelible mark on Indian societies and cultures and helped create the stereotype of warlike Indians that Europeans and later Americans invoked to justify treating them as "savages."

European involvement also sometimes undercut the influence of Indian women in councils and decision making. Traditionally, Iroquois men did the hunting, fighting, trading, and diplomacy, which took them away from the villages and into the forest, but an Iroquois town "was largely a female world," perhaps increasingly so as men went away to war more often. Men cleared the fields but women did the planting, cultivating, and harvesting, and women possessed the power attributed to fertility that was necessary in performing rituals that ensured successful crops. Men built them, but women controlled the longhouses that sheltered Iroquois clans and families. Women's economic power gave them considerable political power. Clan mothers could decide the fate of captives, elect and remove council chiefs, and influence decisions for war or peace: "the Elders decide no important affair without their advice," noted one seventeenth-century French missionary.[58] Women in other eastern tribes exercised similar influence. A Quaker missionary at a Conestoga town on the Susquehanna River in 1706 was surprised to see women speaking in council; he was told "That some Women were wiser than some Men" and that the Conestogas never did anything without the advice of one particular old woman.[59]

Europeans were troubled by the influence and independence that Indian women displayed in public meetings as well as in their private lives, and they tried to curb it.[60] Europeans were primarily interested in Indians as allies (or enemies) in war and as customers in the fur and deerskin trades; consequently they expected to deal with men, the warriors and hunters, not women, who traditionally were peacemakers and farmers. Even Sir William Johnson, who married the Mohawk woman Molly Brant and who understood the role of women in Iroquois politics, tried to ignore them. At a council meeting in the spring of 1762, Johnson barred women and children and invited "none but those who were Qualified for, and Authorized to proceed on business." When the Iroquois men reminded him that it was customary for their women to be present on such occasions "being of Much Estimation Amongst Us, in that we proceed from them," Johnson replied that, while he appreciated the women's "Zeal & Desire to promote a good work," it was his wish that "no more persons would Attend any meeting than were necessary for the Discharge of the business on Which they were Summoned." In the eyes of the British superintendent, Indian women were politically unnecessary.[61] But European males failed to eradicate the influence of Iroquois clan mothers; Molly Brant's influence actually increased as a result of her connection to Sir William Johnson. She remained a considerable presence in British Iroquois diplomacy even after his death in 1774: an officer rated "Miss Molly Brant's Influence" over her people as "far superior to that of all their Chiefs put together."[62] In some ways, the changes bombarding Indian society affected women's lives less than men's. Many women "continued to hoe their corn, raise their children, and exercise traditional kinds of power just as they always had."[63]

Captives Taken, Captives Returned

While thousands of Indians were enslaved in the Spanish, French, and English colonies, Europeans who fell into Indian hands as war captives sometimes experienced a different fate. In February 1704 a war party of Abenakis, Mohawks from Kahnawake, and Hurons from Lorette (both on the St. Lawrence in Quebec), together with their French allies, sacked the town of Deerfield, Massachusetts, and carried off 112 people, including the town's minister, the Rev. John Williams, and his family. As the Indians fled north along the frozen Connecticut River, they tomahawked Williams's wife who had recently given birth and could not keep up the pace. But as they continued the three-hundred-mile trek through the snow to Canada, they carried the captive children or pulled them along on toboggans. One of the children was Williams's seven-year-old daughter, Eunice. When they reached Canada, many of the captives were adopted into French or Indian communities. John Williams was liberated after two and a half years in captivity and wrote an account of his experiences, *The Redeemed Captive Returning to Zion.* In it, he expounded the Puritan view of captivity as a testing of good Protestants, an ordeal which, with God's help, they survived by resisting the torments of Indian savages and the inducements of evil Jesuit priests who tried to turn them into Catholics. But Eunice's fate said something different about the experiences of some captives in Indian society. She stayed with the Indians, converted to Catholicism, and married a Mohawk of Kahnawake. Despite repeated entreaties from her father and brother, she refused to return home. One emissary reported that Eunice was "thoroughly naturalized" to the Indian way of life and "obstinately resolved to live and dye here." Another reported that the Indians "would as soon part with their hearts" as let Eunice return home. To her family's dismay and her countrymen's consternation, Eunice Williams — although she later visited her New England relatives — lived with the Indians for more than eighty years and died among the people with whom she had made her life, her home, and her own family.[64] For patriarchal Puritans like John Williams, a wife or daughter taken into captivity who became a baptized Catholic, married a French or Indian man, and refused to return to New England threatened an Englishman's masculinity, the safety of his household, and the stability of the social order.[65]

◆ **Ernest Smith, *Washing Corn after Leaching***
This picture by Seneca artist Ernest Smith portrays how Seneca women might have dressed in Mary Jemison's time. Captured by Indians in 1758 at age fifteen, Mary Jemison was adopted by Senecas and spent the rest of her life as an Iroquois woman. Her life story, which she related in her old age, was first published in 1824 and has been reprinted more than thirty times. *Watercolor painting by Ernest Smith, 1937. Courtesy of the Rochester Museum & Science Center, Rochester, New York.*

Other captives at other times and places followed Eunice's example. During the French and Indian War in the Ohio valley, British and French soldiers seldom took Indian captives but, even as the fighting escalated, Indians continued to take captives, and adopted many of them into their clans and communities.[66] Mary Jemison, who was captured and adopted by the Senecas as a teenager in 1758, married

◆ **The Indians Delivering Up the English Captives to Colonel Bouquet**

"Liberating" young captives in compliance with the terms of the peace treaty proved to be a heartbreaking experience for the captives and for their adoptive Shawnee and Delaware families. This engraving by Benjamin West accompanied William Smith's *An Historical Account of the Expedition against the Ohio Indians in the Year 1764,* published in 1766. *Dartmouth College Library.*

an Indian husband and raised a family. In time, she came to share fully in the lives of Seneca women (see Mary Jemison's account on pages 184–87). Captives had to adjust to new ways in their new situations, but they often brought new ideas and technologies to their captors' societies.[67]

Indians also, when occasion demanded, returned captives. Captives who returned to colonial society did not always come home happily. Hans Fife, a German captured by the Senecas and then delivered up to the British, "immediately made his Escape to the Senecas" and joined them fighting the British in Pontiac's War in 1763 (see pages 201–3). After Colonel Henry Bouquet defeated the Indians of the Ohio valley at Bushy Run later that year he dictated peace terms that required the Indians to hand over all of the captives they had taken during the recent war. The Shawnees and Delawares complied, but they reminded Bouquet that the captives "have been all tied to us by Adoption. . . . we have taken as much care of these Prisoners, as if they were [our] own Flesh, and blood." Many of the Shawnees' captives resisted their "liberation." An observer who was present when the Indians delivered their captives to Bouquet said that the children had become "accustomed to look upon the Indians as the only connexions they had, having been tenderly treated by them, and speaking their language," and "they considered their new state in the light of a captivity, and parted from the savages with tears." Some of the adult captives were equally reluctant to return, and the Shawnees "were obliged to bind several of their prisoners and force them along to the camp; and some women, who had been delivered up, afterwards found means to escape and run back to the Indian towns. Some, who could not make their escape, clung to their savage acquaintances at parting, and continued many days in bitter lamentations, even refusing sustenance."[68]

Women and children were more likely to remain with their Indian captors than were men, but Eunice Williams and Mary Jemison were not typical. Many women clung to hopes of returning home and gathering back their children.

Nevertheless, white captives who "went Indian" remained a recurrent, and for Euro-Americans a troubling, occurrence on the frontier.

RESPONSES TO CHANGE IN THE WEST: INDIAN POWER ON THE PLAINS

While countless Indians were displaced from their homelands elsewhere during the colonial era, the Great Plains was becoming a magnet for Indian peoples (Map 3.4). As horses, introduced by Spanish invaders to the south, and guns and trade goods from French and British traders to the east and northeast spread across the Plains, many groups migrated on to the open grasslands, taking advantage of new conditions and embracing new sources of power in building a new way of life. The image of the horse-riding, buffalo-hunting Plains Indian is an enduring stereotype, but that culture emerged in response to forces unleashed by European invasion and colonialism.

By the end of the eighteenth century, two broad categories of Indian peoples lived on the Great Plains: sedentary farming tribes and mobile buffalo hunters. The Mandans, Hidatsas, and Arikaras, for instance, had lived alongside the Missouri River for hundreds of years. They inhabited earth-lodge villages, cultivated extensive acreage of crops, practiced elaborate rituals, and observed rank and status within their societies. British, French, and Spanish merchants traded in their villages. Many of the nomadic buffalo-hunting peoples, such as the Lakota Sioux, Cheyennes, Kiowas, and Comanches, arrived much later.

Horses Transform the Plains

The Plains Indians' way of life was the product of interplay between their grasslands environment, vast herds of roaming buffalo, and horses. Spreading by trade and raids, horses reached virtually every tribe on the Plains by the mid-eighteenth century (Map 3.5). Apaches traded horses to Pueblos; Kiowas and Kiowa-Apaches traded them to Caddos; Wichitas and Pawnees traded them to Osages; Comanches and Utes traded them to Shoshonis. Shoshonis then traded them to Crows and to the Flatheads and Nez Perces in the Plateau region, who traded them to the Blackfeet. Blackfeet traded them to Assiniboines. Crows, Kiowas, Arapahos, Cheyennes, and other tribes brought horses to the villages of the Mandans, Hidatsas, and Arikaras. The Lakotas, the western Sioux, obtained horses at the Arikara villages and traded them to their eastern Yankton and Dakota relatives.[69] *Sunkawakan,* the Lakota word for horse, means sacred or powerful dog. Lakota writer Joseph M. Marshall III remarks that horses did not create Lakota culture, but they "took it to levels never dreamed of."[70]

Horses transformed Plains Indians into mobile communities, capable of traveling great distances and fully exploiting the rich resources of their environment. In Cheyenne tradition, the prophet Sweet Medicine foretold the coming of the horse and how it would change people's lives: "This animal will carry you on his back and help you in many ways," he said. "Those far hills that seem only a blue

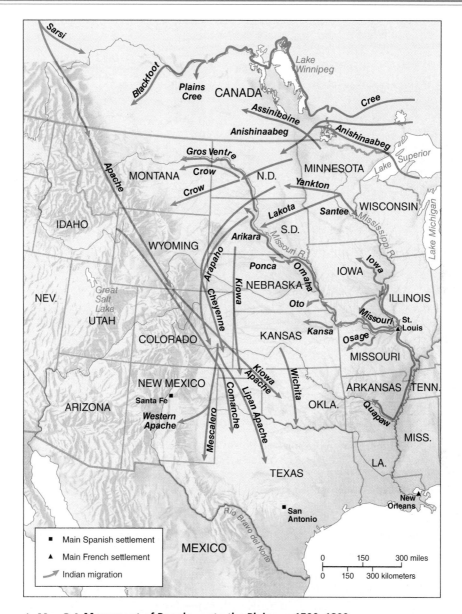

◆ **Map 3.4 Movement of Peoples onto the Plains, c. 1500–1800**

Long before Euro-Americans pushed west onto the Great Plains, Indian peoples had been moving into and across the vast grasslands. Some peoples, like the Quapaws, Osages, Omahas, and Poncas, followed river valleys west before horses reached the Plains. Others, like the Cheyennes, Comanches, and Lakotas, migrated deep into the Plains to take advantage of new opportunities presented by the spread of horses. Some peoples were still in motion and competing for position on the Plains when the Euro-Americans arrived.

SOURCE: Adapted from *The Settling of North America: The Atlas of the Great Migrations into North America from the Ice Age to Ellis Island and Beyond* by Helen Hornbeck Tanner, Janice Reiff, and John H. Long, eds. Copyright © 1995 by Swanston Publishing Ltd.

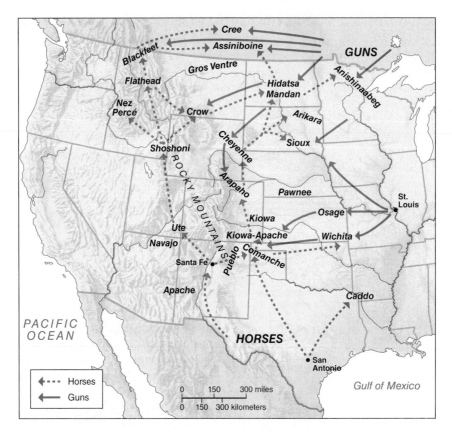

◆ **Map 3.5 The Diffusion of Guns and Horses across the Plains, 1680–1750**
In the late seventeenth and eighteenth centuries, Indian peoples on the Great Plains incorporated into their cultures major factors of change brought by Europeans: horses, introduced by Spaniards in the Southwest, and firearms, introduced primarily by French and British traders to the northeast.

vision in the distance take many days to reach now; but with this animal you can get there in a short time, so fear him not." When the first Cheyenne saw horses, sometime in the early eighteenth century, "he thought of the prophecy of Sweet Medicine, that there would be animals with round hoofs and shaggy manes and tails, and men could ride on their backs into the Blue Vision. He went back to the village and told the old Indians, and they remembered."[71]

The buffalo that Plains Indians now hunted from horseback provided the tribes with food, shelter, clothing, tools, and weapons; it became the economic and cultural base of the societies that developed on the Plains. Women dressed and prepared the meat, made tools from the bones, and tanned the hides, producing tipis, clothing, moccasins, and other articles. The Crow woman Pretty Shield recalled her grandmothers' talk about the hard lives they had lived before horses and decided that horses had changed everything for the better: "there was always fat meat, glad singing, and much dancing in our villages," she remembered nostalgically.[72] The new way of life emphasized the man's role as warrior and hunter and seems to have brought an increase in polygyny in some societies, as successful hunters could afford more wives.

Although there was great diversity among the equestrian hunting tribes in their languages, social structures, and historical experiences, in comparison with the farming peoples of the Missouri River they shared some common characteristics. They depended on the buffalo for subsistence. Easily transportable skin tipis and a fluid band structure (living most of the year in relatively small bands and coming together in larger gatherings only at certain times) enabled them to follow the herds at will, and restraints on individual freedom were kept to a minimum. Public opinion and tradition exerted more influence than the words of chiefs, whose positions depended on their own prestige and the example they set. The new horse-buffalo complex was the source of power, prosperity, and freedom for Plains societies.

Jostling for Position on the Plains

Horses were not an unmixed blessing. They brought new wealth and power but they also brought ecological instability, economic disruption, and social inequality.[73] The horse-buffalo complex was also the source of escalating conflict as the Great Plains was transformed into a huge arena of competition between rival tribes jostling for position and rich hunting territories. When the first Europeans arrived on the northern Plains in the eighteenth century they met many Shoshoni or Snake Indians. Descendants of peoples who once inhabited the Great Basin region of Nevada, the Shoshonis had moved north and east. They acquired horses early in the eighteenth century from Ute and Comanche relatives to the south and pushed onto the northern Plains. But as other groups edged onto the Plains and as the Blackfeet to the north acquired both horses and guns, the Shoshonis pulled back into the Rocky Mountains. Some Kiowa and Comanche bands were still on the northern Plains at the end of the century, but they continued their migration southward to the area of present-day Texas and Oklahoma. En route, the Comanches came into conflict with Apache bands, whom they pushed west off the Plains and into areas of Arizona and New Mexico. The Apaches and Navajos had themselves migrated from the north several hundred years before, coming into contact and conflict with the Pueblo Indians of the Southwest and with the northern frontier of Spain's empire.

Other groups entered the Plains from the east. The Crow Indians split off from their Hidatsa relatives sometime before 1700, moved onto the Plains, and eventually took up residence in the rich hunting territory of the Yellowstone region. The Cheyennes, who once lived in sedentary farming villages in Minnesota and then North Dakota, crossed the Missouri River and took up life as mounted hunters on the Plains in the late 1700s. Moving first to the Black Hills, they swung south to the central Plains after 1800. Like American settlers who came later, the Cheyennes were drawn westward by new opportunities, but in their case the opportunities were the vast buffalo herds and "the chance to become middlemen in a sprawling trading system that reached from New Mexico to Canada."[74]

At the Confluence of Guns and Horses

By the eighteenth century the Great Plains had become a battleground. Warriors raided for horses and fought for honor; tribes clashed over hunting grounds and resources. War became an integral part of Plains Indian life. Young men sought visions that would bring them success in battle against their enemies, joined warrior societies that encouraged and sustained their martial spirit, and participated in elaborate rituals in preparation for war. Success in war brought status and prestige. Counting coup on an enemy — touching or striking an enemy without necessarily harming him — or stealthily stealing horses from an enemy camp carried more prestige than killing or conquering. However, as intertribal competition intensified on the Plains, warfare became more deadly. European and American traders introduced a lethal new element: guns. As had Eastern Woodland peoples in the seventeenth century, Plains Indians in the eighteenth century found that they had to have guns to survive in an increasingly dangerous world.

Guns dispersed across the Plains through a series of networks. Like other Indians in North America, Plains Indians were accustomed to trading over long distances. Indian hunters living deep in the Plains already traveled to the Missouri River trading centers to exchange meat and leather for the corn, tobacco, and other crops grown by women in the Mandan, Hidatsa, and Arikara villages; now bands of Crows, Cheyennes, and other tribes brought horses and meat to the villages, traded for guns and manufactured goods, and then headed back to the Plains where they traded those guns and goods to more distant neighbors (see Map 3.5, "The Diffusion of Guns and Horses across the Plains, 1680–1750," page 168). Crow traders often traveled to a rendezvous with the Shoshonis in southwestern Wyoming; the Shoshonis in turn traded with the Nez Perces, Flatheads, and other groups in the mountains. Many of those mountain groups were in contact with Native traders at The Dalles, the great salmon fishing site on the Columbia River, who in turn dealt with European and American maritime traders on the Pacific coast.

The Sioux, living in Minnesota around the headwaters of the Mississippi, had fought for hunting territories in the western Great Lakes region against Anishinaabe and Cree enemies armed with guns. Pressured by firearms in the forests and beckoned by horses and buffalo on the Plains, some Sioux began to move west. While the eastern Sioux — the Dakotas — remained in their Minnesota homelands, the western Sioux — the Lakotas — migrated out onto the northern and central plains, where they began to pressure other tribes and wrest control of new hunting territories there.[75]

War and Diplomacy on the Southern Plains

Europeans imagined extending their empires into the trans-Mississippi West although their knowledge of the physical and human geography of the vast interior remained vague and their imperial ambitions depended on establishing and maintaining alliances with powerful Indian nations.[76] At the end of the seventeenth century, France and Spain both had their eyes on Texas. The French saw it as an area into which they could extend the network of Indian trade and alliances they had already established in the Mississippi valley. For Spain, Texas represented a northern periphery of a great American empire, a vast borderland that might be used to thwart French intrusions and protect more valuable holdings to the south, particularly the silver mines of Mexico. Both powers had aspirations in the area, but real power lay with the Indian peoples who lived there. To a large extent, they determined which Europeans entered and operated in their country.

The Caddos were farming peoples living in what is now eastern Texas and Louisiana. In the century and a half since Spaniards from the de Soto expedition wandered through their country in 1542, epidemic diseases had cut their population dramatically, perhaps from as many as 200,000 to as few as 10,000 by the late seventeenth century. A huge smallpox epidemic struck the Caddos in 1691, and diseases continued to thin their numbers through the next century. Some twenty-five Caddoan communities in several geographic groupings formed three loose confederacies: the Hasinais (whom the Spaniards called *Tejas*) lived in the Neches and Angelina river valleys of eastern Texas; the Cadodachos and Nachitoches inhabited the Red River region in the north. Despite falling populations and increasing pressure from mounted Apache and Osage enemies, the Caddos remained a powerful force. They were strategically located, and far-reaching trade routes ran in and out of their villages. The French and Spanish each recognized the Caddos's position and power and courted their allegiance.

The Caddos were not unreceptive. Accustomed to making pacts of friendship with other tribes, they extended their network of trade and alliance to include Europeans, who might provide merchandise and military assistance against their enemies. When they met Europeans, Caddos smoked the calumet pipe with them, gave them gifts, and offered them their women. Europeans frequently misinterpreted this as evidence that Indians had no morals. Caddo women often functioned as diplomatic mediators, but Europeans saw their dress, body tattoos, and ritualized greetings that involved touching as evidence of promiscuity. Frenchmen who entered Caddo country, however, seem to have overcome their qualms, easing their relationships with the local Caddos. Spain tried to break the connections that the French in Louisiana had forged with the Caddos and made efforts to win them over to a Spanish alliance. But Indian, not Spanish, power determined what happened in Texas.[77]

Increasingly, Spain found itself confronting a new and growing power on the southern Plains, one produced and propelled by the horses the Spaniards had introduced. Comanches and Utes advanced together on to the southern Plains out of the foothills of the Rockies. They drove most of the Apache bands off the Plains, into the Southwest desert and against the Spanish frontier. They captured and enslaved women and children from other tribes, and, like the Apaches they displaced, developed raiding economies that preyed on Spanish (and later Mexican) societies. As the Comanches and Utes consolidated their position as horse and buffalo Indians on the rich grasslands of the southern Plains, they also incorporated other peoples and built exchange networks with other tribes that enabled them to dominate trade between New Mexico and French Louisiana. By mid-century, the Ute–Comanche alliance had dissolved, and the Comanches were the dominant and growing power on the southern Plains.[78]

When Tomás Vélez Cachupín became governor of the Spanish province of New Mexico in 1749, he inherited a colony beset by Indian enemies on all sides. Mounted Utes, Navajos, Comanches, and Apaches raided Spanish and Pueblo communities alike. Lacking the manpower and resources to maintain a constant war effort, Vélez Cachupín turned to diplomacy to secure the protection his province needed. In 1751 he defeated a large Comanche war party, pinning it down at a waterhole and killing almost one hundred warriors. Then he made peace, sitting down and smoking with the Comanche chiefs who visited trade fairs at the Pueblo towns. He made peace with the Utes, Navajos, and Apaches as well. He maintained that Spain had been too quick to respond with force and had alienated Indians whose friendship might have been secured by trade and diplomacy. He said, "There is not a nation among the numerous ones which live around this government in which a kind word does not have more effect than the execution of the sword." He had employed both.[79] But the peace did not hold, and Spanish–Comanche relations oscillated between open conflicts and cautious truces.

◆ **George Catlin, *His-oo-san-chees***
By the middle of the eighteenth century the Comanches were emerging as the dominant power on the southern Plains. This Comanche warrior, known as His-oo-san-chees or Little Spaniard, was painted by the American artist George Catlin in the 1830s. *Smithsonian American Art Museum, Washington, DC/Art Resource, NY.*

DOCUMENTS

An English Treaty and a Penobscot Response

EARLY TREATIES INVOLVED A BLENDING of European and Native American traditions of conducting diplomacy. Indian nations had their own ways of establishing, maintaining, and renewing relationships with other nations, and their negotiations involved rituals of exchanging gifts, wampum, and words. When Indian peoples met Europeans in treaty councils, they attached importance to the protocols, to what was said, and to the agreements that were reached. The "treaty" was the whole meeting and they would remember, and retell for future generations, what was said and done there. For Europeans, what mattered most was what was written down; for them the treaty was the document that recorded the terms of the agreement and bore the signatures of the participants, and they would refer to the written treaty as a legal document that gave them title to Indian lands and that bound the Indian peoples to its terms.

Treaty documents drawn up by Europeans constituted only the summary of lengthy proceedings with Indian delegates in formal councils. Misunderstandings, mistranslations, and even deliberate distortions and deceptions sometimes crept into the final text. In 1727, the English finalized a treaty with several bands of Abenaki Indians at Casco Bay in what is now Maine. As was usual in English treaties with Eastern Indians, the language and the terms of the treaty placed blame for past hostilities squarely on the shoulders of the Indians and depicted the Indians as rebellious subjects begging peace from their sovereign King George. This testimony by a Penobscot who participated in the Casco Bay negotiations is extremely valuable in that it gives a detailed account of the deliberations from the Indians' perspective and points to the gulf that could exist between what Indian delegates remembered saying and what English treaty makers recorded. Loron, alias Sauguaarum or Sagourrab, Alexis, François Xavier, Meganumbee, and others were delegates from the Penobscot, Norridgewock, Passamaquoddy, Maliseet, and other tribes that the English called "Eastern Indians."

Treaty between the Abenaki Indians and the English at Casco Bay (1727)

THE SUBMISSION AND AGREEMENT OF THE DELEGATES OF THE EASTERN INDIANS

Whereas the several Tribes of the Eastern Indians Viz. The Penobscot, Nerridgawock, St. Johns, Cape Sables, and other Tribes Inhabiting within His Majesties Territories of *New England* and *Nova Scotia*, who have been engaged in the present War, from whom we, Saguaarum alias Loron, Arexis, Francois Xavier, & Meganumbee, are Delegated and fully Impowered to enter into Articles of Pacification with His Majesties Governments of the *Massachusetts-Bay, New-Hampshire* and *Nova Scotia*, have contrary to the several Treaties they have Solemnly entred into with the said Governments, made an Open Rupture, and have continued some Years in Acts of Hostility against the Subjects of His Majesty King GEORGE within the said Governments.

They being now sensible of the Miseries and Troubles they have involved themselves in, and being desirous to be restored to His Majesties Grace and Favour, and to Live in Peace with all His Majesties Subjects of the said Three Governments, and the Province of *New York* and Colonies of *Connecticut* and *Rhode Island* and that all former Acts of Injury be forgotten, have Concluded to make, and we do by these Presents in the Name and Behalf of the said Tribes, make Our Submission unto His most Excellent Majesty GEORGE by the Grace of GOD of *Great Britain, France* and *Ireland,* KING Defender of the Faith, &c. in as Full and Ample Manner, as any of our Predecessors have heretofore done.

And we do hereby promise and engage with the Honourable WILLIAM DUMMER Esq; as he is Lieutenant Governour and Commander in Chief of His Majesties Province of the *Massachusetts Bay* and with the Governours or Commanders in Chief of the said Province for the Time being, *That is to say.*

We the said Delegates for and in behalf of the several Tribes abovesaid, Do Promise and Engage, that at all times for Ever, from and after the Date of these Presents, We and They will Cease and Forbear all Acts of Hostility, Injuries and Discords towards all the Subjects of the Crown of *Great Britain*, and not offer the least Hurt, Violence or Molestation to them or any of them in their Persons or Estates, But will hence forward hold and maintain a firm and constant Amity and Friendship with all the English, and will never confederate or combine with any other Nation to their Prejudice.

That all the Captives taken in this present War, shall at or before, the Time of the further Ratification of this Treaty be restored without any Ransom or Payment to be made by them or any of them.

That His Majesty's Subjects the English shall and may peaceably and quietly enter upon, improve and for ever enjoy all and singular their Rights of Land and former Settlements, Properties and Possessions within the Eastern parts of the said Province of the *Massachusetts Bay*, together with all Islands, Isletts, Shoars, Beaches and Fishery within the same, without any Molestation or Claims by us or any other Indians, and be in no ways Molested, Interrupted or Disturbed therein. Saving unto the *Penobscot, Nerridgawock,* and other Tribes within His Majesties Province aforesaid, and their Natural Decendants repectively, all their Lands, Liberties and Properties not by them conveyed or Sold to or Possessed by any of the English subjects as aforesaid, as also the Priviledge of Fishing, Hunting, and Fowling as formerly.

That all Trade and Commerce which hereafter may be Allowed betwixt the English and Indians, shall be under such Management and Regulation as the Government of the *Massachusetts* Province shall Direct.

If any Controversie or Difference at any time hereafter happen to arise between any of the English and Indians for any real or supposed Wrong or Injury done on either side, no Private Revenge

---

SOURCE: "Indian Treaties," *Collections of the Maine Historical Society* (1856), 4:118–84.

shall be taken for the same but proper Application shall be made to His Majesties Government upon the place for Remedy or Redress thereof in a due course of Justice.

We Submitting Our selves to be Ruled and Governed by His Majesty's Laws, and desiring to have the Benefit of the same.

We also the said Delegates, in Behalf of the Tribes of Indians, inhabiting within the French Territories, who have Assisted us in this War, for whom we are fully Impowered to Act in this present Treaty, Do hereby Promise and Engage, that they and every of them shall henceforth Cease and Forbear all Acts of Hostility Force and Violence towards all and every the Subjects of His Majesty the King of Great Britain.

We do further in Behalf of the Tribe of the *Penobscot* Indians, promise and engage, that if any of the other Tribes intended to be Included in this Treaty, shall notwithstanding refuse to Confirm and Ratifie this present Treaty entred into on their Behalf and continue or Renew Acts of Hostility against the English, in such case the said *Penobscot* Tribe shall joine their Young Men with the English in reducing them to Reason.

In the next place we the aforenamed Delegates Do promise and engage with the Honourable John Wentworth Esq; as He is Lieut. Governour and Commander in Chief of His Majesties Province of *New Hampshire,* and with the Governours and Commader in Chief of the said Province for the time being, that we and the Tribes we are deputed from will henceforth cease and forbear all Acts of Hostility, Injuries & Discords towards all the Subjects of His Majesty King GEORGE within the said Province. And we do understand and take it that the said Government of *New Hampshire* is also included and comprehended in all and every the Articles aforegoing excepting that respecting the regulating the Trade with us.

And further we the aforenamed Delegates do Promise and Engage with the Honourable Lawrance Armstrong Esq; Lieutenant Governour and Commander in Chief of His Majesties Province of *Nova Scotia* or *L'Acadie* to live in peace with His Majesties Good Subjects and their Dependants in that Government according to the Articles agreed on with Major Paul Mascarene commissioned for that purpose, and further to be Ratified as mentioned in the said Articles.

That this present Treaty shall be Accepted Ratified and Confirmed in a Publick and Solemn manner by the Chiefs of the several Eastern Tribes of Indians included therein at *Falmouth* in *Casco Bay* some time in the Month of *May* next. *In Testimony* whereof we have Signed these Presents, and Affixed Our Seals. Dated at the Council Chamber in *Boston* in *New England*, this Fifteenth Day of December, Anno Domini, One Thousand Seven Hundred and Twenty-five, Annoque Regni Regis GEORGIJ, Magnæ Britanniæ, &c. Duodecimo.

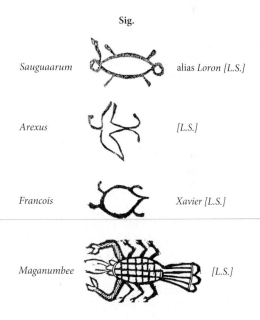

Sig.

Sauguaarum   alias *Loron [L.S.]*

Arexus   *[L.S.]*

Francois   Xavier *[L.S.]*

Maganumbee   *[L.S.]*

SOURCE: Collections of the Maine Historical Society, Series 1, Volume III.

Done in the presence of the Great and General Court or Assembly of the Province of the *Massachusetts Bay* aforesaid, being first Read distinctly, and Interpreted by Capt. *John Gyles*, Capt. *Samuel Jordan*, and Capt. *Joseph Bane*, Sworn Interpreters.

Attest J. Willard, Secr.

LORON SAUGUAARUM
An Account of Negotiations Leading to the Casco Bay Treaty (1727)

I Panaouamskeyen, do inform ye—ye who are scattered all over the earth take notice—of what has passed between me and the English in negotiating the peace that I have just concluded with them. It is from the bottom of my heart that I inform you; and, as a proof that I tell you nothing but the truth, I wish to speak to you in my own tongue.

My reason for informing you, myself, is the diversity and contrariety of the interpretations I receive of the English writing in which the articles of peace are drawn up that we have just mutually agreed to. These writings appear to contain things that are not, so that the Englishman himself disavows them in my presence, when he reads and interprets them to me himself.

I begin then by informing you; and shall speak to you only of the principal and most important matter.

First, that I did not commence the negotiation for a peace, or settlement, but he, it was, who first spoke to me on the subject, and I did not give him any answer until he addressed me a third time. I first went to Fort St. George to hear his propositions, and afterwards to Boston, whither he invited me on the same business.

We were two that went Boston: I, Laurance Sagourrab, and John Ehennekouit. On arriving there I did indeed salute him in the usual mode at the first interview, but I was not the first to speak to him. I only answered what he said to me, and such was the course I observed throughout the whole of our interview.

He began by asking me, what brought me hither? I did not give him for answer—I am come to ask your pardon; nor, I come to acknowledge you as my conqueror; nor, I come to make my submission to you; nor, I come to receive your commands.

All the answer I made was that I was come on his invitation to me to hear the propositions for a settlement that he wished to submit to me.

Wherefore do we kill one another? he again asked me. 'Tis true that, in reply, I said to him—You are right. But I did not say to him, I acknowledge myself the cause of it, nor I condemn myself for having made war on him.

He next said to me—Propose what must be done to make us friends. 'Tis true that thereupon I answered him—It is rather for you to do that. And my reason for giving him that answer is, that having himself spoken to me of an arrangement, I did not doubt but he would make me some advantageous proposals. But I did not tell him that I would submit in every respect to his orders.

Thereupon, he said to me—Let us observe the treaties concluded by our Fathers, and renew the ancient friendship which existed between us. I made him no answer thereunto. Much less, I repeat, did I, become his subject, or give him my land, or acknowledge his King as my King. This I never did, and he never proposed it to me. I say, he never said to me—Give thyself and thy land to me, nor acknowledge my King for thy King, as thy ancestors formerly did.

He again said to me—But do you not recognize the King of England as King over all his states? To which I answered—yes, I recognize him King of all his lands; but I rejoined, do not hence infer that I acknowledge thy King as my King, and king of my lands. Here lies my distinction—my Indian distinction. God hath willed that I have no King, and I be master of my lands in common.

He again asked me—Do you not admit that I am at least master of the lands I have purchased? I answered him thereupon, that I admit nothing, and that I knew not what he had reference to.

He again said to me—If, hereafter, any one desire to disturb the negotiation of the peace we are

SOURCE: E. B. O'Callaghan, ed., *Documents Relative to the Colonial History of the State New York*, 15 vols. (Albany, N.Y.: Weed, Parsons, 1855), 9:966–67.

at present engaged about, we will join together to arrest him. I again consented to that. But I did not say to him, and do not understand that he said to me, that we should go in company to attack such person, or that we should form a joint league, offensive and defensive, or that I should unite my brethren to his. I said to him only, and I understand him to say to me, that if any one wished to disturb our negotiation of peace, we would both endeavor to pacify him by fair words, and to that end would direct all our efforts.

He again said to me — In order that the peace we would negotiate be permanent, should any private quarrel arise hereafter between Indians and Englishmen, they must not take justice into their own hands, nor do any thing, the one to the other. It shall be the business of us chiefs to decide. I again agreed with him on that article, but I did not understand that he alone should be judge. I understood only that he should judge his people, and that I would judge mine.

Finally he said to me — There's our peace concluded; we have regulated every thing.

I replied that nothing had been yet concluded, and that it was necessary that our acts should be approved in a general assembly. For the present, an armistice is sufficient. I again said to him — I now go to inform all my relatives of what has passed between us, and will afterwards come and report to you what they'll say to me. Then he agreed in opinion with me.

Such was my negotiation on my first visit to Boston.

As for any act of grace, or amnesty, accorded to me by the Englishman, on the part of his King, it is what I have no knowledge of, and what the Englishman never spoke to me about, and what I never asked him for.

On my second visit to Boston we were four: I, Laurence Sagourrab, Alexis, Francois Xavier and Migounambe. I went there merely to tell the English that all my nation approved the cessation of hostilities, and the negotiation of peace, and even then we agreed on the time and place of meeting to discuss it. That place was Caskebay, and the time after Corpus Christi.

Two conferences were held at Caskebay. Nothing was done at these two conferences except to read the articles above reported. Every thing I agreed to was approved and ratified, and on these conditions was the peace concluded.

One point only did I regulate at Caskebay. This was to permit the Englishman to keep a store at St. Georges; but a store only, and not to build any other house, nor erect a fort there, and I did not give him the land.

These are the principal matters that I wished to communicate to you who are spread all over the earth. What I tell you now is the truth. If, then, any one should produce any writing that makes me speak otherwise, pay no attention to it, for I know not what I am made to say in another language, but I know well what I say in my own. And in testimony that I say things as they are, I have signed the present minute which I wish to be authentic and to remain for ever.

QUESTIONS FOR CONSIDERATION

1. What are the terms of the treaty that the Indians, by affixing their marks, appear to have agreed to?

2. What is the tone of the language in the treaty? Does it seem to be an agreement between equals?

3. How does Loron Sauguaarum critique and "correct" the terms written down in the formal document of the treaty? How does his response alter our understanding of the treaty?

4. What factors might explain the discrepancies between what the Indians said they said and what the English wrote down in the final treaty?

Indian Foreign Policies and Imperial Rivalries

H ISTORIES OF THE "FRENCH AND INDIAN WARS" often depict Indians as willing pawns or unthinking mercenaries who followed French orders and French agendas. Depictions of negotiations between English colonists and Indians often portray Englishmen speaking from positions of power and dictating terms to defeated and dispirited Indians. The following documents reveal that Indians who fought in the colonial wars were neither pawns nor powerless. They assessed the situations, weighed their options, and made their own decisions, and the foreign policies of Indian nations played a large part in shaping the outcome of imperial conflicts.

In 1752 the governor of Massachusetts dispatched Captain Phineas Stevens as his emissary to meet with the Abenakis in Canada. Stevens had been captured as a boy in Massachusetts by an Abenaki raiding party and had lived with the Abenakis for several years. He had learned their language and customs, and on his return from captivity he ran a trading post at Fort Number Four near Charlestown, New Hampshire, where Abenakis, including his former adoptive relatives, exchanged pelts for merchandise, powder, and ammunition. As commander of the fort, Stevens had withstood a French and Indian siege during King George's War. The Abenakis knew him well.

They also knew well English intentions and ambitions in Abenaki country. As Anglo-French tensions simmered, the English wanted to build a fort at Cowass on the upper Connecticut River. Many Abenakis had migrated northward to escape the pressure of English settlement, and their raids down the Connecticut valley had kept English expansion at bay for years. They were not about to let the English push farther north without a fight, and they still possessed the power to defend their homelands. In a series of meetings with Stevens, Abenaki delegates insisted that the English proposal was unacceptable. In the presence of the French governor of Montreal and other Indians from Kahnawake and Lake of the Two Mountains (Oka), the Abenaki speaker Ateawaneto refused to be browbeaten and asserted Abenaki sovereignty and independence. Stevens blamed Abenaki hostility toward the English on the French: "were it not for ye French," he said in the early 1750s, "it would be Easy to Live at peace with ye Indians."[80] The Abenakis did not agree. Ateawaneto made it clear to Stevens that the Abenakis believed the causes of conflict lay elsewhere.

The forks of the Ohio were the gateway to the West and the focus of imperial ambitions. Indian peoples in the Ohio country were caught between the British and the French but they often played the French and the British against each other to secure their own goals. General Edward Braddock failed to take the French fort at the forks (Fort Duquesne) in 1755 because he failed to recognize the importance of Indian diplomacy and alienated his Indian allies. General John Forbes succeeded in capturing the fort three years later because he recognized the importance of Indian diplomacy and saw that taking Fort Duquesne required the cooperation, or at least the noninterference, of the Indian nations in the Ohio valley.[81] Forbes neutralized Indian power in the struggle by promising that Indian lands would be protected when the war was over, something that Braddock had adamantly refused to do. Forbes sent a Moravian missionary named Christian Frederick Post as an envoy to get the Indians to attend a treaty conference at Easton, Pennsylvania. Post had lived almost ten years among the Delawares and spoke their language. As the following excerpts from Post's journal reveal, the Indian peoples were deeply suspicious of British intentions — a Delaware named Daniel accused him of telling "nothing but idle lying stories" and said "D — n you, why do not you and the *French* fight on the sea? You come here only to cheat the poor *Indians*, and take their land from them."[82] But, working with the Delaware chiefs Pisquetomen, Shingas, and Tamaqua (Beaver), Post managed to convince the Indians that their homelands would be protected once Britain was victorious.

Five hundred Indians attended the treaty at Easton in October. The British promised no settlements would be made west of the mountains without the Indians' consent and promised to establish fair and regulated trade. Having achieved protection for their land and continued access to trade goods, the Ohio valley Indians made peace and Forbes was free to march on Fort Duquesne. Unable to hold the fort without Indian support, the French abandoned it and blew it up. Three days after Fort Duquesne fell, Tamaqua advised Forbes "in a most soft, loving and friendly manner, to go back over the mountains and stay there." Another was more blunt: if the British settled west of the mountains, he warned, "all the nations would be against them; . . . It would be a great war, and never come to peace again."[83] In one of his last letters before he died, Forbes warned General Jeffery Amherst that he must "not think trifflingly of the Indians or their friendship" if Britain hoped to retain its hold on the Ohio country.[84] Instead, the British built Fort Pitt on the ruins of Fort Duquesne, British soldiers and settlers continued to threaten Indian homelands, and Amherst treated the Indians with disdain. Pontiac's War erupted in 1763. "You marched your armies into our country, and built forts here," a Delaware chief named Turtle's Heart told the British at Fort Pitt, "though we told you, again and again, that we wished you to move. My Brothers, this land is ours, and not yours."[85]

ATEAWANETO
Speech Defying the English (1752)

Brother, We speak to you as if we spoke to your Governor of Boston. We hear on all sides that this Governor and the Bostonians say that the Abenakis are bad people. 'Tis in vain that we are taxed with having a bad heart. It is you, brother, that always attack us; your mouth is of sugar but your heart of gall. In truth, the moment you begin we are on our guard.

Brothers, We tell you that we seek not war, we ask nothing better than to be quiet, and it

SOURCE: E. B. O'Callaghan, ed., *Documents Relative to the Colonial History of the State of New York* (Albany, N.Y.: Weed, Parsons, 1853–87), 10:252–54.

depends, brothers, only on you English, to have peace with us.

We have not yet sold the lands we inhabit, we wish to keep the possession of them. Our elders have been willing to tolerate you, brothers Englishmen, on the seabord as far as Sawakwato, as that has been so decided, we wish it to be so.

But we will not cede one single inch of the lands we inhabit beyond what has been decided formerly by our fathers.

You have the sea for your share from the place where you reside; you can trade there. But we expressly forbid you to kill a single beaver, or to take a single stick of timber on the lands we inhabit. If you want timber we'll sell you some, but you shall not take it without our permission.

Brothers, Who hath authorized you to have those lands surveyed? We request our brother, the Governor of Boston, to have those surveyors punished, as we cannot imagine that they have acted by his authority.

Brother, You are therefore masters of the peace that we are to have with you. On condition that you will not encroach on those lands we will be at peace, as the King of France is with the King of Great Britain.

By a Belt.

I repeat to you Brothers, by this belt, that it depends on yourselves to be at peace with the Abenakis.

Our Father who is here present has nothing to do with what we say to you; we speak to you of our own accord, and in the name of all our allies. We regard our Father, in this instance, only as a witness of our words.

We acknowledge no other boundaries of yours than your settlements whereon you have built, and we will not, under any pretext whatsoever, that you pass beyond them. The lands we possess have been given us by the Master of Life. We acknowledge to hold only from him.

We are entirely free. We are allies of the King of France, from whom we have received the Faith and all sorts of assistance in our necessities. We love that monarch, and we are strongly attached to his interests.

Let us have an answer to the propositions we address you, as soon as possible. Take this message in writing to give to your Governor. We also shall keep a copy of it to use in case of need.

Without stirring a step it is easy for your Governor to transmit his answer to us; he will have merely to address it to our Father who will have the goodness to send it to us.

CHRISTIAN FREDERICK POST
Negotiations with the Delawares (1758)

September 1ft. — *Shingas*, King *Beaver, Delaware George*, and *Pifquetumen*, with feveral other captains faid to me,

"Brother, We have thought a great deal fince God has brought you to us; and this is a matter of great confequence, which we cannot readily anfwer; we think on it, and will anfwer you as foon as we can. Our feaft hinders us; all our young men,

women and children are glad to fee you; before you came, they all agreed together to go and join the *French*; but fince they have feen you, they all draw back; though we have great reafon to believe you intend to drive us away, and fettle the country; or elfe, why do you come to fight in the land that God has given us?"

I faid, we did not intend to take the land from them; but only to drive the *French* away. They faid, they knew better; for that they were informed fo by our greateft traders; and fome Juftices of the

SOURCE: Reuben Gold Thwaites, ed., *Early Western Travels, 1748–1846* (Cleveland: Arthur H. Clark, 1904), 1: 213–16.

Peace had told them the fame, and the *French*, faid they, tell us much the fame thing, — "that the *Englifh* intend to deftroy us, and take our lands;" but the land is ours, and not theirs; therfor, we fay, if you will be at peace with us, we will fend the *French* home. It is you that have begun the war, and it is neceffary that you hold faft, and be not difcouraged, in the work of peace. We love you more than you love us; for when we take any prifoners from you, we treat them as our own children. We are poor, and yet we clothe them as well as we can, though you fee our children are as naked as at the firft. By this you may fee that our hearts are better than yours. It is plain that you white people are the caufe of this war; why do not you and the *French* fight in the old country, and on the fea? Why do you come to fight on our land? This makes every body believe, you want to take the land from us by force, and fettle it.°

I told them, "Brothers, as for my part, I have not one foot of land, nor do I defire to have any; and if I had any land, I had rather give it to you, than take any from you. Yes, brothers, if I die, you will get a little more land from me; for I fhall then no longer walk on that ground, which God has made. We told you that you fhould keep nothing in your heart, but bring it before the council fire, and before the Governor, and his council; they will readily hear you; and I promife you, what they anfwer they will ftand to. I further read to you what agreements they made about *Wioming*,° and they ftand to them."

They faid, "Brother, your heart is good, you fpeak always fincerely; but we know there are always a great number of people that want to get rich; they never have enough; look, we do not want to be rich, and take away that which others have. God has given you the tame creatures; we do not want to take them from you. God has given to us the deer, and other wild creatures, which we muft feed on; and we rejoice in that which fprings out of the ground, and thank God for it. Look now, my brother, the white people think we have no brains in our heads; but that they are great and big, and that makes them make war with us: we are but a little handful to what you are; but remember, when you look for a wild turkey you cannot always find it, it is fo little it hides itfelf under the bufhes: and when you hunt for a rattlefnake, you cannot find it; and perhaps it will bite you before you fee it. However, fince you are fo great and big, and we fo little, do you ufe your greatnefs and ftrength in compleating this work of peace. This is the firft time that we faw or heard of you, fince the war begun, and we have great reafon to think about it, fince fuch a great body of you comes into our lands.° It is told us, that you and the *French* con-trived the war, to wafte the *Indians* between you; and that you and the *French* intended to divide the land between you: this was told us by the chief of the *Indian* traders; and they faid further, brothers, this is the laft time we fhall come among you; for the *French* and the *Englifh* intend to kill all the *In-dians*, and then divide the land among themfelves.

Then they addreffed themfelves to me, and faid, "Brother, I fuppofe you know fomething about it; or has the Governor ftopped your mouth, that you cannot tell us?"

Then I faid, "Brothers, I am very forry to fee you fo jealous. I am your own flefh and blood, and fooner than I would tell you any ftory that would be of hurt to you, or your children, I would

---

° The Indians, having plenty of land, are no niggards of it. They fometimes give large tracts to their friends freely; and when they fell it, they make moft generous bargains. But fome *fraudulent purchafes*, in which they were groffly impofed on, and fome *violent intrufions*, imprudently and wickedly made without purchafe, have rendered them jeal-ous that we intend finally to take all from them by force. We fhould endeavour to recover our credit with them by fair purchafes and honeft payments; and then there is no doubt but they will readily fell us, at reafonable rates, as much, from time to time, as we can poffibly have occafion for. — [C.T.?] [C.T. was Charles Thomson, secretary at the Treaty of Easton.]

° The agreement made with *Teedyujcung*, that he fhould enjoy the *Wioming* lands, and have houfes built there for him and his people. — [C.T.?]

° The army under *General Forbes*. — [C.T.?]

fuffer death: and if I did not know that it was the defire of the Governor, that we fhould renew our old brotherly love and friendfhip, that fubfifted between our grandfathers, I would not have undertaken this journey. I do affure you of mine and the people's honefty. If the *French* had not been here, the *Englifh* would not have come; and confider, brothers, whether, in fuch a cafe, we can always fit ftill."

Then they faid, "It is a thoufand pities we did not know this fooner; if we had, it would have been peace long before now."

QUESTIONS FOR CONSIDERATION

1. With what tone do Ateawaneto and the Delaware chiefs talk to the British emissaries?

2. How do the Abenakis and Delawares view alliance with the French?

3. What are the causes of tension, and who is responsible for the conflict, in the Indians' view?

4. Indians who fought in the so-called French and Indian War sided mainly with the French, sometimes with the British, sometimes with one then the other. Do these documents reveal any consistent motivations and strategies in the Indians' war efforts and foreign policies?

A Captive with the Senecas

PEOPLE WHO HAD ENDURED AND SURVIVED CAPTIVITY often wrote or related narratives of their experiences in which they, or their editors, portrayed Indians as bloodthirsty savages who scalped and tortured men, tomahawked children indiscriminately, and subjected women to "unspeakable horrors." Some twentieth-century writers and filmmakers perpetuated such images of Indian savagery. Although many captives suffered violent treatment, Indian captors often had another purpose. They frequently took captives with the intention of adopting them into their family and community.

Indians in the northeastern woodlands took captives to assuage the grief of bereaved relatives and appease the spirits of deceased kinsfolk. War parties often made raids for the specific purpose of taking captives, and they sometimes brought extra clothing and moccasins for the prisoners they expected to seize. With escalating losses to war and diseases in the wake of European invasion, captive-taking became a way of maintaining population levels as well as patching holes torn in the social fabric of kin- and clan-based Indian communities: captives were often adopted to fill the specific place of a deceased relative. The imperial wars waged between England and France from 1689 to 1763 introduced an additional incentive for taking captives, as the French bought prisoners to ransom to the English. During the French and Indian War, Indians abducted more than 1,600 people from New England alone, carrying them north to Canada. Some of the captives did not survive the ordeal — they succumbed to hardships of travel, hunger, and disease or were killed by their captors. Many of those who survived the grueling journey northward were sold to the French and later ransomed to the English. Some made new lives for themselves in Canada. Others were adopted into Indian communities.

The captives' fates and experiences varied according to their age, gender, and health; the character and feelings of their captors; and chance. Older people, adult males, and crying infants might be tomahawked and left for dead, but women and children were often treated with consideration once the raiding party escaped pursuit. Indian warriors generally treated kindly those captives who were likely to be adopted. Contrary to popular fears, Indian warriors in the Eastern Woodlands did not rape female captives. Warriors ritually prepared for war and invoked spiritual assistance; preserving the purity of their war medicine demanded sexual abstinence, while intercourse with someone who might be adopted into one's clan constituted incest. "None of the Indians were disposed to show insults of any nature," former captive Susanna Johnson recalled.[86] Hard travel in moccasins in harsh weather and over rugged terrain, irregular meals and unfamiliar diet, and separation from family and home all took a toll on captives. But these experiences also initiated them into a new way of life.

Once the trek into Indian country was over, captives faced new ordeals. Arriving at a village, they might be made to run a gauntlet between two ranks of Indians brandishing sticks and clubs. Indians mourning relatives might vent their grief by demanding that a captive be tortured to death. But often they dressed and painted the captives in Indian style and ritually adopted them into a family. Time and the wealth of kinship relations that captives found in Indian society healed many wounds. Some captives preferred not to return home even when the opportunity arose, and most found things they admired in Indian society. Many women appear to have found life in an Indian community more rewarding than the isolation and hard work that was the common lot of a wife on the colonial frontier.

Children proved especially susceptible to adoptive "Indianization." Titus King, captured by Abenakis in Massachusetts, saw many English children held by Indians in Canada. He estimated it took only six months for children to forsake their parents, forget their homes, refuse to speak their own language, and "be holley swollowed up with the Indians" and adopt their ways.[87] Susanna Johnson's son, Sylvanus, whom she described as having become "a perfect Indian" after three years with the Abenakis, apparently never lost his Indian ways. According to the nineteenth-century town history of Charlestown, New Hampshire, "he so much preferred the modes of Indian life to the customs of civilization that he often expressed regret at having been ransomed. He always maintained, and no arguments could convince him to the contrary, that the Indians were a far more moral race than the whites."[88] Captives who returned home were permanently changed by the experience. For some, it was a nightmare never to be forgotten. Others retained lasting connections to Indian communities and real affection for the families that had adopted them. It was not unusual for former captors to visit former captives in the English settlements, bringing news of Indian friends and relatives. Some former captives became intermediaries between Indians and whites.

Accurate information about and viewpoints from Native American women in colonial times are extremely scarce, and historians usually have tried to reconstruct the experiences of Indian women through words written by European men. One of the few exceptions is the life story of Mary Jemison (c. 1742–1833), a white woman who was captured by Shawnees and adopted by the Senecas at about age fifteen in 1758. The Iroquois traditionally adopted captives into their society to fill the place of deceased relatives. Mary Jemison married an Indian husband and raised a family. In time and in cultural allegiance she became a Seneca, sharing fully the lives of eighteenth-century Seneca women. She lived most of her life in the Genesee country of western New York, the Seneca heartland, and became known as the "white woman of the Genesee." In her old age, she dictated her story. Though the narrative of her life is flawed by the intrusive influence of her nineteenth-century writer, it nevertheless provides us with a rare opportunity to read the words of a woman who was living in Indian country in times of dramatic change.

These extracts from the autobiography of Mary Jemison give insights into the ways in which — by adoption, acceptance, kind treatment, and family ties — one woman came to be a "white Indian." After the American Revolution, Mary Jemison had the chance to return to white society but refused. By the time she died, she had had two husbands (one a Delaware, the other a Seneca), she had borne eight children (only three of whom survived her), and she had thirty-nine grandchildren and fourteen great-grandchildren. Jemison is still a prominent name among the Senecas.

MARY JEMISON (DICKEWAMIS)
A Narrative of Her Life (1824)

At night we arrived at a small Seneca Indian town, at the mouth of a small river, that was called by the Indians, in the Seneca language, She-nan-jee, where the two Squaws to whom I belonged resided. There we landed, and the Indians went on; which was the last I ever saw of them.

Having made fast to the shore, the Squaws left me in the canoe while they went to their wigwam or house in the town, and returned with a suit of Indian clothing, all new, and very clean and nice. My clothes, though whole and good when I was taken, were now torn in pieces, so that I was almost naked. They first undressed me and threw my rags into the river; then washed me clean and dressed me in the new suit they had just brought, in complete Indian style; and then led me home and seated me in the center of their wigwam.

I had been in that situation but a few minutes, before all the Squaws in the town came in to see me. I was soon surrounded by them, and they immediately set up a most dismal howling, crying bitterly, and wringing their hands in all the agonies of grief for a deceased relative.

Their tears flowed freely, and they exhibited all the signs of real mourning. At the commencement of this scene, one of their number began, in a voice somewhat between speaking and singing, to recite some words to the following purport, and continued the recitation till the ceremony was ended; the company at the same time varying the appearance of their countenances, gestures and

SOURCE: Colin G. Calloway, *The World Turned Upside Down: Indian Voices from Early America* (Boston: Bedford Books, 1994), 73–77.

tone of voice, so as to correspond with the sentiments expressed by their leader:

"Oh our brother! Alas! He is dead—he has gone; he will never return! Friendless he died on the field of the slain, where his bones are yet lying unburied! Oh, who will not mourn his sad fate? No tears dropped around him; oh, no! No tears of his sisters were there! He fell in his prime, when his arm was most needed to keep us from danger! Alas! he has gone! and left us in sorrow, his loss to bewail: Oh where is his spirit? His spirit went naked, and hungry it wanders, and thirsty and wounded it groans to return! Oh helpless and wretched, our brother has gone! No blanket nor food to nourish and warm him; nor candles to light him, nor weapons of war:—Oh, none of those comforts had he! But well we remember his deeds!—The deer he could take on the chase! The panther shrunk back at the sight of his strength! His enemies fell at his feet! He was brave and courageous in war! As the fawn he was harmless: his friendship was ardent: his temper was gentle: his pity was great! Oh! Our friend, our companion is dead! Our brother, our brother, alas! he is gone! But why do we grieve for his loss? In the strength of a warrior, undaunted he left us, to fight by the side of the Chiefs! His warwhoop was shrill! His rifle well aimed laid his enemies low: his tomahawk drank of their blood: and his knife flayed their scalps while yet covered with gore! And why do we mourn? Though he fell on the field of the slain, with glory he fell, and his spirit went up to the land of his fathers in war! Then why do we mourn? With transports of joy they received him, and fed him, and clothed him, and welcomed him there! Oh friends, he is happy; then dry up your tears! His spirit has seen our distress, and sent us a helper whom with pleasure we greet. Dickewamis has come: then let us receive her with joy! She is handsome and pleasant! Oh! she is our sister, and gladly we welcome her here. In the place of our brother she stands in our tribe. With care we will guard her from trouble; and may she be happy till her spirit shall leave us."

In the course of that ceremony, from mourning they became serene—joy sparkled in their countenances, and they seemed to rejoice over me as over a long lost child. I was made welcome amongst them as a sister to the two Squaws before mentioned, and was called Dickewamis; which being interpreted, signifies a pretty girl, a handsome girl, or a pleasant, good thing. That is the name by which I have ever since been called by the Indians.

I afterwards learned that the ceremony I at that time passed through, was that of adoption. The two squaws had lost a brother in Washington's war,° sometime in the year before, and in consequence of his death went up to Fort Pitt, on the day on which I arrived there, in order to receive a prisoner or an enemy's scalp, to supply their loss.

It is a custom of the Indians, when one of their number is slain or taken prisoner in battle, to give to the nearest relative to the dead or absent, a prisoner, if they have chanced to take one, and if not, to give him the scalp of an enemy. On the return of the Indians from conquest, which is always announced by peculiar shoutings, demonstrations of joy, and the exhibition of some trophy of victory, the mourners come forward and make their claims. If they receive a prisoner, it is at their option either to satiate their vengeance by taking his life in the most cruel manner they can conceive of; or, to receive and adopt him into the family, in the place of him whom they have lost. All the prisoners that are taken in battle and carried to the encampment or town by the Indians, are given to the bereaved families, till their number is made good. And unless the mourners have but just received the news of their bereavement, and are under the operation of a paroxysm of grief, anger and revenge; or, unless the prisoner is very old, sickly, or homely, they generally save him, and treat him kindly. But if their mental wound is fresh, their loss so great that they deem it irreparable, or if their prisoner or prisoners

---

° The Seven Years' War, although in Iroquois memory, Washington is more often associated with the war of the Revolution, during which he earned the name "Town Destroyer."

do not meet their approbation, no torture, let it be ever so cruel, seems sufficient to make them satisfaction. It is family, and not national, sacrifices amongst the Indians, that has given them an indelible stamp as barbarians, and identified their character with the idea which is generally formed of unfeeling ferocity, and the most abandoned cruelty.

It was my happy lot to be accepted for adoption; and at the time of the ceremony I was received by the two squaws, to supply the place of their brother in the family; and I was ever considered and treated by them as a real sister, the same as though I had been born of their mother.

During my adoption, I sat motionless, nearly terrified to death at the appearance and actions of the company, expecting every moment to feel their vengeance, and suffer death on the spot. I was, however, happily disappointed, when at the close of the ceremony the company retired, and my sisters went about employing every means for my consolation and comfort.

Being now settled and provided with a home, I was employed in nursing the children, and doing light work about the house. Occasionally I was sent out with the Indian hunters, when they went but a short distance, to help them carry their game. My situation was easy; I had no particular hardships to endure. But still, the recollection of my parents, my brothers and sisters, my home, and my own captivity, destroyed my happiness, and made me constantly solitary, lonesome and gloomy.

My sisters would not allow me to speak English in their hearing; but remembering the charge that my dear mother gave me at the time I left her, whenever I chanced to be alone I made a business of repeating my prayer, catechism, or something I had learned in order that I might not forget my own language. By practising in that way I retained it till I came to Genesee flats, where I soon became acquainted with English people with whom I have been almost daily in the habit of conversing.

My sisters were diligent in teaching me their language; and to their great satisfaction I soon learned so that I could understand it readily, and speak it fluently. I was very fortunate in falling into their hands; for they were kind good natured women; peaceable and mild in their dispositions; temperate and decent in their habits, and very tender and gentle towards me. I have great reason to respect them, though they have been dead a great number of years.

The town where they lived was pleasantly situated on the Ohio, at the mouth of the Shenanjee: the land produced good corn; the woods furnished a plenty of game, and the waters abounded with fish. Another river emptied itself into the Ohio, directly opposite the mouth of the Shenanjee. We spent the summer at that place, where we planted, hoed, and harvested a large crop of corn, of an excellent quality.

I had then been with the Indians four summers and four winters, and had become so far accustomed to their mode of living, habits and dispositions, that my anxiety to get away, to be set at liberty, and leave them, had almost subsided. With them was my home; my family was there, and there I had many friends to whom I was warmly attached in consideration of the favors, affection and friendship with which they had uniformly treated me, from the time of my adoption. Our labor was not severe; and that of one year was exactly similar, in almost every respect, to that of the others, without that endless variety that is to be observed in the common labor of the white people. Notwithstanding the Indian women have all the fuel and bread to procure, and the cooking to perform, their task is probably not harder than that of white women, who have those articles provided for them; and their cares certainly are not half as numerous, nor as great. In the summer season, we planted, tended and harvested our corn, and generally had all our children with us; but had no master to oversee or drive us, so that we could work as leisurely as we pleased. We had no ploughs on the Ohio; but performed the whole process of planting and hoeing with a small tool that resembled, in some respects, a hoe with a very short handle.

Our cooking consisted in pounding our corn into samp or hommany, boiling the hommany, making now and then a cake and baking it in the ashes, and in boiling or roasting our venison. As our cooking and eating utensils consisted of a hommany block and pestle, a small kettle, a knife or two, and a few vessels of bark or wood, it required but little time to keep them in order for use.

Spinning, weaving, sewing, stocking knitting, and the like, are arts which have never been practised in the Indian tribes generally. After the revolutionary war, I learned to sew, so that I could make my own clothing after a poor fashion; but the other domestic arts I have been wholly ignorant of the application of, since my captivity. In the season of hunting, it was our business, in addition to our cooking, to bring home the game that was taken by the Indians, dress it, and carefully preserve the eatable meat, and prepare or dress the skins. Our clothing was fastened together with strings of deer skin, and tied on with the same.

In that manner we lived, without any of those jealousies, quarrels, and revengeful battles between families and individuals, which have been common in the Indian tribes since the introduction of ardent spirits amongst them.

The use of ardent spirits amongst the Indians, and the attempts which have been made to civilize and christianize them by the white people, has constantly made them worse and worse; increased their vices, and robbed them of many of their virtues; and will ultimately produce their extermination. I have seen, in a number of instances, the effects of education upon some of our Indians, who were taken when young, from their families, and placed at school before they had had an opportunity to contract many Indian habits, and there kept till they arrived to manhood; but I have never seen one of those but what was an Indian in every respect after he returned. Indians must and will be Indians, in spite of all the means that can be used for their cultivation in the sciences and arts.

One thing only marred my happiness, while I lived with them on the Ohio; and that was the recollection that I had once had tender parents, and a home that I loved. Aside from that consideration, or, if I had been taken in infancy, I should have been contented in my situation. Notwithstanding all that has been said against the Indians, in consequence of their cruelties to their enemies — cruelties that I have witnessed, and had abundant proof of — it is a fact that they are naturally kind, tender and peaceable towards their friends, and strictly honest; and that those cruelties have been practiced, only upon their enemies, according to their idea of justice.

QUESTIONS FOR CONSIDERATION

1. European males typically depicted Indian women as living in unremitting hardship, and colonial literature often told of European women being raped and abused when captured by Indians. What indications does Mary Jemison give that the lives of women — Indian or European — in Seneca society were rather different?

2. What information does Jemison offer about Indian societies and intercultural interaction in early America?

3. What value can the narrative of a captive have as a historical source?

4. If Jemison did not speak the Seneca language at the time of her capture, how might she recollect scenes such as the grieving ceremony?

PICTURE ESSAY

Atlantic Travelers: Indians in Eighteenth-Century London

·⋅⟡⟨⟩⟡⟨⟩⟡⟨⟩⟡⟨⟩⟡⟨⟩⟡⟨⟩⟡⟨⟩⟡⋅·

Pocahontas was the most famous Indian visitor to England, but she was not the first. Pocahontas and the Powhatan delegation in 1616 followed on the heels of three captured Mi'kmaqs presented to the king in 1502; four Inuit (all of whom died) in 1576–77; three Virginia Indians in the 1580s; five Wabanakis kidnapped on the coast of Maine in 1605; an Indian abducted from Martha's Vineyard in 1611; and Squanto a few years later (see page 107). In the eighteenth century, Indian delegates visited London, Paris, and Madrid, where powers competed for their allegiance. Among the Indian emissaries to London were four "Mohawk Kings" in 1710; delegations of Creeks, Cherokees, and Mohegans in the 1730s; more Cherokees in 1762; Samson Occom (raising funds for the future Dartmouth College) several years later; and Joseph Brant (Molly Brant's brother) before and after the American Revolution. Through the nineteenth century London saw Indian ministers, delegates, and members of various troupes and Wild West shows. Like early explorers and colonists in America, Indians who crossed the Atlantic to England "discovered" new lands and people. In the streets, factories, pubs, palaces, and churches of Britain they experienced new frontiers and zones of contact. The British press covered their visits, often in considerable detail. Indians were curiosities and sometimes celebrities. In some cases, they had their portraits painted.[89]

In 1710 "four Mohawk kings" visited the court of Queen Anne, on an embassy designed to secure Mohawk allegiance for a pending British invasion of Canada. They were not kings (and one of them was actually a Mahican), but they were treated as visiting dignitaries. In addition to their audience with the queen, they met with representatives of the Church of England, attended the theater and opera, and saw the sights. The queen commissioned John Verelst, a Dutch artist working in England, to paint individual portraits of each chief. The paintings were then engraved in mezzotint and sold. The engraving of Tac Yec Neen Ho Gar Ton, or Hendrick, "Emperor of the Six Nations" (Figure 3.1), shows him dressed "in the English manner," with black coat, breeches, and buckled shoes, and wearing a scarlet cloak trimmed with gold; the forested background suggests the North American "wilderness," and the wolf behind his leg conveys his clan. The wampum belt signifies the alliance being cemented by the visit.[90]

In 1730 a delegation of seven Cherokees visited London to make a treaty of alliance, and once again an engraving was made to commemorate the occasion (Figure 3.2). The original caption below the picture informed viewers that the delegates were "Cloth'd with these Habits out of the Royal Wardrobe" for a visit

◆ **Figure 3.1** **John Verelst, *Tac Yec Neen Ho Gar Ton* (Hendrick, *"Emperor of the Six Nations")* (1701)**
Tac Yec Neen Ho Gar Ton, Emperor of the Six Nations, 1701, oil on canvas, Johannes or Jan
Verelst (b. 1648–fl.1719). Private Collection/Bridgeman Images.

◆ Figure 3.2 **Isaac Basire, *Seven Cherokees* (1730)**
The Cherokee Embassy to England, 1730, line engraving by Isaac Basire, 1730. Granger, NYC.

to Windsor Castle. The Cherokees were also identified individually by name. The youth at the far right is Attakullakulla, the Little Carpenter (see page 161). As an adult, Attakullakulla frequently expressed his desire to visit England again.

In 1734 a delegation of Creek Indians led by the Yamacraw chief Tomochichi traveled to London with General James Oglethorpe to meet the Trustees of Georgia and King George II. In this section of a larger group portrait painted over the course of several weeks by William Verelst (Figure 3.3), Tomochichi stands in the center with right arm extended, while Oglethorpe hands a book to Tomochichi's nephew, Toonahowi. Tomochichi's wife, Senaukey, accompanied her husband on his transatlantic voyage. Like earlier visitors, the Creek delegates toured London and went to the theater. For their audience with the king they were prevailed upon to shed their Native clothing and dress "appropriately." The Indians evidently were impressed by London, but not too impressed. According to one earl, Tomochichi "observed we knew many things his Country men did not, but doubted if we were happier, Since we live worse than they, and they more innocently."[91] One of the delegates died in London.

After the Anglo-Cherokee War of 1759–61, Lieutenant Henry Timberlake accompanied three Cherokee chiefs to London to help secure the peace that had been made. In addition to the usual attentions, the three young men apparently attracted

◆ Figure 3.3 **William Verelst, _Creek Delegation Meets the Trustees of Georgia_ (1734)**
Creek Delegation Meets the Trustees of Georgia, 1734, painting by William Verelst. Granger, NYC.

"groupies" and inspired ribald verse.[92] As this portrait of Cunne Shote by Francis Parsons shows (Figure 3.4), the Cherokees were given white English shirts and red cloaks, and Cunne Shote wears a gorget around his neck engraved with "G. R. III." ([King] George III Reigns). Yet the scalp lock, lacerated ear lobe, and clutched knife convey Cunne Shote's Cherokee identity, or his exoticism for English audiences.

Samson Occom was a Mohegan Indian minister who had been educated by the Rev. Eleazar Wheelock at his Indian Charity School in Lebanon, Connecticut. In 1765 Wheelock sent Occom to Britain on a preaching tour to raise money for a new school to be built in the heart of the Indian country. Sailing from Boston two days before Christmas, Occom spent six weeks at sea (about average for the time; the westward voyage across the Atlantic took even longer) and arrived in London in February. Taking a walk on his first Sunday evening in the city, he "Saw

Such Confusion as I never Dreamt of—there was Some at Churches Singing & Preaching, in the Streets some Cursing, Swaring & Damning one another, others was hollowing, Whestling, talking, gigling, & Laughing, & Coaches and footmen passing and repassing, Crossing and Cross-Crossing, and the poor Begars Praying, Crying, and Beging upon their knees."[93] He met King George III and the arch-bishops of Canterbury and York and saw the city's sights (Westminster Abbey, the Tower of London). He was the first Indian minister to visit Britain, and he attracted large congregations wherever he preached. In all, Occom delivered more than three hundred sermons in England and Scotland and raised about £12,000 for Wheelock's new school—the future Dartmouth College. This portrait of Occom (Figure 3.5), likely commissioned by the Earl of Dartmouth, was painted while he was in England and was later made into a print for mass distribution.

◆ Figure 3.4 **Francis Parsons,**
***Cunne Shote* (1762)**
Cunne-Shote (c. 1715–1810), oil on
canvas, Francis Parsons (fl. 1760–80).
Private Collection/Peter Newark
American Pictures/Bridgeman Images.

◆ **Figure 3.5 Jonathan Spilsbury, after Mason Chamberlain,** *The Reverend Mr. Samson Occom* **(1768)**
The Reverend Samson Occom (1723–92), 1768, Jonathan Spilsbury, British, 1737–1812/ after Mason Chamberlain, British, 1727–87/ Mezzotint on laid paper/Hood Museum of Art, Dartmouth College, Hanover, New Hampshire; gift of Mrs. Robert White Birch, Class of 1927W.

QUESTIONS FOR CONSIDERATION

1. Few Indian visitors recorded their impressions on paper, but what might eighteenth-century London have looked like to Native Americans? Like the United States in later years, the British government assumed that Indian visitors to the nation's capital would be awed by the power, wealth, and population of the city, but what things in eighteenth-century London might Indian visitors have been less impressed by?

2. What meanings might the British have attached to adorning Indian visitors in scarlet cloaks and other items of European clothing? What do other symbols in the portraits stand for?

3. What do these images reveal, or fail to reveal, about the relationships between these Indian travelers and their British hosts?

REFERENCES

1. Patrick Wolfe, "Settler Colonialism and the Elimination of the Native," *Journal of Genocide Research* 8 (December 2006), 387–409.

2. Stuart Banner, *How the Indians Lost Their Land: Law and Power on the Frontier* (Cambridge, Mass.: Harvard University Press, 2005); Colin G. Calloway and Neal Salisbury, eds., *Reinterpreting New England Indians and the Colonial Experience* (Boston: Colonial Society of Massachusetts, 2003); Walter R. Echo-Hawk, *In the Courts of the Conqueror: The 10 Worst Indian Law Cases Ever Decided* (Golden, Colo.: Fulcrum, 2010); Waziyatawin Angela Wilson and Michael Yellow Bird, eds., *For Indigenous Eyes Only: A Decolonizing Handbook* (Santa Fe: School of American Research Press, 2005), 1.

3. Colin G. Calloway, *New Worlds for All: Indians, Europeans, and the Remaking of Early America* (Baltimore: Johns Hopkins University Press, 1997; 2nd ed., 2013); Kathleen DuVal, *The Native Ground: Indians and Colonists in the Heart of the Continent* (Philadelphia: University of Pennsylvania Press, 2006); Juliana Barr, *Peace Came in the Form of a Woman: Indians and Spaniards in the Texas Borderlands* (Chapel Hill: University of North Carolina Press, 2007); Joseph M. Hall Jr., *Zamumo's Gifts: Indian-European Exchange in the Colonial Southeast* (Philadelphia: University of Pennsylvania Press, 2009); Sophie White, *Wild Frenchmen and Frenchified Indians: Material Culture and Race in Colonial Louisiana* (Philadelphia: University of Pennsylvania Press, 2012).

4. James Axtell, *The Invasion Within: The Contest of Cultures in Colonial North America* (New York: Oxford University Press, 1985).

5. Jerald T. Milanich, *Laboring in the Fields of the Lord: Spanish Missions and Southeastern Indians* (Washington, D.C.: Smithsonian Institution Press, 1999).

6. James H. Merrell, *The Indians' New World: Catawbas and Their Neighbors from European Contact through the Era of Removal* (Chapel Hill: University of North Carolina Press, 1989), 210.

7. Gunlög Fur, *A Nation of Women: Gender and Colonial Encounters among the Delaware Indians* (Philadelphia: University of Pennsylvania Press, 2009), p. 43 (quote) and chap. 4; Joel W. Martin and Mark A. Nicholas, eds., *Native Americans, Christianity, and the Reshaping of the American Religious Landscape* (Chapel Hill: University of North Carolina Press, 2010); Rachel Wheeler, *To Live upon Hope: Mohicans and Missionaries in the Eighteenth-Century Northeast* (Ithaca, N.Y.: Cornell University Press, 2008); Richard W. Pointer, *Encounters of the Spirit: Native Americans and European Colonial Religion* (Bloomington: Indiana University Press, 2007); Julius H. Rubin, *Tears of Repentance: Christian Indian Identity and Community in Colonial Southern New England* (Lincoln: University of Nebraska Press, 2013). Linford D. Fisher, *The Indian Great Awakening: Religion and the Shaping of Native Cultures in Early America* (New York: Oxford University Press, 2012), recommends "affiliation" as a better term than conversion for understanding the varied, changing engagements of Indian peoples with Christianity in a colonial world.

8. Colin G. Calloway, ed., *The World Turned Upside Down: Indian Voices from Early America* (Boston: Bedford Books, 1994), 101–4; Franklin's version is in Leonard W. Labaree, ed., *The Papers of Benjamin Franklin*. 39 vols. (New Haven: Yale University Press, 1959--.), 4:483. For a complete study of this treaty, see James H. Merrell, ed., *The Lancaster Treaty of 1744, with Related Documents* (Boston: Bedford/St. Martin's, 2008). For broader coverage of Indian education, see Margaret Connell Szasz, *Indian Education in the American Colonies, 1607–1783* (Albuquerque: University of New Mexico Press, 1988); Axtell, *The Invasion Within*; Colin G. Calloway, *The Indian History of an American Institution: Native Americans and Dartmouth* (Hanover, N.H.: University Press of New England, 2010); and Craig Steven Wilder, *Ebony and Ivy: Race, Slavery, and the Troubled History of America's Universities* (New York: Bloomsbury Press, 2013).

9. Daniel H. Usner Jr., *Indians, Settlers, and Slaves in a Frontier Exchange Economy: The Lower Mississippi Valley before 1783* (Chapel Hill: University of North Carolina Press, 1992); White, *Wild Frenchmen and Frenchified Indians*.

10. J. B. Tyrrell, ed., *Journals of Samuel Hearne and Philip Turnor between the Years 1774 and 1792* (Toronto: The Champlain Society, 1934), 534.

11. Labaree, *The Papers of Benjamin Franklin*, 4:481–83.

12. David L. Preston, *The Texture of Contact: European and Indian Settler Communities on the Frontier of Iroquoia, 1667–1783* (Lincoln: University of Nebraska Press, 2009).

13. Clara Sue Kidwell, "Indian Women as Cultural Mediators," *Ethnohistory* 39 (Spring 1992), 97–107. On cultural mediators more generally, see Margaret Connell Szasz, ed., *Between Indian and White Worlds: The Cultural Broker* (Norman: University of Oklahoma Press, 1994).

14. Jacqueline Peterson and Jennifer S. H. Brown, eds., *The New Peoples: Being and Becoming Métis in North America* (Lincoln: University of Nebraska Press, 1985); Susan Sleeper-Smith, *Indian Women and French Men: Rethinking Cultural Encounter in the Western Great Lakes* (Amherst: University of Massachusetts Press, 2001). For a broader survey of the offspring of intermarriage, see Thomas N. Ingersoll, *To Intermix with Our White Brothers: Indian Mixed Bloods in the United States from Earliest Times to the Indian Removals* (Albuquerque: University of New Mexico Press, 2005).

15. Colin G. Calloway, *White People, Indians, and Highlanders: Tribal Peoples and Colonial Encounters in Scotland and America* (New York: Oxford University Press, 2008); Michelle LeMaster, *Brothers Born of One Mother: British–Native American Relations in the Colonial Southeast* (Charlottesville: University of Virginia Press, 2012).

16. Christopher L. Miller and George R. Hamell explore the spiritual associations of glass beads and other trade items in "A New Perspective on Indian-White Contact: Cultural Symbols and Colonial Trade," *Journal of American History* 73 (September 1986), 311–28.

17. Quoted in Colin G. Calloway, *The American Revolution in Indian Country: Crisis and Diversity in Native American Communities* (Cambridge: Cambridge University Press, 1995), 11.

18. Richard White, *The Roots of Dependency: Subsistence, Environment, and Social Change among the Choctaws, Pawnees, and Navajos* (Lincoln: University of Nebraska Press, 1983).

19. Hugh Talmage Lefler, ed., *A New Voyage to Carolina by John Lawson* (Chapel Hill: University of North Carolina Press, 1967), 211.

20. Quoted in Calloway, *World Turned Upside Down*, 108.

21. Peter C. Mancall, *Deadly Medicine: Indians and Alcohol in Early America* (Ithaca, N.Y.: Cornell University Press, 1995), esp. 5–8.

22. Alan Gallay, *The Indian Slave Trade: The Rise of the English Empire in the American South, 1670–1717* (New Haven: Yale University Press, 2002); Alan Gallay, ed., *Indian Slavery in Colonial America* (Lincoln: University of Nebraska Press, 2009); Christina Snyder, *Slavery in Indian Country: The Changing Face of Captivity in Early America* (Cambridge, Mass.: Harvard University Press, 2010).

23. Robbie Ethridge and Sheri M. Shuck-Hall, eds., *Mapping the Mississippian Shatter Zone: The Colonial Indian Slave Trade and Regional Instability in the American South* (Lincoln: University of Nebraska Press, 2009).

24. Eric Bowne, *The Westo Indians: Slave Traders of the Early Colonial South* (Tuscaloosa: University of Alabama Press, 2005).

25. Robbie Ethridge, "The Making of a Militaristic Slaving Society: The Chickasaws and the Colonial Indian Slave Trade," in Gallay, *Indian Slavery*; Robbie Etheridge, *From Chicaza to Chickasaw: The European Invasion and the Transformation of the Mississippian World, 1540–1715* (Chapel Hill: University of North Carolina Press, 2010); Richebourg Gaillard McWilliams, trans. and ed., *Iberville's Gulf Journals* (Tuscaloosa: University of Alabama Press, 1981), 119.

26. Paul Kelton, *Epidemics and Enslavement: Biological Catastrophe in the Native Southeast, 1492–1715* (Lincoln: University of Nebraska Press, 2007); Lefler, *New Voyage to Carolina*, 17, 232; William L. Ramsey, *The Yamasee War: A Study of Culture, Economy, and Conflict in the Colonial South* (Lincoln: University of Nebraska Press, 2008); Gallay, *Indian Slave Trade*, 299.

27. Snyder, *Slavery in Indian Country*.

28. Ned Blackhawk, *Violence over the Land: Indians and Empires in the Early American West* (Cambridge, Mass.: Harvard University Press, 2006).

29. Brett Rushforth, *Bonds of Alliance: Indigenous and Atlantic Slaveries in New France* (Chapel Hill: University of North Carolina Press, 2012); Carl J. Ekberg, *Stealing Indian Women: Native Slavery in the Illinois Country* (Urbana: University of Illinois Press, 2007).

30. Hall, *Zamumo's Gifts*.

31. Colin G. Calloway, *Pen and Ink Witchcraft: Treaties and Treaty Making in American Indian History* (New York: Oxford University Press, 2013); Tom Arne Midtrød, *The Memory of All Ancient Customs: Native American Diplomacy in the Colonial Hudson Valley* (Ithaca, N.Y.: Cornell University Press, 2012).

32. Usner, *Indians, Settlers, and Slaves*, 29.

33. Edward P. Hamilton, trans. and ed., *Adventure in the Wilderness: The American Journals of Louis Antoine de Bougainville, 1756–1760* (Norman: University of Oklahoma Press, 1964), 170.

34. Alfred Barnaby Thomas, ed., *The Plains Indians and New Mexico, 1751–1778: A Collection of Documents Illustrative of the History of the Eastern Frontier of New Mexico* (Albuquerque: University of New Mexico Press, 1940), 137.

35. Wilbur R. Jacobs, ed., *The Appalachian Indian Frontier: The Edmond Atkin Report and Plan of 1755* (Lincoln: University of Nebraska Press, 1967), 3–4.

36. Stephen Craig Harper, *Promised Land: Penn's Holy Experiment, the Walking Purchase, and the Dispossession of Delawares, 1600–1763* (Bethlehem, Pa.: Lehigh University Press, 2006).

37. James H. Merrell, *Into the American Woods: Negotiators on the Pennsylvania Frontier* (New York: W. W. Norton, 1999), quote at 38; Kevin Kenny, *Peaceable Kingdom Lost: The Paxton Boys and the Destruction of William Penn's Holy Experiment* (New York: Oxford University Press, 2009).

38. Timothy J. Shannon, *Iroquois Diplomacy on the Early American Frontier* (New York: Viking Penguin, 2008), 62; Timothy J. Shannon, *Indians and Colonists at the Crossroads of Empire: The Albany Congress of 1754* (Ithaca, N.Y.: Cornell University Press, 2000).

39. Fintan O'Toole, *White Savage: William Johnson and the Invention of America* (New York: Farrar, Straus, and Giroux, 2005).

40. Steven C. Hahn, *The Invention of the Creek Nation, 1760–1763* (Lincoln: University of Nebraska Press, 2004); Joshua Piker, *Okfuskee: A Creek Indian Town in Colonial America* (Cambridge, Mass.: Harvard University Press, 2004).

41. Quoted in Daniel K. Richter, *The Ordeal of the Longhouse: The Peoples of the Iroquois League in the Era of European Colonization* (Chapel Hill: University of North Carolina Press, 1992), 206.

42. James H. Merrell, " 'Minding the Business of the Nation': Hagler as Catawba Leader," *Ethnohistory* 33 (Winter 1986), 55–70; quote from Merrell, *Indians' New World*, 166.

43. Francis Parkman, *Montcalm and Wolfe: The French and Indian War* (New York: Da Capo Press, 1995), 452–53.

44. David LaVere, *The Tuscarora War: Indians, Settlers, and the Fight for the Carolina Colonies* (Chapel Hill: University of North Carolina Press, 2014).

45. Sami Lakomäki, *Gathering Together: The Shawnee People through Diaspora and Nationhood, 1600–1870* (New Haven: Yale University Press, 2014); Stephen Warren, *The Worlds the Shawnees Made: Migration and Violence in Early America* (Chapel Hill: University of North Carolina Press, 2014); Michael N. McConnell, *A Country Between: The Upper Ohio Valley and Its Peoples, 1724–1774* (Lincoln: University of Nebraska Press, 1992).

46. Calloway, *World Turned Upside Down*, 133–34.

47. Tanaghrisson quoted in *The Journal of Major George Washington* (Williamsburg: Colonial Williamsburg Foundation, 1959), 7.

48. Shingas related his account of the exchange with Braddock to a captive: Beverley W. Bond Jr., ed., "The Captivity of Charles Stuart, 1755–57," *Mississippi Valley Historical Review* 13 (June 1926), 63–64.

49. Matthew C. Ward, *Breaking the Backcountry: The Seven Years' War in Virginia and Pennsylvania, 1754–1765* (Pittsburgh: University of Pittsburgh Press, 2003); Peter Silver, *Our Savage Neighbors: How Indian War Transformed Early America* (New York: W. W. Norton, 2008).

50. Ian K. Steele, *Betrayals: Fort William Henry and the "Massacre"* (New York: Oxford University Press, 1990).

51. Fred Anderson, *Crucible of War: The Seven Years' War and the Fate of Empire in British North America, 1754–1766* (New York: Alfred A. Knopf, 2000), chap. 28.

52. Stephen Brumwell, *White Devil: A True Story of War, Savagery, and Vengeance in Colonial America* (Cambridge, Mass.: Da Capo Press, 2005); John F. Ross, *War on the Run: The Epic*

Story of Robert Rogers and the Conquest of America's First Frontier (New York: Bantam Books, 2009).

53. Duane H. King, ed., *The Memoirs of Lt. Henry Timberlake: The Story of a Soldier, Adventurer, and Emissary to the Cherokees, 1756–1765* (Cherokee, N.C.: Museum of the Cherokee Indian Press, 2007), 35.

54. Tom Hatley, *The Dividing Paths: Cherokees and South Carolinians through the Era of Revolution* (New York: Oxford University Press, 1993), chap. 10.

55. Gregory Evans Dowd, *A Spirited Resistance: The North American Indian Struggle for Unity, 1745–1815* (Baltimore: Johns Hopkins University Press, 1992).

56. *Minutes of the Provincial Council of Pennsylvania (Colonial Records of Pennsylvania),* 16 vols. (Philadelphia: Jo. Severns [and other printers], 1851–53), 5:146–47.

57. Quoted in Calloway, *American Revolution in Indian Country,* 7, 59.

58. Richter, *Ordeal of the Longhouse,* 22–23, 43.

59. Fur, *Nation of Women,* 40.

60. Fur, *Nation of Women,* chap. 3.

61. James Axtell, ed., *The Indian Peoples of Eastern America: A Documentary History of the Sexes* (New York: Oxford University Press, 1981), 156–57.

62. Quoted in Lois M. Feister and Bonnie Pulis, "Molly Brant: Her Domestic and Political Roles in Eighteenth-Century New York," in *Northeastern Indian Lives, 1632–1816,* ed. Robert S. Grumet (Amherst: University of Massachusetts Press, 1996), 313.

63. Theda Perdue, *Cherokee Women: Gender and Culture Change, 1700–1835* (Lincoln: University of Nebraska Press, 1998), 186.

64. John Demos, *The Unredeemed Captive: A Family Story from Early America* (New York: Alfred A. Knopf, 1994); Evan Haefeli and Kevin Sweeney, *Captors and Captives: The 1704 French and Indian Raid on Deerfield* (Amherst: University of Massachusetts Press, 2003); Evan Haefeli and Kevin Sweeney, *Captive Histories: English, French, and Native Narratives of the 1704 Deerfield Raid* (Amherst: University of Massachusetts Press, 2006). For multiple perspectives on the raid, see www.1704.deerfield.history.museum.

65. Ann M. Little, *Abraham in Arms: War and Gender in Colonial New England* (Philadelphia: University of Pennsylvania Press, 2007).

66. Ian K. Steele, *Setting All the Captives Free: Capture, Adjustment, and Recollection in Allegheny Country* (Montreal: McGill-Queens University Press, 2013).

67. Catherine Cameron, *Invisible Citizens: Captives and Their Consequences* (Salt Lake City: University of Utah Press, 2008); Cameron, "Captives and Culture Change," *Current Anthropology* 52 (2011), 169–209.

68. Armand Francis Lucier, comp., *Pontiac's Conspiracy and Other Indian Affairs: Notices Abstracted from Colonial Newspapers, 1763–1765* (Bowie, Md Heritage Books, 2000), 146 (Hans Fife); William Smith, *An Historical Account of the Expedition against the Ohio Indians in the Year 1764* (Cincinnati, 1868), 80–81.

69. Loretta Fowler, "The Great Plains from the Arrival of the Horse to 1885," in *The Cambridge History of the Native Peoples of the Americas,* vol. 1, pt. 2, ed. Bruce G. Trigger and Wilcomb E. Washburn (Cambridge: Cambridge University Press, 1996), 2–8.

70. Joseph M. Marshall III, *The Day the World Ended at Little Bighorn: A Lakota History* (New York: Viking Penguin, 2006), 39, 41.

71. John Stands In Timber and Margot Liberty, *Cheyenne Memories* (Lincoln: University of Nebraska Press, 1972), 40, 117.

72. Frank B. Linderman, *Pretty-shield, Medicine Woman of the Crows* (Lincoln: University of Nebraska Press, 1972), 83.

73. Pekka Hämäläinen, "The Rise and Fall of Plains Indian Horse Cultures," *Journal of American History,* 90 (2003), 833–66.

74. Elliott West, *The Way to the West: Essays on the Central Plains* (Albuquerque: University of New Mexico Press, 1995), 15; West, "Called Out People: The Cheyennes and the Central Plains," *Montana: The Magazine of Western History* 48 (Summer 1998), 2–15.

75. Richard White, "The Winning of the West: The Expansion of the Western Sioux in the Eighteenth and Nineteenth Centuries," *Journal of American History* 65 (September 1978), 319–43.

76. On the limitations of European knowledge about the West, see Paul W. Mapp, *The Elusive West and the Contest for Empire, 1713–1763* (Chapel Hill: University of North Carolina Press, 2011).

77. Colin G. Calloway, *One Vast Winter Count: The Native American West before Lewis and Clark* (Lincoln: University of Nebraska Press, 2003), 250–60; Juliana Barr, "Diplomatic Ritual in the 'Land of the Tejas,'" chap. 1 in *Peace Came in the Form of a Woman*; Juliana Barr, "Beyond Their Control: Spaniards in Native Texas," in *Choice, Persuasion, and Coercion: Social Control on Spain's North American Frontiers,* ed. Jesús F. de la Teja and Ross Frank (Albuquerque: University of New Mexico Press, 2005), 154–58.

78. Pekka Hämäläinen, *The Comanche Empire* (New Haven: Yale University Press, 2008); Blackhawk, *Violence over the Land,* 35–54.

79. Thomas, ed., *The Plains Indians and New Mexico, 1751–1778,* 63–156, quote at 132.

80. Colin G. Calloway, *The Western Abenakis of Vermont, 1600–1800: War, Migration, and the Survival of an Indian People* (Norman: University of Oklahoma Press, 1990), Stevens quote at p. 162.

81. Anderson, *Crucible of War,* chap. 28.

82. Reuben Gold Thwaites, ed., *Early Western Travels, 1748–1846* (Cleveland: Arthur H. Clark, 1904), 1: 212.

83. Thwaites, ed., *Early Western Travels,* 1: 274, 278.

84. Anderson, *Crucible of War,* 284.

85. Quoted in Francis Parkman, *The Conspiracy of Pontiac.* (New York: E. P. Dutton, 1908) 2: 15.

86. "A Narrative of the Captivity of Mrs. Johnson," in Colin G. Calloway, comp., *North Country Captives: Selected Narratives of Indian Captivity from Vermont and New Hampshire* (Hanover, N.H.: University Press of New England, 1992), 62.

87. Colin G. Calloway, ed., *Dawnland Encounters: Indians and Europeans in Northern New England* (Hanover, N.H.: University Press of New England, 1991), 239.

88. Rev. Henry H. Saunderson, *History of Charlestown, New Hampshire* (Claremont, N.H.: The Claremont Manufacturing Company, 1876).

89. Alden T. Vaughan, *Transatlantic Encounters: American Indians in Britain, 1500–1776* (Cambridge: Cambridge University

Press, 2006); Christian F. Feest, ed., *Indians and Europe: An Interdisciplinary Collection of Essays* (1989; repr., Lincoln: University of Nebraska Press, 1999); Kate Fullagar, *The Savage Visit: New World People and Popular Imperial Culture in Britain, 1710–1795* (Berkeley: University of California Press, 2012).
90. Eric Hinderaker, *The Two Hendricks: Unraveling a Mohawk Mystery* (Cambridge, Mass.: Harvard University Press, 2010). Hinderaker distinguishes between this individual and a later chief of the same name who was an ally of Sir William Johnson and died at the battle of Lake George in 1755.

91. Nancy Shoemaker, "Wonder and Repulsion: North American Indians in Eighteenth-Century Europe," in *Europe Observed: Multiple Gazes in Early Modern Encounters,* ed. Kumkum Chatterjee and Clement Hawes (Lewisburg: Bucknell University Press, 2008), 173–97, quote at 185.
92. Stephanie Pratt, *American Indians in British Art, 1700–1840* (Norman: University of Oklahoma Press, 2005), 54–57.
93. Joanna Brooks, ed., *The Collected Writings of Samson Occom, Mohegan: Leadership and Literature in Eighteenth-Century Native America* (New York: Oxford University Press, 2006), 266–67.

SUGGESTED READINGS

Anderson, Fred. *Crucible of War: The Seven Years' War and the Fate of Empire in British North America, 1754–1766.* New York: Alfred A. Knopf, 2000.

Anderson, Gary Clayton. *The Indian Southwest, 1530–1830: Ethnogenesis and Reinvention.* Norman: University of Oklahoma Press, 1999.

Axtell, James. *The European and the Indian: Essays in the Ethnohistory of Colonial North America.* New York: Oxford University Press, 1981.

———. *The Invasion Within: The Contest of Cultures in Colonial North America.* New York: Oxford University Press, 1985.

———. *Natives and Newcomers: The Cultural Origins of North America.* New York: Oxford University Press, 2001.

Barr, Juliana. *Peace Came in the Form of a Woman: Indians and Spaniards in the Texas Borderlands.* Chapel Hill: University of North Carolina Press, 2007.

Blackhawk, Ned, ed. *Ethnohistory* 54, no. 4, "Between Empires: Indians in the American West during the Age of Empire" (Fall 2007).

Blackhawk, Ned. *Violence over the Land: Indians and Empires in the Early American West.* Cambridge, Mass.: Harvard University Press, 2006.

Bowne, Eric. *The Westo Indians: Slave Traders of the Early Colonial South.* Tuscaloosa: University of Alabama Press, 2005.

Brooks, Joanna, ed. *The Collected Writings of Samson Occom, Mohegan: Leadership and Literature in Eighteenth-Century Native America.* New York: Oxford University Press, 2006.

Brooks, Lisa. *The Common Pot: The Recovery of Native Space in the Northeast.* Minneapolis: University of Minnesota Press, 2008.

Calloway, Colin G., ed. *Dawnland Encounters: Indians and Europeans in Northern New England.* Hanover, N.H.: University Press of New England, 1991.

———. *New Worlds for All: Indians, Europeans, and the Remaking of Early America.* Baltimore: Johns Hopkins University Press, 1997.

———, comp. *North Country Captives: Selected Narratives of Indian Captivity from Vermont and New Hampshire.* Hanover, N.H.: University Press of New England, 1992.

———. *One Vast Winter Count: The Native American West before Lewis and Clark.* Lincoln: University of Nebraska Press, 2003.

———. *Pen and Ink Witchcraft: Treaties and Treaty Making in American Indian History.* New York: Oxford University Press, 2013.

———. *The Shawnees and the War for America.* New York: Viking Penguin, 2007.

———. *The Western Abenakis of Vermont, 1600–1800: War, Migration, and the Survival of an Indian People.* Norman: University of Oklahoma Press, 1990.

———, ed. *The World Turned Upside Down: Indian Voices from Early America.* Boston: Bedford Books, 1994.

Cayton, Andrew R. L., and Fredrika J. Teute, eds. *Contact Points: American Frontiers from the Mohawk Valley to the Mississippi, 1750–1830.* Chapel Hill: University of North Carolina Press, 1998.

Demos, John. *The Unredeemed Captive: A Family Story from Early America.* New York: Alfred A. Knopf, 1994.

Dolin, Eric Jay. *Fur, Fortune, and Empire: The Epic History of the Fur Trade in America.* New York: W. W. Norton, 2010.

Dowd, Gregory Evans. *A Spirited Resistance: The North American Indian Struggle for Unity, 1745–1815.* Baltimore: Johns Hopkins University Press, 1992.

Downes, Randolph C. *Council Fires on the Upper Ohio: A Narrative of Indian Affairs in the Upper Ohio Valley until 1795.* Pittsburgh: University of Pittsburgh Press, 1940.

DuVal, Kathleen. *The Native Ground: Indians and Colonists in the Heart of the Continent.* Philadelphia: University of Pennsylvania Press, 2006.

Ethridge, Robbie. *From Chicaza to Chickasaw: The European Invasion and the Transformation of the Mississippian World, 1540–1715.* Chapel Hill: University of North Carolina Press, 2010.

Ethridge, Robbie, and Sheri M. Shuck-Hall, eds. *Mapping the Mississippian Shatter Zone: The Colonial Indian Slave Trade and Regional Instability in the American South.* Lincoln: University of Nebraska Press, 2009.

Fisher, Linford D. *The Indian Great Awakening: Religion and the Shaping of Native Cultures in Early America.* New York: Oxford University Press, 2012.

Fur, Gunlög. *A Nation of Women: Gender and Colonial Encounters among the Delaware Indians.* Philadelphia: University of Pennsylvania Press, 2009.

Gallay, Alan, ed. *Indian Slavery in Colonial America.* Lincoln: University of Nebraska Press, 2009.

———. *The Indian Slave Trade: The Rise of the English Empire in the American South, 1670–1717.* New Haven: Yale University Press, 2002.

Grumet, Robert S. *The Munsee Indians: A History.* Norman: University of Oklahoma Press, 2009.

Haefeli, Evan, and Kevin Sweeney. *Captors and Captives: The 1704 French and Indian Raid on Deerfield.* Amherst: University of Massachusetts Press, 2003.

Hall, Joseph M., Jr. *Zamumo's Gifts: Indian-European Exchange in the Colonial Southeast.* Philadelphia: University of Pennsylvania Press, 2009.

Hämäläinen, Pekka. *The Comanche Empire.* New Haven: Yale University Press, 2008.

Harper, Stephen Craig. *Promised Land: Penn's Holy Experiment, the Walking Purchase, and the Dispossession of Delawares, 1600–1763.* Bethlehem, Pa.: Lehigh University Press, 2006.

Hatley, Tom. *The Dividing Paths: Cherokees and South Carolinians through the Era of Revolution.* New York: Oxford University Press, 1993.

Hinderaker, Eric. *Elusive Empires: Constructing Colonialism in the Ohio Valley, 1673–1800.* Cambridge: Cambridge University Press, 1997.

———. *The Two Hendricks: Unraveling a Mohawk Mystery.* Cambridge, Mass.: Harvard University Press, 2010.

Juricek, John T. *Colonial Georgia and the Creeks: Anglo-Indian Diplomacy on the Southern Frontier, 1733–1763.* Gainesville: University Press of Florida, 2010.

Kalter, Susan, ed. *Benjamin Franklin, Pennsylvania, and the First Nations: The Treaties of 1736–62.* Urbana: University of Illinois Press, 2006.

Kelton, Paul. *Cherokee Medicine, Colonial Germs: An Indigenous Nation's Fight against Smallpox, 1518–1824.* Norman: University of Oklahoma Press, 2015.

———. *Epidemics and Enslavement: Biological Catastrophe in the Native Southeast, 1492–1715.* Lincoln: University of Nebraska Press, 2007.

Kenny, Kevin. *Peaceable Kingdom Lost: The Paxton Boys and the Destruction of William Penn's Holy Experiment.* New York: Oxford University Press, 2009.

Kugel, Rebecca, and Lucy Eldersveld Murphy, eds. *Native Women's History in Eastern North America before 1900: A Guide to Research and Writing.* Lincoln: University of Nebraska Press, 2007.

Lakomäki, Sami. *Gathering Together: The Shawnee People through Diaspora and Nationhood, 1600–1870.* New Haven: Yale University Press, 2014.

LaVere, David. *The Tuscarora War: Indians, Settlers, and the Fight for the Carolina Colonies.* Chapel Hill: University of North Carolina Press, 2014.

Little, Ann M. *Abraham in Arms: War and Gender in Colonial New England.* Philadelphia: University of Pennsylvania Press, 2007.

MacLeitch, Gail D. *Imperial Entanglements: Iroquois Change and Persistence on the Frontiers of Empire.* Philadelphia: University of Pennsylvania Press, 2011.

Mancall, Peter C. *Deadly Medicine: Indians and Alcohol in Early America.* Ithaca, N.Y.: Cornell University Press, 1995.

Mancall, Peter C., and James H. Merrell, eds. *American Encounters: Natives and Newcomers from European Contact to Indian Removal, 1500–1850.* 2nd ed. New York: Routledge, 2007.

Mandell, Daniel R. *Behind the Frontier: Indians in Eighteenth-Century Eastern Massachusetts.* Lincoln: University of Nebraska Press, 1996.

Mapp, Paul W. *The Elusive West and the Contest for Empire, 1713–1763.* Chapel Hill: University of North Carolina Press, 2011.

Martin, Joel W., and Mark A. Nicholas, eds. *Native Americans, Christianity, and the Reshaping of the American Religious Landscape.* Chapel Hill: University of North Carolina Press, 2010.

Merrell, James H. *The Indians' New World: Catawbas and Their Neighbors from European Contact through the Era of Removal.* Chapel Hill: University of North Carolina Press, 1989; 2nd ed., 2009.

———. *Into the American Woods: Negotiators on the Pennsylvania Frontier.* New York: W. W. Norton, 1999.

———, ed. *The Lancaster Treaty of 1744, with Related Documents.* Boston: Bedford/St. Martin's, 2008.

Merritt, Jane T. *At the Crossroads: Indians and Empires on a Mid-Atlantic Frontier, 1700–1763.* Chapel Hill: University of North Carolina Press, 2003.

Midtrød, Tom Arne, *The Memory of All Ancient Customs: Native American Diplomacy in the Colonial Hudson Valley.* Ithaca, N.Y.: Cornell University Press, 2012.

Namias, June, ed. *A Narrative of the Life of Mrs. Mary Jemison.* Norman: University of Oklahoma Press, 1992.

———. *White Captives: Gender and Ethnicity on the American Frontier.* Chapel Hill: University of North Carolina Press, 1993.

O'Brien, Jean M. *Dispossession by Degrees: Indian Land and Identity in Natick, Massachusetts, 1650–1790.* Cambridge: Cambridge University Press, 1997.

Oliphant, John. *Peace and War on the Anglo-Cherokee Frontier, 1756–63.* Baton Rouge: Louisiana State University Press, 2001.

O'Toole, Fintan. *White Savage: William Johnson and the Invention of America.* New York: Farrar, Straus, and Giroux, 2005.

Parmenter, Jon. *The Edge of the Woods: Iroquoia, 1534–1701.* East Lansing: Michigan State University Press, 2010.

Perdue, Theda. *Cherokee Women: Gender and Culture Change, 1700–1835.* Lincoln: University of Nebraska Press, 1998.

Piker, Joshua. *Okfuskee: A Creek Indian Town in Colonial America.* Cambridge, Mass.: Harvard University Press, 2004.

Preston, David L. *The Texture of Contact: European and Indian Settler Communities on the Frontier of Iroquoia, 1667–1783.* Lincoln: University of Nebraska Press, 2009.

Richter, Daniel K. *Before the Revolution: America's Ancient Pasts.* Cambridge, Mass.: Harvard University Press, 2011.

———. *Facing East from Indian Country: A Native History of Early America.* Cambridge, Mass.: Harvard University Press, 2001.

————. *The Ordeal of the Longhouse: The Peoples of the Iroquois League in the Era of European Colonization*. Chapel Hill: University of North Carolina Press, 1992.

————. *Trade, Land, Power: The Struggle for Eastern North America*. Philadelphia: University of Pennsylvania Press, 2013.

Rubin, Julius H. *Tears of Repentance: Christian Indian Identity and Community in Colonial Southern New England*. Lincoln: University of Nebraska Press, 2013.

Rushforth, Brett. *Bonds of Alliance: Indigenous and Atlantic Slaveries in New France*. Chapel Hill: University of North Carolina Press, 2012.

Schutt, Amy C. *Peoples of the River Valleys: The Odyssey of the Delaware Indians*. Philadelphia: University of Pennsylvania Press, 2007.

Shannon, Timothy J. *Indians and Colonists at the Crossroads of Empire: The Albany Congress of 1754*. Ithaca, N.Y.: Cornell University Press, 2000.

————. *Iroquois Diplomacy on the Early American Frontier*. New York: Viking Penguin, 2008.

Silver, Peter. *Our Savage Neighbors: How Indian War Transformed Early America*. New York: W. W. Norton, 2008.

Sleeper-Smith, Susan, ed. *Rethinking the Fur Trade: Cultures of Exchange in an Atlantic World*. Lincoln: University of Nebraska Press, 2009.

Snyder, Christina. *Slavery in Indian Country: The Changing Face of Captivity in Early America*. Cambridge, Mass.: Harvard University Press, 2010.

Steele, Ian K. *Setting All the Captives Free: Capture, Adjustment, and Recollection in Allegheny Country*. Montreal: McGill-Queens University Press, 2013.

Szasz, Margaret Connell. *Indian Education in the American Colonies, 1607–1783*. Albuquerque: University of New Mexico Press, 1988.

Tanner, Helen Hornbeck, ed. *Atlas of Great Lakes Indian History*. Norman: University of Oklahoma Press, 1987.

Usner, Daniel H., Jr. *Indians, Settlers, and Slaves in a Frontier Exchange Economy: The Lower Mississippi Valley before 1783*. Chapel Hill: University of North Carolina Press, 1992.

Vaughan, Alden T. *Transatlantic Encounters: American Indians in Britain, 1500–1776*. Cambridge: Cambridge University Press, 2006.

Vaughan, Alden T., and Edward W. Clark, eds. *Puritans among the Indians: Accounts of Captivity and Redemption, 1676–1724*. Cambridge, Mass.: Harvard University Press, 1981.

Warren, Stephen. *The Worlds the Shawnees Made: Migration and Violence in Early America*. Chapel Hill: University of North Carolina Press, 2014.

Wheeler, Rachel. *To Live upon Hope: Mohicans and Missionaries in the Eighteenth-Century Northeast*. Ithaca, N.Y.: Cornell University Press, 2008.

White, Richard. *The Middle Ground: Indians, Empires, and Republics in the Great Lakes Region, 1650–1815*. Cambridge: Cambridge University Press, 1991.

————. "The Winning of the West: The Expansion of the Western Sioux in the Eighteenth and Nineteenth Centuries." *Journal of American History* 65 (September 1978): 319–43.

White, Sophie. *Wild Frenchmen and Frenchified Indians: Material Culture and Race in Colonial Louisiana*. Philadelphia: University of Pennsylvania Press, 2012.

Witgen, Michael J. *An Infinity of Nations: How the Native New World Shaped Modern America*. Philadelphia: University of Pennsylvania Press, 2012.

Wood, Peter H., Gregory A. Waselkov, and M. Thomas Hatley, eds. *Powhatan's Mantle: Indians in the Colonial Southeast*. Lincoln: University of Nebraska Press, 1989.

4

Revolutions East and West

1763–1800

FOCUS QUESTIONS

1. What was the purpose and effect of the Royal Proclamation of 1763?

2. Who was vying for Indian support before and during the American Revolution, and what did each potential ally offer or threaten?

3. How did Indian nations unify or divide in response to American land policy?

4. What distinguished Native American experiences in the East from those in the West in the latter half of the eighteenth century?

WORLDS TURNED UPSIDE DOWN

BY 1763 DIRECT AND INDIRECT CONTACT with Europeans had generated far-reaching changes throughout the Eastern Woodlands and across the Great Plains. Conflict and competition had escalated everywhere, as Indians resisted increasing encroachment on their lands and ways of life, as tribes fought for hunting territories and slaves and for access to trade goods, firearms, and horses, and as European wars for empire spilled over into Indian country and involved Indian warriors. After more than half a century of conflict with France, Britain emerged as the victorious colonial power in eastern North America. At the Peace of

Paris in 1763, more American territory changed hands than at any other treaty, before or since. France ceded Canada and its claims east of the Mississippi to Britain, and it transferred Louisiana to Spain, mainly to keep it out of the hands of the British. The European nations exchanged huge swaths of territory without consulting the indigenous nations who lived there but they could not ignore the reality that Indian peoples and Indian power still dominated most of the continent.[1] Britain and Spain both set about trying to govern their hugely expanded empires in North America, and in doing so, both had to try and regulate the frontier and deal with Indian nations that were also adjusting to, and in some cases, creating far-reaching changes. Britain's efforts initiated a series of unanticipated events that culminated in the American Revolution.[2]

Pontiac's War: Indians Confront a New Empire

Indian tribes east of the Mississippi that had traded and allied with the French now found that they had to deal with the representatives of King George. Many British officials regarded the Indians as a defeated people and, with the war won, saw little reason to cultivate their allegiance. The Iroquois could no longer play the English and the French against each other, and with peace a flood of English settlers invaded Indian lands. Inevitably, conflict ensued. In one of the most famous Indian wars for independence, named after the Ottawa chief Pontiac, tribes in the Great Lakes and the Ohio valley regions rallied against the British.

Indians resented the new British presence and power. They had expected the British to enhance their diplomacy with gifts, as the French had, but Britain, on the brink of financial ruin at the end of the most expensive war it had ever fought, cut back on what it considered to be extraneous and costly niceties. Jeffery Amherst, the commander of the British army in North America at the end of the French and Indian War, exacerbated the Indians' worst fears. Arrogant and ignorant of Indian ways, Amherst viewed an empire as something to be governed, not negotiated over and cultivated by maintaining a mutually beneficial relationship with Indians. He demanded the return of prisoners, many of whom had been adopted and were now, in Indian eyes, Indians. His soldiers and

1787	Northwest Ordinance pledges United States to conduct Indian affairs with "the utmost good faith"
1789	Congress assigns Indian affairs to the War Department
1789	U.S. Constitution gives Congress sole power to regulate commerce with Indian tribes
1790	Congress passes the first Indian Trade and Intercourse Act
1790	Northwestern tribes defeat General Josiah Harmar
1791	Northwestern tribes defeat General Arthur St. Clair
1791–1793	George Vancouver trades with Indian peoples on Pacific Northwest Coast
1794	Anthony Wayne defeats northwestern tribes at Fallen Timbers
1794	First U.S.–Indian treaty providing education for Indians (Oneidas, Tuscaroras, and Stockbridges)
1795	Treaty of Greenville: northwestern tribes cede most of Ohio to United States
1799	The Russian American Company takes control of the Alaskan coast

his forts threatened Indian lands, and British traders entered Indian villages for profit, not for an exchange between allies. Amherst prohibited all gift giving at the western posts and placed restrictions on the amounts of powder and lead traded to Indians. By sending in troops and withholding gifts, he sent a clear message, reinforced by the language of British officers: Britain intended to reduce the Indians to submission and take over their land. But Indians were not about to accept Englishmen in the place of the French who had been ousted from their lands.[3]

A Delaware prophet named Neolin gave spiritual force to Indian discontent and gained a following, preaching that the Indians could redeem themselves only by casting off alien influences and returning to traditional ways.[4] Pontiac turned

Sinclair's Lith. Phil.ᵃ
EVENTS OF INDIAN HISTORY.
Massacre of the Indians at Lancaster by the Paxton boys in 1763.

◆ ***Massacre of the Indians at Lancaster by the Paxton Boys in 1763*** **(1841)**
Two days after Christmas 1763, the "Paxton Boys," who had killed six Indians at Conestoga two weeks earlier, rode into Lancaster, Pennsylvania, and murdered fourteen Indians who had taken refuge in the workhouse. *The Library Company of Philadelphia, www.librarycompany.org.*

growing anti-British sentiment into direct action by calling for the expulsion of the redcoats from Indian country. Most of the western posts were garrisoned by a handful of soldiers, isolated from supply and support and often dependent on Indian hunters for provisions. In 1763 Indian warriors responding to Pontiac's call captured every British fort west of the Appalachians except Niagara, Detroit, and Fort Pitt, to which they laid siege. Indians in the borderlands around Michilimackinac, where Lakes Huron and Michigan meet, prevented the war from spreading because they were more concerned with maintaining trade networks than with the threat of settlers on their lands,[5] but elsewhere the Indians drove the redcoats back on almost every front, and backcountry settlers fled east to escape Indian raiding parties. However, the combination of European military superiority and disease among the Indian forces eventually turned the tide. Colonel Henry Bouquet and his troops fought off an Indian attack at the Battle of Bushy Run in western Pennsylvania in October 1763, and in an act of germ warfare, Indians who came to the besieged garrison at Fort Pitt were given blankets from a smallpox hospital. Indian hating escalated: in December 1763 Scotch-Irish frontiersmen in Pennsylvania known as the Paxton Boys slaughtered peaceful Conestoga Indians in an act of racial hatred and later marched on Philadelphia in an act of frustration at their colonial government's failure to defend its frontiers.[6]

Normally considered an aftermath to the Seven Years' War, Pontiac's War was really a continuation of that conflict, as Indian fighters who had not been defeated refused to accept the conditions of peace that Britain imposed and France accepted. A dozen years before American colonists declared independence, American Indians fought for their independence against the British and compelled them to think seriously about the place of Native peoples in the British Empire. Britain's response prompted another war of independence.

Attempting to Draw a Line

In 1763 the British attempted to regulate the frontier and avoid further Indian wars of resistance by prohibiting settlement on Indian lands west of the Appalachian Mountains. The Royal Proclamation issued in October of that year established the Appalachians as the boundary line between Indian and colonial lands and stipulated "that no private Person do presume to make any Purchase from the said Indians"[7] (Map 4.1). Only the crown's representatives acting in formal council with Indian nations could negotiate land transfers, and only licensed traders would be permitted to operate in Indian country. The government hoped such measures would prevent future Indian wars. But, like the Indian chiefs who were unable to control their young warriors, the distant British government was unable to prevent its subjects from encroaching on Indian lands. British armed forces in the West constituted a very thin red line, and even when the army tried to eject squatters, its efforts were inadequate to the task.

The Royal Proclamation did little to placate Indian-hating frontier settlers, and it infuriated members of the colonial elite who had investments in western lands that could not be realized now that the sale of those lands was illegal.

◆ **Map 4.1 Proclamation Line of 1763**

At the Treaty of Paris in 1763, which ended the Seven Years' War, France ceded its North American territorial claims to Britain. France had already ceded its lands west of the Mississippi to Spain to keep them out of British hands.

Investors such as George Washington, Thomas Jefferson, Arthur Lee, and Patrick Henry saw tyranny in Britain's interference with their freedom to make a fortune out of Indian lands; a new British and Indian barrier threatened to replace the old French and Indian barrier. Washington began to contemplate separating from the empire he had served in the French and Indian War. Writing to a friend and business associate in 1767, he said:

> I can never look upon that Proclamation in any other light (but this I may say between ourselves) than as a temporary expedient to quiet the Minds of the Indians & [one that] must fall of course in a few years especially when those Indians are consenting to our Occupying the Lands. [A]ny Person therefore who neglects the present opportunity of hunting out good Lands & in some Measure Marking & distinguishing them for their own (in order to keep others from settling them) will never regain it.[8]

The British themselves did not intend the proclamation line to be a permanent barrier. The king's agents, meeting with Indian tribes in formal and open council, could negotiate cessions of land to the crown that would push the line westward. However, when Sir William Johnson met with the Iroquois at Fort Stanwix in 1768, he exceeded his authority and purchased a huge tract of land from the assembled Indian delegates. Most of the land the Iroquois sold was south of the Ohio River — hunting territory claimed by the Shawnees and Cherokees, who were not at the treaty negotiations. The Iroquois delegates deftly diverted colonial expansion away from their own land but lost prestige among western tribes who regarded the Fort Stanwix treaty as an act of betrayal.[9] (See Map 4.7, "Cherokee Land Cessions in the Colonial and Revolutionary Eras, 1721–1785," page 235.) Combined with new boundary lines negotiated with the Cherokees at the Treaty of Hard Labor that same year and at the Treaty of Lochaber in 1770, the Fort Stanwix cession thrust a wedge into the heart of Indian country. Colonists swarmed into Kentucky, confident that these lands had been duly ceded, and clashed with Shawnee and Cherokee warriors determined to defend their hunting grounds against trespassers.

Continued encroachment on Shawnee land produced open conflict with the Virginians in 1774 in a war named after Lord Dunmore, the colonial governor of Virginia. The Shawnee chief Cornstalk argued against war but led his warriors at the Battle of Point Pleasant at the junction of the Ohio and Kanawha rivers in present-day West Virginia. After a day-long battle the Shawnees were defeated and made peace, reaffirming the Ohio River as their boundary, but hostilities had hardly ceased before the American Revolution broke out. The Shawnees and their neighbors would once again fight for their lands.

INDIANS AND THE AMERICAN REVOLUTION

Indians during the Revolution were fighting for their freedom just as much as Americans were. But from the very start of the conflict, Americans portrayed Indians as enemies of freedom. In the Declaration of Independence, Thomas Jefferson clearly described their role. Jefferson wrote that among his other oppressive acts, Britain's King George III had "endeavoured to bring on the inhabitants of our frontiers, the merciless Indian Savages whose known rule of warfare, is an undistinguished destruction of all ages, sexes and conditions." Inscribed in the founding document of the United States, almost a sacred text, Jefferson's words placed Indians on the wrong side of the struggle for liberty and on the wrong side of history from the very beginning of the Revolution. In this view, while Americans fought for their rights and freedoms, Native Americans, the vicious pawns of a tyrannical king, fought against them. The reality was much more complex.

Indian Loyalties Divided

The Declaration of Independence announced the separation of thirteen former colonies from the British Empire. It took eight years of often bitter fighting to make independence a reality. Many men who had fought for the crown in the French and Indian War now fought against the king's troops; others remained loyal to the king, and still others found themselves undecided, caught between the two sides. Both the Americans and the British tried to enlist Indian allies. The American Revolution was a source of considerable confusion to Indian peoples: the British appeared to have fallen to fighting among themselves. At first most Indians chose to remain neutral in what they regarded as a family quarrel. "We must be Fools indeed to imagine that they regard us or our Interest who want to bring us into an unnecessary War," said the Seneca chief Guyasuta or Kayashuta.[10] But diplomatic and economic pressures rendered neutrality difficult and dangerous. Different motives prompted different groups, but most Indians who fought in the Revolution sided with the British. They recognized that the war was a contest for Indian land as well as for American independence, and their experiences of the land hunger of American settlers convinced them that their best hopes of survival lay in supporting the crown. In Indian eyes, aggressive Americans posed a greater threat than did a distant king to their land, their liberty, and their way of life.

While most Indians eventually allied with the British, Indians in New England who were surrounded by American neighbors mostly supported the Patriot cause. Indians from Massachusetts and Connecticut fought at Bunker Hill. Rebecca Tanner, a Mohegan, lost five sons who served in the American army during the war.[11] Warriors from the mission town of Stockbridge in western Massachusetts were among the first Indians to fight in the conflict, joining Washington's army at the siege of Boston in 1775. They suffered heavy casualties throughout the war, only to find that their American neighbors had taken over their lands and most of their town while they were away fighting. Other Indian towns in New England also sustained heavy casualties but secured few rewards for their services.

Indians knew that Indian lands were at stake in the Revolution. By the war's outbreak in 1776, the Cherokees in the Southeast had seen their territory whittled away in a series of treaties (see Map 4.7, page 235), and land speculators and settlers were swarming the ceded lands. Young Cherokee men, frustrated by their fathers' policies of selling land and determined to prevent further erosion of the

Cherokee homeland, seized the outbreak of the Revolution as an occasion to drive trespassers off their lands and staged a coup during the war negotiations at Chota in May 1776, joining northern Shawnee, Delaware, and Mohawk delegates who called for resistance against the revolutionary colonists (see "Report from Cherokee Country," pages 238–40). Cherokee warriors attacked frontier settlements the following month, but they did so on their own, without British support and against the advice of British agents who urged them to wait until they could coordinate with His Majesty's troops. American forces immediately retaliated, burning Cherokee towns and forcing Cherokee chiefs to sue for peace, which they did at the cost of ceding even more land.[12]

Many Cherokees, led by a war chief named Dragging Canoe, migrated rather than make peace with the Americans and kept up the fight from new towns they built around Chickamauga Creek in southwestern Tennessee. American campaigns against the Chickamauga Cherokees sometimes struck the villages of those Cherokees who had made peace, which were closer and offered easier targets than those of the Chickamauga. The Revolution left the Cherokee Nation devastated and divided, but the Chickamaugas remained defiant and continued to fight against American dominance until 1795.

The Revolution also shattered the unity of the Iroquois Confederacy, the Six Nations in upstate New York who had managed to keep their ancient league intact throughout the French and Indian wars. The Mohawks, led by war chief Joseph Brant, supported the crown, as did most of the Onondagas, Cayugas, and Senecas, but the Oneidas and Tuscaroras leaned toward the colonists, due in no small measure to the influence of their missionary, Samuel Kirkland, who favored breaking with the Church of England. (See "An Oneida Declaration of Neutrality (1775)," pages 237–38). At the Battle of Oriskany in 1777, Oneidas fought alongside the Americans, while Mohawks and Senecas fought with the British, a devastating development in Iroquois society that was built around clan and kinship ties. Like the Cherokees, many Iroquois lost their homes during the Revolution. Mohawks were driven from the Mohawk Valley, and Oneidas fleeing retaliation lived in squalid refugee camps around Schenectady, New York. In the fall of 1779, responding to raids on the frontiers of New York and Pennsylvania, George Washington dispatched an American expedition to burn out the Iroquois. General John Sullivan's army marched through the heart of Iroquois country, burned some forty towns, cut down orchards, destroyed crops, "and left nothing but the bare soil and timber." The Indians pulled back as Sullivan advanced but returned to find their homes laid waste. Mary Jemison, who was living with the Senecas at the time, remembered in her old age that "we found that there was not a mouthful of any kind of sustenance left, not even enough to keep a child one day from perishing with hunger." That winter, the snow fell to a depth of five feet, and the weather became so bitterly cold "that almost all the game upon which the Indians depended for subsistence, perished, and reduced them almost to a state of starvation through that and three or four succeeding years."[13] (For more of Mary Jemison's experience, see "A Narrative of Her Life," pages 184–87.) Deprived of food and shelter, Iroquois refugees crowded around the British garrison at Fort Niagara. But Niagara stood at the end of a long supply line that was closed during the winter months when vessels from Montreal and Quebec could not navigate the ice-bound Great Lakes. The refugees at Niagara endured exposure, starvation, sickness, and misery during one of the coldest winters on record.

At the end of the war, many Iroquois relocated north of the new border to Canada rather than stay in New York and deal with the Americans. Joseph Brant and his followers settled on lands set aside for them by the British government on the Grand River in Ontario, the genesis of the Six Nations Reserve. Others — Senecas at Tonawanda and Buffalo Creek, for example — remained on their ancestral homeland and rebuilt their communities. American soldiers who had accompanied Sullivan told of the fertile lands they had marched through, and American settlers and land speculators eagerly awaited the end of the war. Former masters of the region, the Iroquois soon were struggling to survive in a new world dominated by Americans.

The Revolution turned the Ohio valley into a fiercely contested war zone. Henry Hamilton, the British commander at Detroit, and George Morgan, the American agent at Fort Pitt, competed for the allegiance of the tribes. The

◆ *Joseph Brant* **(c. 1797) by Charles Willson Peale**
The Mohawk Joseph Brant (1743–1807) was probably the most famous Indian of his day. He sat for portraits by such noted artists as George Romney and Gilbert Stuart, as well as by Peale. Educated at Eleazar Wheelock's Indian Charity School in Connecticut, Brant was bilingual and literate, and assisted in translating the gospel into Mohawk. He visited England twice, was received at court, and befriended the Prince of Wales. He was the protégé of Sir William Johnson, who married Brant's sister Molly. Brant became a war leader on the British side during the Revolution and led his people to the Grand River after the war. Though bitterly disappointed by Britain's abandonment of its Indian allies in 1783, he continued to play a pivotal role in relations between the northeastern Indians, the British, and the new United States. *Granger, NYC.*

Shawnee chief Cornstalk had led his warriors in Lord Dunmore's War, but now he counseled a neutral stance and worked to cultivate peaceful relations with the Americans. Seized under a flag of truce at Fort Randolph, Cornstalk was murdered by American militia in 1777. Most Shawnees made common cause with the British, who had been telling them they could expect nothing less than annihilation at the hands of the Americans, although Cornstalk's sister, Nonhelema, continued to work for peace and assisted the Americans. Kentucky militia crossed the Ohio River almost every year to raid Shawnee villages. In 1782 the Indians lured Daniel Boone and the Kentucky militia into an ambush and routed them at the Battle of Blue Licks. About half of the Shawnees migrated west to present-day Missouri, which was claimed by Spain. Those who remained moved their villages farther and farther away from American assault. By the end of the Revolution most Indians living in Ohio were concentrated in the northwestern region.

Like their Shawnee neighbors, the Delawares were initially reluctant to take up arms or support the British. In fact, the Delaware chief White Eyes led his people in making the Treaty of Fort Pitt in 1778, the first written Indian treaty concluded by the new United States. The Delawares and the U.S. Congress agreed to a defensive alliance, but that alliance was short-lived: later that year, American militiamen, who evidently regarded all Indians as enemies, murdered White Eyes, their best friend in the Ohio Indian country. The government claimed that he had died of smallpox, but the damage was done. Like the Shawnees, Delawares took up the hatchet and made Britain's war their own. Americans struck back, blindly. In 1782 a force of Pennsylvania militia marched into the town of Gnadenhütten in Ohio, a community of Delaware Indians who had converted to the Moravian faith. The Delawares were Christians and pacifists, but the militia recognized them only as their Delaware enemy. The Americans divided the residents into three groups — men, women, and children. Then, with the Indians kneeling before them singing hymns, the militiamen took up butchers' mallets and bludgeoned to death ninety-six people. Delaware warriors exacted brutal revenge when American soldiers fell into their hands.

Treaties of Peace and Conquest

In the East, the fighting between the redcoats, the rebels, and their Indian allies effectively ended after the British general Lord Cornwallis surrendered to Washington's army and their French allies at Yorktown in 1781. In the West, Indians continued their wars for independence, but in 1783, at the Treaty of Paris, an exhausted Britain recognized the independence of the United States and acknowledged American sovereignty over all territory south of the Great Lakes, east of the Mississippi, and north of Florida. There were no Indians at the Peace of Paris and Indians were not mentioned in its terms. In effect, Britain abandoned its Indian allies to the mercy of the Americans. Indians were furious and incredulous when they learned that their allies had sold them out and given away their lands. Many Indians had fought for the king throughout the war, but they were neither

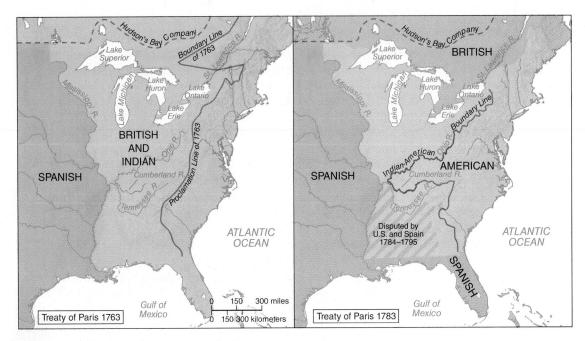

◆ **Map 4.2** **Changing Territorial Claims, 1763–1783**
Twenty years after the treaty that ended the Seven Years' War, another Treaty of Paris ended
the War of American Independence, and Britain ceded territory east of the Mississippi, south
of the Great Lakes, and north of Florida to the new United States. In all of these agreements,
the bulk of the territories transferred were Indian homelands, and Indian power stood
between paper claims and actual possession of the lands.

represented nor included in the peace treaty. Now they faced a new power that
regarded them as defeated enemies who had forfeited both lands and rights
(Map 4.2). The Iroquois were "thunderstruck" when they heard of the peace terms,
and the Mohawk chief Joseph Brant, who had fought for the British throughout
the war, was enraged and "cast down" to be betrayed by "Our Allies for whom we
have so often freely Bled."[14]

The Peace of Paris brought little peace in Indian country. In the summer of
1784, more than two hundred Indians—Iroquois, Shawnees, Cherokees, Creeks,
and others—who were visiting St. Louis told the Spanish governor they were
already feeling the effects of the American victory: "The Americans, a great deal
more ambitious and numerous than the English, put us out of our lands, forming
therein great settlements, extending themselves like a plague of locusts in the territories of the Ohio River which we inhabit." For them, the American victory meant
continued warfare and hunger; it was, they said, "the greatest blow that could have
been dealt us."[15] American veterans who had seen fertile lands while campaigning
in Indian country were eager to return and occupy them.

European colonial powers had learned to deal with Indian peoples by mastering their languages and the protocols of council-fire diplomacy, dealing with the Indians on their own terms, and lubricating negotiations with a steady supply of gifts and alcohol. Like the French before them, the British had come to understand that compromise, conciliation, and respectful dealings were generally more effective than force (or the threat of force) in a world where Indian power was significant and where Indian nations usually had a choice of European allies. The British had developed a policy whereby transfers of Indian lands were supposed to occur only in open council between tribal delegates and the king's authorized agents, although the crown was unable to enforce this policy on the borders of colonial settlement. The American colonists had fought for independence from Britain in part for the freedom to acquire Indian lands that had been barred to them by British policies. Like Britain before it, the new United States preferred to achieve its goals by treaty rather than by war and to obtain Indian lands by purchase rather than by risky and expensive military action, and it too lacked the ability to enforce its policies on distant and turbulent frontiers. Older Indian chiefs and federalist leaders tried to counsel moderation and restore order to the frontier after the bloodletting of the Revolution, but militants on both sides resented and resisted their efforts.[16]

With the British defeated, the United States was eager to impress on the Indians that a new era had dawned, and that the Americans were people not to be trifled with. Commissioners from "the Thirteen Fires" (the original thirteen states) traveled into Indian country and employed the rhetoric and symbols of council-fire diplomacy, but they never deviated from their purpose: to obtain tribal acquiescence to the claim that the United States had acquired all territory

◆ **F. Bartoli, *Portrait of Ki-on-twog-ky* (1796)**
The Allegany Seneca chief Ki-on-twog-ky or Cornplanter (c. 1740–1836) was also sometimes called John Abeel or Obail after his father, a Dutch trader. He fought against the Americans during the Revolution but then pursued a policy of cooperation with the new nation, signing treaties and helping to keep the Iroquois neutral in the war with the Northwestern confederacy in the 1790s. For his services, Pennsylvania granted Cornplanter "and his heirs forever" 1,500 acres of former Seneca land. This "Cornplanter grant," as it was known, was flooded by the Kinzua Dam in 1965 (see page 465). *Portrait of Ki-on-twog-ky, 1796 (oil on canvas), Bartoli, F. (fl. 1796)/© Collection of the New-York Historical Society, USA/Bridgeman Images.*

east of the Mississippi by right of conquest (see the scale of their success on Map 4.3, page 214). At Fort Stanwix, New York, in the fall of 1784, U.S. commissioners with troops at their backs met with the Seneca chief Cornplanter and other delegates from the Six Nations. Eighteen years earlier, the Iroquois had been co-participants in the largest Indian treaty council in colonial America and had transferred lands they claimed but did not occupy. Now commissioners from the United States, New York, and Pennsylvania were after Iroquois land and told the Iroquois, "You are a subdued people." The Americans said they were masters of all Indian lands "and can dispose of the Lands as we think proper or most convenient to ourselves." They demanded huge cessions of Iroquois country as the price of peace. Still divided by the war and now abandoned by their British allies, the Iroquois delegates agreed to cede much of the Seneca land in western New York and Pennsylvania as well as all their territory west of Pennsylvania, giving six hostages to guarantee their compliance.[17] When the Iroquois returned home they were met with scorn. The Six Nations in council refused to ratify the proposed treaty, but the United States proceeded as if the treaty were valid. Even the Oneidas and Tuscaroras, two of the Iroquois nations that had supported the Americans during the war, found their lands, too, were soon under pressure from settlers, land speculators, and state and federal agents. Indians from Stockbridge and elsewhere in New England moved west at the end of the war and built new Christian Indian communities on land set aside for them by the Oneidas, but they too were dispossessed and pushed farther west, first to Indiana and then to Wisconsin. As New Yorkers gobbled up Indian lands by treaty and chicanery, Indian communities showed signs of collapse and racial attitudes became entrenched. It became commonplace for "white people to say 'dirty as an Indian,' 'as lazy as an Indian,' 'as drunk as an Indian,' 'lie like Indians,'" reported an Oneida who saw what was happening. "And we Indians can only say 'Cheat like a white man.'"[18]

In January 1785 at Fort McIntosh in western Pennsylvania, U.S. commissioners met with delegates from the Wyandots, Anishinaabeg, Delawares, and Ottawas and demanded large cessions of land. When the Indians objected that the king of England had no right to transfer their lands to the United States, the Americans reminded them they were a defeated people. The Indian delegates attached their names to a treaty that was dictated to them. However, the Shawnees refused to attend. They had resisted expansion across the Ohio since the 1760s and knew from past experience that peace could only be bought with land. The Americans realized that no peace in the West would last if it did not include the Shawnees and dispatched emissaries to Shawnee villages.

In January 1786 more than two hundred Shawnees finally met the American commissioners at Fort Finney, where the Great Miami River meets the Ohio River in southwestern Ohio. Most of them were Maquachakes, the most conciliatory division of the tribe whose traditional responsibilities included healing and negotiation. The negotiations at Fort Finney graphically illustrate the contrast between the old and new ways of conducting diplomacy in Indian country. The Shawnees approached the treaty grounds in ceremonial fashion, and the proceedings opened with traditional speeches of welcome, smoking peace pipes, and dining. But this was not a meeting between equals, and the American commissioners were in no mood for conciliation. General Richard Butler had fought with Colonel Bouquet against the Shawnees and Delawares in 1764 and was a veteran of the Revolutionary War. George Rogers Clark, the other American commissioner, had made a name for himself as an Indian fighter during the Revolution and led assaults on Shawnee villages in 1780 and 1782. At the siege of Vincennes in 1779 he had tomahawked Indian prisoners within sight of the British garrison and tossed their still-kicking bodies into the river. "To excel them in barbarity," Clark declared, "is the only way to make war upon Indians."[19] He had little patience for the protocols of Indian diplomacy as practiced by the British and the French, preferring instead to dictate terms with the threat of force. "I am a man and a Warriour and not a councillor," he told Indians on the Wabash River in 1778; "I carry in my Right hand war and Peace in my left."[20] The Americans were determined to negotiate from a position of strength. When the Shawnees balked at the terms of the treaty, the Americans threw the Shawnees' wampum belt onto the table and threatened them with destruction. Moluntha, a Maquachake chief, urged his people to reconsider, and they grudgingly accepted the American terms.

But there was to be no peace for the Shawnees. Many who did not attend the treaty were outraged by the terms, and some refused to give up their captives as required by the treaty. Younger warriors accused Moluntha and the older chiefs of selling out to the Americans. Before the year was over, Kentucky militia raided Shawnee country again. At Moluntha's village, the old chief, carrying a copy of the treaty he had made at Fort Finney, met the militia, while his people hoisted an American flag. The Kentuckians destroyed the town and killed Moluntha in cold blood.

In the South, Alexander McGillivray of the Creeks headed a confederacy of tribes whose united power represented a considerable force in the decade after the Revolution. McGillivray was the son of a Scottish trader who provided him an education in Charleston, South Carolina, and a French-Creek mother who gave him membership in the influential Wind clan. McGillivray tried to protect Creek lands and independence in a region of competing and threatening international, intertribal, and state ambitions. He refused to recognize any claims of the United States to Creek lands based on the 1783 treaty with Britain because the Indians took no part in the treaty. In 1784 he signed a treaty with Spain at Pensacola, securing Spanish trade and protection of Creek lands. The United States signed its first treaty with the other major southeastern tribes — the Cherokees, Choctaws, and Chickasaws — at Hopewell in Georgia in 1785–86, reaffirming tribal boundaries in an effort to avoid all-out war on the southern frontier. In 1790 McGillivray led a delegation of Creek chiefs to New York, where they signed a treaty in which the United States guaranteed Creek territorial boundaries. But the southern states posed a more immediate threat than Congress, and Georgia continued to encroach on Creek and Cherokee lands (Map 4.3).

◆ **Map 4.3 United States Treaties and Indian Land Cessions to 1810**
Although individual states exerted pressure on the southern tribes, the new U.S. government
devoted most of its energy to acquiring Indian lands beyond the Ohio River and to defeating
the multitribal coalitions that resisted American expansion there. Treaties, by which Indian
nations sold lands or ceded them in return for peace, became major instruments in the
United States' policy of national expansion.

INDIANS CONFRONT AN EXPANDING NATION

Fully expecting another war with the young republic, the British in Canada maintained
alliances with Indians for years after the Revolution, but tribes south of the new international border now had to deal primarily with the United States. At the start of the
Revolution, despite American entreaties and assurances, the Indians had worried and
the British had warned that the Americans were only interested in taking the Indians'
lands and lives. The Shawnees' experiences in 1786 demonstrated that those worries
and warnings were well founded. Shawnees became leaders in forming a multitribal
coalition that resisted American expansion for a dozen years after the Revolution.

The United States Develops an Indian — and a Land — Policy

Once the United States had won its liberty from Britain, it began to build its own domain in the territory that Britain had transferred at the Peace of Paris in 1783 — lands inhabited by Indian peoples but which the United States now claimed by right of conquest. These territories were a vital national resource that would provide land for the new nation's citizens, fill an empty treasury, and guarantee a future of continuous growth and prosperity. But the government's formulation and implementation of national policy was frequently hampered and frustrated.

The United States regarded its expansion as inevitable, even divinely ordained, and recognized that its growth would entail dispossessing the original Indian inhabitants. Many government leaders were conscious of their country's position as the only republic on the world stage and wanted to ensure that national expansion was pursued honorably, but the drive to acquire land overwhelmed most moral scruples. Although George Washington, his secretary of war Henry Knox, Thomas Jefferson, and other good men of the founding fathers' generation wrestled with how to deal honorably with Indian people, the taking of Indian land was never in doubt. After the long war against Britain, the United States government had no money; its only resource was the land the British had ceded. Acquiring actual title to that land and transforming it into "public land" that could be sold to settlers was vital to the future, even the survival, of the new republic. Having won its independence from the British Empire, the United States turned to building an empire of its own — "an empire of liberty," Jefferson called it. In this empire, all citizens shared the benefits. But — and this was a question that plagued the nation and the national conscience for generations — who qualified as citizens? Did African Americans? Did women? Did Native Americans? And how could Americans claim to deal honorably with Indian people at the same time as they built their nation on Indian lands?

The Declaration of Independence provided answers: hadn't Indians fought against American rights and freedoms at the moment of the nation's birth? They could not now expect to share those rights and freedoms that had been won at so much cost. The United States had no obligation to include Indians in the body politic or to protect Indian lands. But the Declaration also made clear that Indians were "savages," and Washington, Jefferson, and others believed that the United States did have an obligation to "civilize" them. The United States must and would take the Indians' lands; that was inevitable. But it would give them civilization in return, and that was honorable. In the years following the Revolution, American settlers invaded Indian country; so too, at different times and places, did American soldiers, Indian agents, land speculators, treaty commissioners, and missionaries.

The new United States followed the British example in Indian relations: they set up an Indian department, established rules for the sale and transfer of Indian lands, and tried to regulate the advance of the frontier. The U.S. Constitution established national authority over the conduct of Indian relations, permitting only the federal government to negotiate and make treaties with Indian nations. The War Department assumed responsibility for Indian affairs, and the first

◆ **John Vanderlyn, *The Death of Jane McCrea* (1804)**
Americans used various forms of propaganda to gain support for their national policies
regarding Indian rights and land ownership. In John Vanderlyn's 1804 painting *The Death
of Jane McCrea*, the artist's depiction of a historical event — the alleged 1777 murder of a
European woman by the Indian allies of a British general — reflected and fueled popular stereotypes and fears about the victimization of innocent Americans by cruel Indian warriors. It
graphically imprinted on the minds of generations of Americans the notion embodied in the
Declaration of Independence, that Native Americans were "merciless Indian savages, whose
known rule of warfare is an undistinguished destruction of all ages, sexes, and conditions."
Granger, NYC.

secretary of war, Henry Knox, proved relatively humanitarian in his dealings
with Indians. In the 1780s, with dust from the Revolution not quite settled on the
frontiers, it made sense for Indian affairs to be under the jurisdiction of the War
Department. Furthermore, the United States in the 1780s was still an infant power,
with hostile European neighbors on its northern and southern borders. Both the

British in Canada and the Spanish in Florida continued to encourage and support Indians living within the United States' territory in resisting American expansion, while the young nation lacked the military resources and economic strength to establish control over its frontiers. The Indian Office, later known as the Bureau of Indian Affairs, was established in 1824; not until 1849 was it transferred from the War Department to the Department of the Interior.

Indian policy and the machinery for conducting Indian relations evolved slowly over time.[21] However, a clear and consistent objective of the United States' Indian policy from the end of the American Revolution to the Indian removals of the 1830s was the acquisition of lands between the Appalachians and the Mississippi, lands that the federal government bought "parcel by parcel." Like Europeans before them, Americans not only acquired the land but also established the legal framework by which they, and not the Indians, would own it.[22]

Further complicating the government's land policy were conflicting colonial charters; because of them, seven of the original states had land claims stretching to the Mississippi valley. The parties involved agreed that these claims should be ceded to the national government for the common good before the Articles of Confederation went into effect in 1781, and that the lands lying beyond those boundaries should fall into the public domain. By 1786 the states had ceded most of the lands north of the Ohio River. Southern states proved less compliant, however. Virginia retained claims to Kentucky, North Carolina did not cede Tennessee until 1789, and Georgia did not relinquish its claims to the territory of Alabama and Mississippi until 1802. In the early years of the republic, national expansion focused north of the Ohio, since the government had no lands to sell in the South.

In 1787 the Northwest Ordinance proclaimed that the United States would observe "the utmost good faith" in its dealings with Indian people and that their lands would not be invaded or taken except in "just and lawful wars authorized by Congress." But the ordinance also laid out a blueprint for national expansion: the Northwest Territory was to be divided into districts that, after passing through territorial status, would become states. Ohio, Indiana, Illinois, Michigan, and Wisconsin eventually entered the Union as states carved from the Northwest Territory. Indians who resisted American expansion soon found themselves subjected to "just and lawful wars."

In an effort to regulate conditions on the frontier and reaffirm that conduct of Indian affairs was reserved to the federal government, not the states, Congress passed the Indian Trade and Intercourse Act in 1790. Only licensed traders were permitted to operate in Indian country, and no transfers of Indian land were valid without congressional approval. The Trade and Intercourse Acts were renewed periodically until 1834. But, like the British after 1763, the fledgling U.S. government failed to control its own citizens on distant frontiers. Frontier settlers, squatters, and speculators seldom shared their government's concern for expansion with honor — all they wanted was expansion. Individual states, resentful of attempts by the federal government to restrict their rights, frequently made treaties that never received congressional approval.

Indians Build a United Defense

For Native Americans, the policies of the new nation translated into a dual assault on their lands and cultures, which were inextricably linked. They fought back, challenging the policies that threatened to transform their homelands into national real estate. "Our lands are our life and our breath," declared the Creek chief Hallowing King in 1787. "If we part with them, we part with our blood."[23] Giving up land meant more than shrinking a tribe's territorial base: it reduced the people's mobility and restricted the range of resources available to them, and it uprooted them from ancestral places to which they felt bound by communal traditions and stories. Tribes disputed American claims to their homelands, killed trespassers, and sometimes inflicted stunning defeats on American armies. Indian resistance continued to limit American expansion for many years. While American power was relatively weak after the Revolution, Indian power remained formidable in much of the western territory the United States claimed. Indian tribes usually acted in the specific interests of family and band rather than as a "race," but in times of crisis, Indian peoples often cooperated in impressive displays of unity.

In the 1780s a confederacy of northwestern tribes rejected treaties signed by individual tribes and refused to accept any American settlement west of the Ohio River. Delegates from the Iroquois, Hurons, Delawares, Shawnees, Ottawas, Anishinaabeg, Potawatomis, Miamis, and Wabash River tribes assembled in council at the mouth of the Detroit River in December 1786. They sent a message to Congress, assuring the Americans of their desire for peace, but insisting that "as landed matters are often the subject of our councils with you, a matter of the greatest importance and of general concern to us," any cession of lands "should be made in the most public manner, and by the united voice of the confederacy; holding all partial treaties as void and of no effect."[24] The confederacy prepared to resist American expansion, by armed force if necessary.

Early American efforts at a military solution met with little success. In 1790 General Josiah Harmar invaded Indian country with some 1,500 men, but the warriors of the western tribes, ably led by the Miami war chief Little Turtle and Blue Jacket of the Shawnees, inflicted a decisive defeat. Worse was to come. In 1791 the Indian confederacy routed an American army under General Arthur St. Clair in the heaviest defeat Indians ever inflicted on the United States. St. Clair suffered over nine hundred casualties, with some six hundred dead, at a time when the young republic had neither the manpower nor the resources to sustain such losses.[25] American claims to Indian land by right of conquest looked empty. For a time it seemed as if the United States would negotiate a compromise agreement with the Indian tribes of the Old Northwest. However, while the Americans rebuilt their army, deep divisions appeared in Indian ranks, divisions that American commissioners exacerbated. Cornplanter led a Seneca delegation to meet with Washington in Philadelphia and Joseph Brant recommended that the western tribes reach a settlement with the United States. Brant and the Iroquois continued to exert influence in Indian country after the Revolution, but many of the western tribes regarded them with increasing suspicion. Western warriors who had already defeated two American armies rejected the idea of compromise (see "Message to the Commissioners of the United States," pages 242–44).

Meanwhile, Congress was appropriating $1 million to raise, equip, and train a new army, the Legion of the United States, to be led by General Anthony Wayne against the Indian alliance. Little Turtle began to incline toward peace and his son-in-law William Wells, a white captive who had been adopted and fought against the Americans in St. Clair's defeat, switched sides and served as a scout and interpreter for Wayne.[26] By the time Wayne and his army entered Indian country in 1794, the confederacy of northwestern tribes was no longer united. On the west bank of the Maumee River, south of Lake Erie, a reduced Indian force confronted Wayne's troops in a tangle of trees felled by a tornado. Outnumbered and out-gunned, the Indians were driven from the field by the American cannon, cavalry, and bayonets. "We were driven by the sharp end of the guns of the Long Knives," recalled one Indian leader. "Our moccasins trickled with blood in the sand, and the water was red in the river."[27]

◆ *The Treaty of Greenville, August 1795*
The artist, who may have been a member of Wayne's staff, depicts the Miami chief Little Turtle addressing Wayne and his officers, while a scribe takes notes on bended knee. © *Chicago History Museum, USA/Bridgeman Images.*

They fled to a nearby British fort, where they believed they would receive assistance. They were mistaken. Britain, faced with trouble in Europe and a revolutionary government in France, was not interested in another war in America. The fleeing Indians found the gates of the fort barred against them. The lack of British support dispirited the Indians more than the actual battle at Fallen Timbers, where their losses were relatively light. In 1795, at the Treaty of Greenville, more than a thousand Indian delegates accepted Wayne's terms and ceded to the United States two-thirds of present-day Ohio and part of Indiana. In return, the Indians were promised a lasting boundary between their lands and American territory. With the war for the Ohio country over, many Indians turned to more subtle forms of resistance in what remained of their homelands, compromising where they had no choice, adapting and adjusting to changes, and preserving what they could of Indian life and culture in a nation that was intent on eradicating both.

UPHEAVALS IN THE WEST

The era that brought the Revolution in the East also brought revolutionary changes to the West. The Spanish monarchy implemented a series of reforms, and Spanish colonial officials in the late eighteenth century tried to develop more enlightened Indian policies.[28] Indian nations empowered with guns and horses altered balances of power on the Great Plains. Indians in California entered Franciscan missions amid a world of disrupted lifeways and plummeting populations. Indians on the Northwest Coast became involved in a rush for sea otter pelts that brought the outside world to their shores. They witnessed the clash of imperial ambitions at their coastline, dealt with Russian, Spanish, British, and American ships, and became connected to a trade network that embraced Europe, Hawaii, and China. Like other peoples throughout the West, they also died in huge numbers as a massive smallpox epidemic raged from Mexico to Canada, a human catastrophe that occurred at the same time as the American Revolution but that has been largely ignored in American history.

Emerging and Colliding Powers on the Plains

Indian power had always limited European ambitions and affected European decisions in the interior of the continent. The Osages dominated the region between the Arkansas and Red rivers for much of the eighteenth century. They exploited their trade with the French to expand their power over rival tribes and dictated the terms on which Europeans entered their domain. Spaniards and French alike treated the Osages with healthy respect and courted their friendship.[29] When Spain attempted to solidify and extend imperial authority on its northern frontiers, it collided with an emerging Comanche empire on the southern plains. It was not an empire like the British imperial system or the "empire of liberty" that Jefferson envisioned; Comanche dominance rested on buffalo, horses, and grasslands, operated along networks of exchange and kinship, and relied on coexistence and coercion rather than conquest and colonization. Nevertheless, Comanche military prowess, commercial reach and economic power, incorporation of other peoples, and political and cultural influence challenged and eclipsed Spain's empire. The Comanches maintained alliances with the Wichitas, confined the Osages to the east, and pushed the Apaches south and west. They raided at will deep into Texas, New Mexico, and Spain's other northern provinces, carrying off captives and livestock and draining and diverting the limited resources Spain could afford for frontier defense.[30]

Despite Governor Cachupín's efforts to cultivate peace with the Comanches, Spanish–Comanche relations continued to be marred by hostilities. In 1779 Governor Juan Bautista de Anza defeated and killed the Comanche chief Cuerno Verde (Green Horn). Realizing that years of fighting could have been avoided if Spain had always treated the Comanches "with gentleness and justice," Anza quickly moved to restore peace.[31] Following Native diplomatic protocols that involved exchanging gifts and having Comanche women act as mediators, Spaniards and Comanches made peace in Texas in 1785 and in New Mexico the following year.[32] Peace may also have been tied to recent Comanche losses to disease (see page 231).

Spaniards then enlisted Comanche support in a no-holds-barred war against the Apaches, who had been pushed up against Spain's northern frontier by Comanche expansion and who raided Spanish settlements as an essential part of their economy. Spaniards paid bounties for Apache ears, shipped Apache captives to slavery in the Caribbean, and tried to resettle Apache people. Spain supported those Apaches who agreed to live in peace near presidios and accepted Christian "civilization," but waged unrelenting war against "hostiles" and deported those who were captured. Chain gangs of Apache prisoners trekked south to Mexico City; from there, many were sent to Vera Cruz and on to Havana.[33] But Western Indian resistance, though shifting in its composition and power balance, remained a formidable force against Spanish expansion, and Comanche and Apache raids would continue long after Mexico won its independence from Spain in 1821.

Farther north, another growing Native power that would come to match Comanche dominance in the South was pushing west and establishing its hold on the northern and central Plains. According to a Sioux winter count° kept by American Horse, in 1775–76, while George Washington was capturing Boston and Congress was declaring independence, a Lakota named Standing Bull discovered the Black Hills, a site of sacred significance and spiritual power for the Sioux. As the Lakota bands—the Oglala, Hunkpapa, Brulé or Sicangu, Miniconjou, Sans Arc, Two Kettle, and Sihaspa or Blackfeet Sioux—asserted their power, they pushed Omahas, Otos, Missouris, Iowas, Pawnees, and Cheyennes to the south and west, seizing hunting territories to support their large populations.[34]

Horses and guns also shifted the balance of power on the northwestern plains. Although the Shoshonis originated in the Great Basin area of Nevada, a great drought in the area triggered a series of population movements. Groups of Shoshoni speakers drifted across the Rocky Mountains in the early sixteenth century.

°Calendars, usually on hide, that marked each year with the symbol for a memorable event. See Dohasan calendar on page 340 for an example.

While their Comanche relatives moved south, the Shoshonis moved north and east. They obtained horses from Utes and Comanches by about 1700 and moved onto the buffalo-rich plains of Wyoming and Montana in increasing numbers. They appear to have extended as far north as the Saskatchewan River, where they came into conflict with the Blackfeet by the 1730s. At first, the Shoshoni cavalry had the advantage and pushed the Blackfeet northwards. However, firearms soon offset Shoshoni wealth in horses.

As the Blackfeet began to close the gap on the Shoshonis in terms of horse power, they built up their arsenals of firearms and steel weapons, trading first with Cree and Assiniboine middlemen and then directly with the French, British, and

◆ **Karl Bodmer, *Blackfeet Warrior on Horseback* (c. 1833–43)**
Mounted and well-armed Blackfeet warriors defeated the Shoshonis and established themselves as the most formidable power on the northern Plains by 1800. *Karl Bodmer (1809–93),
c. 1833–43 (pencil, pen, and w/c on paper)/Newberry Library, Chicago, Illinois, USA/Bridgeman Images.*

Canadian traders who came to their country in growing numbers. After the French ceded Canada, British fur trading companies had an open field and competition flourished. The Northwest Company challenged the monopoly of the old Hudson's Bay Company by sending traders west to seek out new customers and new sources of furs. The Hudson's Bay Company followed suit. In 1774 it established Cumberland House on the border of Saskatchewan and Manitoba, and by the 1790s rival Northwest and Hudson's Bay Company posts were competing for trade with the Blackfeet. Cree and Assiniboine Indians who had operated as middlemen between western tribes and trading posts on the shores of Hudson Bay now moved west to maintain their role in the expanding fur trade.[35] With plenty of access to trade, the powerful Blackfeet played off rival traders to their advantage and controlled the trade routes, preventing guns from reaching the Shoshonis. Smallpox hit both the Blackfeet and the Shoshonis in 1781 (see page 231), killing between one-third and one-half of the people and interrupting hostilities for several years. However, by 1800, the Blackfeet and their allies had succeeded in pushing the Shoshonis off the Plains and into the Rocky Mountain ranges of western Wyoming and Idaho, where the American explorers Meriwether Lewis and William Clark met them five years later. The Shoshonis welcomed American traders into their country; the new source of firearms allowed them to confront Blackfeet and other enemies on equal terms again in the nineteenth century.[36]

California Missions

California Indians did not feel the full impact of European contact until 1769. That year the Franciscan missionary Father Junípero Serra founded the first Catholic mission in Upper California, at San Diego. By 1823 there were twenty-one missions between San Diego and San Francisco (Map 4.4). Many Indians moved to the missions to seek refuge from the devastating demographic and ecological disruptions that followed in the wake of European contact. In the missions they lived a regulated existence that revolved around work and religion: breakfast, religious instruction, Mass, morning work, noon prayer and meal, siesta, afternoon work, choir or catechism, dinner, and evening activities. Priests imposed Catholic family structures and rules on Indians who had previously lived in extended kin groups. They segregated unmarried men and women into separate dormitories at night to enforce Catholic moral codes, imposed strict labor regimens, and resorted to whipping, branding, and solitary confinement to keep Indians on the path to "civilization and salvation." Indians at the missions were a source of labor: "nearly everything grown, manufactured, or consumed in the region's missions, presidios, and pueblos was to a great extent produced by laboring Indians." But Indians at the missions managed to hold on to important elements of their culture, and they also developed their own forms of labor. Many made their own economic arrangements with soldiers and settlers, working as blacksmiths, carpenters, potters, and masons in California's emerging colonial society.[37] As it had among the Pueblos in 1680, Franciscan oppression, backed by the Spanish military and combined with the disruption of traditional lifeways

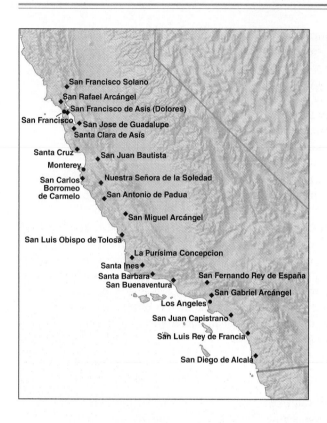

◆ **Map 4.4 Franciscan Missions in California**
The chain of twenty-one missions established by Franciscans between 1769 and 1823.
SOURCE: © MAPS.com/CORBIS.

and economies, produced suffering and resentment that occasionally burst out into open violence.

Missionaries labored to save Indian souls but brought misery to Indian lives. Missionaries pictured their neophytes as docile and submissive and themselves as benevolent fathers, but the mission system was backed by force and violence. Many Indians saw the missionaries as thieves, witches, and sexual predators. Priests tried to alter Native patterns of sexuality and marriage and ostensibly enforced strict moral codes, but they also sometimes abused Indian women. Spanish soldiers often committed rape. Venereal disease spread through mission communities. Mission Indians were usually powerless to resist but not always. Many ran away, while others turned to violence. Kumeyaay warriors attacked the settlement at San Diego in 1769, and in 1775 about eight hundred Indians from a number of villages attacked the mission in an outbreak sparked at least in part by Spanish abuses of Indian women.[38]

Mission populations rose between 1769 and the end of the century, but the increase stemmed from congregating converts in one place and masked a broader demographic collapse. Mission Indians died in epidemics of measles (in 1769) and smallpox (in 1781–82). Social controls and social disruption produced psychological trauma. Abortions, miscarriages, and deaths in childbirth reduced fertility rates among women. Poor diet, overcrowding, and unsanitary conditions produced appalling infant mortality rates, often with nine out of ten children dying before the age of eight. At the San Francisco mission, an Indian named Uichase buried four wives, whom he had married one after the other as each died, and had ten children, none of whom lived past the age of three. In places where mortality rates were so high, the missions depended on recruitment to maintain population levels.[39] As had Indians in New England, New Mexico, and elsewhere, Indians in California often adapted to (and in turn adapted) the new religion to help them survive in a chaotic new world, but the treatment accorded Indian people in the California missions prompted outrage and controversy when Serra, the founder of the California mission system, was considered for canonization in the late twentieth century.

◆ Mission Indians of California
Indian converts at the Spanish mission at Carmel, California, line up to receive visiting Frenchmen in 1786. Spanish priests worked to produce dutiful congregations of "mission Indians." However, beneath the appearance of order and contentment depicted on occasions such as this, Indians in Spanish missions often suffered hunger, disease, and abuse. One of the French visitors compared the mission to a slave plantation. Indians frequently ran away from the missions and sometimes resorted to violent resistance. *Granger, NYC.*

The Pacific Northwest Pelt Rush

Farther north on the Pacific Coast, Native peoples had little direct contact with Europeans and Americans until the late eighteenth century, and the intruders there came for the Indians' furs rather than their souls. Long and hazardous routes around Cape Horn at the southern tip of South America protected the Indians from European and Yankee seaborne traffic; vast distances and mountain walls limited contact by land. Chinook and Clatsop Indians at the mouth of the Columbia, however, moved easily across the water in long, sturdy canoes. They traded inland with other Indian peoples and acquired items from half a continent away at the busy portage market at The Dalles.[40] Northwest Coast people were not isolated, but they were isolated for a time from direct contact with Europeans. That changed dramatically in the last quarter of the eighteenth century.

The Spanish had sent occasional voyages up the Pacific Coast, but Russian activity in the area prompted them to focus their attention. Russian interest in the Northwest Coast represented the culmination of an expansion eastward across Siberia that had begun in the seventeenth century. Vitus Bering, a Dane in the czar's service who explored the Asian shoreline northward and gave his name to the straits, reached the Aleutian Islands off the coast of present-day Alaska in 1741. The expedition traded for sea otter pelts from the Natives and sold them for nearly one thousand rubles each in Chinese markets. The profits to be made unleashed a rush of *promyshleniki*, Russian fur traders, mainly from Siberia, to the Aleutian chain. They abused the Natives and forced the men to hunt for sea otter pelts by holding their women hostage.

Spanish expeditions sailed north from Monterey in response to rumors of Russians on the coast of what Spain regarded as part of Alta, California. In an international chain reaction, the British set sail to find out what the Spaniards were up to, and to assert their claims to the area and search for the western opening of the Northwest Passage that was believed to provide an all-water route to the Pacific and the wealth of the Orient.[41] In July 1776, just days after American colonists signed the Declaration of Independence in Philadelphia, Captain James Cook left England with two ships, *Resolution* and *Discovery*. Cook's crews sailed around the Cape of Good Hope, past Australia and Tasmania and on to New Zealand; dropped anchor at Tahiti; and then sailed to Hawaii, becoming the first Europeans to visit the islands. They reached the northwest coast of America in the spring of 1778. The local Indians came alongside the ships in their canoes and traded sea otter pelts. Cook then pushed north along the coast of Alaska. When the ships returned to Hawaii, Cook was killed by angry Natives, but his crew carried on to Siberia and China, where they sold fifteen hundred beaver pelts as well as sea otter furs. Returning to England after fifty months at sea, they completed what has been called the greatest voyage in the age of sail. They also returned with news that there were fortunes to be made in the sea otter trade.[42] John Ledyard, a young New Englander who had sailed with Cook, published his own account of the voyage in an effort to promote American participation; "[S]kins which did not cost the purchaser sixpence sterling sold in China for 100 dollars," he announced.[43]

Sea otters became the key to great fortunes in England and New England, and Northwest Coast Indian villages were soon busy ports of call in an enormous trade network involving three continents (Map 4.5). British and Yankee merchants loaded ships with manufactured goods, sailed around the tip of South America and up to the Pacific Northwest Coast, and exchanged their goods for sea otter pelts. When their holds were stuffed with pelts, the merchants sailed their ships to Hawaii, where they often spent the winter, and then on to Chinese ports. In China,

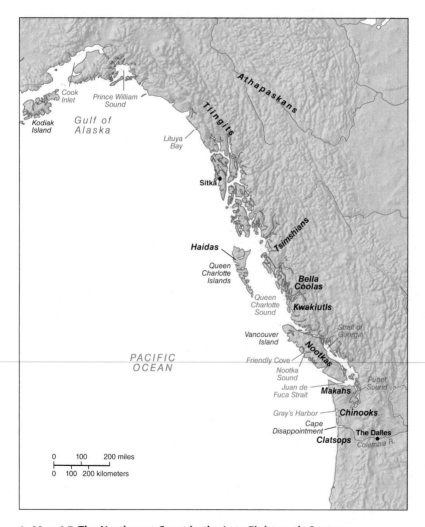

◆ **Map 4.5 The Northwest Coast in the Late Eighteenth Century**
The Northwest Coast in the late eighteenth century, showing major Native groups and key locations in the sea otter trade.
SOURCE: Reprinted from *One Vast Winter Count: The Native American West before Lewis and Clark* by Colin G. Calloway by permission of the University of Nebraska Press. Copyright 2003 by the University of Nebraska Press.

warm and glossy sea otter fur became a status symbol of the royal family, mandarins, and wealthy classes. The sea captains sold their otter skins at huge profits and bought silks, spices, and tea, items that commanded high prices back home.[44] As the competition increased, the countries vying for a stake sometimes clashed. In 1789 English and Spanish claims collided in Nootka Sound, off the coast of British Columbia. Spaniards seized English ships, and for a moment the two nations were poised on the brink of war. Even so, the influx of sailors on the coast continued unabated. By one count, at the height of the maritime trade in 1792, thirty-two vessels visited the coastal area: eight Spanish, thirteen British, five American, four Portuguese, one French, and one ship sailing under the Swedish flag, with an unknown number of Russian vessels operating off the coast of Alaska.[45] Northwest Coast Indians came into contact with crews that included Russians, English, Scots, "Boston men" from coastal New England, Spaniards, Portuguese, Hawaiians, Hindus, Filipinos, Malays, and Chinese.

As other nations probed the coasts of Alaska, Russia redoubled its efforts to secure the sea otter trade. In 1784 Grigory Shelikhov established a settlement on Kodiak Island after subjugating the Alutiiq inhabitants. He petitioned the Russian government to grant his company a monopoly and asked that missionaries be sent. The first group of Russian Orthodox missionaries arrived at Kodiak in 1794, and in 1799 the state granted a monopoly to the Russian American Company (RAC). The RAC took control, but government regulations prohibiting abuse of the Natives were regularly ignored. Pushing southeast along the coast, Russians opened trade relations with the Tlingits in the late 1780s. In 1799 Alexander Baranov, general manager of the RAC, shifted the company's base of operations to a site a few miles north of present-day Sitka. But the powerful Tlingits, who numbered some ten thousand at the turn of the century, proved formidable customers and adversaries. In 1802 Tlingits attacked and burned the Russian outpost at St. Michael.[46]

The world began to close in from land and sea. Scotsman Alexander Mackenzie, in the employ of the Northwest Company, became the first white man to cross the continent north of Mexico when he reached the Pacific in July 1793.[47] But the Americans ultimately dominated. In 1792 Captain Robert Gray, the first American to circumnavigate the globe, became the first non-Indian to enter the mouth of the Columbia River.[48] By 1800 the Americans had transformed the Northwest Coast into what one historian called a trade suburb of Boston. The next year, American vessels outnumbered British ships on the coast twenty-two to one.[49] By the time Lewis and Clark reached the Pacific in 1805, Northwest Coast peoples were used to seeing Americans.

Indians embraced the maritime trade. The new materials, tools, and goods contributed to an artistic blossoming even as their cultures experienced the shock of contact. Many goods were acquired as prestige items to be given away at potlatches. Northwest Coast peoples quickly became shrewd dealers and discriminating consumers. They obliged ships' captains to participate in, or at least tolerate, a considerable amount of ceremony as a prerequisite to trade and to accede to the custom of reciprocal gift giving. They might accept beads and trinkets as gifts, but once they got down to business they wanted metal goods and clothing. Native chiefs manipulated competition between different traders, monopolized profitable roles as middlemen by preventing tribes farther inland from dealing directly with the ships, and sometimes resorted to violence to protect their borderlands, resources, and trading positions.[50]

Yet no matter how Northwest Coast Indians endeavored to direct the tide, the floodgates of change were open. Along with tools and goods, they acquired alcohol, guns, and new diseases. Overhunting produced glutted markets, fluctuating prices, and depletion of the very source on which the trade rested. Before the mid-eighteenth century, sea otters ranged from Baja California to Alaska; by the turn of the century they were on the way to becoming an endangered species. As Indian men devoted more energy to hunting and chiefs traded pelts for sheets of copper and other goods that could be given away for status at potlatch ceremonies, they spent less time whaling and salmon fishing, which meant they stored less food for the winter.[51] Native women played prominent roles in the trade, although Europeans most often commented on their sexual roles. Some Euro-American seafarers reported that Northwest Coast women displayed chastity before contact with the trade ships, and there is no evidence that prostitution existed in these societies before the sea otter trade created the demand, but Northwest Coast women quickly became renowned for easy sex and sex in trade. Northwest Coast Indians often held war captives and their descendants as slaves, and as demand increased, they began trafficking in the sexual services of their slave women, providing sexual laborers as an item of trade and perhaps also diverting the worst consequences of colonial sexual encounters away from their own families.[52] Venereal disease became rampant among the Natives of the lower Columbia. Alcohol also made deadly inroads.

When George Vancouver sailed through the Strait of Juan De Fuca in 1792, he found grim evidence of diseases imported from the outside world. Many of the Indians bore the marks of smallpox, and Vancouver's crew found abandoned villages littered with bones and skeletons scattered along the beach of Discovery Bay. It was obvious that some disaster had struck the region.[53] From a conservative estimate of more than 180,000 in 1774, the Indian population of the Northwest Coast had dropped to 35,000 or 40,000 just a century later.[54] What had started as a limited, mutually beneficial trade relationship had spiraled into a cataclysmic upheaval for the peoples of the Northwest Coast.

Smallpox Used Them Up

Disease caused upheaval throughout the West. During the American Revolution, while rebels and redcoats killed each other by the hundreds in the East, a great smallpox pandemic killed Indian people by the thousands in the West. As it had in colonial times, smallpox plagued Boston, Philadelphia, Charleston, and other eastern cities and struck American armies and Woodland Indian villages. But death tolls in the East paled in comparison to the horrors in the West. Between 1779 and 1784 smallpox reached from South America to the Saskatchewan River, from Puget Sound to Hudson Bay (Map 4.6). It was certainly not the first epidemic to ravage the West, but it was more extensive than any before or since.

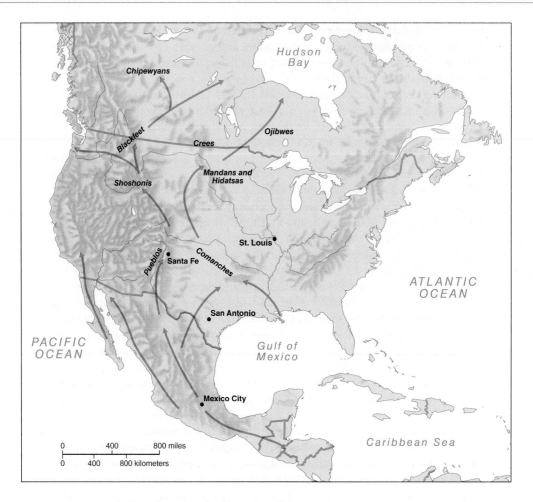

◆ **Map 4.6 The Smallpox Pandemic, 1779–1784**
After a smallpox epidemic broke out in Mexico City late in 1779, the disease spread rapidly
across the West, often following the same routes by which horses had spread northward.
SOURCE: Adapted from Elizabeth Fenn, *Pox Americana: The Great Smallpox Epidemic of 1775–82*
(New York: Hill and Wang, 2001), 7. Copyright © 2002 by Elizabeth Fenn. Reprinted by permission of
Hill and Wang, a division of Farrar, Straus and Giroux, LLC.

The epidemic struck first in Mexico City, where it killed an estimated eighteen
thousand people between September and December 1779. From there it spread
in all directions: to the silver mining districts of northern Mexico; to Guatemala
in 1780–81; to Colombia in 1781–83; to Ecuador in 1783.[55] Infected families from
Sonora carried the disease to Baja California. Spanish priests watched it spread
like wildfire through the missions; some inoculated their congregations, but most
watched helplessly as people died of starvation and disease. Indians who fled from
the mission deathtraps into the mountains carried smallpox to the non-Christian
Indians who lived there. The disease spread from Mexico along the *camino real*

and other trails to New Mexico, where more than five thousand people died in 1780–81. So many people perished that Governor Anza urged reducing the number of missions in New Mexico. Hopis there told Anza they expected the epidemic to exterminate them. In 1785 a band of Comanches reported that two-thirds of their people had recently died of smallpox.[56]

The disease spread far and fast along well-traveled trade routes, following roughly the same routes by which horses spread across the West and racing across two-thirds of the continent in two to three years. Shoshonis in the foothills of the Rocky Mountains in present-day Idaho told the explorers Lewis and Clark that they could travel to Spanish trade sites in just ten days; a Shoshoni who became infected with smallpox while trading for horses could be back home before the symptoms erupted. And the Shoshonis were major traders in the diffusion of horses through the Northwest. As horses spread north across the West, manufactured goods filtered in via the Mandan and Hidatsa villages on the Missouri, from French traders operating among the Wichitas and Caddos, and from British and Yankee merchant ships on the Northwest Coast. Indian middlemen shuttled between Indians and Europeans and between Indians and Indians. Traditional trading centers became the hubs of vast exchange networks that connected Indian peoples across half a continent and beyond. When the rival Hudson's Bay and Northwest companies built a string of trading posts stretching west to the Saskatchewan River, they created a series of stepping-stones by which disease would leap from the northern Plains back to the bay. When smallpox hit village farmers, they died in huge numbers; when it hit mobile hunters, they carried it to other groups. People who fled the dreaded disease infected their allies and the relatives who took them in.

The epidemic became a turning point in relations between the semi-sedentary farming tribes on the upper Missouri and the Sioux. The Mandans, Hidatsas, and Arikaras held a commanding position on the Great Bend of the upper Missouri prior to 1780 and their power and numbers had blocked Sioux expansion. An estimated twenty-four thousand Arikaras lived in numerous villages in the mid-eighteenth century, but they lost 75 to 80 percent of their population in the epidemic, and the survivors huddled into just a couple of villages. The Mandans, who numbered about nine thousand people in the middle of the eighteenth century, told Lewis and Clark in 1805 that twenty-five years before they had inhabited half a dozen villages but had been reduced to just two by repeated attacks from Sioux and smallpox. Reeling from massive losses and internal discord, the survivors retreated north, opening the way for the Sioux to circumvent them, move west across the Missouri, and establish themselves as the dominant power on the northern and central Plains.[57]

Once smallpox hit the Missouri River trading villages, it spread quickly to the Indians of the northern forests. Sioux winter counts referred to 1779–80 as "Smallpox Used Them Up Winter."[58] The Crows, regular visitors to the Hidatsa villages, caught the disease. They told traders that they had totaled two thousand lodges before smallpox came and were since reduced to three hundred lodges.[59] From the Crows the disease appears to have spread west to the Flatheads or Salish, although Shoshonis just as likely transmitted it there. As much as half of the Salish population died. The Salish passed it on to the Pend d'Oreilles, Kalispels, Kutenais, Spokanes, and Colvilles, and on down the Columbia River to the Northwest Coast. The Shoshonis transmitted it to the Blackfeet. "We had no belief that one Man could give it to another, any more than a wounded Man could give his wound to another," recalled one of the Blackfeet who survived. "Our hearts were low and dejected, and we shall never again be the same people."[60] Thousands of Indians died on the Canadian plains. The Chipewyans in the central subarctic lost about 90 percent of their population. It spread east to Hudson Bay, where traders' journals recorded Indians dying every day.

Smallpox was especially deadly for children and pregnant women. When Englishman Nathaniel Portlock arrived in the Sitka area of Alaska in 1787, he met an old Tlingit man who had pockmarks on his face and "ten strokes tattooed on one of his arms, which I understood were marks for the number of children he had lost."[61] Children who survived the disease itself often died of starvation and neglect when smallpox claimed their parents. Deaths in the younger population reduced the number of individuals surviving to reproductive age and produced a decrease in births twenty or twenty-five years later. The survivors of the 1779–83 epidemic acquired immunity, thus they were spared when another epidemic hit later on, but their children were not. Traditional healers and healing rituals were powerless in the face of the disaster; in fact, the common medical treatment of sweating in a lodge and then plunging into cold water often proved fatal to smallpox victims. Survivors had to regroup socially and politically as well as psychologically and emotionally. Sometimes small groups of survivors from larger stricken populations congregated to form new communities. Some communities tried to rebuild their populations through large-scale adoptions. Societies struggled to redefine their political structures and patterns of leadership. Despair added to the death toll, as many survivors without family or community lost the will to live. An Oglala winter count by American Horse marks the year 1784 with the suicide of a smallpox victim: the man sat in his tipi, sang his death song, then shot himself.[62]

After the Revolution, the new American nation turned its eyes west, but the West was a very different place from what it had been just a generation earlier. It had felt the reverberations of revolution in the East. Missionaries and traders had reached the Pacific Coast. Balances of power had shifted between Indian nations as well as between European nations. And smallpox had ravaged the country. To Americans who had just won their independence from the British Empire, it seemed that God had cleared the way for His chosen people to build their own empire in the West, just as He had when the Pilgrims landed in Massachusetts Bay in 1620 in the wake of an epidemic that had depopulated the East Coast.

DOCUMENTS

The Revolution Divides the Iroquois and the Cherokees

··•·✕✕✕✕✕◆✕◆✕✕✕✕✕·•··

IN THE MONTHS LEADING UP TO the Revolution, most Indians hoped to stay out of the struggle. Tribal circumstances differed but eventually most Native peoples were pushed or pulled into the conflict and most suffered disastrous consequences. Among the Iroquois, the Seneca chief Guyasuta, who had played a leading role in Pontiac's War, worked tirelessly to keep his people out of this war and rejected British efforts to enlist Iroquois support. "We must be fools indeed to imagine that they regard us or our Interest who want to bring us into an unnecessary War," he said. "We will not suffer either the English or Americans to march an army through our country," he declared; "we will mind our Business and not join either side."[63] The Oneidas were also determined to stay out of the war, and in June 1775, their chiefs issued a declaration of neutrality. Neutrality had served the Iroquois well in past conflicts between Britain and France, but it did not work this time. As one Onondaga chief explained: "Times are altered with us Indians. Formerly the Warriors were governed by the wisdom of their uncles the Sachems but now they take their own way & dispose of themselves without consulting their uncles the Sachems—while we wish for peace and they are for war."[64]

The Oneidas' neutrality quickly broke down. Their geographic location meant they had had long contact with colonists and developed close ties with them as the Oneidas came to rely more on farming, animal husbandry, and trade. (Of the Iroquois tribes only the Mohawks were farther to the east and the Oneidas occupied a key portage site known as the Carrying Place.) In addition, as the document reprinted here shows, the Oneidas' missionary Samuel Kirkland was an important conduit between the Oneidas and the Americans. As teenagers, Kirkland and the Mohawk chief Joseph Brant had been friends at Eleazar Wheelock's school in Lebanon, Connecticut. But as tensions escalated between Britain and its American colonies, Brant reaffirmed his ties to the Crown and the Church of England while Kirkland adhered to the Congregationalist religion and the Patriot cause. With the outbreak of the Revolution, Brant and Kirkland became bitter enemies. Each exerted his influence in the tug-of-war for Indian allegiance: Brant helped to bring the Mohawks out for the King's cause; Kirkland generated divisions within the Oneidas but swayed the tribe to support the colonists.[65] Ultimately, the Oneidas felt they had no choice: they split with most of the Iroquois confederacy and sided with the patriots.

In the summer of 1775 an Oneida chief named Skenandoah accompanied Kirkland to Boston, where George Washington was besieging a British army. In the summer of 1777 when the British launched a campaign to cut off New England from the other colonies, Oneida warriors rallied to assist their patriot neighbors and resist the invasion of the Oneida homeland. Ambushed by the British and their Mohawk and Seneca allies at the Battle of Oriskany, the Americans suffered heavy casualties and as many as thirty Oneidas died in a fight that pitted Iroquois against Iroquois. Mohawks and Oneidas subsequently destroyed one another's villages and, although Iroquois warriors generally avoided killing one another during the remainder of the war, the American Revolution became an Iroquois civil war.[66] In the spring of 1778, a group of Oneida Indians journeyed more than 250 miles from their homes in upstate New York to join Washington's bedraggled little army at Valley Forge. They brought corn to the starving troops and, so the story goes, an Oneida woman named Polly Cooper showed Continental soldiers how to prepare hulled corn soup. In 1779 American armies invaded Iroquois country and burned the towns and crops of the Oneidas' former allies. The Oneidas did not fare much better. The war forced them from their towns and, contrary to the assurances of their American allies, they lost most of their New York homelands in the postwar land rush.

In the southeast, the Cherokee Indians experienced revolutionary changes long before the American Revolution. Traditional subsistence practices and settlement patterns changed as Cherokees participated in the deerskin trade and adopted English styles of farming and domesticating animals. English traders funneled new goods, new values, and deadly alcohol into Cherokee communities. Some Cherokees began to traffic in and eventually own African slaves. Cherokee political structure became more unified as English colonial governments insisted that the various Cherokee towns function as a single tribe. Smallpox hit the Cherokee population hard in 1738, and it returned in 1759. British armies burned Cherokee crops and villages in 1760 and 1761. And Cherokee lands were steadily whittled away (Map 4.7).

The tempo of Cherokee land loss increased dramatically in the decade before the Revolution. In 1768 Iroquois delegates to the Treaty of Fort Stanwix with Sir William Johnson handed away Cherokee hunting lands north of the Tennessee River. That same year, the Treaty of Hard Labor in South Carolina fixed boundaries to Cherokee territory. Cherokee chiefs met with colonial officials from North and South Carolina and drew a border between their respective lands by burning marks on a strip of trees, but constant pressure from colonial settlers compelled the Cherokees to agree to new limits two years later at the Treaty of Lochaber. The surveyors lopped off another chunk of Cherokee land when they ran the treaty line. In 1772, Virginia demanded another cession of everything east of the Kentucky River. No matter how much land Cherokees gave up, settlers kept coming: Cherokees complained that they could "see the smoke of the Virginians from their doors."[67]

In March 1775, a group of North Carolina land speculators led by Richard Henderson pulled off one of the biggest real estate deals in frontier history at Sycamore Shoals on the Watauga River in Tennessee. The Cherokee chiefs Attakullakulla (Little Carpenter), Oconostota, and Savunkah (the Raven of Chota) sold Henderson 27,000 square miles of territory between the Cumberland River in the south and the Kentucky River in the north in exchange for a cabin full of trade goods. The deal contravened the Royal Proclamation of 1763 as well as Cherokee tribal law, and

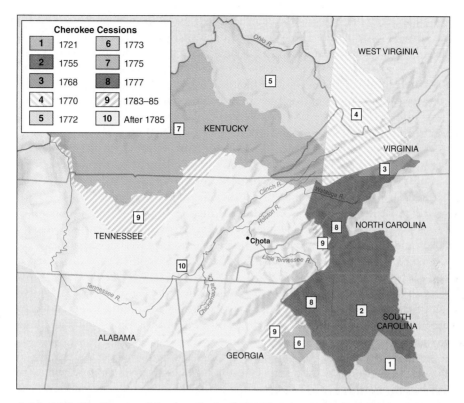

◆ **Map 4.7 Cherokee Land Cessions in the Colonial and Revolutionary Eras, 1721–1785**
By the outbreak of the American Revolution, when their delegates assembled at Chota, the
Cherokees had seen their lands whittled away in a series of treaties. The Treaty of Sycamore
Shoals in 1775 that gobbled up most of the remaining Cherokee land in Kentucky (No. 7) was
especially devastating. The Cherokee decision to go to war, and the restoration of peace, did
little to stem the pressures on Cherokee land.
SOURCE: Adapted from Charles C. Royce, *The Cherokee Nation of Indians* (Washington, D.C.: U.S.
Government Printing Office, 1887), 256.

the chiefs later declared that Henderson had deceived them as to what they were
signing. Settlers were soon filling up the ceded lands, and the Cherokees found
themselves cut off from both the Ohio River and their Kentucky hunting grounds.
Even then the invasion of Cherokee lands did not stop: settlers encroached on
the Watauga and upper Holston rivers in northeastern Tennessee. (See Map 4.3,
"United States Treaties and Indian Land Cessions to 1810," page 214.)

The older chiefs may have been trying to buy time for their people by creating a buffer zone of ceded territory between Cherokees and colonists, but younger
Cherokees bitterly resented the recurrent sacrifice of homeland and hunting
grounds. Attakullakulla's son, Dragging Canoe (Chincanacina), stormed out of the
negotiations at Sycamore Shoals and is reputed to have warned Henderson that he
would make the lands "dark and bloody." He told British deputy superintendent

of Indian affairs Henry Stuart "that he had no hand in making these Bargains but blamed some of their Old Men who he said were too old to hunt and who by their Poverty had been induced to sell their Land but that for his part he had a great many young fellows that would support him and that were determined to have their Land."[68] The outbreak of the American Revolution seemed to offer the younger warriors the opportunity, with British support, to drive invaders off their homelands, but first they had to challenge the authority of the older chiefs and gain the upper hand in the councils of the Cherokee Nation.

Their opportunity to make this challenge came in May 1776 when a delegation of Shawnee, Delaware, Mohawk, and other Indians from the north arrived at Chota, the Cherokee capital or "beloved town" on the Little Tennessee River. Their faces painted black, they urged the Cherokees to join them in a war of united resistance against the Americans. Delegates from the various Cherokee towns assembled at the council house to hear the northern Indians' talk. Henry Stuart and Alexander Cameron, the British agent to the Overhill Cherokees, were also there.° John Stuart, British superintendent for the Southern Indians, who had taken refuge at St. Augustine, had sent his brother Henry to Chota. Henry had a difficult mission: to arm the Cherokees in readiness for war against the colonists, but to restrain them until the British could coordinate their attacks in the southern colonies. Like the older chiefs, the British did not want the Cherokees to go to war — yet.

But recurrent losses of Cherokee territory had undermined the prestige of the older chiefs. When Dragging Canoe and the younger warriors accepted the war belt the northern Indians offered them, they seized authority from the chiefs and reversed their policies of appeasement. Cherokee warriors attacked American settlements on the Watauga River the following month.

The war was a disaster for the Cherokees. American expeditions from Georgia, Virginia, and the Carolinas marched into Cherokee country, burning towns and destroying cornfields. As Cherokee refugees fled the smoking ruins of their towns, the compromising older chiefs began to reassert their influence and open negotiations for peace. The Americans granted them peace, but at a price: the Cherokees lost more than five million acres in treaties with Georgia, Virginia, North Carolina, and South Carolina. Dragging Canoe and his followers refused to be party to the treaties and retreated to the southwestern reaches of Cherokee country, building new towns on the Chickamauga River and fracturing the ancient balance between old and young in Cherokee society. The Chickamauga Cherokees, as they became known, continued their war against the Americans. The Americans retaliated, often without making a distinction between different groups of Cherokees: in 1780 they burned Chota itself.

By the end of the Revolution, the Cherokees' population had dropped to perhaps ten thousand people; they had lost three-quarters of their territory and

---

° The British divided the Cherokees into four main divisions: the Overhill Towns in the north on the Little Tennessee and Tellico rivers, the Valley and Middle Towns in the Blue Ridge region, and the Lower Towns in South Carolina.

more than half of their towns had been destroyed. Their world was in chaos. The Chickamaugas made common cause with militant factions among the Creeks and Shawnees and continued to resist American expansion. Other Cherokees, closer to the Americans and with bitter memories of the war, preferred to try to survive by peace. In 1785 the Cherokees signed the Treaty of Hopewell, their first treaty with the United States. Many tried to earn themselves a place in the new nation by following a path of accommodation and controlled change. It worked — for a time.

Henry Stuart's presence at Chota in May 1776 and his report on the momentous council meeting that occurred there affords us a rare glimpse of the change that the American Revolution generated in Cherokee society. Stuart clearly wanted to portray his own efforts in a good light, but his account reminds us that Indian people who fought in the American Revolution did so for their own, not for British, reasons. Cherokees were struggling to survive in a world that was crumbling around them, and they attempted different strategies in their struggle. Continued pressure on their lands had pushed the Cherokees to the brink of disintegration by 1776. The traditional division between young and old, warrior and councillor, that had served for generations to preserve balance in Cherokee society became the fault line around which the nation split and from which a new tribe would emerge.

An Oneida Declaration of Neutrality (1775)

A Speech of the Chiefs and Warriors of the ONEIDA *Tribe of* INDIANS, *to the four* NEW-ENGLAND *Provinces, directed to Governour* TRUMBULL; *and by him to be communicated:*

As our younger brothers of the *New-England Indians*, (who have settled in our vicinity) are now going down to visit their friends, and to move up parts of their families that were left behind, with this belt by them, we open the road wide, clearing it of all obstacles, that they may visit their friends and return to their settlements here in peace, We *Oneidas* are induced to this measure on account of the disagreeable situation of affairs that way; and we hope, by the help of *God*, that they may go and return in peace.

We earnestly recommend them to your charity through their long journey.

Now we more immediately address you, our brother, the Governour and the Chiefs of *New-England*.

Brothers! We have heard of the unhappy differences and great contention betwixt you and old *England*. We wonder greatly, and are troubled in our minds.

Brothers! Possess your minds in peace respecting us *Indians*. We cannot intermeddle in this dispute between two brothers. The quarrel seems to be unnatural; you are two brothers of one blood. We are unwilling to join on either side in such a contest, for we bear an equal affection to both of you, *Old* and *New-England*. Should the great King of *England* apply to us for our aid, we shall deny him. If the Colonies apply, we will refuse. The present situation of you two brothers is new and strange to us. We *Indians* cannot find

SOURCE: Peter Force, ed. *American Archives* (Washington, D.C., 1837–52), series 4, vol. 2: 1116–7. https://archive.org/details/AmericanArchives-FourthSeriesVolume2peterForce?

nor recollect in the traditions of our ancestors the like case or a similar instance.

Brothers! For these reasons possess your minds in peace, and take no umbrage that we *Indians* refuse joining in the contest; we are for peace.

Brothers! Was it an alien, a foreign Nation, which struck you, we should look into the matter. We hope, through the wise government and good pleasure of *God*, your distresses may soon be removed, and the dark cloud be dispersed.

Brothers! As we have declared for peace, we desire you will not apply to our *Indian* brethren in *New-England* for their assistance. Let us *Indians* be all of one mind, and live in peace with one another, and you white people settle your own disputes betwixt yourselves.

Brothers! We have now declared our minds; please write to us that we may know yours.

We, the sachems, warriors, and female governesses of *Oneida*, send our love to you, brother Governour, and all the other chiefs in *New-England*.

Signed by

Chief Warriors of *Oneida*.

William Sunoghsis

Viklasha Watshaleagh

William Kanaghquassea

Peter Thayehcase

Germine Tegayavher

Nickhes Ahsechose

Thomas Yoghtanawca

Adam Ohonwano

Quedellis Agwerondongwas

Handerchiko Tegahpreahdyen

Johnks Skeanender

Thomas Teorddeatha

Caughnawaga, June 19, 1775.
Interpreted and wrote by *Samuel Kirkland*, Missionary

HENRY STUART
Report from Cherokee Country (1776)

The principal Deputy for the Mohawks and six Nations began. He produced a belt of white and purple Whampum with strings of white beads and purple whampum fixed to it; He said he supposed there was not a man present that could not read his Talk; the back settlers of the Northern Provinces whom he termed the Long Knife had without any provocation come into one of their Towns and murdered their people and the son of their Great Beloved Man; that what was their case one day might be the case of another Nation another day; That his Nation was fighting at this time and that he was sent by them to secure the friendship of all Nations for he considered their interests as one, and that at this time they should forget all their quarrels among themselves and turn their eyes and their thoughts one way. The Belt was delivered to Chincanacina.

The principal Deputy of the Ottowas produced a white Belt with some purple figures; they expressed their desire of confirming a lasting bond of true friendship with all their red Brethren; that they were almost constantly at war one Nation against another, and reduced by degrees, while their common enemies were taking the

SOURCE: William L. Saunders, ed., *The Colonial Records of North Carolina*, vol. 10 (Raleigh, N.C.: State Printer, 1890), 777–84.

advantage of their situation; that they were willing & they hoped every Nation would be the same to drop all their former quarrels and to join in one common cause, and that altho' the Trade to their Nation and all the other Northern Nations had been stopped, that their friends, the French in Canada, had found means to supply them and would assist them. Chincanacina received this Belt.

The Talk of the Nations was much to the same effect, he produced a white Belt and it was received by the Raven.

There was only a boy of the Delaware Nation. The Talk was now to be finished by the Shawnees Deputy, formerly (as I am informed) a noted French partizan. He produced a War Belt about 9 feet long and six inches wide of purple Whampum strewed over with vermilion. He began with pathetically enumerating the distresses of his own and other Nations. He complained particularly of the Virginians who after having taken away all their Lands and cruelly and treacherously treated some of their people, had unjustly brought war upon their Nation and destroyed many of their people; that in a very few years their Nation from being a great people were now reduced to a handful; that their Nation possessed Lands almost to the Sea Shore and that the red people who were once Masters of the whole Country hardly possessed ground enough to stand on; that the Lands where but lately they hunted close to their Nations were thickly inhabited and covered with Forts & armed men; that wherever a Fort appeared in their neighbourhood, they might depend there would soon be Towns and Settlements; that it was plain, there was an intention to extirpate them, and that he thought it better to die like men than to diminish away by inches; That their Fathers the French who seemed long dead were now alive again; that they had supplied them plentifully with ammunition, arms and provisions and that they promised to assist them against the Virginians; that their cause was just and that they hoped the Great Being who governs everything would favour their cause; that now is the time to

begin; that there is no time to be lost, and if they fought like men they might hope to enlarge their Bounds; that the Cherokees had a Hatchett which was brought in six years ago & desired that they would take it up and use it immediately; That they intended to carry their Talks through every Nation to the Southward and that that Nation which should refuse to be their Friends on this occasion should forever hereafter be considered as their common enemy and that they would all fall on them when affairs with the White People should be settled.

The Belt was received by Chincanacina. It was some minutes before any one got up to give his Assent which was to be done by laying hold of the Belt. At last a Head man of Chilhowie who had lived long in the Mohawk Nation and whose wife had constantly lived in Sir William Johnson's house was the first who rose up to take the Belt from Chincanacina. He sung the war song and all the Northern Indians joined in the chorus. Almost all the young warriors from the different parts of the Nation followed his example, though many of them expressed their uneasiness at being concerned in a war against the white people. But the principal Chiefs, who were averse to the measure and remembered the Calamities brought on their Nation by the last war, instead of opposing the rashness of the young people with spirit, sat down dejected and silent. The Deputies proposed that Mr. Cameron and I with all the white People that were present should take up the Belt as the King's friends among them and all the French had done, which we refused. We told them that Indians did not understand our written Talks and we did not understand their Beads, nor what were their intentions; That for my part I was determined not to give any sanction to a war that was likely to bring destruction on their Nation, especially as I had not forgot the use that they made of my telling them that the King should expect their assistance if it should be asked to bring his disobedient and obstinate children to order; That the Virginians when they were not above half the number that they are at present had withstood the French and the combined Force of all the Indian Nations when they were twice as numerous as they are at present and that now they are in Arms ready to go against the King's forces; that if they went to war they had no white People to direct them against their proper Enemy as the Northern Tribes had, and if they should go over the Boundary Line or fall on indiscriminately to kill women and children and to attack the King's friends as well as his enemies, they would draw on themselves all the force that was intended against the King's Troops and the resentment of those that otherwise would have been their friends, and would have assisted them; that their Father was willing to support them and supply them with ammunition while they paid regard to our Talks, But that we did not yet think it time for them to go out unless they were certain that there was an Army coming against them and therefore could not give our consent, as it was your desire that they should remain quiet until they should hear from you.

Cahetoy delivered this very distinctly. The Raven of Chote told them that they would consider of their Talks before they gave them a full answer and a meeting was appointed next day at Settico [Tellico,] where we were told the young fellows expressed a great deal of dissatisfaction at our not laying hold of their Belt, and from what we were afterwards informed passed there, and from the insinuations of one James Branham a half breed who had been in the settlements and was sent in with a design to injure Mr. Cameron, that our lives and the lives of all the white people of the Nation had been in great danger. . . .

It was in vain to talk any more of Peace, all that could now be done was to give them strict charge not to pass the Boundary Line, not to injure any of the King's faithful subjects, not to kill any women and children, and to stop hostilities when you should desire it notwithstanding any promises to the contrary given to the Shawnese. All these instructions they promised strictly to adhere to, and they begged that I would acquaint you of this, and that altho' they had been rash and listened too readily to the Talks of the Northward Indians, that the usage you had received, the threats against Mr. Cameron, and the cruelty used to Sir William Johnson's son were the causes that spurred them on and they therefore hoped that you would not be angry with them nor cast them off, but continue your assistance & support. They blamed Chincanacina the Warrior of Chilhowie as the cause of their beginning before they received your Orders.

QUESTIONS FOR CONSIDERATION

1. What do these documents reveal about the pressures and dilemmas Indian communities faced at the beginning of the Revolution?

2. What do the documents reveal about the workings of inter- and intratribal politics in an era of crisis?

3. Was neutrality ever a viable option for Indian peoples during the Revolution? What would you have done in their situation?

4. Henry Stuart was watching events from the wings but was vitally interested in their outcome; in what ways could this have affected the reliability of his report? Samuel Kirkland served as interpreter for the Oneidas on this and many other occasions; in what ways might Kirkland have affected the tone and content of the Oneidas' communications with the Americans?

An Indian Solution to the Conflict over Indian Lands

IN 1791 THE NORTHWEST INDIAN CONFEDERACY smashed Arthur St. Clair's army. As Anthony Wayne rebuilt the army and prepared for another invasion, the United States pursued diplomatic options in the hope of avoiding war by wringing concessions from the Indians, or simply to divide the confederacy in preparation for the next round of conflict. In the fall of 1792, the noted Seneca orator Red Jacket carried a message to the western tribes, saying the Americans would be willing to compromise and might accept the Muskingum River as the boundary line. But the Shawnees and their allies had defeated both Harmar's and St. Clair's armies and saw no need to compromise now. A Shawnee chief named Painted Pole told Red Jacket to "speak from your heart and not from your mouth," and, picking up the strings of wampum on which Red Jacket had spoken, he threw them at the feet of the Seneca delegation.

In the spring of 1793, while Wayne advanced into Indian country, three American commissioners traveled north to meet the Indian nations in council at Lower Sandusky in northwestern Ohio. Delegates from the various tribes held their own discussions before meeting with the commissioners. Joseph Brant suggested ceding land east of the Muskingum River as a compromise solution, but few other Indians were prepared to back down now from their insistence on the Ohio River boundary. Two British Indian agents, Alexander McKee and Matthew Elliott, both of whom had Shawnee wives, were present at the councils and evidently exerted their influence to back Indian resistance. Messages passed back and forth between the Indians and the commissioners, but the talks went nowhere. The Americans were not likely to concede while General Wayne was preparing for war, and with Wayne's army on the move, the Indian peoples suspected the United States was not serious about making peace. The Shawnees demanded that the Ohio boundary established at Fort Stanwix in 1768 be restored and that American settlements north of the Ohio be removed. The commissioners said that was out of the question: the Indians had ceded the lands north of the Ohio by treaty, and American settlers were already living there.

After two weeks of fruitless negotiations, the Indians sent the commissioners a message in which they reviewed the recent history of treaty relations with the United States and then, tongue in cheek, offered a formula for peace. Delegates from all the tribes, except for Brant and the Iroquois, affixed their marks to the message. The American commissioners promptly packed their bags and left. "The Indians have refused to make peace," they reported to the secretary of war. Having tried and failed to reach an agreement with the tribes, the government now turned to General Wayne's army to resolve the issue.[69]

WESTERN INDIANS
Message to the Commissioners of the United States (1793)

Brothers,

We have received your speech dated the 31st of last month, and it has been interpreted to all the different nations. We have been long in sending you an answer, because of the great importance of the subject. But we now answer it fully, having given it all the consideration in our power.

Brothers,

You tell us that after you had made peace with the king, our Father, about [ten] years ago, "it remained to make peace between the United States and the Indian Nations who had taken part with the king; for this purpose Commissioners were appointed, who sent messages to all those nations, inviting them to come and make peace;" and after reciting the periods at which you say treaties were held at Fort Stanwix, Fort McIntosh, and Miami, all which treaties, according to your own acknowledgement, were for the sole purpose of making peace; you then say, "Brothers, the Commissioners who conducted these treaties in behalf of the United States, sent the papers containing them to the general council of the States, who, supposing them satisfactory to the nations treated with, proceeded to dispose of the lands thereby ceded."

Brothers,

This is telling us plainly what we always understood to be the case, and it agrees with the declarations of those few who attended these treaties, viz. that they went to meet your Commissioners to make peace, but, through fear, were obliged to sign any paper that was laid before them; and it has since appeared, that deeds of cession were signed by them, instead of treaties of peace.

Brothers,

You say "after some time it appeared that a number of people in your nations were dissatisfied with the treaties of Fort McIntosh, and Miami. Therefore the council of the United States appointed Governor St. Clair their Commissioner with full power, for the purpose of removing all causes of controversy relating to trade and settling boundaries between the Indian nations in the northern department of the United States. He accordingly sent messages, inviting all the nations concerned to meet him at a council-fire he kindled at the falls of Muskingum. While he was waiting for them, some mischief happened at that place, and the fire was put out, so he kindled a fire at Fort Harmar, where near six hundred Indians of different nations attended. The Six Nations then renewed and confirmed the Treaty of Fort Stanwix, and the Wyandots and Delawares renewed and confirmed the treaty of Fort McIntosh. Some Ottawas, Chippeways, Potawatamies and Sacs were also parties to the treaty of Fort Harmar." Now brothers, these are your words, and it is necessary for us to make a short reply to them.

Brothers,

A general council of all the Indian confederacy was held, as you well know, in the fall of the year 1788, at this place; and that general council was invited by your Commissioner, General St. Clair, to meet him for the purpose of holding a treaty with regard to the lands mentioned by you to have been ceded by the treaties of Fort Stanwix and Fort McIntosh.

Brothers,

We are in possession of the speeches and letters which passed on that occasion between those deputed by the confederate Indians, and Governor St. Clair, the Commissioner of the United States. These papers prove that your said Commissioner, in the beginning of the year 1789,

SOURCE: "Journal of a Treaty held in 1793, with the Indian Tribes northwest of the Ohio by Commissioners of the United States," *Collections of the Massachusetts Historical Society*, series 3, vol. 5 (1836), 163–67.

after having been informed by the general council of the preceding fall, that no bargain or sale of any part of these Indian lands would be considered as valid or binding, unless agreed to by a general council, nevertheless persisted in collecting a few chiefs of two or three nations only, and with them held a treaty for the cession of an immense country, in which they were no more interested than a branch of the general confederacy, and who were in no manner authorized to make any grant or cession whatever.

Brothers,

How then was it possible for you to expect to enjoy peace, and quietly hold these lands, when your Commissioner was informed, long before he held the treaty of Fort Harmar, that the consent of a general council was absolutely necessary to convey any part of these lands to the United States? The part of these lands which the United States wish us to relinquish, and which you say are settled, have been sold by the United States since that time.

Brothers,

You say "the United States wish to have confirmed all the lands ceded to them by the treaty of Fort Harmar, and also a small tract at the Rapids of the Ohio, claimed by General Clark for the use of himself and his warriors. And in consideration thereof the United States would give such a large sum in money or goods as was never given at any one time for any quantity of Indian lands since the white people first set their feet on this island. And because those lands did every year furnish you with skins and furs, with which you bought clothing and other necessaries, the United States will now furnish the constant supplies. And therefore, besides the great sum to be delivered at once, they will every year deliver you a large quantity of such goods as are best fitted to the wants of yourselves, your women and children."

Brothers,

Money to us is of no value, and to most of us unknown; and as no consideration whatever can induce us to sell our lands, on which we get sustenance for our women and children, we hope we may be allowed to point out a mode by which your settlers may be easily removed, and peace thereby obtained.

Brothers,

We know that these settlers are poor, or they would never have ventured to live in a country which has been in continual trouble ever since they crossed the Ohio. Divide therefore this large sum of money, which you have offered to us, among these people; give to each also a proportion of what you say you would give us annually, over and above this very large sum of money; and we are persuaded they would most readily accept of it in lieu of the lands you sold to them. If you add also the great sums you must expend in raising and paying armies with a view to force us to yield you our country, you will certainly have more than sufficient for the purposes of repaying these settlers for all their labor and improvements.

Brothers,

You have talked to us about concessions. It appears strange that you should expect any from us, who have only been defending our just rights against your invasions. We want peace. Restore to us our country, and we shall be enemies no longer.

Brothers,

You make one concession to us by offering to us your money, and another by having agreed to do us justice, after having long and injuriously withheld it; we mean in the acknowledgement you have now made that the king of England never did, nor ever had a right to give you our country by the treaty of peace. And you want to make this act of common justice a great part of your concession, and seem to expect that because you have at last acknowledged our independence, we should for such a favor surrender to you our country.

Brothers,

You have also talked a great deal about preemption, and your exclusive right to purchase Indian lands, as ceded to you by the king at the treaty of peace.

Brothers,

We never made any agreement with the king, nor with any other nation, that we would give to either the exclusive right to purchase our lands, and we declare to you that we consider ourselves free to make any bargain or cession of lands whenever and to whomsoever we please. If the white people, as you say, made a treaty that none of them but the king should purchase of us, and he has given that right to the United States, it is an affair which concerns you and him, and not us. We have never parted with such a power.

Brothers,

At our general council held at the Glaise last fall, we agreed to meet Commissioners from the United States for the purpose of restoring peace, provided they consented to acknowledge and confirm our boundary line to be the Ohio; and we determined not to meet you, until you gave us satisfaction on that point. That is the reason we have never met.

We desire you to consider, brothers, that our only demand is the peaceable possession of a small part of our once great country. Look back and view the lands from whence we have been driven to this spot. We can retreat no farther, because the country behind hardly affords food for its present inhabitants, and we have therefore resolved to leave our bones in this small space, to which we are now consigned.

Brothers,

We shall be persuaded that you mean to do us justice, if you agree that the Ohio shall remain the boundary line between us. If you will not consent thereto, our meeting will be altogether unnecessary. This is the great point, which we hoped would have been explained before you left your homes; as our message last fall was principally directed to obtain that information.

Done in general council at the foot of the Miami Rapids, the 13th day of August, 1793.

[Nations.]	Marks.
Wyandots,	A Bear.
Seven Nations of Canada,	A Turtle.
Delawares,	A Turtle.
Shawanese,	
Miamis,	A Turtle.
Ottawas,	A Fish.
Chippeways,	A Crane.
Senecas of the Glaise,	A Turtle.
Potawatamies,	A Fish.
Connoys,	A Turkey.
Munsees,	
Nantikokes,	A Turtle.
Mohegans [Mohicans],	{ A Turkey. { A Turtle.
Messasaguas,	
Creeks,	
Cherokees	

QUESTIONS FOR CONSIDERATION

1. How did the western Indians view U.S. dealings with the Indians in the decade after the end of the American Revolution?

2. What was the policy of the Northwest Indian confederacy with regard to land sales?

3. What, from the Indians' perspective, were the key causes of conflict?

PICTURE ESSAY

Northwest Coast Indians on the Brink: The Drawings of John Webber

✦ ✕✕✕✕✕✕✕✦✕✕✕✕✕✕✕ ✦

M ANY EUROPEANS WHO TRAVELED to the Northwest Coast in the sea otter
trade also recorded detailed accounts of the Native peoples they met: Chinooks on the Columbia, Nootkas on the west coast of Vancouver, Haidas on the
Queen Charlotte Islands, and Tlingits in southeastern Alaska. Euro-American
observers rarely displayed much cultural sensitivity toward the coastal peoples,
some of whom practiced ornamental head deformation and wore labrets inserted
in their lower lips as marks of status. But seamen's journals provide valuable
ethnographic information, and in some cases shipboard artists created invaluable
visual records of the Native cultures of the Northwest. They also provide insights
into the cataclysmic changes they themselves initiated.[70]

John Webber (1751–93) was the official artist on Captain James Cook's third
voyage. Cook was the greatest seaman of his age. By the time of his death in 1779
he had sailed more than 200,000 miles, the equivalent of circling the equator eight
times or traveling to the moon, and his voyages brought his crews into contact
with Native peoples around the world.[71] On Cook's third and final voyage, which
reached the Northwest Coast in the spring of 1778, Webber composed an impressive collection of drawings of Native people in Hawaii, British Columbia, Alaska,
Siberia, Tonga, Tahiti, and New Zealand, in many cases sketching their portraits
when they came on board ship.[72] He also sketched houses, artifacts, kayaks, and
landscapes. He drew people whose world was about to change forever. Indians
paddled cedar canoes out to ships (Figure 4.1) that carried cloth and copper; but
those ships also carried guns, alcohol, syphilis, and smallpox. When Lewis and
Clark reached the Pacific Coast thirty years later, they found abandoned villages,
people with pockmarked faces and venereal diseases, and Indians who swore like
sailors.

Webber's drawing of the interior of a Native plank house at Nootka Sound
shows living arrangements, methods of cooking, racks of smoked salmon under
the ceiling, baskets and cedar storage boxes, and carved posts at the rear of the
room (Figure 4.2). Northwest Coast Indians became famous for their elaborately
carved totem poles, and Native wood carvers were eager to trade for metal chisels
and other new tools.

The woman from Nootka (Figure 4.3) is wearing a rain cape of woven
cedar and a woven hat on which are depicted whale hunting scenes. Whale

◆ **Figure 4.1 John Webber, *A View in Ship Cove, Nootka Sound* (1778)**
© British Library Board/Robana/Art Resource, NY.

hunting was a male activity, and such hats were normally worn by men of high status, so the woman may have donned the hat at Webber's request to enrich the portrait.[73]

The man from Nootka (Figure 4.4) also wears a rain cape, but Webber is especially interested in and meticulously records the man's facial ornaments and facial markings, made with a mixture of paint, fish oil, and rue. Traveling north to the Gulf of Alaska, Webber sketched a Native woman from Prince William Sound, again paying particular attention to face ornamentations and the custom of slitting the underlip to insert pieces of bone (Figure 4.5). In Alaska, Webber sketched Aleutian hunters paddling sealskin kayaks. The Aleutian hunter (Figure 4.6) wears a glare visor decorated with painted designs, feathers, amulets, and seal and sea lion whiskers. The groups of sea lion whiskers indicate the number of marine mammals taken.[74]

◆ **Figure 4.2 John Webber, *Interior of Habitation at Nootka Sound* (1778)**
Granger, NYC.

◆ **Figure 4.3 John Webber, *A Woman of Nootka Sound* (1778)**
Washington State Historical Society/Art Resource, NY.

◆ **Figure 4.4 John Webber, *A Man of Nootka Sound* (1778)**
De Agostini Picture Library/Granger, NYC.

◆ **Figure 4.5 John Webber, *A Woman of Prince William's Island* (1778)**

Granger, NYC.

◆ **Figure 4.6 John Webber, *A Man of Oonalashka* (1778)**

De Agostini Picture Library/Granger, NYC.

QUESTIONS FOR CONSIDERATION

1. Webber was clearly interested in Native customs, government, clothing, religion, and lifeways, but he also viewed Native peoples with many of the prejudices of his age and society. How are these interests and attitudes revealed in his drawings?

2. What purposes might the facial markings and the designs on the conical hat and visor have served, besides pure decoration?

3. Webber drew Northwest Coast Indians just as the sea otter trade was about to boom. What changes might his pictures and portraits have shown had he sketched them twenty years later?

REFERENCES

1. See, e.g., Michael J. Witgen, *An Infinity of Nations: How the Native New World Shaped Modern America* (Philadelphia: University of Pennsylvania Press, 2012).

2. Colin G. Calloway, *The Scratch of a Pen: 1763 and the Transformation of North America* (New York: Oxford University Press, 2006).

3. William R. Nester, *"Haughty Conquerors": Amherst and the Great Indian Uprising of 1763* (Westport, Conn.: Praeger, 2000), 50–52; Wilbur R. Jacobs, *Wilderness Politics and Indian Gifts: The Northern Colonial Frontier, 1748–1763* (1950; repr., Lincoln: University of Nebraska Press, 1966), 180–85; Gregory Evans Dowd, *War under Heaven* (Baltimore: Johns Hopkins University Press, 2002).

4. Gregory Evans Dowd, *A Spirited Resistance: The North American Indian Struggle for Unity, 1745–1815* (Baltimore: Johns Hopkins University Press, 1992), 33–36.

5. Keith R. Widder, *Beyond Pontiac's Shadow: Michilimackinac and the Anglo-Indian War of 1763* (East Lansing: Michigan State University Press, 2013).

6. Peter Silver, *Our Savage Neighbors: How Indian War Transformed Early America* (New York: W. W. Norton, 2008); Kevin Kenny, *Peaceable Kingdom Lost: The Paxton Boys and the Destruction of William Penn's Holy Experiment* (New York: Oxford University Press, 2009).

7. Reprinted in Adam Shortt and Arthur G. Doughty, eds., *Documents Relating to the Constitutional History of Canada, 1759–1791* (Ottawa: Historical Documents Publication Board, 1918), 1:163–68.

8. Quoted in Fred Anderson, *Crucible of War: The Seven Years' War and the Fate of Empire in British North America, 1754–1766* (New York: Alfred A. Knopf, 2000), 740.

9. William J. Campbell, *Speculators in Empire: Iroquoia and the 1768 Treaty of Fort Stanwix* (Norman: University of Oklahoma Press, 2012); Colin G. Calloway, *Pen and Ink Witchcraft: Treaties and Treaty Making in American Indian History* (New York: Oxford University Press, 2013), chap. 2.

10. Quoted in Colin G. Calloway, *The American Revolution in Indian Country: Crisis and Diversity in Native American Communities* (Cambridge: Cambridge University Press, 1995), 29–30.

11. George Quintal Jr., *Patriots of Color: African Americans and Native Americans at Battle Road and Bunker Hill* (Boston: Boston National Historical Park, 2002), 30–31.

12. Nadia Dean, *A Demand of Blood: The Cherokee War of 1776* (Cherokee, N.C.: Valley River Press, 2012).

13. Quoted in Colin G. Calloway, ed., *The World Turned Upside Down: Indian Voices from Early America* (Boston: Bedford Books, 1994), 159–60.

14. Calloway, *World Turned Upside Down*, 167–69.

15. Quoted in Calloway, *American Revolution*, vi, 281.

16. Andrew Nichols, *Red Gentlemen and White Savages: Indians, Federalists, and the Search for Order on the American Frontier* (Charlottesville: University of Virginia Press, 2008).

17. Colin G. Calloway, ed., *Revolution and Confederation*, vol. 18 of *Early American Indian Documents: Treaties and Laws, 1607–1789*, ed. Alden T. Vaughan (Bethesda, Md.: University Publications of America, 1994), 284, 313–27.

18. Karim M. Tiro, *People of the Standing Stone: The Oneida Indian Nation from Revolution through Removal* (Amherst: University of Massachusetts Press, 2011); David J. Silverman, *Red Brethren: The Brothertown and Stockbridge Indians and the Problem of Race in Early America* (Ithaca, N.Y.: Cornell University Press, 2010), Oneida quote at 140.

19. Quoted in Calloway, *American Revolution*, 48.

20. Quoted in Calloway, *Revolution and Confederation*, 158.

21. Francis Paul Prucha, *American Indian Policy in the Formative Years: The Indian Trade and Intercourse Acts, 1790–1834* (Lincoln: University of Nebraska Press, 1970), vii, 1–2.

22. Stuart Banner, *How the Indians Lost Their Land: Law and Power on the Frontier* (Cambridge, Mass.: Harvard University Press, 2005), quote at 146.

23. Quoted in Calloway, *Revolution and Confederation*, xxv.

24. Calloway, *World Turned Upside Down*, 175–76.

25. Colin G. Calloway, *Victory with No Name: The Native American Defeat of the First American Army* (New York: Oxford University Press, 2015).

26. William Heath, *William Wells and the Struggle for the Old Northwest* (Norman: University of Oklahoma Press, 2015).

27. Dresden W. H. Howard, "The Battle of Fallen Timbers as Told by Chief Kin-Jo-I-No," *Northwest Ohio Quarterly* 20, no. 1 (1948), 37–49, quotes at 46–47.

28. David J. Weber, *Bárbaros: Spaniards and Their Savages in the Age of Enlightenment* (New Haven: Yale University Press, 2005).

29. Kathleen DuVal, chap. 4 in *The Native Ground: Indians and Colonists in the Heart of the Continent* (Philadelphia: University of Pennsylvania Press, 2006); Willard H. Rollings, *The Osage: An Ethnohistorical Study of Hegemony on the Prairie-Plains* (Columbia: University of Missouri Press, 1992).

30. Pekka Hämäläinen, *The Comanche Empire* (New Haven: Yale University Press, 2008).

31. Alfred Barnaby Thomas, trans. and ed., *Forgotten Frontiers: A Study of the Spanish Indian Policy of Don Juan Bautista de Anza, Governor of New Mexico, 1777–1787* (Norman: University of Oklahoma Press, 1932), 317.

32. Juliana Barr, *Peace Came in the Form of a Woman: Indians and Spaniards in the Texas Borderlands* (Chapel Hill: University of North Carolina Press, 2007), 276–86.

33. Mark Santiago, *The Jar of Severed Hands: Spanish Deportation of Apache Prisoners of War 1770–1810* (Norman: University of Oklahoma Press, 2011).

34. Claudio Saunt, *West of the Revolution* (New York: W. W. Norton, 2014), 150–51; Richard White, "Winning the West: The Expansion of the Western Sioux in the Eighteenth and Nineteenth Centuries," *Journal of American History* 65 (1978), 319–43.

35. Saunt, *West of the Revolution*, chap. 5; Arthur J. Ray, *Indians in the Fur Trade: Their Role as Hunters, Trappers, and Middlemen in the Lands Southwest of Hudson Bay, 1660–1870* (Toronto: University of Toronto Press, 1974).

36. Colin G. Calloway, "Snake Frontiers: The Eastern Shoshones in the Eighteenth Century," *Annals of Wyoming* 63 (Summer 1991), 82–92.

37. James A. Sandos, *Converting California: Indians and Franciscans in the Missions* (New Haven: Yale University Press, 2004); Steven W. Hackel, *Children of Coyote, Missionaries of Saint Francis: Indian-Spanish Relations in Colonial California, 1769–1850* (Chapel Hill: University of North Carolina Press, 2005), quote at 280.

38. Albert L. Hurtado, "Sexuality in California's Franciscan Missions: Cultural Perceptions and Sad Realities," *California History* 71 (Fall 1992), 371–85; Robert H. Jackson and Edward Castillo, *Indians, Franciscans, and Spanish Colonization: The Impact of the Mission System on California Indians* (Albuquerque: University of New Mexico Press, 1995); Virginia M. Bouvier, chaps. 3, 5–7 in *Women and the Conquest of California, 1542–1840: Codes of Silence* (Tucson: University of Arizona Press, 2001).

39. Robert H. Jackson, *Indian Population Decline: The Missions of Northwestern New Spain, 1687–1840* (Albuquerque: University of New Mexico Press, 1994); Quincy D. Newell, *Constructing Lives at Mission San Francisco: Native Californians and Hispanic Colonists, 1776–1821* (Albuquerque: University of New Mexico Press, 2009).

40. Robert H. Ruby and John A. Brown, chap. 1 in *The Chinook Indians: Traders of the Lower Columbia River* (Norman: University of Oklahoma Press, 1976); Robert T. Boyd, Kenneth M. Ames, and Tony A. Johnson, eds., *Chinookan Peoples of the Lower Columbia* (Seattle: University of Washington Press, 2013).

41. Warren L. Cook, chap. 3 in *Flood Tide of Empire: Spain and the Pacific Northwest, 1543–1819* (New Haven: Yale University Press, 1973); Barry Gough, *Distant Dominion: Britain and the Northwest Coast of North America, 1579–1809* (Vancouver: University of British Columbia Press, 1980).

42. J. C. Beaglehole, ed., *The Journals of Captain James Cook on His Voyages of Discovery*, vol. 3 (Cambridge: Cambridge University Press for the Hakluyt Society, 1967).

43. John Ledyard, *A Journal of Captain Cook's Last Voyage to the Pacific Ocean, and in Quest of a Northwest Passage, Performed in the Years 1776–79* (Hartford, Conn.: Nathaniel Patten, 1783), 70.

44. Thomas Vaughan and Bill Holm, eds., *Soft Gold: The Fur Trade and Cultural Exchange on the Northwest Coast of America* (Portland: Oregon Historical Society, 1982); James R. Gibson, *Otter Skins, Boston Ships, and China Goods: The Maritime Fur Trade of the Northwest Coast, 1785–1841* (Montreal: McGill-Queens University Press; Seattle: University of Washington Press, 1992).

45. Cook, chap. 8 in *Flood Tide*, figures on vessels at p. 551; Gibson, *Otter Skins*, 299–310.

46. Sergei Kan, *Memory Eternal: Tlingit Culture and Russian Orthodox Christianity through Two Centuries* (Seattle: University of Washington Press, 1999), 34–65.

47. W. Kaye Lamb, ed., *Journals and Letters of Sir Alexander Mackenzie* (Cambridge: Published for the Hakluyt Society at the University Press, 1970), 375–76.

48. John Scofield, *Hail, Columbia: Robert Gray, John Hendrick, and the Pacific Fur Trade* (Portland: Oregon Historical Society Press, 1993); Frederic W. Howay, ed., *Voyages of the Columbia to the Northwest Coast* (1941; repr., Portland: Oregon Historical Society, 1990).

49. Frederic W. Howay, "Early Days of the Maritime Fur Trade on the Northwest Coast," *Canadian Historical Review* 4 (March 1923), 26–44 (Boston suburb quote at 41–42); Gibson, chap. 3 in *Otter Skins*.

50. Robin Fisher, chap. 7 in *Contact and Conflict: Indian-European Relations in British Columbia, 1774–1890* (Vancouver: University of British Columbia Press, 1977); Gibson, chap. 6 in *Otter Skins*; Joshua L. Reid, *The Sea Is My Country: The Maritime World of the Makahs* (New Haven: Yale University Press, 2015).

51. Cook, *Flood Tide*, 313.

52. Mary C. Wright, "Economic Development and Native American Women in the Early Nineteenth Century," *American Quarterly* 33 (Winter 1981), 525–36, esp. 534–35; Gray Whaley, "'Complete Liberty'? Gender, Sexuality, Race, and Social Change on the Lower Columbia River, 1805–1838," *Ethnohistory* 54 (Fall 2007), 669–95.

53. W. Kaye Lamb, ed., *George Vancouver: A Voyage of Discovery to the North Pacific Ocean and Round the World, 1791–1795* (London: Hakluyt Society, 1984), 2:516–17, 528, 538–40, 559.

54. Robert Boyd, *The Coming of the Spirit of Pestilence: Introduced Infectious Diseases and Population Decline among the Northwest Coast Indians, 1774–1874* (Seattle: University of Washington Press, 1999).

55. For additional information on the course of the epidemic and on the sources for tracing it, see Elizabeth E. Fenn, *Pox Americana: The Great Smallpox Epidemic of 1775–82* (New York: Hill and Wang, 2001), and Colin G. Calloway, *One Vast Winter Count: The Native American West before Lewis and Clark* (Lincoln: University of Nebraska Press, 2003), 415–26.

56. Fenn, *Pox Americana*, 163, 214–15; Thomas, *Forgotten Frontiers*, 244–45.

57. Elizabeth A. Fenn, *Encounters at the Heart of the World: A History of the Mandan People* (New York: Hill and Wang, 2014), chap. 7; Alfred Bowers, *Hidatsa Social and Ceremonial Organization* (1963; repr., Lincoln: University of Nebraska Press, 1992), 214–15, 486; Annie Heloise Abel, ed., *Tabeau's Narrative of Loisel's Expedition to the Upper Missouri* (Norman: University of Oklahoma Press, 1939), 123–24; Gary E. Moulton, ed., *The Journals of the Lewis and Clark Expedition*. 13 vols. (Lincoln: University of Nebraska Press, 1983–2001), 3:161, 163, 197, 201–2, 205–7, 233, 312, 401–5; Adam R. Hodge, "Pestilence and Power: The Smallpox Epidemic of 1780–1782 and Intertribal Relations on the Northern Great Plains," *The Historian* 72 (2010), 543–67.

58. Linea Sundstrom, "Smallpox Used Them Up: References to Epidemic Disease in Northern Plains Winter Counts, 1714–1920," *Ethnohistory* 44 (Spring 1997), 330–40.

59. W. Raymond Wood and Thomas D. Thiessen, eds., *Early Fur Trade on the Northern Plains: Canadian Traders among the Mandan and Hidatsa Indians, 1738–1818* (Norman: University of Oklahoma Press, 1985), 206.

60. Colin G. Calloway, ed., *Our Hearts Fell to the Ground: Plains Indian Views of How the West Was Lost* (Boston: Bedford/St. Martin's, 1996), 46–47.

61. Quoted in Boyd, *Coming of the Spirit*, 23–24, and Fenn, *Pox Americana*, 227.

62. Sundstrom, "Smallpox Used Them Up."
63. Calloway, ed. *Confederation and Revolution*, 121–22, 134–36.
64. Maryly B. Penrose, ed., *Indian Affairs Papers: American Revolution* (Franklin Park, N.J.: Liberty Bell Associates, 1981), 115.
65. Alan Taylor, *The Divided Ground: Indians, Settlers, and the Northern Borderland of the American Revolution* (New York: Alfred A. Knopf, 2006); Martin and Glatthaar, *Forgotten Allies*, 78–85; Tiro, *People of the Standing Stone*, 45–47.
66. Tiro, *People of the Standing Stone*, 48–49; Calloway, *American Revolution*, 33–34.
67. Quoted in Calloway, *American Revolution*, 189.
68. William L. Sanders, ed., *The Colonial Records of North Carolina*, vol. 10 (Raleigh: State Printer, 1890), 764; Colin G. Calloway, "Declaring Independence and Rebuilding a Nation: Dragging Canoe and the Chickamauga Revolution," in Alfred F. Young, Gary B. Nash, and Ray Raphael, eds., *Revolutionary Founders: Rebels, Radicals, and Reformers in the Making of the Nation* (New York: Knopf, 2011), 185–98.
69. Colin G. Calloway, *The Shawnees and the War for America* (New York: Viking Penguin, 2007), 94–101.
70. Erna Gunther, *Indian Life on the Northwest Coast of North America, as Seen by the Early Explorers and Fur Traders during the Last Decades of the Eighteenth Century* (Chicago: University of Chicago Press, 1972).
71. Frank McLynn, *Captain Cook: Master of the Seas* (New Haven: Yale University Press, 2011), 411.
72. Rüdiger Joppien and Bernard Smith, *The Art of Captain Cook's Voyages*, vol. 3, *The Voyage of the Resolution and Discovery, 1776–1780* (New Haven: Yale University Press, 1988).
73. Vaughan and Holm, *Soft Gold*, 187.
74. Vaughan and Holm, *Soft Gold*, 199.

SUGGESTED READINGS

Banner, Stuart. *How the Indians Lost Their Land: Law and Power on the Frontier*. Cambridge, Mass.: Harvard University Press, 2005.

Blackhawk, Ned, ed. *Ethnohistory* 54, no. 4, "Between Empires: Indians in the American West during the Age of Empire" (Fall 2007).

———. *Violence over the Land: Indians and Empires in the Early American West*. Cambridge, Mass.: Harvard University Press, 2006.

Bouvier, Virginia M. *Women and the Conquest of California, 1542–1840: Codes of Silence*. Tucson: University of Arizona Press, 2001.

Boyd, Robert. T*he Coming of the Spirit of Pestilence: Introduced Infectious Diseases and Population Decline among the Northwest Coast Indians, 1774–1874*. Seattle: University of Washington Press, 1999.

Calloway, Colin G. *The American Revolution in Indian Country: Crisis and Diversity in Native American Communities*. Cambridge: Cambridge University Press, 1995.

———. *Crown and Calumet: British-Indian Relations, 1783–1815*. Norman: University of Oklahoma Press, 1987.

———. *One Vast Winter Count: The Native American West before Lewis and Clark*. Lincoln: University of Nebraska Press, 2003.

———. *Pen and Ink Witchcraft: Treaties and Treaty Making in American Indian History*. New York: Oxford University Press, 2013.

———, ed. *Revolution and Confederation*. Vol. 18 of *Early American Indian Documents: Treaties and Laws, 1607–1789*, edited by Alden T. Vaughan. Bethesda, Md.: University Publications of America, 1994.

———. *The Scratch of a Pen: 1763 and the Transformation of North America*. New York: Oxford University Press, 2006.

———. *The Shawnees and the War for America*. New York: Viking Penguin, 2007.

———. *Victory with No Name: The Native American Defeat of the First American Army*. New York: Oxford University Press, 2015.

———, ed. *The World Turned Upside Down: Indian Voices from Early America*. Boston: Bedford/St. Martin's, 1994.

Campbell, William J. *Speculators in Empire: Iroquoia and the 1768 Treaty of Fort Stanwix*. Norman: University of Oklahoma Press, 2012.

Cook, Warren L. *Flood Tide of Empire: Spain and the Pacific Northwest, 1543–1819*. New Haven: Yale University Press, 1973.

Dean, Nadia. *A Demand of Blood: The Cherokee War of 1776*. Cherokee, N.C.: Valley River Press, 2012.

Dowd, Gregory Evans. *A Spirited Resistance: The North American Indian Struggle for Unity, 1745–1815*. Baltimore: Johns Hopkins University Press, 1992.

———. *War under Heaven: Pontiac, the Indian Nations, and the British Empire*. Baltimore: Johns Hopkins University Press, 2002.

Downes, Randolph C. *Council Fires on the Upper Ohio: A Narrative of Indian Affairs in the Upper Ohio Valley until 1795*. Pittsburgh: University of Pittsburgh Press, 1940.

DuVal, Kathleen. *The Native Ground: Indians and Colonists in the Heart of the Continent*. Philadelphia: University of Pennsylvania Press, 2006.

Fenn, Elizabeth A. *Encounters at the Heart of the World: A History of the Mandan People*. New York: Hill and Wang, 2014.

———. *Pox Americana: The Great Smallpox Epidemic of 1775–82*. New York: Hill and Wang, 2001.

Gibson, James R. *Otter Skins, Boston Ships, and China Goods: The Maritime Fur Trade of the Northwest Coast, 1785–1841*.

Montreal: McGill-Queens University Press; Seattle: University of Washington Press, 1992.

Glatthaar, Joseph T., and James Kirby Martin. Forgotten *Allies: The Oneida Indians and the American Revolution*. New York: Hill and Wang, 2006.

Gough, Barry. *Distant Dominion: Britain and the Northwest Coast of North America, 1579–1809*. Vancouver: University of British Columbia Press, 1980.

Griffin, Patrick. *American Leviathan: Empire, Nation, and Revolutionary Frontier*. New York: Hill and Wang, 2007.

Gunther, Erna. *Indian Life on the Northwest Coast of North America, as Seen by the Early Explorers and Fur Traders during the Last Decades of the Eighteenth Century*. Chicago: University of Chicago Press, 1972.

Hackel, Steven W. *Children of Coyote, Missionaries of Saint Francis: Indian-Spanish Relations in Colonial California, 1769–1850*. Chapel Hill: University of North Carolina Press, 2005.

Hämäläinen, Pekka. *The Comanche Empire*. New Haven: Yale University Press, 2008.

Harjo, Suzan Shown, ed. *Nation to Nation: Treaties between the United States and American Indian Nations*. Washington, D.C.: Smithsonian Institution, 2014.

Hatley, Tom. *The Dividing Paths: Cherokees and South Carolinians through the Era of Revolution*. New York: Oxford University Press, 1993.

Heath, William. *William Wells and the Struggle for the Old Northwest*. Norman: University of Oklahoma Press, 2015.

Hinderaker, Eric. *Elusive Empires: Constructing Colonialism in the Ohio Valley, 1673–1800*. Cambridge: Cambridge University Press, 1997.

Horsman, Reginald. *Expansion and American Indian Policy, 1783–1812*. Reprint, Norman: University of Oklahoma Press, 1992.

Jackson, Robert H. *Indian Population Decline: The Missions of Northwestern New Spain, 1687–1840*. Albuquerque: University of New Mexico Press, 1994.

Jackson, Robert H., and Edward Castillo. *Indians, Franciscans, and Spanish Colonization: The Impact of the Mission System on California Indians*. Albuquerque: University of New Mexico Press, 1995.

Kenny, Kevin. *Peaceable Kingdom Lost: The Paxton Boys and the Destruction of William Penn's Holy Experiment*. New York: Oxford University Press, 2009.

Lakomäki, Sami. *Gathering Together: The Shawnee People through Diaspora and Nationhood, 1600–1870*. New Haven: Yale University Press, 2014.

Mann, Barbara Alice. *George Washington's War on Native America*. Westport, Conn.: Praeger, 2005.

Middleton, Richard. *Pontiac's War: Its Causes, Course and Consequences*. New York: Routledge, 2007.

Newell, Quincy D. *Constructing Lives at Mission San Francisco: Native Californians and Hispanic Colonists, 1776–1821*. Albuquerque: University of New Mexico Press, 2009.

Nichols, David Andrew. *Red Gentlemen and White Savages: Indians, Federalists, and the Search for Order on the American Frontier*. Charlottesville: University of Virginia Press, 2008.

O'Brien, Greg. *Choctaws in a Revolutionary Age, 1750–1830*. Lincoln: University of Nebraska Press, 2002.

Perdue, Theda. *Cherokee Women: Gender and Culture Change, 1700–1835*. Lincoln: University of Nebraska Press, 1998.

Prucha, Francis Paul. *American Indian Policy in the Formative Years: The Indian Trade and Intercourse Acts, 1790–1834*. Lincoln: University of Nebraska Press, 1970.

Reid, Joshua L. *The Sea Is My Country: The Maritime World of the Makahs*. New Haven. Yale University Press, 2015.

Sandos, James A. *Converting California: Indians and Franciscans in the Missions*. New Haven: Yale University Press, 2004.

Saunt, Claudio. *West of the Revolution: An Uncommon History of 1776*. New York: W. W. Norton, 2014.

Silver, Peter. *Our Savage Neighbors: How Indian War Transformed Early America*. New York: W. W. Norton, 2008.

Silverman, David J. *Red Brethren: The Brothertown and Stockbridge Indians and the Problem of Race in Early America*. Ithaca, N.Y.: Cornell University Press, 2010.

Snapp, J. Russell. *John Stuart and the Struggle for Empire on the Southern Frontier*. Baton Rouge: Louisiana State University Press, 1996.

Sugden, John. *Blue Jacket: Warrior of the Shawnees*. Lincoln: University of Nebraska Press, 2000.

Sundstrom, Linea. "Smallpox Used Them Up: References to Epidemic Disease in Northern Plains Winter Counts, 1714–1920." *Ethnohistory* 44 (Spring 1997), 330–40.

Sword, Wiley. *President Washington's Indian War*. Norman: University of Oklahoma Press, 1985.

Tanner, Helen Hornbeck, ed. *Atlas of Great Lakes Indian History*. Norman: University of Oklahoma Press, 1987.

Taylor, Alan. *The Divided Ground: Indians, Settlers, and the Northern Borderland of the American Revolution*. New York: Alfred A. Knopf, 2006.

Thomas, Alfred Barnaby, trans. and ed. *Forgotten Frontiers: A Study of the Spanish Indian Policy of Don Juan Bautista de Anza, Governor of New Mexico, 1777–1787*. Norman: University of Oklahoma Press, 1932.

Tiro, Karim M. *People of the Standing Stone: The Oneida Indian Nation from Revolution through Removal*. Amherst: University of Massachusetts Press, 2011.

Usner, Daniel H., Jr. *Indians, Settlers, and Slaves in a Frontier Exchange Economy: The Lower Mississippi Valley before 1783*. Chapel Hill: University of North Carolina Press, 1992.

Vaughan, Thomas, and Bill Holm, eds. *Soft Gold: The Fur Trade and Cultural Exchange on the Northwest Coast of America*. Portland: Oregon Historical Society, 1982.

Weber, David J. *Bárbaros: Spaniards and Their Savages in the Age of Enlightenment*. New Haven: Yale University Press, 2005.

White, Richard. *The Middle Ground: Indians, Empires, and Republics in the Great Lakes Region, 1650–1815.* Cambridge: Cambridge University Press, 1991.

Widder, Keith R. *Beyond Pontiac's Shadow: Michilimackinac and the Anglo-Indian War of 1763.* East Lansing: Michigan State University Press, 2013.

Willig, Timothy D. *Restoring the Chain of Friendship: British Policy and the Indians of the Great Lakes, 1783–1815.* Lincoln: University of Nebraska Press, 2008.

Witgen, Michael J. *An Infinity of Nations: How the Native New World Shaped Modern America.* Philadelphia: University of Pennsylvania Press, 2012.

Wood, Raymond, and Thomas D. Thiessen, eds. *Early Fur Trade on the Northern Plains: Canadian Traders among the Mandan and Hidatsa Indians, 1738–1818.* Norman: University of Oklahoma Press, 1985.

5

American Indians and the New Nation

1800–1840

FOCUS QUESTIONS

1. What were the various responses of Indian peoples to the social, cultural, and religious pressures imposed on them by the new United States?

2. What kinds of Indian worlds did Lewis and Clark encounter, and in what ways did their expedition affect Indians west of the Mississippi?

3. What methods of removal did the United States implement, and where? What forms of resistance and support formed in response to the removal policy?

ACCOMMODATING AND RESISTING CHANGE

BETWEEN 1800 AND 1840, the new American nation grew dramatically in size, population, and power. It acquired vast new territory in the West, defeated the final efforts at united Indian resistance in the East, and extended the Cotton Kingdom and African slave labor across the South. Indian peoples east of the Mississippi responded to this pressure in a variety of ways, from selective accommodation to outright resistance, but always in an effort to preserve their homelands and communities. Ultimately, however, it made little difference: the United States determined that Indian peoples in the East should be relocated to new lands in the West, and their homelands turned over to American settlers.

Adapting to New Ways

Although the United States sent armies into Indian country on occasion, its assault on Indian culture was constant and pervasive. Americans sought to eradicate the Indians' way of life at the same time as they took away their lands. Indian agents and missionaries attempted to impose a social revolution in Indian communities, organize Indian economic life around intensive agriculture, and redefine gender roles in Indian families. Most Eastern Woodland peoples had farmed for centuries, but in the American program, men, not women, were to do the farming and were to give up hunting for a life behind a plow. Women were to take up spinning, weaving, and other "domestic chores." As Indians spent less time hunting, they would need less land and could sell the "surplus" land to the United States. As men spent more time at home, the nuclear family, with the male at its head, would supplant the clans, which in many Indian tribes were matrilineal. As families acquired more property, they would adopt Anglo-American principles of ownership and inheritance. Unfortunately, such plans were more likely to produce hunger and poverty than self-sufficiency and prosperity because by 1800 many Indians hunted for trade rather than for food. At the same time as the government was trying to get Indian women to stop farming and take up spinning, Anglo-American women were giving up homespun cloth for store-bought cloth.[1]

Some chiefs attempted to lead their people along the paths of change mandated by the United States. Little Turtle, Black Hoof, Blue Jacket, and others who had fought against the Americans since the days of the Revolution — kept the peace they made at the Treaty of Greenville, which had created a boundary between Indian and American territory while ceding huge tracts of Indian land in present-day Ohio and Indiana (see page 200). Aided by William Wells who now served as an Indian agent for the United States, Little Turtle urged the Miamis to make the transition to a new way of life. Many Shawnees left Ohio and moved to Missouri, but most of those who stayed followed the lead of their principal chief, Black Hoof, in adapting to a changing world.[2]

In the South, many Cherokees, Creeks, Chickasaws, and Choctaws accommodated to American ways as the best way to survive in the new nation. They wore European styles of clothing, plowed fields and fenced lands, and cultivated corn and cotton. Some were Christian and were literate in English. Influential sons of Scottish traders and Creek mothers had

◆ **Benjamin Hawkins and the Creeks**
U.S. Indian agent Benjamin Hawkins is shown introducing Creek Indians to plows, steel tools, and Euro-American farming techniques. For Hawkins, promoting agriculture meant transforming Indian men from hunters to farmers; Indian women, who produced the cornucopia portrayed here, were to be allotted more "domestic" chores. *Granger, NYC.*

already begun inculcating property values and reorienting Creek society toward a market economy. Traders had entered Creek country along old paths in the eighteenth century, but new roads opened the land to growing numbers of settlers and slaves in the early nineteenth century.[3] The Creeks, encouraged by official U.S. Indian agents, attempted to diversify their economy to include farming and ranching. The goal of agent Benjamin Hawkins, concludes one scholar, was that the Creeks "would become good yeoman farmers, settlers with a slightly darker skin and some quaint ethnic memories. The men would display 'the manners of a well bred man,' the women the 'neatness and economy of a white woman.'"[4]

One marker of southern "civilization" that some Indians adopted was slaveholding. As slave labor became the foundation of tobacco and cotton production in the South and slaves became a symbol of status, southern Indians also held African slaves — an estimated ten thousand between the late 1700s and the end of the Civil War. Indian history is usually written in terms of relations with white people, but black people constituted an "invisible third element" among the southeastern tribes. Many Indians and Africans had shared lives of enslavement in the colonial South, and they had built relationships, shared aspects of their cultures, and sometimes made families. But in the early nineteenth century, as more southeastern Indians became slaveholders, Creeks and Cherokees adopted increasingly racial attitudes toward Africans that conflicted with traditional notions of kinship. James Vann, a Cherokee chief, established a plantation and a manor and by 1809 owned more than one hundred slaves, which not only made him probably the wealthiest man in the Cherokee Nation but also placed him among the elite of southern planters. Vann bought and sold slaves and by all accounts treated them as harshly as any white slave owner. Intermarriage with African Americans added a complicated and often divisive strand to southeastern Indian history. Interracial families sometimes split as the United States moved toward a rigidly biracial society.[5]

Missionaries and other groups in American society believed it was their duty to "civilize" the Indians by destroying their traditions and culture and transforming them into Christians. Some Indians were quick to point out what they saw as the Americans' hypocrisy. The Seneca chief Red Jacket, for example, asked missionaries to explain why they were so sure that theirs was the one true religion. The Great Spirit had made Indians and white men different in many respects, so why not accept that He had given them different religions to suit their needs? The Indians might be more inclined to accept Christianity, he said, if the Christians they saw around them served as better examples. But since they saw lying, cheating, drunkenness, and theft, the Indians thought they were better off with their own religion.[6]

As Native American homelands eroded under intense American pressure, individuals and communities experienced crisis. Many of the dispossessed sought refuge in alcohol; others found solace in new forms of religion. Time and again, Indian people turned to ritual and belief to restore balance and harmony to a world that had gone chaotic. The Delaware prophet Neolin had headed one such movement in the 1760s; his renunciation of European material goods and influences helped fuel Pontiac's war of resistance against the British (see page 201). Other prophets stepped forward in the early nineteenth century as land dispossession intensified.[7]

By 1800, the Iroquois Confederacy was broken. Iroquois people who had once dominated the northeastern United States were now confined to reservations in small areas of their traditional homelands or lived in exile in Canada. The Senecas once held some 4 million acres of western New York and Pennsylvania; now they lived on fewer than 200,000 acres divided into ten separate tracts. They rebuilt their communities but were under pressure from missionaries, land speculators, settlers, and the state and federal governments. In 1799, a hard-drinking Seneca named Handsome Lake, who lay ill and apparently close to death, experienced a vision in which the Creator awakened him to a new religion and a new way of life for Iroquois people. Handsome Lake renounced his former life of drunkenness and embarked on a mission to bring his teachings, *Gaiwiio,* or "the Good Message," to his people. The "Longhouse Religion" that developed based on his teachings combined traditional beliefs with some Christian additions, which he adopted from Quaker missionaries to the Senecas. Handsome Lake preached that Iroquois people should live in peace with the United States and with one another and based many of his teachings on the Great Law of Peace (see "The Iroquois Great League of Peace," pages 52–61). He denounced alcohol, factionalism, and the breakdown of family life, and he emphasized the importance of education and farming. In place of a society based on matrilineal, extended families that traditionally inhabited the clan mothers' longhouses, and in

◆ *Handsome Lake Preaching*

Handsome Lake preaches his new religion in the Seneca longhouse at Tonawanda, New York, in a twentieth-century watercolor by Ernest Smith, who was born at Tonawanda. Handsome Lake's teachings resulted in the Longhouse Religion, which many Iroquois people still practice. *Handsome Lake Preaching, painting by Ernest Smith, Tonawanda Reservation. From the Rochester Museum & Science Center, Rochester, NY.*

which women were allowed to divorce their husbands simply by excluding them from their houses, Handsome Lake espoused a new social gospel in which men now did the farming, and husbands headed the nuclear family.[8] At the same time, his teachings incorporated thanksgiving festivals and other ceremonies from the old religion and denounced the sale of lands.

For many, the new religion meant a new way of living, and it met opposition from both traditionalists and Christians. But by reviving and reshaping traditional morality and values, Handsome Lake offered hope in a time of spiritual crisis and staggering transformations, and a way for Senecas to preserve their identity, autonomy, and lands through resilience and adaptation rather than outright resistance. The Longhouse Religion and the code of values Handsome Lake preached was a source of endurance, and it had enduring appeal: it continues as a way of life for many Iroquois people today.[9]

The Last Phases of United Indian Resistance

Like the Iroquois, the Shawnee Indians had lost lands, suffered defeat in battle, and seen their culture assaulted. In the first decade of the nineteenth century, however, while Black Hoof tried to make the transition to a new way of life, two Shawnees emerged as leaders in a pan-Indian religious and political movement. Like Handsome Lake, the Shawnee Prophet, Tenskwatawa, lived an early life of drunkenness and debauchery. Like Handsome Lake, he fell into a trance and experienced a vision in 1805, which caused him to transform his life and bring a message of hope to his people. Tenskwatawa preached that the Master of Life had selected him to spread the new religion among the Indians. Indian people were warned to avoid contact with the Americans, who were "children of the Evil Spirit." They were urged to give up alcohol, refuse intermarriage, reject Christianity, lay down manufactured tools, and throw off white man's clothing. Instead of eating the meat of domesticated animals, they should return to a diet of corn, beans, maple sugar, and other traditional foods. They should avoid intertribal conflict and practice communal ownership of property. Tenskwatawa's teachings promised a revitalization of Shawnee culture, but his message also drew adherents from the Delawares, Kickapoos, Ottawas, Potawatomis, Anishinaabeg, and other tribes, especially after he accurately predicted a total eclipse of the sun on June 16, 1806. Many Indians rejected his message, but hundreds of others flocked to the village he established at Prophetstown on the Tippecanoe River in Indiana.

However, it was the Shawnee Prophet's brother, Tecumseh, who gave strongest direction to the developing movement of Indian unity. Tecumseh had fought at the Battle of Fallen Timbers in 1794 (see page 219), but he refused to sign the Treaty of Greenville. Identifying American expansion and piecemeal cessions of land as the major threat to Indian survival, Tecumseh argued that no tribe had the right to sell their lands, because the lands belonged to all Indians. He denounced older chiefs who signed away tribal territory, and his influence soared after pro-American chiefs ceded more than three million acres to the United States at a "whiskey treaty" at Fort Wayne in 1809. Tecumseh traveled from the Great Lakes to Florida, carrying his message of pan-Indian land tenure

◆ **Tenskwatawa**

Although Tenskwatawa, the Shawnee Prophet, was later eclipsed as leader by his brother Tecumseh, his vision of cultural and spiritual revitalization was crucial in forging the intertribal confederacy Tecumseh led. *Tenskwatawa (1775–1836) (color litho.), King, Charles Bird (1785–1862)/Private Collection/Peter Newark American Pictures/Bridgeman Images.*

and preaching a vision of an independent Indian nation stretching from Canada to the Gulf of Mexico.

Tenskwatawa's teachings and Tecumseh's vision alarmed the U.S. government, especially the governor of Indiana Territory, General William Henry Harrison, who had built his career advancing Jefferson's policies of national expansion and Indian dispossession.[10] In 1811 Harrison led an army in a preemptive strike against the Prophet's village at Tippecanoe while Tecumseh was away in the South.[11] The battle was a relatively minor affair — Tecumseh dismissed it as "a scuffle between children" — but the Americans claimed a victory, the Prophet lost prestige, and Tecumseh's confederacy suffered a setback and loss of momentum. When the War of 1812 broke out between Britain and the United States, Tecumseh sided with the British in a last attempt to stem the tide of American expansion. The British–Indian alliance scored some early victories, but Britain was distracted by its involvement in European resistance to Napoleon. When Tecumseh was killed fighting Harrison's army at the Battle of the Thames in Ontario in 1813, the last hope of Indian unity east of the Mississippi also died.

In the South, Alexander McGillivray of the Creeks had led his confederacy of tribes in dealing with Spain, the United States, and Georgia in the decade after the Revolution (see page 213) but his death in 1793 created room for division within the confederacy. Tensions escalated after Tecumseh traveled the Southeast with his message of united Indian resistance in 1811. Upper Creek towns tended to favor adopting a militant stance in dealing with the United States; Lower Creek towns tended to advocate peace and accommodation. Conflicts within the Creek confederacy spilled over into attacks on American settlers, and the United States responded with swift military action against the militant Creeks, or "Red Sticks." In the Creek War of 1813–14, General Andrew Jackson directed a series of devastating campaigns that culminated in the slaughter of some eight hundred Creek warriors at the Battle of Tohopeka, or Horseshoe Bend, on the Tallapoosa River in present-day Alabama in March 1814.[12] About five hundred Cherokees and one hundred Lower Creeks helped Jackson win his victory. But at the Treaty of Fort Jackson the general dictated punitive terms that divested the Creek Nation of 23 million acres, or two-thirds of their tribal domain, much of it taken from Jackson's Lower Creek allies. It was the single largest cession of territory ever made in the Southeast and initiated a boom in land sales and cotton production in the Deep South. Jackson confirmed American control of the region by defeating a British army at the Battle of New Orleans in January 1815 — although the treaty ending the War of 1812 had been signed in Ghent, Belgium, two weeks earlier.

The age of Indian confederacies in the East and of Indian power that delayed American expansion was over by the end of the War of 1812, but Indians did not disappear just because they stopped fighting. As the deerskin trade declined and the Cotton Kingdom expanded into new lands in Mississippi, the Choctaws and Chickasaws adjusted to new economic conditions. They changed their farming and settlement patterns, raised more stock, mingled with African American slaves, and grew cotton for the market, even as they retained core cultural values.[13]

LEWIS AND CLARK IN INDIAN COUNTRY

But the United States was already looking farther West. In 1803 American emissaries in Paris purchased the Louisiana Territory from its French holders. Acquired for a mere $15 million, the 827,000 square miles of territory between the Mississippi and the Rocky Mountains doubled the size of the United States overnight (Map 5.1). Even before the United States completed the Louisiana Purchase, President Thomas Jefferson was making plans for an American expedition to explore the Missouri River to its sources and from there to the Pacific. After becoming the first European to cross the continent north of Mexico in 1793, Scotsman Alexander Mackenzie published *Voyages from Montreal* (1801), which not only described his travels from Saskatchewan to the Pacific but also spelled out his ideas for British settlement in the West. Jefferson read this book and was galvanized into action. He chose two Virginians, Meriwether

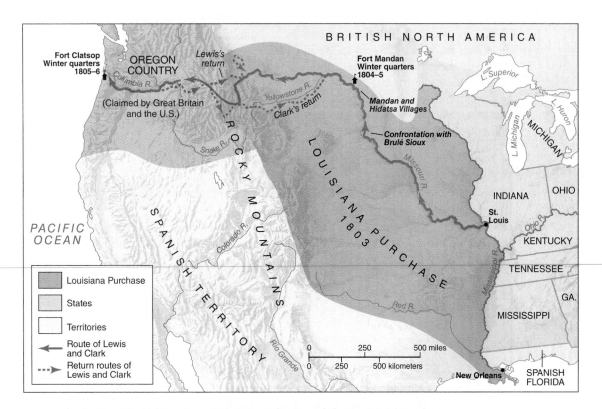

◆ **Map 5.1 The Lewis and Clark Expedition and the Louisiana Purchase**
The Louisiana Purchase (1803) added to the United States an enormous amount of land inhabited by a great variety of Indian peoples. In their expedition across and beyond that territory in 1804–6, Lewis and Clark encountered many Indians who had plenty of experience dealing with European traders, but for most of the Indians in the West the expedition marked their first encounter with representatives of the new American nation that now laid claim to their lands.

Lewis and William Clark, to lead an American expedition from St. Louis to the Pacific and back. They were to proclaim American sovereignty over the area, prepare the way for American commerce with the tribes, and gather as much information as possible about this "new land" and the many Indian peoples who inhabited it.

France, Spain, and now the United States had all laid claim to Louisiana Territory, and so the presence of British, French, and Spanish traders and the aspirations of competing European nations had been felt there for some time. St. Louis, the departure point of the Lewis and Clark expedition, had started life forty years earlier as a French trading post, dealing with the powerful Osages, and some of the first people whom Lewis and Clark encountered on their trek west were French, not Indians.[14] Nevertheless, it was Indian country, where Indian people and Indian power still dominated. Lewis and Clark had to deal with Indian tribes and develop a working knowledge of Indian politics. The success of the expedition depended on cultivating amicable relations: "In all your intercourse with the natives," Jefferson instructed Lewis, "treat them in the most friendly and conciliatory manner which their own conduct will permit."[15]

On the whole, the expedition succeeded in doing so. The explorers carried with them flags and gifts to present to Indian chiefs; they met and smoked with Indians in council after council, proclaiming the new era of peace and prosperity that would surely come to the Indians now that their land "belonged" to the Great Father in Washington. Lewis and Clark painstakingly gathered information on the names, numbers, and customs of the tribes they encountered. Indian knowledge, guidance, assistance, transportation, and food helped the expedition trek to the Pacific and back.

Encounters on the Missouri

Things did not get off to an auspicious start, however. Leaving St. Louis in June 1804, the explorers headed up the Missouri River — about fifty men,° including Clark's African American servant, York, who was to cause quite a stir among the Indians — in half a dozen canoes and two pirogues. They tested their skills at Indian diplomacy among the Otos, Omahas, and Missouris, once-powerful tribes already badly reduced by the ravages of disease. Then in September, they encountered a band of Brulé or Sicangu Sioux — "a Stout bold looking people," said Clark. The Sioux were accustomed to levying tribute from St. Louis traders and were not about to allow the American strangers to pass upriver to other tribes without exacting some share of their cargo. Clark called them "the pirates of the Missouri." Eager to demonstrate that the United States would not be bullied, the Americans were equally determined not to concede. There was a tense scene in which each side stood to arms. "I felt my Self warm & Spoke in verry [sic] positive terms," wrote Lewis with characteristic understatement. Only the presence of Indian women and children and the quick-thinking statesmanship of the Brulé chief Black Buffalo averted conflict. The Americans tossed the Indians some tobacco as a token tribute, and the Sioux allowed them to proceed.[16] But it was touch and go. Lewis and Clark failed the first

---

° That number included St. Louis boatmen and U.S. soldiers attached to the expedition as far as the Mandan villages, as well as the core party of twenty-nine.

serious test of their Indian diplomacy. They had a lot to learn if the expedition was to navigate successfully the turbulent waters of inter- and intratribal politics. A winter in the Mandan villages — the first major objective in Lewis and Clark's transcontinental odyssey — provided an invaluable crash course.

Surrounded by extensive fields of corn, beans, squash, and sunflowers that the women cultivated and that were the basis of their prosperity and trade, the villages of the Mandans and their Hidatsa (also known as Gros Ventre or Minnetaree)

◆ **Bird's-Eye View of the Mandan Village, 1,800 Miles above St. Louis**
On the edges of the Great Plains, Mandans, Hidatsas, Arikaras, Pawnees, Omahas, and other people inhabited earth-lodge villages for hundreds of years before whites saw them. Lewis and Clark headed for the Mandan villages on the first leg of their trek in 1804, knowing that there they would find the food and shelter to get them through a winter on the northern Plains. By the time George Catlin painted this village in the 1830s, the Mandans, Hidatsas, and Arikaras on the upper Missouri had been ravaged by recurrent epidemics. *Smithsonian American Art Museum, Washington, D.C./Art Resource, NY.*

neighbors straddled the great bend of the Missouri in present-day North Dakota. They were a great marketplace and crossroads, the hub of a huge intertribal trading network in which Plains Indians exchanged horses and the products of buffalo hunting for guns, trade goods, and agricultural produce. Indian traders from deep in the Plains traveled to the upper Missouri villages, then returned home to trade the goods they had acquired to other Indian peoples. Spanish, British, and French-Canadian traders operated in and around the Missouri villages. Unfortunately, the same location and circumstances that made the villages a gathering place of nations guaranteed that they would be transformed into deathtraps when epidemic diseases raced along the trade routes: the smallpox epidemic of 1779–81 had hit the villagers hard; there were other outbreaks on the Missouri early in the nineteenth century, and the epidemic of 1837 virtually destroyed the Mandans.[17]

The winter spent with the Mandans was one of the high points of the expedition. In Mandan lodges, the Americans found shelter from winter on the northern Plains and corn to get them through the season. From Mandan people they learned about tribes they could expect to encounter when they resumed their journey westward in the spring. One chief drew Clark a sketch of the country as far as the Rocky Mountains. Mandans and Americans visited back and forth, joined in each other's dances, hunted buffalo together, and together pursued Sioux horse raiders. Members of the expedition slept with Mandan women, and the expedition blacksmith mended Mandan axes and hoes in exchange for corn. With no other group did Lewis and Clark's men live so closely, for so long, and on such good terms. They enjoyed good relations with other Indian peoples — the Shoshonis and Nez Perces, in particular — but their months with the Mandans demonstrated the capacity of one group of humans to coexist harmoniously with another, at least for a time. It was not an experience repeated often in subsequent relations between the United States and the Indian peoples of the West.

Over the Mountains and Back

Despite the warmth of Mandan hospitality, Lewis and Clark were eager to be on their way. They left the Mandan villages in April, as soon as the ice broke on the Missouri. They were "now about to penetrate a country at least two thousand miles in width, on which," wrote Lewis, "the foot of civilized man had never trodden."[18] They hoped to locate a Northwest Passage that would provide a water route across the continent to the Pacific. The maps available at the time showed the Rockies to be a thin line of mountains not far from the Pacific; once they reached the headwaters of the Missouri, a short portage over the crest of the mountains would bring them to another river that would carry them down to the ocean. But when Lewis and his companions reached that crest, all they saw was range after range of mountains. The maps were wrong; there was no Northwest Passage, and the very survival of the expedition was in jeopardy if they did not make it over those mountain barriers before winter.

While the expedition was at the Mandan villages, they had been joined by a Shoshoni woman — actually a teenager — whom the neighboring Hidatsas had captured in a raid as a child. Sacagawea or Sakakawea was married to Toussaint Charbonneau, a French-Canadian trader, who became one of the expedition's interpreters. She proved invaluable when the Americans made contact with the Shoshonis in the Rocky Mountains. The Shoshonis provided them with horses and guides to get them over the mountains. The Nez Perces took them in and fed them when they came staggering down the Lolo Trail, starved and half-frozen.[19] Rejuvenated, the expedition put canoes into the mighty Columbia River and, speeding past the massive rapids and salmon fishing grounds at The Dalles, paddled hard for the Pacific.[20]

Their winter on the Pacific Coast was miserable. Far from home, wet and dispirited, they did not like the Chinooks and Clatsops who lived near the mouth of the Columbia, nor did they find the women attractive: the tribes practiced ornamental head flattening, they were rife with venereal disease, and marks of smallpox were common. They also drove hard bargains, and some swore like sailors. The Indians in turn had little time for the expedition: they were used to dealing with merchants who arrived from the ocean in ships laden with cargo, and they paid scant regard to a bunch of disheveled Americans who arrived from the mountains with little but the buttons on their coats to trade. Thirty years of contact with maritime crews had produced new forms of sex labor and new forms of exploiting slave women (see page 229), and Lewis complained that the Clatsop and Chinook men would prostitute their wives and daughters "for a fishing hook or a stran [sic] of beads." He explained that "in common with other savage nations they make their women perform every species of domestic drudgery." But in the same journal entry he acknowledged that because the women shared equally in procuring food they were treated with a measure of respect. "The females are permitted to speak freely before the men, whom, indeed, they sometimes address in a tone of authority," he wrote. "On many subjects their judgments and opinions are respected, and in matters of trade their advice is generally asked and followed."[21] The fact that Lewis reported this as noteworthy suggests that such was not the case for women in American society at the time.

When spring came, Lewis and Clark were anxious to depart for home. Trudging back across the mountains, they made their way through countless Indian groups. Although relations were not always harmonious — their tempers flared often, and they were now more interested in putting Indians behind them than in conducting diplomacy with them — they avoided conflict with the Indian peoples they encountered, except for one occasion when Lewis separated from Clark and ran into a party of Blackfeet (see "An Account of His Fight with the Blackfeet," pages 283–86). By April 1806, they were back in St. Louis.

The Lewis and Clark expedition was not a total success. It failed to find a water route to the Pacific — the fabled Northwest Passage giving access to the markets of the Far East that had been the dream of empire builders for generations — because none existed. It failed to establish intertribal peace on the Missouri River, and instead cemented Sioux and Blackfeet hostility toward the United States. But it did put the West on the American map. The Lewis and Clark expedition is often seen as marking the beginning of the history of the West, but it should more accurately be understood as the beginning of U.S. history in the West, where Indian peoples had lived for thousands of years and where French and Spaniards had lived for generations. Direct and indirect contact with the outside world had transformed the Indian West long before Lewis and Clark arrived. At the time, many Americans imagined the country beyond the Mississippi to be barren and virtually empty. It was not particularly attractive to American settlers. Still, it might serve as a place to which Indians from the East could be removed.

INDIAN REMOVALS

The state of Oklahoma today is home to numerous tribes—Cherokee, Creek, Chickasaw, Choctaw, Seminole, Caddo, Comanche, Southern Cheyenne, Southern Arapaho, Kiowa, Apache, Shawnee, Potawatomi, Wyandot, Quapaw, Osage, Peoria, Ottawa, Seneca, Pawnee, Ponca, Oto, Kansa, Tonkawa, Kickapoo, Modoc, Wichita, Iowa, and Sauk & Fox—as well as to members and descendants of many other tribes. Few of these peoples were indigenous to the Oklahoma region; most live there because nineteenth-century United States policies designated the region "Indian Territory" and relocated thousands of Indian people there from other areas of the country.

The policy of removing Indian peoples from their eastern homelands to the West was implemented in the late 1820s and 1830s, but it originated in earlier periods when Americans had considered various solutions to the problem of what to do with Indians in the eastern United States. The government could try to destroy the Indians, assimilate them into American society, protect them on their ancestral lands, or remove them to more distant lands. Most Americans favored the last option as the only practical course. Removal became a policy on which almost all sectors of American society could agree. Even some Indians came to believe that removal represented their best strategy for survival.

Roots of the Removal Policy

The beginnings of removals went back to the presidency of Thomas Jefferson. In 1802, the state of Georgia ceded its western land claims to the federal government, and in return Congress agreed to secure on "reasonable and peaceful" terms title to Cherokee and Creek lands within the state as soon as possible.

In the winter of 1802–3 President Jefferson told Delaware and Shawnee delegates in Washington that he would "pay the most sacred regard to existing treaties between your respective nations and ours, and protect your whole territories against all intrusions that may be attempted by white people." At the same time, Jefferson was implementing plans to dispossess the Indians of their lands.[22] Jefferson and others easily solved the dilemma of how to take Indian lands with honor by determining that too much land was a disincentive for Indians to become "civilized." Ignoring the role of agriculture in Eastern Woodland societies, they argued that Indians would continue to hunt rather than settle down as farmers unless their options were restricted. Taking their lands forced Indians into a settled, agricultural, and "civilized" way of life and was, therefore, good for them in the long run. As Indians took up farming, Jefferson wrote in 1803 to William Henry Harrison, governor of Indiana Territory, "they will perceive how useless to them are their extensive forests, and will be willing to pare them off from time to time in exchange for necessaries for their farms and families." To promote this process "we shall push our trading houses, and be glad to see the good and influential individuals . . . run into debt, because we observe that when these debts get beyond what the individuals can pay, they become willing to lop them off by a cession of lands." In this way, American settlements would gradually surround the Indians, "and they will in time either incorporate with us as citizens of the United States, or remove beyond the Mississippi."[23] The process of dispossession could be comfortably accomplished within Jefferson's philosophy of minimal government. The government could do little to regulate the frontier and protect Indian lands, causing Indians to fight for their land (Map 5.2). The government would then have no choice but to invade

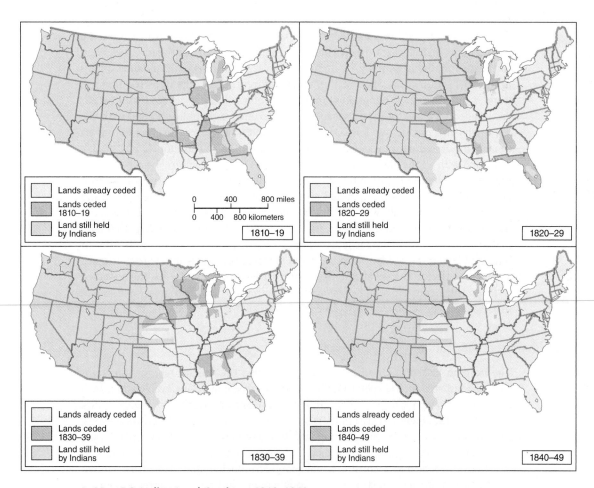

◆ **Map 5.2 Indian Land Cessions, 1810–1849**
Between 1810 and 1849, the United States quashed the final Indian military resistance east of the Mississippi and implemented the policy of removing eastern Indian peoples to west of the Mississippi. The result was massive loss of Indian homelands.

Indian country, suppress the uprising, and dictate treaties in which defeated Indians signed away land. The stage was then set for the process to repeat itself. Jefferson's strategy for acquiring Indian lands resulted in some thirty treaties with a dozen or so tribal groups and the cession of almost 200,000 square miles of Indian territory in nine states. Jefferson regretted that Indians seemed doomed to extinction, but he showed little compunction in taking away their homelands.[24]

Some Indians moved west voluntarily; others determined never to abandon their ancestral lands. But in the early decades of the century the pressure to move west mounted steadily. Americans who hated Indians and desired their lands favored removal as a means of freeing up territory. Although many New Englanders denounced the removal policies in the South, many other Americans who were sympathetic to the Indians also favored removal as the only way to protect them from their rapacious neighbors. Proremoval forces received a boost when Andrew Jackson, a renowned Indian fighter and a staunch advocate of removal, was elected president in 1828. Jackson knew the settled and agriculturally based Creeks and Cherokees firsthand — many of them had served alongside him as allies in his campaigns — but in his State of the Union address in 1830 he depicted them as wandering hunters: "What good man would prefer a country covered with forests and ranged by a few thousand savages to our extensive republic studded with cities, towns and prosperous farms, embellished with all the improvements that art can devise or industry execute, occupied by more than 12 million happy people and filled with all the blessings of civilization, liberty and religion?" he asked.[25] The Indians would be better off in the West, where they could live undisturbed, Jackson argued. Other politicians expressed similar views, declaring that a few thousand Indians could not be allowed to stand in the way of human progress. Indians did not put the land to good use, they said, and could not be allowed to deny that land to American farmers. Thomas Jefferson had regarded Indians as culturally inferior but capable of improvement with the proper instruction; Jackson regarded Indians as racially inferior and incapable of change. In Jackson's view, even the so-called civilized tribes must, in fact, be "savages." "Civilization" and "progress" demanded that "savages" be removed. Today, we would call such a policy "ethnic cleansing."[26]

The Cherokee Resistance

The irony in Jackson's argument lay in the fact that the Indians whom Americans seemed most anxious to expel from their lands were people whom, even by their own definition, Americans termed civilized. A census taken among the Cherokees in 1825 showed that they owned 33 grist mills, 13 saw mills, 1 powder mill, 69 blacksmith shops, 2 tan yards, 762 looms, 2,486 spinning wheels, 172 wagons, 2,923 plows, 7,683 horses, 22,531 cattle, 46,732 pigs, and 2,566 sheep.[27] In 1827 the Cherokees restructured their tribal government into a constitutional republic modeled after that of the United States, with a written constitution, an independent judiciary, a supreme court, a principal chief, and a two-house legislature. They had a written language based on the syllabary developed by Sequoyah (a.k.a. George Gist, c. 1770–1843), who devoted a dozen years to creating a written version of the Cherokee language.[28] In 1828 they

Cherokee Alphabet.

◆ **Cherokee Syllabary**

Developed over twelve years and introduced in 1821, Sequoyah's syllabary became widely used within a few years and allowed Cherokees to read and write in their own language. *Cherokee Alphabet, developed in 1821 (print), American School (nineteenth century)/Private Collection/Peter Newark American Pictures/Bridgeman Images.*

established a newspaper, the *Cherokee Phoenix,* which was published in both Cherokee and English. The editor of the *Phoenix,* Elias Boudinot, originally called Buck Watie, had received an education at a Moravian school in North Carolina and at the American Board's Foreign Mission School in Cornwall, Connecticut. Boudinot and his cousin John Ridge — the son of Major Ridge, speaker of the Cherokee Council who had fought as an ally of Andrew Jackson during the Creek War—attended the Mission School together. When the two young men fell in love with women in the town and proposed marriage, the citizens of Cornwall responded with an outburst of racist attacks and the school was forced to close.[29] The young people married anyway, with John Ridge taking Sarah Bird Northrup as his wife.

Despite such setbacks, the Cherokees seemed to have everything the United States required of them to take their place in the new nation as a self-supporting, functioning republic of farmers. Some Cherokees displayed more of the attributes of supposedly "civilized" society than did many of the American frontiersmen who were so eager to occupy their lands. John Ridge wrote for the *Phoenix* and served as an interpreter and secretary in delegations to Washington. "You asked us to throw off the hunter and warrior state," said Ridge in a speech in Philadelphia in 1832. "We did so—you asked us to form a republican government: We did so—adopting your own as a model. You asked us to cultivate the earth, and learn the mechanic arts: We did so. You asked us to learn to read: We did so. You asked us to cast away our idols, and worship your God: We did so."[30]

But it did not save them. Indeed, their very success and prosperity only increased pressure from neighbors eager to get their hands on Cherokee land. Cherokee territory originally extended into five southeastern states, but by the 1820s most of the remaining Cherokees were confined to Georgia (read more about Cherokee removals before 1820 in "Cherokee and white Women Oppose Removal," pages 286–91). Gold was discovered in Cherokee country in 1827 and prospectors flooded into the area. In December the Georgia legislature passed a resolution asserting its sovereignty over Cherokee lands within the state's borders. Georgia demanded that the U.S. government begin negotiations to compel the Cherokees to cede their land: "The lands in question *belong* to Georgia," the legislators asserted. "She *must* and *will* have them."[31] Georgia subjected the Cherokees to a systematic campaign of harassment, intimidation, and deception, culminating in a sustained assault on their government. The state applied to the Cherokees not only general laws governing all citizens but also special laws aimed only at Cherokees with "a direct intent to destroy the political, economic, and social infrastructure of the nation."[32] It prohibited meetings of the tribal council and closed down the tribal courts. It deprived Cherokees of their right to legal protest and made it illegal for Cherokees to testify in court against whites, dig for gold, or try to dissuade other Cherokees from moving west. In 1830, Georgia created a police force—the Georgia Guard—to patrol Cherokee country. Over the next few years the guard harassed Cherokee people, arrested Principal Chief John Ross and seized his papers, and confiscated the Cherokee printing press. Elias Boudinot appealed to Washington in words that proved prophetic:

> The State of Georgia has taken a strong stand against us, and the United States must either defend us in our rights, or leave us to our foe. In the former case, the General Government will redeem her pledge solemnly given in treaties. In the latter, she will violate her promise of protection, and we cannot, in future, depend consistently, upon any guarantee made by her to us, either here or beyond the Mississippi.[33]

◆ **John Ross, Principal Chief of the Cherokees (1790–1866)**
Ross was a steadfast opponent of removal, lobbying in Congress and taking the Cherokee case to the U.S. Supreme Court. In Indian Territory, he set about rebuilding the Cherokee Nation and his own fortune. The divisions occasioned by removal persisted, however, and surfaced again during the Civil War. Ross first advocated neutrality but later supported the Union. A regular visitor to Washington, Ross died there in 1866 while serving in a treaty delegation. *Archiv Gerstenberg-ullstein bild/Granger, NYC.*

Implementing Removal in the South

In May 1830, after extensive debate and a close vote in both houses, and despite widespread opposition from church and reform groups throughout much of the country, Congress passed the Indian Removal Act, authorizing the president to negotiate treaties of removal with all Indian tribes living east of the Mississippi. Almost immediately, surveyors and squatters entered Cherokee country and Georgia stepped up its campaign of harassment. The Cherokees decided to fight Georgia in the federal courts. In 1830 John Ross hired William Wirt, the former U.S. attorney general, and other lawyers to represent his people's interests. Wirt filed a series of test cases. He first obtained a writ of error from Supreme Court justice John Marshall to stay the execution of a Cherokee named Corn Tassel.

Corn Tassel had been sentenced to death by a Georgia court for killing another Indian in Cherokee country, a crime the Cherokees and their supporters argued should fall under Indian jurisdiction. In a special session, the Georgia legislature voted to defy the writ, and Corn Tassel was hanged. "The conduct of the Georgia Legislature is indeed surprising," wrote Elias Boudinot in another prophetic passage. "[T]hey . . . authorize their governor to hoist the flag of rebellion against the United States! If such proceedings are sanctioned by the majority of the people of the U. States, the Union is but a tottering fabric which will soon fall and crumble into atoms."[34]

In 1831 the Cherokee Nation brought suit against the state of Georgia in the U.S. Supreme Court (see "Foundations of Federal Indian Law and a Native Response," pages 291–98). Chief Justice John Marshall declared that the Court lacked jurisdiction over the case since the Cherokees were neither U.S. citizens nor an independent nation; they (and all other Indian tribes residing within the United States) were "domestic dependent nations." The next year, however, a Vermont missionary brought suit challenging Georgia's right to exert its authority over him in Cherokee country. Because the suit involved a U.S. citizen, it fell within the Supreme Court's jurisdiction. In *Worcester v. Georgia* the Court found that the Cherokee Nation was "a distinct community, occupying its own territory" in which "the laws of Georgia can have no force."[35] The Court's decision was one of the most important in the history of U.S.–Indian relations, but it was not enough to save the Cherokees. Georgia would not tolerate a sovereign Cherokee nation within its boundaries nor would it tolerate federal protection of that sovereignty. Georgia ignored the Supreme Court's ruling.

By the 1830s, the South was producing about half the cotton consumed in the world and growing rich exporting most of it to the cotton mills of northern England. In the view of southerners, Indian lands were too valuable to be left in Indian hands. Southern Indians faced a choice between gradual destitution and removal. Most bowed to the inevitable. As early as 1820, the Choctaw chief Pushmataha made a treaty with Andrew Jackson at Doak's Stand, ceding lands in Mississippi to the United States and accepting new lands in the West in return. Ten years later, the Choctaws signed the Treaty of Dancing Rabbit Creek, ensuring the removal of most of the tribe, although some Choctaws remained in Mississippi. The Creeks tried to resist: a Creek chief named William McIntosh was executed by fellow tribesmen in 1825 for selling lands in contravention of tribal law. But in 1836 the Creeks embarked on a bitter march west.

In 1835 the United States signed the Treaty of New Echota with a minority of Cherokees who agreed to move west voluntarily. The "Treaty Party" included Major Ridge, John Ridge, Elias Boudinot, his brother Stand Watie, and others who had formerly resisted removal but now felt they had no alternative but to migrate. Major Ridge had executed a Cherokee chief named Doublehead for selling tribal land in 1806 and had authored the Cherokee law prohibiting land sales. He knew what the consequences of his action were likely to be. "I have signed my death warrant," he said as he put his name to the treaty.[36] Principal Chief John Ross and the majority of his people denounced the treaty as fraudulent and refused to abide by it. In 1838, citing the Treaty of New Echota, federal troops rounded up most of the Cherokees, placed them in stockaded internment camps, and then relocated them across the Mississippi. About one quarter of the Cherokees, including John Ross's wife, died on the aptly named "Trail of Tears" (Map 5.3). Thousands of other Indian people perished on their journeys west. Alexis de Tocqueville, a French visitor to the United States, witnessed the removal process and concluded that, whereas the Spaniards had earned a reputation for brutality in their dispossession of the Indians, the Americans had attained the same objective under the pretense of legality and philanthropy. It was, he wrote, "impossible to destroy men with more respect to the laws of humanity."[37]

For most of the Cherokees, the march west to Indian Territory was the beginning of a new era in which they would have to adjust to life in a strange land and re-create their societies in the area that became the state of Oklahoma. In 1839

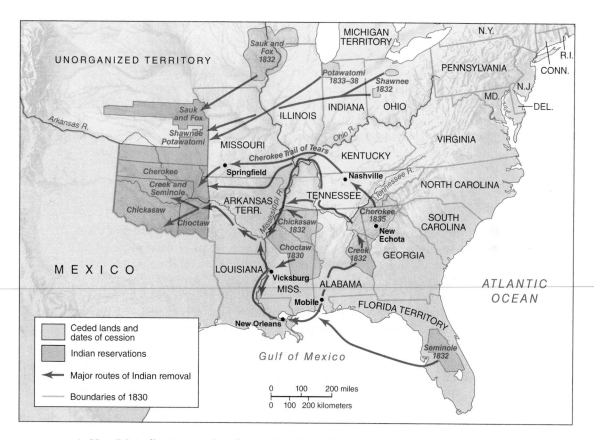

◆ **Map 5.3 Indian Removal and the Trail of Tears in the 1830s**
The U.S. government policy of removing Indians to west of the Mississippi brought tremendous suffering to the uprooted people and disrupted the lives of the people already inhabiting the region to which they moved. As many as a quarter of the Cherokees died on their Trail of Tears in 1838. But not all Indians were removed: groups of Cherokees, Seminoles, and Choctaws still live in their traditional homelands.

unknown assailants killed Major Ridge, John Ridge, and Elias Boudinot, the leaders of the Treaty Party who had ceded Cherokee land. John Ridge was dragged from his bed and beaten to death in front of his wife and children. The assassinations sparked a cycle of revenge killings and plunged the Cherokees into a state of virtual civil war. The situation became so bad that President James Polk recommended permanently dividing the Cherokee Nation, which forced the two sides to patch together an uneasy truce in 1846. Nevertheless, the Cherokees rebuilt their nation in the West. They reestablished their political institutions, centering their government at Tahlequah, in northeastern Oklahoma. They established churches and Protestant seminaries for both men and women and provided free coeducation in their public schools — the first west of the Mississippi. Once again, Cherokees were the vanguard of "civilization." Other facets of their southern culture persisted as well. They took their slaves with them, and African Cherokees not only had to adjust to life in Indian Territory but in time also had to negotiate their changing status both within the United States and within the Cherokee Nation.[38]

Some southern Indians managed to stay in their traditional lands. Some Choctaws stayed in Mississippi. Some Cherokees evaded the American drive west and survived in North Carolina as the Eastern Band of Cherokees. Florida Seminoles refused to remove and, in the Second Seminole War (1835–42), fought the U.S. army to a standstill from their stronghold in the Everglades. The federal government spent millions of dollars, deployed thousands of troops, and lost 1,500 men. Despite the capture by treachery of their leader, Chief Osceola, under a flag of truce and his subsequent death in prison, some Seminoles remained defiant in their Florida homelands.

Removal in the North

In the North, implementing the removal policy meant dealing with a variety of tribes and bands, many of which had migrated from one region to another, and many of which were already living on a fraction of their former lands. Between 1829 and 1851, the United States signed eighty-six treaties with twenty-six northern tribes between New York and the Mississippi. Sometimes several tribes participated in a treaty; sometimes a single tribe signed several treaties.[39] Ohio Shawnees moved west in 1832, although their principal chief, Black Hoof, who had encouraged his tribe to adapt to the new ways of life, did not live to see it. After a harrowing removal to Kansas, the migrant Shawnees began the difficult task of rebuilding their nation as they reunited with other Shawnees who had moved west before them.[40] In New York, pressure to remove the remaining Indians mounted steadily. In the years between the Revolution and the Civil War, New York politicians, transportation interests, and land speculators conspired to convert Iroquois homelands into American real estate. Canals, railroads, the massive influx of settlers, and the rapid growth of cities like Buffalo transformed what had once been Iroquoia. In 1838 sixteen Seneca chiefs signed the fraudulent Treaty of Buffalo Creek. Coerced by threats, bribery, and alcohol, they agreed to sell their remaining lands in New York to the Ogden Land Company, give up their four reservations, and move to Kansas. But charges of bribery and fraud by the commissioners impeded the treaty's ratification by the

U.S. Senate, and the Senecas were able to negotiate a compromise treaty four years later that allowed most of them to stay in western New York.[41] In the Great Lakes region, the Potawatomis alone participated in nineteen treaties. At the treaty of Chicago in 1833 they ceded 5 million acres on the west shore of Lake Michigan; in 1836 alone they signed nine treaties, each one committing them to removal within two years. While the Cherokees walked the Trail of Tears in 1838, the Potawatomis trekked west along their Trail of Death. Most Anishinaabe bands managed to preserve reservations in their Michigan, Wisconsin, and Minnesota homelands. Often they signed treaties that ceded large chunks of territory but guaranteed their rights to continue hunting, fishing, and gathering wild rice on the ceded lands and the rivers and lakes — rights that they had to reassert in confrontations and court cases in the late twentieth century. Some Potawatomis, Anishinaabeg, and Ottawas moved north into Canada rather than go west to Kansas and Oklahoma.[42]

Other tribes joined the general pattern of coerced migration beyond the Mississippi. In 1832 the Sauk chief Black Hawk returned with his people to plant corn in their Illinois homelands after wintering in Iowa. American settlers occupying the area claimed that they were being invaded. The Illinois militia (including a young Abraham Lincoln, although he saw no combat) was called out, federal troops were brought in, and many of the Sauks' enemies made common cause with the Americans. The so-called Black Hawk War culminated at the Battle of Bad Axe as Black Hawk's band tried to escape across the Mississippi. Caught between American riflemen on the shore and an American steamboat spewing grapeshot from its cannon, at least 150 men, women, and children were shot down, many in cold blood. Others who escaped the slaughter and made it across the river were killed by Sioux. Black Hawk was captured and imprisoned, but later was taken on a tour of the East and related his autobiography.[43] Citing the "unprovoked" war as justification, the United States stripped the Sauks of their lands in treaties in 1833, 1836, 1837, and 1842. Most Sauks eventually removed to new homes in Kansas.

Contrary to what some Americans asserted, the country to which the eastern tribes were removed was not empty. The United States carved its "Indian Territory" out of the homelands of Omahas, Otos, Missouris, Kansas, Pawnees, and Osages, who regarded the newcomers as invaders. The Osages, who had dominated the southern prairies in the eighteenth century, clashed repeatedly with Cherokees in the Arkansas country. Relations between Native inhabitants and Native immigrants from the East remained tense for years. The Osages were also coming under increasing pressure from the United States to give up their lands and their way of life, although they fended off missionaries' attempts to change them and held on to their traditional beliefs.[44]

Surviving behind the Frontier: Race, Class, and History in Nineteenth-Century New England

Despite the pressures to remove west, many Indian people remained on their traditional homelands throughout the eastern United States. They continued the fight to remain Indian in the midst of an alien society that denied the validity of their culture and in time ignored their very presence. In New England, Indian people remained long after New Englanders believed they had resolved their Indian "problem." Confined to tiny reservations and subjected to increasing regulation by individual states, they saw their lands whittled away. In Vermont and New Hampshire, as Americans

◆ Mohongo

At a time when her people were coming under increasing pressure from immigrant Indians moving west, the Osage woman Mohongo, pictured here with her child, traveled east. She and her husband were part of a troupe taken to Europe as "show Indians" by an unscrupulous entrepreneur: they sailed from New Orleans to France in 1827, traveled through Holland and Germany, and finished up in Paris where their visit attracted considerable attention.[45] Several of the party, including Mohongo's husband, died of smallpox. The survivors made it back to America, where Mohongo was received at the White House in 1830. In this portrait, she wears trade silver jewelry around her neck; her child clutches the peace medal presented to her by the president. *Illustration from* The Indian Tribes of North America, *Vol. 1, by Thomas L. McKenney and James Hall, pub. by John Grant (color litho.), after Charles Bird King (1785–1862)/Private Collection. Photo © Christie's Images/Bridgeman Images.*

◆ **Cornelius Krieghoff (1815–1872), Canadian,**
The Basket Seller **(c. 1850)**

With traditional economies disrupted and their men often away from home, many Indian women in New England and eastern Canada found that making and selling baskets offered a way of both preserving traditional craft skills and making ends meet. Some women peddled their wares from village to village and house to house, often a humiliating experience. William Apess's (see pages 279–81) grandmother barely earned enough to feed her family. A minister in Ledyard, Connecticut, recalled, as a small boy, seeing an Indian woman named Anne Wampy every spring selling baskets she had made during the winter. "When she started from home she carried upon her shoulders a bundle of baskets so large as almost to hide her from view," he wrote. Her fine baskets found customers at almost every house. After two or three days her load would be sold, but "sad to relate," noted the minister, she would spend much of her earnings on strong drink before she reached home.[47] *The Basket Seller, c. 1850 (oil on board), Krieghoff, Cornelius (1815-72)/ Art Gallery of Ontario, Toronto, Canada/Gift from the fund of the T. Eaton Co. Ltd for Canadian works of Art, 1951/Bridgeman Images.*

occupied their lands, Abenakis pulled back into the farthest reaches of their territory or maintained a low profile on the peripheries of the new towns, villages, and farms. Newcomers assumed that Indians were fast disappearing from the region, or insisted that those they saw were from St. Francis and belonged in Canada, not in Vermont.[46] In Maine, Penobscots and Passamaquoddies, who had supported the American cause during the Revolution, appealed to Congress for justice as their former allies invaded their hunting territories. But, in defiance of the Indian Trade and Intercourse Act of 1790, first Massachusetts and then after 1820 the new state of Maine imposed treaties that gobbled up huge areas of Indian land without obtaining congressional approval. In 1794 the Passamaquoddies ceded more than 1 million acres to Massachusetts. Two years later, the Penobscots ceded almost 200,000 acres in the Penobscot valley; in 1818 they relinquished all their remaining lands except an island in the Penobscot River and four six-mile-square townships. In 1833 Maine bought the four townships for $50,000. By midcentury, the Penobscots were confined to Indian Island at Old Town, near Orono, Maine, and the Passamaquoddies were reduced to two reservations.

Massachusetts reinstituted a guardian system for Indians after the Revolution, placing Indian communities and lands under the supervision of state-appointed overseers who were entrusted with protecting Indian interests but who often exploited their position for their own ends. At places like Natick and Stockbridge where Indians and Anglo-Americans shared the same town, Indians were edged out of town offices and off the land. Stephen Badger, minister at Natick, reported in 1798 that Indians were "generally considered by white people, and placed, as if by common consent, in an inferiour and degraded situation, and treated accordingly." Covetous neighbors "took every advantage of them that they could, under colour of legal authority . . . to dishearten and depress them."[48]

Indian people who had once moved seasonally for subsistence purposes were now compelled to move about by poverty and the search for either work or displaced relatives. New England towns added to the numbers of Indian people traveling the roads by withholding poor relief from needy people who could not prove they were town residents. Many Indian men went away to sea, often on lengthy whaling voyages, pursuing income and status denied to people of color in New England.[49] Their wives had to assume the burden of supporting the family and many women married non-Indians. Some Mashpee women of Cape Cod married Africans, Portuguese sailors, or German veterans of the Revolutionary War. Indian people who moved to Boston, Providence, Worcester, and other cities often took up residence among the growing African American population.

◆ **Captain Amos Haskins: Daguerreotype by an Unknown Photographer**
Haskins (1815–61), a Wampanoag Indian from Mattapoisett, just east of New Bedford, Massachusetts, was one of many New England Indians who worked in deep-sea whaling in the nineteenth century. He undertook his first whaling voyage at 18 in 1834. This picture was most likely taken in the mid-1850s, by which time he had achieved the rank of ship's captain and made his fortune. Few Indian whalers were so fortunate, and whaling was always a perilous occupation. A few years after this picture was taken, Haskins himself was lost at sea with his crew when their ship went down on a homeward voyage.[50] *Courtesy of the New Bedford Whaling Museum, www.whalingmuseum.org.*

Indian people became increasingly invisible to New Englanders who embraced romantic notions of Indians as a tragically vanishing race. Most New Englanders believed that Indians had, for all intents and purposes, disappeared from the region after King Philip's War, and that the few who remained were "degenerating" as a result of intermarriage with African Americans. Erasing Native Americans from their view of New England's past and present, they saw only poor people of color where Indian people survived and reshaped their communities to accommodate African Americans.[51] Stephen Badger said in 1798 that the Indians of Natick were "frequently shifting their place of residence, and are intermarried with blacks, and some with whites; and the various shades between these, and those that are descended from them." Indians in some parts of Massachusetts had become "almost extinct," and seemed to "vanish" among "people of color."[52] Former president John Adams, writing to Thomas Jefferson in 1812, recalled growing up in Massachusetts seventy years earlier with Indians as neighbors and visitors to his father's house. "But the Girls went out to Service and the Boys to Sea, till not a Soul is left," he wrote. "We scarcely see an Indian in a year."[53] In his *Report on Indian Affairs,* submitted to the secretary of war in 1822, Jedidiah Morse portrayed the Indian communities in New England as a "few feeble remnants" teetering on the brink of extinction.[54] Writing in 1833, after his visit to the United States, French historian Alexis de Tocqueville declared, "All the Indian tribes who once inhabited the territory of New England — the Narragansetts, the Mohicans, the Pequots — now live only in men's memories."[55] Indian people and communities in New England who survived conquest struggled against constructions of history created by non-Indians, who wrote them out of history and essentially out of existence.[56] The prevailing view among Anglo-Americans was that Indians were a doomed race — an idea embodied in James Fenimore Cooper's *The Last of the Mohicans* (1826).

They were wrong. Many Indian people maintained their communities, kinship networks, and core aspects of their cultures while they lived and worked in Anglo-American society. Some moved back and forth between rural tribal reserves and cities. The same year that Tocqueville pronounced them gone, the Mashpee Indians openly defied the authority of Massachusetts and staged a "revolt" that, though never violent, did win them a measure of self-government and that was a limited victory for Indian rights.[57] William Apess (1798–1839), a Pequot Indian and Methodist minister, took an active role in the revolt and worked hard to make sure that Americans did not forget that New England had once been, and still was, Indian country.

Apess was born into an Indian world of poverty, marginalization, and racism. The Pequot tribe was supposed to have been all but exterminated in 1637 and was now confined to two small reservations in southeastern Connecticut. Apess was the product of a broken home, was beaten as a child by his drunken grandmother, and himself succumbed to alcoholism. As a young man he served in the American army in the War of 1812. He later became a Methodist preacher, married, and,

Mr. WILLIAM APES,

A NATIVE MISSIONARY OF THE PEQUOT TRIBE

OF INDIANS.

◆ **William Apess**
Pequot William Apess was, at one time or another, a soldier, a Methodist preacher, a writer, and a leading figure in an Indian "rebellion" in Massachusetts. This undated portrait was imprinted on a card with a ticket for the lecture "Eulogy on King Philip," which he delivered in Boston in 1836. *Portrait of William Apess, engraved by Illman and Pilbrow (litho.), Paradise, John (1783–1833) (after)/ American Antiquarian Society, Worcester, Massachusetts, USA/Bridgeman Images.*

despite having only a rudimentary education, began to write, publishing five books between 1829 and 1836.

The 1830s were not a good time to be an Indian, as U.S. policy mandated the removal of all Indians from east of the Mississippi, and thousands were forced out of their ancestral homelands. In New England, where Indians had been dispossessed long before, many people criticized the government's policies and opposed the actions of the southern states, but few sought justice for Native people closer to home. Rather than keep his head down or curry favor with New Englanders by expressing gratitude for their antiremoval stance, Apess confronted them with their own history, hypocrisy, and racism. Having experienced that racism firsthand, he "understood that the Revolution, which enshrined republican principles in the American commonwealth, also excluded African Americans and Native Americans from their reach."[58] Addressing those New Englanders who protested against Georgia's treatment of the Cherokees,

Apess reminded his readers that the new American nation was built on Indian land and with African slave labor. White society misrepresented both races to justify their continued oppression; skin color was not a marker of inferiority. In 1833 Apess wrote "An Indian's Looking Glass for the White Man," an essay in which he contrasted white Americans' professed Christianity with their treatment of nonwhite people.

> Assemble all nations together in your imagination, and then let the whites
> be seated among them, and then let us look for the whites, and I doubt not
> it would be hard finding them; for to the rest of the nations, they are still but

a handful. Now suppose these skins were put together, and each skin had its national crimes written upon it — which skin do you think would have the greatest? I will ask one question more. Can you charge the Indians with robbing a nation almost of their whole continent, and murdering their women and children, and then depriving the remainder of their lawful rights, that nature and God require them to have? And to cap the climax, rob another nation to till their grounds and welter out their days under the lash with hunger and fatigue under the scorching rays of a burning sun? I should look at all the skins, and I know that when I cast my eye upon that white skin, and if I saw those crimes written upon it, I should enter my protest against it immediately and cleave to that which is more honorable. And I can tell you that I am satisfied with the manner of my creation, fully — whether others are or not.[59]

In 1836, 160 years after Metacomet's death, Apess delivered a remarkable speech in Boston eulogizing Metacomet and giving a very different view of King Philip's War. He portrayed Metacomet as a patriot like George Washington who, after having made every possible compromise, fought to defend his people's rights and freedom. "Does it not appear," he asked, "that the whites have always been the aggressors, and the wars, cruelties, and bloodshed is a job of their own seeking, and not the Indians? . . . Let us have principles that will give everyone his due; and then shall wars cease, and the weary find rest. Give the Indian his rights, and you may be assured war will cease."[60] In New England, as in the rest of the country, the Indians, struggles for those rights continued.

DOCUMENTS

A Double Homicide at Two Medicine

IN JULY 1806 THE BLACKFEET DISCOVERED AMERICANS. Looking down from a hillside they observed Meriwether Lewis and his companions, George Drouillard and the brothers Joseph and Reuben Field, scouting in the valley of the Two Medicine River in Montana. During the return journey from the Pacific, Lewis's party had separated from the main body of the expedition to explore the Marias River. Lewis thought the Indians were "Minnetares of Fort de Prarie" — in other words, Gros Ventres or Atsina, a tribe allied with the Blackfeet. (The Gros Ventres of Montana were a different people from the Gros Ventres of the Missouri.) In fact they were Piegans, members of the southernmost division of the Blackfoot Confederacy that stretched from Alberta and Saskatchewan down into Montana, and the group who were described as "always the Frontier Tribe" in the wars with the Shoshonis.[61]

The Blackfeet may not have met Americans before, but they had already had plenty of contact with non-Indians. Traders from the Hudson's Bay Company and the Northwest Company had pushed west in the second half of the eighteenth century, establishing posts in Blackfeet country, and for more than twenty years the Blackfeet had had access to supplies of guns via the Canadian fur trade. While the Shoshonis had obtained horses before the Blackfeet, guns enabled the Blackfeet to turn the tables on their enemies, and they drove the Shoshonis from the northern Plains and into the foothills of the Rockies, where Lewis and Clark had met them (see page 265). The Blackfeet made sure that the flow of guns stopped with them; they monopolized the gun trade in the North and effectively blocked the supply of guns from reaching their enemies to the south and west. The Shoshonis, Flatheads, Kutenais, Nez Perces, and others lived in fear of well-armed Blackfeet raiding parties and ventured on to the Plains to hunt buffalo at their peril.

The Blackfeet were the dominant power on the northern Plains, and their reputation as fearsome warriors made Lewis and Clark apprehensive about meeting them. They expected trouble. It is not known whether the Blackfeet had heard rumors or reports about the Americans, but the appearance of these new white men in their territory was clearly a cause for attention and concern. Their first encounter with Americans, described here in Lewis's journal, earned the Blackfeet a reputation for treachery and hostility toward Americans and set the stage for decades of conflict during the Rocky Mountain fur trade. For most of the expedition Lewis and Clark got along peacefully with the Indian people they met. Lewis's encounter with the Blackfeet produced the only bloodshed, and Lewis's journal is the only firsthand written account of what happened.

MERIWETHER LEWIS
An Account of His Fight with the Blackfeet (1806)

July 26, 1806

[Lewis] I had scarcely ascended the hills before I discovered to my left at the distance of a mile an assembleage of about 30 horses, I halted and used my spye glass by the help of which I discovered several indians on the top of an eminence just above them who appeared to be looking down towards the river I presumed at Drewyer.° about half the horses were saddled. this was a very unpleasant sight, however I resolved to make the best of our situation and to approach them in a friendly manner. I directed J. Fields to display the flag which I had brought for that purpose and advanced slowly toward them, about this time they discovered us and appeared to run about in a very confused manner as if much allarmed, their attention had been previously so fixed on Drewyer that they did not discover us untill we had began to advance upon them, some of them decended the hill on which they were and drove their horses within shot of its summit and again returned to the hight as if to wate our arrival or to defend themselves. I calculated on their number being nearly or quite equal to that of their horses, that our runing would invite pursuit as it would convince them that we were their enimies and our horses were so indifferent that we could not hope to make our escape by flight; added to this Drewyer was seperated from us and I feared that his not being apprized of the indians in the event of our attempting to escape he would most probably fall a sacrefice. under these considerations I still advanced towards them; when we had arrived within a quarter of a mile of them, one of them mounted his horse and rode full speed towards us, which when I discovered I halted and alighted from my horse; he came within a hundred paces halted looked at us and turned his horse about and returned as briskly to his party as he had advanced; while he halted near us I held out my hand and becconed to him to approach but he paid no attention to my overtures. on his return to his party they all decended the hill and mounted their horses and advanced towards us leaving their horses behind them, we also advanced to meet them. I counted eight of them but still supposed that there were others concealed as there were several other horses saddled. I told the two men with me that I apprehended that these were the Minnetares of Fort de Prarie and from their known character I expected that we were to have some difficulty with them; that if they thought themselves sufficiently strong I was convinced they would attempt to rob us in which case be their numbers what they would I should resist to the last extremity prefering death to that of being deprived of my papers instruments and gun and desired that they would form the same resolution and be allert and on their guard. when we arrived within a hundred yards of each other the indians except one halted I directed the two men with me to do the same and advanced singly to meet the indian with whom I shook hands and passed on to those in his rear, as he did also to the two men in my rear; we now all assembed and alighted from our horses; the Indians soon asked to smoke with us, but I told them that the man whom they had seen pass down the river had my pipe and we could not smoke untill he joined us. I requested as they had seen which way he went that they would one of them go with one of my men in surch of him, this they readily concented to and a young man set out with R. Fields in surch of Drewyer. I now asked them by sighns if they were the Minnetares of the North which they answered in the affirmative; I asked if there was any cheif among them and they pointed out 3 I did not believe them however I

° George Drouillard.

SOURCE: Gary E. Moulton, ed., *The Journals of Lewis and Clark: An American Epic of Discovery* (Lincoln: University of Nebraska Press, 2003), 341–45.

thought it best to please them and gave to one a medal to a second a flag and to the third a handkercheif, with which they appeared well satisfyed. they appeared much agitated with our first interview from which they had scarcely yet recovered, in fact I beleive they were more allarmed at this accedental interview than we were. from no more of them appearing I now concluded they were only eight in number and became much better satisfyed with our situation as I was convinced that we could mannage that number should they attempt any hostile measures. as it was growing late in the evening I proposed that we should remove to the nearest part of the river and encamp together, I told them that I was glad to see them and had a great deel to say to them. we mounted our horses and rode towards the river which was at but a short distance, on our way we were joined by Drewyer Fields and the indian. we decended a very steep bluff about 250 feet high to the river where there was a small bottom of nearly ½ a mile in length and about 250 yards wide in the widest part . . . in this bottom there stand t[h]ree solitary trees near one of which the indians formed a large simicircular camp of dressed buffaloe skins and invited us to partake of their shelter which Drewyer and myself accepted and the Fieldses lay near the fire in front of the sheter. with the asistance of Drewyer I had much conversation with these people in the course of the evening. I learned from them that they were a part of a large band which lay encamped at present near the foot of the rocky mountains on the main branch of Maria's river one ½ days march from our present encampment; that there was a whiteman with their band; that there was another large band of their nation hunting buffaloe near the broken mountains and were on there way to the mouth of Maria's river where they would probably be in the course of a few days. they also informed us that from hence to the establishment where they trade on the Suskasawan river is only 6 days easy march or such as they usually travel with their women and childred which may be estimated at about 150 ms. that from these traders they obtain arm amunition

sperituous liquor blankets &c in exchange for wolves and some beaver skins. I told these people that I had come a great way from the East up the large river which runs towards the rising sun, that I had been to the great waters where the sun sets and had seen a great many nations all of whom I had invited to come and trade with me on the rivers on this side of the mountains, that I had found most of them at war with their neighbours and had succeeded in restoring peace among them, that I was now on my way home and had left my party at the falls of the missouri with orders to decend that river to the entrance of Maria's river and there wait my arrival and that I had come in surch of them in order to prevail on them to be at peace with their neighbours particularly those on the West side of the mountains and to engage them to come and trade with me when the establishment is made at the entrance of this river to all which they readily gave their assent and declared it to be their wish to be at peace with the Tushepahs whom they said had killed a number of their relations lately and pointed to several of those present who had cut their hair as an evidince of the truth of what they had asserted. I found them extreemly fond of smoking and plyed them with the pipe untill late at night. I told them that if they intended to do as I wished them they would send some of their young men to their band with an invitation to their chiefs and warriors to bring the whiteman with them and come down and council with me at the entrance of Maria's river and that the ballance of them would accompany me to that place, where I was anxious now to meet my men as I had been absent from them some time and knew that they would be uneasy untill they saw me. that if they would go with me I would give them 10 horses and some tobacco. to this proposition they made no reply, I took the first watch tonight and set up untill half after eleven; the indians by this time were all asleep, I roused up R. Fields and laid down myself; I directed Fields to watch the movements of the indians and if any of them left the camp to awake us all as I apprehended they would attempt to s[t]eal our horses. this being done I fell into a profound sleep and did not wake untill the noise of the men and indians awoke me a little after light in the morning. . . .

July 27, 1806
[Lewis] This morning at day light the indians got up and crouded around the fire, J. Fields who was on post had carelessly laid his gun down behind him near where his brother was sleeping, one of the indians the fellow to whom I had given the medal last evening sliped behind him and took his gun and that of his brothers unperceived by him, at the same instant two others advanced and seized the guns of Drewyer and myself, J. Fields seing this turned about to look for his gun and saw the fellow just runing off with her and his brothers he called to his brother who instantly jumped up and pursued the indian with him whom they overtook at the distance of 50 or 60 paces from the camp sized their guns and rested them from him and R Fields as he seized his gun stabed the indian to the heart with his knife the fellow ran about 15 steps and fell dead; of this I did not know untill afterwards, having recovered their guns they ran back instantly to the camp; Drewyer who was awake saw the indian take hold of his gun and instantly jumped up and s[e]ized her and rested her from him but the indian still retained his pouch, his jumping up and crying damn you let go my gun awakened me I jumped up and asked what was the matter which I quickly learned when I saw drewyer in a scuffle with the indian for his gun. I reached to seize my gun but found her gone, I then drew a pistol from my holster and terning myself about saw the indian making off with my gun I ran at him with my pistol and bid him lay down my gun which he was in the act of doing when the Fieldses returned and drew up their guns to shoot him which I forbid as he did not appear to be about to make any resistance or commit any offensive act, he droped the gun and walked slowly off, I picked her up instantly, Drewyer having about this time recovered his gun and pouch asked me if he might

not kill the fellow which I also forbid as the indian did not appear to wish to kill us, as soon as they found us all in possession of our arms they ran an indeavored to drive off all the horses I now hollowed to the men and told them to fire on them if they attempted to drive off our horses, they accordingly pursued the main party who were dr[i]ving the horses up the river and I pursued the man who had taken my gun who with another was driving off a part of the horses which were to the left of the camp, I pursued them so closely that they could not take twelve of their own horses but continued to drive one of mine with some others; at the distance of three hundred paces they entered one of those steep nitches in the bluff with the horses before them being nearly out of breath I could pursue no further, I called to them as I had done several times before that I would shoot them if they did not give me my horse and raised my gun, one of them jumped behind a rock and spoke to the other who turned arround and stoped at the distance of 30 steps from me and I shot him through the belly, he fell to his knees and on his wright elbow from which position he partly raised himself up and fired at me, and turning himself about crawled in behind a rock which was a few feet from him. he overshot me, being bearheaded I felt the wind of his bullet very distinctly. not having my shotpouch I could not reload my peice and as there were two of them behind good shelters from me I did not think it prudent to rush on them with my pistol which had I discharged I had not the means of reloading untill I reached camp; I therefore returned leasurely towards camp, on my way I met with Drewyer who having heared the report of the guns had returned in surch of me and left the Fieldes to pursue the indians, I desired him to haisten to the camp with me and assist in catching as many of the indian horses as were necessary and to call to the Fieldes if he could make them hear to come back that we still had a sufficient number of horses, this he did but they were too far to hear him. we reached the camp and began to catch the horses and saddle them and put on the pcks. the reason I had not my pouch with me was that I had not time to return about 50 yards to camp after geting my gun before I was obliged to pursue the indians or suffer them to collect and drive off all the horses. we had caught and saddled the horses and began to arrange the packs when the Fieldses returned with four of our horses; we left one of our horses and took four of the best of those of the indian's; while the men were preparing the horses I put four sheilds and two bows and quivers of arrows which had been left on the fire, with sundry other articles; they left all their baggage at our mercy.

they had but 2 guns and one of them they left the others were armed with bows and arrows and eyedaggs.° the gun we took with us. I also retook the flagg but left the medal about the neck of the dead man that they might be informed who we were. we took some of their buffaloe meat and set out ascending the bluffs by the same rout we had decended last evening leaving the ballance of nine of their horses which we did not want. . . .

_____

° A type of dagger with a hole in the handle.

QUESTIONS FOR CONSIDERATION

1. In light of Blackfeet foreign policy and the military situation on the northern Plains at the time of this encounter, what might Lewis have said to incite the Blackfeet to turn against him?

2. Remembering that the Blackfeet had a reputation as formidable warriors and that Lewis produced the only written record of the event, what things in the report might appear not to "add up"?

3. Blackfeet oral tradition tells that the warriors in this encounter were in fact boys returning home from their first horse raid. How might this information clarify Lewis's account and help in understanding it?

Cherokee and White Women Oppose Removal

THE POLICY AND PROCESS OF INDIAN REMOVAL generated heated debate and widespread opposition in American as well as Indian societies. Many white Americans denounced it as immoral and inhumane, a stain on the nation's honor, and a breach of sacred treaty pledges. Some feared divine retribution. Many associated the removal of Indian peoples with the expansion of slavery onto the newly emptied lands. Students protested and sent petitions to Congress. Church and reform groups organized massive pamphlet and petition campaigns. Some American women, who did not yet have the right to vote, took the only political action available to them and organized their own national petition campaign. Invoking the concept of republican motherhood, they assumed the responsibility to act as moral guardians of the nation's virtue. Almost 1,500 American women from the northern states submitted petitions to Congress opposing Indian removal.

The largest petition, submitted to the Senate from Pittsburgh, contained 670 signatures. Like other women opposing removal, the ladies of Steubenville, Ohio, took an unprecedented step and made their voices heard in the national debate. They failed to stop removal from going ahead but they and their reform-minded allies later applied the same tactics in the fight to abolish slavery.[62] However, the first women to petition against removal were Cherokees, a dozen years earlier.

European males encountering Native peoples often missed, misunderstood, or ignored the roles of women in Native American society, but gender played a key role in how most Native American societies organized themselves.[63] Among the Cherokees, the importance of women as producers of corn meant that they enjoyed considerable influence, a status reflected in the Green Corn Ceremony, the key ritual which marked the social and spiritual regeneration of the community. "By honoring the corn," explains historian Theda Perdue, "the Cherokees paid homage to women." Cherokee society was matrilineal; children inherited clan membership from their mothers. Cherokee men assisted in clearing the fields for planting, but their primary roles took them away from the village, to hunt and to fight. Women gave life, raising children and corn; men took life in hunting and war. Even though they lived together, women and men each had separate roles, separate spaces, and distinct sources of power. Women not only grew corn, but "the land on which corn grew was a uniquely female space."[64]

Since war and diplomacy were typically male responsibilities. Europeans who entered Indian country looking for allies or land tended to ignore the women, but women sometimes actively participated in making war and making treaties on occasion, and they sat in council meetings. The Cherokee chief Attakullakulla, or Little Carpenter, once expressed surprise to see no women present during a council with South Carolina. He said "that the White Men as well as the Red were born of Women and that it was Customary for them to admit the Women into their Councils and desired to know if that was not the Custom of the White People also."[65] (It was not.) As a young woman, Nanye-hi (also known as Nancy Ward) of the Cherokee earned the title of War Woman for fighting alongside her husband and rallying the warriors after his death. In the Revolution she opposed Dragging Canoe's decision for war (see page 236), and later in life she became a "Beloved Woman," a title reserved for highly regarded female elders. At the Treaty of Hopewell in 1785, she addressed the American and Cherokee negotiators as a "mother of warriors." Indian women did not normally sign treaties, but they sometimes signed and presented petitions while treaties were in process, and they occasionally challenged — and even threatened — male speakers. As wives and mothers, they spoke for future generations and demanded respect.[66]

In the past, town councils in Cherokee society had usually been composed of men, but women had their own town council that acted in an advisory role. As the Cherokee Nation began to fracture over the difficult issue of removal, and some tribe members began to move west, Cherokee women submitted petitions to the Cherokee National Council, the all-male governing body of the tribe, making clear their position on removal, land sales, and individual allotments. In 1817 the Cherokees were being pressured to accept a plan by which 13,000 of their people would move west to Arkansas at Congress's expense. Before the Cherokee National Council met to consider the issue, a group of senior Cherokee women held their own council and then sent representatives to the National Council with a petition signed by Nancy Ward and a dozen other women. The men agreed with the women, but Andrew Jackson and the U.S. commissioners convinced a group of chiefs to sign a treaty whereby individual Cherokees could choose between moving to Arkansas or staying in the East on allotment. The Cherokee women submitted a second petition in 1818. Although addressed to the Cherokee National Council, it was actually intended for the white men pushing for removal.

These women had lived through huge reductions in the Cherokees' homelands (see Map 4.7, "Cherokee Land Cessions in the Colonial and Revolutionary Eras, 1721–1785," page 235). Hunting territories were the domain of Cherokee men, but, while Cherokees technically held land in common, the fields around Cherokee villages belonged to the matrilineal households of the women who tended and grew the crops. As mothers, Cherokee women also raised past and future generations of Cherokee children on those same lands. Cherokee women spoke with a special authority and concern over sales of the land. In their second petition, addressing white men as well as Cherokee men, the women again argued the primacy of motherhood but also invoked Christian morality and pointed to the Cherokees' progress toward civilization.[67] It is unclear how much of an impact the women's petitions had on the National Council, but after 1819 the Cherokees ceded no more land until the fraudulent Treaty of New Echota in 1835, which the United States negotiated with a proremoval minority (see page 272). The political structures and practices established by the Cherokee constitution adopted in 1827 emulated those of the United States: women were barred from voting in elections and from holding political office.

CHEROKEE WOMEN
Petition (May 2, 1817)

The Cherokee ladys now being present at the meeting of the chiefs and warriors in council have thought it their duty as mothers to address their beloved chiefs and warriors now assembled.

Our beloved children and head men of the Cherokee Nation, we address you warriors in council. We have raised all of you on the land which we now have, which God gave us to inhabit and raise provisions. We know that our country has once been extensive, but by repeated sales has become circumscribed to a small track, and [we] never have thought it our duty to interfere in the disposition of it till now. If a father or mother was to sell all their lands which they had to depend on, which their children had to raise their living on, which would be indeed bad & to be removed to another country. We do not wish to go to an unknown country [to] which we have understood some of our children wish to go over the Mississippi, but this act of our children would be like destroying your mothers.

Your mothers, your sisters ask and beg of you not to part with any more of our land. We say ours. You are our descendants; take pity on our request. But keep it for our growing children, for it was the good will of our creator to place us here, and you know our father, the great president,° will not allow his white children to take our country away. Only keep your hands off of paper talks for its our own country. For [if] it was not, they would not ask you to put your hands to paper, for it would be impossible to remove us all. For as soon as one child is raised, we have others in our arms, for such is our situation & will consider our circumstance.

Therefore, children, don't part with any more of our lands but continue on it & enlarge your

---

° James Monroe.

farms. Cultivate and raise corn & cotton and your mothers and sisters will make clothing for you which our father the president has recommended to us all. We don't charge any body for selling any lands, but we have heard such intentions of our children. But your talks become true at last; it was our desire to forwarn you all not to part with our lands.

Nancy Ward to her children: Warriors to take pity and listen to the talks of your sisters. Although I am very old yet cannot but pity the situation in which you will here of their minds. I have great many grand children which [I] wish them to do well on our land.

CHEROKEE WOMEN
Petition (June 30, 1818)

Beloved Children,
We have called a meeting among ourselves to consult on the different points now before the council, relating to our national affairs. We have heard with painful feelings that the bounds of the land we now possess are to be drawn into very narrow limits. The land was given to us by the Great Spirit above as our common right, to raise our children upon, & to make support for our rising generations. We therefore humbly petition our beloved children, the head men & warriors, to hold out to the last in support of our common rights, as the Cherokee nation have been the first settlers of this land; we therefore claim the right of the soil.

We well remember that our country was formerly very extensive, but by repeated sales it has become circumscribed to the very narrow limits we have at present. Our Father the President advised us to become farmers, to manufacture our own clothes, & to have our children instructed. To this advice we have attended in every thing as far

---

SOURCE: Theda Perdue and Michael D. Green, eds., *The Cherokee Removal: A Brief History with Documents* (Boston: Bedford/St. Martin's, 2005), 131–33.

as we were able. Now the thought of being compelled to remove the other side of the Mississippi is dreadful to us, because it appears to us that we, by this removal, shall be brought to a savage state again, for we have, by the endeavor of our Father the President, become too much enlightened to throw aside the privileges of a civilized life.

We therefore unanimously join in our meeting to hold our country in common as hitherto.

Some of our children have become Christians. We have missionary schools among us. We have hard the gospel in our nation. We have become civilized & enlightened, & are in hopes that in a few years our nation will be prepared for instruction in other branches of sciences & arts, which are both useful & necessary in civilized society.

There are some white men among us who have been raised in this country from their youth, are connected with us by marriage, & have considerable families, who are very active in encouraging the emigration of our nation. These ought to be our truest friends but prove our worst enemies. They seem to be only concerned how to increase their riches, but do not care what becomes of our Nation, nor even of their own wives and children.

Petition from the Women of Steubenville, Ohio (1830)

"Memorial of the Ladies of Steubenville, Ohio, Against the forcible removal of the Indians without the limits of the United States." *February 15, 1830*
Read:–ordered that it lie upon the table.

To the Honorable the Senate and House of Representatives of the United States.

The memorial of the undersigned, residents of the state of Ohio, and town of Steubenville, Respectfully Sheweth:

That your memorialists are deeply impressed with the belief, that the present crisis in the affairs of the Indian nations, calls loudly on *all* who can feel for the woes of humanity, to solicit, with earnestness, your honorable body to bestow on this subject, involving, as it does, the prosperity and happiness of more than fifty thousand of our fellow Christians, the immediate consideration demanded by its interesting nature and pressing importance.

It is readily acknowledged, that the wise and venerated founders of our country's free institutions have committed the powers of Government to those whom nature and reason declare the best fitted to exercise them; and your memorialists would sincerely deprecate any presumptuous interference on the part of their own sex with the ordinary political affairs of the country, as wholly unbecoming the character of the American females. Even in private life, we may not presume to direct the general conduct, or control the acts of those who stand in the near and guardian relations of husbands and brothers; yet all admit that *there are times* when duty and affection call on us to *advise* and *persuade*, as well as to cheer or console. And if we approach the public Representatives of our husbands and brothers, only in the humble character of suppliants in the cause of mercy and humanity, may we not hope that even the small voice of *female* sympathy will be heard?

Compared with the estimate placed on woman, and the attention paid to her on other nations, the generous and defined deference shown by all ranks and classes of men, in this country, to our sex, forms a striking contrast; and as an honorable and distinguishing trait in the American Character, has often excited the admiration of intelligent foreigners. Nor is this general kindness lightly regarded or coldly appreciated; but, with warm feelings of affection and pride, and hearts swelling with gratitude, the mothers and daughters of America bear testimony to the generous nature of their countrymen.

When, therefore, injury and oppression threaten to crush a hapless people within our borders, we, the feeblest of the feeble, appeal with confidence to those who should be representatives of national virtues as they are the depositaries of national powers, and implore them to succor the weak and unfortunate. In despite of the *undoubted national right* which the Indians have to the land of their forefathers, and in the face of solemn treaties, pledging the faith of the nation for their secure possession of those lands, it is intended, we are told, to force them from their native soil, to compel them to seek new homes in a distant and dreary wilderness. To you, then, as the constitutional protectors of the Indians within our territory, and as the peculiar guardians of our national character, and our country's welfare, we solemnly and honestly appeal, to save this remnant of a much injured people from annihilation, to shield our country from the curses denounced on the cruel and ungrateful, and to shelter the American character from lasting dishonor.

And your petitioners will ever pray.

Frances Norton, Catharine Norton, Mary A. Norton, M. J. Hodge, Emily N. Page, Rachel Mason, E. Anderson, S. Ashburn, A. Wilson,

SOURCE: Transcription of primary source, 21st Congress, 1st Session, Report no. 209, House of Representatives, U.S. Docs. Serial Vol. 0200 Doc. 209 (Washington, D.C.: U.S. Government, 1830).

S. J. Walker, E. J. Porter, A. Cushener, M. J. Kelly, Frances P. Wilson, Eliza M. Rogers, Ann Eliza Wilson, Sarah Moodey, Mary Jenkinson, Jane Wilson, Editha Veirs, Mary Veirs, Nancy Fuston, Sarah Hoghland, Nancy Laremore, Nancy Wilson, Elizabeth Sheppard, Mary C. Green, Anna Woods, Anna Dike, Margaretta Woods, Margaret Larimore, Maria E. Larimore, Sarah S. Larimore, Martha E. Leslie, Catharine Slacke, W. D. Andrews, P. Lord, Eliza S. Wilson, Sarah Wells, Rebecca R. Morse, Hetty E. Beatty, Caroline S. Craig, Elizabeth Steenrod, Elloisa Lefflen, Lucy Whipple, N. Kilgore, C. Colwell, E. Brown, M. Patterson, R. Craig, J. M. Millan, Betsey Tappan, Margaret M. Andrews, Sarah Spencer, Mary Buchannan, do., Rebecca J. Buchannan, do., Hetty Collier, Eunice Collier, Elizabeth Beatty, Jane Beatty, Sarah Means, Elizabeth Sage.

QUESTIONS FOR CONSIDERATION

1. What reasons did the Cherokee and American women present to support their positions and to justify their participation in the political debate?

2. What language did the Cherokee petitioners employ to represent their special, even sacred, relationship to the land? What did they mean when they wrote that moving west would be "like destroying your mothers"? What language did the American women employ and what were the "natural rights" they invoked?

3. In each case, the women addressed their petitions to the male leaders of their government. Does the tone of the petitions suggest anything about gender relations and the relative positions of Cherokee and American women in their respective societies?

Foundations of Federal Indian Law and a Native Response

AMERICANS WHO ADVOCATED THE REMOVAL of the Cherokees and their neighbors from the southeastern United States to new homes west of the Mississippi often justified that removal on the grounds that the Indians were, after all, "savages." Such assertions ignored the realities of Cherokee culture, Cherokee history, and Cherokee success in adapting to the demands of American mores in the early nineteenth century. The Cherokees created and participated in a republican form of government modeled on the U.S. Constitution, and they built a capital at New Echota with impressive public buildings. Their response to Georgia's assault on their society and government was to provide testimony to the degree to which Cherokees had adapted and incorporated the "civilized ways" of their non-Indian neighbors. The Cherokees did not resort to violence, striking the war post as Dragging Canoe and his followers had done more than half a century earlier — they took Georgia to court.

Since colonial times, Indians had used British colonial and U.S. courts to seek legal protection and redress of grievances. But the Cherokees were the first to bring a case to the U.S. Supreme Court. They hired as their lawyer former attorney general of the United States William Wirt. Wirt sought an injunction to stop Georgia from executing or enforcing its laws in Cherokee country. The sitting chief justice, John Marshall, had presided over the Supreme Court since 1801, and he consciously used his position to mold the evolving law of the young nation. Despite the precedents of English, colonial, natural, and international law, Marshall believed that "the United States had to have an *American* law developed by American jurists attending to American needs." The Cherokee cases — *Cherokee Nation v. Georgia* (1831) and *Worcester v. Georgia* (1832) — have been called "the central fury of . . . one of the greatest constitutional crises in the history of the nation." Marshall used the Cherokee cases that came before the Court "to establish the legal doctrine . . . of an American law of United States–Native American relations."[68]

In an earlier case, *Johnson v. McIntosh* (1823), Marshall had restricted tribal rights to transfer lands only to the U.S. government. In a case marked by collusion, Marshall declared that Indians possessed only a right of occupancy but that Europeans had acquired ownership by right of discovery and that the United States had inherited that ownership. "Discovery converted the indigenous owners of discovered lands into tenants on those lands." They could lease or sell land, but only to the discovering sovereign. In 1823 that meant they could sell their lands only to the United States. It was a doctrine with disastrous consequences for Native people in America and around the world.[69] In *Cherokee Nation v. Georgia,* the Supreme Court found that it lacked original jurisdiction, but Justice Marshall tried to define the exact status of the Cherokees — and by extension all Indian tribes — within the United States. The Cherokees and other Native tribes in the United States, he decided, were "domestic dependent nations" who had retained some aspects of their sovereignty through treaties. He likened the Indians' relationship to the government to that between a ward and a guardian. However, without a strong show of federal power to enforce U.S. laws protecting tribal sovereignty, the Cherokees were vulnerable to Georgia's strong antisovereignty position. "Marshall's opinion," writes one legal scholar, "was a feeble gesture compared with Georgia's dramatic assertion of state power when it hung Corn Tassel."[70] (For more on the case of Corn Tassel, see page 271–72.)

In 1832 the Cherokees succeeded in getting their case into the Supreme Court via a U.S. citizen. Samuel Worcester, a missionary from Vermont, defied a law passed by the Georgia legislature requiring non-Indians living in Cherokee country to take an oath of allegiance to Georgia. Worcester and another missionary, Elihu Butler, were arrested and sentenced to four years of hard labor. Worcester and Butler petitioned the Supreme Court, which accepted the case. As in *Cherokee Nation,* Georgia refused to appear. Marshall, seventy-five-years old and in poor health, took just two weeks to write the Court's opinion. In March 1832 the Supreme Court rendered its decision in *Worcester v. Georgia.* Worcester's arrest, said Marshall, was illegal. Georgia had no authority to execute its laws within an Indian nation protected under the treaty clause of the U.S. Constitution. The Cherokee

Nation was "a distinct community, occupying its own territory . . . in which the law of Georgia can have no right to enter but with the assent of the Cherokees."

The cases clearly asserted the authority of the federal government, but where did they leave the legal status of the Cherokees? Georgia refused to release the missionaries and openly defied the Court. President Andrew Jackson had no intention of executing the law in this case, and the two missionaries remained in prison until 1833, when a new governor released them. Georgia continued its campaign to undermine Cherokee government. Many Cherokees and their supporters came to believe that in winning their Supreme Court victory they had, in fact, lost their last battle.

Even so, John Marshall's opinions established the legal foundation for the existence of Indian tribes within the borders of the United States. Indians were to be considered domestic, dependent nations, but Indian country had distinct legal boundaries within which state law did not apply. As John Wunder notes in his study of Indians and the Bill of Rights, some of the chickens hatched in *Cherokee Nation v. Georgia* came home to roost in modern times: "Whereas nineteenth-century law focused on defining 'domestic' and 'dependent' for nineteenth-century audiences anxious to take Indian lands, twentieth-century courts after World War II expanded the meaning of 'nation.'"[71] Law professor Charles F. Wilkinson regards *Worcester* as "one of the Supreme Court's most lasting statements." Its principles are fundamental to understanding modern Indian law and the modern Court's protective stance toward Indian self-government: "Tribes are sovereign nations with broad inherent powers that, almost without exception, exist by dint of inherent right, not by delegation."[72]

Marshall's opinions in *Cherokee Nation* and *Worcester* thus define the status of Indian tribes in the United States. *Cherokee Nation* defines the tribes' relationship to the federal government, *Worcester* their relationship to the states. Tribes are under the protection of the federal government, but they possess sufficient sovereignty to defend themselves from intrusion by the states.[73] The federal government, of course, has not always carried out its responsibility to protect tribal sovereignty against state encroachment, but legal relationships — and the existence of federal, state, and tribal jurisdictions — laid out in *Cherokee Nation* and *Worcester* are keys to understanding many aspects of U.S.–Indian affairs in the past and many developments in Indian country today.

Marshall's ruling in *Worcester* represented a major — but short-lived — victory for Cherokee chief John Ross, who had fought long and hard against passage of the Indian Removal Act. As he wrote to Davy Crockett, who as Democratic congressman from Tennessee had broken party ranks and voted against the removal bill, Ross lived in hope that humanity and justice would ultimately prevail over greed, intrigue, and corruption. "Whether this day will come in time to save the suffering Cherokees from violence and fraud, it is for wisdom, magnanimity & justice of the United States to determine."[74] The Supreme Court decision was a victory for justice, but Ross knew all too well the forces and interests arrayed against the Cherokees.

In 1992, the Georgia State Board of Pardons and Paroles acted "to remove a stain on the history of criminal justice in Georgia"; 160 years after *Worcester v. Georgia,* the board issued full and unconditional pardons to Samuel Worcester and Elihu Butler.[75]

JOHN MARSHALL
Cherokee Nation v. State of Georgia (1831)
and Worcester v. Georgia (1832)

CHEROKEE NATION V. STATE OF GEORGIA

Mr. Chief Justice *Marshall* delivered the opinion of the court:

This bill is brought by the Cherokee Nation, praying an injunction to restrain the State of Georgia from the execution of certain laws of that State, which as it is alleged, go directly to annihilate the Cherokees as a political society, and to seize, for the use of Georgia, the lands of the nation which have been assured to them by the United States in solemn treaties repeatedly made and still in force.

If the courts were permitted to indulge their sympathies, a case better calculated to excite them can scarcely be imagined. A people once numerous, powerful, and truly independent, found by our ancestors in the quiet and uncontrolled possession of an ample domain, gradually sinking beneath our superior policy, our arts and our arms, have yielded their lands by successive treaties, each of which contains a solemn guarantee of the residue, until they retain no more of their formerly extensive territory than is deemed necessary to their comfortable subsistence. To preserve this remnant the present application is made.

Before we can look into the merits of the case, a preliminary inquiry presents itself. Has this court jurisdiction of the cause?

The third article of the Constitution describes the extent of the judicial power. The second section closes an enumeration of the cases to which it is extended, with "controversies" "between the State or the citizens thereof, and foreign states, citizens, or subjects." A subsequent clause of the same section gives the Supreme Court original jurisdiction in all cases in which a state shall be a party. The party defendant may

SOURCE: Supreme Court of the United States, 1831. 30 U.S. (5 Pet.) 1, 8 L.Ed. 25. Supreme Court of the United States, 1832. 31 U.S. (6 Pet.) 515, 8 L.Ed. 583.

then unquestionably be sued in this court. May the plaintiff sue in it? Is the Cherokee Nation a foreign state in the sense in which that term is used in the Constitution?

The counsel for the plaintiffs have maintained the affirmative of this proposition with great earnestness and ability. So much of the argument as was intended to prove the character of the Cherokees as a State, as a distinct political society separated from others, capable of managing its own affairs and governing itself, has, in the opinion of a majority of the judges, been completely successful. They have been uniformly treated as a State from the settlement of our country. The numerous treaties made with them by the United States recognize them as a people capable of maintaining the relations of peace and war, of being responsible in their political character for any violation of their engagements, or for any aggression committed on the citizens of the United States by any individual of their community. Laws have been enacted in the spirit of these treaties. The acts of our government plainly recognize the Cherokee Nation as a State, and the courts are bound by those acts.

A question of much more difficulty remains. Do the Cherokees constitute a foreign state in the sense of the Constitution?

The counsel have shown conclusively that they are not a State of the Union, and have insisted that individually they are aliens, not owing allegiance to the United States. An aggregate of aliens composing a State must, they say be a foreign state. Each individual being foreign, the whole must be foreign.

This argument is imposing, but we must examine it more closely before we yield to it. The condition of the Indians in relation to the United States is perhaps unlike that of any other two people in existence. In the general, nations not owing a common allegiance are foreign to each other. The term "foreign nation" is, with strict propriety, applicable by either to the other. But the relation of the Indians to the United States is marked by peculiar and cardinal distinctions which exist nowhere else.

The Indian Territory is admitted to compose part of the United States. In all our maps, geographical treaties, histories and laws, it is so considered. In all our intercourse with foreign nations, in our commercial regulations, in any attempt at intercourse between Indians, and foreign nations, they are considered as within the jurisdictional limits of the United States, subject to many of those restraints which are imposed upon our own citizens. They acknowledge themselves in their treaties to be under the protection of the United States; they admit that the United States shall have the sole and exclusive right of regulating the trade with them, and managing all their affairs as they think proper; and the Cherokees in particular were allowed by the treaty of Hopewell, which preceded the Constitution, "to send a deputy of their choice, whenever they think fit, to Congress." Treaties were made with some tribes by the State of New York under a then unsettled construction of the confederation, by which they ceded all their lands to that State, taking back a limited grant to themselves, in which they admit their dependence.

Though the Indians are acknowledged to have an unquestionable, and, heretofore, unquestioned right to the lands they occupy until that right shall be extinguished by a voluntary cession to our government, yet it may well be doubted whether those tribes which reside within the acknowledged boundaries of the United States can, with strict accuracy, be denominated foreign nations. They may, more correctly, perhaps, be denominated domestic dependent nations. They occupy a territory to which we assert a title independent of their will, which must take effect in point of possession when their right of possession ceases. Meanwhile they are in a state of pupilage. Their relation to the United States resembles that of a ward to his guardian.

They look to our government for protection; rely upon its kindness and its power; appeal to it for relief to their wants; and address the President as their great father. They and their country are considered by foreign nations, as well as by ourselves, as being so completely under the sovereignty and dominion of the United States, that any attempt to acquire their lands, or to form a political connection with them, would be considered by all as an invasion of our territory, and an act of hostility.

These considerations go far to support the opinion that the framers of our Constitution had not the Indian tribes in view when they opened the courts of the Union to controversies between a State or the citizens thereof, and foreign states.

In considering this subject, the habits and usages of the Indians in their intercourse with their white neighbors ought not to be entirely disregarded. At the time the Constitution was framed, the idea of appealing to an American court of justice for an assertion of right or a redress of wrong, had perhaps never entered the mind of an Indian or of his tribe. Their appeal was to the tomahawk, or to the government. This was well understood by the statesmen who framed the Constitution of the United States, and might furnish some reason for omitting to enumerate them among the parties who might sue in the courts of the Union. Be this as it may, the peculiar relations between the United States and the Indians occupying our territory are such that we should feel much difficulty in considering them as designated by the term "foreign State," were there no other part of the Constitution which might shed light on the meaning of these words. But we think that in construing them, considerable aid is furnished by that clause in the eighth section of the third article, which empowers Congress to "regulate commerce with foreign nations, and among the several States, and with the Indian tribes."

In this clause they are as clearly contradistinguished by a name appropriate to themselves from foreign nations as from the several States composing the Union. They are designated by a distinct appellation; and as this appellation can be applied to neither of the others, neither can the appellation distinguishing either of the others be in fair construction applied to them. The objects to which the power of regulating commerce might be directed, are divided into three distinct classes — foreign nations, the several States, and Indian tribes. When forming this article, the convention considered them as entirely distinct. We cannot assume that the distinction was lost in framing a subsequent article, unless there be something in its language to authorize the assumption.

WORCESTER V. GEORGIA

The Indian nations had always been considered as distinct, independent political communities, retaining their original natural rights, as the undisputed possessors of the soil from time immemorial, with the single exception of that imposed by irresistible power, which excluded them from intercourse with any other European potentate than the first discoverer of the coast of the particular region claimed: and this was a restriction which those European potentates imposed on themselves, as well as on the Indians. The very term "nation," so generally applied to them, means "a people distinct from others." The Constitution, by declaring treaties already made, as well as those to be made, to be the supreme law of the land, has adopted and sanctioned the previous treaties with the Indian nations, and consequently admits their rank among those powers who are capable of making treaties. The words "treaty" and "nation" are words of our own language, selected in our diplomatic and legislative proceedings, by ourselves, having each a definite and well understood meaning. We have applied them to Indians, as we have applied them to the other nations of the earth. They are applied to all in the same sense.

Georgia herself has furnished conclusive evidence that her former opinions on this subject concurred with those entertained by her sister States, and by the government of the United States. Various acts of her Legislature have been cited in the argument, including the contract of cession made in the year 1802,° all tending to

prove her acquiescence in the universal conviction that the Indian nations possessed a full right to the lands they occupied, until that right should be extinguished by the United States, with their consent; that their territory was separated from that of any State within whose chartered limits they might reside, by a boundary line, established by treaties; that, within their boundary, they possessed rights with which no State could interfere, and that the whole power of regulating the intercourse with them was vested in the United States. A review of these acts, on the part of Georgia, would occupy too much time, and is the less necessary because they have been accurately detailed in the argument at the bar. Her new series of laws, manifesting her abandonment of these opinions, appears to have commenced in December, 1828.

In opposition to this original right, possessed by the undisputed occupants of every country; to this recognition of that right, which is evidenced by our history, in every change through which we have passed, is placed the charters granted by the monarch of a distant and distinct region, parceling out a territory in possession of others whom he could not remove and did not attempt to remove, and the cession made of his claims by the Treaty of Peace.

The actual state of things at the time, and all history since, explain these charters; and the King of Great Britain, at the Treaty of Peace, could cede only what belonged to his crown. These newly asserted titles can derive no aid from the articles so often repeated in Indian treaties; extending to them, first, the protection of Great Britain, and afterwards that of the United States. These articles are associated with others, recognizing their title to self-government. The very fact of repeated treaties with them recognizes it; and the settled doctrine of the law of nations is that a weaker power does not surrender its independence — its right to self-government, by associating with a stronger and taking its protection. A weak State in order to provide for its safety, may place itself under the protection of one more powerful without stripping

---

° The Compact of 1802, by which Georgia ceded her western land claims to the federal government. See page 266.

itself of the right of government, and ceasing to be a State. Examples of this kind are not wanting in Europe. "Tributary and feudatory states," says Vattel,° "do not thereby cease to be sovereign and independent states so long as self-government and sovereign and independent authority are left in the administration of the state." At the present day, more than one State may be considered as holding its right of self-government under the guaranty and protection of one or more allies.

° Emer de Vattel (1714–67), a Swiss diplomat.

The Cherokee nation, then, is a distinct community, occupying its own territory, with boundaries accurately described, in which the laws of Georgia can have no force, and which the citizens of Georgia have no right to enter but with the assent of the Cherokees themselves or in conformity with treaties and with the acts of Congress. The whole intercourse between the United States and this nation is, by our Constitution and laws, vested in the government of the United States.

The act of the State of Georgia under which the plaintiff in error was prosecuted is consequently void, and the judgment a nullity.

John Ross
Reactions to Worcester v. Georgia:
Letter to Richard Taylor, John Baldridge, Sleeping Rabbit, Sicketowee, and Wahachee (April 28, 1832)

My Friends,

. . . The Supreme Court in the case of Worcester & Butler vs. the State of Georgia has determined the question of our national rights as fully as can be. The decision is final & cannot be revoked: but the course of legal proceedings is necessarily attended with tardiness, consequently should the authorities of Georgia, refuse, as they have done, to release immediately those much injured imprisoned gentlemen, and continue still to arrest & oppress our citizens, we should not be discouraged, because the President, out of his disappointment, may still pursue a political course towards us, under the hope that by withholding from us the protection of the government, a Treaty may yet be effected previous to the time when it shall become his imperious duty to act for the enforcement of this decision of the Supreme Court [in *Worcester v.*

SOURCE: John Ross, *The Papers of Chief John Ross* (Norman: University of Oklahoma Press, 1985), 2:242–43. Reproduced with permission of University of Oklahoma Press in the format Republish in a book via Copyright Clearance Center.

Georgia]. The conflict is now between the United States & Georgia. The final issue ere long will be seen. Should Georgia prevail, the Union of the States is dissolved: but should the United States regard the constitutional liberties guaranteed to their citizens, Georgia must submit to see the Cherokees triumph over their oppressions under her usurped authority; therefore, let the people endure patiently to await the final result. We have gained a great point and they should be watchful over the conduct of such disappointed traitors as may be found amongst them. Thro' the false impressions made by them upon the government, our sufferings have been prolonged, and protections withheld from us. Our country is again full of surveyors who are engaged by the authorities of Georgia, to run out a large portion of our Territory into small lots. This illegal proceeding can have no effect to weaken our national rights, even should they proceed so far as to draw for the lands: the title granted by the drawer of lots° will not be valid, unless our

---

° Georgia awarded Cherokee lands to its citizens by lottery.

national title be first extinguished by a Treaty with the United States, which contingency can never take place, if our people continue to remain firm & be united in the support of our common interests. I cannot believe that the General Government would allow Georgia to go so far as to draw for and *occupy our lands by force.* The President has repeatedly said to us, that the Cherokees will be *protected in their territorial possessions;* and he has also boasted of never having told a red brother a lie, nor ever having spoke to them with a forked tongue. We have a right, however, to judge of this bravado for ourselves from his own acts. The decision of the Supreme Court, under the Treaties, Laws & Constitution, is the strong shield by which our rights must be respected & protected; and under any other administration than Gen. Jackson, there would be no trouble or difficulty on the subject. Even under his, the crisis is at hand to induce him to act otherwise than he had done, or else his political career will be prostrated. I beseech the people to continue to be patient, firm & united & to have as little intercourse with the white intruders in our country as possible, & above all things, to discountenance & refrain from the introduction & use of ardent spirits. A tippling shop is the fountain from which every species of evil that befalls our citizens & our country flows; and it should be spurned & shunned as the bosom of desolation, by every true friend to humanity & patriotism.

Your friend

Jno Ross

QUESTIONS FOR CONSIDERATION

1. What do the Marshall and Ross documents reveal about the status of Indian nations in the United States? Identify key passages and consider their bearing on the standing and sovereignty of Indian tribes.

2. How does John Marshall define the place of Indian tribes in the federal constitutional system?

3. Which of Marshall's statements about Indian rights and sovereignty seem to be most important — and most relevant to the political aspirations of Indian peoples today?

PICTURE ESSAY

Indian Life on the Upper Missouri:
A Catlin/Bodmer Portfolio

THEIR CENTRAL IMPORTANCE AS THE HUB of intersecting trade networks ensured that the villages of the Mandans and Hidatsas received a regular stream of visitors. Indians from dozens of other tribes went there to trade and smoke; French, Canadian, and Spanish traders centered their operations there; and Lewis and Clark wintered there in 1804–5. In the early 1830s, the Swiss artist Karl Bodmer and the American artist George Catlin both traveled up the Missouri River, stopped off at the Mandan villages and other locations, and painted portraits of Indian people and scenes of Indian life much as Lewis and Clark would have seen them thirty years earlier.

Catlin, a Pennsylvania lawyer-turned-artist, made several trips to the West, including a voyage up the Missouri River in 1832. In 1837–38, he exhibited more than six hundred paintings and his collection of Indian artifacts in eastern cities, and he hoped to sell his "Indian gallery" to Congress for a national museum. Failing to gain congressional support, he tried his luck in Europe, but was finally forced to sell his collection to meet his debts. Many of his sketches and paintings appeared as illustrations to his published accounts of travel among the Indians of the West.[76]

Karl Bodmer traveled up the Missouri in 1833. He had been hired by a German prince, Maximilian of Wied, to accompany him on a scientific tour of the United States. Bodmer's watercolors and sketches illustrated the prince's account of his travels, published in German in 1839 and in English in 1840.[77]

Between them, these two artists left an invaluable visual record of Indian life on the upper Missouri in the years just before the smallpox epidemic of 1837 devastated the tribes and virtually annihilated the Mandans. They depicted the earth-lodge villages of the Mandans and their neighbors and scenes of everyday life inside these lodges, such as Lewis and Clark would have experienced during their winter sojourn.

Bodmer's painting of the interior of a Mandan earth lodge (Figure 5.1) shows the occupants sitting on buffalo robes between the four central posts and under the open skylight. (Figure 5.2 is a diagrammatic sketch of the interior of such a lodge, which shows how space was organized and allocated in these communities.) The lodge housed an extended family and contains their valued possessions, including prized horses. The men's weapons lean against a post in

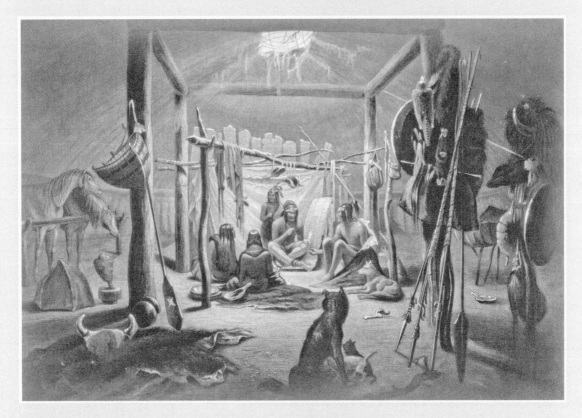

◆ Figure 5.1 **Karl Bodmer, *The Interior of the Hut of a Mandan Chief***
DEA Picture Library/Granger, NYC.

the foreground. Mandan women were the producers of food — a wooden mortar
and pestle used for grinding corn and large baskets in the background testify to
the food supplies that supported the tribe's prosperity and trade system. Catlin
and Bodmer both recorded pictures of Mandan women. Shakoha, or Mint,
whom Catlin calls "a pretty girl with piercing black eyes" (Figure 5.3), was twelve
years old when Catlin painted her in 1832, but he said she was already famous
for her conquests.[78]

In his painting of Pehriska-Ruhpa or Two Ravens, Bodmer shows a Hidatsa
warrior of the Dog Society (Figure 5.4). Two Ravens wears a headdress of owl,
raven, and magpie feathers, designed to be seen in motion, an eagle bone whistle
hangs from his neck, and he carries a rattle made of small hooves in one hand
and bow and arrows in the other. Bodmer did a watercolor of the subject but
reworked it for publication as an engraving, adding motion to the figure and

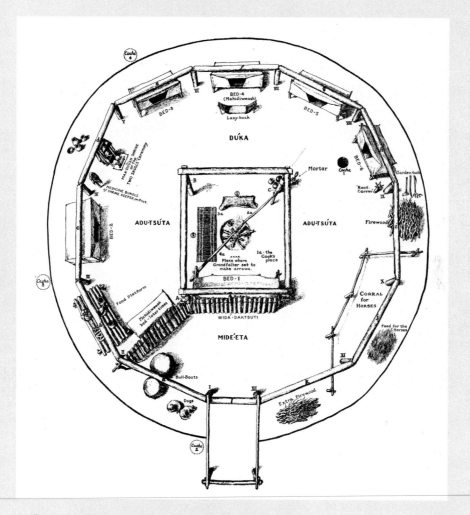

◆ **Figure 5.2 Diagram of the Interior of an Earth Lodge**
Image #2A19110, American Museum of Natural History Library.

meticulous detail to the costume. "I have long considered this the finest full-length portrait of an Indian I have seen," wrote a scholar of northern Plains art and history.[79]

No matter their firsthand experiences, the artists also shared and shaped the prejudices and perspectives of their time. They regarded Indians as part of a vanishing frontier, doomed as "civilization" engulfed their world. Catlin's paintings of the Assiniboine chief Ah-jon-jon (Figure 5.5), also known as the Light (or, according to Catlin, Pigeon's Egg Head), exemplify this view.

◆ Figure 5.3 **George Catlin, *Mint, a Pretty Girl***
Smithsonian American Art Museum, Washington, D.C./Art
Resource, NY.

◆ Figure 5.4 **Karl Bodmer, *Pehriska-Ruhpa, Moen-
nitarri Warrior, in the Costume of the Dog Dance***
Medicine Man of the Mandan Tribe in the Costume of the
Dog Dance, 1834 (color litho.), Bodmer, Karl (1809–93)/Private
Collection/Peter Newark American Pictures/Bridgeman
Images.

Catlin saw Ah-jon-jon in St. Louis in 1832 when the chief was on his way to
Washington as part of a delegation from the upper Missouri; he saw him again
as a fellow-passenger on the steamboat *Yellow Stone,* heading back up the Missouri on his return home. Struck by the transformation in Ah-jon-jon, Catlin
painted a full-length, two-figure oil portrait depicting the contrast. Military
coat, top hat, high-heeled boots, and white gloves have replaced buckskins,
headdress, and moccasins. In Catlin's portrait, the Indian has lost his dignified
bearing and cuts a ridiculous figure as he returns home with an umbrella, a fan,
and a rum bottle in his coat pocket. In Catlin's view, Ah-jon-jon was an Indian
"betrayed by civilization."

   Ah-jon-jon came to a tragic end. He acted as the government hoped Indian
delegates to the capital would and tried to convince his people of the superiority
of American power by describing the wonders he had seen in the East. His people
came to regard him as a braggart, and the chief was eventually killed by one of

◆ Figure 5.5 George Catlin, *Pigeon's Egg Head (The Light) Going to and Returning from Washington*

Smithsonian American Art Museum, Washington, D.C./Art Resource, NY.

his own tribe.[80] It seemed as if Catlin's assessment of the impact of contact with "civilization" was accurate. Ah-jon-jon passed into recorded history as a victim and as something of a fool.

Ah-jon-jon's present-day descendants remember a different man and a more complex personality, however, and Catlin's assumption that outward forms of cultural borrowing represent cultural suicide was too simple. Ah-jon-jon may have alienated people with his stories and his boasting, but he discarded his fancy clothes soon after he returned home. Every year thousands of people from the eastern United States visit the West and stagger home in cowboy hats and boots without abandoning their eastern way of life. It might be more accurate to see Ah-jon-jon as a tourist rather than a symbol of a disappearing way of life.

QUESTIONS FOR CONSIDERATION

1. What do the pictures and diagram reveal about Mandan and Hidatsa social organization?
2. What do Catlin and Bodmer, two outsiders, manage to convey about Indian life on the upper Missouri?
3. Which aspects of Indian life do the artists seem to have been most interested in?

REFERENCES

1. Daniel K. Richter, *Trade, Land, Power: The Struggle for Eastern North America* (Philadelphia: University of Pennsylvania Press, 2013), chap. 11.

2. Stephen Warren, *The Shawnees and Their Neighbors, 1795–1870* (Urbana: University of Illinois Press, 2005), chap. 2; Colin G. Calloway, *The Shawnees and the War for America* (New York: Viking Penguin, 2007), chap. 6; Sami Lakomäki, *Gathering Together: The Shawnee People through Diaspora and Nationhood, 1600–1870* (New Haven: Yale University Press, 2014), chap. 5.

3. Angela Pulley Hudson, *Creek Paths and Federal Roads: Indians, Settlers, and Slaves and the Making of the American South* (Chapel Hill: University of North Carolina Press, 2010).

4. Joel Martin, *Sacred Revolt: The Muskogees' Struggle for a New World* (Boston: Beacon Press, 1991), quote at 98; Robbie Ethridge, *Creek Country: The Creek Indians and Their World* (Chapel Hill: University of North Carolina Press, 2003); Claudio Saunt, *A New Order of Things: Property, Power, and the Transformation of the Creek Indians, 1733–1816* (Cambridge: Cambridge University Press, 1999).

5. Gabrielle Tayac, ed., *IndiVisible: African-Native American Lives in the Americas* (Washington, D.C.: National Museum of the American Indian, 2009), slave numbers at 149; Tiya Miles, *Ties That Bind: The Story of an Afro-Cherokee Family in Slavery and Freedom* (Berkeley: University of California Press, 2005), "invisible third element" quote at 24; Tiya Miles, *The House on Diamond Hill: A Cherokee Plantation Story* (Chapel Hill: University of North Carolina Press, 2010), Vann's slave wealth at 79; James F. Brooks, ed., *Confounding the Color Line: The Indian-Black Experience in North America* (Lincoln: University of Nebraska Press, 2002); Theda Perdue, *"Mixed Blood" Indians: Racial Construction in the Early South* (Athens: University of Georgia Press, 2003); Claudio Saunt, *Black, White, and Indian: Race and the Unmaking of an American Family* (New York: Oxford University Press, 2005); Claudio Saunt et al., "Rethinking Race and Culture in the Early South," *Ethnohistory* 53 (Spring 2006), 399–407; Barbara Krauthamer, *Black Slaves, Indian Masters: Slavery, Emancipation, and Citizenship in the Native American South* (Chapel Hill: University of North Carolina Press, 2013).

6. Quoted in Peter Nabokov, ed., *Native American Testimony* (New York: Harper and Row, 1978), 69–70.

7. Gregory Evans Dowd, *A Spirited Resistance: The North American Indian Struggle for Unity, 1745–1815* (Baltimore: Johns Hopkins University Press, 1992); Alfred A. Cave, *Prophets of the Great Spirit: Native American Revitalization Movements in Eastern North America* (Lincoln: University of Nebraska Press, 2006).

8. Joy Bilharz, "First Among Equals? The Changing Status of Seneca Women," in Laura F. Klein and Lillian A. Ackerman, eds., *Women and Power in Native North America* (Norman: University of Oklahoma Press, 1995), 108.

9. Matthew Dennis, *Seneca Possessed: Indians, Witchcraft, and Power in the Early American Republic* (Philadelphia: University of Pennsylvania Press, 2010).

10. Robert M. Owens, *Mr. Jefferson's Hammer: William Henry Harrison and the Origins of American Indian Policy* (Norman: University of Oklahoma Press, 2007); David Curtis Skaggs, *William Henry Harrison and the Conquest of the Ohio Country* (Baltimore: Johns Hopkins University Press, 2014).

11. Adam Jortner, *The Gods of Prophetstown: The Battle of Tippecanoe and the Holy War for the American Frontier* (New York: Oxford University Press, 2012).

12. Gregory A. Waselkov, *A Conquering Spirit: Fort Mims and the Redstick War of 1813–1814* (Tuscaloosa: University of Alabama Press, 2006); Martin, *Sacred Revolt*; Kathryn E. Holland Braund, ed., *Tohopeka: Rethinking the Creek War and the War of 1812* (Tuscaloosa: University of Alabama Press, 2012).

13. Daniel H. Usner Jr., "American Indians on the Cotton Frontier: Changing Economic Relations with Citizens and Slaves in the Mississippi Territory," *Journal of American History* 72 (September 1985), 297–317; James Taylor Carson, *Searching for the Bright Path: The Mississippi Choctaws from Prehistory to Removal* (Lincoln: University of Nebraska Press, 1999), chap. 4.

14. Shirley Christian, *Before Lewis and Clark: The Story of the Chouteaus, the French Dynasty That Ruled America's Frontier* (New York: Farrar, Straus and Giroux, 2004); Jay Gitlin, *The Bourgeois Frontier: French Towns, French Traders, and American Expansion* (New Haven: Yale University Press, 2010).

15. James P. Ronda, *Lewis and Clark among the Indians* (Lincoln: University of Nebraska Press, 1984), quote at 1.

16. Gary E. Moulton, ed., *The Lewis and Clark Journals: An American Epic of Discovery* (Lincoln: University of Nebraska Press, 2003), chap. 2, quotes at 41 and 48. Chapter 2 of Ronda's *Lewis and Clark among the Indians* provides an excellent account of the confrontation with the Brulé Sioux.

17. Raymond W. Wood and David D. Thiessen, eds., *Early Fur Trade on the Northern Plains: Canadian Traders among the Mandan and Hidatsa Indians, 1738–1818* (Norman: University of Oklahoma Press, 1985); John C. Ewers, "The Indian Trade of the Upper Missouri before Lewis and Clark," in *Indian Life on the Upper Missouri* (Norman: University of Oklahoma Press, 1968), 14–34; Elizabeth A. Fenn, *Encounters at the Heart of the World: A History of the Mandan People* (New York: Hill and Wang, 2014); *The History and Culture of the Mandan, Hidatsa, Sanhnish (Arikara)* (Bismarck: North Dakota Department of Public Instruction, 2002).

18. Moulton, *Lewis and Clark Journals*, 93.

19. Allen V. Pinkham and Steven Ross Evans, *Lewis and Clark among the Nez Perce: Strangers in the Land of the Nimiipuu* (Washburn, N.D.: The Dakota Institute Press, 2013), distributed by University of Oklahoma Press.

20. David L. Nicari, *River of Promise: Lewis and Clark on the Columbia* (Washburn, N.D.: The Dakota Institute Press, 2009), distributed by University of Oklahoma Press.

21. Gray Whaley, "'Complete Liberty'? Gender, Sexuality, Race, and Social Change on the Lower Columbia River, 1805–1838," *Ethnohistory* 54 (Fall 2007), 669–95; Moulton, *Lewis and Clark Journals*, 259.

22. Henry Harvey, *History of the Shawnee Indians* (Cincinnati: Ephraim Morgan and Sons, 1855), 130.

23. Quoted in Francis Paul Prucha, ed., *Documents of United States Indian Policy* (Lincoln: University of Nebraska Press, 1975), 22–23.

24. Anthony F. C. Wallace, *Jefferson and the Indians: The Tragic Fate of the First Americans* (Cambridge, Mass.: Harvard University Press, 1999).

25. Quoted in Theda Perdue and Michael D. Green, eds., *The Cherokee Removal: A Brief History with Documents*, 2nd ed. (Boston: Bedford/St. Martin's, 2005), 127.

26. Perdue and Green, *Cherokee Removal*, 114–23; Gary Clayton Anderson, *Ethnic Cleansing and the Indian: The Crime That Should Haunt America* (Norman: University of Oklahoma Press, 2014), chaps. 6–8.

27. Virgil J. Vogel, ed., *This Country Was Ours: A Documentary History of the American Indian* (New York: Harper and Row, 1972), 289.

28. Ellen Cushman, *The Cherokee Syllabary: Writing the People's Perseverance* (Norman: University of Oklahoma Press, 2011).

29. John Demos, *The Heathen School: A Story of Hope and Betrayal in the Early Republic* (New York: Alfred Knopf, 2014).

30. Quoted in John Ehle, *Trail of Tears: The Rise and Fall of the Cherokee Nation* (New York: Doubleday, 1988), 254.

31. Quoted in William G. McLoughlin, *Cherokee Renascence in the New Republic* (Princeton, N.J.: Princeton University Press, 1986), 412.

32. Sidney L. Harring, *Crow Dog's Case: American Indian Sovereignty, Tribal Law, and United States Law in the Nineteenth Century* (Cambridge: Cambridge University Press, 1994), 32.

33. Theda Perdue, ed., *Cherokee Editor: The Writings of Elias Boudinot* (Knoxville: University of Tennessee Press, 1983), 105–6.

34. Perdue, *Cherokee Editor*, 121.

35. Perdue and Green, *Cherokee Removal*, 83.

36. Thanks to Jace Weaver for drawing my attention to Ridge's record on tribal land sales; Perdue and Green, eds., *Cherokee Removal*, 145–54; Colin G. Calloway, *Pen and Ink Witchcraft: Treaties and Treaty Making in American Indian History* (New York: Oxford University Press, 2013), chap. 4.

37. Alexis de Tocqueville, *Democracy in America*, ed. J. P. Mayer (New York: Harper and Row, 1966), 339.

38. Celia E. Naylor, *African Cherokees in Indian Territory: From Chattel to Citizens* (Chapel Hill: University of North Carolina Press, 2008); Krauthamer, *Black Slaves, Indian Masters*.

39. Francis Paul Prucha, *American Indian Treaties: The History of a Political Anomaly* (Lincoln: University of Nebraska Press, 1994), 184.

40. Lakomäki, *Gathering Together*, chaps. 6–7.

41. Laurence M. Hauptman, *Conspiracy of Interests: Iroquois Dispossession and the Rise of New York State* (Syracuse, N.Y.: Syracuse University Press, 1999).

42. John Bowes, *This Land Is Too Good for Indians: Histories of Northern Indian Removal* (Norman: University of Oklahoma Press, 2015).

43. Kerry Trask, *Black Hawk: The Battle for the Heart of America* (New York: Henry Holt, 2006); Donald Jackson, ed., *Black Hawk: An Autobiography* (Urbana: University of Illinois Press, 1964); Patrick J. Jung, *The Black Hawk War of 1832* (Norman: University of Oklahoma Press, 2007); John W. Hall, *Uncommon Defense: Indian Allies in the Black Hawk War* (Cambridge, Mass.: Harvard University Press, 2009).

44. For an Osage account of the troubles, see John Joseph Matthews, *The Osages: Children of the Middle Waters* (Norman: University of Oklahoma Press, 1961), chaps. 44–45. See also Willard Hughes Rollings, *Unaffected by the Gospel: Osage Resistance to the Christian Invasion, 1673–1906: A Cultural Victory* (Albuquerque: University of New Mexico Press, 2004).

45. William Least Heat-Moon and James K. Wallace, trans. and ed., *An Osage Journey to Europe, 1827–1830: Three French Accounts* (Norman: University of Oklahoma Press, 2014).

46. Colin G. Calloway, *The Western Abenakis of Vermont, 1600–1800: War, Migration, and the Survival of an Indian People* (Norman: University of Oklahoma Press, 1990).

47. Quoted in Barry O'Connell, ed., *On Our Own Ground: The Complete Writings of William Apess, a Pequot* (Amherst: University of Massachusetts Press, 1992), 153.

48. Stephen Badger, "Historical and Characteristic Traits of the American Indians in General, and Those of Natick in Particular," *Collections of the Massachusetts Historical Society*, 1st series, 5 (1798), 38–39.

49. Nancy Shoemaker, "Mr. Tashtego: Native American Whalemen in Antebellum New England," *Journal of the Early Republic* 33 (Spring 2013), 109–32; Nancy Shoemaker, ed., *Living with Whales: Documents and Oral Histories of Native New England Whaling History* (Amherst: University of Massachusetts Press, 2014).

50. Shoemaker, "Mr. Tashtego," 129–32.

51. Daniel R. Mandell, *Tribe, Race, History: Native Americans in Southern New England, 1780–1880* (Baltimore: Johns Hopkins University Press, 2008); Jean M. O'Brien, *Firsting and Lasting: Writing Indians Out of Existence in New England* (Minneapolis: University of Minnesota Press, 2010).

52. Badger, "Historical and Characteristic Traits," 35, 43; Mandell, *Tribe, Race, History*.

53. Lester J. Cappon, ed., *The Adams-Jefferson Letters: The Complete Correspondence between Thomas Jefferson and Abigail and John Adams* (Chapel Hill: University of North Carolina Press, 1959), 2:310–11.

54. Rev. Jedidiah Morse, *A Report to the Secretary of War of the United States, on Indian Affairs* (New Haven, Conn.: S. Converse, 1822), 64–75.

55. Tocqueville, *Democracy in America*, 321.

56. Colin G. Calloway, ed., *After King Philip's War: Presence and Persistence in Indian New England* (Hanover, N.H.: University Press of New England, 1997); Amy E. Den Ouden, *Beyond Conquest: Native Peoples and the Struggle for History in New England* (Lincoln: University of Nebraska Press, 2005); O'Brien, *Firsting and Lasting*.

57. Donald M. Nielsen, "The Mashpee Indian Revolt of 1833," *New England Quarterly* 58 (September 1985), 400–420.

58. O'Connell, *On Our Own Ground*, lxxiii.

59. O'Connell, *On Our Own Ground*, 155–57.

60. O'Connell, *On Our Own Ground*, 276–310.

61. Richard Glover, ed., *David Thompson's Narrative, 1784–1812* (Toronto: Champlain Society, 1962), 240.

62. Mary Hershberger, "Mobilizing Women, Anticipating Abolition: The Struggle against Indian Removal in the 1830s," *Journal of American History* 86 (June 1999), 15–40. I am grateful to Jacquelynn Allen and Jason Lemieux, who, as students at Oregon State University, urged me to consider including this and other petitions against Cherokee Removal.

63. Gunlög Fur, "'Some Women Are Wiser than Some Men': Gender and Native American History," in Shoemaker, *Clearing a Path*, 75–103.

64. Theda Perdue, *Cherokee Women: Gender and Culture Change, 1700–1835* (Lincoln: University of Nebraska Press, 1998), 26; Rebecca Kugel and Lucy Eldersveld Murphy, eds., *Native Women's History in Eastern North America before 1900: A Guide to Research and Writing* (Lincoln: University of Nebraska Press, 2007), xiv.

65. Quoted in Michelle LeMaster, *Brothers Born of One Mother: British–Native American Relations in the Colonial Southeast* (Charlottesville: University of Virginia Press, 2012), 38.

66. Nancy Shoemaker, "The Rise or Fall of Iroquois Women," and Michelene E. Pesantubbee, "Beyond Domesticity: Choctaw Women Negotiating the Tension between Choctaw Culture and Protestantism," both in Kugel and Murphy, *Native Women's History in Eastern North America*, 309–10, 442–43.

67. Tiya Miles, "Circular Reasoning: Recentering Cherokee Women in the Antiremoval Campaigns," *American Quarterly* 61 (June 2009), 221–43; Theda Perdue, "Cherokee Women and the Trail of Tears," *Journal of Women's History* 1 (Spring 1989), 14–30.

68. David H. Getches, Charles F. Wilkinson, and Robert A. Williams Jr., eds. *Cases and Materials on Federal Indian Law*, 4th ed. (St. Paul, Minn.: West Group, 1998), 102.

69. Lindsay G. Robertson, *Conquest by Law: How the Discovery of America Dispossessed Indigenous Peoples of Their Lands* (New York: Oxford University Press, 2005); Blake A. Watson, *Buying America from the Indians*: Johnson v. McIntosh *and the History of Native Land Rights* (Norman: University of Oklahoma Press, 2012).

70. Harring, *Crow Dog's Case*, 31–32.

71. John R. Wunder, *"Retained by the People": A History of American Indians and the Bill of Rights* (New York: Oxford University Press, 1994), 27.

72. Charles F. Wilkinson, *American Indians, Time, and the Law* (New Haven: Yale University Press, 1987), 30, 95–96.

73. Vine Deloria Jr. and Clifford M. Lytle, *American Indians, American Justice* (Austin: University of Texas Press, 1983), 33.

74. Gary E. Moulton, ed., *The Papers of Chief John Ross* (Norman: University of Oklahoma Press, 1985), 1:210.

75. Quoted in Jill Norgren, *The Cherokee Cases: The Confrontation of Law and Politics* (New York: McGraw-Hill, 1996), 1–2.

76. George Catlin, *Letters and Notes on the Manners, Customs, and Conditions of North American Indians* (London: printed by author, 1844); Brian W. Dippie, *Catlin and His Contemporaries: The Politics of Patronage* (Lincoln: University of Nebraska Press, 1990).

77. "Prince Maximilian of Wied's Travels in the Interior of North America, 1832–1834," in Reuben G. Thwaites, ed., *Early Western Travels, 1748–1846*, vols. 22–25 (Cleveland: Arthur H. Clark, 1906).

78. John C. Ewers, *Views of a Vanishing Frontier* (Lincoln: University of Nebraska Press and Joslyn Art Museum, 1984), 65.

79. Ewers, *Views of a Vanishing Frontier*, 65.

80. John C. Ewers, "When the Light Shone in Washington," in *Indian Life on the Upper Missouri* (Norman: University of Oklahoma Press, 1968), 75–90.

SUGGESTED READINGS

Ambrose, Stephen E. *Undaunted Courage: Meriwether Lewis, Thomas Jefferson, and the Opening of the American West.* New York: Simon and Schuster, 1996.

Anderson, Gary Clayton. *Ethnic Cleansing and the Indian: The Crime That Should Haunt America.* Norman: University of Oklahoma Press, 2014.

Banner, Stuart. *How the Indians Lost Their Land: Law and Power on the Frontier.* Cambridge, Mass.: Harvard University Press, 2005.

Barth, Gunther, ed. *The Lewis and Clark Expedition: Selections from the Journals, Arranged by Topic.* Boston: Bedford Books, 1998.

Benn, Carl. *Native Memoirs from the War of 1812: Black Hawk and William Apess.* Baltimore: Johns Hopkins University Press, 2014.

Bowes, John P. *Exiles and Pioneers: Eastern Indians in the Trans-Mississippi West.* Cambridge: Cambridge University Press, 2007.

———. *This Land Is Too Good for Indians: Histories of Northern Indian Removal.* Norman: University of Oklahoma Press, 2015.

Braund, Kathryn E. Holland, ed. *Tohopeka: Rethinking the Creek War and the War of 1812.* Tuscaloosa: University of Alabama Press, 2012.

Calloway, Colin G., ed. *After King Philip's War: Presence and Persistence in Indian New England.* Hanover, N.H.: University Press of New England, 1997.

———. *One Vast Winter Count: The Native American West before Lewis and Clark.* Lincoln: University of Nebraska Press, 2003.

———. *Pen and Ink Witchcraft: Treaties and Treaty Making in American Indian History.* New York: Oxford University Press, 2013.

———. *The Shawnees and the War for America.* New York: Viking Penguin, 2007.

Cushman, Ellen. *The Cherokee Syllabary: Writing the People's Perseverance.* Norman: University of Oklahoma Press, 2011.

Deloria, Vine, Jr., and Clifford M. Lytle. *American Indians, American Justice.* Austin: University of Texas Press, 1983.

Demos, John. *The Heathen School: A Story of Hope and Betrayal in the Early Republic.* New York: Alfred Knopf, 2014.

Dennis, Matthew. *Seneca Possessed: Indians, Witchcraft, and Power in the Early American Republic.* Philadelphia: University of Pennsylvania Press, 2010.

Dowd, Gregory Evans. *A Spirited Resistance: The North American Indian Struggle for Unity, 1745–1815.* Baltimore: Johns Hopkins University Press, 1992.

Duncan, Dayton, and Ken Burns. *Lewis and Clark: The Journey of the Corps of Discovery.* New York: Alfred A. Knopf, 1997.

Edmunds, R. David. *The Shawnee Prophet.* Lincoln: University of Nebraska Press, 1983.

Fenn, Elizabeth A. *Encounters at the Heart of the World: A History of the Mandan People.* New York: Hill and Wang, 2014.

Garrison, Tim Alan. *The Legal Ideology of Removal: The Southern Judiciary and Native American Nations.* Athens: University of Georgia Press, 2002.

Getches, David H., Charles F. Wilkinson, et al., eds. *Cases and Materials on Federal Indian Law.* 4th ed. St. Paul, Minn.: West Group, 1998; 5th ed. 2005; 6th ed. 2011.

Hall, John W. *Uncommon Defense: Indian Allies in the Black Hawk War.* Cambridge: Harvard University Press, 2009.

Harjo, Suzan Shown. *Nation to Nation: Treaties Between the United States and American Indian Nations.* Washington, D.C.: National Museum of the American Indian and Smithsonian Books, 2014.

Hauptman, Laurence M. *Conspiracy of Interests: Iroquois Dispossession and the Rise of New York State.* Syracuse, N.Y.: Syracuse University Press, 1999.

Heath, William. *William Wells and the struggle for the Old Northwest.* Norman: University of Oklahoma Press, 2015.

Heidler, David S., and Jeanne T. Heidler. *Indian Removal.* New York: W. W. Norton, 2007.

Hicks, Brian. *Toward the Setting Sun: John Ross, the Cherokees, and the Trail of Tears.* New York: Atlantic Monthly Press, 2011.

Horsman, Reginald. *Expansion and American Indian Policy, 1783–1812.* Reprint, Norman: University of Oklahoma Press, 1992.

Hoxie, Frederick E., and Jay T. Nelson, eds. *Lewis and Clark and the Indian Country: The Native American Perspective.* Urbana: University of Illinois Press, 2007.

Hudson, Angela Pulley. *Creek Paths and Federal Roads: Indians, Settlers, and Slaves and the Making of the American South.* Chapel Hill: University of North Carolina Press, 2010.

Hurt, R. Douglas. *The Indian Frontier, 1763–1846.* Albuquerque: University of New Mexico Press, 2002.

Jackson, Donald, ed. *Black Hawk: An Autobiography.* Urbana: University of Illinois Press, 1964.

Jones, Landon Y. *William Clark and the Shaping of the West.* New York: Hill and Wang, 2004.

Jortner, Adam. *The Gods of Prophetstown: The Battle of Tippecanoe and the Holy War for the America Frontier.* New York: Oxford University Press, 2012.

Jung, Patrick J. *The Black Hawk War of 1832.* Norman: University of Oklahoma Press, 2007.

Keating, Ann Durkin. *Rising Up from Indian Country: The Battle of Fort Dearborn and the Birth of Chicago.* Chicago: University of Chicago Press, 2012.

Krauthamer, Barbara. *Black Slaves, Indian Masters: Slavery, Emancipation, and Citizenship in the Native American South.* Chapel Hill: University of North Carolina Press, 2013.

Lakomäki, Sami. *Gathering Together: The Shawnee People through Diaspora and Nationhood, 1600–1870.* New Haven: Yale University Press, 2014.

Mandell, Daniel R. *Tribe, Race, History: Native Americans in Southern New England, 1780–1880.* Baltimore: Johns Hopkins University Press, 2008.

Martin, Joel. *Sacred Revolt: The Muskogees' Struggle for a New World.* Boston: Beacon Press, 1991.

McLoughlin, William G. *Cherokee Renascence in the New Republic.* Princeton, N.J.: Princeton University Press, 1986.

Miles, Tiya. "'Circular Reasoning': Recentering Cherokee Women in the Antiremoval Campaigns," *American Quarterly* 61 (June 2009), 221–43.

———. *The House on Diamond Hill: A Cherokee Plantation Story.* Chapel Hill: University of North Carolina Press, 2010.

———. *Ties That Bind: The Story of an Afro-Cherokee Family in Slavery and Freedom.* Berkeley: University of California Press, 2005.

Miller, Robert J. *Native America, Discovered and Conquered: Thomas Jefferson, Lewis and Clark, and Manifest Destiny.* Westport, Conn.: Praeger, 2006.

Moulton, Gary E., ed. *The Journals of the Lewis and Clark Expedition.* 13 vols. Lincoln: University of Nebraska Press, 1986–2001.

———, ed. *The Lewis and Clark Journals: An American Epic of Discovery.* Lincoln: University of Nebraska Press, 2003.

———, ed. *The Papers of Chief John Ross.* 2 vols. Norman: University of Oklahoma Press, 1985.

Nicari, David L. *River of Promise: Lewis and Clark on the Columbia.* Washington, ND.: The Dakota Institute Press, 2009. Distributed by University of Oklahoma Press.

Norgren, Jill. *The Cherokee Cases: The Confrontation of Law and Politics.* New York: McGraw-Hill, 1996.

O'Brien, Jean M. *Firsting and Lasting: Writing Indians out of Existence in New England.* Minneapolis: University of Minnesota Press, 2010.

O'Connell, Barry, ed. *On Our Own Ground: The Complete Writings of William Apess, a Pequot.* Amherst: University of Massachusetts Press, 1992.

Owens, Robert M. *Mr. Jefferson's Hammer: William Henry Harrison and the Origins of American Indian Policy.* Norman: University of Oklahoma Press, 2007.

Perdue, Theda. *Cherokee Women: Gender and Culture Change, 1700–1835.* Lincoln: University of Nebraska Press, 1998.

Perdue, Theda, and Michael D. Green. *The Cherokee Nation and the Trail of Tears.* New York: Viking Penguin, 2007.

———, eds. *The Cherokee Removal: A Brief History with Documents.* 2nd ed. Boston: Bedford/St. Martin's, 2005.

Pinkham, Allen V., and Steven Ross Evans, *Lewis and Clark among the Nez Perce: Strangers in the Land of the Nimiipuu.* Washburn, N.D.: The Dakota Institute Press, 2013. Distributed by University of Oklahoma Press.

Prucha, Francis Paul. *The Great Father: The United States Government and the American Indians*. 2 vols. Lincoln: University of Nebraska Press, 1984.

Richter, Daniel K., *Trade, Land, Power: The Struggle for Eastern North America*. Philadelphia: University of Pennsylvania Press, 2013.

Robertson, Lindsay G. *Conquest by Law: How the Discovery of America Dispossessed Indigenous Peoples of Their Lands*. New York: Oxford University Press, 2006.

Ronda, James P. *Finding the West: Explorations with Lewis and Clark*. Albuquerque: University of New Mexico Press, 2001.

———. *Lewis and Clark among the Indians*. Lincoln: University of Nebraska Press, 1984.

Saunt, Claudio. *Black, White, and Indian: Race and the Unmaking of an American Family*. New York: Oxford University Press, 2005.

———. *A New Order of Things: Property, Power, and the Transformation of the Creek Indians, 1733–1816*. Cambridge: Cambridge University Press, 1999.

Sheehan, Bernard W. *Seeds of Extinction: Jeffersonian Philanthropy and the American Indian*. Chapel Hill: University of North Carolina Press, 1973.

Shoemaker, Nancy, ed. *Living with Whales: Documents and Oral Histories of Native New England Whaling History*. Amherst: University of Massachusetts Press, 2014.

———. "Mr. Tashtego: Native American Whalemen in Antebellum New England," *Journal of the Early Republic* 33 (Spring 2013), 109–32.

Silverman, David J. *Red Brethren: The Brothertown and Stockbridge Indians and the Problem of Race in Early America*. Ithaca, N.Y.: Cornell University Press, 2010.

Smith, Daniel Blake. *An American Betrayal. Cherokee Patriots and the Trail of Tears*. New York: Henry Holt, 2011.

Sugden, John. *Blue Jacket: Warrior of the Shawnees*. Lincoln: University of Nebraska Press, 2000.

———. *Tecumseh: A Life*. New York: Henry Holt, 1998.

Swagerty, William R. The Indianization of Lewis and Clark. 2 vols. Norman: University of Oklahoma Press, 2012.

Tanner, Helen Hornbeck, ed. *Atlas of Great Lakes Indian History*. Norman: University of Oklahoma Press, 1987.

Tayac, Gabrielle, ed. *IndiVisible: African–Native American Lives in the Americas*. Washington, D.C.: National Museum of the American Indian, 2009.

Tiro, Karim M. *People of the Standing Stone: The Oneida Indian Nation from Revolution through Removal*. Amherst: University of Massachusetts Press, 2011.

Treuttner, William H. *Painting Indians and Building Empires in North America, 1710–1840*. Berkeley: University of California Press, 2010.

Wallace, Anthony F. C. *The Death and Rebirth of the Seneca*. New York: Alfred A. Knopf, 1969.

———. *Jefferson and the Indians: The Tragic Fate of the First Americans*. Cambridge, Mass.: Harvard University Press, 1999.

———. *The Long, Bitter Trail: Andrew Jackson and the Indians*. New York: Hill and Wang, 1993.

Warren, Stephen. *The Shawnees and Their Neighbors, 1795–1870*. Urbana: University of Illinois Press, 2005.

Watson, Blake A. *Buying America from the Indians: Johnson V. McIntosh and The History of Native Land Rights*. Norman: University of Oklahoma Press, 2012.

Wilkins, David E. *American Indian Sovereignty and the U.S. Supreme Court: The Masking of Justice*. Austin: University of Texas Press, 1997.

Wilkinson, Charles F. *American Indians, Time, and the Law*. New Haven: Yale University Press, 1987.

Wood, W. Raymond, and Thomas D. Thiessen, eds. *Early Fur Trade on the Northern Plains: Canadian Traders among the Mandan and Hidatsa Indians, 1738–1818*. Norman: University of Oklahoma Press, 1985.

6

Defending the West

1840–1890

FOCUS QUESTIONS

1. Where and in what ways did American expansion affect western Indian peoples before the mid-nineteenth century?

2. What factors determined the defeat of the Plains Indians in their wars against the United States?

3. Why did the United States relocate and confine Indian people to reservations?

4. How did different tribes, and different individuals at different times, respond to American expansion and colonialism?

INVADERS FROM THE EAST: INCURSIONS BEFORE THE AMERICAN CIVIL WAR

THE AMERICAN WEST IN 1840 was still Indian country. But as American expansion gathered pace, the doctrine of Manifest Destiny° proclaimed that Americans had a God-given right to occupy all land west to the Pacific and a duty to extend the blessings of American democracy to the peoples already living there, whether Mexican or Indian. Between 1840 and 1890, when the U.S. Census Bureau declared the frontier officially "closed," the American nation underwent massive and rapid expansion

---

° The term "manifest destiny" was first coined by newspaperman John L. Sullivan in 1845, but it was a concept that had grown from the beginning of the century.

across the trans-Mississippi West. American forces defeated Indians and Mexicans, American settlers and ranchers occupied the lands of displaced peoples, American miners extracted resources, American railroad companies linked East and West, and American hunters cleared the plains of buffalo, making way for American cattle. In many history books and in popular culture, these events represented the *winning* of the West; the people who were pushed aside, however, saw their West being lost, not won. Americans then and since depicted Indian resistance as a futile effort to stem the tide of civilization and hold back the future; Indians who fought and died, however, did so to defend their homelands, families, and ways of life and to try to ensure that their people survived in the future.

Coronado's Spaniards had invaded New Mexico and the Great Plains from the South in the 1540s, and European traders in the eighteenth century and then American explorers in the early nineteenth century penetrated the West in small numbers, but the first invaders to come from the East in force were Indians. In the 1830s, Indians expelled from their eastern homelands by U.S. removal policies migrated into areas of present-day Oklahoma, Arkansas, Kansas, and Missouri. Like the Americans who followed, the Cherokee, Creek, Shawnee, Potawatomi, and other Indian emigrants did not enter a static situation; they added to the far-reaching changes already taking place in Indian country and encountered Indian peoples who had been contesting among themselves for generations. They came into conflict with local tribes like the Osages, who were pushed into increased conflict with Comanche enemies to their southwest. Southern Plains Indians resisted the invasion of their homelands by the "Five Civilized Tribes"° from the Southeast.[1] But white Americans were not far behind: the expanding power of the Comanches on the southern Plains and of the Lakota Sioux in the north would soon clash head-on with the expanding power of the United States. As Americans spread from coast to coast, they seized Indian lands by war and treaties until only a small fraction of the tribal homelands remained in Native possession (Map 6.1).

° The Five Civilized Tribes comprised the Cherokees, Creeks, Choctaws, Chickasaws, and Seminoles.

1869	Ely S. Parker becomes the first Indian to head the BIA
1869	First transcontinental railroad completed
1869–1870	Smallpox epidemic on the northern Plains
1870	Marias River massacre of Blackfeet in Montana
1871	Congress terminates treaty making with Indian tribes
1871	Over one hundred Aravaipa Apaches murdered at Camp Grant
1872–1873	Modoc War in California and Oregon
1874–1875	Red River War on the southern Plains
1876	Sioux and Cheyenne defeat Seventh Cavalry at Little Bighorn
1876	American troops destroy Cheyenne villages in Montana and Wyoming, send surviving Cheyennes to Indian Territory
1877	Crazy Horse assassinated
1877	Congress annexes the Black Hills
1877	Nez Perce War and flight
1877	U.S. government forcibly removes members of the Ponca tribe from Nebraska to Indian Territory
1878	Northern Cheyennes attempt to return north to Montana
1881	Sitting Bull surrenders
1886	End of Apache military resistance; U.S. military conquest of the West is complete
1890	Ghost Dance religion spreads to the Lakotas
1890	Sitting Bull assassinated
1890	Wounded Knee massacre

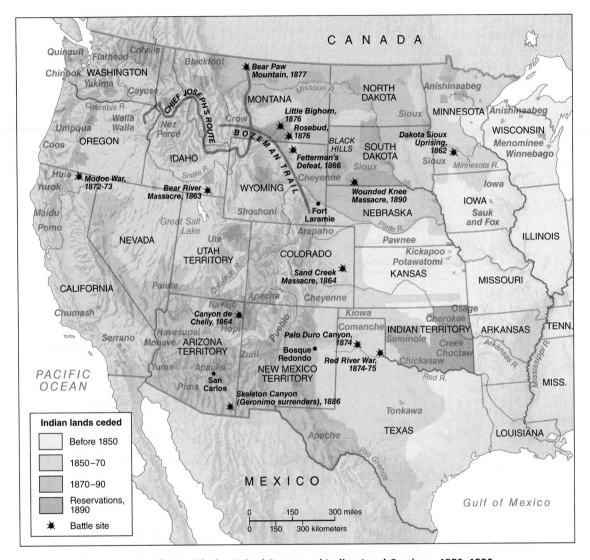

◆ **Map 6.1 Conflicts with the United States and Indian Land Cessions, 1850–1890**
The rapid expansion of the United States in the second half of the nineteenth century
demanded the defeat and dispossession of the Indian peoples living in the West. By 1890,
Indian military resistance was broken, and Indian homelands were reduced to a fraction of
their original size.

The Ravages of Disease

Smallpox was a regular visitor to the American West after the great pandemic of
1779–84, repeatedly devastating Indian communities (see "Smallpox Used Them
Up," pages 229–32). Smallpox struck the Missouri valley again in 1801–2: Lewis and

Clark passed deserted villages on their voyage upriver in 1804. Disease struck the sedentary tribes harder than the nomads, further shifting the balance of power in the region from river peoples like the Mandans and Hidatsas to Plains groups like the Lakotas. But nomads also suffered terribly. As many as 4,000 Comanches died in a smallpox epidemic in 1816; another epidemic hit the Sioux in 1819. Half of the Pawnees died in an epidemic on the central Plains in the early 1830s.

The Mandan trading villages along the upper Missouri River in North Dakota were particularly susceptible. Their location at the center of a trade network on the Missouri River guaranteed that Mandans received germs as well as goods from Europeans. The Mandans' population, as many as 15,000 when the French met them in 1738, declined steadily. They suffered heavily during the 1779–81 pandemic and probably numbered no more than 2,000 by the summer of 1837. Then, in June 1837, an American steamboat carrying smallpox docked at the Mandan villages. Within a few weeks, fever appeared. Soon people were dying by the hundreds. "I Keep no a/c of the dead, as they die so fast it is impossible," wrote Francis Chardon, a trader at Fort Clark near the Mandan villages, as he watched his customers succumb to the epidemic. By October only 138 Mandans remained.[2]

Between 1837 and 1840 the disease spread thousands of miles and killed thousands of people: half of the Assiniboines, two-thirds of the Blackfeet, half of the Arikaras, a third of the Crows, and perhaps a quarter of the Pawnees. At Fort Union, where the Yellowstone River meets the Missouri, a trader reported "such a stench in the fort that it could be smelt at a distance of 300 yards." So many Assiniboines died that bodies were buried in large pits until the ground froze, after which there was no choice but "to throw them into the river."[3] A Kiowa winter count recorded 1839–40 as a year of smallpox on the southern Plains (see "Sixty Years of Kiowa History," pages 336–41).

The discovery of gold in California in 1848 brought increased migrant traffic across the Plains. European immigrants on the overland trails brought more diseases to the Indians. Cholera, measles, and scarlet fever were soon adding to the toll of Indian deaths. "If I could see this thing, if I knew where it came from, I would go there and fight it," cried an anguished Cheyenne warrior as cholera raged through the tribe in 1849.[4] Smallpox hit the Blackfeet again in 1869 and continued to ravage Indian country into the next century. The American military conquest of the West took place in the wake of biological disasters that had reduced Indian power to resist and, for some pockmarked survivors who watched these horrible deaths, the will to live. Those who did survive had to deal with more and more American intruders as the United States pushed west to realize its "Manifest Destiny" and occupy the continent from the Atlantic to the Pacific.

Ethnic Cleansing in Texas, c. 1836–48

Before the war with Mexico in 1846–48, the region that today constitutes the American Southwest was claimed first by Spain, then Mexico, when in reality the land had long belonged to Indians. In Texas, in addition to farming tribes like the Caddos with a deep historic presence in the area, nomadic peoples like the

◆ **John Mix Stanley, *The Last of Their Race* (1857)**
Euro-Americans who headed west into Indian country carried with them assumptions that
Indians were, at best, noble but tragic figures who would inevitably disappear as civilization
advanced, and at worst, vicious savages who should be hunted to extinction. Assuming that
Indian extinction was assured, some American artists also indulged in nostalgic mourning
for a passing way of life. In 1857, John Mix Stanley's *The Last of Their Race* allegorically depicted
a group of Indians driven to the Pacific, where they await and contemplate their final extinction against a setting sun. *Buffalo Bill Center of the West, Cody, Wyoming, USA; Museum
Purchase, 5.75.*

Kiowas, Comanches, and Lipan Apaches vied for dominance. Not only did these
Indian nations remain independent on the northern frontiers of Mexico, but they
also were actually expanding. They incorporated other Native peoples into their
societies and, in some cases, pushed back the Hispanic frontier. The movement
of Indian nations, the emergence and competition of the Mexican and American nation-states, and the intrusion of new economic forces made the southern
Plains a volatile region in which people shifted loyalties, and sometimes identities,
according to changing circumstances, opportunities, and imperatives.[5] As it had
throughout the eighteenth century, Indian power shaped the outcome of imperial

struggles. Comanches and neighboring tribes who had raided south of the Rio Grande for years escalated their incursions in the 1830s and 1840s. Their attacks diverted and drained Mexican resources, drove away Mexican settlers, left whole areas devastated, and generated political instability. By the time American armies marched in, the Comanches, Kiowas, and Apaches had rendered Mexico's northern provinces ripe for conquest.[6]

After Texans won their independence from Mexico in 1836, Sam Houston became the first president of the Republic of Texas. Houston tried to pursue a policy of negotiation in dealing with Indians, especially with immigrant Cherokees, Shawnees, and Delawares, whom he hoped might form a buffer between Texan settlements and raiding Comanches, Kiowas, and other Plains tribes. But in 1838 Mireau B. Lamar, a Texan from Georgia, became president. Lamar despised Houston and his conciliatory Indian policy, and he initiated a policy of ethnic cleansing to drive all Indians out of Texas. Indians and whites could not live side by side, said Lamar; "the proper policy to be pursued toward the barbarian race is absolute expulsion from the country."

Anglo-Texans drove the Cherokees and Shawnees north into what is now Oklahoma and pushed the Comanches and other Plains tribes into western Texas. A Texan army routed the Cherokees, and when a delegation of thirty-five Comanches came with their women and children to a peace council at San Antonio in 1840, Texans first seized the chiefs and then, in the ensuing fight, killed the delegates. Texas plunged into bitter warfare. Comanche raiders struck settlements, killing people and carrying off captives and livestock; Texas Rangers struck Comanche villages, looting and killing indiscriminately. Houston returned as president in 1841, but he could do little to stem the tide of violence.

The Texas Rangers are often regarded as a heroic frontier police force, but many were vigilante companies motivated by hatred of Indians and a desire for plunder. In an environment of intense racial violence, fueled by fear, rumors, and reports of atrocities, rangers often fell on camps of peaceful Caddos rather than pursuing Comanches who remained beyond their reach on the high Plains. After Texas entered the Union in 1845, the U.S. cavalry carried out a policy of driving the Comanches onto reservations. Indians who were not on reservations were assumed to be "hostile." The cavalry hunted Indians on the Plains and attacked them in their villages. Some northern Comanches clung to the Panhandle, but dozens of tribes, both immigrants and those indigenous to Texas, were forced out; by 1859, writes one historian, "Texas had become a conquered land." The campaigns against the Kiowas and Comanches continued. In 1835 some 35,000 Indians lived in Texas; forty years later, they were all but gone.[7]

At the Treaty of Guadalupe Hidalgo ending the war with Mexico in 1848, the United States acquired California, Arizona, New Mexico, and parts of Utah and Colorado. It acquired additional Indian lands from Mexico by the Gadsden Purchase in 1853. Americans were soon encroaching on lands that the Indians of the Southwest regarded as their own, not to be transferred from Mexico to the United States without their consent. Pueblo Indians had seen Spanish, Mexican, and now American invaders claim their land and they once again revolted in 1847. Apaches watched with concern as American surveyors ran a boundary line between the United States and Mexico, and wondered where Apache country figured into the picture.[8]

American Empire Reaches the Pacific Northwest, 1846–56

Indians in the Pacific Northwest had dealt with maritime traders since the late eighteenth century, but in the 1840s their homelands became a contested zone between the British Empire in the form of the Hudson's Bay Company in the North and the forerunners of American empire in the form of immigrant settlers from the East. In 1846 Britain and the United States agreed to divide the Oregon Territory along the forty-ninth parallel. This agreement confirmed American possession of the lands south of the line and opened Native homelands to transformation at the hands of an empire that demanded Indian land rather than Indian furs.[9]

The Indians of the region had experienced epidemics in the late eighteenth century and again in the 1830s, and they continued to suffer from newly introduced diseases. When a measles epidemic hit the Cayuse Indians in 1847, American missionary Marcus Whitman and his wife treated Indian as well as non-Indian children, but the Cayuse children died while others recovered. The Cayuses feared the Whitmans were poisoning their children and murdered them and a dozen other settlers. The ensuing war lasted until 1850. Such "Indian massacres" were used to justify military reprisals and dispossessions.

Oregon Territory was organized in 1848; five years later, it was divided into the territories of Washington and Oregon. Between 1853 and 1855 Governor Joel Palmer of Oregon and Governor Isaac Stevens of Washington negotiated a string of treaties with the Walla Wallas, Umatillas, Cayuses, Yakamas, and others. The Indians ceded millions of acres of tribal homelands to the United States, but unrelenting American pressure produced conflicts, most notably in the Rogue River War in southwestern Oregon and the Yakima War. By 1856, most of the Native population of western Oregon had been removed to new reservations.

Genocide and Exploitation in California

In California, the Indian population was shattered by the massive upheavals that followed the discovery of gold in 1848. As many as 300,000 people lived in the area at the time of first contact with Spaniards. By 1848, the Indian numbers had been cut in half at least. Disease, starvation, exploitive labor systems, enslavement, and murder reduced them to a mere 30,000 by 1861.[10] Americans in California routinely depicted the Native inhabitants as degenerate and primitive, little better than wild animals.[11] Miners, settlers, and "volunteer companies" hunted down Indians in systematic campaigns of extermination. When Pomo Indians killed two avaricious miners who had ruthlessly exploited their Indian laborer, American soldiers retaliated in 1850, killing more than one hundred Pomo men, women, and children, "a perfect slaughter pen" according to the officer commanding the troops.[12] Historians disagree about whether it is appropriate to use the term "genocide" in American Indian history. Those who address the question head-on have often tended to be polemical; their work has been suggestive and provocative but of uneven quality and limited usefulness. Other historians have too easily dismissed the term as not applicable to the United States. But "genocide studies" is now an established field of scholarship and scholars of Native American genocide now engage in painstaking accumulation of evidence rather than sweeping generalizations.

If genocide occurred anywhere in the United States, it seems, it occurred in California in the wake of the gold rush. "*Genocide* is a term of awful significance," wrote the late historian Tom Hagan, "but one which has application to the story of California's Native Americans." Many scholars today agree. Whether it is called genocide, ethnic cleansing, or simply murder, there seems little doubt that California became a killing field, where white vigilante groups carried out mass killings and many more people "through apathy, inaction, or tacit support" allowed it to happen.[13]

The influx of thousands of single men to work the gold fields put Indian women in a precarious and often perilous position. Some men turned to Native women for companionship and lasting relationships. But unlike fur traders, miners did not need to establish long-term relationships with Native women or kinship ties with Native communities to achieve their economic goals.[14] Many men turned on Indian women in acts of sexual violence. Poverty and starvation forced some women into prostitution.[15] Thousands of women and children throughout California were sold into slavery.

Many white Californians depended on Indian labor on their ranches, and capturing and indenturing or selling Indian children was common. When California achieved statehood in 1850, ranchers lobbied hard to get the state to implement an "Indian code," which like the slave codes in the South would regulate and control the labor force. The delegates to California's constitutional convention voted unanimously to prohibit slavery in California, but they were thinking of black slavery, not Indian slavery. California Indians were to remain a subservient class of laborers without political rights and with inferior legal rights. Contemporary stereotypes depicted California Indians as dissolute and idle. Under California's laws, Indians were free, but "they were not free to be idle."[16]

The first session of the California state legislature passed an Act for the Government and Protection of Indians. As historian Albert Hurtado points out, few people believed "that paper guarantees could have protected Indians caught in the maw of the gold rush." In reality, the law served white ranchers more than Indians, "by providing a legal process . . . to procure Indian workers and Indian land." Indian vagrants, Indians convicted of crimes (including specifically "Indian" practices, such as "loitering or strolling about"), and even orphaned Indian children could be contracted out to ranchers to pay off their fines. Ostensibly for the "Protection of Indians," the law actually forced many Indians into servitude and protected white ranchers' access to their labor. It also stipulated that white men could not be convicted of any offense on the testimony of an Indian. Despite repeated genocidal acts against the Indian peoples of California, many whites

◆ **Mono Women**

Mono women photographed in front of a bark lodging in the late nineteenth century. Native women in California were often vulnerable to acts of sexual violence after thousands of single men arrived to work the gold fields. *Courtesy of the California History Room, California State Library, Sacramento, California.*

preferred to keep them as a subservient workforce rather than see them exterminated. The act was amended in 1860 and repealed in 1863.[17]

In January 1851, federal treaty commissioners published an address to the people of California in the *Daily Alta California* newspaper. With Indian people being pushed to extinction, the commissioners advocated a policy of moderation:

> As there is now *no further west* to which they *can* be removed, the General Government and the people of California appear to have left but one alternative in relation to these remnants of once numerous and powerful tribes. viz: *extermination* or *domestication*. As the latter includes all proper measures for their protection and gradual improvement, and secures to the people of the State an element greatly needed in the development of its resources, viz: cheap labor — it is the one which we deem the part of wisdom to adopt.[18]

The U.S. government created a series of reservations. Operating in a period of massive upheaval and casualties, these reservations have been likened to refugee camps.

With ongoing white migration to the Pacific after the gold rush, California Indians struggled to remain on their traditional lands. Debris from mining and logging operations choked fishing streams; the newcomers' fences and "property rights" kept Indians from places where they had formerly fished, hunted, and gathered. Cahuilla Indians sent a petition to the U.S. commissioner of Indian affairs in 1856, complaining that the Americans not only took their best farming and grazing lands but also diverted the water they needed for irrigation. In some instances the water had been "wholly monopolized by the white settlers thereby depriving us of the most essential means for the successful cultivation of our crops," and forcing them "to abandon portions of our improved lands greatly to the detriment and distress of our people."[19] As in other areas of the country, Indians who survived in California did so by adapting to harsh new circumstances. Many became part of the market economy and the agricultural labor force. Indians, said one California farmer in 1851, were "all *among* us, *around* us, *with* us — hardly a farm house — a kitchen without them."[20]

Opening Clashes on the Plains, 1851–56

Contrary to Hollywood's obsession with Indian raids on wagon trains, emigrants crossing the Plains to Oregon and California experienced relatively little hostility from Indians. Of 250,000 emigrants who crossed the Plains between 1840 and 1860, only 362 died in all of the recorded conflicts with Indians. More often, Indians acted as pilots and guides, aided emigrants at river crossings, and traded horses and food for guns and cloth. But tensions were inevitable. The Indians regarded the emigrants as trespassers and expected them to pay tribute. "The Indians say that the whites have no right to be in their country without their consent," reported Thomas H. Harvey, the superintendent of Indian affairs at St. Louis in 1845. They "complain that the buffalo are wantonly killed and scared off, which renders their only means of subsistence every year more precarious."[21]

It was only a matter of time before the United States clashed headlong with the Sioux. The Lakotas, the western Sioux° who had established themselves as the dominant Native power on the northern and central Plains, built alliances with the Northern Cheyennes and Arapahos and pushed aside weaker tribes. At first the United States hoped to create safe passage for white immigrants and to reduce conflict among settlers and tribes: at the first Treaty of Fort Laramie in 1851, delegates from all the major tribes on the northern Plains came together in a huge council and heard American proposals that Indians recognize and respect tribal boundaries. The United States wanted to restrict the tribes to designated areas in an effort to reduce intertribal conflict and prevent confrontations with Americans,

---

° The Lakotas comprised the Oglala, Hunkpapa, Miniconjou, Brulé (Sicangu), Blackfeet (Sihaspa), Two Kettle, and Sans Arc tribes.

but fighting broke out only a few years later. In 1854 a young army officer overreacted when a Brulé Sioux Indian killed an immigrant's cow. Lieutenant John Grattan led his command to the Indian village, demanded the killer be delivered up, and opened fire: when the smoke cleared, Grattan and his men lay dead. General William Harney retaliated by destroying a Brulé village at Ash Hollow in Nebraska the following year. The stage was set for more than twenty years of open warfare between the Sioux and the U.S. army.

WARS AND TREATIES, 1861–74

In 1861 the southern states seceded from the United States in an effort to preserve and protect their way of life from what they perceived as northern aggression, and the North went to war to ensure that the Union would endure. In the aftermath of the Civil War many Americans believed that "Winning the West" could help restore the nation's unity and heal its wounds. Rebuilding and expansion required constructing transcontinental railroads across Indian lands, replacing Indian hunters and buffalo with American ranchers and cattle, confining Indians to reservations, and exercising control over Indian lives as Native Americans were brought around to live like white Americans. Many Indians resisted American efforts to absorb them and their homelands into the reunited nation, but the forces arraigned against them were overwhelming. "The whites are as numerous as the years," said one Sioux chief.[22]

Indian Experiences during the American Civil War

The American Civil War, 1861–65, temporarily slowed migration westward and called most troops away from the frontier. But conflicts between Indians and whites continued with little respite, and many Indians were pulled into the nation's strife. Some 20,000 Indians enlisted, serving on both the Union and Confederate sides. Confederate agents made overtures to many of the tribes on the southern Plains and signed nine treaties with tribes in Indian Territory, the area to which many eastern Indians had been removed. Many Cherokees fought for the South and many more sympathized with the southern cause, but others supported the Union. Old divisions from the removal era persisted. For example, Stand Watie had signed the Treaty of New Echota (see page 272) and his brother, Elias Boudinot, was assassinated by followers of Chief John Ross. Watie became a Cherokee general in the Confederate army, and in 1863 he burned John Ross's home. The American Civil War became a Cherokee civil war and undid much of the rebuilding Cherokees had accomplished in Indian Territory after the Trail of Tears. Ely S. Parker, a Seneca, was military secretary to General Ulysses S. Grant and drew up the articles of surrender signed by General Robert E. Lee at Appomattox in 1865. Stand Watie surrendered later, one of the last Confederate generals to surrender. At the end of the war, at Fort Smith, Arkansas, federal officials told the Five Civilized Tribes that since some of them had supported the Confederacy, they had all broken their treaties with the United States and forfeited their treaty rights.[23]

◆ *Little Crow*

Artist Frank Blackwell Mayer sketched this portrait of the Mdwekanton chief Taoyateduta, or Little Crow (c. 1810–63), during negotiations of the Treaty of Traverse des Sioux in 1851, in which the Dakotas ceded much of their land to the United States. Mayer described Little Crow as an intelligent man in his forties, with a "very determined & ambitious nature, but withall exceedingly gentle and dignified in his deportment." His whole bearing, said Mayer, was "that of a gentleman." After attempting accommodation with the United States for a decade, Little Crow led his young men to war in 1862. The next year, he was shot dead by an American settler while picking raspberries with his son. His body was then scalped and dismembered by Americans. Little Crow, 1851 *(pencil on paper), Mayer, Frank Blackwell (1827–89) / Newberry Library, Chicago, Illinois, USA/Bridgeman Images.*

In Minnesota, the Dakota Sioux,° eastern relatives of the Lakota Sioux, were on the verge of starvation when the Civil War began. Their chief Little Crow for years pursued a policy of accommodation in dealing with the United States and took the lead in signing treaties selling Dakota lands. But the Americans failed to deliver the annuities, and the Indian agent told the hungry Dakotas to eat grass. In 1862 Little Crow agreed to lead his angry warriors in a desperate war against the Americans. The war tore apart kinship and other relationships that had evolved over years as Dakota people intermarried and co-existed with white traders and neighbors. Families of mixed heritage faced divided loyalties. Dakota warriors killed more than one thousand settlers. But, as Little Crow had warned his angry young men when they demanded he lead them to war, the Americans were as thick as locusts in flight: "Count your fingers all day long and white men with guns . . . will come faster than you can count." American troops quelled the "Great Sioux Uprising." About 1,700 Sioux were marched to Fort Snelling and confined in a wooden stockade. Four hundred Indians were put on trial for murder, and thirty-eight were eventually executed at Mankato in the largest public hanging in American history.[24] Some Dakota refugees fled west to join their Lakota relatives on the Plains.

° The Dakota Sioux comprised the Mdwekantons, Wahpetons, Wahpekutes, and Sissetons.

Two of the worst massacres of the wars for the West occurred during the Civil War. In January 1863, Colonel Patrick Connor and a force of California Volunteers struck a Shoshoni–Bannock village on Bear River in present-day Idaho, killing more than two hundred men, women, and children. The following year witnessed the infamous Sand Creek massacre. In 1858 gold was discovered in Colorado. Thousands of settlers poured into the area, transforming the front range of the Rockies and the Plains and destroying the Cheyenne Indians' way of life. Tensions escalated, heightened by settlers' fears during the Civil War that the withdrawal of American troops east for war duty would precipitate an Indian uprising. In 1864 Black Kettle's band of Cheyennes and some Southern Arapahos were camped at Sand Creek near Fort Lyon, Colorado, on land set aside by, and supposedly under the protection of, the U.S. government. On a November morning, Colonel J. M. Chivington and the Third Colorado Cavalry attacked the village. Black Kettle raised an American flag and a white flag, but the soldiers butchered between 150 and 270 people, mostly women and children. Some soldiers refused to shoot or participate in the slaughter, but most appear to have gone on a rampage of killing. Black Kettle's wife, who survived, sustained nine gunshot wounds. According to testimony gathered for a congressional investigation, the victims of the Sand Creek massacre "were mutilated in the most horrible manner." In the Treaty of Little Arkansas the following year the United States apologized to the Cheyennes and Arapahos and promised reparations for what happened, but as word of the massacre spread across the Plains, Indian warriors retaliated and the war that settlers feared became a reality. A Civil War monument erected in 1909 on the steps of the state capitol in Denver included Sand Creek in its list of "battles" in which Coloradoans had fought. It has since been erased but the site of the massacre — and how to remember what happened there — continues to be a source of controversy and contention.[25]

In the Southwest, Colonel Edward Canby, General James Carleton, and Colonel Christopher (Kit) Carson, accompanied by Ute Indian allies, campaigned vigorously and mercilessly against the Navajos, destroying sheep herds and homes. Finally, many Navajos surrendered, and in 1864 thousands of Navajos were removed to Bosque Redondo Reservation at Fort Sumner, New Mexico, a four-hundred-mile trek that cost some two hundred lives and that the Navajos called their "Long Walk." Carleton hoped that relocating the Navajos to Bosque Redondo would create a buffer zone protecting New Mexicans from Comanche raids. Confined to barren lands, the Navajos endured malnutrition and disease, bad water, drought, and swarms of grasshoppers. The government provided rations that were sometimes unfit for human consumption, and there were tensions with New Mexicans and raids by the local Comanches. As many as two thousand Navajos died during their imprisonment at Bosque Redondo. Meanwhile, the government tried to transform Navajos into farmers. The Navajo chief Manuelito, who had been one of the last to surrender, traveled to Washington, D.C., to plead that his people be permitted to return home. After four years, the Navajos were allowed to return to their traditional homes with 15,000 head of sheep and goats as breeding stock to replenish their severely depleted herds. In return for being given a chance to rebuild their communities, they promised to stay on their reservation, to stop raiding, and to become farmers and ranchers. Like the Trail of Tears for the Cherokees, the "Long Walk" remained a traumatic and defining event in Navajo history.[26]

Final Treaties and Ongoing Conflicts, 1866–74

While conflict raged on the southern Plains in the wake of the Sand Creek massacre, in the immediate aftermath of the Civil War the Lakotas fought to protect their lands in the northern Plains against the building of the Bozeman Trail, which was to run from Fort Laramie in eastern Wyoming to gold fields in Montana. The Oglala chief Red Cloud fought the U.S. army to a standstill in 1866–67. His warriors annihilated Captain William Fetterman's entire command in December 1866. With American expansion stalled by Indian resistance on both the northern and southern Plains, the U.S. Congress responded by establishing the Indian Peace Commission in 1867. The commissioners were to make treaties that would end the fighting and prevent future conflicts by confining the Indians on reservations where they could be segregated, supervised, and educated in "civilized" ways, leaving the way open for the construction of the railroads that drove American expansion across the west.[27]

The U.S. peace commissioners met first with delegates of the Kiowas, Comanches, Plains Apaches, Southern Cheyennes, and Southern Arapahos at Medicine Lodge in Kansas in 1867. At Medicine Lodge, the Kiowa chief, Satanta, declared, "All the land south of the Arkansas belongs to the Kiowas and Comanches, and I don't want to give away any of it. I love the land and the buffalo, and will not part with any."[28] But the commissioners promised the Indians they could continue to hunt buffalo as long as the herds existed "in sufficient numbers to justify the chase" and induced the tribes to accept reservation lands in Indian Territory. Tensions persisted, and the army launched a series of campaigns to punish Indian raids and "bring in" tribes who refused to accept confinement. In 1868 George Armstrong Custer attacked Black Kettle's Southern Cheyenne village on the Washita River in the dead of winter. Black Kettle and his wife had survived Sand Creek, but they both died at the Washita, along with more than one hundred people. In addition, Custer's command slaughtered hundreds of Indian ponies: an Indian on foot was immobilized and easily defeated. The government failed to deliver the annuities promised under the Treaty of Medicine Lodge and failed to keep buffalo hunters out of the lands guaranteed to the Indians. Faced with chronic food shortages on the reservations, Kiowas, Comanches, and Apaches turned to hunting the same buffalo that white hunters were slaughtering, but they could do so only with the Indian agents' permission. Young men resumed raiding for horses and mules, an activity that had long been part of their economy and which the United States had previously ignored when the raiders targeted Mexico, or Texas when it was a Republic or part of the Confederacy. Now the government declared the raids acts of war and further reduced rations on the reservations in an effort to force the outlaws to "come in."[29] Escalating tensions on the southern Plains erupted in the

Red River War, or Buffalo War, of 1874. In September 1874, at the Battle of Palo Duro Canyon in Texas, Colonel Ranald Mackenzie attacked an encampment of Comanches, Kiowas, and Southern Cheyennes, burning four hundred lodges and slaughtering 1,400 ponies. That winter starving Indians drifted into the reservations from the snow-covered Plains. Seventy-five of the alleged "ringleaders" were sent as prisoners of war to Fort Marion in Florida (see Chapter 7 Picture Essay, "The Fort Marion Artists," pages 433–38).

After the Medicine Lodge treaty, the members of the Peace Commission traveled north to deal with the Sioux. At the second Treaty of Fort Laramie in 1868 (see "The Sioux, the Treaty of Fort Laramie, and the Black Hills," pages 341–55), Lakota spokesmen like Iron Shell and One Horn made clear the Indians' reason for going to war, and the United States agreed to abandon the Bozeman Trail, although by that time it had built a railroad beyond the contested area, rendering the trail obsolete and no longer worth fighting for.[30] Having won his war, Red Cloud kept his word and kept the peace. But American pressures on the Sioux only intensified: "We are melting like snow on the hillside, while you are grown like spring grass," Red Cloud told the secretary of the interior during a visit to Washington, D.C., in 1870. "When the white man comes in my country he leaves a trail of blood behind him."[31] Leadership of the Sioux warriors gradually passed to younger men like Crazy Horse and Sitting Bull, who advocated uncompromising resistance against American expansion and colonialism.

Elsewhere in the West, Colonel Eugene Baker led his U.S. cavalry in a dawn attack on a village of Blackfeet on the Marias River in Montana in January 1870. The inhabitants were huddled in their tipis, cold and reeling from a recent smallpox epidemic. The soldiers killed 173 people, mostly old men, women, and children, and slaughtered 300 horses. It was the wrong village. The cavalry were after Mountain Chief's band; this was Heavy Runner's village.[32] And in 1872–73, the United States defeated the Modocs of southern Oregon and northern California in a brutal war.

LAND SEIZURE AND REMOVAL TO RESERVATIONS

For almost a century, the United States made treaties with Indian nations. But there was growing sentiment that the United States should treat Indians as wards of the government, not as independent nations. The House of Representatives, which was left out of the treaty-making process — the Senate, not the House, ratified treaties — also wanted change, and in 1871 Congress declared an end to making treaties. In the years that followed, treaties that had already been made also came under attack. But the United States still needed mechanisms by which to deal with Indian tribes and create Indian reservations, and they did so by agreements, statutes, and presidential executive orders.[33] Indian people continued to resist the assault on their lands and, in many cases, fought rather than succumbed to the reservation system (Map 6.2).

Other forces, more powerful than army bullets, were at work bringing an end to the Plains Indians' world. The first transcontinental railroad was completed

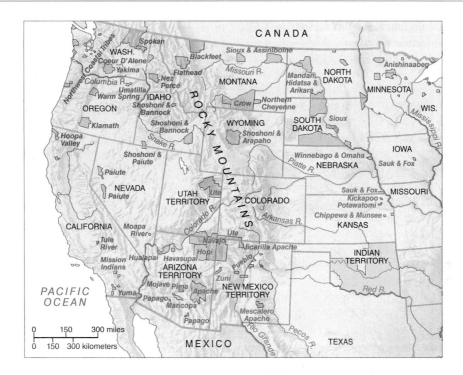

◆ **Map 6.2 Indian Reservations in the West, 1890**

When Lewis and Clark journeyed across the West in the first decade of the nineteenth century, they entered an Indian world through which they traveled at their risk and by Indian tolerance and guidance. By the end of the century, that world was transformed, and Indian peoples were confined on patches of the lands they once occupied or were removed to Indian Territory. (See Map 6.4, page 346, for the Lakota Sioux reservations.)

SOURCE: Based on maps by Harry Scott taken from *The Indian Frontier of the American West, 1846–1890,* by Robert Utley. Copyright © 1984 University of New Mexico Press. Used by permission.

in 1869; other lines proliferated in the years that followed, bringing more immigrants west and facilitating the movement of troops and supplies. At the same time the buffalo herds — the staple diet of the Plains Indians and the basis of their culture — were systematically slaughtered between 1867 and 1883. Some estimates based on the reports of travelers across the Plains in the early nineteenth century put buffalo numbers as high as 40 million or more. The influx of Indian peoples onto the Plains and the development of more efficient hunting techniques from horseback placed the herds under substantial pressure. Hunting for the American hide market, together with a drought in the 1840s and the possible impact of bovine diseases, further reduced buffalo populations, and there were reports of Indians starving even before 1850.[34] And the herds received no relief, as another pressure arose in the wake of the immigrants.

In 1871 a Pennsylvania tannery found that buffalo hides could be used to manufacture belts for industrial machinery. Roads and railroads brought immigrants and hide hunters by the hundreds to the Indians' hunting grounds, and in just a few short years American buffalo hunters, with the support and encouragement of the U.S. army, brought the species to the brink of extinction. Colonel Richard Irving Dodge, stationed in Kansas, witnessed the slaughter. In 1871 the buffalo seemed limitless. The hunting was sufficient the next year. But by 1873 everything had changed. "Where there were myriads of buffalo the year before, there were now myriads of carcasses. The air was foul with sickening stench, and the vast plain, which only a short twelvemonth before teemed with animal life, was a dead, solitary, putrid desert." A year later, there seemed to be more buffalo hunters than buffalo. Fewer than a thousand buffalo survived in 1895.[35] "We believed for a long time that the buffalo would again come to us," recalled a Crow woman, Pretty Shield, "but they did not." Crow hunters rode far and wide looking for buffalo but came back empty-handed. "'Nothing; we found nothing,' they told us; and then, hungry, they stared at the empty plains, as though dreaming."[36] With their food supply gone, Indians faced a choice between starvation and the reservation.

◆ **Buffalo Skulls to Be Sold as Fertilizer, c. 1880**
The slaughter of the buffalo herds in the late nineteenth century struck at the core of Plains Indian life and reduced once-independent peoples to dependence on government rations.
Courtesy of the Burton Historical Collection, Detroit Public Library.

Battles for Sacred Lands and Homelands, 1875–78

Indian people felt the outside world rushing in on them. Red Dog, a Sioux chief who had visited Washington, told U.S. commissioners that when he was there he did not pull a twig from a tree or disturb anything, but Americans entering Indian land did not treat it with the same respect. "This is our country," he said, "and when white men come into it, it makes our hearts beat fast."[37] Red Dog had good reason to be anxious. In 1874 George Custer led an expedition into the Black Hills of South Dakota that verified reports of gold in the region. The Black Hills were sacred to the Sioux and had been guaranteed to them in the Treaty of Fort Laramie. Prospectors who trespassed there were killed. The government offered to purchase the Black Hills, but the Sioux dismissed their offers. Sitting Bull said that the Black Hills were simply not for sale.[38]

The United States resolved to take them anyway. The army sent an ultimatum ordering all Sioux and Northern Cheyenne bands onto the reservations by January 31, 1876, and then launched a three-pronged "pacification campaign" against the "hostiles" who refused to come in. Crazy Horse, the renowned Oglala war chief, turned back one prong, led by General George Crook, at the Battle of the Rosebud in South Dakota. A week later, Custer and the Seventh Cavalry, approaching from the east, came upon a huge Indian village in the valley of the Little Bighorn and rashly attacked it. The Hunkpapa chief Sitting Bull had had a vision of soldiers without ears — indicating that they refused to listen — falling into the Indians' camp. When the cavalry's attack came, Sitting Bull's vision seemed to be coming true. The Lakotas and Cheyennes wiped out Custer's command in a battle that was commemorated in countless movies and paintings (see Picture Essay, "The Battle of the Little Bighorn in Myth and History," pages 367–71).

This most famous Indian victory occurred when Indians were nearing the end of fighting for their freedom. The bands that had congregated at the Little Bighorn split up and were tracked down and rounded up in the next year or two. Sitting Bull fled to Canada; Crazy Horse surrendered in 1877 and was bayoneted to death while "trying to escape."[39] The Lakotas were confined to reservations (see Map 6.4, "The Lakota Reservations, 1890," page 346), and Congress passed a law taking the Black Hills and extinguishing all Lakota rights outside the Great Sioux Reservation. American troops destroyed the Northern Cheyenne village of Dull Knife and Little Wolf on the Powder River in Wyoming in November 1876. Fifty years later, a Northern Cheyenne woman named Iron Teeth remembered the attack: "They killed our men, women, and children," she said. Her husband died in the fighting. Afterward, with men dying from their injuries and women and children freezing to death without blankets or shelter, Cheyenne mothers "killed some of their ponies, removed the entrails, and placed their [infants] inside the steaming carcasses to keep them from freezing."[40] The surviving Cheyennes were shipped to Indian Territory, where they began to die of malaria. After repeated pleas that they be allowed to return to their tribal lands, in September 1878 about three hundred Cheyennes began a desperate attempt to go home. Hungry, sick, and exhausted, they made their way north through Kansas, Nebraska, and Dakota, finally reaching Montana after traveling 1,500 miles across the Plains in the fall and winter. Most were captured and many were killed, but some eventually were allowed to return home to a reservation in southern Montana.[41]

In 1877 Chief Joseph and the Nez Perces of Oregon also made a 1,500-mile bid for freedom, trying to reach Canada rather than go to a reservation. They defeated and eluded various American armies sent in pursuit but were caught just short of the border and exiled to Indian Territory (see "Chief Joseph's Plea for Freedom," pages 356–66). Also in 1877, the government forcibly removed members of the Ponca tribe from Nebraska to Indian Territory. (The Poncas' land had been as-signed to them by treaty in 1865 but was subsequently included in the reservation area ceded to the Sioux by the Treaty of Fort Laramie in 1868.) The following year Ponca chief Standing Bear and a small group set off on a six-hundred-mile walk to carry the body of his only son back home to Nebraska for burial. When he reached his destination, he was arrested and imprisoned. Standing Bear brought a habeas corpus suit° in federal district court, arguing in effect that an Indian was a person under federal law. The judge concurred, and Standing Bear ultimately won his freedom. His case sparked controversy, generated national publicity, and fueled demands for reform in Indian policy.[42]

The End of Apache Resistance

In Arizona and New Mexico, Apaches continued to raid into Mexico as they had for generations and steadfastly resisted American invasion of their homeland after 1848. Apache warriors fought with ferocity and Americans responded with equal ferocity. American soldiers killed the Mimbreño Apache chief, Mangas Coloradas, while he was shackled and under guard and they botched an attempt to capture the Chiricahua chief, Cochise, under a flag of truce. As the Mexicans had done for generations, Americans offered bounties on Apache scalps. "When I was young I walked all over this country, east and west, and saw no other people than the Apaches," said Cochise in 1866. "After many summers I walked again and found another race of people had come to take it. How is it? Why is it that the Apaches wait to die?"[43] Even Apaches who attempted to live in peace found no safe haven. In 1871 a group comprising Mexicans, Tohono O'odam Indians, and American citizens of Tucson massacred more than one hundred Aravaipa Apaches who had settled at Camp Grant under the protection of the army.[44]

Eventually, most Apache bands were confined on a reservation at San Carlos, Arizona Territory. Daklugie, an Apache who lived there as a child, told researcher Eve Ball in the 1940s that San Carlos was "the worst place in all the great territory stolen from the Apaches." The only vegetation was cacti. "Where there is no grass there is no game. . . . The heat was terrible. The insects were terrible. The water was terrible." Rattlesnakes and mosquitoes thrived there, but Apaches died of "the shaking sickness," malaria. San Carlos, said Daklugie, "was considered a good place for the Apaches — a good place for them to die." Daklugie was the son of an

---

° A legal action by which prisoners may seek release from unlawful imprisonment.

Apache chief named Juh and retained an implacable hatred for white Americans. Even though he had spent a dozen years at Carlisle boarding school and worked as an interpreter, he pretended he could not speak English. "It took four years to get him to talk," said Ball.[45]

Not surprisingly, many Apaches rebelled against reservation confinement, preferring death in battle to a slow death at San Carlos. Victorio led his Warm Springs people off the reservation in 1877. "I will not go to San Carlos," he said. "I will not take my people there. We prefer to die in our own land under the tall cool pines. We will leave our bones with those of our people. It is better to die fighting than to starve."[46] For three years he outwitted, outmaneuvered, and out-fought the troops sent against him. In 1880, driven across the Mexican border by pursuing American troops, Victorio's band clashed with a force of Mexicans and Tarahumara Indians in a two-day battle in Chihuahua. When the smoke cleared, Victorio lay dead.

The United States also spent years chasing down a small band of Chiricahuas led by Geronimo and Naiche. General Crook, whom Crazy Horse turned back at the Battle of the Rosebud, employed Chiricahua scouts and always maintained that they "did most excellent service, and were of more value in hunting down and compelling the surrender of the renegades, than all other troops engaged in operations against them combined." Two Chiricahua scouts, Martine and Kay-itah, risked their lives to get Geronimo to surrender to General Nelson Miles in 1886. Miles had five thousand soldiers, one-fourth of the regular army, under his command. Geronimo's band consisted of only eighteen warriors and some women and children. Even so, Geronimo and other Apaches agreed that Miles had to lie to them to get their surrender. Jasper Kanseah, Geronimo's nephew who was about fifteen at the time of the surrender and had been fighting with Geronimo for three years, said, "Nobody ever captured Geronimo. I know. I was with him. Anyway," he added, "who can capture the wind?"[47]

After Geronimo and his band of Chiricahua Apache holdouts surrendered in September 1886, they were sent to Fort Pickens, Florida. The rest of the Chirica-huas, most of whom had not supported Geronimo's war and some of whom had served the U.S. army as scouts against him, were also loaded on to trains to Fort Marion, a military prison in Florida. Martine and Kayitah, who had risked their lives to bring peace, were thrown on the train still wearing their army uniforms. Crowded into the rundown old fortress at Fort Marion, the Chiricahuas endured an unfamiliar climate and malaria. "We were accustomed to dry heat," said James Kaywaykla, "but in Florida the dampness and the mosquitoes took toll of us until it seemed that none would be left. Perhaps we were taken to Florida for that pur-pose."[48] Army officers who had fought alongside the Apache scouts and the Indian Rights Association took up the Chiricahuas' cause, but they succeeded only in hav-ing them removed to Alabama. In 1894 the surviving Chiricahuas were relocated to the Kiowa and Comanche Reservation in Indian Territory. There Geronimo died of pneumonia in 1909. Not until 1913 were the Chiricahuas allowed to return to the Southwest, many of them joining the Mescalero Apaches in New Mexico.[49] With the Apaches' defeat, American military conquest of the West was complete.

◆ **Apache Leaders before Surrender**

Geronimo, Naiche (wearing brimmed hat), and Naiche's son (standing next to Naiche), with an unidentified Apache and child in a photograph taken by C. S. Fly of Tombstone, Arizona, shortly before the Apaches first surrendered to General Crook in March 1886. *Granger, NYC.*

DIFFERENT STRATEGIES FOR SURVIVAL

Not all Indians resisted American expansion westward; some participated in it and played an active role in bringing change to the West. One Delaware, Black Beaver (1806–80), lived through the era of American exploration, conquest, and settlement of the West and participated in almost every phase of it. Born in Illinois in the year that Lewis and Clark returned from their western travels, Sekettu Maquah, or Black Beaver, became a trapper and trader, a guide, an army scout, and an interpreter. As a young man, he traveled west. Along with many other Delaware and Iroquois Indians, he worked as a trapper in the Rocky Mountain fur trade. He never learned to read or write but mastered the sign language of the Plains Indians and could speak several Indian languages as well as English, French, and Spanish. In 1834 he served as interpreter for an expedition led by Colonel Richard Dodge to the Red River country of the Comanches, Kiowas, and Wichitas. A dozen years later, he was a scout for the U.S. army during the war with Mexico and commanded a company of thirty-five Delawares and Shawnees. He guided Captain Randolph Marcy and a company of dragoons° in establishing a route to Santa Fe and accompanying a wagon train of five hundred emigrants across the Southwest. Marcy said Black Beaver "had visited nearly every point of interest within the limits of our unsettled territory. . . . His life is that of a veritable cosmopolite, filled

---

° Heavily armed troops on horseback.

with scenes of intense and startling interest, bold and reckless adventure." In the 1850s, Black Beaver worked as a farmer, trader, and guide. By the Civil War, he had a ranch on the Wichita Agency in Indian Territory (Oklahoma). Along with many other Delawares, he served the Union; as a result, Confederates seized his cattle and horses and destroyed his ranch. He acted as an interpreter in negotiations with the tribes of the southern Plains, and in 1872 he was a member of an Indian delegation from the Wichita Agency to Washington, D.C. Toward the end of his life he became a Baptist minister. When he died in 1880, he had outlived most of the people he had known and whose roles in westward expansion were far more renowned.[50]

Indian Scouts and Allies

Like Black Beaver, some leaders opted for accommodation and attempted to control the pace of change. Washakie of the Shoshonis, Ouray of the Utes, Plenty Coups of the Crows, Red Cloud of the Oglalas after his successful war of resistance in the 1860s, and many others realized that the survival of their people depended upon dealing with the reality of American power and presence. They attempted to cooperate with government agents in the hope of securing better food, clothing, and shelter for their people, but continued the fight to be Indian. Some men who found themselves deprived of their traditional roles in society as warriors and hunters joined the Indian police as a means of attaining status and a way of helping their people make the transition through hard times.

American expansion and wars against the Sioux offered some Indian peoples an opportunity to secure powerful allies in their own struggles. Crows, Arikaras, Pawnees, and Shoshonis all, at one time or another, fought alongside the U.S. army in its battles against the Lakota Sioux and their allies. The Pawnees, for example, formed a battalion of scouts that served alongside U.S. troops during the height of the Plains wars between 1864 and 1877.[51] The westward expansion of the Lakotas in the late eighteenth and early nineteenth centuries had placed all these tribes on the defensive, and many of them had lost lands and relatives to the Lakotas. The Crows' rich hunting territories had come under virtual siege from neighboring tribes as buffalo herds in these tribes' lands diminished: "Look at our country, and look at our enemies," Crow chiefs declared in 1870, "they are all around it; the Sioux, Blackfeet, Cheyennes, Arapahos, and Flatheads, all want our country, and kill us when they can." It made sense for the Crows to align themselves with the Lakotas' new enemies, the Americans. In June 1876, Crows and Shoshonis fought with General Crook against Crazy Horse at the Battle of the Rosebud, where a Crow woman named Other Magpie fought to avenge her brother's death at the hands of the Lakotas. Crow and Arikara scouts guided Custer to the Little Bighorn. Before the so-called Sioux War of 1876–77 was over, Crows, Shoshonis, Arikaras, Utes, Bannocks, Pawnees, and even some Arapahos, Cheyennes, and Sioux had all served with the U.S. army.

The Crows and Shoshonis each managed to secure and retain a reservation in their traditional homelands in the late nineteenth century, when many Indian peoples were being uprooted and shipped off to Indian Territory. In later life, the Crow chief Plenty Coups explained that his people allied with the United States "not because we loved the whiteman [*sic*] who was already crowding other tribes into our country, or because we hated the Sioux, Cheyenne, and Arapaho, but because we plainly saw that this course was the only one which might save our beautiful country for us. When I think back my heart sings because we acted as we did. It was the only way open to us." Tribal historian Joe Medicine Crow agreed: "We were looking for survival and I think we played it smart." Like the Shoshonis, they used the United States as allies, and doing so brought short-term gains.[52] The Crows survived their long military struggle against the Lakotas with the help of American allies, but the Americans would soon pose a greater threat to the Crows' country and culture.

◆ **A Crow Delegation to Washington, D.C., Spring 1880**
The chiefs (from left to right) are Old Crow, Medicine Crow, Two Belly, Long Elk, Plenty Coups, and Pretty Eagle. Indian delegations to Washington were a regular feature of U.S.–Indian relations in the second half of the nineteenth century, as the government conducted negotiations with key chiefs and tried to impress them with American power. For the delegates, visiting the nation's capital offered an opportunity to represent their people's interests to the president, Congress, and senior officials. *National Archives.*

Return of the Prophets

For most Indian people, the hard times following defeat and dispossession proved traumatic. They suffered defeat in war, saw their subsistence base destroyed, and lost most of their lands. Once prosperous and powerful, the Plains tribes were reduced to poverty, forced to rely on government handouts and the assistance of the agents. Once free and mobile, they were confined to arid, nonproductive reservations, which they could not leave without permission. Poor health and diet, a high mortality rate, and a low life expectancy became the norm on many Indian reservations. Even the environment was transformed as Americans pushed relentlessly to master the West and exploit its resources. The United States demanded that the defeat of the western tribes involve the destruction of their way of life as well as their military subjugation.

Some people sought escape from the harsh reality of their situation and succumbed to alcoholism. Others looked inward and tried to restore harmony and meaning to their world through religion and ritual. As had Handsome Lake and the Shawnee Prophet at the beginning of the century, new prophets were believed to have died, traveled to heaven, and returned with divine messages that promised deliverance from suffering and oppression and a new era for Indian people. The prophets initiated religious movements that combined old beliefs and new teachings and offered an outlet for frustration and a source of solace for people in crisis. In the 1850s, Smohalla, a Wanapum Indian from the Columbia River region, began prophesying a restoration of the Indian world and the destruction of whites. He taught his followers to abstain from alcohol, to revive the old ways, and to purify themselves of white influences. His religion became known as the Dreamer religion, with believers spending long periods in meditation. Smohalla opposed the government's program of converting his people into farmers — "You ask me to plow the ground. Shall I take a knife and tear my mother's bosom?" — and rejected the Protestant work ethic promoted by Christian missionaries and Indian agents: "My young men shall never work. Men who work can not dream, and wisdom comes to us in dreams." Smohalla was persecuted and jailed, but the Dreamer religion he founded spread across the Pacific Northwest and survives today.[53]

Another Northwest Coast prophet, Squsachtun or John Slocum, founded the Indian Shaker religion in the Puget Sound region in 1881. Squsachtun, a Nisqually Indian, experienced trances in which he received divine messages on how Indian people could survive the trauma of reservation life. He taught his followers to believe in God and Christ, heaven and hell, but to rely on his prophecies for sacred guidance. His followers, who shook their bodies while ritually brushing away their sins, became known as Shakers. Like Smohalla, Squsachtun was harassed and imprisoned, but, like the Dreamer religion, the Shaker sect survived. The religion spread through the Northwest and northern California, and the Indian Shaker Church was incorporated in 1910.

Prophetic movements on the northern Plains produced different, tragic results. A young Crow medicine man named Sword Bearer gained a following of frustrated young Crows who could no longer subsist by warring or hunting. He was reputed to have great power and preached an apocalyptic vision that alarmed the government and the citizens of Montana. The army was sent in, Sword Bearer was killed, and the potential movement was crushed. A possible bloodbath was averted. Three years later the Lakotas were not so fortunate.

The Ghost Dance religion that swept the Plains at the end of the 1880s originated in the Nevada region. A Paiute Indian named Wovoka preached a religion that promised a return of the old ways that would reunite its practitioners with departed ancestors if they abstained from alcohol, lived in peace, and followed a prescribed ritual, including a dance in a circle called the Ghost Dance. It also promised that the white man would disappear. The religion spread rapidly on the Plains. The Lakotas sent messengers who traveled by train to receive the new religion.

Many Lakotas embraced the Ghost Dance as a religious response to the harsh conditions on the reservations. The Ghost Dancers harmed no one and destroyed no property — they hoped to restore their world by dancing, not fighting — but non-Indians became alarmed by reports of warriors performing a strange new dance that was supposed to result in the disappearance of whites and the return of the buffalo. Inexperienced Indian agents tried in vain to stop the dancing and began to see it as preparation for an uprising. By November, they were warning Washington of an impending war. With midterm elections looming (including the election of a senator from South Dakota, which had become a state in 1889), President Benjamin Harrison's Republican administration likely wanted to be seen as protecting South Dakota's citizens against an Indian uprising, and mobilizing troops would also give a timely boost to the local economy. General Miles ordered troops onto the Pine Ridge and Rosebud reservations.[54]

Sitting Bull had returned from Canada and surrendered to U.S. forces in 1881, but he was always regarded as a potential "troublemaker" by the authorities. He was killed by Indian police as they tried to arrest him at his cabin on the Standing Rock Reservation in mid-December 1890. Two weeks later, perhaps still smarting from their defeat at the Little Bighorn fourteen years before, the Seventh Cavalry intercepted Big Foot's band of Miniconjou Lakotas at Wounded Knee in South Dakota as they were making their way to the Pine Ridge Reservation. After a botched attempt to disarm the Indians, the soldiers opened fire on the encampment and massacred between two and three hundred men, women, and children. Many wounded people left to die on the site of the massacre succumbed to subzero temperatures as a blizzard hit the Plains. Charles Eastman, the Sioux doctor who had returned to Pine Ridge as agency physician (see Chapter 7, page 401), treated wounded and mutilated survivors in a makeshift hospital in a chapel. On New Year's Day 1891, after the blizzard had ended, Eastman and others combed the "battlefield" searching for survivors. He found a woman's body three miles from the site of the massacre, "and from this point on we found them scattered along as they had been relentlessly hunted down and

◆ **A Lakota Baby Bonnet, c. 1875–1900**
This baby's bonnet, beaded with love and attention to detail by a Lakota woman in the late nineteenth or early twentieth century, shows the incorporation of a stars and stripes design into Plains Indian beadwork. A baby wearing a similar bonnet was found after the massacre at Wounded Knee. *Thaw Collection, Fenimore Art Museum, New York State Historical Association, Cooperstown, NY. Photograph by John Bigelow Taylor, NYC/The New York State Historical Association.*

slaughtered while fleeing for their lives." He found a little girl about a year old, warmly wrapped and still alive, lying near her dead mother. The child was wearing a fur bonnet beaded with an American flag. Standing amid the fragments of burned tipis and the frozen bodies was, Eastman wrote with considerable understatement, "a severe ordeal for one who had so lately put all his faith in the Christian love and lofty ideals of the white man."[55]

The Oglala holy man Black Elk, a young man at the time of the massacre, later reflected on the events at Wounded Knee. His words, as recorded by poet John G. Neihardt, have often been cited as elegiac testimony to the end of a way of life.

> When I look back now from this high hill of my old age, I can still see the butchered women and children lying heaped and scattered all along the crooked gulch as plain as when I saw them with eyes still young. And I can see that something else died there in the bloody mud, and was buried in the blizzard. A people's dream died there.

The "nation's hoop"—Lakota society—was "broken and scattered," concluded Black Elk. Wounded Knee put a grisly end to armed conflict on the northern Plains, but Indian people around the country were already engaged in another desperate struggle. In time, the hoop of the Lakota Nation would be mended.[56]

DOCUMENTS

Sixty Years of Kiowa History

•••✕✕✕✕✕◆✕✕✕✕✕✕•••

ALL PEOPLES DEVISE WAYS OF RECORDING their history and preserving for posterity the events that give meaning to their collective lives. In oral cultures like those of the Plains Indians, the memories of the elders served as repositories of tribal histories. Retellings of significant events fastened them into the communal memory, just as songs, stories, dances, and other public performances fastened traditions in the lives of successive generations. Tribal historians on the Plains also compiled calendars of events — often called winter counts — significant to the community as a whole.

Usually painted on a buffalo robe in a spiral denoting successive years, these calendars chronicle the people's history with each year marked by a pictographic device symbolizing a memorable event. The symbols functioned as mnemonic devices, allowing the keeper of the chronicle at some future date to draw on his fund of memory and knowledge, recalling more details and other events. Sometimes a single individual would compile a winter count, recording the years of his own life; other calendars would be made over two or three generations, or compiled by one person in consultation with elders who remembered the events or who had received knowledge of them from people long since dead. The keepers of the chronicles would bring them out to be displayed and discussed around the campfires during winter evenings.

Winter counts are of great value to modern ethnohistorians when used in conjunction with documentary evidence. Most calendars record outbreaks of smallpox and other epidemics, and most note "the winter when the stars fell," the meteor shower visible throughout the western United States in November 1833. But sometimes these tribal records make no reference to things outsiders might assume would be significant: they contain many references to horse raids, the Sun Dance, battles with enemy tribes, deaths of prominent chiefs, and domestic squabbles that resulted in violence — things that were noteworthy in the community and also served to jog the memory about other events — but might ignore major battles and treaties with the United States.[57]

Like other historical sources, winter counts have limitations: their chronology usually cannot be established without cross-referencing to other sources. Interpretation of the mnemonic devices can vary considerably, and when winter counts were explained to outsiders in the early twentieth century it was not always clear how much of the interpretation came from the keeper of the calendar, how much from the translator, and how much from the ethnologist or other scholar who then transferred what he had been told into a written chronology of events. Nevertheless, they provide scholars with a unique research tool and, properly analyzed, allow integration of Indian and non-Indian records to create a richer story of the past.[58]

◆ **Sam Kills Two**

The Lakota Sam Kills Two adds the symbol of another year to a winter count documenting 130 years of tribal history. The chronicles created and preserved by tribal recordkeepers such as Sam Kills Two supplemented oral histories handed down from generation to generation. *Nebraska State Historical Society, photo no. RG2969. Copy and reuse restrictions apply.*

Moreover, winter counts are by no means the only source of history for the Plains Indian societies who created and kept them. Lakota author Mary Crow Dog, recounting her life in the twentieth century, commented on some of the ways through which history survived among a people who did not record it in writing: "The Sioux used to keep winter counts, picture writings on buffalo skin, which told our people's story from year to year," she said. "Well, the whole country is one vast winter count. You can't walk a mile without coming to some family's sacred vision hill, to an ancient Sun Dance circle, an old battleground, a place where something worth remembering happened."[59]

The chronicle reproduced here records Kiowa history during sixty years of calamitous change. Kiowa traditions tell that the people entered the world through a hollow log "in the bleak northern mountains" in western Montana. Life there was hard, and in the late seventeenth century they began to migrate southward (Map 6.3). "The great adventure of the Kiowas was a going forth into the heart of the continent," wrote Kiowa author N. Scott Momaday. They began a long migration from the headwaters of the Yellowstone River, east to the Black Hills, where they befriended the Crows. They acquired horses, "and their ancient nomadic spirit was suddenly free of the ground." They acquired Tai-me, the sacred Sun Dance doll, and with it "the religion of the Plains." And they acquired "a love and possession of the open land." Pushed out of the Black Hills by the Lakotas and Cheyennes, they moved south through Wyoming along the Front Range of the Rockies and toward the Ouachita Mountains in Oklahoma. By the time they reached the southern Plains, they had been transformed. "In the course of that long migration they had come of age as a people," said Momaday. "They had conceived a good idea of themselves; they had dared to imagine and determine who they were."[60]

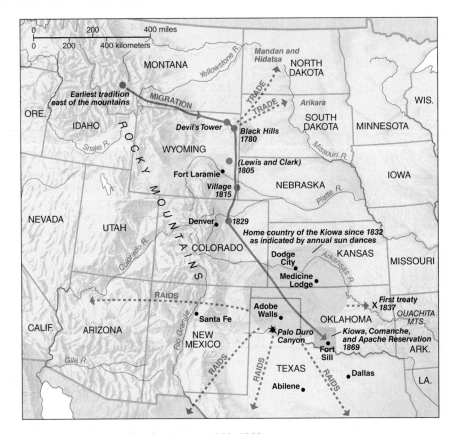

◆ **Map 6.3 Kiowa Migration Route, 1832–1869**

Migration south across the Great Plains brought the Kiowas to new homes and a new way of life. But as they journeyed, the Kiowas encountered Americans, whose growing presence would soon change forever the way of life the Kiowas created on the Plains and who would eventually confine them on a reservation.

SOURCE: James Mooney, *Calendar History of the Kiowa Indians* (Washington, D.C.: U.S. Government Printing Office, 1898).

By the early nineteenth century, the Kiowas were ranging across western Oklahoma, northern Texas, northeastern New Mexico, southeastern Colorado, and southwestern Kansas. They became allied with the Comanches sometime around 1790, and together they dominated the southern Plains. Kiowas traded with Pueblo peoples in New Mexico, but as the calendar indicates, they were also far-ranging raiders, striking deep into Mexico as well as against other Indian tribes. They lived in small, independent bands. But each summer the people came together for the Sun Dance, the central ceremony of the tribe, where they reaffirmed their unity, renewed relationships, and hunted buffalo, the foundation of Kiowa economy and culture. That way of life collapsed under the onslaught of American expansion and the assaults of American colonialism in the years documented by the calendar.

The Dohasan Calendar (1832–92)

This calendar was begun by a Kiowa chief named Dohasan, whom the artist George Catlin met and painted in 1834 and described as "a very gentlemanly and high minded man."[61] When Dohasan died in 1866, the calendar was continued to 1892 by his nephew, also called Dohasan. It contains two pictorial devices for each year — one representing the winter and one the summer. The chronicle was originally painted on hides that were renewed from time to time as they became worn out from age and handling, but Dohasan drew a copy with colored pencils on paper which he gave to Captain Hugh L. Scott of the Seventh Cavalry at Fort Sill in 1892. Four years later anthropologist James Mooney compiled an explanation of the events associated with each picture, primarily from information supplied to Scott by Dohasan before his death in 1893, and supplemented with information from other Kiowa chronicles.

The pictographs are arranged in a continuous spiral. The calendar begins in the winter of 1832–33 at the lower left-hand corner (1), when a man (indicated by his breech cloth) named Black Wolf (identified by the symbol above his head) was killed in an encounter with a party of Americans.[62] The next symbol (2) refers to an Osage attack on a Kiowa camp that summer, when the Osages cut off the heads of their victims.[63] Then, three stars (3) indicate the meteor shower in the winter of 1833, which, according to Momaday, "has a special place in the memory of the Kiowa people" and "marks the beginning as it were of the historical period in the tribal mind."[64] Black bars, representing dead vegetation, mark the winters; summers are usually indicated by a Sun Dance lodge with a door. (In years when the Sun Dance was not held, the season is marked by a tree in leaf or simply by the symbol for that summer's event

between the two winter bars.) The major event of the season is indicated by a pictograph above or beside the winter mark or the Sun Dance lodge.[65]

The story recorded here is a familiar one in the histories of other peoples on the Plains. New diseases scythed the Kiowa population as American immigrants encroached on their territory. (The calendar records epidemics among the Kiowas in the winters of 1839–40 [4] and 1861–62 [6], and cholera in the summer of 1849 — the figure over the central Sun Dance lodge is doubled over with the pangs of cholera [5].)[66] Escalating tensions exploded in outbursts of sporadic violence and occasional pitched conflicts. The superior numbers, resources, and firepower of the United States compelled the Kiowas and their neighbors to contemplate an unknown kind of life: in the Treaty of Medicine Lodge in 1867 ("Timber Hill winter" indicated by the large black tree [7]),[67] Kiowas, Comanches, Southern Cheyennes, Southern Arapahos, and Plains Apaches agreed to move on to a reservation in what is now Oklahoma. Meanwhile, the slaughter of the southern herds continued without respite, and in 1874 Kiowa and other southern Plains warriors went to war rather than die of hunger. The U.S. army responded with overwhelming force and destroyed the Kiowas' lodges and horse herds at the Battle of Palo Duro Canyon. The Kiowas surrendered to the army at Fort Sill, Oklahoma, and seventy-two "ringleaders" of the southern Plains Indians were shipped to Florida as prisoners of war. (The calendar records clashes with Texans and U.S. soldiers, and the arrests of chiefs.) "The young Plains culture of the Kiowas," wrote Momaday, "withered and died like grass that is burned in the prairie wind."[68]

The summer of 1879, marked by a horse head above a Sun Dance lodge (8), was remembered as the "Horse-Eating Sun Dance." The buffalo were so scarce that the Kiowas had to kill and eat their horses to keep from starving. "This may be recorded as the date of the disappearance

SOURCE: *A Chronicle of the Kiowa Indians, 1832–1892* (1968). Courtesy of Phoebe A. Hearst Museum of Anthropology and the Regents of the University of California.

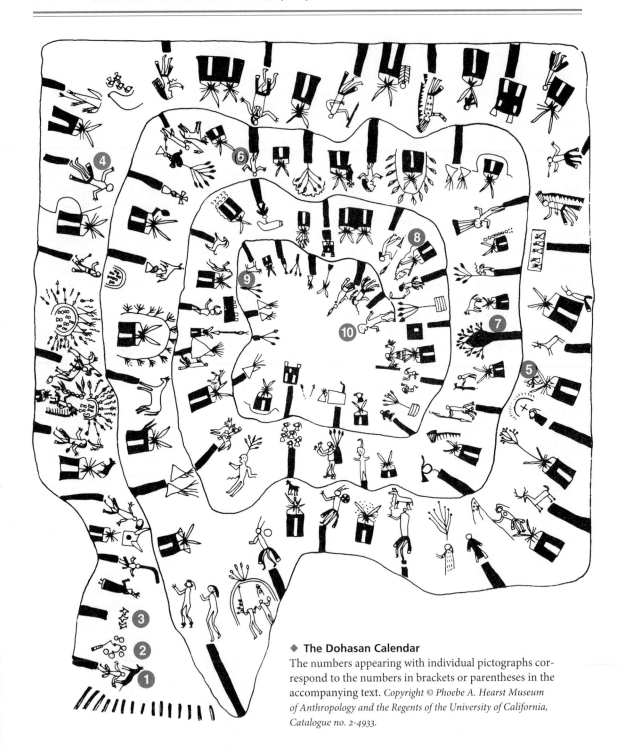

◆ **The Dohasan Calendar**
The numbers appearing with individual pictographs correspond to the numbers in brackets or parentheses in the accompanying text. *Copyright © Phoebe A. Hearst Museum of Anthropology and the Regents of the University of California, Catalogue no. 2-4933.*

of the buffalo from the Kiowa country," wrote Mooney. "Thenceforth the appearance of even a single animal was a rare event."[69] In subsequent years, as indicated by trees in leaf rather than Sun Dance lodges, the Sun Dance sometimes could not be held, because of the lack of buffalo. The last Kiowa Sun Dance in the nineteenth century was held in 1887. The buffalo and the Sun Dance were the anchors of Kiowa culture and experience. "Those were the two things that were always there. Things changed around them, but the buffalo and the Sun Dance stayed the same. Now they were both gone, together."[70] With buffalo gone, Kiowas began to lease grasslands to cattlemen, as indicated by the drawing of a cow (9).

The calendar ends with a measles epidemic in 1892 (10). The epidemic broke out at the reservation school and spread rapidly when the school superintendent sent the sick children home. When James Mooney visited the Kiowas in early summer the disease had spent its force, but deaths were still occurring every day or two and its impact was evident everywhere: "nearly every woman in the tribe had her hair cut off close to her head and her face and arms gashed by knives, in token of mourning, while some had even chopped off a finger as a sign of grief at the loss of a favorite child. The men also had their hair cut off at the shoulders and had discarded their usual ornaments and finery." Bereaved relatives wailed, burned blankets, tipis, and other property, and shot horses and dogs over the graves of their owners, "to accompany them to the world of shades." The scenes of mourning continued for months.[71]

The calendar provides a tribal record of the years when "the West was lost," when peoples like the Kiowas went from a life of mobility and independence to one of confinement and dependence. Those Kiowas who survived the wars and diseases of the nineteenth century had to learn new ways to survive in the world that had been imposed on them.[72]

QUESTIONS FOR CONSIDERATION

1. What does the Dohasan Calendar suggest about different ways of understanding and remembering history?

2. What things seem to have been important to the Kiowas? Are they the same kind of things that non-Indians might have recalled and recorded during these years?

3. What does the calendar tell us about Kiowa relations with other Indian tribes and about how the Kiowas witnessed their world changing before their eyes?

The Sioux, the Treaty of Fort Laramie, and the Black Hills

LAKOTA PEOPLE MAINTAIN THAT THEY EMERGED into this world from the Black Hills in western South Dakota. French sources and most historians locate the Sioux on the headwaters of the Mississippi in Minnesota at the time of first contact with Europeans, and the Crows, Kiowas, and other tribes have historical connections to the Black Hills. But whenever and however they arrived there, the Lakotas came to regard the Black Hills, Paha Sapa, as sacred ground, the center of their universe, "the heart of everything that is." The Sioux struggle to keep and to recover the Black Hills has been and remains at the heart of their relations with the United States.

In the first Treaty of Fort Laramie in 1851, the United States recognized the territory of the Lakotas or Teton Sioux as covering most of the present-day states of North and South Dakota and parts of Nebraska, Montana, and Wyoming, an enormous expanse of territory constituting approximately 5 percent of the continental United States. The Black Hills lay within that territory.

When the United States attempted to establish the Bozeman Trail through Sioux Territory to gold mines in Montana (see Map 6.1, "Conflicts with the United States and Indian Land Cessions, 1850–1890," page 312), the Lakotas and their Northern Cheyenne and Arapaho allies fought the army to a standstill in the so-called Red Cloud's War, which took its name from the Oglala Sioux chief who led the charge. They laid siege to the posts the army built along the trail at Fort Reno, Fort Phil Kearny, and Fort C. F. Smith, and in December 1866 they annihilated the entire command of Captain William Fetterman, who had boasted that with eighty men he could ride through the Sioux Nation. Faced with embarrassing defeats, the United States looked for peace. The result was the second Treaty of Fort Laramie in 1868, one of the most significant and controversial treaties in the history of Indian–U.S. relations. It ended the war, planted the seeds for another war, and provided the legal foundation for Sioux claims to the Black Hills for more than a hundred years.

The U.S. Peace Commission consisted of military men — Generals William Tecumseh Sherman, William S. Harney, Alfred H. Terry, Christopher C. Augur, and John B. Sanborn — and politicians and reformers — Commissioner of Indian Affairs Nathaniel G. Taylor, Senator John B. Henderson, and Indian agent Samuel F. Tappan. The commission's goals were to end warfare on the Plains and to consolidate the Indians on reservations.

In the spring of 1868, the commissioners dispatched messengers to the Indian encampments in the Powder River country, inviting Red Cloud, Old Man Afraid of His Horses, and their followers to meet them at Fort Laramie. The more compliant bands who lived close to the fort — nicknamed the "Laramie loafers" — were happy to sign the treaty and receive gifts. Spotted Tail's Brulés met the commissioners in April. "I have helped you to make peace and I will help you again," Spotted Tail told them. Another Brulé, Baptiste, made clear that the United States had caused the war by placing soldiers and forts in Sioux country. Remove them, he said. "I do not want them to stay another night. . . . As long as they remain here it will look as if this road is a warpath."[73] Red Cloud and the more militant Oglalas remained aloof: "We are on the mountains looking down on the soldiers and the forts," he said. "When we see the soldiers moving away and the forts abandoned, then I will come down and talk."[74]

Over a six-month period, 159 chiefs from ten Sioux bands "touched the pen" to the treaty. The commissioners left in May without meeting Red Cloud. Only after the forts were abandoned and burned did Red Cloud ride into Fort Laramie and sign the treaty with the post commander in November. Having signed the treaty, Red Cloud kept it. The United States did not.

By the terms of the treaty, both sides agreed to end the war and live in peace. But the treaty also contained the seeds of future conflicts and included contradictory provisions. The government undertook to punish persons under U.S. jurisdiction who committed offenses against the Indians, but it also secured agreement that any Indians committing offenses against American citizens should be delivered to the United States for punishment. The Americans agreed to close the Bozeman Trail, but, having just fought and won a war to close one road, the Lakotas now agreed to allow other roads and railroads to be built through their hunting grounds. The government set aside South Dakota west of the Missouri River as the "Great Sioux Reservation" and confirmed the country north of the North Platte River and east of the Bighorn Mountains as unceded hunting territory. But Article 11 of the treaty stipulated that, at some future date, the Indians "will relinquish all right to occupy permanently the territory outside their reservation." The treaty guaranteed the Indians the right to hunt north of the North Platte "so long as the buffalo may range thereon in sufficient numbers to justify the chase"; but the campaign to exterminate the buffalo herds was already under way on the southern Plains and would soon spread north. The treaty contained provisions for transforming the Indians into farmers who would "compel" their children to attend schools where they would be educated out of Lakota ways and into American ways. The treaty supposedly guaranteed the northern Plains to the Lakotas, but Congress created Wyoming Territory that same year. The treaty also stipulated that no further cessions of reservation lands would be valid unless agreed to by three-quarters of the adult male Indian population.

The treaty's true purpose is clear. Military historian John Gray described it as "so exclusively a white man's device . . . that it served primarily as an instrument of chicanery and a weapon of aggression." He had no doubt that the contradictions contained in the Fort Laramie treaty were inserted deliberately, to obtain from the Indians in peace what the army had been unable to seize in war:

> Here is a solemn treaty that cedes territory admittedly unceded; that confines the Indian to a reservation while allowing him to roam elsewhere; and that guarantees against trespass, unless a trespasser appears! The Indian was given to understand that he retained his full right to live in the old way in a vast unceded territory without trespass or molestation from whites. The treaty does indeed say precisely this. The fact that it also denies it, was no fault of the Indian. It was the Commission that wrote in the contradictions. There can be only one explanation — they designed one set of provisions to beguile and another to enforce.

Proof of Gray's contention came the year after the treaty was signed. In June 1869, General Philip Sheridan issued a general order: all Indians on reservations were under the control and jurisdiction of their agents; outside the limits of their reservations they were under military jurisdiction "and as a rule will be considered hostile." The "unceded territory" had become "white territory."[75]

As had been the case in treaty councils between eastern Indians and European colonists, the Treaty of Fort Laramie represented a diplomatic forum that the participants approached with different expectations and understandings. For the Indians, who lived in an oral culture, the council, the spoken words, and the accompanying rituals of smoking together in peace were the important things. For the Americans, these parleys were just the prelude to the "real thing": a written document on which the Indian delegates recorded their agreement by "touching the pen" or making an X after their names.[76] As in the forest diplomacy of the eighteenth century, so in the Plains diplomacy of the nineteenth century, Indians affixed their names to documents that sometimes differed greatly from what they had said in council. Sometimes Indian delegates changed their minds or succumbed to persuasion or coercion. Sometimes errors in translation created genuine misunderstandings. Sometimes Indians were deceived into signing documents that contained statements they were not aware of, and to which they would never have agreed. "In 1868, men came out and brought papers. We could not read them and they did not tell us truly what was in them," said Red Cloud in a speech to the Cooper Union in New York in 1870. "We thought the treaty was to remove the forts and for us to cease from fighting." Another Sioux delegate, Bear in the Grass, said "these words of the treaty were never explained. It was merely said that the treaty was for peace and friendship among the whites. When we took hold of the pen they said they would take the troops away so we could raise our children."[77] From that day to this, Sioux people have been convinced that the treaty was altered after the delegates signed it. At a gathering of Northern Plains Native Nations at Fort Laramie in 1996, tribal elder Homer Whirl Wind Horse accused white men of always speaking with duplicity. "With one of their tongues they tell us good things, and the other tongue is a pencil," he said. "We understood the words of the treaty, but when they wrote it down, the pencil changed it."[78]

Whatever contradictions and deceptions the Treaty of Fort Laramie contained, it soon became quite clear that the United States would break it. In 1873 Pierre Jean De Smet, a Jesuit missionary, reported that there was gold in the Black Hills. The next year, George Armstrong Custer led a military expedition into the hills and confirmed the news. The United States was in the grip of a severe depression; it would not leave the Lakotas in undisturbed possession of the gold-rich Black Hills, no matter what the Fort Laramie treaty said.

As miners began to risk their lives by trespassing on Lakota hunting grounds, the government tried to buy the Black Hills. A commission traveled to Lakota country but met stiff opposition. Some chiefs refused to discuss selling the hills; Little Big Man threatened to kill the first Indian who even spoke of doing so. Others asked for far more than the United States was prepared to offer: Red Cloud demanded enough money to feed his people for seven generations. The commission returned to Washington and the army took over.

The Northwest Ordinance of 1787 had declared that the United States would not disturb Indians in the rightful possession of their lands, except in "just and lawful wars authorized by Congress." The army withdrew the troops that, under the terms of the Fort Laramie treaty, were supposed to prevent miners from entering the Black Hills. An ultimatum ordered all Lakota and Cheyenne bands to report to the agencies by January 31, 1876, and then declared that those who failed to come in were "hostile." The war against them *would* be just and lawful.

The army launched a three-pronged invasion to trap and crush Lakota resistance, but things did not go according to plan. Crazy Horse and his warriors turned back General George Crook's army at the Battle of the Rosebud in mid-June. Eight days later, on June 25, the Lakotas and Cheyennes routed an attack on their village in the Little Bighorn valley and annihilated Custer's immediate command. (See Picture Essay, "The Battle of the Little Bighorn in Myth and History," pages 367–71.) The army won its war, but it did so in a series of mopping-up operations, chasing scattered Indian bands over the northern Plains, attacking winter encampments, and killing women, children, and ponies in the snow. Crazy Horse surrendered and was killed. Sitting Bull fled to Canada.

With Lakota resistance broken, another commission, this one led by George Manypenny, arrived on the reservations to obtain consent to the transfer to the United States of the "unceded territory" that included the Black Hills. Congress cut funding for rations to the agencies until the Lakotas agreed to cede the land. Lakota people recalled having to negotiate under the guns of American soldiers. The Lakotas protested but the reservation chiefs signed. The commissioners managed to secure the agreement of only about 10 percent of the adult males — about 65 percent short of what the Treaty of Fort Laramie required — but, in the wake of the "Custer Massacre," the government was in no mood to worry about such niceties. In February 1877 Congress passed a law taking the Black Hills and extinguishing all Sioux rights outside the Great Sioux Reservation.

The "Great Sioux Nation" had shrunk in less than twenty years from about 134 million acres as recognized in the 1851 Treaty of Fort Laramie to less than 15 million acres. It continued to shrink. The Sioux Act of 1888 applied the Dawes Allotment Act (see pages 385–87) to the Great Sioux Reservation, opening "surplus lands" to settlement and dividing the Lakotas into six separate reservations (Map 6.4).

Congress passed another Sioux Act in 1889 and dispatched another commission. This one included General George Crook, a veteran of wars against both the Apaches and the Sioux. Crook told the Indians there was a flood coming and they must save what they could or see it all swept away. He applied divide-and-conquer tactics. The commission found that "it was impossible to deal with the Indians as a body in general councils." The Lakotas in their own councils had already decided against agreement with the U.S. government, and they presented the commissioners with a united front. The commissioners then "endeavored to convince individuals that substantial advantages to the Indians as a whole would result from an acceptance of the bill." For a time, they said in their report, "the task seemed almost hopeless, but persistence prevailed and interest was awakened. As soon as the question became debatable the situation changed and success was assured."[79] Congress cut the amount of rations the commission promised, and another

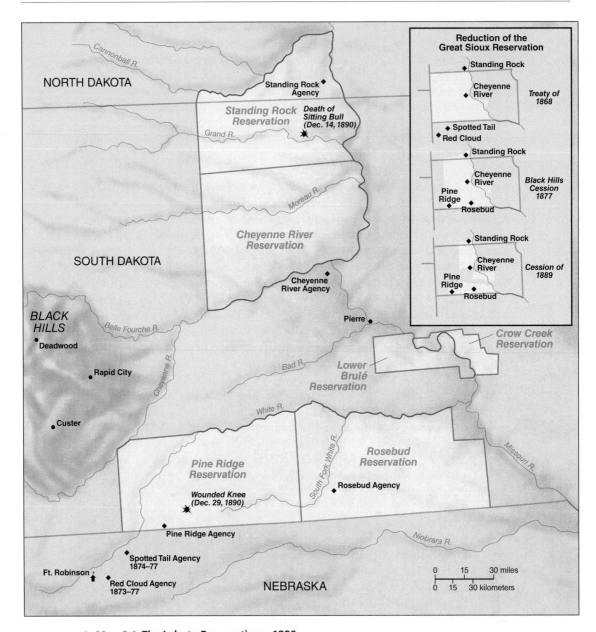

◆ Map 6.4 **The Lakota Reservations, 1890**

The Treaty of Fort Laramie in 1868 recognized the territory west of the Missouri River in South Dakota as the Great Sioux Reservation. Following the discovery of gold in the Black Hills and the defeat of the Sioux after the Little Bighorn, the United States systematically reduced Sioux territory, depriving the Lakotas of the sacred Black Hills and dividing them into six separate reservations.

SOURCE: Based on maps by Harry Scott taken from *The Indian Frontier of the American West, 1846–1890*, by Robert Utley. Copyright © 1984 University of New Mexico Press. Used by permission.

nine million acres was stripped away from the reservation. Angry and divided, Lakota people watched as settlers moved onto lands that less than twenty-five years earlier had been set apart for their "absolute and undisturbed use and occupation."

The Sioux never accepted the loss of the Black Hills.[80] In 1923 they filed suit with the U.S. Court of Claims demanding compensation. The Court of Claims dragged its feet until 1942 and then dismissed the claim. The U.S. Supreme Court refused to review the decision of the Court of Claims. With the creation of the Indian Claims Commission in 1946, the Sioux tried again, but in 1954 the commission dismissed the case on the grounds that the claim had already been denied. In 1956, the Sioux fired their lawyer and had their claim reinstated on the basis that they had been represented by "inadequate counsel." Despite the Justice Department's attempt to secure a ruling granting "extraordinary relief" from continued litigation, in 1974 the Indian Claims Commission decided that the government had taken the land in violation of the Fifth Amendment because it had not paid just compensation. The commission awarded the Sioux $17.5 million plus interest. The government appealed, and the Court of Claims reversed the decision on the basis of *res judicata,* stating that the claim had already been litigated and decided back in 1942. But the court declared that "a more ripe and rank case of dishonorable dealings will never, in all probability, be found in our history," and opened the door for the Sioux to seek compensation on the grounds of dishonorable dealings.[81] In 1978 Congress passed an act enabling the Court of Claims to rehear the case. The Court of Claims found that the United States had taken the Black Hills unconstitutionally and reinstated the $17.5 million award, plus 5 percent interest, for a total of $122.5 million. The Justice Department appealed the decision, and finally, in 1980 — fifty-seven years after the Sioux first brought suit — the Supreme Court heard the Black Hills case. It found that the annexation act of 1877 constituted "a taking of tribal property which had been set aside by the treaty of Fort Laramie for the Sioux's exclusive occupation" and upheld the award.

The Sioux, having won their long-sought victory, turned down the money. T-shirts and bumper stickers echoed their position that "The Black Hills Are Not For Sale." Instead, Sioux people demanded that the United States return the Black Hills to them and pay the money as compensation for the billions of dollars of wealth that had been extracted and the damages done while whites illegally occupied the hills. In 1981 Russell Means and other activists established Yellow Thunder Camp in the Black Hills and announced it was the first step in reoccupying the land. Senator Bill Bradley of New Jersey and others proposed compromises, but most Sioux remained adamant that the Black Hills must be returned. The award remains uncollected and, with accumulated interest, now stands at more than $1.5 billion. The conflict between the Sioux and the United States remains unresolved.

By reprinting a Sioux statement from the councils that preceded the Treaty of Fort Laramie, as well as the final treaty itself, the following selections provide a sense of the concerns the Indians voiced as well as the written articles by which they signified their agreement to live within reservation boundaries and embark on the "white man's road."

IRON SHELL, BRULÉ SIOUX
"We want you to take away the forts from the country." (April 28, 1868)

I am getting to be an old man. . . . My father and grandfather used to be with the whites, and I have been with them, too. We used to treat them well, I do not recollect that there was any war while we were with the whites. We used to take pity on one another and did nothing bad to each other while we were together. I know that the whites are like the grass on the prairie. Anybody that takes anything from the whites must pay for it. You have come into my country without my consent and spread your soldiers all over it. I have looked around for the cause of the trouble and I can not see that my young men were the cause of it. All the bad things that have been done, you have made the road for it. That is the truth. I love the whites. You whites went all over my country, killing my young men, and disturbing everything in my country. My heart is not made out of rock, but of flesh, but I have a strong heart. All the bad deeds that have been done I have had no hand in, neither have any of our young men. I want to hear you give us good advice. I came here for that purpose. We helped you to stop this war between us and the whites. You have put us in misery; also these old traders whom the war has stopped. We want you to set us all right and put us back the same as in old times.

We want you to take away the forts from the country. That will leave big room for the Indians to live in. If you succeed about the forests all the game will come back and we will have plenty to eat. If you want the Indian to live do that and we will have a chance to live. One above us has created all of us, the whites the same as the Indians, and he will take pity on us. Our God has put us on earth to live in the way we do, to live on game. Our great father we depend on at Washington. We do not deliberate for ourselves, and we want him to take pity on us. Do you think that our God is for us the same as for the whites? I have prayed to God and asked him to make me succeed, and He has allowed it to me. I succeeded often. Your commissioners want to make peace and take pity on the Indians. Take away all these things if you intend to make peace, and we will live happy and be at peace. All we have is the land and the sky above. This war has set an example to our young men to make war on the whites. If it had not been for that we should have been at peace all the time.

You generally pick on bad white men to give them office which is the cause of our being put in trouble. From this our young men have learned all these bad things and we are in misery and have a hard time. Me and some others of the sensible men have been put in trouble by you. I have listened to your advice, General Sanborn, and I told the others to listen to you. You sent messengers to us last winter and we have come in to you. A few of us are inclined to do well out of way that are for war, and we have pushed for you to make peace with you. The Single Horn [a chief, probably Lone Horn or One Horn] went to the Missouri. I brought a chief of the Sans Arcs to you, and I want you to send word by him to the Sans Arcs when he goes away.

You are passing over the foolish acts of our young men, and we are pleased at that. Try to get all the Indians in and give them good advice and it will be all right. Push, push as hard as you can, and in that way you will take great pity on me. I want to live. It goes slow, and there are a great many Indians who are pushing for peace. Go slow yourselves and you will succeed. Get through with the Brulés at once. I want to go

SOURCE: Vine Deloria Jr. and Raymond De Mallie, intro., *Proceedings of the Great Peace Commission of 1867–1868* (Washington, D.C.: Institute for the Development of Indian Law, 1975), 106–9, 117–20; Charles J. Kappler, ed., *Indian Affairs, Laws and Treaties.* 2 vols. (Washington, D.C.: U.S. Government Printing Office, 1904), 2:998–1007.

home. You will have plenty of Indians in and will have enough to do. You will hear pretty much the same from the different tribes of Indians as you have heard from me. Three moons is too long in which to move the forts. I would like them to be moved before. Winter will come before that time. . . .

Those forts are all that is in the way — wagons coming backward and forward. You have taken Spotted Tail away from me and have him to go around with you. That is good. I expect you will listen to him when he talks with you. You are right in bringing him here. There are a very few who are out yet. Often when you are persecuting me and the Indians with papers we do not get well thought of. I have one recommendation which I take good care of. I always talk to the whites in a good way and they generally listen to me. Today you tell us you will take pity on us. I have listened to it all. I will recollect all you have to say.

Our country is filling up with whites. Our great father has no sense; he lets our country be filled up. That is the way I think sometimes. Our great father is shutting up on us and making us a very small country. That is bad. For all that I have a strong heart. I have patience and pass over it, although you come over here and get all our gold, minerals, and skins. I pass over it all and do not get mad. I have always given the whites more than they have given me.

Yesterday you tell us we would have a council and last night I did not sleep; I was so glad. Now, I would like you to pick some good sensible young men, from one to four, and send them out, men who can be depended upon. I name Blue Horse, myself, and I want him to pick the others. We have been speaking very well together, and I am glad we get along so smoothly. The last thing I have to ask you about are the forts. This is sufficient and all right. We have got through talking. Give us our share of the goods and send them over to our village. We want to get back immediately as our children are crying for food. What you are doing with the Brulés will be a good example to the others. It will encourage them. We do not want to stay here and loaf upon you. . . .

I will always sign any treaty you ask me to do, but you have always made away with them, broke them. The whites always break them, and that is the way that war has come up.

(The treaty was here signed by the chiefs and head soldiers of the Brulés.)

Treaty with the Sioux — Brulé, Oglala, Miniconjou, Yanktonai, Hunkpapa, Blackfeet, Cuthead, Two Kettle, Sans Arcs, and Santee — and Arapaho (1868)

Apr. 29, 1868.
15 Stats., 635.
Ratified,
Feb. 16, 1869.
Proclaimed,
Feb. 24, 1869.

Articles of a treaty made and concluded by and between Lieutenant-General William T. Sherman, General William S. Harney, General Alfred H. Terry, General C. C. Augur, J. B. Henderson, Nathaniel G. Taylor, John B. Sanborn, and Samuel F. Tappan, duly appointed commissioners on the part of the United States, and the different bands of the Sioux Nation of Indians, by their chiefs and headmen, whose names are hereto subscribed, they being duly authorized to act in the premises.

War to cease and peace to be kept.

ARTICLE 1. From this day forward all war between the parties to this agreement shall forever cease. The Government of the United States desires peace, and its honor is hereby pledged to keep it. The Indians desire peace, and they now pledge their honor to maintain it.

Offenders against the Indians to be arrested, etc.

If bad men among the whites, or among other people subject to the authority of the United States, shall commit any wrong upon the person or property of the Indians, the United States will, upon proof made to the agent and forwarded to the Commissioner of Indian Affairs at Washington City, proceed at once to cause the offender to be arrested and punished according to the laws of the United States, and also reimburse the injured person for the loss sustained.

Wrongdoers against the whites to be punished.

Damages.

If bad men among the Indians shall commit a wrong or depredation upon the person or property of any one, white, black, or Indian, subject to the authority of the United States, and at peace therewith, the Indians herein named solemnly agree that they will, upon proof made to their agent and notice by him, deliver up the wrong-doer to the United States, to be tried and punished according to its laws; and in case they wilfully refuse so to do, the person injured shall be reimbursed for his loss from the annuities or other moneys due or to become due to them under this or other treaties made with the United States. And the President, on advising with the Commissioner of Indian Affairs, shall prescribe such rules and regulations for ascertaining damages under the provisions of this article as in his judgment may be proper. But no one sustaining loss while violating the provisions of this treaty or the laws of the United States shall be reimbursed therefor.

Reservation boundaries.

Certain persons not to enter or reside thereon.

ARTICLE 2. The United States agrees that the following district of country, to wit, viz: commencing on the east bank of the Missouri River where the forty-sixth parallel of north latitude crosses the same, thence along low-water mark down said east bank to a point opposite where the northern line of the State of Nebraska strikes the river, thence west across said river, and along the northern line of Nebraska to the one hundred and fourth degree of longitude west from Greenwich, thence north on said meridian to a point where the forty-sixth parallel of north latitude intercepts the same, thence due east along said parallel to the place of beginning; and in addition thereto, all existing reservations on the east bank of said river shall be, and the same is, set apart for the absolute and undisturbed use and occupation of the Indians herein named, and for such other friendly tribes or individual Indians as from time to time they may be willing, with the consent of the United States, to admit amongst them; and the United States now solemnly agrees that no persons except those herein designated and authorized so to do, and except such officers, agents and employés of the Government as may be authorized to enter upon Indian reservations in discharge of duties enjoined by law, shall ever be permitted to pass over, settle upon, or reside in the territory described in this article, or in such territory as may be added to this reservation for the use of said Indians, and henceforth they will and do hereby relinquish all claims or right in and to any portion of the United States or Territories, except such as is embraced within the limits aforesaid, and except as hereinafter provided.

Additional arable land to be added, if, etc.

ARTICLE 3. If it should appear from actual survey or other satisfactory examination of said tract of land that it contains less than one hundred and sixty acres of tillable land for each person who, at the time, may be authorized to reside on it under the provisions of this treaty, and a very considerable number of such persons shall be disposed to commence cultivating the soil as farmers, the United States agrees to set apart, for the use of said Indians, as herein provided, such additional quantity of arable land, adjoining to said reservation, or as near to the same as it can be obtained, as may be required to provide the necessary amount.

Buildings on reservation.   ARTICLE 4. The United States agrees, at its own proper expense, to construct at some place on the Missouri River, near the center of said reservation, where timber and water may be convenient, the following buildings, to wit: a warehouse, a store-room for the use of the agent in storing goods belonging to the Indians, to cost not less than twenty-five hundred dollars; an agency-building for the residence of the agent, to cost not exceeding three thousand dollars; a residence for the physician, to cost not more than three thousand dollars; and five other buildings, for a carpenter, farmer, blacksmith, miller, and engineer, each to cost not exceeding two thousand dollars; also a school-house or mission-building, so soon as a sufficient number of children can be induced by the agent to attend school, which shall not cost exceeding five thousand dollars.

The United States agrees further to cause to be erected on said reservation, near the other buildings herein authorized, a good steam circular-saw mill, with a grist-mill and shingle-machine attached to the same, to cost not exceeding eight thousand dollars.

Agent's residence, office, and duties.   ARTICLE 5. The United States agrees that the agent for said Indians shall in the future make his home at the agency-building; that he shall reside among them, and keep an office open at all times for the purpose of prompt and diligent inquiry into such matters of complaint by and against the Indians as may be presented for investigation under the provisions of their treaty stipulations, as also for the faithful discharge of other duties enjoined on him by law. In all cases of depredation on person or property he shall cause the evidence to be taken in writing and forwarded, together with his findings, to the Commissioner of Indian Affairs, whose decision, subject to the revision of the Secretary of the Interior, shall be binding on the parties to this treaty.

Heads of families may select lands for farming.   ARTICLE 6. If any individual belonging to said tribes of Indians, or legally incorporated with them, being the head of a family, shall desire to commence farming, he shall have the privilege to select, in the presence and with the assistance of the agent then in charge, a tract of land within said reservation, not exceeding three hundred and twenty acres in extent, which tract, when so selected, certified, and recorded in the "land-book," as herein directed, shall cease to be held in common, but the same may be occupied and held in the exclusive possession of the person selecting it, and of his family, so long as he or they may continue to cultivate it.

Others may select land for cultivation.   Any person over eighteen years of age, not being the head of a family, may in like manner select and cause to be certified to him or her, for purposes of cultivation, a quantity of land not exceeding eighty acres in extent, and thereupon be entitled to the exclusive possession of the same as above directed.

Certificates.   For each tract of land so selected a certificate, containing a description thereof and the name of the person selecting it, with a certificate endorsed thereon that the same has been recorded, shall be delivered to the party entitled to it, by the agent, after the same shall have been recorded by him in a book to be kept in his office, subject to inspection, which said book shall be known as the "Sioux Land-Book."

Surveys. The President may, at any time, order a survey of the reservation, and, when so surveyed, Congress shall provide for protecting the rights of said settlers in their improvements, and may fix the character of the title held by each. *Alienation and descent of property.* The United States may pass such laws on the subject of alienation and descent of property between the Indians and their descendants as may be thought proper. And it is further stipulated that any male Indians, over eighteen years of age, of any band or tribe that is or shall hereafter become a party to this treaty, who now is or who shall hereafter become a resident or occupant of any reservation or Territory not included in the tract of country designated and described in this treaty for the permanent home of the Indians, which is not mineral land, nor reserved by the United States for special purposes other than Indian occupation, and who shall have made improvements thereon of the value of two hundred dollars or more, and continuously occupied the same as a homestead for the term of three years, shall be entitled to receive from the *Certain Indians may receive patents for 160 acres of land.* United States a patent for one hundred and sixty acres of land including his said improvements, the same to be in the form of the legal subdivisions of the surveys of the public lands. Upon application in writing, sustained by the proof of two disinterested witnesses, made to the register of the local land-office when the land sought to be entered is within a land district, and when the tract sought to be entered is not in any land district, then upon said application and proof being made to the Commissioner of the General Land-Office, and the right of such Indian or Indians to enter such tract or tracts of land shall accrue and be perfect from the date of his first improvements thereon, and *Such Indians receiving patents to become citizens of the United States.* shall continue as long as he continues his residence and improvements, and no longer. And any Indian or Indians receiving a patent for land under the foregoing provisions, shall thereby and from thenceforth become and be a citizen of the United States, and be entitled to all the privileges and immunities of such citizens, and shall, at the same time, retain all his rights to benefits accruing to Indians under this treaty.

Education. ARTICLE 7. In order to insure the civilization of the Indians entering into this treaty, the necessity of education is admitted, especially of such of them as are or may be settled on said agricultural reservations, and they therefore pledge *Children to attend school.* themselves to compel their children, male and female, between the ages of six and sixteen years, to attend school; and it is hereby made the duty of the agent for said Indians to see that this stipulation is strictly complied with; and the United States *Schoolhouses and teachers.* agrees that for every thirty children between said ages who can be induced or compelled to attend school, a house shall be provided and a teacher competent to teach the elementary branches of an English education shall be furnished, who will reside among said Indians and faithfully discharge his or her duties as a teacher. The provisions of this article to continue for not less than twenty years.

Seeds and agricultural implements. ARTICLE 8. When the head of a family or lodge shall have selected lands and received his certificate as above directed, and the agent shall be satisfied that he intends in good faith to commence cultivating the soil for a living, he shall be entitled to receive seeds and agricultural implements for the first year, not exceeding in value one hundred dollars, and for each succeeding year he shall continue to farm, for a period of three years more, he shall be entitled to receive seeds and implements as aforesaid, not exceeding in value twenty-five dollars.

*Instructions in farming.*And it is further stipulated that such persons as commence farming shall receive instruction from the farmer herein provided for, and whenever more than one hundred persons shall enter upon the cultivation of the soil, a second blacksmith shall be provided, with such iron, steel, and other material as may be needed.

Instructions in farming.

Second blacksmith.

Physician, farmer, etc., may be withdrawn.

Additional appropriation in such cases.

ARTICLE 9. At any time after ten years from the making of this treaty, the United States shall have the privilege of withdrawing the physician, farmer, blacksmith, carpenter, engineer, and miller herein provided for, but in case of such withdrawal, an additional sum thereafter of ten thousand dollars per annum shall be devoted to the education of said Indians, and the Commissioner of Indian Affairs shall, upon careful inquiry into their condition, make such rules and regulations for the expenditure of said sum as will best promote the educational and moral improvement of said tribes.

Delivery of goods in lieu of money or other annuities.

ARTICLE 10. In lieu of all sums of money or other annuities provided to be paid to the Indians herein named, under any treaty or treaties heretofore made, the United States agrees to deliver at the agency-house on the reservation herein named, on or before the first day of August of each year, for thirty years, the following articles, to wit:

Clothing.

For each male person over fourteen years of age, a suit of good substantial woolen clothing, consisting of coat, pantaloons, flannel shirt, hat, and a pair of home-made socks.

For each female over twelve years of age, a flannel skirt, or the goods necessary to make it, a pair of woolen hose, twelve yards of calico, and twelve yards of cotton domestics.

For the boys and girls under the ages named, such flannel and cotton goods as may be needed to make each a suit as aforesaid, together with a pair of woolen hose for each.

Census.

And in order that the Commissioner of Indian Affairs may be able to estimate properly for the articles herein named, it shall be the duty of the agent each year to forward to him a full and exact census of the Indians, on which the estimate from year to year can be based.

Other necessary articles.

And in addition to the clothing herein named, the sum of ten dollars for each person entitled to the beneficial effects of this treaty shall be annually appropriated for a period of thirty years, while such persons roam and hunt, and twenty dollars for each person who engages in farming, to be used by the Secretary of the Interior in the purchase of such articles as from time to time the condition and necessities of the Indians may indicate to be proper. And if within the thirty years, at any time, it shall appear that the amount of money needed for clothing under this article can be appropriated to better uses for the Indians named herein, Congress may, by law, change the appropriation to other purposes; but in no event shall the amount of this appropriation be withdrawn or discontinued for the

Appropriation to continue for thirty years.

Army officer to
attend the
delivery.

period named. And the President shall annually detail an officer of the Army to be present and attest the delivery of all the goods herein named to the Indians, and he shall inspect and report on the quantity and quality of the goods and the manner of their delivery. And it is hereby expressly stipulated that each Indian over the age of four years, who shall have removed to and settled permanently upon said reservation and complied with the stipulations of this treaty, shall be entitled to receive from the United States, for the period of four years after he

Meat and flour.

shall have settled upon said reservation, one pound of meat and one pound of flour per day, provided the Indians cannot furnish their own subsistence at an earlier date. And it is further stipulated that the United States will furnish and deliver to each lodge of Indians or family of persons legally incorporated with them, who shall remove to the reservation herein described and commence

Cows and oxen.

farming, one good American cow, and one good well-broken pair of American oxen within sixty days after such lodge or family shall have so settled upon said reservation.

Right to occupy
territory outside
of the reservation
surrendered.

ARTICLE 11. In consideration of the advantages and benefits conferred by this treaty, and the many pledges of friendship by the United States, the tribes who are parties to this agreement hereby stipulate that they will relinquish all right to occupy permanently the territory outside their reservation as herein defined, but

Right to hunt
reserved.

yet reserve the right to hunt on any lands north of North Platte, and on the Republican Fork of the Smoky Hill River, so long as the buffalo may range thereon in such numbers as to justify the chase. And they, the said Indians, further expressly agree:

Agreements as
to railroads.

1st. That they will withdraw all opposition to the construction of the railroads now being built on the plains.

2d. That they will permit the peaceful construction of any railroad not passing over their reservation as herein defined.

Emigrants, etc.

3d. That they will not attack any persons at home, or travelling, nor molest or disturb any wagon-trains, coaches, mules, or cattle belonging to the people of the United States, or to persons friendly therewith.

Women and
children.

4th. They will never capture, or carry off from the settlements, white women or children.

White men.

5th. They will never kill or scalp white men, nor attempt to do them harm.

Pacific Railroad,
wagon roads, etc.

6th. They withdraw all pretence of opposition to the construction of the railroad now being built along the Platte River and westward to the Pacific Ocean, and they will not in future object to the construction of railroads, wagon-roads, mail-stations, or other works of utility or necessity, which may be ordered or permitted by the laws of the United States. But should such roads or other works be constructed on the lands of their reservation, the Government will pay the tribe

Damages for
crossing their
reservation.

whatever amount of damage may be assessed by three disinterested commissioners to be appointed by the President for that purpose, one of said commissioners to be a chief or head-man of the tribe.

Military posts
and roads.

7th. They agree to withdraw all opposition to the military posts or roads now established south of the North Platte River, or that may be established, not in violation of treaties heretofore made or hereafter to be made with any of the Indian tribes.

No treaty for cession of reservation to be valid unless, etc.

ARTICLE 12. No treaty for the cession of any portion or part of the reservation herein described which may be held in common shall be of any validity or force as against the said Indians, unless executed and signed by at least three-fourths of all the adult male Indians, occupying or interested in the same; and no cession by the tribe shall be understood or construed in such manner as to deprive, without his consent, any individual member of the tribe of his rights to any tract of land selected by him, as provided in Article 6 of this treaty.

United States to furnish physician, teachers, etc.

ARTICLE 13. The United States hereby agrees to furnish annually to the Indians the physician, teachers, carpenter, miller, engineer, farmer, and blacksmiths as herein contemplated, and that such appropriations shall be made from time to time, on the estimates of the Secretary of the Interior, as will be sufficient to employ such persons.

Presents for crops.

ARTICLE 14. It is agreed that the sum of five hundred dollars annually, for three years from date, shall be expended in presents to the ten persons of said tribe who in the judgment of the agent may grow the most valuable crops for the respective year.

Reservation to be permanent home of tribes.

ARTICLE 15. The Indians herein named agree that when the agency house or other buildings shall be constructed on the reservation named they will regard said reservation their permanent home, and they will make no permanent settlement elsewhere; but they shall have the right, subject to the conditions and modifications of this treaty, to hunt, as stipulated in Article 11 hereof.

Unceded Indian territory.

ARTICLE 16. The United States hereby agrees and stipulates that the country north of the North Platte River and east of the summit of the Bighorn Mountains shall be held and considered to be unceded Indian territory, and also stipulates and agrees that no white person or persons shall be permitted

Not to be occupied by whites, etc.

to settle upon or occupy any portion of the same; or without the consent of the Indians first had and obtained, to pass through the same; and it is further agreed by the United States that within ninety days after the conclusion of peace with all the bands of the Sioux Nation, the military posts now established in the territory in this article named shall be abandoned, and that the road leading to them and by them to the settlements in the Territory of Montana shall be closed.

Effect of this treaty upon former treaties.

ARTICLE 17. It is hereby expressly understood and agreed by and between the respective parties to this treaty that the execution of this treaty and its ratification by the United States Senate shall have the effect, and shall be construed as abrogating and annulling all treaties and agreements heretofore entered into between the respective parties hereto, so far as such treaties and agreements obligate the United States to furnish and provide money, clothing, or other articles of property to such Indians and bands of Indians as become parties to this treaty, but no further.

QUESTIONS FOR CONSIDERATION

1. Which parts of the treaty are the ones the Lakota delegates were least likely to have agreed to or understood?

2. What issues did Indians and treaty commissioners view differently?

3. What do Iron Shell's talk and the text of the treaty suggest about the mechanics of treaty making and the problems and pitfalls of translation?

Chief Joseph's Plea for Freedom

WHEN LEWIS AND CLARK STUMBLED DOWN from the Lolo Trail across the Bitterroot Mountains on their way west to the Columbia River in the fall of 1805, they met the Nee-me-poo Indians, whom the French called Nez Perces (pierced noses). The Nez Perces had heard of Americans, but few if any had seen them. They could have killed the hungry and exhausted explorers, but instead they welcomed them, fed them, and helped them on their way. Lewis and Clark developed respect and admiration for them. In part, the Nez Perces were extending traditional hospitality to strangers; in part, they were eager to receive the trade, and especially the guns, that Lewis and Clark promised to bring them in return. Like their Shoshoni neighbors, the Nez Perces were hard pressed by well-armed Blackfeet who ranged to their north and kept British guns out of their reach.

The Nez Perces lived where the present states of Washington, Idaho, and Oregon meet. After they acquired horses early in the eighteenth century, they built up huge herds and gained a reputation as skilled riders and breeders. From their first meeting with Americans in 1805, they pursued policies of peaceful coexistence with the newcomers. They traded with American fur traders and attended trappers' rendezvous in the 1820s. In 1831 they sent a delegation to St. Louis searching for the "book of heaven." Presbyterian missionaries Reverend Henry Spalding and his wife answered their call and went to live and work among the Nez Perces; other missionaries followed.[82]

In 1855 the Nez Perces signed a treaty with Governor Isaac Stevens of Washington Territory that set aside a large reservation for the tribe. But immigrants pressed in ever-growing numbers and miners encroached on the reservation after gold was discovered in 1860. In 1863 the Americans negotiated a new treaty with a chief named Lawyer. The Nez Perces lost 90 percent of their land and were assigned to a reservation at Lapwai on the Clearwater River in Idaho (see Map 6.2, "Indian Reservations in the West, 1890," page 325). Like most of the Nez Perce chiefs, Tu-ke-kas, whom the whites called Old Joseph, refused to sign the treaty; his band continued to live in the Wallowa valley in northeastern Oregon. Just before he died in 1871, Old Joseph made his son promise never to sell his homeland.

Young Joseph (In-mut-too-yah-lat-lat) came under almost immediate pressure to break his promise. Settlers encroached on the Wallowa valley, and the

United States dispatched commissioners, first to investigate the situation and then to persuade Joseph to sell and join the "treaty party" on the Lapwai Reservation. The commissioners, led by Oliver Otis Howard, a one-armed Civil War general and founder of Howard University for African American students, declared that the Nez Perces who had not signed the 1863 treaty must come into the reservation or be moved there by force. The Indians pleaded to be allowed to remain on their homelands, but Howard lost patience and had one old chief, Toohoolhoolzote, arrested and thrown into the guardhouse. The Nez Perces were given until April 1, 1877, to complete the move. According to Nez Perce warrior Yellow Wolf, "That was what brought war, the arrest of this chief and showing us the rifle."[83]

Despite his promise to his father, Joseph persuaded his angry people to move rather than go to war. "None of the chiefs wanted war," said Yellow Wolf, one of the last survivors of the conflict, who related his story in 1931.[84] But events were moving beyond their control. Three young warriors killed some men along the Salmon River in revenge for the murder of a chief called Tipyahlanah Siskon, or Eagle Robe. The U.S. army was quick to respond and attacked the Nez Perces at White Bird Canyon. The Nez Perces routed the soldiers. It was the first of a series of embarrassing defeats for the United States, and the beginning of a fifteen-hundred-mile odyssey for the Nez Perces. Ably led by Joseph, his younger brother Ollokot, and the war chief Looking Glass, some eight hundred Nez Perces fled east. Fighting off Howard's troops, they crossed the Bitterroot Mountains into Montana, where they hoped to find refuge with the Crows. They rested at the Big Hole River, but Colonel John Gibbon struck them in a surprise dawn attack,

◆ **Chief Joseph**
Joseph (c. 1840–1904) is seen here shortly after his surrender to General Miles in 1877. Handsome and dignified in defeat, Joseph came to symbolize the heroic resistance of the Nez Perces. *Chief Joseph (1840–1904) 1878 (color photo), Jackson, William Henry (1843–1942)/Private Collection/Peter Newark American Pictures/Bridgeman Images.*

killing men, women, and children. The warriors rallied and fought off Gibbon's troops until their families could escape. With American troops at their backs and news that Crow scouts were riding for the army, the Nez Perces decided to head for Canada (Map 6.5). Passing through the newly created park, they frightened tourists in Yellowstone. They defeated General Samuel Sturgis's cavalry at Canyon Creek. Time and again they fended off pursuing troops. Reaching the Bear Paw Mountains, about thirty miles from the Canadian border, they halted in exhaustion, confident they had shaken off their pursuers.

But General Nelson Miles and six hundred men were rushing to head them off. Miles's Cheyenne scouts found the Nez Perces' tipis and the general attacked immediately. Caught off guard, the Nez Perces were split into groups and lost most of their horses. Ollokot and Toohoolhoolzote died in the fight. The survivors dug rifle pits and settled down for a siege. It began to snow. "Most of our few warriors left from the Big Hole had been swept as leaves before the storm," recalled Yellow Wolf. He looked around: "Children crying with cold. No fire. There could be no light. Everywhere the crying, the death wail. . . . I felt the coming end."[85] Looking Glass was killed. White Bird and about three hundred people slipped past the army

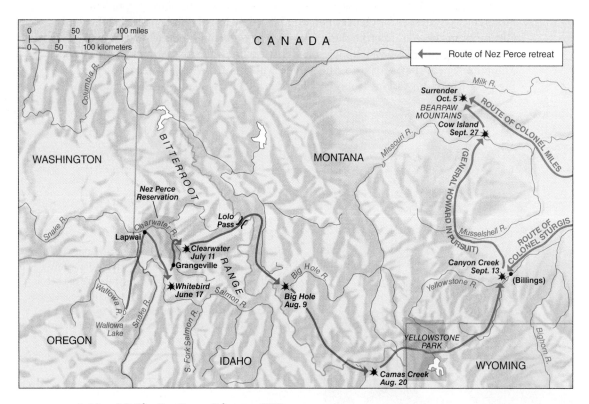

◆ **Map 6.5 The Nez Perce Odyssey, 1877**
Nez Perce men, women, and children trekked 1,500 miles and fought off pursuing American armies in a desperate but ultimately unsuccessful bid to reach freedom in Canada.

and made it to Canada. After five days of fighting and a botched attempt to take him prisoner, Joseph finally accepted Miles's entreaties to surrender. His surrender speech, as reported or attributed to him by Lieutenant Charles Erskin Wood, General Howard's aide, has become famous.

"I am tired of fighting," he said as he handed Miles his rifle. "Our chiefs are killed. Looking Glass is dead. Toohoolhoolzote is dead. The old men are all dead. It is the young men who say 'yes' or 'no.' He who led the young men [Ollokot] is dead. It is cold, and we have no blankets. The little children are freezing to death. . . . I want to have time to look for my children, and see how many of them I can find. Maybe I shall find them among the dead. Hear me, my chiefs! I am tired. My heart is sick and sad. From where the sun now stands, I will fight no more forever."[86]

The Nez Perces' epic trek and Joseph's dignified conduct and tragic speech all captured public attention. Newspapers across the country carried reports of the war and of the Nez Perces' military exploits. Even their adversaries expressed admiration. General William Tecumseh Sherman admitted that they "displayed a courage and skill that elicited universal praise; they abstained from scalping, let captive women go free, did not commit indiscriminate murder of peaceful families which is usual, and fought with almost scientific skill, using advance and rear guards, skirmish-lines and field-fortifications."[87] Ollokot and Looking Glass had been the masterminds behind the military retreat, but they were dead. Joseph, handsome and dignified in defeat, became a celebrity.

Nevertheless, the Nez Perces were betrayed again. Contrary to Miles's assurances that they would be allowed to return home if they surrendered, they were loaded on trains and sent first to Fort Leavenworth, then to Indian Territory (Oklahoma). Miles's role in the betrayal is uncertain (he argued consistently that the Nez Perces be allowed to return home, but the promises made and broken when Joseph surrendered to him are strikingly similar to the promises made and broken when Geronimo surrendered to him seven years later). Secretary of the Interior Carl Schurz and Commissioner of Indian Affairs Ezra Hayt concurred with General Sherman and General Philip Sheridan that the Nez Perces should not be allowed to return home.

Four hundred eighteen Nez Perces arrived at Fort Leavenworth in late November and were put in a winter camp close to the Missouri River. Commissioner Hayt described it as "the worst possible place that could have been selected." "We were not badly treated in captivity," said Yellow Wolf. "Only the climate killed many of us. All the newborn babies died, and many of the old people too. It was the climate. Everything so different from our old homes. No mountains, no springs, no clear running rivers. We called where we were Eeikish Pah [Hot Place]."[88] In the summer of 1878, the Nez Perces were moved to the northeastern corner of present-day Oklahoma. Huddled in refugee camps, they endured hunger, misery, and malaria. By the end of the year, reported Hayt, more than a quarter of them had died.[89]

Joseph tried to secure relief for his people. In January 1879, he and another chief, Yellow Bull, were permitted to travel to Washington to plead that the Nez Perces be sent home. Arthur Chapman accompanied them as interpreter. Chapman was a rancher who had fought against the Nez Perces during the war, but he had an Indian wife, spoke Nez Perce fluently, and was Joseph's friend. They met President Rutherford B. Hayes and Secretary Schurz and received a sympathetic hearing in the East. Joseph made a two-hour speech to a gathering of cabinet members, congressmen, and others in Lincoln Hall and received a standing ovation. In March he met with Commissioner Hayt. A month later his speech was published in the *North American Review*. Some critics have suggested that Chapman, or even the periodical's editor, embellished Joseph's words. Joseph, of course, spoke in his own language, not in English, and the speech that was printed in the *Review* may have been inspired by Joseph's talks on several occasions rather than an accurate record of a single speech. The speech clearly conveys Nez Perce views and focuses public attention on the injustices suffered by the Nez Perces, but, like the surrender speech attributed to Joseph, its language and imagery also suited American tastes and expectations that associated Indian eloquence with defeat and nobility in the face of tragedy.[90] In any case, Western politicians effectively resisted any efforts to let the Nez Perces go home.

In 1885 the Nez Perces were finally allowed to return to the Northwest. One group of about 188 people who agreed to become Christians went to the Lapwai agency. The others, about 150 people including Joseph, were sent to the Colville Reservation in Washington Territory, where they joined San Poils, Okanogans, Colvilles, Palouses, Wenatchees, and other Indians. Joseph continued the fight to be allowed to return home to the land where his father had died, the land he had promised never to sell. In 1897 he traveled to Washington again to plead his case with President William McKinley. In 1903 he met with President Theodore Roosevelt. In 1904 he had his photograph taken with his old enemy, General Howard. But Joseph did not get to return home. He died that fall, at sixty-four, probably of a heart attack, and was buried on the Colville Reservation.

CHIEF JOSEPH
An Indian's View of Indian Affairs (1879)

The United States claimed they had bought all the Nez Percés country outside the Lapwai Reservation, from Lawyer and other chiefs, but we continued to live on this land in peace until eight years ago, when white men began to come inside the bounds my father had set. We warned them against this great wrong, but they would not leave our land, and some bad blood was raised. The white men represented that we were going upon the warpath. They reported many things that were false.

SOURCE: "An Indian's Views of Indian Affairs," *North American Review*, April 1879.

The United States Government again asked for a treaty council. My father had become blind and feeble. He could no longer speak for his people. It was then that I took my father's place as chief. In this council I made my first speech to white men. I said to the agent who held the council:

"I did not want to come to this council, but I came hoping that we could save blood. The white man has no right to come here and take our country. We have never accepted any presents from the Government. Neither Lawyer nor any other chief had authority to sell this land. It has always belonged to my people. It came unclouded to them from our fathers, and we will defend this land as long as a drop of Indian blood warms the hearts of our men."

The agent said he had orders, from the Great White Chief at Washington, for us to go upon the Lapwai Reservation, and that if we obeyed he would help us in many ways. "You must move to the agency," he said. I answered him: "I will not. I do not need your help; we have plenty, and we are contented and happy if the white man will let us alone. The reservation is too small for so many people with all their stock. You can keep your presents; we can go to your towns and pay for all we need; we have plenty of horses and cattle to sell, and we won't have any help from you; we are free now; we can go where we please. Our fathers were born here. Here they lived, here they died, here are their graves. We will never leave them." The agent went away, and we had peace for a little while.

Soon after this my father sent for me. I saw he was dying. I took his hand in mine. He said: "My son, my body is returning to my mother earth, and my spirit is going very soon to see the Great Spirit Chief. When I am gone, think of your country. You are the chief of these people. They look to you to guide them. Always remember that your father never sold this country. You must stop your ears whenever you are asked to sign a treaty selling your home. A few years more, and white men will be all around you. They have their eyes on this land. My son, never forget my dying words. This country holds your father's body. Never sell the bones of your father and your mother." I pressed my father's hand and told him I would protect his grave with my life. My father smiled and passed away to the spirit land.

I buried him in that beautiful valley of winding waters. I love that land more than all the rest of the world. A man who would not love his father's grave is worse than a wild animal.

For a short time we lived quietly. But this could not last. White men had found gold in the mountains around the land of winding water. They stole many horses from us, and we could not get them back because we were Indians. The white

men told lies for each other. They drove off a great many of our cattle. Some white men branded our young cattle so they could claim them. We had no friend who would plead our cause before the law councils. It seemed to me that some of the white men in Wallowa were doing these things on purpose to get up a war. They knew that we were not strong enough to fight them. I labored hard to avoid trouble and bloodshed. We gave up some of our country to the white men, thinking that then we could have peace. We were mistaken. The white man would not let us alone. We could have avenged our wrongs many times, but we did not. Whenever the Government has asked us to help them against other Indians, we have never refused. When the white men were few and we were strong we could have killed them all off, but the Nez Percés wished to live at peace.

If we have not done so, we have not been to blame. I believe that the old treaty has never been correctly reported. If we ever owned the land we own it still, for we never sold it. In the treaty councils the commissioners have claimed that our country had been sold to the Government. Suppose a white man should come to me and say, "Joseph, I like your horses, and I want to buy them." I say to him, "No, my horses suit me, I will not sell them." Then he goes to my neighbor, and says to him: "Joseph has some good horses. I want to buy them, but he refuses to sell." My neighbor answers, "Pay me the money, and I will sell you Joseph's horses." The white man returns to me, and says, "Joseph, I have bought your horses, and you must let me have them." If we sold our lands to the Government, this is the way they were bought.

On account of the treaty made by the other bands of the Nez Percés, the white men claimed my lands. We were troubled greatly by white men crowding over the line. Some of these were good men, and we lived on peaceful terms with them, but they were not all good.

Nearly every year the agent came over from Lapwai and ordered us on to the reservation. We always replied that we were satisfied to live in

Wallowa. We were careful to refuse presents or annuities which he offered.

Through all the years since the white men came to Wallowa we have been threatened and taunted by them and the treaty Nez Percés. They have given us no rest. We have had a few good friends among white men, and they have always advised my people to bear these taunts without fighting. Our young men were quick-tempered, and I have had great trouble in keeping them from doing rash things. I have carried a heavy load on my back ever since I was a boy. I learned then that we were but few, while the white men were many, and that we could not hold our own with them. We were like deer. They were like grizzly bears. We had a small country. Their country was large. We were contented to let things remain as the Great Spirit Chief made them. They were not; and would change the rivers and mountains if they did not suit them.

Year after year we have been threatened, but no war was made upon my people until General Howard came to our country two years ago and told us he was the white war-chief of all that country. He said: "I have a great many soldiers at my back. I am going to bring them up here, and then I will talk to you again. I will not let white men laugh at me the next time I come. The country belongs to the Government, and I intend to make you go upon the reservation." . . .

I knew I had never sold my country, and that I had no land in Lapwai; but I did not want bloodshed. I did not want my people killed. I did not want anybody killed. Some of my people had been murdered by white men, and the white murderers were never punished for it. I told General Howard about this, and again said I wanted no war. I wanted the people who lived upon the lands I was to occupy at Lapwai to have time to gather their harvest.

I said in my heart that, rather than have war, I would give up my country. I would give up my father's grave. I would give up everything rather than have the blood of white men upon the hands of my people.

General Howard refused to allow me more than thirty days to move my people and their stock. I am sure that he began to prepare for war at once.

When I returned to Wallowa I found my people very much excited upon discovering that the soldiers were already in the Wallowa Valley. We held a council and decided to move immediately, to avoid bloodshed.

Too-hool-hool-suit, who felt outraged by his imprisonment, talked for war, and made many of my young men willing to fight rather than be driven like dogs from the land where they were born. He declared that blood alone would wash out the disgrace General Howard had put upon him. It required a strong heart to stand up against such talk, but I urged my people to be quiet, and not to begin a war.

We gathered all the stock we could find, and made an attempt to move. We left many of our horses and cattle in Wallowa, and we lost several hundred in crossing the river. All of my people succeeded in getting across in safety. Many of the Nez Percés came together in Rocky Cañon to hold a grand council. I went with all my people. This council lasted ten days. There was a great deal of war talk, and a great deal of excitement. There was one young brave present whose father had been killed by a white man five years before. This man's blood was bad against white men, and he left the council calling for revenge.

Again I counseled peace, and I thought the danger was past. We had not complied with General Howard's order because we could not, but we intended to do so as soon as possible. I was leaving the council to kill beef for my family, when news came that the young man whose father had been killed had gone out with several other hot-blooded young braves and killed four white men. He rode up to the council and shouted: "Why do you sit here like women? The war has begun already." I was deeply grieved. All the lodges were moved except my brother's and my own. I saw clearly that the war was upon us when I learned that my young men had been secretly buying ammunition. I heard then that Too-hool-hool-suit, who had been imprisoned by General Howard, had succeeded in organizing a war party. I knew that their acts would involve all my people. I saw that the war could not be prevented. The time had passed. I counseled peace from the beginning. I knew that we were too weak to fight the United States. We had many grievances, but I knew that war would bring more. We had good white friends, who advised us against taking the war path. My friend and brother, Mr. Chapman, who has been with us since the surrender, told us just how the war would end. Mr. Chapman took sides against us, and helped General Howard. I do not blame him for doing so. He tried hard to prevent bloodshed. We hoped the white settlers would not join the soldiers. Before the war commenced we had discussed this matter all over, and many of my people were in favor of warning them that if they took no part against us they should not be molested in the event of war being begun by General Howard. This plan was voted down in the war council.

There were bad men among my people who had quarreled with white men, and they talked of their wrongs until they roused all the bad hearts in the council. Still I could not believe that they would begin the war. I know that my young men did a great wrong, but I ask, Who was first to blame? They had been insulted a thousand times; their fathers and brothers had been killed; their mothers and wives had been disgraced; they had been driven to madness by whisky sold to them by white men; they had been told by General Howard that all their horses and cattle which they had been unable to drive out of Wallowa were to fall into the hands of white men; and, added to all this, they were homeless and desperate.

I would have given my own life if I could have undone the killing of white men by my people. I blame my young men and I blame the white men. I blame General Howard for not giving my people time to get their stock away from Wallowa. I do not acknowledge that he had the right to order me to leave Wallowa at any time. I deny that either my father or myself ever sold that land. It is still our land. It may never again be our home, but

my father sleeps there, and I love it as I love my mother. I left there, hoping to avoid bloodshed.

If General Howard had given me plenty of time to gather up my stock, and treated Too-hool-hool-suit as a man should be treated, there would have been no war.

My friends among white men have blamed me for the war. I am not to blame. When my young men began the killing, my heart was hurt. Although I did not justify them, I remembered all the insults I had endured, and my blood was on fire. Still I would have taken my people to the buffalo country without fighting, if possible.

I could see no other way to avoid a war. We moved over to White Bird Creek, sixteen miles away, and there encamped, intending to collect our stock before leaving; but the soldiers attacked us, and the first battle was fought. We numbered in that battle sixty men, and the soldiers a hundred. The fight lasted but a few minutes, when the soldiers retreated before us for twelve miles. They lost thirty-three killed, and had seven wounded. When an Indian fights, he only shoots to kill; but soldiers shoot at random. None of the soldiers were scalped. We do not believe in scalping, nor in killing wounded men. Soldiers do not kill many Indians unless they are wounded and left upon the battle field. Then they kill Indians.

Seven days after the first battle, General Howard arrived in the Nez Percés country, bringing seven hundred more soldiers. It was now war in earnest. . . .

We heard nothing of General Howard, or Gibbon, or Sturgis. We had repulsed each in turn, and began to feel secure, when another army, under General Miles, struck us. This was the fourth army, each of which outnumbered our fighting force, that we had encountered within sixty days.

We had no knowledge of General Miles' army until a short time before he made a charge upon us, cutting our camp in two, and capturing nearly all of our horses. About seventy men, myself among them, were cut off. My little daughter, twelve years old, was with me. I gave her a rope, and told her to catch a horse and join the others who were cut off from the camp. I have not seen her since, but I have learned that she is alive and well.

I thought of my wife and children, who were now surrounded by soldiers, and I resolved to go to them or die. With a prayer in my mouth to the Great Spirit Chief who rules above, I dashed unarmed through the line of soldiers. It seemed to me that there were guns on every side, before and behind me. My clothes were cut to pieces and my horse was wounded, but I was unhurt. As I reached the door of my lodge, my wife handed me my rifle, saying: "Here's your gun. Fight!"

The soldiers kept up a continuous fire. Six of my men were killed in one spot near me. Ten or twelve soldiers charged into our camp and got possession of two lodges, killing three Nez Percés and losing three of their men, who fell inside our lines. I called my men to drive them back. We fought at close range, not more than twenty steps apart, and drove the soldiers back upon their main line, leaving their dead in our hands. We secured their arms and ammunition. We lost, the first day and night, eighteen men and three women. General Miles lost twenty-six killed and forty wounded. The following day General Miles sent a messenger into my camp under protection of a white flag. I sent my friend Yellow Bull to meet him.

Yellow Bull understood the messenger to say that General Miles wished me to consider the situation; that he did not want to kill my people unnecessarily. Yellow Bull understood this to be a demand for me to surrender and save blood. Upon reporting this message to me, Yellow Bull said he wondered whether General Miles was in earnest. I sent him back with my answer, that I had made up my mind, but would think about it and send word soon. A little later he sent some Cheyenne scouts with another message. I went out to meet them. They said they believed that General Miles was sincere and really wanted peace. I walked on to General Miles' tent. He met me and we shook hands. He said, "Come, let us sit down by the fire and talk this matter over." I remained with him all

night; next morning Yellow Bull came over to see if I was alive, and why I did not return.

General Miles would not let me leave the tent to see my friend alone.

Yellow Bull said to me: "They have got you in their power, and I am afraid they will never let you go again. I have an officer in our camp, and I will hold him until they let you go free."

I said: "I do not know what they mean to do with me, but if they kill me you must not kill the officer. It will do no good to avenge my death by killing him."

Yellow Bull returned to my camp. I did not make any agreement that day with General Miles. The battle was renewed while I was with him. I was very anxious about my people. I knew that we were near Sitting Bull's camp in King George's land, and I thought maybe the Nez Percés who had escaped would return with assistance. No great damage was done to either party during the night.

On the following morning I returned to my camp by agreement, meeting the officer who had been held a prisoner in my camp at the flag of truce. My people were divided about surrendering. We could have escaped from Bear Paw Mountain if we had left our wounded, old women, and children behind. We were unwilling to do this. We had never heard of a wounded Indian recovering while in the hands of white men.

On the evening of the fourth day General Howard came in with a small escort, together with my friend Chapman. We could now talk understandingly. General Miles said to me in plain words, "If you will come out and give up your arms, I will spare your lives and send you to your reservation." I do not know what passed between General Miles and General Howard.

I could not bear to see my wounded men and women suffer any longer; we had lost enough already. General Miles had promised that we might return to our own country with what stock we had left. I thought we could start again. I believed General Miles, or I never would have surrendered. I have heard that he has been censured for making the promise to return us to Lapwai. He could not have made any other terms with me at that time. I would have held him in check until my friends came to my assistance, and then neither of the generals nor their soldiers would have ever left Bear Paw Mountain alive.

On the fifth day I went to General Miles and gave up my gun, and said, "From where the sun now stands I will fight no more." My people needed rest — we wanted peace.

I was told we could go with General Miles to Tongue River and stay there until spring, when we would be sent back to our country. Finally it was decided that we were to be taken to Tongue River. We had nothing to say about it. After our arrival at Tongue River, General Miles received orders to take us to Bismarck. The reason given was, that subsistence would be cheaper there.

General Miles was opposed to this order. He said: "You must not blame me. I have endeavored to keep my word, but the chief who is over me has given the order, and I must obey it or resign. That would do you no good. Some other officer would carry out the order."

I believe General Miles would have kept his word if he could have done so. I do not blame him for what we have suffered since the surrender. I do not know who is to blame. We gave up all our horses — over eleven hundred — and all our saddles — over one hundred — and we have not heard from them since. Somebody has got our horses.

General Miles turned my people over to another soldier, and we were taken to Bismarck. Captain Johnson, who now had charge of us, received an order to take us to Fort Leavenworth. At Leavenworth we were placed on a low river bottom, with no water except river water to drink and cook with. We had always lived in a healthy country, where the mountains were high and the water was cold and clear. Many of my people sickened and died, and we buried them in this strange land. I can not tell how much my heart suffered for my people while at Leavenworth. The Great Spirit Chief who rules above seemed to be looking some other way, and did not see what was being done to my people.

During the hot days (July, 1878) we received notice that we were to be moved farther away from our own country. We were not asked if we were willing to go. We were ordered to get into railroad cars. Three of my people died on the way to Baxter Springs. It was worse to die there than to die fighting in the mountains.

We were moved from Baxter Springs (Kansas) to the Indian Territory, and set down without our lodges. We had but little medicine, and we were nearly all sick. Seventy of my people have died since we moved there.

We have had a great many visitors who have talked many ways. . . .

At last I was granted permission to come to Washington and bring my friend Yellow Bull and our interpreter with me. I am glad we came. I have shaken hands with a great many friends, but there are some things I want to know which no one seems able to explain. I can not understand how the Government sends a man out to fight us, as it did General Miles, and then breaks his word. Such a government has something wrong about it. I can not understand why so many chiefs are allowed to talk so many different ways, and promise so many different things. I have seen the Great Father Chief (the President), the next Great Chief (Secretary of the Interior), the Commissioner Chief (Hayt), the Law Chief (General Butler), and many other law chiefs (Congressmen), and they all say they are my friends, and that I shall have justice, but while their mouths all talk right I do not understand why nothing is done for my people. I have heard talk and talk, but nothing is done. Good words do not last long unless they amount to something. Words do not pay for my dead people. They do not pay for my country, now overrun by white men. They do not protect my father's grave. They do not pay for all my horses and cattle. Good words will not give me back my children. Good words will not make good the promise of your War Chief General Miles. Good words will not give my people good health and stop them from dying. Good words will not get my people a home where they can live in peace and take care of themselves. I am tired of talk that comes to nothing. It makes my heart sick when I remember all the good words and all the broken promises. There has been too much talking by men who had no right to talk. Too many misrepresentations have been made, too many misunderstandings have come up between the white men about the Indians. If the white man wants to live in peace with the Indian he can live in peace. There need be no trouble. Treat all men alike. Give them the same law. Give them all an even chance to live and grow. All men were made by the same Great Spirit Chief. They are all brothers. The earth is the mother of all people, and all people should have equal rights upon it. You might as well expect the rivers to run backward as that any man who was born a free man should be contented when penned up and denied liberty to go where he pleases. If you tie a horse to a stake, do you expect he will grow fat? If you pen an Indian up on a small spot of earth, and compel him to stay there, he will not be contented, nor will he grow and prosper. I have asked some of the great white chiefs where they get their authority to say to the Indian that he shall stay in one place, while he sees white men going where they please. They can not tell me.

I only ask of the Government to be treated as all other men are treated. If I can not go to my own home, let me have a home in some country where my people will not die so fast. I would like to go to Bitter Root Valley. There my people would be healthy; where they are now they are dying. Three have died since I left my camp to come to Washington.

When I think of our condition my heart is heavy. I see men of my race treated as outlaws and driven from country to country, or shot down like animals.

I know that my race must change. We can not hold our own with the white men as we are. We only ask an even chance to live as other men live. We ask to be recognized as men. We ask that the same law shall work alike on all men. If the Indian breaks the law, punish him by the law. If the white man breaks the law, punish him also.

Let me be a free man — free to travel, free to stop, free to work, free to trade where I choose, free to choose my own teachers, free to follow the religion of my fathers, free to think and talk and act for myself — and I will obey every law, or submit to the penalty.

Whenever the white man treats an Indian as they treat each other, then we will have no more wars. We shall all be alike — brothers of one father and one mother, with one sky above us and one country around us, and one government for all. Then the Great Spirit Chief who rules above will smile upon this land, and send rain to wash out the bloody spots made by brothers' hands from the face of the earth. For this time the Indian race are waiting and praying. I hope that no more groans of wounded men and women will ever go to the ear of the Great Spirit Chief above, and that all people may be one people.

In-mut-too-yah-lat-lat has spoken for his people.

QUESTIONS FOR CONSIDERATION

1. What do the extracts from Chief Joseph's speech tell about the war's causes and the conduct of United States Indian policy?

2. What does his speech reveal about the options and strategies and the role and authority of an Indian leader in a time of crisis?

3. To what extent does Joseph seem to be speaking in a context and terms defined by whites? What metaphors and expressions might reflect romantic American stereotypes about defeated and disappearing Indians?

PICTURE ESSAY

The Battle of the Little Bighorn in Myth and History

••✕✕✕✕✕✕✕✕✕✕✕••

T HE BATTLE OF THE LITTLE BIGHORN is the exception to the rule that the winners write history. In this case the losers transformed a defeat into a mythic symbol of nation building. Almost immediately after the death of George Custer and his men on June 25, 1876, Americans began to construct an image of the battle that became part of a national mythology. Even among people who know little or nothing of the battle or its historical circumstances, the very words "Custer's Last Stand" conjure up images of the blond-haired officer and his gallant band of soldiers surrounded by hordes of Indian warriors.

For many Americans then and since, the battle was the epic struggle of Western history, a final clash between two ways of life, between the old and the new, between "savagery" and "civilization." It is the soldiers, not the Indians whose land is invaded and whose villages are attacked, who are fighting for their lives. Surrounded and doomed, they become martyrs to the cause of westward expansion, and their deaths justify the eventual victory of the United States over the Indians. Even as society's values have changed and Custer in some circles has tumbled from gallant hero, to bumbling incompetent, to genocidal maniac, the central image of the battle — beleaguered soldiers on the hilltop — has endured.[91]

Yet this enduring image of the battle was created by people who were not there. The only survivors and eyewitnesses were Indians, most of whom remained tight-lipped about the battle and their role in it, fearing retribution even into the twentieth century. Stories and memories of what really happened survived among the Lakotas and Cheyennes, but most Americans imagined or preferred a different story, one perpetuated in countless books, paintings, and movies.

Less than a month after the battle, William Cary sketched the first image of the fight, subtitled *The Death Struggle of General Custer* (Figure 6.1). It set the standard for subsequent portrayals. The Anheuser-Busch Brewing Association distributed lithographs of Custer's Last Stand that decorated countless barrooms across the country, and Buffalo Bill Cody got in on the act by staging reenactments that both perpetuated and popularized the heroic image of the battle in his Wild West shows (Figure 6.2). Twentieth-century movie audiences saw numerous heroic renditions of the battle in films but by the time of *Little Big Man* (1970), Custer's reputation was at a low ebb. Few Americans who anguished about their country's actions in Vietnam could admire the Indian-killing Custer. The film

◆ **Figure 6.1 William Cary, *The Death Struggle of General Custer* (1876)**
Library of Congress.

portrayed him, like his country, as bloodthirsty, arrogant, and ultimately mad (Figure 6.3). The hero turned villain still died alone on the hill.[92]

But other images of the battle existed. Lakota and Cheyenne participants, in keeping with the traditional practice of recording and recounting warriors' heroic deeds, produced pictographic accounts of the fight. These pictures, like the oral traditions of the battle passed down within the tribes, usually depict it as a rout rather than a heroic last stand (Figure 6.4). Increasingly sophisticated battlefield archaeology that employs metal detectors and forensic techniques, together with the very placement of the grave markers where the bodies of dead soldiers were found, suggest an interpretation of the battle that more closely resembles that offered by the Indians than that presented by Buffalo Bill or Hollywood: a breakdown of command occurred, discipline disintegrated, and the men of the Seventh Cavalry died in a series of desperate, piecemeal actions — plenty of tragedy, but little heroism.

◆ Figure 6.2 *Custer's Last Stand* **(1904)**
Buffalo Bill Center of the West/The Art Archive at Art Resource, NY.

Yet the old images endure and will continue to do so, and they are historically significant. They may distort understanding of what really happened at the Battle of the Little Bighorn, but they have become historical documents in their own right, showing how people view the past and exerting powerful influences even to this day.

After Gettysburg, the Little Bighorn is probably America's most famous battlefield, and it continues to generate heated emotions more than 140 years after the event. Events in the late twentieth century—the appointment of the first Indian (a woman) as National Parks superintendent of the site, the renaming of the battlefield the Little Bighorn instead of the Custer Battlefield, and the erection of a monument to the Indians (Figure 6.5) alongside the monument to the Seventh Cavalry—raised controversy and also helped to heal wounds for some people. The battle means different things to different people, and the battlefield has become a contested site of historical memories, but it remains a defining event in American history.

◆ Figure 6.3 *Little Big Man* (1970)
Photofest.

◆ Figure 6.4 **Lakotas Fighting Custer's Command**
National Anthropological Archives, Smithsonian Institution [NAA INV 08569200].

◆ Figure 6.5 **Indian Memorial at Little Bighorn**
© Universal Images Group Limited/Alamy.

QUESTIONS FOR CONSIDERATION

1. What do the images in this picture essay suggest about the power of art — and more recently the movies — in shaping history?

2. What do the changing images indicate about how, even when one side controls the interpretations, those interpretations change over time?

3. How do the American and Lakota images differ in their depiction of the battle?

4. Why would adding a memorial to the Indians who fought and died at the battle be controversial? What do memorials say about how we remember historic events and why do they matter?

REFERENCES

1. David La Vere, *Contrary Neighbors: Southern Plains and Removed Indians in Indian Territory* (Norman: University of Oklahoma Press, 2000).

2. Annie Heloise Abel, ed. *Chardon's Journal at Fort Clark, 1834–1839* (1932; repr., Lincoln: University of Nebraska Press, 1997), 126; Elizabeth A. Fenn, *Encounters at the Heart of the World: A History of the Mandan People* (New York: Hill and Wang, 2014), chap. 14.

3. Russell Thornton, *American Indian Holocaust and Survival: A Population History since 1492* (Norman: University of Oklahoma Press, 1987), 94–99; Clyde D. Dollar, "The High Plains Smallpox Epidemic of 1837–38," *Western Historical Quarterly* 8 (January 1977), 15–38.

4. George Bird Grinnell, *The Cheyenne Indians: Their History and Ways of Life* (Lincoln: University of Nebraska Press, 1972), 2:165.

5. Andrés Reséndez, *Changing National Identities at the Frontier: Texas and New Mexico, 1800–1850* (Cambridge: Cambridge University Press, 2005). On Comanche expansion and incorporation of other peoples, see Gary Clayton Anderson, *The Indian Southwest, 1580–1830: Ethnogenesis and Reinvention* (Norman: University of Oklahoma Press, 1999).

6. Pekka Hämäläinen, *The Comanche Empire* (New Haven: Yale University Press, 2008), 357–59; Brian DeLay, *War of a Thousand Deserts: Indian Raids and the U.S.–Mexican War* (New Haven: Yale University Press, 2008).

7. Gary Clayton Anderson, *The Conquest of Texas: Ethnic Cleansing in the Promised Land, 1820–1875* (Norman: University of Oklahoma Press, 2005), quote at 324; see also David La Vere, *The Texas Indians* (College Station: Texas A&M University Press, 2004). For a white woman's account of the "Council House Fight," see Mercy Maverick in *Major Problems in Texas History*, ed. Sam W. Haynes and Cary D. Wintz (Boston: Houghton Mifflin, 2002), 153–56.

8. John C. Cremony, *Life among the Apaches* (San Francisco: A. Roman & Co., 1868), chaps. 3–7.

9. Gray H. Whaley, *Oregon and the Collapse of Illahee: U.S. Empire and the Transformation of an Indigenous World, 1792–1859* (Chapel Hill: University of North Carolina Press, 2010).

10. Kathleen L. Hull, *Pestilence and Persistence: Yosemite Indian Demography and Culture in Colonial California* (Berkeley: University of California Press, 2009), traces the massive impact of disease and other factors on the culture of the Awahnichi Indians after the Gold Rush.

11. James J. Rawls, *Indians of California: The Changing Image* (Norman: University of Oklahoma Press, 1984).

12. Peter Nabokov, ed., *Native American Testimony* (New York: Harper and Row, 1979), 125–32.

13. Tom Hagan, "How the West Was Lost," in *Indians in American History*, ed. Frederick E. Hoxie (Arlington Heights, Ill.: Harlan Davidson, 1988), 193; Benjamin Madley, *American Genocide: The California Indian Catastrophe, 1846–1873* (New Haven: Yale University Press, 2015); Madley, "Califonia's Yuki Indians: Defining Genocide in Native American History," *Western Historical Quarterly* 39 (2008), 303–8; Brendan C. Lindsay, *Murder State: California's Native American Genocide, 1846–1873* (Lincoln: University of Nebraska Press, 2012), apathy quote at 9. Gary Clayton Anderson maintains that American atrocities constituted ethnic cleansing, not genocide, and argues that the population collapse in California has been exaggerated by scholars who accept inflated population estimates for the period before the gold rush; his evidence suggests that "only" about 2,000 Indians were murdered during and after the gold rush. Anderson, *Ethnic Cleansing and the Indian* (Norman: University of Oklahoma Press, 2014), chap. 10.

14. Lucy Eldersveld Murphy, "To Live among Us: Accommodation, Gender, and Conflict in the Western Great Lakes Region, 1760–1832," in *Native Women's History in Eastern North America before 1900: A Guide to Research and Writing*, ed. Rebecca Kugel and Lucy Eldersveld Murphy (Lincoln: University of Nebraska Press, 2007), 368–97.

15. Albert L. Hurtado, *Indian Survival on the California Frontier* (New Haven: Yale University Press, 1988), chap. 9.

16. Rawls, *Indians of California*, 82–86.

17. Chapter 122, Statutes of California, April 22, 1850, reprinted in Robert F. Heizer, ed., *The Destruction of California Indians* (1933, 1974; Lincoln: University of Nebraska Press, 1993), 220–24; Hurtado, *Indian Survival*, 129–31; Benjamin Madley, "'Unholy Traffic in Human Blood and Souls': Systems of California Indian Servitude under U.S. Rule," *Pacific Historical Review* 83 (2014), 626–67.

18. Clifford E. Trafzer and Joel R. Hyer, eds., *Exterminate Them! Written Accounts of the Murder, Rape, and Enslavement of Native Americans during the California Gold Rush* (East Lansing: Michigan State University Press, 1999), 139.

19. Robert F. Heizer, ed., *The Destruction of the California Indians: A Collection of Documents from the Period 1847 to 1865* (Santa Barbara and Salt Lake City: Peregrine Smith, 1974), 201.

20. Quoted in Hurtado, *Indian Survival*, 193; William J. Bauer Jr., *We Were All Like Migrant Workers Here: Work, Community, and Memory on California's Round Valley Reservation, 1850–1941* (Chapel Hill: University of North Carolina Press, 2009).

21. John D. Unruh Jr., *The Plains Across: The Overland Emigrants and the Trans-Mississippi West, 1840–60* (Urbana: University of Illinois Press, 1979), quote at 128, figures at 144; Michael L. Tate, *Indians and Emigrants: Encounters on the Overland Trails* (Norman: University of Oklahoma Press, 2005).

22. Henry M. Stanley, *My Early Travels and Adventures in America and Asia* (London: Sampson, Low, Marston, 1895), 1:206.

23. Laurence M. Hauptman, *Between Two Fires: American Indians in the Civil War* (New York: Free Press, 1995); Clarissa W. Confer, *The Cherokee Nation in the Civil War* (Norman: University of Oklahoma Press, 2007).

24. Gary Clayton Anderson and Alan R. Woolworth, eds., *Through Dakota Eyes: Narrative Accounts of the Minnesota*

Indian War of 1862 (St. Paul: Minnesota Historical Society Press, 1988), quote at 40; Scott W. Berg, *38 Nooses: Lincoln, Little Crow, and the Beginning of the Frontier's End* (New York: Pantheon, 2012); Dakota Kaskapi Okicize Wowapi, *The Dakota Prisoner of War Letters* (St. Paul: Minnesota Historical Society Press, 2013).

25. Elliott West, *The Contested Plains: Indians, Goldseekers, and the Rush to Colorado* (Lawrence: University Press of Kansas, 1998); Stan Hoig, *The Sand Creek Massacre* (Norman: University of Oklahoma Press, 1961), 180; Ari Kelman, *A Misplaced Massacre: Struggling Over the Memory of Sand Creek* (Cambridge, Mass.: Harvard University Press, 2013).

26. Jennifer Denetdale, *The Long Walk: The Forced Navajo Exile* (New York: Chelsea House, 2007); Jennifer Nez Denetdale, *Reclaiming Diné History: The Legacies of Navajo Chief Manuelito and Juanita* (Tucson: University of Arizona Press, 2007), provides a Navajo perspective on these events by a direct descendant of Chief Manuelito and Juanita.

27. Richard White, *Railroaded: The Transcontinentals and the Making of Modern America* (New York: W. W. Norton, 2011).

28. Colin G. Calloway, ed., *Our Hearts Fell to the Ground: Plains Indian Views of How the West Was Lost* (Boston: Bedford Books, 1996), 114; Colin G. Calloway, *Pen and Ink Witchcraft: Treaties and Treaty Making in American Indian History* (New York: Oxford University Press, 2013), chap. 6.

29. Jacki Thompson Rand, *Kiowa Humanity and the Invasion of the State* (Lincoln: University of Nebraska Press, 2008), chap. 4; Calloway, *Pen and Ink Witchcraft*, chap. 6.

30. Jill St. Germain, *Indian Treaty-Making Policy in the United States and Canada, 1867–1877* (Lincoln: University of Nebraska Press, 2001), 36.

31. *First Annual Report of the Board of Indian Commissioners for 1870* (Washington, D.C.: U.S. Government Printing Office, 1871), 41.

32. Calloway, *Our Hearts Fell*, 105–10; Blanca Tovías, "Diplomacy and Contestation before and after the 1870 Massacre of Amskapi Pikuni," *Ethnohistory* 60 (2013), 269–93.

33. Francis Paul Prucha, *American Indian Treaties: The History of a Political Anomaly* (Berkeley: University of California Press, 1994), chaps. 12–13.

34. Dan Flores, "Bison Ecology and Bison Diplomacy: The Southern Plains from 1800 to 1850," *Journal of American History* 78 (September 1991), 465–85.

35. Thornton, *American Indian Holocaust*, 52; Andrew C. Isenberg, *The Destruction of the Bison: An Environmental History, 1750–1920* (Cambridge: Cambridge University Press, 2000), chap. 5; Richard Irving Dodge, *Our Wild Indians: Thirty-Three Years' Personal Experience among the Red Men of the Great West* (1882; repr., Freeport, N.Y.: Books for Libraries Press, 1970), 293–96.

36. Frank B. Linderman, *Pretty-shield, Medicine Woman of the Crows* (Lincoln: University of Nebraska Press, 1972), 250–51.

37. *Annual Report of the Commissioner of Indian Affairs for 1873* (Washington, D.C.: U.S. Government Printing Office, 1874), 166.

38. Jeffrey Ostler, *The Lakotas and the Black Hills: The Struggle for Sacred Ground* (New York: Viking Penguin, 2010).

39. Thomas Powers, *The Killing of Crazy Horse* (New York: Alfred A. Knopf, 2010). For biographies of the famous Oglala, see Joseph Marshall III, *The Journey of Crazy Horse: A Lakota History* (New York: Penguin, 2005), and Kingsley M. Bray, *Crazy Horse: A Lakota Life* (Norman: University of Oklahoma Press, 2006).

40. John H. Monnett, "'My heart now has become changed to softer feelings': A Northern Cheyenne Woman and Her Family Remember the Long Journey Home," *Montana, the Magazine of Western History* 59 (Summer 2009), quote at 49.

41. Alan Boye, *Holding Stone Hands: On the Trail of the Cheyenne Exodus* (Lincoln: University of Nebraska Press, 1999); James N. Leiker and Ramon Powers, *The Northern Cheyenne Exodus in History and Memory* (Norman: University of Oklahoma Press, 2011).

42. Valerie Sherer Mathes and Richard Lowitt, *The Standing Bear Controversy: Prelude to Indian Reform* (Urbana: University of Illinois Press, 2003); Joe Starita, *I Am a Man: Chief Standing Bear's Journey for Justice* (New York: St. Martin's Press, 2009).

43. W. C. Vanderwerth, comp., *Indian Oratory: Famous Speeches by Noted Indian Chieftains* (Norman: University of Oklahoma Press, 1971), 125.

44. On the massacre, its context, and how it has been remembered (and forgotten), see Karl Jacoby, *Shadows at Dawn: A Borderlands Massacre and the Violence of History* (New York: Penguin, 2008); Ian W. Record, *Big Sycamore Stands Alone: The Western Apaches, Aravaipa, and the Struggle for Place* (Norman: University of Oklahoma Press, 2008); Chip Colwell-Chanthaphonh, *Massacre at Camp Grant: Forgetting and Remembering Apache History* (Tucson: University of Arizona Press, 2007).

45. Eve Ball, *Indeh: An Apache Odyssey* (Provo, Utah: Brigham Young University Press, 1980; Norman: University of Oklahoma Press, 1988), xv, 37.

46. Eve Ball, *In the Days of Victorio: Recollections of a Warm Springs Apache* (Tucson: University of Arizona Press, 1970; London: Corgi Books, 1973), 69.

47. General Crook is quoted in Dan L. Thrapp, *The Conquest of Apacheria* (Norman: University of Oklahoma Press, 1967), 364. S. M. Barrett, *Geronimo: His Own Life Story* (New York: Penguin, 1996), 132–38; Ball, *Indeh: An Apache Odyssey*, 106–12, quote at 110. For a detailed narrative of events, see Edwin R. Sweeney, *From Cochise to Geronimo: The Chiricahua Apaches, 1874–1886* (Norman: University of Oklahoma Press, 2010) and Robert M. Utley, *Geronimo* (New Haven: Yale University Press, 2012).

48. Ball, *In the Days of Victorio*, 210.

49. Alicia Delgadillo, ed., *From Fort Marion to Fort Sill: A Documentary History of the Chiricahua Prisoners of War, 1886–1913* (Lincoln: University of Nebraska Press, 2013).

50. Dee Brown, "Black Beaver," *American History Illustrated* 2 (May 1967), 32–40; Carolyn Thomas Foreman, "Black Beaver," *Chronicles of Oklahoma* 24 (August 1946), 269–92.

51. Mark van de Logt, *War Party in Blue: Pawnee Scouts in the U.S. Army* (Norman: University of Oklahoma Press, 2010);

Thomas W. Dunlay, *Wolves for the Blue Soldiers: Indian Scouts and Auxiliaries with the United States Army, 1860–90* (Lincoln: University of Nebraska Press, 1982), chap. 9.

52. Colin G. Calloway, "Army Allies or Tribal Survival? The 'Other Indians' in the 1876 Campaign," in *Legacy: New Perspectives on the Battle of the Little Bighorn,* ed. Charles E. Rankin (Helena: Montana Historical Society Press, 1996), 62–81; quotes at 71 and 75–76. See also David D. Smits, "Fighting Fire with Fire: The Frontier Army's Use of Indian Scouts and Allies in the Trans-Mississippi Campaigns, 1860–1890," *American Indian Culture and Research Journal* 22, no. 1 (1998), 73–116, and Dunlay, *Wolves.*

53. Clifford E. Trafzer and Margery Ann Beach, "Smohalla, the Washani, and Religion as a Factor in Northwestern Indian History," in "American Indian Prophets: Religious Leaders and Revitalization Movements," ed. Clifford E. Trafzer, special issue, *American Indian Quarterly* 9 (Summer 1985), 309–24; quotes at 316, 320.

54. Heather Cox Richardson, *Wounded Knee: Party Politics and the Road to an American Massacre* (New York: Basic Books, 2010), 198–203; Jerome A. Greene, *American Carnage: Wounded Knee, 1890* (Norman: University of Oklahoma Press, 2014).

55. Charles A. Eastman, *From the Deep Woods to Civilization: Chapters in the Autobiography of an Indian* (1916; repr., Lincoln: University of Nebraska Press, 1977), 111–14.

56. John G. Neihardt, *Black Elk Speaks: Being the Life Story of a Holy Man of the Oglala Sioux* (Lincoln: University of Nebraska Press, 1988), 270. Mario Gonzalez and Elizabeth Cook-Lynn, *The Politics of Hallowed Ground: Wounded Knee and the Struggle for Indian Sovereignty* (Urbana: University of Illinois Press, 1999), provides a Sioux interpretation of the massacre and describes efforts by the Survivors' Association to secure a formal apology from the U.S. government and recognition of the Wounded Knee massacre site as a national American monument.

57. See, for example, Candace S. Greene and Russell Thornton, eds., *The Year the Stars Fell: Lakota Winter Counts at the Smithsonian* (Washington, D.C.: Smithsonian Institution Press, 2007); Garrick Mallery, *Picture Writing of the American Indians, Tenth Annual Report of the Bureau of American Ethnology, 1888–89* (Washington, D.C.: U.S. Government Printing Office, 1893), 266–328; James Mooney, *Calendar History of the Kiowa Indians, Seventeenth Annual Report of the Bureau of American Ethnology, 1895–96,* pt. 1 (Washington, D.C.: U.S. Government Printing Office, 1898), 129–445.

58. Melburn D. Thurman, "Plains Indian Winter Counts and the New Ethnohistory," *Plains Anthropologist* 27 (May 1982), 173–75.

59. Mary Crow Dog, with Richard Erdoes, *Lakota Woman* (New York: HarperPerennial, 1991), 11.

60. Mooney, *Calendar History,* 152–64; quotations from N. Scott Momaday, *The Way to Rainy Mountain* (Albuquerque: University of New Mexico Press, 1969), 4, 6–7.

61. George Catlin, *Letters and Notes on the Manners, Customs, and Conditions of North American Indians* (London: printed by author, 1844; repr., New York: Dover, 1973), 2:74 and plate 178.

62. Mooney, *Calendar History,* 254–55.

63. Mooney, *Calendar History,* 257–60.

64. Momaday, *Way to Rainy Mountain,* 85.

65. Mooney, *Calendar History,* 143–44.

66. Mooney, *Calendar History,* 289.

67. Mooney, *Calendar History,* 320.

68. Momaday, *Way to Rainy Mountain,* 1.

69. Mooney, *Calendar History,* 344.

70. Alice Marriott, *The Ten Grandmothers* (Norman: University of Oklahoma Press, 1945), 144.

71. Mooney, *Calendar History,* 362–63.

72. For a Kiowa calendar drawn by the noted Kiowa artist Silver Horn, see Candace S. Greene, *One Hundred Summers: A Kiowa Calendar Record* (Lincoln: University of Nebraska Press, 2009).

73. Vine Deloria Jr. and Raymond DeMallie, introduction to *Proceedings of the Great Peace Commission of 1867–1868* (Washington, D.C.: Institute for the Development of Indian Law, 1975), 103.

74. James C. Olson, *Red Cloud and the Sioux Problem* (Lincoln: University of Nebraska Press, 1965), 74–75.

75. John S. Gray, *Centennial Campaign: The Sioux War of 1876* (Norman: University of Oklahoma Press, 1988), 11, 15.

76. For an excellent discussion of Indian treaties, and of the 1851 Treaty of Fort Laramie in particular, see Raymond J. DeMallie, "Touching the Pen: Plains Indian Treaty Councils in Ethnohistorical Perspective," in *Ethnicity on the Great Plains,* ed. Frederick C. Luebke (Lincoln: University of Nebraska Press, 1980), 38–51.

77. Quoted in Edward Lazarus, *Black Hills/White Justice: The Sioux Nation versus the United States, 1775 to the Present* (New York: HarperCollins, 1991), 61–62. A full version of Red Cloud's Cooper Union speech as reported in the *New York Times* is in Wayne Moquin and Charles Van Doren, eds., *Great Documents in American Indian History* (New York: Praeger, 1973), 211–13.

78. *Indian Country Today* 16 (Oct. 7–14, 1996), A2 (incorrectly identified as George Whirl Wind Horse).

79. Quoted in Robert M. Utley, *The Last Days of the Sioux Nation* (New Haven: Yale University Press, 1963), 53.

80. For a thorough account of the history of the Black Hills land claim, see Lazarus, *Black Hills,* and Ostler, *Lakotas and the Black Hills.*

81. Quoted in Lazarus, *Black Hills,* 344.

82. Albert Fortwangler, *Bringing Indians to the Book* (Seattle: University of Washington Press, 2005).

83. L. V. McWhorter, *Yellow Wolf: His Own Story* (Caldwell, Idaho: Caxton Printers, 1940, 1995), 41.

84. McWhorter, *Yellow Wolf,* 42.

85. McWhorter, *Yellow Wolf,* 211–12.

86. Quoted in Alvin M. Josephy Jr., *The Nez Perce Indians and the Opening of the Northwest* (New Haven: Yale University Press, 1965), 630.

87. Quoted in Bruce Hampton, *Children of Grace: The Nez Percé War of 1877* (New York: Henry Holt, 1994), 311.

88. *Annual Report of the Commissioner of Indian Affairs for 1878* (Washington, D.C.: U.S. Government Printing Office, 1879), 464; quoted in Hampton, *Children of Grace,* 321–22. See also McWhorter, *Yellow Wolf,* 289.

89. *Annual Report of the Commissioner of Indian Affairs for 1878,* 464; quoted in Hampton, *Children of Grace,* 323; J. Diane Pearson, *The Nez Percés in the Indian Territory: Nimiipuu Survival* (Norman: University of Oklahoma Press, 2008).

90. Thomas H. Guthrie, "Good Words: Chief Joseph and the Production of Indian Speech(es), Texts, and Subjects," *Ethnohistory* 54 (Summer 2007), 509–46.

91. For further discussion of the issues surrounding the battle, see the essays in Rankin, *Legacy*; on the lasting fascination with Custer and the iconic battle see Michael A. Elliott, *Custerology: The Enduring Legacy of the Indian Wars and George Armstrong Custer* (Chicago: University of Chicago Press, 2007).

92. On Custer imagery in art and film, see the essays by Brian W. Dippie and Paul Andrew Hutton in Rankin, *Legacy,* 206–70, and Brian W. Dippie, *Custer's Last Stand: The Anatomy of an American Myth* (1976; repr., Lincoln: University of Nebraska Press, 1994).

SUGGESTED READINGS

Anderson, Gary Clayton. *The Conquest of Texas: Ethnic Cleansing in the Promised Land, 1820–1875.* Norman: University of Oklahoma Press, 2005.

———. *Ethnic Cleansing and the Indian: The Crime That Should Haunt America.* Norman: University of Oklahoma Press, 2014.

———. *Little Crow: Spokesman for the Sioux.* St. Paul: Minnesota Historical Society Press, 1986.

Ball, Eve. *Indeh: An Apache Odyssey.* Norman: University of Oklahoma Press, 1988.

Barrett, S. M. *Geronimo: His Own Story.* New York: Penguin, 1996.

Bauer, William J., Jr. *We Were All Like Migrant Workers Here: Work, Community, and Memory on California's Round Valley Reservation, 1850–1941.* Chapel Hill: University of North Carolina Press, 2009.

Beal, Merrill D. *"I Will Fight No More Forever": Chief Joseph and the Nez Percé War.* Seattle: University of Washington Press, 1963.

Berg, Scott W. *38 Nooses: Lincoln, Little Crow, and the Beginning of the Frontier's End.* New York: Pantheon, 2012.

Blackhawk, Ned. *Violence over the Land: Indians and Empires in the Early American West.* Cambridge, Mass.: Harvard University Press, 2006.

Bray, Kingsley M. *Crazy Horse: A Lakota Life.* Norman: University of Oklahoma Press, 2006.

Calloway, Colin G., ed. *Our Hearts Fell to the Ground: Plains Indian Views of How the West Was Lost.* Boston: Bedford Books, 1996.

———. *Pen and Ink Witchcraft: Treaties and Treaty Making in American Indian History.* New York: Oxford University Press, 2013.

Clements, William M. *Imagining Geronimo: An Apache Icon in Popular Culture.* Albuquerque: University of New Mexico Press, 2013.

Confer, Clarissa W. *The Cherokee Nation in the Civil War.* Norman: University of Oklahoma Press, 2007.

DeLay, Brian. *War of a Thousand Deserts: Indian Raids and the U.S.–Mexican War.* New Haven: Yale University Press, 2008.

Delgadillo, Alicia, ed. *From Fort Marion to Fort Sill: A Documentary History of the Chiricahua Prisoners of War, 1886–1913.* Lincoln: University of Nebraska Press, 2013.

Deloria, Vine, Jr., and Raymond DeMallie. Introduction to *Proceedings of the Great Peace Commission of 1867–1868.* Washington, D.C.: Institute for the Development of Indian Law, 1975.

Denetdale, Jennifer. *The Long Walk: The Forced Navajo Exile.* New York: Chelsea House, 2007.

———. *Reclaiming Diné History: The Legacies of Navajo Chief Manuelito and Juanita.* Tucson: University of Arizona Press, 2007.

Dunlay, Thomas W. *Wolves for the Blue Soldiers: Indian Scouts and Auxiliaries with the United States Army, 1860–90.* Lincoln: University of Nebraska Press, 1982.

Elliott, Michael A. *Custerology: The Enduring Legacy of the Indian Wars and George Armstrong Custer.* Chicago: University of Chicago Press, 2007.

Fenn, Elizabeth A. *Encounters at the Heart of the World: A History of the Mandan People.* New York: Hill and Wang, 2014.

Getches, David H., Charles F. Wilkinson, et al. *Cases and Materials on Federal Indian Law.* 4th ed. St. Paul, Minn.: West Group, 1998; 5th ed., 2004; 6th ed., 2011.

Gonzalez, Mario, and Elizabeth Cook-Lynn. *The Politics of Hallowed Ground: Wounded Knee and the Struggle for Indian Sovereignty.* Urbana: University of Illinois Press, 1999.

Greene, Candace S. *One Hundred Summers: A Kiowa Calendar Record.* Lincoln: University of Nebraska Press, 2009.

Greene, Candace S., and Russell Thornton, eds. *The Year the Stars Fell: Lakota Winter Counts at the Smithsonian.* Washington, D.C.: Smithsonian Institution Press, 2007.

Greene, Jerome A. *American Carnage: Wounded Knee, 1890.* Norman: University of Oklahoma Press, 2014.

———, ed. *Lakota and Cheyenne Indian Views of the Great Sioux War, 1876–1877.* Norman: University of Oklahoma Press, 1994.

Guthrie, Thomas H. "Good Words: Chief Joseph and the Production of Indian Speech(es), Texts, and Subjects." *Ethnohistory* 54 (Summer 2007), 509–46.

Hämäläinen, Pekka. *The Comanche Empire.* New Haven: Yale University Press, 2008.

———. "The Rise and Fall of Plains Indian Horse Cultures." *Journal of American History* 90 (December 2003), 833–62.

Hampton, Bruce. *Children of Grace: The Nez Percé War of 1877.* New York: Henry Holt, 1994.

Harjo, Suzan Shown. *Nation to Nation: Treaties between the United States and American Indian Nations.* Washington, D.C.: Smithsonian Books, 2014.

Hoxie, Frederick E. *Parading through History: The Making of the Crow Nation in America, 1805–1935.* Cambridge: Cambridge University Press, 1995.

Hurtado, Albert L. *Indian Survival on the California Frontier.* New Haven: Yale University Press, 1988.

Isenberg, Andrew C. *The Destruction of the Bison.* Cambridge: Cambridge University Press, 2000.

Jacoby, Karl. *Shadows at Dawn: A Borderlands Massacre and the Violence of History.* New York: Penguin, 2008.

Josephy, Alvin M., Jr. *The Nez Perce Indians and the Opening of the Northwest.* New Haven: Yale University Press, 1965.

Kelman, Ari. *A Misplaced Massacre: Struggling Over the Memory of Sand Creek.* Cambridge, Mass.: Harvard University Press, 2013.

Lazarus, Edward. *Black Hills/White Justice: The Sioux Nation versus the United States, 1775 to the Present.* New York: HarperCollins, 1991.

Leiker, James N., and Ramon Powers, *The Northern Cheyenne Exodus in History and Memory* Norman: University of Oklahoma Press, 2011.

Lindsay, Brendan C. *Murder State: California's Native American Genocide, 1846–1873.* Lincoln: University of Nebraska Press, 2012.

Madley, Benjamin. *American Genocide: The California Indian Catastrophe, 1846–1873.* New Haven: Yale University Press, 2016.

Mallery, Garrick. *Picture Writing of the American Indians, Tenth Annual Report of the Bureau of American Ethnology, 1888–89.* Washington, D.C.: U.S. Government Printing Office, 1893. Reprint, New York: Dover, 1972.

Marshall, Joseph M., III. *The Day the World Ended at Little Bighorn: A Lakota History.* New York: Viking Penguin, 2007.

McWhorter, L. V. *Yellow Wolf: His Own Story.* Caldwell, Idaho: Caxton Printers, 1940, 1995.

Momaday, N. Scott. *The Way to Rainy Mountain.* Albuquerque: University of New Mexico Press, 1969.

Mooney, James. *Calendar History of the Kiowa Indians, Seventeenth Annual Report of the Bureau of American Ethnology, 1895–96.* Part 1. Washington, D.C.: U.S. Government Printing Office, 1898. Reprint, Washington, D.C.: Smithsonian Institution Press, 1979, 129–445.

———. "The Ghost-Dance Religion and the Sioux Outbreak of 1890." *Fourteenth Annual Report of the Bureau of American Ethnology, 1892–93.* Part 2. Washington, D.C.: U.S. Government Printing Office, 1896.

Moore, John H. *The Cheyenne.* Cambridge, Mass.: Blackwell, 1996.

Nabokov, Peter. *Two Leggings: The Making of a Crow Warrior.* Lincoln: University of Nebraska Press, 1982.

Olson, James C. *Red Cloud and the Sioux Problem.* Lincoln: University of Nebraska Press, 1965.

Ostler, Jeffrey. *The Lakotas and the Black Hills: The Struggle for Sacred Ground.* New York: Viking Penguin, 2010.

———. *The Plains Sioux and U.S. Colonialism from Lewis and Clark to Wounded Knee.* Cambridge: Cambridge University Press, 2004.

Pearson, J. Diane. *The Nez Perces in the Indian Territory: Nimiipuu Survival.* Norman: University of Oklahoma Press, 2008.

Philbrick, Nathaniel. *The Last Stand: Custer, Sitting Bull, and the Battle of the Little Bighorn.* New York: Viking Penguin, 2010.

Powers, Thomas. *The Killing of Crazy Horse.* New York: Alfred A. Knopf, 2010.

Price, Catherine. *The Oglala People, 1841–1879: A Political History.* Lincoln: University of Nebraska Press, 1996.

Rand, Jacki Thompson. *Kiowa Humanity and the Invasion of the State.* Lincoln: University of Nebraska Press, 2008.

Robinson, Charles M., III. *A Good Year to Die: The Story of the Great Sioux War.* New York: Random House, 1995.

Rzeczkowski, Frank. *Uniting the Tribes: The Rise and Fall of Pan-Indian Community on the Crow Reservation.* Lawrence: University Press of Kansas, 2012.

Scott, Douglas D. *Uncovering History: Archaeological Investigations at the Little Bighorn.* Norman: University of Oklahoma Press, 2013.

Slickpoo, Allen P., Sr., and Deward E. Walker Jr. *Noon Nee-Me-Poo (We, the Nez Percés): Culture and History of the Nez Percés.* Nez Percé Tribe of Idaho, 1973.

Smoak, Gregory. *Ghost Dances and Identity: Prophetic Religion and American Indian Ethnogenesis in the Nineteenth Century.* Berkeley: University of California Press, 2006.

St. Germain, Jill. *Indian Treaty-Making Policy in the United States and Canada, 1867–1877.* Lincoln: University of Nebraska Press, 2001.

Stands In Timber, John, and Margot Liberty. *Cheyenne Memories.* Lincoln: University of Nebraska Press, 1972.

Sweeney, Edwin R. *From Cochise to Geronimo: The Chiricahua Apaches, 1874–1886.* Norman: University of Oklahoma Press, 2010.

Tate, Michael L. *Indians and Emigrants: Encounters on the Overland Trails.* Norman: University of Oklahoma Press, 2005.

Thomas, Rodney G., comp. *Rubbing Out Custer: The American Indian Story of the Little Big Horn in Art and Word.* Washington: Elk Plain Press, 2010.

Utley, Robert M. *Geronimo.* New Haven: Yale University Press, 2012.

———. *The Indian Frontier of the American West, 1846–1890.* Albuquerque: University of New Mexico Press, 1984.

———. *The Lance and the Shield: The Life and Times of Sitting Bull.* New York: Henry Holt, 1993.

van de Logt, Mark. *War Party in Blue: Pawnee Scouts in the U.S. Army.* Norman: University of Oklahoma Press, 2010.

VenDevelder, Paul. *Savages and Scoundrels: The Untold Story of America's Road to Empire through Indian Territory.* New Haven: Yale University Press, 2009.

West, Elliott. *The Contested Plains: Indians, Goldseekers, and the Rush to Colorado.* Lawrence: University Press of Kansas, 1998.

———. *The Last Indian War: The Nez Percé Story.* New York: Oxford University Press, 2009.

Westerman, Gwen, and Bruce White. *Mni Sota Makoce: The Land of Dakota.* Minneapolis: Minnesota Historical Society, 2012.

Whaley, Gray H. *Oregon and the Collapse of Illahee: U.S. Empire and the Transformation of an Indigenous World, 1792–1859.* Chapel Hill: University of North Carolina Press, 2010.

White, Richard. *Railroaded: The Transcontinentals and the Making of Modern America.* New York: W. W. Norton, 2011.

Wooster, Robert. *The American Military Frontiers: The United States Army in the West, 1783–1900.* Albuquerque: University of New Mexico Press, 2010.

7

"Kill the Indian and Save the Man"

1870s–1920s

FOCUS QUESTIONS

1. How did the U.S. government control Indian life on the reservations, and how did Indian people adjust and resist?

2. What were the goals of Indian boarding schools, and in what ways did Native students use the kind of education they received there?

3. How did Indians and their leaders maintain aspects of their culture in the face of acculturation?

AMERICANIZING THE AMERICAN INDIAN

AS THE WARS FOR THE WEST CAME TO AN END and various organizations mobilized for a reform of Indian policies, Indian people found themselves subjected to attacks of a different kind. After waging war to defeat Indian military resistance and take Indian lands, the United States now waged war on Indian cultures, values, and families. U.S. Indian policy as it evolved after the Civil War was often contentious. Different groups—the Army, the Indian Office, business interests, the states, humanitarian reformers, and Indian people themselves—competed for control and influence, and the so-called Indian problem attracted national attention: between 1860 and 1900 the *New York Times* published almost 1,000 editorials related to Native Americans.[1]

President Ulysses S. Grant (in office 1869–77) had established precedent by using churchmen as officials and agents as part of his "peace policy," and some of his appointees had brought an element of humanitarianism to Indian affairs. To implement his peace policy, Grant appointed as commissioner of Indian Affairs Ely S. Parker, author of the Confederate surrender terms at Appomattox and the first Native American to hold the position. In the late 1870s and 1880s, groups which saw themselves as the "friends of the Indian" attempted to take things further. Tragic events such as the pursuit and relocation of the Nez Perces in 1877, the uprooting of the Ponca tribe to make room for new Sioux reservations the same year, and the desperate flight in 1878 of some three hundred Northern Cheyennes from a reservation in Indian Territory had left an ugly taste in the mouths of those who believed the United States should be extending the blessings of civilization to Indian people, not shooting them down in the snow (see Chapter 6, pages 327–28). Reformer and activist Helen Hunt Jackson, who had heard Ponca chief Standing Bear speak in Boston, related these and other events in moving terms in her book *A Century of Dishonor*, published in 1881. She described the history of the government's relations with the Indians as "a shameful record of broken treaties and unfulfilled promises" and called for a radical change of Indian policy. She sent a copy of her book to every congressman.[2]

The need for a thorough reform of Indian affairs was clear. The Board of Indian Commissioners, established by Congress in 1869 to curb mismanagement in the Bureau of Indian Affairs, investigated conditions on the reservations, where corruption was notorious. The Indian Rights Association, founded in 1882, pledged to protect the rights and interests of the Indians; its reformers attended annual conferences at Lake Mohonk in upstate New York where they discussed what was best for "the Indian." The Indian Rights Association did champion Indian causes and on occasion backed Indian cases in the courts, but it shared the commitment of other reform groups to "saving" the Indians by assimilating them. Captain Richard Henry Pratt, founder of Carlisle Indian boarding school, coined the phrase "Kill the Indian and Save the Man," but he and his fellow reformers targeted women and children as well as men in their efforts to save Indians by destroying their Indianness.

1900	Recorded Indian population in the United States reaches all-time low of 237,000
1903	Supreme Court in *Lone Wolf v. Hitchcock* rules Congress has power to break treaties with Indian tribes
1906	Burke Act, amending Dawes Act, allows "competent" Indians to sell allotments
1906	Alaska Native Allotment Act
1907	Indian Territory and Oklahoma Territory combined to form the state of Oklahoma
1908	*Winters v. United States* defines federally reserved water rights for Indian tribes
1911	Society of American Indians formed in Columbus, Ohio
1912	Jim Thorpe wins pentathlon and decathlon at Stockholm Olympic Games
1912	Alaska Native Brotherhood established
1913	Commissioner of Indian Affairs establishes "competency commissions"
1914–1918	World War I (for United States, 1917–18); more than 12,000 Native men serve in the armed forces
1918	Native American Church incorporated
1919	United States grants citizenship to honorably discharged Indian veterans
1923	New England Indian Council formed
1924	Indian Citizenship Act extends citizenship to all Indians
1928	Meriam Report published

American continental expansion officially ended in 1890 when the Census Bureau declared that the western "frontier" no longer existed, but the United States began to extend its colonial reach beyond its shores and over other Native peoples. In 1893 plantation owners in Hawaii, acting in conjunction with the U.S. minister to Hawaii and U.S. military forces, overthrew the Hawaiian monarchy and assumed control of the government; five years later the United States annexed Hawaii as a territory. Also, the Spanish-American War in 1898 resulted in the United States' occupation of Cuba and its acquisition of Guam, Puerto Rico, and the Philippines. Meanwhile, Native people in the continental United States continued to experience, adjust to, and resist multiple forms of American colonialism.

Relating his life story in old age, Two Leggings, a Crow warrior, concentrated on his search for a vision and his aspirations and achievements as a warrior. He ended his story at the point when his people were confined to the reservation. Nothing in his warrior tradition and training prepared him for reservation life. "Nothing happened after that," he said. "We just lived. There were no more war parties, no capturing of horses from the Piegans and the Sioux, no buffalo to hunt. There is nothing more to tell."[3] But Two Leggings lived for another forty years after the end of the old days. There was plenty more to tell.

Policies of Detribalization

Influential groups in American society combined with the federal government in a sustained campaign to remake Indians in the image of white American citizens. Like earlier generations of Euro-Americans, they wanted to "civilize" Indians and have them lead sedentary lives on fixed plots of land, be self-supporting, and practice Christianity. As the first step in this transformation, American reformers believed it was necessary to eradicate all vestiges of tribal life. Powerful forces acted to suppress Indian culture, undermine tribal ways, and destroy the economic base of tribal communities. The American government and reformers sought to apply a single model of transformation to all tribes, regardless of their differences. Like the European immigrants who were streaming into eastern cities, the first peoples in America were to be made into "Americans." The result was tremendous suffering and hardship for Indian peoples who saw their land domains diminish, their heritage distorted, and their certainties questioned. But tribal culture and society proved more resilient than the reformers imagined. They could not predict the extent of the "Indian problem"—the failure or refusal of Indians to stop being Indians.

With the defeat of the resistant groups, many of the Indian "ringleaders" were rounded up and sent away as prisoners of war, while their people were herded onto reservations. In 1875, seventy-two southern Plains war leaders were loaded on to trains and transported across the country to St. Augustine, Florida, where they were incarcerated in Fort Marion, a military prison. There, Captain Richard Henry Pratt, the same man responsible for the first off-reservation boarding school, subjected them to an experimental program of "civilization by immersion." Pratt took off their shackles, cut their hair, gave them army uniforms, and attempted to prepare them for complete assimilation.

At the same time, the government in the late nineteenth century refined its policies for dealing with the Indians already on its nearly two hundred reservations. The new Indian policies employed a hierarchy of command that ran from the Department of the Interior, down through the Indian Office to the regional superintendents, and on to the Indian agents on the reservations. The reservation was the context in which the process of detribalization was to occur. But in the long-term policy of assimilating Indians, reservations were regarded as

◆ **Apache Reservation c. 1899**
With their traditional economies destroyed, Indian people were reduced to unaccustomed poverty and dependence on government rations. Here, Apache men, women, and children wait in line for their rations outside the agency building at San Carlos, Arizona. *Granger, NYC.*

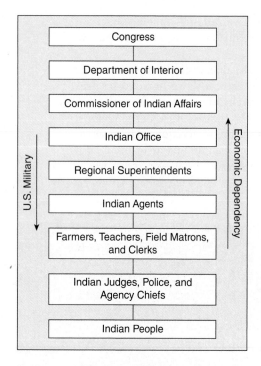

◆ **Chart 7.1 The Reservation System**

temporary, a stage on the road to incorporating Indians into mainstream American society. The agents were the key figures in the administration and enforcement of the government's Americanization program on the reservations. They relied for assistance on the clerks, doctors, field matrons, farmers, teachers, and blacksmiths who worked with the agencies; they also relied on the reservation police and the Courts of Indian Offenses, both of which were staffed by Indians and designed to enforce the suppression of tribal culture and traditional activities. In this way, resentment against government policies at the community level often became channeled against the Indians charged with implementing those policies rather than against the federal government or its agents. The Indians' new dependence on the government for rations of food and clothing helped keep them in line. If the system failed and resentment erupted in open resistance, the army could be called in to restore order and enforce compliance.

Some agents were dedicated and honest men who worked hard to ease the Indians' transition to a new way of life and who displayed genuine sympathy for their charges. Many were not. Often, agents were political appointees in a system that encouraged graft and corruption, and they made matters worse for the people they were supposed to administer.

Resistance Takes New Forms

As Indian peoples confronted new and renewed assaults, they developed new ways to protest and resist. In public and in print, men like Ely S. Parker and Carlos Montezuma (see pages 420–22), did what they could to shape or temper U.S. policies. On the reservations, people found ways to shield their lives and values from the prying eyes of Indian agents and maintain ties of family, clan, and community.

The U.S. government regarded Indian tribes as "domestic nations" and set about reducing tribal people to "domestic subjects." To "civilize" the Indians, it launched a full-scale assault on their cultures, communal homelands, community values, and family structures, and on how they lived and how they taught their children. Transforming Indians into Americans involved rendering Indian women politically and economically subordinate to men and making sure that their roles as wives and mothers fit contemporary American conventions of female domesticity. The government pursued a strategy of "intimate colonialism," employing field matrons on the reservations who supervised and attempted to change family life, child-rearing, and even sexual practices.[4] For example, Indian mothers placed their babies in cradle boards; propped against a tree or rock while the mother worked, a cradle board allowed the baby to see the world from an upright position, rather than lying down, and provided security and protection for the baby's head. Cradle boards were one of the "evils" that government-appointed field matrons sought to eradicate from Indian women's lives.[5] Indian women often accepted and sometimes cooperated with change — after all, not all changes were bad: advancements in sanitation, nursing, and child care could reduce infant mortality and improve women's health. But few women succumbed completely to the new policies, and many continued to play key roles in reservation economies, to exert political influence, to participate in communal activities, and to preserve and pass on cultural traditions.[6]

Sarah Winnemucca refused to be a "domestic subject." Born in 1844, she saw her Paiute people decline into poverty after they were confined to a Nevada reservation created by presidential order in 1860 and then relocated to the Yakima Reservation in Oregon in 1879. In her book *Life among the Piutes: Their Wrongs and Claims* (1883), which was clearly intended for a white audience, she described the brutality of American expansion, the immorality and hypocrisy of American "civilization" policies, and the greed and corruption of Indian agents. Indians will "never be civilized," she wrote, "if you keep on sending us such agents as have been sent to us year after year, who do nothing but fill their pockets, and the pockets of their wives and sisters, who are always put in as teachers, . . . and yet they do not teach." Indians complained regularly to the government about corrupt agents, "Yet it goes on, just the same, as if they did not know." The first known Native woman to publish a book, Sarah Winnemucca went on the lecture circuit, dressed as a Paiute "princess," to denounce the government's policies and to call attention to her people's plight. In historian Frederick Hoxie's words, "She exposed the violence and injustice that accompanied the 'winning' of the West and provided the public with a dramatic substitute for the white male voices that previously had dominated discussions of Indian policy making."[7] Though she met the president, she died in 1891 without seeing the Paiutes receive justice.

On the reservations, Indian officials sometimes evaded or diluted the impact of the laws they were supposed to enforce: Wooden Leg, a Northern Cheyenne who had fought at the Little Bighorn and later served as a tribal judge, sent away one of his two wives in compliance with the government's ban on polygyny, but when he heard that some of the older men refused to obey the order he "just listened, said nothing, and did nothing." The government originally conceived of Indian judges as men who would simply enforce the rules, but many judges had other ideas. In time, notes one historian, Crow judges evolved into "government-sanctioned elders who worked to reconcile their oaths of office with individual behavior and the standards of their communities."[8]

◆ **Sarah Winnemucca as Paiute "Princess" While Lecturing in Boston**
Sarah Winnemucca gave more than four hundred speeches in the United States and Europe in an effort to improve conditions for her people. *Granger, NYC.*

As they had in the East and California in colonial times, missionaries on the reservations tried to get Indians to reject their "heathen" ways and embrace Christianity, and the government outlawed or discouraged many traditional religious ceremonies such as the Sun Dance. But efforts at suppression did not match Indian insistence on preservation. Indians continued to practice their religious ceremonies illegally and found ways to covertly evade government regulations and hold dances. Kiowas, for instance, transferred elements from the Sun Dance, which was banned, into the new Gourd Dance, which was not.[9] As the practice of Native ceremonies on reservations today indicates, the government's attempts at "cultural genocide" and religious oppression were only partially successful at best. Still, some Indian people became Christians or at least embraced elements of Christian teachings, and in some cases Indian people actively sought missionaries as allies in a changing world. On the Crow Creek Reservation in South Dakota, for example, tribal leaders asked for a Catholic mission school to help teach their children.[10]

On the neighboring Pine Ridge Reservation, with the buffalo herds all but exterminated and government beef rations woefully inadequate, the Oglala Lakotas turned to building their own cattle herd. But instead of becoming American-style cattle ranchers, they made cattle an opportunity to maintain a traditional mobile subsistence economy while they adapted to reservation life. They herded cattle communally, branded them with the Pine Ridge "flying O" brand, and when they received shipments of steers would often hunt them from horseback and kill them with arrows, to the dismay of their agents.[11]

Where international borders had cut across tribal spaces and turned Indian homelands into borderlands, some bands — Anishinaabeg on the northern shores of the Great Lakes, for example, and Blackfeet and Sioux on the northern Plains — experienced similar policies emanating from the Canadian government.

Borderland peoples sometimes made strategic use of the white man's "medicine line" to preserve their autonomy, passing back and forth across the U.S.–Canadian border to limit interference by either government in their lives.[12]

American reformers in the East were appalled by the poverty and ill health that typified life on the reservations out west. They were outraged by the corruption and mismanagement they saw in the Indian Service and in the administration of Indian affairs. They also realized that, despite the massive assaults on Indian life and cultures, the reservations were nevertheless failing in one of their primary purposes: Indians were not abandoning the old ways; they refused to stop being Indians. Reservations were supposed to be crucibles of change where tribalism would perish and "civilization" flourish, but Indians made them into homelands where tribal ways refused to die. In the eyes of reformers determined to save Indians from themselves, the reservations came to be "obstacles to progress."

The Dawes Allotment Act (1887)

Since the days of Thomas Jefferson, reservations had been regarded as places where Indians would learn to live more like their white neighbors. In the second half of the nineteenth century, the number of reservations increased, as did demands to speed up the pace of change. But by 1880 reformers, many of whom called themselves "Friends of the Indian," began advocating that reservations be dismantled as the best way to push Indians into the modern world. In some cases, concentrating Indians on reservations stimulated tribal organization and identity — the far-ranging Comanche bands, for example, came together as a nation after they were confined to a reservation in the 1870s (Map 7.1). But reformers wanted to dismantle the *tribes* themselves. "The organization of the Indian tribes is, and has been, one of the most serious hindrances to the advancement of the Indian toward civilization," the Indian Rights Association proclaimed at its 1884 Lake Mohonk Conference: "every effort should be made to secure the disintegration of all tribal organizations."[13] The reformers wanted to grant Indians citizenship and to educate them in Christian and American ways. They rejected the notion that Indians were different; they felt that Indians should dissolve tribal ties and assimilate into American society just as European and Asian immigrants were expected to do. Reformers and federal officials shifted their support from a policy based on reservations to a policy based on *breaking up* reservations.

In 1887 Congress passed the Dawes or General Allotment Act to reduce reservations and allot lands to individual Indians as private property. Reformers saw these provisions as the way to radically change federal Indian policy and initiate a new era for American Indians. Like the Indian removal policy of the 1830s, allotment was a program on which both pro- and anti-Indian groups could agree as a solution to the "Indian problem." The new policy would terminate communal ownership, push Indians into mainstream society, and offer for sale "surplus" land not used by Indians. The law was an attempt to impose

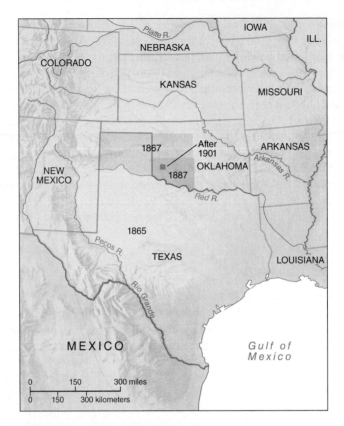

◆ **Map 7.1 Confining the Comanches, 1865–1901**

The Comanche experience dramatically illustrates the impact of the assault on tribal lands that culminated in the 1887 Allotment Act. For much of the nineteenth century, the Comanches ranged across a huge region from north of the Arkansas River to south of the Rio Grande. The Treaty of the Little Arkansas in 1865 began to compress the tribal domain, and the end of the Civil War initiated new pressures on Indian lands. In the Treaty of Medicine Lodge in 1867, the Comanches ceded most of their lands to the United States and agreed to live on a 3-million-acre reservation. After the Allotment Act was applied around the turn of the century, the reservation shrank to a patchwork of holdings. For Indian people, land loss meant a shift from mobility, prosperity, and independence to confinement, poverty, and dependence, and also separation from familiar sites linked to individual, family, and tribal memories.

Source: Adapted from *The American Indian: Prehistory to the Present,* first edition, by Arrell M. Gibson. Copyright © 1980 Wadsworth, a part of Cengage Learning, Inc. Reproduced by permission. www .cengage.com/permissions.

a revolution on Indian societies. Allotment, its advocates believed, would liberate Indians from the stifling hold of community and instill individual ambition, American ideas of property rights, habits of thrift and industry. It would also break up extended families and undermine leaders who worked for the collective good. Indians could progress no further as long as they held land in common, said Senator Henry Dawes of Massachusetts, the main proponent of the Allotment Act. "There is no selfishness, which is at the bottom of civilization."[14] Thus the acquisition of private property was vital if an Indian was to become a fully participating and competing member of American society. "The desire for a home of his own awakens him to new efforts," declared Merrill Gates, a member of the Board of Indian Commissioners. "Discontent with the tepee and the starving rations of the Indian camp in winter is needed to get the Indian out of the blanket and into trousers, — and trousers with a pocket in them, and with a *pocket that aches to be filled with dollars!*"[15] Theodore Roosevelt put it more bluntly: allotment, he said, was "a vast pulverizing engine to break up the tribal mass."[16]

The Dawes Allotment Act passed through Congress and was implemented with speed. It contained the following provisions:

1. The president was authorized to assign allotments of 160 acres to heads of families, with lesser amounts to younger persons and orphans.
2. Indians were to select their own lands, but if they failed to do so, the agent would make the selection for them. Reservations were to be surveyed and rolls of tribal members prepared prior to allotment.
3. The government was to hold title to the land in trust for twenty-five years, preventing its sale until allottees could learn to treat it as real estate.
4. All allottees and all Indians who abandoned their tribal ways and became "civilized" were to be granted citizenship.
5. "Surplus" reservation lands could be sold.

The law remained in force from 1887 to 1934. Its main effect was to strip Indian people of millions more acres of land. Indians whose lands were allotted became U.S. citizens. Their lands could now be taxed by the state in which they lived, and land transfers could be treated as individual sales of property, which allowed Americans to legally purchase even more Native land once its title was handed over to its allottee. Conversely, the protections provided to Indian allottees were steadily whittled away. In 1902 Congress allowed Indian heirs to sell inherited land without approval from the secretary of the interior. In 1906 the Burke Act declared that Indians whom the secretary of the interior deemed "competent" to manage their own affairs could be granted patents in fee simple, which meant they no longer had to wait twenty-five years before they could sell their allotments. In 1913 the Commissioner of Indian Affairs established "competency commissions," which issued fee patents to Indians judged competent to sell their land. Often, "competency" was determined by blood quantum—finding a French-Canadian fur trader in someone's heritage was sufficient evidence of "competency" to issue a patent, and to render land available for purchase.

On the White Earth Reservation in northern Minnesota, American businessmen and speculators steadily eroded the land base of the Anishinaabe residents. The U.S. government had established White Earth in 1867 as a reservation for all

◆ *The Twilight of the Indian* (1897)
Indians who accepted allotment were expected to give up the tipi, bow, and hunting shirt in favor of a cabin, plow, and farming clothes. As Frederic Remington's painting and title indicate, most Americans believed that once Indians lived on and farmed their own plots of land, they embarked on the path to a new life: they would not only cease being hunters, they would also eventually cease being Indian. *Courtesy of the R. W. Norton Art Gallery, Shreveport, Louisiana.*

Anishinaabe people, and the various bands who lived there made a promising start. But the rich timber lands in the eastern part of the reservation and fertile farm lands to the west attracted the attention of outsiders. In 1889 the Nelson Act mandated that all the land be allotted under the terms of the Dawes Act. In 1906 Minnesota senator Moses A. Clapp, a former lumber baron, attached a provision to the annual Indian appropriations bill stating that "mixed-blood" adults on White Earth were "competent" to dispose of their land parcels immediately. One Anishinaabeg, a school superintendent from 1903 to 1911, said that the Clapp amendment "brought grief and happiness to many people." Speculators approached Indian people who knew nothing about the legislation and got witnesses to "subscribe to affidavits that the Indian in question had white blood in his veins and in many cases the white blood ran through the branches of the family . . . for many generations to some remote Canadian Frenchman."[17] Powerful lumber interests bought up timber-rich allotments for a fraction of their value and proceeded to clear the northern forests that had sustained Anishinaabe people for centuries.

As reservation lands and resources dwindled, social and political conflicts within Anishinaabe society increased. Before the 1906 Clapp amendment, the people of White Earth had been adapting relatively well to life on the reservation and to the demands and opportunities of a market economy; an investigation in 1909 found them with "no lands, no money." By 1920, "most of the reservation land base had transferred to Euroamerican hands," and by 1994, "only 7 percent of White Earth's land base remain[ed] under Indian control."[18]

Even as allotment was implemented, however, Indians found ways to evade its assimilationist intent. Some Indians—Jicarilla Apaches and the bands on the Grand Ronde Reservation in western Oregon, for example—actually requested allotment and used it to secure control of land and to build new agricultural communities defined as much by their own choices and standards as by government policies. Others—the Nez Perces, for instance—selected their allotments of land "with agendas other than assimilation in mind." They used space in Indian rather than Euro-American ways, occupied land as families and communities rather than as individual property owners, and perpetuated rather than terminated traditional environmental practices.[19] Kiowas in Indian Territory, who had begun to take up farming after the buffalo herds were destroyed, now had to adjust to allotment and to individual rather than collective farming. Yet most maintained their tribal connections and social bonds even as the outside world pressured them to change.[20]

Indian Territory Becomes Oklahoma

The "Five Civilized Tribes" in Indian Territory were originally excluded from the provisions of the Allotment Act. The Cherokees, Creeks, Choctaws, Chickasaws, and Seminoles had rebuilt their economic, educational, and political structures after removal, had weathered the divisive effects of the Civil War, and functioned as autonomous societies. But in 1890 Indian Territory was divided into Oklahoma Territory and Indian Territory. Congress appointed a commission to negotiate allotment agreements with the five tribes (Map 7.2). Between 1889 and 1893, the "Cherokee Commission" (or the Jerome Commission, as it was often known, after its chairman David H. Jerome) dealt with about twenty tribes in Indian Territory. The commission controlled the negotiations and often resorted to intimidating tactics. The Cherokees, Iowas, Pawnees, Poncas, Tonkawas, Wichitas, Cheyennes, Arapahos, Sauks & Foxes, and others agreed to accept allotment and sell surplus lands at a price set by the government. By 1900, 15 million acres of "surplus land" were opened to white settlers, "making

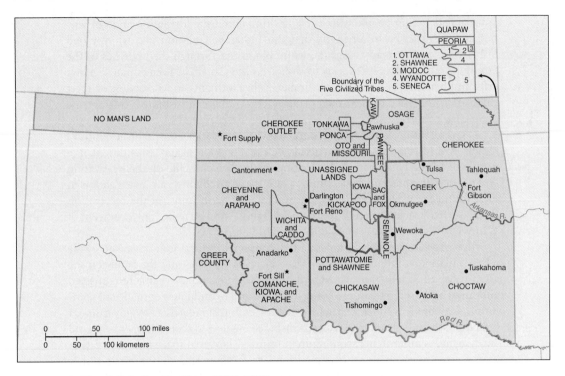

◆ **Map 7.2 Indian Territory, 1866–1889**
Following the Indian Removal Act of 1830, thousands of Indian people from the East were
relocated to Indian Territory. Other peoples from other regions were moved there in later
years. They rebuilt their societies in what was originally supposed to be "permanent" Indian
territory, but allotment produced huge losses of land in what became the state of Oklahoma.
SOURCE: Reprinted from *Atlas of American Indian Affairs* by Francis Paul Prucha by permission of the
University of Nebraska Press. Copyright 1990 by the University of Nebraska Press.

possible . . . the state of Oklahoma." For Indian Territory, the Jerome Commission was a disaster.[21]

Many tribal leaders opposed allotment, but the Curtis Act of 1898 effectively
terminated the Indian governments and allotment proceeded in the remainder
of Indian Territory. In 1907 Congress combined Indian Territory and Oklahoma Territory to create the new state of Oklahoma. Although the Muscogee
(Creek) National Council agreed to allotment, some Creeks followed the lead
of Chitto Harjo, or Crazy Snake, in resisting allotment. After violence erupted
with whites in 1909, the Oklahoma National Guard was called out to quell the
"uprising." In the meantime, fraud and chicanery characterized the allotment
process in Oklahoma. Non-Indians married Indians to get on the tribal rolls and
thereby become eligible for allotments. They cheated the Indians out of their
allotments with words or whiskey, and, in the view of one Oklahoma historian,

"lurked about the Indian nations, a predacious wolf pack lusting for the last parcels of tribal land."[22] When the Osages were forced to accept the allotment of their lands in 1907, they wisely insisted that the tribe continue to own the subsurface materials — oil had been discovered beneath the Osage Reservation ten years before. Jackson Burnett, a Creek Indian, earned so much in royalties from the oil wells on his Oklahoma allotment that by 1917 he was known as "the World's Richest Indian." Claiming Burnett was not competent to manage his own affairs — he was illiterate, and, as was appropriate in Creek culture, he gave money away to friends and relatives — outsiders scrambled to manage his wealth for him. The tangle of litigation and jockeying for control of his estate became a national scandal.[23] The Osages benefited from an oil bonanza, but non-Indians resorted to swindling, bribery, and even a spate of murders in the 1920s. "The Osage Reign of Terror" attracted national attention and federal investigations.[24] The FBI was called in to stop the murders.

In the United States as a whole between 1887 and 1934, tribal landholding was reduced from some 138 million acres to about 48 million acres. In Oklahoma between 1890 and 1940 the lands belonging to the Five Tribes shrank from nearly 20 million acres to 1.8 million acres, a loss of more than 90 percent in fifty years. As Indian allotments moved onto the open market, unscrupulous speculators, many of them leading Oklahoma citizens, snapped them up, an "orgy of theft" courageously detailed by Oklahoma historian Angie Debo in her book *And Still the Waters Run*, published in 1940.[25]

The allotment of 160 acres was often insufficient for Indians to make a living by farming or herding, especially as the lands were usually arid and marginally fertile. By the late nineteenth century many white American farmers were finding it hard to make ends meet, even on good lands. Moreover, the original 160 acres were often broken up into smaller parcels as they were divided among the heirs of the original allottee. Over time, individual Indians were left with joint ownership in tracts of trust land that became "fractionated" among hundreds of owners. Many Indians were persuaded to lease their lands. As non-Indian settlers bought up surplus lands, many reservations assumed a "checkerboard" pattern of Indian and non-Indian property. The Navajo population and reservation increased in the late nineteenth century as the tribe rebuilt their economy around stock raising, but they were an exception to the general rule.[26] With their already reduced tribal domain further diminished and disrupted, most Indians living on allotted reservations endured increasing poverty, despondency, and discrimination.

THE EDUCATIONAL ASSAULT ON INDIAN CHILDREN

While allotment tried to break up the reservations as obstacles to progress, education was seen as the key to making progress and saving the Indian. In the eyes of reformers like Merrill Gates (see "From the Seventeenth Annual Report of the Board of Indian Commissioners," pages 416–20), allotment and education went hand in hand. If necessary, both would be forced upon

Indians. Like the children of European immigrants, Indian children were expected to jettison their old ways and language and become English-speaking "Americans." The Board of Indian Commissioners in 1880 outlined its view of the Indian:

> As a savage we cannot tolerate him any more than as a half-civilized parasite, wanderer or vagabond. The only alternative left is to fit him by education for civilized life. The Indian, though a simple child of nature with mental faculties dwarfed and shriveled, while groping his way for generations in the darkness of barbarism, already sees the importance of education. . . .[27]

Deprived of their lands and reduced to poverty, Indians had to learn to support themselves as wage laborers.

Removing Children from the Tribe

Reformers first aimed to educate Indian adults. Captain Richard Henry Pratt imposed his program of civilization on the Plains Indian prisoners of war in Fort Marion, attempting to immerse them in white culture. But as many adults resisted assimilation, Indian children became the main targets of American education efforts. Congress in 1877 appropriated $20,000 for the express purpose of Indian education. Funding rose and reached almost $3 million by 1900. The numbers of students enrolling in school also increased: 3,598 in 1877; 21,568 in 1900.[28] Some children attended day schools on the reservations, but reformers preferred off-reservation boarding schools where children could be isolated from the "contaminating" influences of parents, friends, and family. The boarding school "was the institutional manifestation of the government's determination to completely restructure the Indians' minds and personalities." "Our purpose," said the superintendent of Rainy Mountain Boarding School in Oklahoma, which hundreds of young Kiowas attended between 1893 and 1920, "is to change them forever."[29]

Some of Pratt's younger Indians at Fort Marion opted to stay and continue their education in the East, and Samuel Armstrong, who in 1868 had founded Hampton Normal and Industrial School in Virginia as a school for former slaves, agreed to take them. The first Indian students arrived in 1878 and more Indian students attended Hampton Institute later. In 1879 Pratt opened the nation's first off-reservation Indian boarding school in Carlisle, Pennsylvania.[30] Two dozen more boarding schools were opened in the next twenty-three years (Map 7.3). These schools became famous, or infamous, and served as models for other Indian educational facilities in their curriculum, discipline, regimen, and goals.

Attendance was mandatory. In 1891 Congress authorized the commissioner of Indian affairs "to make and enforce by proper means" rules and regulations to ensure that Indian children of suitable age attended the schools established for them. Two years later, Congress went further and authorized the Indian Office to

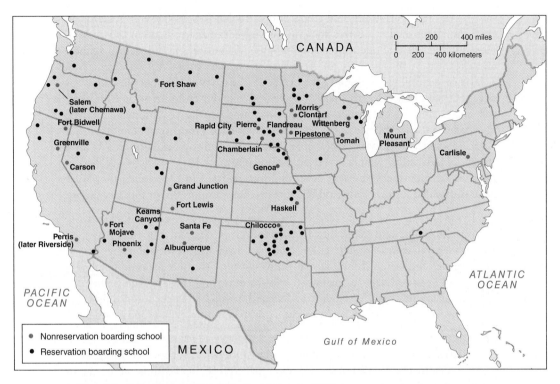

◆ **Map 7.3 U.S. Government Boarding Schools, 1889**
Twenty years after Richard Henry Pratt opened his school at Carlisle, Pennsylvania, Indian country was dotted by two dozen off-reservation boarding schools and many more reservation boarding schools, such as Keams Canyon on the Hopi Reservation, which Helen Sekaquaptewa attended (see page 394).
SOURCE: Reprinted from *Atlas of American Indian Affairs* by Francis Paul Prucha by permission of the University of Nebraska Press. Copyright 1990 by the University of Nebraska Press.

withhold rations and annuities from parents who refused to send their children to school. Many children were hauled off to school by soldiers or Indian police enforcing the agents' instructions. In 1886, the agent at the Mescalero Apache agency reported:

> Everything in the way of persuasion and argument having failed, it became necessary to visit the camps unexpectedly with a detachment of police, and seize such children as were proper and take them away to school, willing or unwilling. Some hurried their children off to the mountains or hid them away in camp, and the police had to chase and capture them like so many wild rabbits. This unusual proceeding created quite an outcry. The men were sullen and muttering, the women loud in their lamentations, and the children almost out of their wits with fright.[31]

When the government built a boarding school at Keams Canyon, Arizona, in 1887, the Hopis at first refused to send their children there. In 1890 the government established a quota system for the attendance of Hopi children in schools and the next year sent African American troops to round up children. Don Talayesva, a Hopi, remembered hearing about it as a child: "The people said it was a terrible sight to see Negro soldiers come and take our children away from their parents." Using African American troops to round up Native American children may have been a deliberate policy to pit one oppressed group against another, but Hopis recognized who was responsible. Talayesva "grew up believing that Whites are wicked, deceitful people."[32] Helen Sekaquaptewa, a Hopi woman, recalled in 1969 the bewilderment she and other children had felt in 1906 when they were lined up, loaded into wagons, and taken from their families under military escort:

> It was after dark when we reached the Keams Canyon boarding school and were unloaded and taken into the big dormitory, lighted with electricity. I had never seen so much light at night. . . . Evenings we would gather in a corner and cry softly so the matron would not hear and scold or spank us. . . . I can still hear the plaintive little voices saying, "I want to go home. I want my mother." We didn't understand a word of English and didn't know what to say or do. . . . We were a group of homesick, lonesome, little girls. . . .[33]

As in Australia, child-removal policies in the United States ruptured indigenous people's ties to place and family, isolating children in institutions, and later in homes, where they were often neglected, abused, and exploited.[34]

Life in the Schools

Schools such as the Carlisle Indian Industrial School were designed not only to educate the Indian students who attended but also to completely transform them. They tried to provide students with the kind of skills that America deemed appropriate and even necessary for their survival and to remake them as individual citizens, not tribal members. To this end, boarding schools imposed militaristic discipline and regimented the students' activities, from morning until prayers before bedtime. When Indian children arrived at the boarding schools, they were given new Anglo-American names. The boys had their hair cut, and all students had to wear stiff uniforms in place of their native clothing. Writing in the 1930s, Luther Standing Bear, a Lakota and one of the first students to attend Carlisle, remembered the discomfort of high collars, stiff shirts, and leather boots; when the students were issued red flannel underwear for the winter "discomfort grew into actual torture."[35] They ate a monotonous diet, endured harsh discipline, and followed daily routines to acquire systematic habits. Educational policy at the boarding schools discouraged — and often prohibited — students from returning home during vacations or at times of sickness and death among family members, to the distress of parents and students alike.[36]

◆ **Chiricahua Apache Children on Arrival at Carlisle School**
National Anthropological Archives, Smithsonian Institution [photo neg. 52, 542].

Most students suffered from homesickness. Basil Johnston, a Canadian Anishinaabeg who attended a Jesuit school in Ontario, remembered the emotional toll on the youngest children. These "babies" clung to one of the Jesuit priests or huddled in the corner; they "seldom laughed or smiled and often cried and whimpered during the day and at night." Some of the older students carved toys for them but the children did not play with them; "they just held on to them, hugged them and took them to bed at night, for that was all they had in the world when the lights went out, and they dared not let it go."[37]° Many students suffered

---

° In 1998 the Canadian government issued a formal apology to the victims of sexual and physical abuse in the residential school system and committed $350 million to support the development of community-based healing to help deal with the legacy of that abuse. In 2006 the government agreed to pay almost $2 billion in damages to 80,000 former students.[38]

◆ **Chiricahua Apache Children after Four Months at Carlisle**
National Anthropological Archives, Smithsonian Institution [photo neg. 53, 599 and 599A].

from trachoma, a contagious viral disease of the eye. Many died of tuberculosis, coughing up blood as the disease attacked their lungs. Between 1885 and 1913, one hundred Indian students, from thirty-seven tribes, were buried in the cemetery at Haskell Institute in Kansas°; others were buried in unmarked graves in the marshland to conceal the high mortality rates at the school. Most of the students who died at the schools were teenagers, but some were only six or seven years old. Some students even committed suicide. "The change in clothing, housing, food, and confinement combined with lonesomeness was too much," recalled Standing Bear. "In the graveyard at Carlisle most of the graves are those of little ones."[39]

° Founded in 1884, the United States Industrial Training School was renamed Haskell Institute three years later.

The ravages of disease were not confined to boarding schools far from home, of course. Don Talayesva attended school at New Oraibi on the Hopi Reservation and recalled hearing just before Christmas 1899 that smallpox was spreading west across Hopi country. "Within a few weeks news came to us that on Second Mesa the people were dying so fast that the Hopi did not have time to bury them, but just pitched their bodies over the cliff." The government employees and some of the teachers fled Oraibi. Another Hopi, Edmund Nequatewa, was at the Keams Canyon boarding school when the epidemic struck: "the whole reservation was condemned," he remembered. "They had to draw the line between the school and the Hopi village. There were guards going back and forth day and night. No one could come in to the school from the Hopi villages." For several months, students at the school were cut off from news of their relatives in the disease-ridden villages. When Nequatewa was allowed home in the spring, he found his parents alive but two aunts dead. "Some of those people that had had smallpox were very hard to recognize," he recalled. "Their faces were all speckled and they looked awful."[40]

In the classroom, teachers taught reading and writing by memorization, pushed "American" values on the children, and taught patriotism and a version of American history that distorted or ignored the Indians' role. Teachers punished those caught speaking their native language. Many parents who had attended missionary or government boarding schools refused to teach their children their native tongue in order to save them from having the language beaten out of them in school. Eleven-year-old Elsie Allen, a Pomo girl, was beaten with a strap for speaking her language at the Covelo boarding school in California. "[E]very night I cried and then I'd lay awake and think and think and think. I'd think to myself, 'If I ever get married and have children I'll *never* teach my children the language or all the Indian things that I know. I'll *never* teach them that, I don't want my children to be treated like they treated me.' That's the way I raised my children."[41]

Inheriting, applying, and fueling racial assumptions about the intellectual inferiority of Indians, boarding school educators taught the boys vocational and manual skills; girls were taught the domestic skills thought appropriate for a Victorian mother and homemaker, or trained for work as maids in middle-class families.[42] In fact, many students found themselves in a twilight world: they were not equipped or allowed to enter American society as equals, yet they had been subjected to sufficient change as to make returning to the reservations difficult and sometimes traumatic.

Surviving the Schools, Using the Education

The boarding school experience and the educational philosophy of the government left a legacy of bitterness, confusion, and heartbreak that continues to affect Indian people as they struggle to revive languages that were almost destroyed and to restore pride in a heritage that was denied any worth for so long. Stripped of much of their traditional culture yet regarded by American society as capable

◆ **Plenty Horses**
What conflicts and contradictions are suggested in this photograph of Plenty Horses, a Carlisle graduate, wearing braids, blanket, and moccasins and standing next to an army gun shortly after the Wounded Knee massacre? *Granger, NYC.*

only of the most menial employment, many students came out of the schools as bewildered as when they went in. The story of Plenty Horses graphically illustrates the plight of many Carlisle graduates. In 1890, during the Ghost Dance troubles on Pine Ridge Reservation (pages 334–35), the twenty-two-year-old Lakota shot and killed an army officer. He was tried for murder. When asked why he killed the officer, Plenty Horses responded: "I am an Indian. Five years I attended Carlisle and was educated in the ways of the white man. . . . I was lonely. I shot the lieutenant so I might make a place for myself among my people. Now I am one of them. I shall be hung and the Indians will bury me as a warrior." The federal court, however, confronted a dilemma: if Plenty Horses was guilty of murdering the army officer, were not the officers and men of the Seventh Cavalry guilty of murdering Lakota men, women, and children at Wounded Knee? The court decided that Plenty Horses had acted as a belligerent during a state of war and acquitted him. The case made legal history but it did not help Plenty Horses, who lived out his life in poverty and despondency.[43]

But the boarding schools were also sites of cultural contests — however unequal — where young Indian people found ways of resisting the educational crusade intended to transform them. They engaged in acts of subversion and rebellion against petty authority, built bonds of loyalty and friendship with other students, and found humor and humanity in the midst of loneliness, hardship, and regimentation. Interviews with alumni from Chilocco Indian School in northeastern Oklahoma convinced one anthropologist, the daughter of a former Chilocco student, that Indians at boarding schools "actively created an ongoing educational and social process." They built their own world within the confines of boarding-school life, and in the process, they turned an institution founded and controlled by the federal government into an Indian school. Some students even had pride in their school, and most found ways to enjoy themselves. Indian people, she concluded, "made Chilocco their own."[44] Students from Haskell—who often used sign language to get around the "English only" rule—told similar stories. Instead of being transformed, the students survived as Indians and transformed the school: in the late twentieth century the former boarding school became Haskell Indian Nations University, an institution dedicated to the survival of Indian cultures and identities.[45]

In 1894 the government arrested nineteen Hopi leaders and sent them to prison in Alcatraz (from January to September 1895) for refusing to send their children to government-run schools. But those Hopis who went to school drew strength from the traditional Hopi education they had received at home on the mesas and were determined to do well as they continued their education at places like Sherman Institute in Riverside, California. Hopi students drew strength from singing traditional Hopi songs but also enjoyed playing Bach, Beethoven, and Mozart in the school orchestra.[46]

As in other eras and areas, Native responses to cultural assault and change in boarding schools did not divide neatly into assimilation and resistance. Things were rarely that simple; individual students often accepted some changes in their lives and rejected others.[47] Many Indian students took the knowledge, experience, and literacy acquired during their school years and applied it in their work, their lives, and their understanding of the world. Like Luther Standing Bear (see "What a School Could Have Been Established," pages 424–28), they saw Western education and traditional education as two systems of knowledge. They tried to combine the best of both systems in adapting to the demands of a rapidly changing world. Many boarding-school alumni returned to reservations as teachers themselves—in 1899, 45 percent of the U.S. Indian School Service employees were Indians.[48] For Wolf Chief, a Hidatsa who went to school for the first time when he was thirty years old, education was a source of power. He learned arithmetic so he could check traders' weights and later operate his own store on the Fort Berthold Reservation in North Dakota. He also employed his literary skills to bombard the Office of Indian Affairs with complaints and concerns: "He has contracted the letter writing habit and cannot be suppressed," said one exasperated agent in 1886. He wrote to newspapers and magazines and even wrote to the president, and his letters got responses.[49] Anna Moore Shaw, a Pima who attended school with Helen Sekaquaptewa and became the first Indian woman high-school graduate in Arizona, wrote that her generation was "the first to be educated in two cultures, the Pima and the white. Sometimes the values were in conflict, but we were learning to put them together to make a way of life different from anything the early Pimas ever dreamed of."[50]

As Indians were forced into American systems of learning, American forms of employment, and American cultural roles, old stereotypes of the savage warrior gave way to the idea of Indians as a "vanishing race," fading into the sunset and out of American consciousness and history, a concept popularized ever since by photographs of Edward Curtis. As "real" Indians disappeared, they were replaced by idealized Natives acting out prescribed roles. At a time when some people feared that influxes of foreign-born immigrants threatened to dilute the American character, images of Indian "primitivism" and Indian warriors could be safely appropriated to represent distinctly American traits. Indians were proud, courageous, and free and had fought heroically against a superior foe. Once obstacles to American nation building, they could now be symbols of American national identity.[51]

Indian intellectuals often used such popular images and stereotypes for their own purposes. Like Sarah Winnemucca (see page 383), some adopted and adapted to public performance as a way to be heard and to help advance Indian causes.[52] Two Omaha sisters, Susan and Suzette LaFlesche, used their education in the non-Indian world to champion Indian rights, lecturing and lobbying Congress, while their brother, Francis, became one of the first Indian anthropologists. Suzette studied at reservation mission schools, private schools in the East, and the University of Nebraska. She worked as a volunteer nurse among the Poncas. After Standing Bear led his people back to their Nebraska homeland in 1879, Suzette and her brother accompanied him on a tour of eastern cities. On the lecture circuit in both America and Great Britain, using the name Bright Eyes and dressed in ceremonial Omaha clothing, she spoke out about the unjust treatment of Indians and the need for Indians to become citizens to gain full protection under the Constitution. Her sister Susan graduated from Hampton Institute in 1886 and the Women's Medical College in Philadelphia in 1889 to become the first female Indian physician. She returned west, serving as the government reservation doctor for the Omahas, and also went on the lecture circuit with her sister. She lobbied for the eradication of tuberculosis and the prohibition of alcohol on reservations. She campaigned against government corruption, incompetence, and unjust laws that kept Indians dependent. She also supported individual ownership of land and believed that Omahas should be allowed to sell and lease their property free from government supervision. Angel De Cora, of Ho-Chunk (Winnebago) and French parentage, was born on the Winnebago Reservation in Nebraska. She attended Hampton Institute, graduated from Smith College in 1896, and later taught at the Carlisle School, where she established the first "Native Indian" art department. She became a noted artist, illustrator, and designer (she did the frontispiece and cover design for Francis LaFlesche's book *The Middle Five,* for instance). Her work was sometimes criticized as western art reflecting romantic stereotypes about Indians, but she was one of the first Native American artists to be recognized and accepted by the mainstream art world.[53]

The Two Worlds of Ohiyesa and Charles Eastman

Perhaps no individual better personified the changing times in which Indians lived than did Charles Alexander Eastman, also known as Ohiyesa. Raised in traditional Dakota ways by his paternal grandmother, as an adult Ohiyesa lived in two worlds and earned distinction in American society as Dr. Charles Eastman, physician, writer, and reformer. He was born in Minnesota in 1858, the youngest of five children, and named Hakadah, "the pitiful last," before earning the name Ohiyesa, "the winner," in a lacrosse game. Ohiyesa's father, Many Lightnings, was a Wahpeton Dakota Sioux; his mother, who died soon after his birth, was

◆ **Charles Eastman**
Charles Eastman (Ohiyesa, 1858–1939) in later life.
Granger, NYC.

Mary Eastman, daughter of soldier-turned-artist Seth Eastman (see his sugar camp image on page 38).

After the Minnesota Sioux uprising of 1862, Many Lightnings was imprisoned and his family fled to Ontario, Canada, where Ohiyesa lived until the age of fifteen. Ohiyesa believed his father had been hanged in the mass execution of Santee Sioux warriors at Mankato, but in 1873 Many Lightnings returned. He had escaped the gallows by President Lincoln's pardon and instead had served three years in jail in Davenport, Iowa. He then converted to Christianity and took the surname of his deceased wife's father, calling himself Jacob Eastman. He renamed his son Charles Eastman and urged him to learn white Americans' ways. "We have now entered upon this life, and there is no going back," he told his son.[54]

Jacob Eastman sent his son to school. "It is the same as if I sent you on your first warpath," he told him. "I shall expect you to conquer."[55] Charles first attended Santee Normal Training School in Nebraska. "I hardly think I was ever tired in my life until those first days of boarding school," he wrote later. "All day things seemed to come and pass with a wearisome regularity, like walking railway ties — the step was too short for me. At times I felt something of the fascination of the new life, and again there would arise in me a dogged resistance, and a voice seemed to be saying, 'It is cowardly to depart from the old things.'"[56] In September 1876, just months after the Battle of the Little Bighorn, Eastman entered Beloit College in Wisconsin. "I was now a stranger in a strange country," he recalled, "and deep in a strange life from which I could not retreat."[57] After stints at Knox College in Illinois and Kimball Union Academy in New Hampshire, he graduated from Dartmouth College in 1887 and went on to earn his medical degree at Boston University.

Committed to using his education and skills for the benefit of his people, Eastman became the agency physician at the Pine Ridge Reservation in 1890, just as the tensions revolving around the Ghost Dance (see pages 334–35) were reaching a breaking point. There he met Elaine Goodale, a young New England woman who was teaching on the reservation and who spoke Sioux. Their courtship was overshadowed by the tragedy at Wounded Knee, but they married in 1891 and had six children. Despite the horrors he witnessed treating the survivors of the massacre, Eastman remained a staunch advocate of educating his people in American ways. Many of his later writings reflected the ideas of the social Darwinism of the time that asserted that unchanging Indians were a vanishing race. "The North American Indian was the highest type of pagan and uncivilized man," he wrote in 1902. "But the Indian no longer exists as a natural and free man. Those remnants which now dwell upon the reservations present only a sort of tableau — a fictitious copy of the past."[58] He became prominent as one of a group of Native reformers known as "Red Progressives," supported the Dawes Allotment Act, and worked for the Office of Indian Affairs. In the age of the self-made man, many whites held him up as a model for what Indians could achieve if they would only abandon their Indian ways and learn to live like other Americans.

But Charles Eastman never entirely stopped being Ohiyesa. Although he worked to bring about assimilation of Indians into mainstream society, he had been raised in the traditional ways and remained strongly attached to Sioux values. He wrote extensively — often in collaboration with his wife — for a non-Indian audience that contained many influential people. To some extent, he told them what they wanted to hear, but he also supported Indian rights and was a founding member of the Society of American Indians in 1911. He criticized American injustice and hypocrisy and insisted that Americans had much to learn from Indian society about morality and spirituality. He attacked corrupt Indian agents and challenged the administration of Indian affairs. Before his death in 1939, Ohiyesa returned to Ontario. There he lived and died in a forest cabin, thereby completing the circle by returning from "civilization" to "the deep woods."[59] In the rapidly changing world of American Indians, Eastman demonstrated that one could adapt without totally assimilating. One biographer wrote that he "could wear both a war bonnet and a high starched collar with equal aplomb."[60] Eastman insisted that he could be both an Indian and an American. "I am an Indian," he wrote at the end of his autobiography, "and while I have learned much from civilization, for which I am grateful, I have never lost my Indian sense of right and justice. I am for development and progress along social and spiritual lines, rather than those of commerce, nationalism, or material efficiency. Nevertheless, so long as I live, I am an American."[61]

NATIVE AMERICANS ENTER THE TWENTIETH CENTURY

In 1900 the United States census estimated there were fewer than 250,000 Indians in the country. Their count was low — the census takers decided who was or was not Indian and recorded many Indians as "black," "mulatto," or "colored," while Indians who could pass as white often found that safer to do than proclaiming their Indian identity and possibly attracting racist attention. Nevertheless the figures reflected four hundred years of demographic decline. In the eyes of most Americans, Indians were doomed to extinction.

At the same time, Indians found themselves with declining legal protection and subjected to increasing state and federal legislation. After the Supreme Court decision in *Ex Parte Crow Dog* in 1883 assured tribes some autonomy in settlement of criminal cases, Congress in 1885 passed the Major Crimes Act, which made it a federal crime for Indians to commit rape, murder, manslaughter, assault with intent to kill, arson, or larceny against another Indian on a reservation. (In later years, the list of crimes was expanded to fourteen with the addition of kidnapping, incest, assault with a dangerous weapon, assault resulting in serious bodily injury, burglary, robbery, and sexual relations with a female under sixteen years of age.) As scholar of federal Indian law N. Bruce Duthu explains, "The jurisdictional intrusiveness of this law cannot be overstated, since it represented the first major attempt by the federal government to regulate the affairs *of* the Indians, rather than *with* the Indians." When an Indian accused of murdering an Indian victim challenged the law as beyond the scope of federal power, the Supreme Court in *United States v. Kagama* (1886) concluded that Congress acted within its powers because "Indian tribes *are* the wards of the nation. They are communities *dependent* on the United States, dependent largely for their daily food; dependent for their political rights."[62] In 1903, with the support of the Indian Rights Association, the Kiowas sued the secretary of the interior to stop the transfer of their lands by a fraudulent agreement that blatantly contravened the Treaty of Medicine Lodge. In *Lone Wolf v. Hitchcock* (1903), the Supreme Court declared that Congress had complete constitutional authority over Indian affairs and could abrogate or break its own treaties. In *Worcester v. Georgia* in 1832 (see "Foundations of Federal Indian Law and a Native Response," pages 291–98), the Court had described Indian tribes as "domestic dependent nations" with the right of self-government; the ruling in *Lone Wolf v. Hitchcock* depicted them as a weak and colonized people, wards of the government ruled by the plenary power of Congress.[63] The Supreme Court in *Winters v. United States* (1908) recognized Indians as having federally reserved water rights, but on the whole Congress had the power to dispose of Indian lands as it saw fit.[64]

"I Still Live": Indians in American Society

In spite of past population losses and legal constraints, the twentieth century was to be a time of endurance and survival, not decline and disappearance, in Indian country and in Indian communities. Indian people not only survived, but they also demonstrated their ability to adapt to new, "American" ways of life — such as playing on sports teams and in bands, driving motorcars, and going to the movies — and still be Indian.[65] Surviving the dark years of the late nineteenth and early twentieth centuries built resources for later resurgence in a different social and political climate. Indian resilience, even in the midst of far-reaching and dramatic change, forced the government and reformers to abandon policies based on the assumption that Indians were "vanishing Americans" and to consider new approaches in their relations with Indian peoples.[66]

With their traditional economies in ruins, many Indian peoples found that they had to find new ways of making a living. Mohawk men from Kahnawake near Montreal helped construct the bridge over the St. Lawrence River, and Iroquois men developed a reputation as steelworkers on high-rise projects. Many Mohawks traveled south to New York during the city's building boom in the 1920s, working on the Empire State Building, the Chrysler Building, and the George Washington Bridge. Railroads brought a flood of immigrants to the Puget Sound region of western Washington after the Civil War. Some Indians were pushed out of their homelands, but others found new opportunities for employment and barter — selling fish, logging and working in lumber mills, cultivating hops — that brought them into daily contact with their new neighbors.[67] In Alaska, Tlingit people continued the subsistence economies of old but also joined the labor market. Tlingit men fished for the canneries and worked in mining and lumbering operations; women sold baskets and handicrafts to tourists on the streets of Sitka or processed fish alongside Chinese immigrant workers.[68] Although exploitation of Indian land, labor, and resources devastated environments, disrupted communities, and generated dependence, some Indian people participated in the market economy in ways that helped fend off white domination. Menominees in Wisconsin who worked as loggers and mill laborers and Metlakatlan Tsimshians who harvested timber and salmon in British Columbia achieved a measure of prosperity but used the proceeds to strengthen their communities and preserve their cultural independence.[69] In northern California, Indians from the Round Valley Reservation took cash-paying jobs as seasonal migrant laborers, picking hops, shearing sheep, and working on ranches. Despite the exploitation inherent in such roles, they were able to provide for their families in hard times, maintain ties to relatives and to the landscape, and build a strong sense of community and identity as agricultural migrant workers.[70] As railroads brought increased traffic to the Southwest, Navajo weavers supplied traders and dealers with blankets to sell to tourists.[71]

In New England, Indian women continued to make traditional baskets, but they sold them door-to-door or to tourists. Many young Indian women found employment in textile mills in Lowell, Massachusetts, or Manchester, New Hampshire. Native American men continued, as they had since the eighteenth century, to go to sea, while others found work closer to home as trappers, as guides (writer Henry David Thoreau had hired Penobscot guides for his excursions through Maine in the mid-nineteenth century), or in the logging industry. Some migrated to the cities. Mi'kmaq Indians from northern Maine and the Maritime Provinces of Canada worked as seasonal laborers, picking potatoes and blueberries. Some traveled west to work on building the Canadian Pacific Railroad. Others moved south to work in Boston. Native people in New England maintained important ties of kinship and community and began to develop regional networks and pan-Indian organizations. During the nineteenth century, Connecticut, Massachusetts, and Rhode Island all took measures to "detribalize" the Indians, essentially

◆ **O-o-be, a Kiowa Woman, Fort Sill, Oklahoma, 1895, and James Earle Fraser's**
End of the Trail

At the end of the nineteenth century, most Americans assumed that Indians were a tragic and vanishing race and that Native cultures were dying out as depicted in Fraser's sculpture *End of the Trail*. O-o-be, a young Kiowa woman wearing a smile and a hide dress decorated with elk teeth, clearly had other ideas. Photo of O-o-be: *National Museum of the American Indian, Smithsonian Institution (catalog number P13149);* Sculpture: © *Peter Harholdt/CORBIS.*

to legislate them out of existence as Indian tribes.[72] But in 1923, when most white Americans assumed Indians had long since disappeared from the area, the New England Indian Council formed, adopting as its motto "I still live."

During the nineteenth century, Native women on the Plains had adapted new materials obtained in trade, such as woolen cloth from England, vermilion from China, and glass beads from Venice, for use with existing materials such as hide, porcupine quills, and elk teeth in making and decorating clothing. They used glass beads to experiment with different colors, techniques, and designs, in some cases incorporating stars and stripes motifs in their beadwork (see the bonnet on page 335). Women of different tribes developed distinct styles, which they passed on to the next generation.[73] Many women earned cash by selling beadwork and other crafts to off-reservation markets. Plains Indian men, whose economy and role had rested so heavily on hunting buffalo, faced a particularly bleak future once the buffalo herds were destroyed. Many adjusted to the new conditions and the post-allotment world by hunting smaller game, herding, gardening, and working for wages. But the government's exhortations to settle down and take up farming on 160 acres of land had little appeal for many young men. Instead, a few found employment in a venture that took them far from the hard times on the reservations and required them to dress and act like Indians "of old."

Cultural Expression and the American Way

Despite the government's determination to eradicate their warrior culture, some Plains Indians entered the twentieth century riding horses, wearing war bonnets, and attacking wagon trains, albeit in places far from the Plains. For a generation after the end of the wars for the Great Plains, entrepreneurs like William F. (Buffalo Bill) Cody hired Indians to travel the East and Europe as members of Wild West shows. They donned headdresses, rode bareback, and danced for audiences in the eastern United States, England, France, Belgium, Germany, Italy, Austria, Poland, Russia, and even Australia. Even Sitting Bull (see pages 327, 334) participated in Buffalo Bill's show for a few months in 1885, and many other Lakotas joined Cody's Wild West show, including two dozen men who had been imprisoned after the Ghost Dance conflict. "Show Indians" earned money and got to see the world; they became tourists as well as entertainers. Some met presidents, queens, and kings; some attended theater and opera; some, like the Oglala Red Shirt, became celebrities on the tour circuit. Black Elk, another Oglala who later became a spiritual leader, joined the show as a young man "for adventure." Inevitably, some of the performers died in cities far from home. Indian commissioners, members of Congress, humanitarian reformers, and some members of the Society of American Indians opposed the shows for exploiting Indians and perpetuating an image of Indian "barbarism." Some scholars view the Indians who participated as victims of commercial capitalism that marginalized Native people. Certainly the Wild West shows and the people who played "hostile Indians" in them helped to create a popular stereotype of all Indians as feather-bonneted, horse-riding warriors. But the Indians who participated in the shows do not seem to have viewed themselves as victims or pawns. They got paid for displaying a part of their history and culture that the government was intent on destroying, and many seem to have enjoyed themselves doing it. As one scholar of the Wild West show concludes, it was "the only place to be an Indian — and defiantly so — and still remain relatively free from the interference of missionaries, teachers, agents, humanitarians, and politicians."[74]

In a similar vein, Indians continued to use music and dancing as ways to express their Indianness. From the nineteenth century through the 1920s, the government saw music as a way to assimilate Indians: Indian dancing and singing on the reservations was banned, while students in boarding-school bands played songs in stage-managed performances that celebrated "Americanness." But student

◆ **Buffalo Bill Cody and Lakotas in Venice, c. 1890**
Plains Indians who joined Wild West shows in the late nineteenth and early twentieth
centuries traveled far from home and, like the Lakotas photographed here with Buffalo Bill
Cody (seated in front) in Venice, "discovered a new world." *Buffalo Bill Center of the West, Cody,
Wyoming, USA; Garlow Collection, P.69.822.*

bands at Carlisle and Haskell became sources of Indian pride, and some students
went on to form "all-Indian bands." Indian dancers, singers, and musicians produced performances that, often in new and creative ways, expressed their enduring
identity as Indians, not their transformation into Americans. On the reservations,
people held giveaway dances to redistribute food to those in need, dances to bring
returning students back into the community, and dances to honor returning soldiers. They often used Fourth of July celebrations and other national holidays,
which were the few occasions when agents permitted dancing on the reservations,
to perform dances that the government was trying to eradicate. Dancing was a

way of reasserting Indian identity and values in defiance of government policies of cultural oppression.[75]

For a few Indians, sports provided access to temporary fame and fortune. Louis Francis Sockalexis, a Penobscot from Maine, played baseball at College of the Holy Cross and Notre Dame. In 1897 he broke into the major leagues, playing for Cleveland. His first season was a runaway success, but alcoholism cut short his career and he died at the age of forty-two in 1913.[76] Another athlete, Jim Thorpe, was born on the Sauk & Fox Reservation in Oklahoma in 1887, the year the Allotment Act was passed. In 1898 his father sent him to the Haskell Institute in Lawrence, Kansas, where the eleven-year-old learned to play football. But Thorpe was a mediocre student at best, so in 1904 his father sent him to Carlisle, partly because it was too far for the youth to run away to home. At Carlisle, Jim found his niche in athletics and earned varsity letters in eleven sports: football, track, baseball, boxing, wrestling, lacrosse, gymnastics, swimming, hockey, handball, and basketball. Relying on speed, skill, and innovative plays rather than brawn, the Carlisle Indians football team defeated Ivy League opponents, trounced an Army team that included future general and president Dwight D. Eisenhower, and revolutionized the way the game was played. The Carlisle Indians football team created a new source of Indian pride and identity in an institution that was designed to eradicate both. In 1912 Thorpe competed for the United States in the Olympic Games in Stockholm, winning a gold medal in both the pentathlon and the decathlon, an achievement unequaled in Olympic history. (The Hopi runner Louis Tewanima won silver in the 10,000 meters.[77]) A year later, however, the U.S. Amateur Athletic Union stripped Thorpe of his medals and erased his name from the record books after discovering that he had once played baseball for a minor-league team in North Carolina for $25 a week and was therefore a professional. Thorpe went on to play baseball for the New York Giants and other teams and then played professional football. In 1920 he became the first president of the American Professional Football Association (now the National Football League). Press polls judged Thorpe the greatest athlete of the first half of the twentieth century, but after he quit football in 1928 his life was marked by failed marriages, struggles with alcohol, and odd jobs, including bit roles in "cowboy and Indian" movies. A movie was made about him in 1951—*Jim Thorpe, All American,* starring Burt Lancaster, an "all-American" actor of Irish descent, in the title role. Thirty years after Thorpe's death in 1953, a court ruled that he had been unjustly stripped of his medals, and duplicate medals were given to his children.[78]

A New Generation of Leaders

In the first decades of the twentieth century, some Indians began to "talk back" to the United States. A new generation of Indians—schooled in American ways, united for the first time by a common language, English, and aware of the challenges confronting their people—subjected American society to searching scrutiny, criticized its inequalities and hypocrisies, and challenged the supposed superiority of "civilization" by pointing out enduring qualities in Indian life and culture.[79]

In 1911 some of these new Native American professionals and intellectuals founded the Society of American Indians (SAI) in Columbus, Ohio. The society's members included some of the more influential Indians of the day: Charles Eastman; the Rev. Sherman Coolidge, an Arapaho Episcopalian minister who had been captured at the age of seven by American troops and raised by an army captain and who had lived in New York City for many years; Carlos Montezuma, a Yavapai Apache who earned a medical degree and became a respected physician in Chicago (see "What Indians Must Do," pages 420–22); Henry Roe Cloud, a Winnebago who obtained bachelor's and master's degrees from Yale and became a Presbyterian minister; Arthur S. Parker, a Seneca anthropologist; Oneida writer and activist Laura Cornelius Kellogg; and the Sioux writer Gertrude Bonnin, also known as Zitkala-Ša (see "The Melancholy of Those Black Days," on pages 428–32). These people — the first generation of modern pan-Indian intellectuals — became known as the "Red Progressives." According to Sherman Coolidge, the establishment of the SAI, an organization "managed solely for and by the Indians," meant that "the hour has struck when the best educated and most cultured of the race should come together to voice the common demands, to interpret correctly the Indians' heart, and to contribute in a more united way their influence and exertion with the rest of the citizens of the United States in all lines of progress and reform, for the welfare of the Indian race in particular, and all humanity in general."[80]

The SAI favored assimilation but also lobbied for citizenship, improved health care on reservations, a special court of claims for Indians, and other reform issues. Disputes over the Bureau of Indian Affairs and the Native American Church caused deep divisions and the society declined in the 1920s, but it represented a first step toward the kind of pan-Indian unity that would play a vital role in the protection of Indian rights and the preservation of Indian culture in later years; in addressing the ambiguous status of Indian people and nations in the United States the SAI tackled issues that remained a century later.[81] Far to the north, Tlingit and other Alaskan communities formed the Alaska Native Brotherhood in 1912 and lobbied to protect Native resources and rights and to end discrimination.

Other individuals who remained on their reservations forged new roles for themselves and found unconventional ways to represent their people. Quanah Parker transformed himself from a nineteenth-century Comanche warrior to a twentieth-century Comanche politician and businessman. The son of captive Cynthia Ann Parker, he fought against the Americans in the Red River War of 1874–75 and rose to prominence as the principal chief and a savvy politician after his people were confined to the reservation. He made himself useful to the U.S. government as a leader who would comply with the new policies being implemented on the reservation. He leased grazing rights on Comanche lands to local

◆ **Quanah Parker**

Quanah Parker (c. 1852–1911) with Tonasa (or To-nar-cy), one of his five wives, outside their house in 1892. Tonasa accompanied her husband on trips to Washington, D.C., and she was with him when he died in 1911. The government worried about what it called Quanah's "much married condition" and pressured him to give wives up in accordance with its regulations but he still had a second wife—named To-pay—at the time of his death. *Granger, NYC.*

cattlemen. He achieved wealth and position, owning a large herd of cattle and living in an impressive house. He sent his children away to receive an American education. But he also used his position to represent his people; he refused to cut his hair or to comply with the government's rules forbidding polygyny, and he became a leader in the Native American Church.[82]

The buttons of the peyote cactus, native to the southwestern United States, produce a psychedelic effect when dried and ingested. Peyote buttons had been used in Mexico and in religious rituals along the Rio Grande for centuries. In the late nineteenth and early twentieth centuries, however, a new religion based on the ritual use of peyote entered Indian Territory in the United States and then spread north across the Plains. It grew to become the Native American Church of the twentieth century. Though some of the rituals differed among regions and tribes, the religion had widespread appeal because it combined Christian elements with ancient tribal roots and provided "a bridge between traditional faiths and the realities of contemporary life."[83] Whereas many older ceremonies, such as the Sun Dance, took place in the open during the day, peyote ceremonies were performed quietly at night and could more easily escape the prying eyes of Indian agents intent on suppressing tribal religions. The religion was opposed by many non-Indians — and by some Indians. But in 1918 the Native American Church was formally organized in Oklahoma. Its declared purpose was to promote Christian religious belief using "the practices of the peyote sacrament" and to teach Christian morality and self-respect. The church prohibited alcohol and advocated monogamy, family responsibility, and hard work as means of combating the social problems that plagued many Indian communities. The use of peyote in ceremonies continued to draw opposition: fourteen states outlawed the drug by 1923; the Navajo tribal council banned it from their reservation in 1940; and it was the subject of a Supreme Court case and new federal legislation in the 1990s. Nevertheless, the Native American Church, with approximately 300,000 members, functions as an important element in the lives of many Indian people today.[84]

Soldiers and Citizens

In the summer of 1914, following the assassination of Archduke Franz Ferdinand, heir to the throne of Austria-Hungary, Europe's balance of powers unraveled, plunging the world into war, with the British Empire, France, the Russian Empire, and their allies pitted against the German Empire, the Austro-Hungarian Empire, the Ottoman Empire, and Bulgaria. The United States stayed out of the conflict for several years, but following German infringements on American neutrality, President Woodrow Wilson asked Congress for a declaration of war in 1917. More than 12,000 Indians served in the armed forces during the First World War, and many more contributed to the cause on the home front. American society, and the press in particular, interpreted the Indians' participation as evidence of their assimilation: "it may seem strange to see an Apache in a sailor's blue uniform," said one paper, "but it merely shows that he has become an American and has passed the tribal stage." That Indians were now fighting for the United States and defending Western values and democracy constituted, in the words of one scholar, "the ultimate vindication of U.S. expansionism, since it proved that the vanquished were better off for having been conquered." But Indians pointed to their patriotism and sacrifice as evidence of their readiness for full citizenship: "Challenged, the Indian has responded and shown himself a citizen of the world," said Seneca Arthur C. Parker, president of the Society for American Indians. Service in the U.S. armed forces offered young men a chance to win war honors, as their fathers and grandfathers had done. They also believed that it would demonstrate their capacity to take care of their own affairs and might help to bring more justice for Indian people.[85] Many served out of devotion to their homeland more than loyalty to the United States. "Our people's devotion to this land is stronger than any piece of paper," said one man who served in the U.S. navy in World War I. "That devotion is deeper than our mistrust," agreed his granddaughter, Roberta Conner, director of the Tamástslikt Cultural Institute of the Confederated Tribes of the Umatilla Indian Reservation. "It is more important than our wounds from past injustices. It is tougher than hatred."[86]

Although many Indians volunteered, some resisted the draft on the basis that they were not citizens and could not vote, or because they saw it as an infringement of their tribal sovereignty and treaty rights. Carlos Montezuma criticized the drafting of Indians as "another wrong perpetrated upon the Indian without FIRST bestowing his just title—THE FIRST AMERICAN CITIZEN."[87] The Iroquois Confederacy made a separate declaration of war against Germany, emphasizing that its members were independent nations and fighting the war as allies, not as subjects, of the United States.°

Whatever their reasons for joining up, Indian soldiers saw plenty of service on the front lines. Most served the infantry and field artillery, many acted as scouts, runners, and snipers, and a contingent of Choctaws using their own language helped ensure the security of battlefield communications and established a precedent for "code talking" that was to prove important in World War II. The casualty rate for Indian soldiers was more than twice the overall rate for American soldiers and sailors.[88] Still, Native Americans who had served and suffered for their country returned home to find little had changed for Indian people.

In 1924 Congress passed the Indian Citizenship Act, extending citizenship and suffrage to all American Indians. Roughly two-thirds of Indian people, including those who had taken allotments or served in World War I, had already been accorded citizenship, but passage of the act affirmed the belief that America's first peoples had become sufficiently assimilated to take up their role as participating American citizens. But things were not that simple. Some states continued to place obstacles in the way of Indian voting, and not all Indians eagerly embraced their new status. "The law of 1924 cannot . . . apply to Indians," declared one Mohawk, "since they are independent nations. Congress may as well pass a law making Mexicans citizens."[89] To some, the Indian Citizenship Act was yet another attempt to control a long-sovereign people.

Indian Affairs on the Eve of the Great Depression

The 1920s were a time of unprecedented affluence for many Americans. Indians became U.S. citizens, but, unlike Jackson Burnett and the Osages (see page 391), few shared in the prosperity that many Americans enjoyed during the "Roaring Twenties." In 1926 the Department of the Interior commissioned a team of scholars, headed by anthropologist Lewis Meriam, to conduct a survey of Indian affairs. Henry Roe Cloud, a Winnebago graduate of Yale University and Auburn Theological Seminary and one of the founding members of the Society of American Indians, was one of the principal investigators. The commission's report, published two years later as *The Problem of Indian Administration* and popularly known as the Meriam Report, detailed the problems confronting American Indians and drew attention to the poverty, ill health, and despair that beset Indian communities. Indians could not, said the report, live in "a glass case" and the clock could not be turned back; the traditional economic foundations of Indian culture could not be restored. Nevertheless, the report recommended reforms in the Bureau of Indian Affairs to increase its efficiency and promote the social and economic advancement of Indians "so that they may be absorbed into the

---

° The Six Nations of Canada sent a delegation to London in 1921 and to the League of Nations in Geneva in 1923 to argue their case that as a sovereign nation they were exempt from Canada's laws.

prevailing civilization or be fitted to live in the presence of that civilization at least in accordance with a minimum standard of health and decency."[90] These minimum goals had rarely been attained since the Allotment Act had weakened the communal and family basis of Indian life. The report called for an end to allotment and advocated phasing out Indian boarding schools, where "provisions for the care of the Indian children . . . are grossly inadequate." The Indian Service, said the report, "has not appreciated the fundamental importance of a family life and community activities in the social and economic development of a people."[91] The place of American Indian citizens in American society and the relations of Indian nations with the United States were far from resolved. While the federal government continued to legislate rules to govern Native peoples, American Indians continued their struggle to persist and thrive in a larger and still often hostile nation.

DOCUMENTS

An American Reformer Views "the Indian Problem" and an Indian Reformer Views the Indian Bureau

LOOKING AT THE DEVASTATING EFFECTS that the policies of the late nineteenth century had on Indian life and lives, it is easy to forget that many of those advocating and implementing these policies believed they were working in the Indians' best interests. It is also easy to depict Indian peoples as only victims of the policies, never as people who debated, resisted, and sometimes shaped them. The two documents reprinted here illustrate how two reformers—one white, one Indian—viewed "the Indian problem."

The assault on tribalism that culminated in the Allotment Act of 1887 stemmed in part from concern that the government was mishandling Indian affairs, mistreating Indian people, and missing the opportunity to transform American Indians into American citizens. Leaders in the movement to reform Indian affairs were "a group of earnest men and women who unabashedly called themselves 'the friends of the Indian,'" wrote historian Father Francis P. Prucha. They "set about to solve the 'Indian problem' in terms of religious sentiment and patriotic outlook that were peculiarly American. They had great confidence in the righteousness of their cause, and they knew that God approved."[92]

Convinced of the superiority of Anglo-Saxon Protestant civilization, the white reformers saw little or nothing of value in Indian civilization. The "Indian problem" would disappear, they believed, when individual Indian people were swallowed up by American society and Indian tribes ceased to exist. The reformers had no compunction about dictating to Indians what was best for them; after all, they believed they were saving the Indians from themselves and from extinction. The reformers championed Indian rights in some important cases, but their main goals were to revolutionize Indian policy and thoroughly assimilate Indians. Private property, citizenship, and education were the keys to "Americanizing" American Indians.

The reformers were organized and vocal, and they exerted tremendous influence in Congress on the direction of Indian policy. To understand the changes in Indian policy and the intensity of the assault on Indian life, we must try to understand the people who spearheaded the movement. We need to consider how they saw things at the end of the nineteenth century. "They were an articulate lot," said Prucha. They "employed rhetoric as a weapon in their crusade" and "hammered incessantly on the public conscience" in speeches, pamphlets, press releases, articles, editorials, and letters to congressmen and government officials. Only by reading their words "can one begin to appreciate the strength of their convictions and the lengths to which they were willing to go in their program of Americanizing the Indians."[93]

Merrill Gates was one of the most prominent Indian reformers of the time. A former president of Rutgers University and of Amherst College, he was appointed to the Board of Indian Commissioners by President Chester Arthur in 1884. Gates served as president of the board and was an active participant at the Lake Mohonk conferences. In 1885 he prepared a long paper on Indian policy that was printed in the *Annual Report of the Board of Indian Commissioners.* The paper exemplifies the attitudes and thinking of the reformers and shows what Indian peoples faced in their struggle to preserve their cultures and communities in late nineteenth-century America — even from the "friends of the Indian."

Carlos Montezuma (c. 1866–1923) was born in central Arizona at a time when the influx of settlers and prospectors was disrupting the world of his Yavapai people. Named Wassaja by his parents, the young boy was captured by Pima Indians in 1871 and sold to an Italian photographer, Carlos Gentile, for thirty dollars.[94] Gentile gave him a new name and an education. Montezuma attended the University of Illinois and graduated from Chicago Medical College in 1889. He took an appointment in the Indian Service and worked at Fort Stevenson Indian School in North Dakota, the Western Shoshone Agency in Nevada, and the Colville Reservation in Washington. He served as medical officer at Richard Henry Pratt's school in Carlisle from 1894 to 1896 and then opened a private practice in Chicago.

Montezuma believed in the values of hard work and individualism espoused by people like Merrill Gates, and he believed Indian people had what it took to achieve great things if given the chance. But he complained bitterly about the government's Indian policies and believed that the Bureau of Indian Affairs stood in the way of the very "progress" that the government claimed to be promoting among Indians. He came into conflict with bureau personnel, gave lectures in which he criticized the bureau and the reservation system it supported, and advocated citizenship for Indian people. He supported assimilation but also argued for taking pride in Indian ways. He was one of the founding members of the Society of American Indians; he published the article "What Indians Must Do," excerpted here, in the society's *Quarterly Journal* in 1914. But not everyone in the SAI agreed with his outspoken views, and he later left the society. In 1916 he founded the magazine *Wassaja* (his Yavapai name) as a forum for his ideas.

Over time, Montezuma rebuilt his ties with the Yavapai community at Fort McDowell in Arizona. He visited when he could and he assisted the community in their fights to preserve their land and water. After he was diagnosed with tuberculosis, he returned to the Southwest and died at Fort McDowell in January 1923 — a year before Congress granted Indians citizenship.

MERRILL E. GATES
From the Seventeenth Annual Report of the Board of Indian Commissioners (1885)

. . . For what ought we to hope as the future of the Indian? What should the Indian become?

To this there is one answer — and but one. He should become an intelligent citizen of the United States. There is no other "manifest destiny" for any man or any body of men on our domain. To this we stand committed by all the logic of two thousand years of Teutonic and Anglo-Saxon history, since Arminius with his sturdy followers made a stand for liberty against the legions of Rome. Foremost champions of that peculiarly Anglo-Saxon idea, that supports a strong central government, moves as a whole, yet protects carefully the local and individual freedom of all the parts, we are, as a matter of course, to seek to fit the Indians among us as we do all other men for the responsibilities of citizenship. And by the stupendous precedent of eight millions of freedmen made citizens in a day, we have committed ourselves to the theory that the way to fit men for citizenship is to make them citizens. The dangers that would beset Indian voters solicited by the demagogue would not be greater than those which now attend him unprotected by law, the prey of sharpers, and too often the pauperized, ration-fed pensioner of our Government, which, when it has paid at all the sums it has promised to pay to Indians, has paid them in such a way as to undermine what manhood and self-respect the Indian had. For one, I would willingly see the Indians run the risk of being flattered a little by candidates for Congress. None of their tribes are destitute of shrewd men who would watch the interests of the race.

Has our Government in its dealings with the Indians hitherto adopted a course of legislation and administration, well adapted to build up their

manhood and make them intelligent, self-supporting citizens?

They are the wards of the Government. Is not a guardian's first duty so to educate and care for his wards as to make them able to care for themselves? It looks like intended fraud if a guardian persists in such management of his wards and such use of their funds intrusted to him as in the light of experience clearly unfits them and will always keep them unfit for the management of their own affairs and their own property. When a guardian has in his hands funds which belong to his wards, funds which have been expressly set apart for the education of those wards, funds which from time to time he has publicly professed himself to be about to use for that particular end, yet still retains the money from year to year while his wards suffer sadly in the utter lack of proper educational facilities, we call his conduct disgraceful — an outrage and a crying iniquity. Yet our Commissioner of Indian Affairs again and again calls attention to the fact that the Government has funds, now amounting to more than $4,000,000, which are by treaty due to Indians for educational purposes alone. Who can doubt that a comprehensive plan looking to the industrial and the general education of all Indians should be undertaken at once? . . .

But it is not merely in neglecting to provide direct means for their education that we have been remiss in our duty to the Indians. The money and care which our Government has given to the Indians in most cases has not been wisely directed to strengthening their manhood, elevating their morals, and fitting them for intelligent citizenship. We have massed them upon reservations, fenced off from all intercourse with the better whites. We have given them no law to protect them against crimes from within the tribe — almost none to protect them against aggression

SOURCE: *Seventeenth Annual Report of the Board of Indian Commissioners* (1885), 17–19, 26–35.

from without. And above all else we have utterly neglected to teach them the value of honest labor. Nay, by rations dealt out whether needed or not, we have interfered to suspend the efficient teaching by which God leads men to love and honor labor. We have taken from them the compelling inspiration that grows out of His law, "if a man will not work, neither shall he eat!" Why, if a race inured to toil were cut off from all intercourse with the outside world, and left to roam at large over a vast territory, regularly fed by Government supplies, how many generations would pass before that race would revert to barbarism?

We have held them at arm's length, cut them off from the teaching power of good example, and given them rations and food to hold them in habits of abject laziness. A civilization like ours would soon win upon the Indians and bring them rapidly into greater harmony with all its ideas if as a nation in our dealings with them we had shown a true spirit of humanity, civilization, and Christianity. But such a spirit cannot be discerned in the history of our legislation for the Indians or our treaties with them. We have never recognized the obligation that rests upon us as a dominant, civilized people, the strong Government, to legislate carefully, honorably, disinterestedly, for these people. We boast of the brilliant adaptations of science to practical ends and everyday uses as the distinctive mark of American progress. Where are the triumphs of social science discernible in the treatment Americans have given to this distinctively American question? We have not shown in this matter anything approaching that patient study of social conditions which England has shown for the uncivilized natives in her domain. The great mass of our legislation regarding Indians has had to do with getting land we had promised them into our possession by the promise of a price as low as we could fix and yet keep them from making border warfare upon us in sheer despair. The time of would-be reformers has been occupied too constantly in devising precautions to keep what

had been appropriated from being stolen before it reached the Indians. And when it has reached them it has too often been in the form of annuities and rations that keep them physically and morally in the attitude of lazy, healthy paupers. We have not seemed to concern ourselves with the question, How can we organize, enforce, and sustain institutions and habits among the Indians which shall civilize and Christianize them? The fine old legend, *noblesse oblige,*° we have forgotten in our broken treaties and our shamefully deficient legislation. . . .

Two peculiarities which mark the Indian life, if retained, will render his progress slow, uncertain and difficult. These are:

(1) The tribal organization.

(2) The Indian reservation.

I am satisfied that no man can carefully study the Indian question without the deepening conviction that these institutions must go if we would save the Indian from himself.

And first, the tribe. Politically it is an anomaly — an *imperium in imperio.*° Early in our history, when whites were few and Indians were relatively numerous and were grouped in tribes with something approaching to a rude form of government, it was natural, it was inevitable, that we should treat with them as tribes. It would have been hopeless for us to attempt to modify their tribal relations. But now the case is entirely different. There is hardly one tribe outside the five civilized tribes of the Indian Territory which can merit the name of an organized society or which discharges the simplest functions of government. Disintegration has long been the rule. Individualism, the keynote of our socio-political ideas in this century, makes itself felt by sympathetic vibrations even in the rude society of the Indian tribes. There is little of the old loyalty to a personal chief as representing a governing authority from the Great Spirit. Perhaps there never was so much of this as some have fancied among the Indians.

° The idea that with privilege comes responsibility.

° A government within a government.

Certainly there are few signs of it now. A passive acquiescence in the mild leadership of the promising son of a former leader, among the peaceable tribes of the southwest, or a stormy hailing by the young braves of a new and reckless leader, blood-thirsty for a raid upon the whites — these are the chief indications of the survival of the old spirit.

Indian chiefs are never law-makers, seldom even in the rudest sense law-enforcers. The councils where the chief is chosen are too often blast-furnaces of anarchy, liquefying whatever forms of order may have established themselves under a predecessor. The Indians feel the animus of the century. As personal allegiance to a chieftain and the sense of tribal unity wanes, what is taking its place? Literally, nothing. In some cases educated but immoral and selfish leaders take advantage of the old traditions to acquire influence which they abuse. On the whole, however, a rude, savage individuality is developing itself, but not under the guidance of law, moral, civil, or religious.

Surely the intelligence of our nation should devise and enforce a remedy for this state of affairs. . . .

The highest right of man is the right to be a man, with all that this involves. The tendency of the tribal organization is constantly to interfere with and frustrate the attainment of his highest manhood. The question whether parents have a right to educate their children to regard the tribal organization as supreme, brings us at once to the consideration of the family.

And here I find the key to the Indian problem. More than any other idea, this consideration of the family and its proper sphere in the civilizing of races and in the development of the individual, serves to unlock the difficulties which surround legislation for the Indian.

The family is God's unit of society. On the integrity of the family depends that of the State. There is no civilization deserving of the name where the family is not the unit of civil government. Even the extreme advocates of individualism must admit that the highest and most perfect personality is developed through those relations which the family renders possible and fosters. . . .

The tribal organization, with its tenure of land in common, with its constant divisions of goods and rations per capita without regard to service rendered, cuts the nerve of all that manful effort which political economy teaches us proceeds from the desire for wealth. True ideas of property with all the civilizing influences that such ideas excite are formed only as the tribal relation is outgrown. . . .

But the tribal system paralyzes at once the desire for property and the family life that ennobles that desire. Where the annuities and rations that support a tribe are distributed to the industrious and the lazy alike, while almost all property is held in common, there cannot be any true stimulus to industry. And where the property which a deceased father has called his own is at the funeral feast distributed to his adult relatives, or squandered in prolonged feasting, while no provision whatever is made for the widow or the children, how can the family be perpetuated, or the ideal of the permanence and the preciousness of this relation become clear and powerful. Yet this is the custom in by far the greater number of the Indian tribes. . . .

As the allegiance to tribe and chieftain is weakened, its place should be taken by the sanctities of family life and an allegiance to the laws which grow naturally out of the family! Lessons in law for the Indian should begin with the developing and the preservation, by law, of those relations of property and of social intercourse which spring out of and protect the family. First of all, he must have land in severalty.°

Land in severalty, on which to make a home for his family. This land the Government should, where necessary, for a few years hold in trust for him or his heirs, inalienable and unchargeable. But it shall be his. It shall be patented to him as an individual. He shall hold it by what the Indians

---

° Individual ownership of a tract of land.

who have been hunted from reservation to reservation pathetically call, in their requests for justice, "a paper-talk from Washington, which tells the Indian what land is his so that a white man cannot get it away from him." "There is no way of reaching the Indian so good as to show him that he is working for a home. Experience shows that there is no incentive so strong as the confidence that by long, untiring labor, a man may secure a home for himself and his family." The Indians are no exception to this rule. There is in this consciousness of a family-hearth, of land and a home in prospect as permanently their own, an educating force which at once begins to lift these savages out of barbarism and sends them up the steep toward civilization, as rapidly as easy divorce laws are sending some sections of our country down the slope toward barbaric heathenism. . . .

Thus the family and a homestead prove the salvation of those whom the tribal organization and the reservation were debasing. It was a step in advance when Agent Miles began to issue rations to families instead of to the headmen of the tribe. Every measure which strengthens the family tie and makes clearer the idea of family life, in which selfish interests and inclinations are sacrificed for the advantage of the whole family, is a powerful influence toward civilization.

In this way, too, family affection and care for the education and the virtue of the young are promoted. Thus such law as is necessary to protect virtue, to punish offenses against purity, and to abolish polygamy, will be welcomed by the Indians. These laws enforced will help still further to develop true family feeling. Family feeling growing stronger and stronger as all the members of the family work on their own homestead for the welfare of the home, will itself incline all toward welcoming the reign of law, and will increase the desire of all for systematic education. The steadying, educating effect of property will take hold upon these improvident children of the West, who have for too long lived as if the injunction, "Take no thought for the morrow," in its literal sense, were their only law.

We must as rapidly as possible break up the tribal organization and give them law, with the family and land in severalty as its central idea. We must not only give them law, we must force law upon them. We must not only offer them education, we must force education upon them. Education will come to them by complying with the forms and the requirements of the law. . . .

While we profess to desire their civilization, we adopt in the Indian reservation the plan which of all possible plans seems most carefully designed to preserve the degrading customs and the low moral standards of heathen barbarism. Take a barbaric tribe, place them upon a vast tract of land from which you carefully exclude all civilized men, separate them by hundreds of miles from organized civil society and the example of reputable white settlers, and having thus insulated them in empty space, doubly insulate them from Christian civilization by surrounding them with sticky layers of the vilest, most designingly wicked men our century knows, the whiskey-selling whites and the debased half-breeds who infest the fringes of our reservations, men who have the vices of the barbarian plus the worst vices of the reckless frontiersman and the city criminal, and then endeavor to incite the electrifying, life-giving currents of civilized life to flow through this doubly insulated mass. If an Indian now and then gets glimpses of something better and seeks to leave this seething mass of in-and-in breeding degradation, to live in a civilized community, give him no protection by law and no hope of citizenship. If he has won his way as many have done through the highest institutions of learning, with honor, tell him that he may see many of our largest cities ruled by rings of men, many of whom are foreigners by birth, ignorant, worthless, yet naturalized citizens, but that he must not hope to vote or to hold office.

If he says "I will be content to accumulate property, then," tell him "you may do so; but any one who chooses may withhold your wages, refuse to pay you money he has borrowed, plunder you as he will, and our law gives you no redress." Thus we drive the honest and ambitious Indian, as we do the criminals, back to the tribe and the reservation; and cutting them off from all hopes of bettering themselves while we feed their laziness on Government rations, we complain that they are not more ambitious and industrious.

Christian missionaries plunge into these reservations, struggle with the mass of evil there, and feeling that bright children can be best educated in the atmosphere of civilization, they send to Eastern institutions these Indian children plucked like fire-stained brands from the reservations. They are brought to our industrial training schools. The lesson taught by the comparison of their photographs when they come and when they go is wonderful.°

The years of contact with ideas and with civilized men and Christian women so transform them that their faces shine with a wholly new light, for they have indeed "communed with God." They came children; they return young men and young women; yet they look younger in the face than when they came to us. The prematurely aged look of hopeless heathenism has given way to that dew of eternal youth which marks the difference between the savage and the man who lives in the thoughts of an eternal future. . . .

° See examples of these photographs on pages 395–96.

Break up the reservation. Its usefulness is past. Treat it as we treat the fever-infected hospital when life has so often yielded to disease within its walls that we see clearly the place is in league with the powers of death, and the fiat goes forth, "though this was planned as a blessing it has proved to be a curse; away with it! burn it!"

Guard the rights of the Indian, but for his own good break up his reservations. Let in the light of civilization. Plant in alternate sections or townships white farmers, who will teach him by example. Reserve all the lands he needs for the Indian. Give land by trust-deed in severalty to each family.

Among the parts of the reservation to be so assigned to Indians in severalty retain alternate ranges or townships for white settlers. Let only men of such character as a suitable commission would approve be allowed to file on these lands. Let especial advantages in price of land, and in some cases let a small salary be offered, to induce worthy farmers thus to settle among the Indians as object-teachers of civilization. Let the parts of the reservations not needed be sold by the Government for the benefit of the Indians, and the money thus realized be used to secure this wise intermingling of the right kind of civilized men with the Indians. Over all, extend the law of the States and Territories, and let Indian and white man stand alike before the law. . . .

CARLOS MONTEZUMA
What Indians Must Do (1914)

We must free ourselves. Our peoples' heritage is freedom. Freedom reigned in their whole makeup. They harmonized with nature and lived

---

Source: Carlos Montezuma, "What Indians Must Do," *Quarterly Journal of the Society of American Indians* 2 (October–December 1914), 294–99; reprinted in Frederick E. Hoxie, ed., *Talking Back to Civilization: Indian Voices from the Progressive Era* (Boston: Bedford/St. Martin's, 2001), 92–95.

accordingly. Preaching freedom to our people on reservations does not make them free any more than you can, by preaching, free those prisoners who are in the penitentiary. Reservations are prisons where our people are kept to live and die, where equal possibilities, equal education and equal responsibilities are unknown. . . .

We must do away with the Indian Bureau. The reservation system has debarred us as a race from acquiring that knowledge to appreciate our property. The government after teaching us how to live without work has come to the conclusion "that the Indians are not commercialists" and, therefore, "we (his guardian) will remove them as we think best and use them as long as our administration lasts and make friends."° The Indian Department has drifted into commercialism at the expense of our poor benighted people. So they go on and say, "Let us not allot those Indians on that sweet flowing water because there are others who will profit by damming it up and selling it out to the newcomers; that the Indians do not use or develop their lands; five acres of irrigated land is all that one Indian can manage, but in order to be generous, we will give him ten acres and close up the books and call it square; that their vast forest does them no good, before the Indian can open his eyes let us transfer it to the Forestry Reserve Department. Never mind, let the Indian scratch for his wood to cook with and to warm himself in the years to come; that the Indians have no use for rivers, therefore, we will go into damming business and build them on their lands without their consent. Pay? No! Why should we?" They give us "C" class water instead of "A" class. They have got us! Why? Because we do not know the difference.

"In this valley the Indians have too much land. We will move them from where they have lived for centuries (by Executive order in behalf of the coming settlers). Even if he had cultivated and claims more than that, we will allot that Indian only ten acres. If he rebels and makes trouble, we will put him in jail until he is ready to behave himself." This poor Indian may try to get an Indian friend to help him out of his predicament. But right there the Indian helper is balked by the Indian Department and is told he is not wanted on the reservation. When an Indian collects money from among his tribe to defray expenses

to Washington and back in order to carry their complaints, and to be heard and considered in their rights, the superintendent with the aid of the Indian policeman takes this Indian, takes the money away from him and gives back the money to those who contributed, put[s] him in jail and brands him a grafter. . . .

The sooner the Government abolishes the Indian Bureau, the better it will be for we Indians in every way. The system that has kept alive the Indian Bureau has been instrumental in dominating over our race for fifty years. In that time the Indian's welfare has grown to the secondary and the Indian Bureau the whole thing, and therefore a necessary political appendage of the government. It sends out exaggerated and wonderful reports to the public in order to suck the blood of our race, so that it may have perpetual life to sap your life, my life and our children's future prospects. There are many good things to say about the Indian Department. It started out right with our people. It fed them, clothed them and protected them from going outside of the reservations. It was truly a place of refuge. Then they were dominated by agents; now they are called superintendents. On the reservation our people did not act without the consent of the Superintendent; they did not express themselves without the approval of the Superintendent, and *they did not dare to think,* for that would be to rival, to the Superintendent. Yesterday, today, our people are in the same benighted condition. As Indians they are considered nonentities. They are not anything to themselves and not anything to the world. . . .

We must be independent. When with my people for a vacation in Arizona I must live outdoors; I must sleep on the ground; I must cook in the fire on the ground; I must sit on the ground, I must eat nature's food and I must be satisfied with inconveniences that I do not enjoy at my Chicago home. Yet those blood relations of mine are independent, happy, because they were born and brought up in that environment, while as a greenhorn I find myself dependent

---

° Apparently these quotations are fictitious. Montezuma used them as rhetorical devices to make his point that the Indian Office cared little for its charges' welfare.[95]

and helpless in such simple life. In order for we Indians to be independent in the whirl of this other life, we must get into it and used to it and live up to its requirements and take our chances with the rest of our fellow creatures. Being caged up and not permitted to develop our facilities has made us a dependent race. We are looked upon as hopeless to save and hopeless to do anything for ourselves. The only Christian way, then, is to leave us alone and let us die in that condition. The conclusion is true that we will die that way if we do not hurry and get out of it and hustle for our salvation. Did you ever notice how other races hustle and bustle in order to achieve independence? Reservation Indians must do the same as the rest of the wide world.

As a full-blooded Apache Indian° I have nothing more to say. Figure out your responsibility and the responsibility of every Indian that hears my voice.

_____

° Yavapais are sometimes referred to as Yavapai Apaches.

QUESTIONS FOR CONSIDERATION

1. What criticisms does Gates level against the U.S. government's Indian policies, and what recommendations does he make for changing them?

2. What does Gates identify as the defining characteristics of tribal life that "hold Indians back," and what are the characteristics of Anglo-Saxon Protestant life with which he seeks to replace them?

3. What does Gates's paper reveal about how reformers, and eventually the federal government, were able to shift from a policy based on reservations to a policy based on dismantling reservations and yet remain consistent in their ultimate goal of "civilizing" Indians?

4. What does Montezuma advocate for Indian people? Do these goals seem attainable as he outlines them?

5. What is the tone of Montezuma's article, and what is its effect? Who is he addressing, and for what purpose?

6. Compare Montezuma's view of Indian society and Indian policy with that expressed by Gates. Where might they have found common ground?

Two Sioux School Experiences

INDIVIDUALS WHO UNDERWENT THE CULTURAL transformation programs at the boarding schools had mixed experiences. For many Indian students, the experience was heartbreaking and humiliating; they left these schools with bitter memories, little education, and few prospects. But some of those who endured the painful process and found fault with the system also learned from it and employed the knowledge and skills they acquired in their subsequent careers. The government viewed a boarding-school education as a powerful weapon of assimilation, and many Indian students rejected it for that same reason. But two Sioux writers, Luther Standing Bear and Gertrude Bonnin (or Zitkala-Ša), illustrate the ambivalent relationships some alumni had with the boarding-school system and their ability to use the education they received for their own purposes.

Born around the time of the Treaty of Fort Laramie in 1868, Plenty Kill was raised in traditional ways during traumatic years for his Lakota Sioux people. He participated in a buffalo hunt as a boy and was trained to become a Lakota warrior, but such male roles were soon precluded as the Lakotas became confined to reservations. In 1879 his father, Standing Bear, enrolled him in the first class at the new boarding school established in Carlisle, Pennsylvania. There his name was changed from Plenty Kill to Luther Standing Bear; he was subjected to the school's assimilationist curriculum, and he endured a sustained assault on his Lakota heritage and identity. But Standing Bear weathered the assault and did well at school.

When he graduated in 1884, he returned to the Rosebud Reservation. At Carlisle he had been trained as a tinsmith, but he found no use for his skills on the reservation. He became an assistant at the government school on the Rosebud reservation and in 1891 was appointed superintendent of one of the day schools on the Pine Ridge Reservation. He did a stint with Buffalo Bill's Wild West show and spent almost a year in England with the troupe. After holding a variety of jobs, he moved to California in 1912 and began a career as a film actor, playing Indian characters in silent movies and low-budget westerns. He became president of the Indian Actors Association.

Standing Bear died in 1939. On the surface, his life and career might point to the success of Carlisle in separating him from his Lakota community and paving the way for assimilation into modern society. He left the reservation and "made it" in modern America. But Standing Bear's writings — *My People the Sioux* (1928), *Indian Boyhood* (1931), *Land of the Spotted Eagle* (1933), and *Stories of the Sioux* (1934) — champion the values of Indian cultures and implicitly reject the assimilationist policies and philosophies that drove Carlisle. He was a severe critic of the government's reservation policies and of the repressive hand of Indian agents on Indian lives.

Zitkala-Ša (Red Bird), a Yankton Sioux, went to Carlisle not as a student but as a teacher. Born Gertrude Simmons (to a Yankton mother and a white father) in 1876, she left her home in South Dakota for Indiana at eight years old, lured by the promise of "red apples" at a Quaker-sponsored school, White's Indian Manual Labor Institute. Despite poor health, she continued her education at Earlham College in Indiana, where she became a skillful orator and musician. She also studied at the New England Conservatory of Music. In 1898 Richard Henry Pratt hired her to teach at Carlisle. Increasingly, however, she found that her education and career were pulling her away from her mother and her people. About this time she published a series of autobiographical essays under her self-given Yankton name, Zitkala-Ša. The essays were later published as *American Indian Stories* (1921) and, in the words of one scholar, "serve as emblems of the experience of many Indians living in transition between two worlds — the remembered past and the alien present, tradition and change."[96] The passages reprinted here recount her experiences as a student and a teacher. In 1902 she left Carlisle and returned to Yankton. She broke her engagement to Carlos Montezuma, who lived in Chicago and was unwilling to relocate, and married a Yankton man, Raymond Bonnin, who worked for the Indian Service.

Their family was assigned to the Uintah Ouray Ute Reservation in Utah, where they lived for fourteen years. Gertrude Bonnin taught, did public speaking, and became active in the Society of American Indians. When she was elected president of the society in 1916, the family moved to Washington, D.C. She edited the society's magazine, lobbied for reform of Indian policies, campaigned for Indian citizenship, and, like Pratt, strongly opposed peyote. She worked with the Indian Rights Association and the American Indian Defense Association, and in 1926 she and her husband formed the National Council of American Indians. She served as president of the council until she died in 1938.[97]

Standing Bear and Bonnin each experienced a personal journey from traditional life to the modern world through the boarding school. They used their literary and oratorical talents to defy, not promote, the assimilationist education policies of the time.

LUTHER STANDING BEAR
What a School Could Have Been Established (1933)

I grew up leading the traditional life of my people, learning the crafts of hunter, scout, and warrior from father, kindness to the old and feeble from mother, respect for wisdom and council from our wise men, and was trained by grandfather and older boys in the devotional rites to the Great Mystery.° This was the scheme of existence as followed by my forefathers for many centuries, and more centuries might have come and gone in much the same way had it not been for a strange people who came from a far land to change and reshape our world.

At the age of eleven years, ancestral life for me and my people was most abruptly ended without regard for our wishes, comforts, or rights in the matter. At once I was thrust into an alien world, into an environment as different from the one into which I had been born as it is possible to imagine, to remake myself, if I could, into the likeness of the invader.

By 1879, my people were no longer free, but were subjects confined on reservations under the rule of agents. One day there came to the agency a party of white people from the East. Their presence aroused considerable excitement when it became known that these people were school teachers who wanted some Indian boys and girls to take away with them to train as were white boys and girls.

° The Lakota term "Wakan Tanka," meaning sacred, divine, or creator, is usually translated as Great Spirit or Great Mystery.

SOURCE: Reprinted from *Land of the Spotted Eagle* by Luther Standing Bear (Lincoln: University of Nebraska Press, 1978), 229–37, by permission of the University of Nebraska Press. Copyright 1933 by Luther Standing Bear and renewed © 1960 by May Jones.

Now, father was a "blanket Indian,"° but he was wise. He listened to the white strangers, their offers and promises that if they took his son they would care well for him, teach him how to read and write, and how to wear white man's clothes. But to father all this was just "sweet talk," and I know that it was with great misgivings that he left the decision to me and asked if I cared to go with these people. I, of course, shared with the rest of my tribe a distrust of the white people, so I know that for all my dear father's anxiety he was proud to hear me say "Yes." That meant that I was brave.

I could think of no reason why white people wanted Indian boys and girls except to kill them, and not having the remotest idea of what a school was, I thought we were going East to die. But so well had courage and bravery been trained into us that it became a part of our unconscious thinking and acting, and personal life was nothing when it came time to do something for the tribe. Even in our play and games we voluntarily put ourselves to various tests in the effort to grow brave and fearless, for it was most discrediting to be called *can'l wanka,* or a coward. Accordingly there were few cowards, most Lakota men preferring to die in the performance of some act of bravery than to die of old age. Thus, in giving myself up to go East I was proving to my father that he was honored with a brave son. In my decision to go, I gave up many things dear to the heart of a little Indian boy, and one of the things over which my child mind grieved was the thought of saying good-bye to my pony. I rode him as far as I could on the journey, which was to the Missouri River, where we took the boat. There we parted from our parents, and it was a heart-breaking scene, women and children weeping. Some of the children changed their minds and were unable to go on the boat, but for many who did go it was a final parting.

On our way to school we saw many white people, more than we ever dreamed existed, and the manner in which they acted when they saw us quite indicated their opinion of us. It was only about three years after the Custer battle, and the general opinion was that the Plains people merely infested the earth as nuisances, and our being there simply evidenced misjudgment on the part of Wakan Tanka. Whenever our train stopped at the railway stations, it was met by great numbers of white people who came to gaze upon the little Indian "savages." The shy little ones sat quietly at the car windows looking at the people who swarmed on the platform. Some of the children wrapped themselves in their blankets, covering all but their eyes. At one place we were taken off the train and marched a distance down the street to a restaurant. We walked down the street between two rows of uniformed men whom we called soldiers, though I suppose they were policemen. This must have been done to protect us, for it was surely known that we boys and girls could do no harm. Back of the rows of uniformed men stood the white people craning their necks, talking, laughing, and making a great noise. They yelled and tried to mimic us by giving what they thought were war-whoops. We did not like this, and some of the children were naturally very much frightened. I remember how I tried to crowd into the protecting midst of the jostling boys and girls. But we were all trying to be brave, yet going to what we thought would end in death at the hands of the white people whom we knew had no love for us. Back on the train the older boys sang brave songs in an effort to keep up their spirits and ours too. In my mind I often recall that scene — eighty-odd blanketed boys and girls marching down the street surrounded by a jeering, unsympathetic people whose only emotions were those of hate and fear; the conquerors looking upon the conquered. And no more understanding us than if we had suddenly been dropped from the moon.

° The term "blanket Indian" was often used to describe a person who adhered to the old ways. In the parlance of white reformers, it carried pejorative connotations, and Indian students who "returned to the blanket" — i.e., went home to live as Indians on the reservation rather than making new lives for themselves in American society — were regarded with particular disdain by people like Richard Pratt.

At last at Carlisle the transforming, the "civilizing" process began. It began with clothes. Never, no matter what our philosophy or spiritual quality, could we be civilized while wearing the moccasin and blanket. The task before us was not only that of accepting new ideas and adopting new manners, but actual physical changes and discomfort has to be borne uncomplainingly until the body adjusted itself to new tastes and habits. Our accustomed dress was taken and replaced with clothing that felt cumbersome and awkward. Against trousers and handkerchiefs we had a distinct feeling — they were unsanitary and the trousers kept us from breathing well. High collars, stiff-bosomed shirts, and suspenders fully three inches in width were uncomfortable, while leather boots caused actual suffering. We longed to go barefoot, but were told that the dew on the grass would give us colds. That was a new warning for us, for our mothers had never told us to beware of colds, and I remember as a child coming into the tipi with moccasins full of snow. Unconcernedly I would take them off my feet, pour out the snow, and put them on my feet again without any thought of sickness, for in that time colds, catarrh, bronchitis, and *la grippe*° were unknown. But we were soon to know them. Then, red flannel undergarments were given us for winter wear, and for me, at least, discomfort grew into actual torture. I used to endure it as long as possible, then run upstairs and quickly take off the flannel garments and hide them. When inspection time came, I ran and put them on again, for I knew that if I were found disobeying the orders of the school I should be punished. My niece once asked me what it was that I disliked the most during those first bewildering days, and I said, "red flannel." Not knowing what I meant, she laughed, but I still remember those horrid, sticky garments which we had to wear next to the skin, and I still squirm and itch when I think of them. Of course, our hair was cut, and then there was much disapproval. But that was part of the transformation process and in

some mysterious way long hair stood in the path of our development. For all the grumbling among the bigger boys, we soon had our heads shaven. How strange I felt! Involuntarily, time and time again, my hands went to my head, and that night it was a long time before I went to sleep. If we did not learn much at first, it will not be wondered at, I think. Everything was queer, and it took a few months to get adjusted to the new surroundings.

Almost immediately our names were changed to those in common use in the English language. Instead of translating our names into English and calling Zinkcaziwin, Yellow Bird, and Wanbli K'leska, Spotted Eagle, which in itself would have been educational, we were just John, Henry, or Maggie, as the case might be. I was told to take a pointer and select a name for myself from the list written on the blackboard. I did, and since one was just as good as another, and as I could not distinguish any difference in them, I placed the pointer on the name Luther. I then learned to call myself by that name and got used to hearing others call me by it, too. By that time we had been forbidden to speak our mother tongue, which is the rule in all boarding-schools. This rule is uncalled for, and today is not only robbing the Indian, but America of a rich heritage. The language of a people is part of their history. Today we should be perpetuating history instead of destroying it, and this can only be effectively done by allowing and encouraging the young to keep it alive. A language, unused, embalmed, and reposing only in a book, is a dead language. Only the people themselves, and never the scholars, can nourish it into life.

Of all the changes we were forced to make, that of diet was doubtless the most injurious, for it was immediate and drastic. White bread we had for the first meal and thereafter, as well as coffee and sugar. Had we been allowed our own simple diet of meat, either boiled with soup or dried, and fruit, with perhaps a few vegetables, we should have thrived. But the change in clothing, housing, food, and confinement combined with lonesomeness was too much, and in three years nearly one half of the children from the

---

° *la grippe:* influenza.

Plains were dead and through with all earthly schools. In the graveyard at Carlisle most of the graves are those of little ones.

I am now going to confess that I had been at Carlisle a full year before I decided to learn all I could of the white man's ways, and then the inspiration was furnished by my father, the man who has been the greatest influence in all my life. When I had been in school a year, father made his first trip to see me. After I had received permission to speak to him, he told me that on his journey he had seen that the land was full of "Long Knives." "They greatly outnumber us and are here to stay," he said, and advised me, "Son, learn all you can of the white man's ways and try to be like him." From that day on I tried. Those few words of my father I remember as if we talked but yesterday, and in the maturity of my mind I have thought of what he said. He did not say that he thought the white man's ways better than our own; neither did he say that I could be like a white man. He said, "Son, try to be like a white man." So, in two more years I had been "made over." I was Luther Standing Bear wearing the blue uniform of the school, shorn of my hair, and trying hard to walk naturally and easily in stiff-soled cowhide boots. I was now "civilized" enough to go to work in John Wanamaker's fine store in Philadelphia.

I returned from the East at about the age of sixteen, after five years' contact with the white people, to resume life upon the reservation. But I returned, to spend some thirty years before again leaving, just as I had gone — a Lakota.

Outwardly I lived the life of the white man, yet all the while I kept in direct contact with tribal life. While I had learned all that I could of the white man's culture, I never forgot that of my people. I kept the language, tribal manners and usages, sang the songs and danced the dances. I still listened to and respected the advice of the older people of the tribe. I did not come home so "progressive" that I could not speak the language of my father and mother. I did not learn the vices of chewing tobacco, smoking, drinking, and swearing, and for all this I am grateful. I have never, in fact, "progressed" that far.

But I soon began to see the sad sight, so common today, of returned students who could not speak their native tongue, or, worse yet, some who pretended they could no longer converse in the mother tongue. They had become ashamed and this led them into deception and trickery. The boys came home wearing stiff paper collars, tight patent-leather boots, and derby hats on heads that were meant to be clothed in the long hair of the Lakota brave. The girls came home wearing muslin dresses and long ribbon sashes in bright hues which were very pretty. But they were trying to squeeze their feet into heeled shoes of factory make and their waists into binding apparatuses that were not garments — at least they served no purpose of a garment, but bordered on some mechanical device. However, the wearing of them was part of the "civilization" received from those who were doing the same thing. So we went to school to copy, to imitate; not to exchange languages and ideas, and not to develop the best traits that had come out of uncountable experiences of hundreds and thousands of years living upon this continent. Our annals, all happenings of human import, were stored in our song and dance rituals, our history differing in that it was not stored in books, but in the living memory. So, while the white people had much to teach us, we had much to teach them, and what a school could have been established upon that idea! However, this was not the attitude of the day, though the teachers were sympathetic and kind, and some came to be my lifelong friends. But in the main, Indian qualities were undivined and Indian virtues not conceded. And I can well remember when Indians in those days were stoned upon the streets as were the dogs that roamed them. We were "savages," and all who had not come under the influence of the missionary were "heathen," and Wakan Tanka, who had since the beginning watched over the Lakota and his land, was denied by these men of God. Should we not have been justified in thinking them heathen? And so the "civilizing" process went on, killing us as it went.

When I came back to the reservation to resume life there, it was too late to go on the warpath to prove, as I had always hoped to prove to my people, that I was a real brave. However, there came the battle of my life — the battle with agents to retain my individuality and my life as a Lakota. I wanted to take part in the tribal dances, sing the songs I had heard since I was born, and repeat and cherish the tales that had been the delight of my boyhood. It was in these things and through these things that my people lived and could continue to live, so it was up to me to keep them alive in my mind.

Now and then the Lakotas were holding their tribal dances in the old way, and I attended. Though my hair had been cut and I wore civilian clothes, I never forsook the blanket. For convenience, no coat I have ever worn can take the place of the blanket robe; and the same with the moccasins, which are sensible, comfortable, and beautiful. Besides, they were devised by people who danced — not for pastime, excitement, or fashion — but because it was an innate urge. Even when studying under the missionary, I went to the dances of my tribe.

Zitkala-Ša
The Melancholy of Those Black Days (1921)

THE SCHOOL DAYS OF AN INDIAN GIRL
The Land of Red Apples

There were eight in our party of bronzed children who were going East with the missionaries. Among us were three young braves, two tall girls, and we three little ones, Judéwin, Thowin, and I.

We had been very impatient to start on our journey to the Red Apple Country, which, we were told, lay a little beyond the great circular horizon of the Western prairie. Under a sky of rosy apples we dreamt of roaming as freely and happily as we had chased the cloud shadows on the Dakota plains. We had anticipated much pleasure from a ride on the iron horse, but the throngs of staring palefaces disturbed and troubled us.

On the train, fair women, with tottering babies on each arm, stopped their haste and scrutinized the children of absent mothers. Large men, with heavy bundles in their hands, halted near by, and riveted their glassy blue eyes upon us.

Source: Reprinted from *American Indian Stories* by Zitkala-Ša (Gertrude Bonnin) (Washington, D.C.: Hayworth Pubtlishing House, 1921; repr., Lincoln: University of Nebraska Press, 1985), 47–51, 65–68, 81–84, 95–99. Reprinted with permission of the University of Nebraska Press.

I sank deep into the corner of my seat, for I resented being watched. Directly in front of me, children who were no larger than I hung themselves upon the backs of their seats, with their bold white faces toward me. Sometimes they took their forefingers out of their mouths and pointed at my moccasined feet. Their mothers, instead of reproving such rude curiosity, looked closely at me, and attracted their children's further notice to my blanket. This embarrassed me, and kept me constantly on the verge of tears.

I sat perfectly still, with my eyes downcast, daring only now and then to shoot long glances around me. Chancing to turn to the window at my side, I was quite breathless upon seeing one familiar object. It was the telegraph pole which strode by at short paces. Very near my mother's dwelling, along the edge of a road thickly bordered with wild sunflowers, some poles like these had been planted by white men. Often I had stopped, on my way down the road, to hold my ear against the pole, and, hearing its low moaning, I used to wonder what the paleface had done to hurt it. Now I sat watching for each pole that glided by to be the last one.

In this way I had forgotten my uncomfortable surroundings, when I heard one of my comrades call out my name. I saw the missionary standing very near, tossing candies and gums into our midst. This amused us all, and we tried to see who could catch the most of the sweetmeats.

Though we rode several days inside of the iron horse, I do not recall a single thing about our luncheons.

It was night when we reached the school grounds. The lights from the windows of the large buildings fell upon some of the icicled trees that stood beneath them. We were led toward an open door, where the brightness of the lights within flooded out over the heads of the excited palefaces who blocked our way. My body trembled more from fear than from the snow I trod upon.

Entering the house, I stood close against the wall. The strong glaring light in the large whitewashed room dazzled my eyes. The noisy hurrying of hard shoes upon a bare wooden floor increased the whirring in my ears. My only safety seemed to be in keeping next to the wall. As I was wondering in which direction to escape from all this confusion, two warm hands grasped me firmly, and in the same moment I was tossed high in midair. A rosy-cheeked paleface woman caught me in her arms. I was both frightened and insulted by such trifling. I stared into her eyes, wishing her to let me stand on my own feet, but she jumped me up and down with increasing enthusiasm. My mother had never made a plaything of her wee daughter. Remembering this I began to cry aloud.

They misunderstood the cause of my tears, and placed me at a white table loaded with food. There our party were united again. As I did not hush my crying, one of the older ones whispered to me, "Wait until you are alone in the night."

It was very little I could swallow besides my sobs, that evening.

"Oh, I want my mother and my brother Dawée! I want to go to my aunt!" I pleaded; but the ears of the palefaces could not hear me.

From the table we were taken along an upward incline of wooden boxes, which I learned afterward to call a stairway. At the top was a quiet hall, dimly lighted. Many narrow beds were in one straight line down the entire length of the wall. In them lay sleeping brown faces, which peeped just out of the coverings. I was tucked into bed with one of the tall girls, because she talked to me in my mother tongue and seemed to soothe me.

I had arrived in the wonderful land of rosy skies, but I was not happy, as I had thought I should be. My long travel and the bewildering sights had exhausted me. I fell asleep, heaving deep, tired sobs. My tears were left to dry themselves in streaks, because neither my aunt nor my mother was near to wipe them away. . . .

Iron Routine

A loud-clamoring bell awakened us at half-past six in the cold winter mornings. From happy dreams of Western rolling lands and unlassoed freedom we tumbled out upon chilly bare floors back again into a paleface day. We had short time to jump into our shoes and clothes, and wet our eyes with icy water, before a small hand bell was vigorously rung for roll call.

There were too many drowsy children and too numerous orders for the day to waste a moment in any apology to nature for giving her children such a shock in the early morning. We rushed downstairs, bounding over two high steps at a time, to land in the assembly room.

A paleface woman, with a yellow-covered roll book open on her arm and a gnawed pencil in her hand, appeared at the door. Her small, tired face was coldly lighted with a pair of large gray eyes.

She stood still in a halo of authority, while over the rim of her spectacles her eyes pried nervously about the room. Having glanced at her long list of names and called out the first one, she tossed up her chin and peered through the crystals of her spectacles to make sure of the answer "Here."

Relentlessly her pencil black-marked our daily records if we were not present to respond to our names, and no chum of ours had done it successfully for us. No matter if a dull headache or the painful cough of slow consumption had delayed the absentee, there was only time enough to mark the tardiness. It was next to impossible to leave the iron routine after the civilizing machine had once begun its day's buzzing; and as it was inbred in me to suffer in silence rather than to appeal to the ears of one whose open eyes could not see my pain, I have many times trudged in the day's harness heavy-footed, like a dumb sick brute.

Once I lost a dear classmate. I remember well how she used to mope along at my side, until one morning she could not raise her head from her pillow. At her deathbed I stood weeping, as the paleface woman sat near her moistening the dry lips. Among the folds of the bedclothes I saw the open pages of the white man's Bible. The dying Indian girl talked disconnectedly of Jesus the Christ and the paleface who was cooling her swollen hands and feet.

I grew bitter, and censured the woman for cruel neglect of our physical ills. I despised the pencils that moved automatically, and the one teaspoon which dealt out, from a large bottle, healing to a row of variously ailing Indian children. I blamed the hard-working, well-meaning, ignorant woman who was inculcating in our hearts her superstitious ideas. Though I was sullen in all my little troubles, as soon as I felt better I was ready again to smile upon the cruel woman. Within a week I was again actively testing the chains which tightly bound my individuality like a mummy for burial.

The melancholy of those black days has left so long a shadow that it darkens the path of years that have since gone by. These sad memories rise above those of smoothly grinding school days. Perhaps my Indian nature is the moaning wind which stirs them now for their present record. But, however tempestuous this is within me, it comes out as the low voice of a curiously colored seashell, which is only for those ears that are bent with compassion to hear it.

AN INDIAN TEACHER AMONG INDIANS
My First Day

Though an illness left me unable to continue my college course, my pride kept me from returning to my mother. Had she known of my worn condition, she would have said the white man's papers were not worth the freedom and health I had lost by them. Such a rebuke from my mother would have been unbearable, and as I felt then it would be far too true to be comfortable.

Since the winter when I had my first dreams about red apples I had been traveling slowly toward the morning horizon. There had been no doubt about the direction in which I wished to go to spend my energies in a work for the Indian race. Thus I had written my mother briefly, saying my plan for the year was to teach in an Eastern Indian school. Sending this message to her in the West, I started at once eastward.

Thus I found myself, tired and hot, in a black veiling of car smoke, as I stood wearily on a street corner of an old-fashioned town, waiting for a car. In a few moments more I should be on the school grounds, where a new work was ready for my inexperienced hands.

Upon entering the school campus, I was surprised at the thickly clustered buildings which made it a quaint little village, much more interesting than the town itself. The large trees among the houses gave the place a cool, refreshing shade, and the grass a deeper green. Within this large court of grass and trees stood a low green pump. The queer boxlike case had a revolving handle on its side, which clanked and creaked constantly.

I made myself known, and was shown to my room,—a small, carpeted room, with ghastly walls and ceiling. The two windows, both on the same side, were curtained with heavy muslin yellowed with age. A clean white bed was in one corner of the room, and opposite it was a square pine table covered with a black woolen blanket.

Without removing my hat from my head, I seated myself in one of the two stiff-backed chairs that were placed beside the table. For several heart throbs I sat still looking from ceiling to floor, from wall to wall, trying hard to imagine years of contentment there. Even while I was wondering if my exhausted strength would sustain me through this undertaking, I heard a heavy tread stop at my door. Opening it, I met the imposing figure of a stately gray-haired man. With a light straw hat in one hand, and the right hand extended for greeting, he smiled kindly upon me. For some reason I was awed by his wondrous height and his strong square shoulders, which I felt were a finger's length above my head.

I was always slight, and my serious illness in the early spring had made me look rather frail and languid. His quick eye measured my height and breadth. Then he looked into my face. I imagined that a visible shadow flitted across his countenance as he let my hand fall. I knew he was no other than my employer.

"Ah ha! so you are the little Indian girl who created the excitement among the college orators!" he said, more to himself than to me. I thought I heard a subtle note of disappointment in his voice. Looking in from where he stood, with one sweeping glance, he asked if I lacked anything for my room.

After he turned to go, I listened to his step until it grew faint and was lost in the distance. I was aware that my car-smoked appearance had not concealed the lines of pain on my face.

For a short moment my spirit laughed at my ill fortune, and I entertained the idea of exerting myself to make an improvement. But as I tossed my hat off a leaden weakness came over me, and I felt as if years of weariness lay like water-soaked logs upon me. I threw myself upon the bed, and, closing my eyes, forgot my good intention. . . .

Retrospection

. . . As months passed over me, I slowly comprehended that the large army of white teachers in Indian schools had a larger missionary creed than I had suspected.

It was one which included self-preservation quite as much as Indian education. When I saw an opium-eater holding a position as teacher of Indians, I did not understand what good was expected, until a Christian in power replied that this pumpkin-colored creature had a feeble mother to support. An inebriate paleface sat stupid in a doctor's chair, while Indian patients carried their ailments to untimely graves, because his fair wife was dependent upon him for her daily food.

I find it hard to count that white man a teacher who tortured an ambitious Indian youth by frequently reminding the brave changeling that he was nothing but a "government pauper."

Though I burned with indignation upon discovering on every side instances no less shameful than those I have mentioned, there was no present help. Even the few rare ones who have worked nobly for my race were powerless to choose workmen like themselves. To be sure, a man was sent from the Great Father to inspect Indian schools, but what he saw was usually the students' sample work *made* for exhibition. I was nettled by this sly cunning of the workmen who hookwinked [sic] the Indian's pale Father at Washington.

My illness, which prevented the conclusion of my college course, together with my mother's stories of the encroaching frontier settlers, left me in no mood to strain my eyes in searching for latent good in my white co-workers.

At this stage of my own evolution, I was ready to curse men of small capacity for being the dwarfs their God had made them. In the process of my education I had lost all consciousness of the nature world about me. Thus, when a hidden rage took me to the small white-walled prison which I then called my room, I unknowingly turned away from my one salvation.

Alone in my room, I sat like the petrified Indian woman of whom my mother used to tell me. I wished my heart's burdens would turn me to unfeeling stone. But alive, in my tomb, I was destitute!

For the white man's papers I had given up my faith in the Great Spirit. For these same papers I had forgotten the healing in trees and brooks. On account of my mother's simple view of life, and my lack of any, I gave her up, also. I made no friends among the race of people I loathed. Like a slender tree, I had been uprooted from my mother, nature, and God. I was shorn of my branches, which had waved in sympathy and love for home and friends. The natural coat of bark which had protected my oversensitive nature was scraped off to the very quick.

Now a cold bare pole I seemed to be, planted in a strange earth. Still, I seemed to hope a day would come when my mute aching head, reared upward to the sky, would flash a zig-zag lightning across the heavens. With this dream of vent for a long-pent consciousness, I walked again amid the crowds.

At last, one weary day in the schoolroom, a new idea presented itself to me. It was a new way of solving the problem of my inner self. I liked it. Thus I resigned my position as teacher; and now I am in an Eastern city, following the long course of study I have set for myself. Now, as I look back upon the recent past, I see it from a distance, as a whole. I remember how, from morning till evening, many specimens of civilized peoples visited the Indian school. The city folks with canes and eyeglasses, the countrymen with sunburnt cheeks and clumsy feet, forgot their relative social ranks in an ignorant curiosity. Both sorts of these Christian palefaces were alike astounded at seeing the children of savage warriors so docile and industrious.

As answers to their shallow inquiries they received the students' sample work to look upon. Examining the neatly figured pages, and gazing upon the Indian girls and boys bending over their books, the white visitors walked out of the schoolhouse well satisfied: they were educating the children of the red man! They were paying a liberal fee to the government employees in whose able hands lay the small forest of Indian timber.

In this fashion many have passed idly through the Indian schools during the last decade, afterward to boast of their charity to the North American Indian. But few there are who have paused to question whether real life or long-lasting death lies beneath this semblance of civilization.

QUESTIONS FOR CONSIDERATION

1. In what ways do these authors "test the chains which tightly bound [their] individuality" (as Zitkala-Ša said) and manage to preserve their individual and tribal identities despite the "iron routine" of the "civilizing machine"?

2. What do their writings reveal about the tensions they experienced in walking between or combining two ways of life? In what ways do they take issue with the educational system and the assimilationist policies of the time?

3. Who is their audience, and why might they also be described as interpreters and culture brokers?

4. Luther Standing Bear envisioned a truly American school. What might it have looked like? What might it look like today?

PICTURE ESSAY

The Fort Marion Artists

W HEN HISTORY BOOKS INCLUDE EXAMPLES OF INDIAN ART or pictographic records, they tend to place them at the beginning, as examples of unchanging Native traditions that would be replaced. But Indian art was constantly evolving. Like Indian cultures generally, it altered as a result of contact with new influences, but it did not disappear or lose touch with its traditional roots. While Plains Indian women worked in abstract, geometric forms, men drew real people and actual events, and warriors depicted their heroic deeds on tipi covers and buffalo robes; when white men arrived with trade beads, paints, pencils, and paper, Indian artists readily employed the new materials. The Mandan chief Four Bears not only posed for George Catlin and Karl Bodmer (see Picture Essay, "Indian Life on the Upper Missouri: A Catlin/Bodmer Portfolio," pages 299–303), he also watched them at work and adopted some of their techniques in his own representational art.

In the late nineteenth century, a new type of Indian art emerged out of circumstances that seemed more likely to stifle than to stimulate artistic creativity: "under the strains and stresses of their disintegrating world, talented Indian artists transformed painting into an expressive and vital art form."[98] Plains Indians acquired new materials with which to work and new subjects to portray. Since many of the sketches they produced were done on pages torn from account books, the new art form became known as ledger art. Warrior-artists produced a rich visual record of coup-counting and combat on the Plains, but some of the most famous and significant Plains Indian ledger art was produced thousands of miles from the Plains.[99] In 1875, seventy-two Southern Cheyenne, Arapaho, Kiowa, and Comanche warriors whom the government identified as "ringleaders" and "murderers" in the Red River War of 1874 were manacled, chained, and loaded on a train bound for exile and imprisonment at Fort Marion, in St. Augustine, Florida. Their jailor, Captain Richard H. Pratt, regarded their incarceration as an opportunity to test his program for assimilating Indians into American society. As he would do later as superintendent of the boarding school at Carlisle, Pennsylvania, Pratt stripped the Indians of their clothes and gave them army uniforms; he cut their long hair short; and he made them follow a regimented routine of working, schooling, eating, and sleeping that he felt would instill the values and industrious habits they needed to become "civilized." He also encouraged them to draw and gave them the materials to do so.

With time on their hands, the Fort Marion prisoners produced hundreds of drawings. Some sold books of their work to tourists. Far from their homes and loved ones, and with no idea of what the future held for them, they were poised on the edge of old and new ways of life. Their drawings reflected that dualism in form and content. Some of the artists painted nostalgic scenes from the old ways—hunting buffalo, raiding for horses, counting coup—and employed traditional conventions. These included right to left flow of action; pictographic shorthand, such as hoof prints to indicate previous movements; and symbols above the head to identify an individual, such as the Cheyenne warrior named Sitting Bull (not the famous Hunkpapa chief) depicted by Howling Wolf in Figure 7.1.

But the heroic feats that warrior-artists had traditionally recorded were events of the past. The artists experimented with new subjects and new forms of composition and introduced elements of personal expression and individual style.

◆ Figure 7.1 **Howling Wolf, Cheyenne Warrior Striking an Enemy**
Pawnees, 1874–75 (pen, ink & w/c on ledger paper), Howling Wolf (1849–1927)/Allen Memorial Art Museum, Oberlin College, Ohio, USA/Gift of Mrs. Jacob D. Cox / Bridgeman Images.

◆ Figure 7.2 **Courtship Scene**
National Anthropological Archives, Smithsonian Institution [NAA INV 08511300].

Far from their homes and their loved ones, warriors who had once been concerned only with depicting heroic deeds drew scenes of courtship (Figure 7.2). They also turned their attention and skills to aspects of the strange world into which they had been thrust, as when the Kiowa Zotom drew the newly arrived prisoners standing on the parapet at Fort Marion, getting their first look at the Atlantic Ocean (Figure 7.3), as well as scenes of the new way of life that was being imposed back home on the reservations, such as the distribution of annuities or treaty goods (Figure 7.4).

At least twenty-six of the Fort Marion prisoners created drawings.[100] The Cheyenne artist Chief Killer seems to have been drawing before he went to Fort Marion. In fact, it was the lead pencils found in his possession along with other items taken from settlers killed in a raid that provided the evidence that led to his imprisonment. Chief Killer recorded aspects of his new life on paper and in considerable detail. In Figure 7.5, he presented his own perspective on the education meted out to the Fort Marion prisoners. The Indians in their army uniforms

◆ **Figure 7.3** **Paul Caryl Zotom, *On the Parapet of Ft. Marion Next Day after Arrival* (c. 1875)**
Granger, NYC.

◆ **Figure 7.4** **Distribution of Goods**
Yale Collection of Western Americana, Beinecke Rare Book and Manuscript Library.

◆ **Figure 7.5 Chief Killer, *Education of the Fort Marion Prisoners* (1875–78)**
Hood Museum of Art, Dartmouth College, Hanover, New Hampshire; Mark Lansburgh Ledger
Drawing Collection; Purchased through the Robert J. Strasenburgh II 1942 Fund.

and short hair (their caps are hanging from pegs on the wall) sit in an orderly
classroom as the teachers read from books and point to words on a chalkboard.
Chief Killer also included captions written by Pratt or others and handwritten
signatures in place of traditional pictographic name glyphs — indications that the
drawing was intended for sale. Chief Killer stopped drawing after he returned
home to the reservation, where he worked as a butcher, policeman, and teamster.
He died in 1922.[101]

Some of the Fort Marion artists continued to draw and paint long after they
had been released and returned home in 1878. Their work constitutes a unique
collection of historical documents, a record of a people experiencing revolutionary change. As the self-portrait of the Kiowa Wo-Haw (Figure 7.6) graphically
illustrates — he has a foot in each world but wears long hair and a traditional
breech cloth — the Fort Marion artists knew their lives were in transition and some
were unsure about their place in the future.

◆ Figure 7.6 **Wo-Haw, Self-Portrait (c. 1875)**
Pencil and crayon on paper by Wo-Haw, ca. 1875. Missouri History Museum, St. Louis.

QUESTIONS FOR CONSIDERATION

1. What do the compositions of these pictures suggest about the artists' purposes?

2. What elements of these pictures suggest that the artists had new materials and time on their hands, as well as new subjects to paint?

3. What value do pictures such as these have in depicting scenes that could be effectively portrayed by American artists and photographers of the time?

REFERENCES

1. C. Joseph Genetin-Pilawa, *Crooked Paths to Allotment: The Fight over Federal Indian Policy after the Civil War* (Chapel Hill: University of North Carolina Press, 2012); Robert Hays, *Editorializing "the Indian Problem": The* New York Times *on Native Americans, 1860–1900* (Carbondale: Southern Illinois University Press, 2007).

2. Helen Hunt Jackson, *A Century of Dishonor: A Sketch of the United States Government's Dealings with Some of the Indian Tribes* (New York: Harper & Bros., 1881).

3. Peter Nabokov, *Two Leggings: The Making of a Crow Warrior* (Lincoln: University of Nebraska Press, 1982), 197.

4. Cathleen D. Cahill, *Federal Fathers and Mothers: A Social History of the United States Indian Service, 1869–1933* (Chapel Hill: University of North Carolina Press, 2011); Beth H. Piatote, *Domestic Subjects: Gender, Citizenship, and Law in Native American Literature* (New Haven: Yale University Press, 2013).

5. Katherine M. B. Osborn, *Southern Ute Women: Autonomy and Assimilation on the Reservation, 1887–1934* (Albuquerque: University of New Mexico Press, 1998), 65.

6. Such patterns of accommodation and resistance continued well into the twentieth century; for examples, see Osborn, *Southern Ute Women,* and Brenda J. Child, *Holding Our World Together: Ojibwe Women and the Survival of Community* (New York: Viking/Penguin, 2012).

7. Sarah Winnemucca Hopkins, *Life among the Piutes: Their Wrongs and Claims* (Reno: University of Nevada Press, 1994), 89–90; Sally Zanjani, *Sarah Winnemucca* (Lincoln: University of Nebraska Press, 2001); Frederick E. Hoxie, *This Indian Country: American Indian Activists and the Place They Made* (New York: Penguin, 2012), chap. 4, quote at 143.

8. Wooden Leg quoted in Colin G. Calloway, ed., *Our Hearts Fell to the Ground: Plains Indian Views of How the West Was Lost* (Boston: Bedford Books, 1996), 159; Frederick E. Hoxie, *Parading through History: The Making of the Crow Nation in America, 1805–1935* (Cambridge: Cambridge University Press, 1995), 309.

9. Clyde Ellis, "'There Is No Doubt . . . the Dances Should Be Curtailed': Indian Dances and Federal Policy on the Southern Plains, 1880–1930," *Pacific Historical Review* 70 (November 2001), 543–69.

10. Robert Galler, "Making Common Cause: Yanktonais and Catholic Missionaries on the Northern Plains," *Ethnohistory* 55 (Summer 2008), 439–64.

11. Jeffrey D. Means, "'Indians shall do things in common': Oglala Lakota Identity and Cattle-Raising on the Pine Ridge Reservation," *Montana, The Magazine of Western History* 61 (Autumn 2011), 3–21.

12. Edmund Jefferson Danziger Jr., *Great Lakes Indian Accommodation and Resistance during the Early Reservation Years, 1850–1900* (Ann Arbor: University of Michigan Press, 2009); Hana Samek, *The Blackfoot Confederacy, 1880–1920: A Comparative Study of Canadian and U. S. Indian Policy* (Albuquerque: University of New Mexico Press, 1987); David G. McCrady, *Living with Strangers: The Nineteenth-Century Sioux and the Canadian-American Borderlands* (Lincoln: University of Nebraska Press, 2006).

13. *Second Annual Address to the Public of the Lake Mohonk Conference* (Philadelphia: Indian Rights Association, 1884), 6–7.

14. D. S. Otis, ed., *The Dawes Act and the Allotment of Indian Lands* (Norman: University of Oklahoma Press, 1973), 10.

15. Quoted in David Wallace Adams, *Education for Extinction: American Indians and the Boarding School Experience, 1875–1928* (Lawrence: University Press of Kansas, 1995), 23.

16. Virgil Vogel, *This Country Was Ours: A Documentary History of the American Indian* (New York: Harper and Row, 1972), 193.

17. Now-ah-quay-gi-shig (N. B. Hurr) quoted in Ignatia Broker, *Night Flying Woman: An Ojibway Narrative* (St. Paul: Minnesota Historical Society Press, 1983), xi–xii.

18. Melissa L. Meyer, *The White Earth Tragedy: Ethnicity and Dispossession at a Minnesota Anishinaabe Reservation, 1899–1920* (Lincoln: University of Nebraska Press, 1994), quotes at 161, 171, 229.

19. The people of the Grand Ronde Reservation made the transition from a hunting and gathering subsistence economy to an agricultural community and accepted allotment before the Dawes Act was passed. Tracy Neal Leavelle, "'We Will Make It Our Own Place': Agriculture and Adaptation at the Grand Ronde Reservation, 1856–1887," *American Indian Quarterly* 22 (Autumn 1998), 433–56; Emily Greenwald, *Reconfiguring the Reservation: The Nez Percés, Jicarilla Apaches, and the Dawes Act* (Lincoln: University of Nebraska Press, 2002).

20. Bonnie Lynn-Sherow, *Red Earth: Race and Agriculture in Oklahoma Territory* (Lawrence: University Press of Kansas, 2004), chap. 7.

21. William T. Hagan, *Taking Indian Lands: The Cherokee (Jerome) Commission, 1889–1893* (Norman: University of Oklahoma Press, 2003).

22. Arrell M. Gibson, *The American Indian: Prehistory to the Present* (Lexington, Mass.: D. C. Heath, 1980), 502.

23. Tanis C. Thorne, *The World's Richest Indian: The Scandal over Jackson Burnett's Oil Fortune* (New York: Oxford University Press, 2003).

24. Terry P. Wilson, *The Underground Reservation: Osage Oil* (Lincoln: University of Nebraska Press, 1985), chap. 6; "FBI File on Osage Indian Murders," 3 rolls of microfilm (Wilmington, Del.: Scholarly Resources, 1986). Charles H. Red Corn's novel *A Pipe for February* (Norman: University of Oklahoma Press, 2002) deals with the experiences of Osage people amid the wealth and murders of the 1920s.

25. Figures and "orgy" quote from Claudio Saunt, *Black, White, and Indian: Race and the Unmaking of an American Family* (New York: Oxford University Press, 2005), 160, 162.

26. Richard White, *The Roots of Dependency: Subsistence, Environment, and Social Change among Choctaws, Pawnees, and Navajos* (Lincoln: University of Nebraska Press, 1983), 212.

27. Francis Paul Prucha, ed., *Americanizing the American Indians: Writings by the "Friends of the Indian," 1880–1920* (Lincoln: University of Nebraska Press, 1978), 194.

28. Adams, *Education for Extinction,* 26–27.

29. Clyde Ellis, *To Change Them Forever: Indian Education at the Rainy Mountain Boarding School, 1893–1920* (Norman: University of Oklahoma Press, 1996); Adams: *Education for Extinction,* 97.

30. Barbara Landis, *Carlisle Indian Industrial School History,* provides an excellent site at http://home.epix.net/~landis/history .html.

31. Adams, *Education for Extinction,* 63, 211.

32. Helen Sekaquaptewa, *Me and Mine: The Life Story of Helen Sekaquaptewa as Told to Louis Udall* (Tucson: University of Arizona Press, 1969), 8; Leo W. Simmons, ed., *Sun Chief: The Autobiography of a Hopi Indian, by Don C. Talayesva* (New Haven: Yale University Press, 1942), 88–89.

33. Sekaquaptewa, *Me and Mine,* 92–93, 96.

34. Margaret D. Jacobs, *White Mother to a Dark Race: Settler Colonialism, Maternalism, and the Removal of Indigenous Children in the American West and Australia, 1880–1940* (Lincoln: University of Nebraska Press, 2009).

35. Luther Standing Bear, *Land of the Spotted Eagle* (Lincoln: University of Nebraska Press, 1978), 232–33.

36. Brenda J. Child, *Boarding School Seasons: American Indian Families, 1900–1940* (Lincoln: University of Nebraska Press, 1998).

37. Basil H. Johnston, *Indian School Days* (Norman: University of Oklahoma Press, 1988), 60.

38. John S. Milloy, *A National Crime: The Canadian Government and the Residential School System, 1879 to 1986* (Winnipeg: University of Manitoba Press, 1999). Milloy's book chronicles the "persistent neglect and abuse."

39. Luther Standing Bear, *Land of the Spotted Eagle,* 234; Child, *Boarding School Seasons,* 66–67, 112–15. Thanks to Don Fixico for the information about the marshland burials at Haskell.

40. Simmons, *Sun Chief,* 90–91; P. David Seaman, ed., *Born a Chief: The Nineteenth Century Hopi Boyhood of Edmund Nequatewa* (Tucson: University of Arizona Press, 1993), 107–9.

41. Malcolm Margolin, ed., *The Way We Lived: California Indian Stories, Songs and Reminiscences* (Berkeley: Heyday Books; San Francisco: California Historical Society, 1993), 182.

42. Jacqueline Fear-Segal, *White Man's Club: Schools, Race, and the Struggle of Indian Acculturation* (Lincoln: University of Nebraska Press, 2007).

43. Robert M. Utley, *The Indian Frontier of the American West, 1846–1890* (Albuquerque: University of New Mexico Press, 1984), 227–28, 245. Roger L. D. Silvestro, *In the Shadow of Wounded Knee: The Untold Final Chapter of the Indian Wars* (New York: Walker, 2005), and Philip J. Deloria, *Indians in Unexpected Places* (Lawrence: University Press of Kansas, 2004), 28–35, also cover the story of Plenty Horses.

44. K. Tsianina Lomawaima, *They Called It Prairie Light: The Story of Chilocco Indian School* (Lincoln: University of Nebraska Press, 1994), 167.

45. Myriam Vučković, *Voices from Haskell: Indian Students between Two Worlds, 1884–1928* (Lawrence: University of Kansas Press, 2008).

46. Matthew Sakiestewa Gilbert, *Education beyond the Mesa: Hopi Students at Sherman Institute, 1902–1929* (Lincoln: University of Nebraska Press, 2010).

47. Vučković, *Voices from Haskell,* 3.

48. Wilbert H. Ahern, "An Experiment Aborted: Returned Indian Students in the Indian School Service, 1881–1908," *Ethnohistory* 44 (Spring 1997), 263–304.

49. Carolyn Gilman and Mary Jane Schneider, *The Way to Independence: Memories of a Hidatsa Indian Family, 1840–1920* (St. Paul: Minnesota Historical Society Press, 1987), 153–54, 226.

50. Quoted in Gretchen M. Bataille and Kathleen Mullen Sands, *American Indian Women: Telling Their Lives* (Lincoln: University of Nebraska Press, 1984), 84.

51. Mick Gidley, *Edward S. Curtis and the North American Indian, Incorporated* (Cambridge: Cambridge University Press, 1998); Timothy Egan, *Short Nights of the Shadow Catcher: The Epic Life and Immortal Photographs of Edward Curtis* (Boston: Houghton, Mifflin, Harcourt, 2012); Sherry L. Smith, *Reimagining Indians: Native Americans through Anglo Eyes, 1880–1940* (New York: Oxford University Press, 2000); Alan Trachtenberg, *Shadows of Hiawatha: Staging Indians, Making Americans, 1880–1930* (New York: Hill and Wang, 2004).

52. Lucy Maddox, *Citizen Indians: Native American Intellectuals, Race and Reform* (Ithaca, N.Y.: Cornell University Press, 2005).

53. Linda M. Waggoner, *Fire Light: The Life of Angel De Cora, Winnebago Artist* (Norman: University of Oklahoma Press, 2008).

54. Charles A. Eastman, *From the Deep Woods to Civilization: Chapters in the Autobiography of an Indian* (1916; repr., Lincoln: University of Nebraska Press, 1977), 25.

55. Eastman, *From the Deep Woods,* 31–32.

56. Eastman, *From the Deep Woods,* 47.

57. Eastman, *From the Deep Woods,* 54.

58. Charles A. Eastman, *Indian Boyhood* (New York: McClure, Phillips, 1902), v.

59. Hertha Dawn Wong, *Sending My Heart Back across the Years: Tradition and Innovation in Native American Autobiography* (New York: Oxford University Press, 1992), 140.

60. Raymond Wilson, *Ohiyesa: Charles Eastman, Santee Sioux* (Urbana: University of Illinois Press, 1983), 191.

61. Eastman, *From the Deep Woods,* 195.

62. N. Bruce Duthu, *Shadow Nations: Tribal Sovereignty and the Limits of Legal Pluralism* (New York: Oxford University Press, 2013), 83–84.

63. Walter R. Echo-Hawk, *In the Courts of the Conqueror: The 10 Worst Indian Law Cases Ever Decided* (Golden, Colo.: Fulcrum, 2010), 180.

64. John Shurts, *Indian Reserved Water Rights: The Winters Doctrine in Its Social and Legal Context, 1880s–1930s* (Norman: University of Oklahoma Press, 2000).

65. Deloria, *Indians in Unexpected Places.*

66. Tom Holm, *The Great Confusion in Indian Affairs: Native Americans and Whites in the Progressive Era* (Austin: University of Texas Press, 2005).

67. Alexandra Harmon, *Indians in the Making: Ethnic Relations and Indian Identities around Puget Sound* (Berkeley: University of California Press, 1998), chap. 4.

68. Sergei Kan, *Memory Eternal: Tlingit Culture and Russian Orthodox Christianity, 1794–1994* (Seattle: University of Washington Press, 1999), chap. 7.

69. Brian C. Hosmer, *American Indians in the Marketplace: Persistence and Innovation among the Menominees and Metlakatlans, 1870–1920* (Lawrence: University Press of Kansas, 1999).

70. William J. Bauer Jr., *We Were All Like Migrant Workers Here: Work, Community, and Memory on California's Round Valley Reservation, 1850–1941* (Chapel Hill: University of North Carolina Press, 2009).

71. Teresa J. Wilkins, *Patterns of Exchange: Navajo Weavers and Traders* (Norman: University of Oklahoma Press, 2008).

72. Jean M. O'Brien, "State Recognition and 'Termination' in Nineteenth-Century New England," in Amy E. Den Ouden and Jean M. O'Brien, eds., *Recognition, Sovereignty, Struggles, and Indigenous Rights in the United States* (Chapel Hill: University of North Carolina Press, 2013), 149–67.

73. Emil Her Many Horses, ed., *Identity by Design: Tradition, Change, and Celebration in Native Women's Dresses* (Washington, D.C.: National Museum of the American Indian, Smithsonian Institution, 2007).

74. L. G. Moses, *Wild West Shows and the Images of American Indians, 1883–1933* (Albuquerque: University of New Mexico Press, 1996), 278; Sam A. Maddra, *Hostiles? The Lakota Ghost Dance and Buffalo Bill's Wild West* (Norman: University of Oklahoma Press, 2006); Linda Scarangella-McNenly, *Native Performers in Wild West Shows: From Buffalo Bill to Euro Disney* (Norman: University of Oklahoma Press, 2012). The late Blackfeet/GrosVentre author James Welch provides a fictional account of a "show Indian" who gets stranded in France in *The Heartsong of Charging Elk* (New York: Random House, 2000).

75. John W. Troutman, *Indian Blues: American Indians and the Politics of Music, 1879–1934* (Norman: University of Oklahoma Press, 2009).

76. Colin G. Calloway, *The Abenaki* (New York: Chelsea House, 1989), 81.

77. Matthew Sakiestewa Gilbert, "Marathoner Louis Tewanima and the Continuity of Hopi Running, 1908–1912," *Western Historical Quarterly* 43 (2012), 325–46.

78. John Bloom, *To Show What an Indian Can Do: Sports at Native American Boarding Schools* (Minneapolis: University of Minnesota Press, 2000); Sally Jenkins, *The Real All Americans: The Team That Changed a Game, a People, a Nation* (New York: Doubleday, 2007); Kate Buford, *Native American Son: The Life and Sporting Legend of Jim Thorpe* (New York: Alfred A. Knopf, 2010).

79. Frederick E. Hoxie, ed., *Talking Back to Civilization: Indian Voices from the Progressive Era* (Boston: Bedford/St. Martin's, 2001).

80. Sherman Coolidge, "The Function of the Society of American Indians," in *The Elders Wrote: An Anthology of Early Prose by North American Indians, 1768–1931,* ed. Bernd Peyer (Berlin: Dietrich Reimer Verlag, 1982), 161.

81. Chadwick Allen and Beth H. Piatote, eds., "The Society of American Indians and Its Legacies: A Special Combined Issue," *Studies in American Indian Literature* 25:2 (2013)/*American Indian Quarterly* 37:3 (2013).

82. William T. Hagan, *Quanah Parker, Comanche Chief* (Norman: University of Oklahoma Press, 1993).

83. Carol Hampton, "Native American Church," in *Encyclopedia of North American Indians,* ed. Frederick E. Hoxie (Boston: Houghton Mifflin, 1996), 418.

84. Thomas C. Maroukis, *The Peyote Road: Religious Freedom and the Native American Church* (Norman: University of Oklahoma Press, 2010).

85. Russel Lawrence Barsh, "American Indians in the Great War," *Ethnohistory* 38 (Summer 1991), 276–303, quotes at 276, 287, 288; Susan Applegate Krouse, *North American Indians in the Great War* (Lincoln: University of Nebraska Press, 2007), chap. 1.

86. Quoted in Alvin M. Josephy Jr., ed., *Lewis and Clark through Indian Eyes* (New York: Alfred A. Knopf, 2006), 119.

87. Hoxie, *Talking Back,* 126.

88. Krouse, *North American Indians,* 80–81.

89. Quoted in Laurence M. Hauptman, *The Iroquois and the New Deal* (Syracuse, N.Y.: Syracuse University Press, 1981), 6.

90. Francis Paul Prucha, ed., *Documents of United States Indian Policy* (Lincoln: University of Nebraska Press, 1975), 219–21.

91. Margaret Connell Szasz, *Education and the American Indian: The Road to Self-Determination since 1928,* 3rd ed. (Albuquerque: University of New Mexico Press, 1999), chap. 3, quote at 34.

92. Prucha, *Documents,* 1.

93. Prucha, *Americanizing the American Indians,* 8–9.

94. Peter Iverson, *Carlos Montezuma and the Changing World of American Indians* (Albuquerque: University of New Mexico Press, 1982), 6.

95. Hoxie, *Talking Back,* 93.

96. Dexter Fisher, foreword to *American Indian Stories* by Zitkala-Ša (Lincoln: University of Nebraska Press, 1985), vi.

97. P. Jane Hafen, "Zitkala-Ša," in Hoxie, *Encyclopedia of North American Indians,* 708–10.

98. Arthur Silberman, "The Art of Fort Marion," in *Making Medicine: Ledger Drawing Art from Fort Marion* (Oklahoma City: Center of the American Indian, 1984), n.p.

99. For studies of Plains Indian ledger art, see Jean Afton, David Fridtjof Halaas, and Andrew E. Masich, *Cheyenne Dog Soldiers: A Ledgerbook History of Coups and Combat* (Denver: Colorado Historical Society; Niwot: University of Colorado Press, 1997); Janet Catherine Berlo, ed., *Plains Indian Drawings, 1865–1935: Pages from a Visual History* (New York: Harry N. Abrams, 1996); Colin G. Calloway, ed., *Ledger Narratives: The Plains Indian Drawings of the Lansburgh Collection at Dartmouth College* (Norman: University of Oklahoma Press, 2012); Evan M. Maurer et al., *Visions of the People: A Pictorial History of Plains Indian Life* (Minneapolis: Minneapolis Institute of Arts, 1992); Castle McLaughlin, *A Lakota War Book from the Little Bighorn: The Pictographic "Autobiogrphy of Half Moon"* (Cambridge, Mass.: Houghton Library/Peabody Museum Press, 2013); Karen Daniels Peterson, *Plains Indian Art from Fort Marion* (Norman: University of Oklahoma Press, 1971); Joyce M. Szabo, *Art from Fort Marion: The Silberman Collection* (Norman: University of Oklahoma Press, 2007); Joyce M. Szabo, *Howling Wolf and the History of Ledger Art* (Albuquerque: University of New Mexico Press, 1994); Herman J. Viola, *Warrior Artists: Historic Cheyenne and Kiowa Indian Ledger Art Drawing by Making Medicine and Zotom* (Washington, D.C.: National Geographic Society, 1998). Various collections of Plains Indian ledger art are available for viewing at https://plainsledgerart.org.

100. Szabo, *Art from Fort Marion,* 29.

101. Peterson, *Plains Indian Art,* 3, 25, 204, 324.

SUGGESTED READINGS

Adams, David Wallace. *Education for Extinction: American Indians and the Boarding School Experience, 1875–1928*. Lawrence: University Press of Kansas, 1995.

Allen, Chadwick, and Beth H. Piatote, eds., "The Society of American Indians and Its Legacies: A Special Combined Issue," *Studies in American Indian Literature* 25:2 (2013)/*American Indian Quarterly* 37:3 (2013).

Archuleta, Margaret L., Brenda J. Child, and K. Tsianina Lomawaima, eds. *Away from Home: American Indian Boarding School Experiences, 1879–2000*. Phoenix: Heard Museum, 2000.

Bauer, William J., Jr. *We Were All Like Migrant Workers Here: Work, Community, and Memory on California's Round Valley Reservation, 1850–1941*. Chapel Hill: University of North Carolina Press, 2009.

Berlo, Janet Catherine, ed. *Plains Indian Drawings, 1865–1935: Pages from a Visual History*. New York: Harry N. Abrams, 1996.

Bloom, John. *To Show What an Indian Can Do: Sports at Native American Boarding Schools*. Minneapolis: University of Minnesota Press, 2000.

Britten, Thomas A. *American Indians in World War I: At War and at Home*. Albuquerque: University of New Mexico Press, 1997.

Buford, Kate. *Native American Son: The Life and Sporting Legend of Jim Thorpe*. New York: Alfred A. Knopf, 2010.

Cahill, Cathleen D. *Federal Fathers and Mothers: A Social History of the United States Indian Service, 1869–1933*. Chapel Hill: University of North Carolina Press, 2011.

Calloway, Colin G., ed. *Ledger Narratives: The Plains Indian Drawings of the Lansburgh Collection at Dartmouth College*. Norman: University of Oklahoma Press, 2012.

Chang, David. *The Color of the Land: Race, Nation, and the Politics of Landownership in Oklahoma, 1832–1929*. Chapel Hill: University of North Carolina Press, 2010.

Child, Brenda J. *Boarding School Seasons: American Indian Families, 1900–1940*. Lincoln: University of Nebraska Press, 1998.

———. *Holding Our World Together: Ojibwe Women and the Survival of Community*. New York: Viking/Penguin, 2012.

Clancy, Diane. *Fort Marion Prisoners and the Trauma of Native Education*. Norman: University of Oklahoma Press, 2014.

Conn, Steven. *History's Shadow: Native Americans and Historical Consciousness in the Nineteenth Century*. Chicago: University of Chicago Press, 2004.

Deloria, Philip. *Indians in Unexpected Places*. Lawrence: University Press of Kansas, 2004.

Eastman, Charles A. *From the Deep Woods to Civilization: Chapters in the Autobiography of an Indian*. Lincoln: University of Nebraska Press, 1977.

Fear-Segal, Jacqueline. *White Man's Club: Schools, Race, and the Struggle of Indian Acculturation*. Lincoln: University of Nebraska Press, 2007.

Genetin-Pilawa, C. Joseph. *Crooked Paths to Allotment: The Fight over Federal Indian Policy after the Civil War*. Chapel Hill: University of North Carolina Press, 2012.

Gilbert, Matthew Sakiestewa, *Education beyond the Mesa: Hopi Students at Sherman Institute, 1902–1929*. Lincoln: University of Nebraska Press, 2010.

Hagan, William T. *The Indian Rights Association*. Tucson: University of Arizona Press, 1985.

Harring, Sidney L. *Crow Dog's Case: American Indian Sovereignty, Tribal Law, and United States Law in the Nineteenth Century*. Cambridge: Cambridge University Press, 1994.

Holm, Tom. *The Great Confusion in Indian Affairs: Native Americans and Whites in the Progressive Era*. Austin: University of Texas Press, 2005.

Hoxie, Frederick E. *The Final Promise: The Campaign to Assimilate the Indians, 1888–1920*. Lincoln: University of Nebraska Press, 1984.

———. *Parading through History: The Making of the Crow Nation in America, 1805–1935*. Cambridge: Cambridge University Press, 1995.

———, ed. *Talking Back to Civilization: Indian Voices from the Progressive Era*. Boston: Bedford/St. Martin's, 2001.

———. *This Indian Country: American Indian Activists and the Place They Made*. New York: Penguin, 2012.

Krouse, Susan Applegate. *North American Indians in the Great War*. Lincoln: University of Nebraska Press, 2007.

Iverson, Peter. *Carlos Montezuma and the Changing World of American Indians*. Albuquerque: University of New Mexico Press, 1982.

Jackson, Helen Hunt. *A Century of Dishonor: A Sketch of the U.S. Government's Dealings with Some of the Indian Tribes*. New York: Harper Bros., 1881.

Jacobs, Margaret D. *White Mother to a Dark Race: Settler Colonialism, Maternalism, and the Removal of Indigenous Children in the American West and Australia, 1880–1940*. Lincoln: University of Nebraska Press, 2009.

Jenkins, Sally. *The Real All Americans: The Team That Changed a Game, a People, a Nation*. New York: Doubleday, 2007.

Keller, Robert H., Jr. *American Protestantism and United States Indian Policy, 1869–1882*. Lincoln: University of Nebraska Press, 1983.

Landis, Barbara. *Carlisle Indian Industrial School History*. http://home.epix.net/~landis/history.html. Accessed November 12, 2014.

Lomawaima, K. Tsianina. *They Called It Prairie Light: The Story of Chilocco Indian School*. Lincoln: University of Nebraska Press, 1994.

Looking Bill, Brad D. *War Dance at Fort Marion: Plains Indian War Prisoners*. Norman: University of Oklahoma Press, 2006.

Maddox, Lucy. *Citizen Indians: Native American Intellectuals, Race and Reform*. Ithaca, N.Y.: Cornell University Press, 2005.

Maddra, Sam A. *Hostiles? The Lakota Ghost Dance and Buffalo Bill's Wild West*. Norman: University of Oklahoma Press, 2006.

Maroukis, Thomas C. *The Peyote Road: Religious Freedom and the Native American Church*. Norman: University of Oklahoma Press, 2010.

Mathes, Valerie Sherer. *Helen Hunt Jackson and Her Indian Reform Legacy*. Austin: University of Texas Press, 1990.

Maurer, Evan M., et al. *Visions of the People: A Pictorial History of Plains Indian Life*. Minneapolis: Minneapolis Institute of Arts, 1992.

McDonnell, Janet A. *The Dispossession of the American Indian, 1887–1934*. Bloomington: Indiana University Press, 1991.

Meyer, Melissa L. *The White Earth Tragedy: Ethnicity and Dispossession at a Minnesota Anishinaabe Reservation, 1889–1920*. Lincoln: University of Nebraska Press, 1994.

Moses, L. G. *Wild West Shows and the Images of American Indians, 1883–1933*. Albuquerque: University of New Mexico Press, 1996.

Moses, L. G., and Raymond Wilson, eds. *Indian Lives: Essays on Nineteenth- and Twentieth-Century Native American Leaders*. Albuquerque: University of New Mexico Press, 1985.

Osburn, Katherine M. B. *Southern Ute Women: Autonomy and Assimilation on the Reservation, 1887–1934*. Albuquerque: University of New Mexico Press, 1998.

Peterson, Karen Daniels. *Plains Indian Art from Fort Marion*. Norman: University of Oklahoma Press, 1971.

Piatote, Beth H. *Domestic Subjects: Gender, Citizenship, and Law in Native American Literature*. New Haven: Yale University Press, 2013.

Pratt, Richard Henry. *Battlefield and Classroom: Four Decades with the American Indian, 1867–1904*. Edited by Robert M. Utley. New Haven: Yale University Press, 1964.

Prucha, Francis Paul. *American Indian Policy in Crisis: Christian Reformers and the Indians, 1865–1900*. Norman: University of Oklahoma Press, 1976.

———, ed. *Americanizing the American Indians: Writings by the "Friends of the Indian," 1880–1900*. Lincoln: University of Nebraska Press, 1978.

———. *The Great Father: The United States Government and the American Indians*. 2 vols. Lincoln: University of Nebraska Press, 1984.

Rzeczkowski, Frank. *Uniting the Tribes: The Rise and Fall of Pan-Indian Community on the Crow Reservation*. Lawrence: University Press of Kansas, 2012.

Smith, Sherry L. *Reimagining Indians: Native Americans through Anglo Eyes, 1880–1940*. New York: Oxford University Press, 2000.

Standing Bear, Luther. *Land of the Spotted Eagle*. Lincoln: University of Nebraska Press, 1978.

———. *My People the Sioux*. Boston: Houghton Mifflin, 1928.

Szabo, Joyce M. *Art from Fort Marion: The Silberman Collection*. Norman: University of Oklahoma Press, 2007.

———. *Howling Wolf and the History of Ledger Art*. Albuquerque: University of New Mexico Press, 1994.

Trachtenberg, Alan. *Shades of Hiawatha: Staging Indians, Making Americans, 1880–1930*. New York: Hill and Wang, 2004.

Trafzer, Clifford E., Jean A. Keller, and Lorene Sisquoc, eds. *Boarding School Blues: Revisiting American Indian Educational Experiences*. Lincoln: University of Nebraska Press, 2006.

Troutman, John W. *Indian Blues: American Indians and the Politics of Music, 1879–1934*. Norman: University of Oklahoma Press, 2009.

Viola, Herman J. *Warrior Artists: Historic Cheyenne and Kiowa Indian Ledger Art Drawn by Making Medicine and Zotom*. Washington, D.C.: National Geographic Society, 1998.

Vučković, Myriam. *Voices from Haskell: Indian Students between Two Worlds, 1884–1924*. Lawrence: University of Kansas Press, 2008.

Winnemucca (Hopkins), Sarah. *Life among the Piutes: Their Wrongs and Claims*. Reno: University of Nevada Press, 1994.

Zitkala-Ša. *American Indian Stories*. Lincoln: University of Nebraska Press, 1985.

8

From the Great Crash to Alcatraz

1929–1969

FOCUS QUESTIONS

1. What was new about the Indian New Deal?

2. Why did Indian people move to the cities in growing numbers after 1950?

3. What changes did militant young Indians demand from federal and tribal governments?

A NEW ERA IN INDIAN AFFAIRS?

IN 1929 THE U.S. STOCK MARKET CRASHED, and the United States entered the worst depression in its history. Throughout the 1920s, America had enjoyed sustained economic growth, but the surface prosperity concealed widening gaps between rich and poor and wild, unregulated speculation in the stock market. When the bubble burst in October 1929, the economy went into a massive downturn. Millions of Americans found themselves unemployed, and stark pictures of breadlines and starving children replaced images of national prosperity. Confident that the American economy would right itself, the Republican administration of Herbert Hoover was unable to meet the challenge or alleviate the suffering. In the 1932 presidential election Democrat Franklin Delano Roosevelt was swept into the Oval Office with a mandate for reform. Roosevelt committed the federal government to unprecedented levels of economic planning and social responsibility. He promised a new deal for "the forgotten man" — and no one was more forgotten than American Indians.

The Great Depression changed the way the U.S. government conceived of its role and responsibilities toward American society and the economy. It also brought changes in U.S. policies toward American Indians. The government shifted course on Indian affairs several times during the twentieth century. Yet, while policies changed, underlying problems often remained the same, as did the underlying goals of assimilating Indian people and gaining access to Indian resources. Indian communities responded to the policy shifts emanating from Washington, D.C., working both within and against the system to effect change. They took increasing responsibility for implementing programs in their own communities and eventually for formulating policies.

John Collier and the Indian New Deal

Franklin Delano Roosevelt's presidency reversed some of the disastrous policies of the previous fifty years. FDR appointed as his commissioner of Indian affairs John Collier, who served from 1933 to 1945. Collier envisioned and implemented far-reaching changes in the relationship between the U.S. government and the Indian tribes within its borders. He attempted to restore an emphasis on community in the government's dealings with Indian peoples.

Collier had been a social worker among immigrants in New York City, where he became concerned with what he saw as the fragmentation of community life and the decline of traditional cultures among immigrants to the United States. He had learned about Indian life primarily from his visits to Pueblo peoples in New Mexico during the early 1920s. At that time many American intellectuals and idealists recoiled from the havoc and horror of the First World War, a product of Western "civilization," and turned to the Indian communities of the Southwest to find balance and harmony. A visit to Taos Pueblo in 1920 changed Collier's life and convinced him that Indian cultures had something fundamental to offer American society. "He saw modernity as a disaster that was defeating man's perfectability," Collier's son recalled. "He saw the Indian as the last remnant of natural perfection, a model that must be preserved for human rejuvenation."[1] Modern American life seemed shallow, materialistic,

1968	Indian Civil Rights Act extends many Bill of Rights protections to tribal citizens
1968	American Indian Movement (AIM) founded in Minneapolis
1969	Vine Deloria Jr. publishes *Custer Died for Your Sins*
1969	N. Scott Momaday's *House Made of Dawn* wins the Pulitzer Prize for Fiction
1969	Indian activists take over Alcatraz

individualistic; Indian life, as evidenced by the Pueblos, seemed deeply spiritual and communal. Despite "repeated and immense historical shocks," wrote Collier in his autobiography, Pueblo communities "were going right on in the production of states of mind, attitudes of mind, earth-loyalties and human loyalties, amid a context of beauty which suffused all the life of the group." He thought that Indians might be the only people in the Western Hemisphere who still possessed "the fundamental secret of human life—the secret of building great personality through the instrumentality of social institutions." But he feared that Indian life might not survive.[2] Collier based his views on his visits to Taos but, as Frederick Hoxie points out, most Indians did not live at Taos and few shared Collier's romantic views of Indian culture.[3]

Like many other idealists before and since, Collier saw in Indian society the chance for the salvation of his own society. Roosevelt put in office a man with a history of Indian advocacy. Collier helped to establish the All-Pueblo Council, which lobbied successfully against the Bursum bill of 1922 that had threatened to deprive the Pueblos of land and water rights by placing jurisdiction over those rights in the state courts and legitimizing the claims of many non-Indians on Pueblo lands. He became executive secretary of the American Indian Defense Association in 1923. As commissioner of Indian affairs, Collier introduced his own beliefs in the formulation of Indian policy. For a century and a half, the federal government had tried to break up and sell off tribal land holdings, dismantle tribal governments, stamp out Native languages, and eradicate tribal cultures. Now the government tried to reverse the assault on Indian lands, rejuvenate tribal governments, preserve Native languages, and revive tribal cultures. Anthropologist D'Arcy McNickle, an enrolled member of the Flathead tribe who worked on Collier's staff, said that the Roosevelt administration, with Collier's prompting, "accepted the radical concept that the Indian race was not headed for early extinction."[4] Instead, it was committed to promoting revitalization of Indian life. The "Indian New Deal," masterminded by Collier, charted a new direction in United States Indian policy that, despite later efforts to reverse it, had a lasting impact throughout Indian America. (See "Two Views of the Indian Reorganization Act," pages 471–81.)

In some ways the Indian New Deal was not new, but rather another attempt by non-Indians to do what they regarded as the right thing for Indians. It was another paternalistic promise to bring a "new era" in Indian affairs, one of many twentieth-century shifts in Indian policy that left Indian people distrustful of anything coming out of Washington. It was another blueprint for reform, mandating one policy for all Indians and making little allowance for the tremendous diversity of Indian America.

Collier was devoted to championing Indian rights as he understood them, and he did so with a zeal that both attracted and alienated others. According to one historian and advisor on Indian policy, Collier possessed "the zeal of a crusader who knew better than the Indians what was good for them."[5] Collier's long-term goals included the eventual absorption of Indian people into mainstream American society, but he opposed his predecessors' concept of rapid assimilation and tried to develop a program that would preserve much more of the tribal heritage. The aims of his Indian New Deal included ending allotment and consolidating tribal lands, allowing Indians to play a more active role in running their own affairs, organizing tribal governments, supporting Indian cultures, ending government suppression of tribal rituals, and allowing Indian children to attend day schools on their home reservations. He was only partially successful in achieving these goals.

To some extent, Indians benefited from Roosevelt's more general New Deal legislation that provided jobs and relief and built schools and hospitals. Collier succeeded in channeling funds from other agencies and programs to benefit Indians. Many Indians were hired under the Civilian Conservation Corps (CCC), and on some reservations that meant Indians started earning a regular paycheck for the first time. Lakota scholar and activist Vine Deloria Jr., who was born during the Depression, called the CCC "the greatest program ever to come along. The Sioux had climbed from absolute deprivation to mere poverty." Ironically, the Great Depression "was the best time the reservation ever had."[6] But Collier also managed to get specific programs passed by Congress. Long-overdue improvements were made in the field of Indian education, with more focus on community, new curricula more suited to the needs of Indian students, and more and better trained teachers. The number of students at boarding schools soared during the Depression as parents sent children away to escape the grinding poverty of reservation life.[7] But the government shifted the emphasis from off-reservation boarding schools — the core of the government's educational crusade for the past fifty years (see Map 7.3, "U.S. Government Boarding Schools, 1889," page 393) — to day schools on reservations; between 1933 and 1941 almost one hundred day schools were built.

Under the Johnson-O'Malley Act of 1934, the secretary of the interior was authorized to negotiate contracts with any state for financial relief in areas of Indian education, medical aid, agricultural assistance, and welfare. The federal government funded school districts to provide services for the Indian children attending public schools. The idea was that state and federal government would work together to improve the quality of Indian education. Only Arizona, California, Minnesota, and Washington made contracts with the federal government in the 1930s. In some areas, the system worked well, but Indian children in public schools still encountered racism and prejudice, and some school districts drew Johnson-O'Malley money without making any provision for the needs of their Indian students. Nevertheless, the Indian New Deal took bold steps by departing from past educational policy and promoting a bilingual and bicultural education that bore fruit in the late 1960s and 1970s.[8] In another federal initiative, the Indian Arts and Crafts Board was established within the Department of the Interior in 1935 to promote and preserve traditional crafts and arts by helping Indian people form craft cooperatives, authenticate items of Indian manufacture, and establish marketing networks.[9]

The Indian Reorganization Act

The centerpiece of Indian New Deal legislation was the Indian Reorganization Act (IRA), passed in 1934. "The repair work authorized by Congress under the terms of the act," Collier said in his report as commissioner that year, "aims at both the economic and the spiritual rehabilitation of the Indian race."[10] The IRA aimed to protect Indians in their religion and lifestyle and represented an open admission that the Dawes Act (see pages 385–89) was a mistake. The original bill stated that:

1. Indians living on reservations would be allowed to establish local self-government and tribal corporations to develop reservation resources. The secretary of the interior would issue a charter of home rule to each Indian community, granting it greater responsibility over its own affairs, and the Indians would vote to accept the charter in tribal elections.

2. The federal government would train Indians in such issues as land management, public health, and law enforcement and prepare them for employment in the Bureau of Indian Affairs (BIA), as well as provide scholarship money for Indian students.

3. The Dawes Act would be terminated. Further allotments of Indian lands would be prohibited. The bill provided for consolidation of allotted lands into units for community use and provided $2 million each year to purchase lands for the tribes. Any "surplus" land remaining from allotment would be restored to the reservations.

4. A special Court of Indian Affairs would be established.

Congress was not prepared to go as far as Collier in promoting Native American independence, and the bill that finally passed Congress was substantially modified,[11] including the deletion of the special court provision.

Tribes were required to accept or reject the IRA by referendum; the establishment of tribal self-government was to be decided the same way. When a majority of adult tribal members approved the IRA, they could then write a constitution, which had to be approved by another majority vote and by the secretary of the interior. Tribes who accepted the IRA could elect a tribal council. The IRA applied only to those tribes that accepted it, and Oklahoma and Alaska were left out of its provisions. (Congress passed laws in 1936 to encourage the establishment of tribal and village governments in those areas.) Collier spent much time and energy promoting his program to Indian communities and held ten regional conferences in the spring of 1934 to explain the philosophy, operation, and importance of the IRA. For the first time, a commissioner of Indian affairs traveled around the country to explain legislation to Indian people.

Opposing and Disputing the IRA

Despite his enthusiasm, Collier encountered opposition, which slowed the progress of his reform program. Many Indians and non-Indians feared that after generations of painful adjustment the reversal of policies would mean turning

◆ **The Flatheads Adopt the IRA**
In 1935, the three Flathead tribes of western Montana—the Bitterroot Salish, Kootenai, and Pend d'Oreilles—were formally organized as the Confederated Salish and Kootenai Tribes of the Flathead Indian Reservation and became the first Indian tribe in the nation to adopt a constitution under the Indian Reorganization Act. In this photograph, Commissioner of Indian Affairs John Collier and chiefs of the tribe look on in Washington, D.C., as Secretary of the Interior Harold Ickes signs the constitution providing for Indian self-government on October 28, 1935. *EOH/AP Photo.*

back the clock and losing ground in the struggle to become full members of American society. Some Indian traditionalists disliked the proposed changes in tribal government. The Indian Rights Association argued that the new legislation perpetuated segregation, and some members of Congress opposed it for protecting communal ownership.

Some tribes were divided over the New Deal. Collier underestimated the diversity of Indian life and wanted Indians to function as unified tribes. In fact, the IRA proposed to impose rigid and alien political and economic systems on Indian communities. Majority rule went against traditional practices in those societies that reached decisions by consensus, and it seemed to ride roughshod over the views of the minority. In Indian country, not voting was often viewed as a negative vote; in Western-style democracy, however, those who do not vote have no voice. From the viewpoint of many Indians, the referenda on the IRA were rigged to produce an affirmative vote. On the Santa Ysabel Reservation in California, for instance, forty-three people voted against the IRA and only nine voted in favor. Sixty-two eligible voters did not vote, but rather than count them as abstentions or negative votes, the government counted them as "yes" votes, and the IRA was applied.[12]

Eventually, some 174 tribes accepted the Indian Reorganization Act, and of those, 135 communities drafted tribal constitutions. The Blackfeet of Montana voted for it, seeing it as the best vehicle for change available at the time. They used it to improve their political and economic situation and to try "to reorganize relations with the federal government on their [own] terms and to construct an American community of their own design."[13] But seventy-eight tribes rejected the IRA. The Seneca activist Alice Lee Jemison was a vocal critic of both Collier and the Indian New Deal and helped found the American Indian Federation, a group that campaigned against Collier's program. The Senecas regarded the Indian New Deal as a threat to their treaty rights and to the elective self-government they had established in 1848. With the other Iroquois tribes of New York, they voted heavily against the IRA (although the Wisconsin Oneidas accepted it). The Crows, unlike most Plains groups, rejected it, despite the influential support of Robert Yellowtail, superintendent of the Crow Indian Reservation. The Navajos rejected it.

After their return from confinement at Bosque Redondo in 1868, the Navajos had rebuilt their communities around sheep and herding. While Plains Indians had experienced population collapse and loss of subsistence base with the slaughter of buffalo herds, Navajo numbers and Navajo herds had grown steadily. The government even enlarged the Navajo Reservation to accommodate the increase of human and animal population. By 1933, the Navajos numbered more than 40,000 and were self-sufficient sheepherders. Issued 14,000 sheep (less than two per capita) with which to rebuild their herds in 1868, the Navajos had increased their stock to about 800,000 sheep and goats (twenty-one per capita) by the eve of the Great Depression.[14] But, combined with natural erosion cycles in the area and the intrusions of Anglo-American cattlemen who restricted Navajo grazing areas, the increase in livestock took a toll on the Navajo environment. A period of severe drought aggravated the problem. The government feared that overgrazing and trampling hooves broke down soils and that accumulations of silt from the reservation threatened the functioning of the huge Boulder Dam (later renamed Hoover Dam). Built on the Colorado River in northwestern Arizona and completed in 1936, the dam provided water, flood control, and electricity to the southwestern United States and Los Angeles, and its maintenance was a high priority. To relieve the stress on the land, the government implemented a program of livestock reduction.[15]

Navajos were not the only ranchers affected by stock reduction programs during the New Deal era — the government imposed livestock reductions on American farmers elsewhere in an effort to limit production and raise prices — but John Collier underestimated the importance of sheep, goats, and horses in Navajo life. He persuaded the Navajo tribal council to accept a program of stock reduction and promised to secure additional lands for the reservation. The tribal council had been formed under government auspices in the 1920s to facilitate access to oil deposits on the reservation; it hardly spoke for the majority of Navajos scattered across a reservation the size of West Virginia. The council agreed to a 10 percent reduction in stock, but this was only the first stage in a program that continued for more than a decade and cut Navajo herds by half. The stock reduction program was economically and emotionally devastating. Navajo families watched the slaughter of their horses, sheep, and goats with outrage and heartbreak. "It haunts me now, more than a half century later," wrote an anthropologist who worked on the Navajo Reservation at the time of the stock reductions, "and it still haunts the Navajos even more profoundly."[16]

Many Navajos held Collier personally responsible for their most bitter experience since the Long Walk to Bosque Redondo. They felt betrayed when he failed to deliver on promises he had made to expand the reservation eastwards. When Collier visited the reservation in 1934 to promote the IRA, he encountered fierce opposition from Navajos led by J. C. Morgan. When the referendum was held, 98 percent of the eligible voters cast ballots. The voting was close, but in the end the largest tribe in the country rejected the IRA and Collier's vision of a new era in Indian affairs. Collier offered his own interpretation of what had happened. (See "Two Views of the Indian Reorganization Act," pages 473–77.)

The Indian Reorganization Act had a mixed legacy. The broader Indian New Deal produced some dramatic changes in government policy. Indian tribes regained several million acres of lands that had been lost under the allotment program and moved forward in the areas of education, cultural preservation, and control of their own affairs. As commissioner of Indian affairs, Collier displayed sympathy for Indian heritage and recognized the importance of allowing Indian tribes a measure of self-determination. However, the IRA perpetuated indirect colonial control from Washington. According to the Harvard Project on American Indian Economic Development, "From the IRA onward, most reservations came to have the feel of branch offices of the federal government, with decision making dominated by the Bureau of Indian Affairs . . . and with tribal governments typically totally dependent on BIA programs and funds."[17] And Collier did not have the chance to finish his work. In December 1941, Japanese planes bombed Pearl Harbor, and the United States entered the Second World War. U.S. concern for righting wrongs at home diminished as the nation focused its energies on winning the war for democracy abroad.

Indians and World War II

The war had broken out in Europe in 1939, when Adolf Hitler ignored a British ultimatum and invaded Poland. Britain and France joined Poland in resisting German aggression, and Nazi Germany formed a coalition with Italy and Japan known as the Axis powers, with a view to world domination. Poland and France soon fell, and by the time the United States declared war, Britain stood virtually alone against Nazi occupation of Europe.

When World War II broke out, Nazi propaganda pitched American Indians as "natural allies," claiming that Germans and Indians had a historic affinity and should make common cause against the oppressive United States.[18] Instead, Indian people rallied to the defense of their country in record numbers. (See Picture Essay, "Indians and World War II," pages 492–97.) About 25,000 Indians served in the armed forces during World War II. Some Indian men were drafted; other men — and women — volunteered. The Iroquois challenged the right of the federal government to compel Indian men to fight, and a group of Iroquois issued a formal declaration of war against the Axis powers in 1942, indicating that they were participating in the war as sovereign nations, not as subordinates of the United States. Still, almost 100 percent of eligible Indians registered for the draft. Several hundred Indian women served in the WACS (Women's Army Corps), WAVES (Women Accepted for Volunteer Emergency Services), and Army Nurse Corps. Another 40,000 Native women and older Native men worked in war-related industries. As occurred in American society as a whole, Indian women took on many traditionally male responsibilities during the war and assumed new duties directly related to the war effort, such as volunteering for civil defense or nursing, and working in aircraft plants. Despite the extreme poverty of most Indian communities, Native Americans purchased about $50 million in war bonds and made donations to the Red Cross and other organizations.

Some Indians won lasting fame in combat. Five won Congressional Medals of Honor, including Lieutenant Ernest Childers (a Creek) and Lieutenant Jack Montgomery (a Cherokee). Major General Clarence Tinker (an Osage), the highest-ranking Indian in the armed forces at the start of the war, was killed at the pivotal 1942 Battle of Midway in the Pacific and was posthumously awarded the Distinguished Service Medal. Navajo code talkers in the Pacific theater baffled the Japanese with a code based on Navajo words, though their achievements were only belatedly recognized by the U.S. government. Ira Hayes, a Pima Indian from Arizona, participated in the famous flag raising by American marines on Iwo Jima (see page 496) and was then dispatched on a tour of the United States as part of the wartime fund-raising effort. More than five hundred Indians gave their lives in the war.

Native Americans suffered losses at home as well, as the government appropriated some tribal lands and resources for the war effort. The air force took possession of more than 340,000 acres of the Pine Ridge Reservation in South Dakota for use as an aerial gunnery and bombing range, leaving behind unexploded ordnance and shrapnel, and some internment camps for Japanese Americans were

◆ **Molly Spotted Elk, c. 1930**

Molly Spotted Elk, a Penobscot Indian living in Paris when the Germans invaded, was caught up in the throes of the war. Molly Spotted Elk: A Penobscot in Paris *by Bunny McBride, published by the University of Oklahoma Press (1995). Photo courtesy of Jean A. Moore, daughter of Spotted Elk.*

located on Indian land. After the Japanese landed troops on two islands in the Aleutian Chain off the Alaska Peninsula, the U.S. government forced Aleutian and Alaska Natives to evacuate their homes on the islands to make way for military defense preparation. More than 850 Aleuts were forcefully evacuated. They lost their homes and belongings and suffered hardship, disease, and misery in hastily constructed camps in southeastern Alaska and Washington State. When they returned home after the war, they found their homes had been used to billet troops and much of their property had been destroyed.[19]

For one Indian woman, the war brought wrenching personal experiences. Born on the Penobscot Reservation at Indian Island in Maine, Molly Spotted Elk (1903–77) became a dancer and starred in a Hollywood movie, *The Silent Enemy,* in 1930. She made her way to Paris, where she married a French journalist. The German occupation of France in 1940 forced her to flee with her young daughter, crossing the Pyrenees Mountains into Spain on foot. She returned safely to the United States but never saw her husband again. Throughout her career, Molly had wrestled with her need to make a living and her desire for a dancing career on the one hand, and her revulsion at having to do so by donning headdresses and skimpy buckskin costumes to act out stereotypes on the other. Back home in rural Maine after travels in New York, California, and Paris, she struggled to readjust. Her childhood home, in the words of her biographer, "was like an old pair of moccasins that one dreamed of during years of high-heeled city life — only to find, upon slipping into them, that they felt less comfortable than remembered because the shape of one's feet had changed."[20] She was not the first Indian to experience the tensions of moving from reservation to city and back again. Molly Spotted Elk completed her life's circle on Indian Island, where she died in 1977.

The war took Indians away from home (often for the first time), brought them into contact with new people and new ideas, and gave them new pride in having helped win the great fight for democracy. Many Native Americans earned a decent living for the first time in their lives, and when the war ended, some opted to stay in the cities, where there was work, rather than return home to the reservation. Many Indian veterans took advantage of the GI Bill, which provided college education and vocational training for returning servicemen, but otherwise they found few opportunities. Those who returned to the reservations expected to see an improvement in living standards, status, and relations with their white neighbors. They believed that their services to the country had earned them a better life and greater self-determination, but they were quickly disappointed. Drained of federal funds, reservation economies and services were often in worse shape after the war than they had been before the war. On the Navajo Reservation, for example, the program of livestock reduction in the 1930s and 1940s had

◆ **Woodrow Wilson Crumbo,** *Land of Enchantment* **(c. 1946)**
Land of Enchantment was painted the year after World War II ended and depicts with wry humor a situation that was becoming increasingly common on the Navajo Reservation. Weaving for the tourist trade offered Navajo women new financial opportunities to help them cope with economic hardship, but as Potawatomi/Creek artist Woody Crumbo makes clear, it also brought new intrusions into Navajo life. *Watercolor on board. Gift of Clark Field, 1946.45.4. © 2014, Philbrook Museum of Art, Inc., Tulsa, Oklahoma.*

eroded the traditional economy and generated widespread poverty. World War II offset some of the worst effects by providing jobs in war-related industries and service in the armed forces, but Navajos who returned home after the war faced an economic crisis. With their traditional economy disrupted, they needed other sources of income. They found the promise of prosperity in what seemed at the time to be attractive offers to develop the coal, oil, gas, and uranium resources of the Navajo Reservation, but their acceptance of those offers would ultimately have a devastating impact on the health and lives of many Navajo people.

Americans who recognized the Indians' wartime service either stereotypically attributed it to their "warrior tradition" or interpreted it to indicate that Indians were ready for complete assimilation into American society. The spirit of national unity that arose during the war and an increasing societal emphasis on conformity in the postwar years allowed little room for cultural difference. Indian people in general faced more hard times and a renewed assault on their tribalism.

TERMINATION

In the late 1940s and the 1950s, the pendulum of public opinion and government support swung away from the reform impetus of the New Deal to conservatism and conformity. Threatened by the power of the Soviet Union and fearful of the spread of communism, Americans reaffirmed their loyalty to their country and regarded with suspicion and resentment those who did not seem to fit in with mainstream society or subscribe absolutely to American values. Native Americans living on reservations, running their own governments, and maintaining their own communal lifeways seemed an anomaly. The U.S. government decided to hasten the process of Indian assimilation by ending, or "terminating," its relationship with Indian tribes. Termination policy aimed to dismantle tribal governments, dissolve tribal land holdings, and end federal services to Indian people.

After the war, the government implemented a three-part program of compensation, termination, and relocation. Acknowledging that injustices had been committed in the past, Congress aimed to "wipe the slate clean" by settling once and for all the claims that Indian tribes had against the government for loss of lands; it wanted to eliminate special tribal status and turn jurisdiction over the Indians to state and local authorities; and it imagined that Indians would more easily enter the mainstream of American life if they moved from their reservations to cities.

The Indian Claims Commission

From 1778 (the first U.S. treaty with the Delawares) to 1871 (when Congress ended the treaty-making process in favor of executive agreements), the United States negotiated nearly four hundred treaties with Indian tribes. However, many of the provisions of these treaties were never implemented, and many tribes never received payment stipulated in treaties for lands they had ceded. In 1946 Congress established the Indian Claims Commission (ICC) to review tribal grievances over treaty enforcement and management of resources and to resolve lingering disputes between Indian tribes and the U.S. government. Tribes were allowed five years in which to file grievances; they had to prove aboriginal title to the lands in question and then bring suit for settlement. The commission would then review their case and assess the amount, if any, to be paid in compensation. The whole process was expected to be completed in ten years.

The work of the Claims Commission was beset with problems. The Justice Department often discouraged or hindered tribes that wanted to file claims. Some Indian groups had conflicting claims to aboriginal occupancy of the same lands. In addition, some Indians rejected the idea that cash payment could settle land issues. Land, not money, was the basis of their culture. For example, the Taos Indians rejected an offer of $10 million for Blue Lake in northwestern New Mexico because it was sacred to them and not "for sale." The Pit River Indians in northern California rejected the offer of a measly 47 cents per acre for the lands they had lost.

The ICC raised hopes and went some way toward righting old wrongs but it could only offer money in compensation, not return any land. When compensation was paid, other problems arose. People often disagreed over whether the payments should be made per capita to individual tribal members or whether they should be invested by tribal officials in the reservation economy. Tribal members who lived off the reservations often disagreed with their relatives who had stayed behind. In the case of per capita payments, tribal rolls had to be drawn up and verified, producing further disputes over who qualified as a member. Different tribes adopted different procedures. The Crows in Montana, for instance, received a $10 million payment and allocated 50 percent for per capita payments and invested the rest in health, housing, education, scholarships, land purchases, and social services.

In 1978 the Indian Claims Commission ended its operations and transferred its unresolved cases to the Court of Claims. In its thirty-two years, the ICC had dismissed 204 cases, made 274 awards, and paid out more than $800 million in settlements. Some Indian people squandered their payments; others were cheated out of them by unscrupulous local businessmen. Sometimes the awards were woefully inadequate and sometimes much of the money ended up in the pockets of the attorneys who represented the tribes. Thomas E. Leubben, an attorney with more than forty years' experience in federal Indian law, concludes that the way Indian land claims were litigated in the ICC was "a scandal of historic proportions" and that the whole process served the needs of the dominant culture "at great cost to Native Americans."[21]

Removing the Government's Trust Responsibilities

The period also saw a growing call in Congress to end federal services to Indian tribes and remove the government's trust relationship established by treaties and the Constitution. Influential western congressmen such as Senator Arthur

Watkins of Utah and Representative E. Y. Berry of South Dakota were among the most vocal advocates of this termination policy. In 1950 Dillon S. Myer, the former head of the War Relocation Authority that had taken thousands of Japanese Americans from the West Coast and put them in internment camps during World War II, became commissioner of Indian affairs. The new commissioner was hostile to many of the reforms implemented by John Collier in the 1930s. In Myer's view, the Bureau of Indian Affairs should "not do anything which others can do as well or better and as cheaply. The Bureau should do nothing for Indians which Indians can do for themselves and we should lean over backward to help them learn to do more things on their own."[22] He began to implement a government policy of termination and relocation of Indian tribes. Glenn Emmons succeeded Myers as commissioner in 1953 and carried on his work.

Tribes deemed to have made the most "progress" were identified as eligible for termination. The government's list included the Six Nations of New York, the Prairie Potawatomis of Kansas, the Menominees of Wisconsin, the Flatheads of Montana, the Klamaths of Oregon, the Hoopas of northern California, and various southern California bands. In 1953, House Concurrent Resolution 108 proposed ending federal relations with a number of these eligible tribes. The goal of termination expressed in House Concurrent Resolution 108 was "as rapidly as possible, to make the Indians within the territorial limits of the United States subject to the same laws and entitled to the same privileges and responsibilities as are applicable to other citizens of the United States, to end their status as wards of the United States, and to grant them all the rights and prerogatives pertaining to American citizenship."[23] The resolution passed both houses of Congress unanimously. Two weeks later, Congress passed Public Law 280, transferring jurisdiction over tribal lands to state and local governments in California, Oregon, Nebraska, Minnesota, and Wisconsin. PL 280 represented a major step toward extending state control over Indian reservations. Other states could unilaterally adopt it if they chose (until 1968, after which the consent of the reservation was required). In 1954 responsibility for Indian health was transferred from the BIA to the U.S. Public Health Service. Between 1953 and 1966 Congress passed laws terminating 109 tribes: it ended the trust relationship between the federal government and the tribes, withdrew federal services from the communities, required the tribes to distribute property among their members, eliminated the tribes' reservations, and rendered tribal members and their lands subject to state laws and taxes.

As had the proponents of allotment in the 1880s, advocates of termination justified their new policy as one that would liberate Indian people from the stifling atmosphere of reservation life and dependence on government support. In fact, termination was often disastrous to the tribes involved: they were now ineligible for health care from the Indian Health Service, they lost federal support of their schools, they were subject to state laws and taxes, and their lands were no longer protected by federal trust status. The Menominees and the Klamaths were especially hard hit. The Menominees were fairly self-sufficient in 1950, with a tribal lumbering operation and sawmill that provided employment and paid for most of their community services. Termination struck at their prosperity and society. In 1953 the Menominees were seeking distribution of an earlier monetary settlement on a per capita basis. Payment required congressional approval; it passed in the House but encountered stiff opposition before the Senate Committee on Interior Affairs. Utah senator Arthur Watkins, a termination advocate, supported an amendment calling for the termination of federal assistance to the Menominees and then informed the Menominees that agreeing to termination was a precondition to obtain the payments in question.[24] With little understanding of the exact termination provisions, most of those Menominees who voted for termination were probably only voting to receive their per capita payments.

In June 1954, President Eisenhower signed the Menominee Termination Act. The law gave the tribe four years in which to establish their own municipal, educational, health, and other services previously provided by the federal government. The Menominees won a deadline extension to 1961. They reorganized the tribe as a corporation, Menominee Enterprises Incorporated, to manage the lands and lumber mill formerly owned and operated by the tribe, and the reservation became a county. Nevertheless, the impact of termination was devastating. The once-thriving tribal lumber industry was deprived of vital federal contracts at a time of a nationwide slump in house building. Menominees had to sell land to pay their taxes. Hospitals closed and health problems increased. A plan designed to save the federal government money cost more than ever in the form of welfare payments to struggling Menominees.[25]

The law terminating the Klamaths was passed in 1954 and went into effect in 1961. Like the Menominees, the Klamaths impressed government officials as a model tribe for termination because of their rich timber resources and relative prosperity, with a gross annual income of $2 million from sale of tribal timber.[26] But the Klamaths relied heavily on federal services and contracts, and, as in the case of the Menominees, termination brought economic disaster. Cutting off health and education services previously provided by the federal government caused additional suffering. Some communities had little choice but to sell lands that the government had previously held in trust. Many Indians regarded termination as another land grab, with lumber interests influencing policy and lumber companies emerging as the actual beneficiaries of a policy that was supposed to "liberate" Indians.[27]

Many tribes opposed termination and PL 280.[28] The National Congress of American Indians (NCAI), founded in 1944 to protect Indian rights, led the fight under its chairman Joseph Garry, a Coeur d'Alene veteran of World War II and an Idaho state legislator. "Reservations do not imprison us," declared the NCAI. "They are our ancestral homelands, retained by us for our perpetual use and enjoyment. We feel we must assert our right to maintain ownership in our own way, and terminate it only by our consent."[29] Both the Menominees and the Klamaths fought for restoration of tribal status. A young Menominee social worker named Ada Deer led the movement to reverse Menominee termination, lobbying in Washington until Congress passed the Menominee Restoration Act, which President Nixon signed in 1973.[30] The Klamaths secured restoration of tribal status in 1986. But the experience of both tribes stood as a warning to

◆ **National Congress of American Indians**

In November 1944 almost eighty delegates from fifty tribes met in Denver, Colorado, and founded the National Congress of American Indians. The NCAI's mission, according to its constitution, was "to secure the rights and benefits to which we are entitled under the laws of the United States, the several states thereof, and the territory of Alaska; to enlighten the public toward a better understanding of the Indian race; to preserve cultural values; to seek an equitable adjustment to tribal affairs; to secure and to preserve rights under Indian treaties with the United States; and to otherwise promote the common welfare of the American Indians." *National Anthropological Archives, Smithsonian Institution [NAA Photo Lot 75–33].*

others: economic success could bring termination. Most of the tribes terminated in the 1950s and 1960s were eventually restored to tribal status, but others — the mixed-blood Utes, for example — were not so fortunate.[31]

Indian people in the South during this era faced other threats to their identity. In addition to dealing with the Indian policies of the federal government, they confronted "Jim Crow" policies that mandated segregation in public facilities in the states in which they lived. The Lumbees of Robeson County in North Carolina, the largest tribe east of the Mississippi, had a long history of intermarrying with people of European or African origin, and in the biracial South of the nineteenth century they were classified as "nonwhite." Like African Americans, they were treated as second-class citizens — separate, but certainly not equal. Nevertheless, in an era defined by racial segregation, the Lumbees crafted and asserted a distinct Indian identity and steadfastly maintained their community. They attempted to gain federal recognition as an Indian tribe by organizing under the 1934 Indian Reorganization Act but were not successful; however, they achieved state recognition in 1953. And in 1958 they drove the Ku Klux Klan out of Robeson County.[32]

In 1960 John F. Kennedy was elected president. He spoke of a "new frontier" with challenges to meet and opportunities to seize at home, abroad, and in space, but his words brought little comfort to Indian people "who had bad memories of the old frontier."[33] Kennedy had little real interest in Indians, and termination remained the official policy throughout his administration.

◆ **Ada Deer**

Social worker Ada Deer (b. 1935) lobbied in Washington against the Menominee Termination Act. In 1973 President Nixon signed the Menominee Restoration Act, redesignating the Menominees as a federally recognized tribe. Deer served as chairperson of the Menominee Restoration Committee from 1973 to 1976 and became the first Native American woman to head the BIA. Milwaukee Journal, *January 31, 1974. Copyrighted photograph, Journal Sentinel, Inc. Reproduced with permission.*

Relocation and Urban Indians

Since colonial times, some Indians had moved to cities in the wake of dispossession and the disruption of their traditional economies. After the Allotment Act placed them on small plots of land, more Indians began to leave the reservations and look for work elsewhere. During World War II, large numbers of Indians moved to the cities to work in war-related industries. The Indian population of Minneapolis, for example, rose from less than 1,000 in the 1920s to more than 6,000 by the end of World War II in 1945.[34] After the war, endemic unemployment on the reservations and new social and economic opportunities in the cities prolonged the trend all across the country. Kahnawake Mohawks continued to leave their reserve outside Montreal and travel to New York City for jobs in steel construction. Chicago's Indian population jumped twentyfold in the decades after the war, from about 500 in 1945 to 10,000 in 1975.[35] Postwar Los Angeles was "an industrial boom town," offering blue-collar jobs in the petroleum, construction, aircraft, and other manufacturing industries.[36]

The government seized on this trend and initiated its relocation program as the means of ending reservation poverty and accelerating the pace of assimilation. In the nineteenth century the government had tried to absorb Indians into American society by making them farmers; in the mid-twentieth century it tried to do so by making them city dwellers. Many Indians had already relocated from rural reservations to urban areas on their own initiative and successfully adjusted to urban life, and the BIA encouraged other young families to make the move. In 1948 the BIA experimented with a relocation program to move Navajos to Denver, Salt Lake City, and Los Angeles. In 1952 the government launched the Voluntary Relocation Program, and during the next eight years the BIA provided incentives and assistance to move more than 30,000 Indians from their reservations to the cities; by 1973, more than 100,000 Indians had gone on relocation.

Thousands of Indians were given one-way bus tickets to cities where they were expected to live and work like other Americans. Usually, the BIA moved relocatees long distances — Anishinaabe and Sioux people from Minnesota and South Dakota to California, and Alaska Natives and Navajos to Chicago, for instance — to discourage them from returning to their reservation homes. The BIA established relocation centers in key cities, gave help with moving and finding accommodations, offered job training, provided free medical care for one year, and paid a month's subsistence until the relocatees became settled. Relocation officials made arrangements for the move, greeted the relocatees on their arrival in the city, and attempted to prepare them for adjustment to city life. Relocation became a nationwide policy, and Indian people continued to move to the cities, with and without government assistance.

◆ "Come to Denver"
BIA leaflets such as this one promoted the advantages of city life among reservation communities. *National Archives, photo no. 75-N-REL-1G.*

Some Indians experienced real economic gain and built successful new lives in an urban environment. But, like other immigrants from rural areas, many of the newcomers faced new problems. Accustomed to close-knit extended families and small communities, Indian migrants had to adjust to the anonymity of life in a city of millions. Accustomed to a philosophy of communal responsibility and sharing, they had to survive in a world of individual capitalist competition. Accustomed to a slower pace of life on rural reservations where family demands and ceremonial calendars took precedence, many struggled to keep up with the hectic routine and daily time-keeping required by urban employers. Unaccustomed to demanding their rights and not motivated by the financial and property ideals of middle-class America, urban Indians often saw themselves left behind in a race dominated by white Americans. For many Indians, urban life meant poverty, poor housing, and unemployment. "They never told us it would be like this," they said.[37] As many as a third of the relocatees returned to the reservations. Other Indian workers used cities as a source of seasonal labor only, taking paying jobs when they were available and returning home during down times.

Native Americans who stayed in the cities developed new communities and sometimes forged new identities as urban Indians. Newcomers sought out Indian people who had already established themselves in the cities, and Indians tended to concentrate in certain areas, such as the Uptown neighborhood of Chicago and Bell Gardens and Cudahy in Los Angeles County. They built support networks with people who lived in the same neighborhoods, worked at the same jobs, attended the same churches, and frequented the same bars. In many cities they established American Indian centers that provided social services and functioned as a cultural focus. Urban Indians also developed new ways of sustaining ties with their reservation communities. For example, before World War II almost all Comanches lived in southwestern Oklahoma; after the war, about half of the enrolled tribal members left home and took jobs elsewhere. Many Comanches and other Indian groups found that returning home regularly to take part in powwows and social and ceremonial gatherings allowed them to celebrate their culture, express shared tribal values, and reinforce their identity.[38]

After considerable debate and controversy, relocation programs were reduced in the 1970s. But jobs and social opportunities attracted young Indians to urban areas long after the government's program of relocation faded. Los Angeles, Seattle, Albuquerque, Phoenix, Denver, Minneapolis, and Chicago contained large composite Indian communities. There were no more than 5,000 Indians in Los Angeles County before World War II; by 1980, 50,000 lived there.[39] By 1970 Los Angeles had more Native American inhabitants than any place outside the Navajo reservation. The Indian people who moved there were not just victims of federal relocation policy; they also took the initiative to relocate themselves; took advantage of the social, economic, and educational opportunities offered by city life; and created new lives and communities. Like Indian students who had turned their boarding schools into Indian institutions, they remade their city spaces into Indian spaces.[40] In 1950 only 13.4 percent of Indians counted by the U.S. census lived in cities; by 1970, the proportion had risen to 44 percent; by 1980 it was 50 percent.[41] By the end of the twentieth century, more than two-thirds of American Indians lived in urban areas; many of them were third-generation city dwellers. Urbanization was not the death knell of Indian society; it was another phase in an ongoing history of Indian change and adaptation to contact with non-Indian society. Much of Indian America became urban, and parts of urban America became Indian.[42]

Drowning Homelands

Back on the reservations, some Indian peoples faced new assaults on their homelands as well as on their tribal status. They found their homes targeted for flooding, a byproduct of major dam construction. Between 1944 and 1980, the

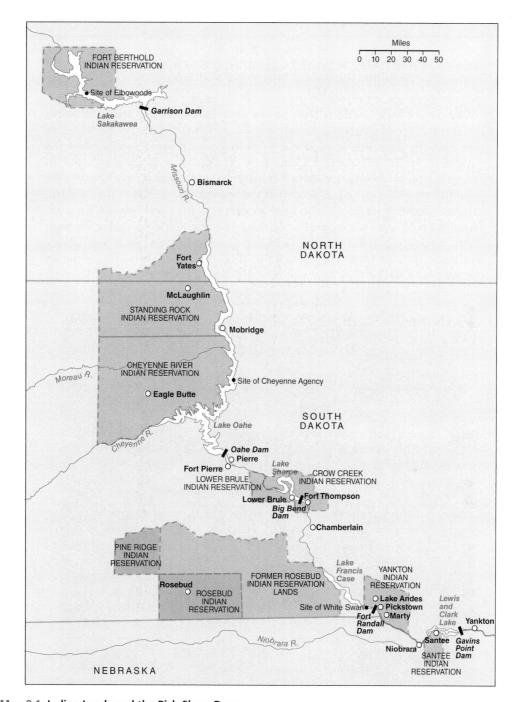

◆ **Map 8.1 Indian Lands and the Pick-Sloan Dams**

In addition to the flooding of Fort Berthold, the dams at Oahe, Big Bend, and Fort Randall, put in place by the Pick-Sloan Missouri River Basin Program, flooded more than 200,000 acres of Sioux land on the Standing Rock, Cheyenne River, Lower Brulé, Crow Creek, and Yankton reservations.

SOURCE: From Michael Lawson, *Dammed Indians Revisited: The Continuing History of the Pick-Sloan Plan and the Missouri River Sioux* (Pierre: South Dakota State Historical Society Press, 2009). Used by permission.

Pick-Sloan Plan flood control and water development program in the Missouri River basin affected Indian peoples along the length of the river (Map 8.1). After a series of floods in the lower basin states in the spring of 1943, the Army Corps of Engineers built Garrison Dam on the Fort Berthold Reservation in North Dakota as part of a massive six-dam project designed to harness the power of the Missouri River and generate energy as well as to provide flood control and irrigation. When the Garrison Dam was completed in 1953, the floodwaters it created covered one-quarter of the total reservation land base, split the reservation in half, and drowned 90 percent of the best agricultural land. The Mandan, Hidatsa, and Arikara people who lived on the reservation had opposed the dam, and now most were forced to relocate. Many became scattered, and many went from supporting their families as farmers to becoming wage laborers or welfare recipients. In 1992 Congress awarded the Three Affiliated Tribes $149.5 million in compensation for their losses and the flooding of their reservation. The Mni

◆ **Losing a Homeland**
Members of the Fort Berthold tribal business council watch — some in tears — as the secretary of the interior signs a contract selling reservation lands to the government for construction of the Garrison Dam in 1950. *AP Photo.*

Sose Intertribal Water Rights Coalition, an alliance of twenty-eight tribes along the Missouri River basin that assists tribes in the protection of their rights to use Missouri River water near and under their reservations, lobbied for an allocation of hydropower to reduce electric utility rates, which remained among the highest in the nation despite the promise of low-cost hydroelectric power from the dams that flooded their homelands.

In Iroquois country, Mohawk communities at Kahnawake and at Akwesasne on the U.S.–Canadian border lost land when the St. Lawrence Seaway was built in the 1950s. The industrialization that followed devastated Akwesasne's dairy industry and left the community with heavily polluted fishing waters. The Senecas fought for years to prevent the Army Corps of Engineers from building the Kinzua Dam on the Allegheny River in northwestern Pennsylvania. But, in contravention of the 1794 Treaty of Canandaigua, which assured the Senecas that the United States would never claim or disturb their reservation lands, the dam was completed in 1965, drowning 10,000 acres. An attempt to halt the dam went all the way to the U.S. Supreme Court, but to no avail. Seneca families were relocated, and the remains of chief Cornplanter, who had led the tribe during and after the American Revolution (see page 211), were removed before the floodwaters covered his grave. The Senecas' Tuscarora relatives and neighbors likewise fought in vain in the Supreme Court to prevent the Federal Power Commission from taking tribal lands by eminent domain for a hydroelectric power project. In the dissenting opinion, Associate Justice Hugo Black criticized the court's decision as another broken promise in a sorry record of treaty violations. "Great nations, like great men, should keep their word," he wrote.[43]

In the Northwest, the Bonneville, Grand Coulee, and Dalles dams destroyed ancient fishing sites and reduced the Columbia River to a shadow of its former power. In the Southeast, Cherokees and environmentalists fought to stop construction of the Tellico Dam on the Little Tennessee River and invoked the American Indian Religious Freedom Act to protect their sacred sites, but the project was pushed through Congress in 1979 and the dam was built. Chota, the site of the old Cherokee capital, and numerous other archaeological sites were flooded. In northern Quebec, Cree Indians in the 1970s saw dams built and lands flooded—and then embarked on a long battle to prevent further destruction of their homelands.

A YOUNGER GENERATION RESPONDS

In 1969 Indian students captured headlines when they took over Alcatraz Island in San Francisco harbor in protest against current government policies and past breaches of treaty rights. In the years that followed, militant young Indian protesters dominated the news coming out of Indian country. Indian activism had a long history, and assertions of tribal sovereignty had taken many forms, from clear political statements to the quiet preservation of cultural practices outlawed by the federal government. Twentieth-century pan-Indian political action started with the work of Charles Eastman, Carlos Montezuma, and the Society of American Indians, but the momentum for change grew steadily after World War II. The National Congress of American Indians fought against termination. In the 1950s and 1960s, Seneca people protested against the Kinzua Dam, and Wallace Mad Bear Anderson, a Tuscarora, helped the Mohawks of St. Regis resist New York State's attempt to impose state income taxes on the reservation and led nonviolent resistance to prevent seizures of Tuscarora land by the New York Power Authority.[44] As the United States wrestled with issues of race, poverty, and foreign policy at home and with anticolonial movements in Asia, Africa, and the Middle East, Indian intellectuals increased the volume on demands for tribal sovereignty and self-determination and moved the debate about the place of American Indians in American society to the center of national politics.[45] Increasing numbers of Indian people insisted on the right to run their own affairs free from the stifling control of the BIA, while holding the government to promises it had made in past treaties, and a growing Red Power movement turned to direct action to achieve its goals.

Upheaval in America

Although their situation and demands were in many ways unique, Native American activists joined a growing chorus for change at home and abroad. As the United States squared off against the Soviet Union in Cold War conflict that usually produced more rhetoric than direct confrontation, each superpower tried to win the hearts, minds, and allegiance of developing nations in the global contest between communism and the free market economy, and each became involved in supporting or suppressing wars of liberation around the world. As they had in two world wars, Native Americans again served their country, fighting in the Korean War between 1950 and 1953 and then the Vietnam War from the 1960s to 1973. Many Native Americans began to relate struggles for independence from colonial rule elsewhere in the world to their own situation in America. Native intellectuals reacted to the threat of termination with an increasingly international perspective and employed the rhetoric of the Cold War in their struggle: how could the United States claim to be defending freedom, justice, and self-determination for peoples abroad when it so clearly denied those same rights to Native Americans at home?[46]

The government's termination and relocation policies largely backfired, generating increased resistance and organization among many American Indian groups. As happened when Indians were sent to boarding schools, a new generation emerged with a new, unifying experience. Mass migrations of Indians fostered a growing pan-Indian identity and a determination to preserve Indian community and heritage (exactly the opposite of what the government relocation program was intended to achieve). Some lobbied effectively in Congress for change; others took to the streets or seized property to confront American society with its shameful record and continuing injustices.

They were not alone. By the late 1960s, American society was in turmoil. The country was divided over the war in Vietnam. People of different generations, genders, ethnicities, and classes clashed over issues of morality, power, and privilege, and they argued about the kind of society America was, or could be. College campuses erupted in protest and violence as students protested against an escalating and agonizing war, denounced the military-industrial complex, and took on bastions of the old order. African Americans demanded their long-deferred civil rights or, increasingly, asserted Black Power, and race riots devastated many American cities. Families split as young people openly rejected the values of their parents' generation and expressed their sexual and cultural revolution in art, literature, and rock music. Like African Americans, college students, and antiwar protesters, young Indians, many of them college educated, declared that it was up to them to bring about change, to save America from itself. Red Power activists added to the cacophony of voices demanding change, and Native American writers and speakers attracted greater attention than ever before. In 1969, Lakota author and activist Vine Deloria Jr. published *Custer Died for Your Sins: An Indian Manifesto* and, for the first time, a Native American writer, Kiowa N. Scott Momaday, won the Pulitzer Prize for Fiction for his novel *House Made of Dawn*.

The Rise of Indian Militancy

The turmoil in American society in the 1960s helped to create a mood for reform in Congress and the courts, and many Native Americans continued the struggle for sovereignty and change by working within the system and at the community level rather than taking to the streets in public protest. But things were not moving quickly enough for many young Indians, who were angry and frustrated by years of dealing with the federal bureaucracy. More vocal and militant than their parents, they insisted on a better deal for Indian people. They demanded that the government cease its assault on Indian tribes and fulfill its treaty obligations; that Indian people be more involved in formulating policy and in running their own affairs; and that the United States respect Indian rights and culture. Like African American civil rights activists and militants who were winning long-denied rights (Congress passed the Civil Rights Act in 1964 and the Voting Rights Act the following year), these young Indians came to believe it was futile to wait patiently for conditions to improve: American society would respond only to political confrontation and the threat of militancy.

In 1961 over four hundred delegates from sixty-five tribes attended the American Indian Chicago Conference and composed a Declaration of Indian Purpose, which they sent to President John F. Kennedy. Later in the year, younger participants from the Chicago conference voiced their discontent and impatience in trying to work with the U.S. government and formed the National Indian Youth Council (NIYC) in Gallup, New Mexico. The NIYC demanded Native American participation in determining the policies that affected Native American

◆ **Billy Frank (1931–2014)**
In the 1960s, Indian people in the Northwest openly asserted their rights to fish despite harassment from state authorities and non-Indian neighbors. Billy Frank Jr., pictured here with a photograph of himself fishing in the 1960s, was arrested more than fifty times fighting for treaty fishing rights on the Nisqually River in Washington State. He died a few months after this photograph was taken.[49] *Ted S. Warren/AP Photo.*

lives. Instead of relying on the government to run their affairs, they sought freedom to make their own decisions, their own futures, their own mistakes.[47] (See "Documents of Indian Militancy," pages 485–90.)

The government was not totally out of step. After President Kennedy's assassination in 1963, President Lyndon Johnson's War on Poverty and his attempts to create a Great Society increased federal assistance programs and prompted greater Indian participation in those programs. In 1964 Congress created the Office of Economic Opportunity, with a special "Indian desk" to administer programs for Native American communities. A year later Congress established the Department of Housing and Urban Development, which assisted many reservation communities in building new housing. Vine Deloria Jr., director of the National Congress of American Indians at the time, said the government's poverty program meant that "for the first time tribes can plan and run their own programs for their people without someone in the BIA dictating to them."[48]

Some of the first causes the NIYC supported occurred on the Northwest Pacific Coast and the Columbia River. Indian peoples there depended on rich and regular harvests of salmon. Salmon were as important in the life and culture of the coastal tribes as buffalo were to the peoples of the Plains or as corn was to the Iroquois. In the 1850s, Governor Isaac Stevens of Washington Territory had secured a series of treaties that deprived the Walla Wallas, Umatillas, Cayuses, Yakamas, and other tribes of most of their lands but that recognized the Indians' right to continue fishing in their "usual and accustomed places." The Americans were interested in farming and lumbering, not in fishing, and they gave little thought to the issue of guaranteeing the Indian fishing rights. In the next century, however, the population of the Northwest increased dramatically. Pollution, dams, and increasing sport and commercial fishing took a heavy toll on salmon runs. Indians struggled to harvest enough fish to live on and found themselves arrested for fishing out of season and without licenses. Denied justice in state courts, they began in the 1960s to stage "fish-ins" to draw public attention to their grievances and publicize their treaty rights. Many Indians went to jail, but their efforts eventually produced some important victories in court (see Chapter 9, page 524).

Many of the young Indian leaders who first articulated and advocated Red Power came from reservations and rural areas, but the movement spread rapidly among young Indians in the cities.[50] About 10,000 Indians, drawn mainly from the Anishinaabe and Sioux populations of Minnesota and the Dakotas, lived in Minneapolis and St. Paul. The Indian community complained frequently of harassment by the police, and Minneapolis Anishinaabeg formed an "Indian patrol" to monitor the activities of police in Indian neighborhoods (much like the Black Panthers did in the ghettos of Oakland, California). Three patrol leaders, Clyde Bellecourt, Dennis Banks, and George Mitchell, went further and in the summer of 1968 organized the American Indian Movement (AIM), which had a more aggressive agenda. Growing urban Indian activism in turn generated a revival of Indian nationalism on many reservations and promoted the Indian identity and culture that the termination and relocation programs were designed to eradicate.

Young urban Indians often returned to their reservations in search of support and spiritual guidance from the traditional people at home and to relearn traditional ways. There they forged new alliances in the struggle for Indian rights.

Confrontations began to flare up from one side of the country to the other. In 1968 Mohawk Indians blockaded the International Bridge between Canada and New York, forcefully protesting the infringement of rights of free passage guaranteed them by the Jay Treaty of 1794. In 1969 a group of young Indians seized Alcatraz Island, a disused federal penitentiary in San Francisco Bay. Under the name "Indians of All Tribes," they issued a "Proclamation to the Great White Father," ironically employing the rhetoric of old treaties to demonstrate their grievances and demand reparations for confiscated land and the hundreds of treaties with Indian nations that the United States had broken. (See "Proclamation to the Great White Father and to All *His* People," page 490.) The takeover of Alcatraz Island ended rather quietly; federal marshals removed the last few protesters in 1971. But it symbolized the dawning of a new era: time and again in the years to come, young Indians would take direct action and mobilize national attention in order to make their voices heard and to confront America with its past and present record of injustice toward Native people.

DOCUMENTS

Two Views of the Indian Reorganization Act

D RAFTED BY JOHN COLLIER AND A TEAM OF LAWYERS, the bill that became the Indian Reorganization Act (IRA) contained forty-eight pages. It was introduced in Congress in February 1934 by Senators Burton K. Wheeler of Montana and Edgar Howard of Nebraska and endured a stormy passage that stripped it of some key provisions — notably, Collier's plans to consolidate Indian landholdings and establish a separate federal court of Indian affairs. President Roosevelt signed the amended bill into law in June. The act ended the policy of allotment and alienation of Indian land; it promoted economic development in Indian communities by establishing a revolving credit fund; and it encouraged tribes to take back responsibility for running their own affairs.

But it was a limited measure of self-government and it often produced unrepresentative minority tribal administrations. The forms of government that the tribes were invited and encouraged to establish and vote on were not their own traditional governments guided by clan or spiritual leaders; they were American-style representative governments and bureaucracies, created and operated under the supervision of the Bureau of Indian Affairs (BIA) and the secretary of the interior. In that sense, the IRA represented a shift in strategy rather than a fundamental change in policy, with assimilation still the ultimate goal. "The IRA and the Indian New Deal set out to grant to Indians a limited but enlarged degree of control over their affairs and destinies," writes one sociologist, "but did so in the service of ends preselected by the dominant society and through methods given by that society, after its own models." Instead of trying to break up tribal communities and assimilate individuals, the IRA sought to make communities the vehicles of assimilation. Indian tribes as political constructs would survive, but as they "voluntarily formed constitutional governments, undertook the development of their own resources, and joined with the federal government in the assault on poverty and ignorance, assimilation would necessarily follow. American economic and political institutions would be reproduced within Indian societies, as a result of Indian efforts."[51]

The IRA revealed and fueled divisions in some Indian communities. Among the Lakotas, some people who became known as "new dealers" enthusiastically embraced Collier's vision of Indian self-government. But others "had their own ideas about what Indian self-government should look like" and wanted nothing to do with a system imposed from Washington.[52] On the Pine Ridge Reservation in South Dakota, only 13 percent of the eligible Oglala voters accepted the IRA in the tribal referendum; 12 percent voted against it. The other 75 percent failed to vote, which from their perspective probably meant voting in the negative by having nothing to do with the process. "But," explained historian Alvin Josephy, "a majority of those who voted had said 'Yes,' and a minority of 13 percent was thus used to foist upon the other 87 percent a form of self-government that White men had chosen for them."[53] The elected BIA-style tribal governments often represented a minority who supported assimilation and acted as rubber stamps for federal policies; many more traditional people continued to look to spiritual leaders and did not participate in, or identify with, the new government. This situation led to open conflict in the early 1970s when traditional Oglalas and American Indian Movement (AIM) militants joined forces to try to oust the corrupt political machine of tribal chair Richard Wilson.

Combative and controversial in his own day, Collier and his legacy as architect of the Indian New Deal remain controversial today. Some people revere Collier for having pulled tribal governments from the brink of extinction; others see him as just another Washington politician who imposed his own ideas on Indian communities with little regard for their needs. Clarence Wesley, a San Carlos Apache leader, said Collier's policy "was the best thing that ever happened to Indian tribes." Rupert Costo, a Cahuilla Indian and president of the American Indian Historical Society, denounced Collier as "vindictive and overbearing," "a rank opportunist" who "betrayed us." For Costo, Collier's Indian New Deal was the "Indian Raw Deal."[54]

Collier had no ambivalence about the IRA. In his view it was the key to the survival of Indian tribes in modern America, and he worked tirelessly for its acceptance and implementation. The original draft of the Wheeler-Howard bill declared "that those functions of government now exercised by the Federal Government through the Department of the Interior and the Office of Indian Affairs shall be gradually relinquished and transferred to the Indians." According to Collier as he left office in 1945, "We tried to extend to the tribes a self-governing self-determination without any limits beyond the need to advance by stages to the goal." As Collier envisioned the IRA, and as he explained it to the tribes, the tribal governments established under the IRA would be allowed to govern in fact, not just in legislation.[55]

Ben Reifel, a Brulé Sioux born in 1906 on the Rosebud Reservation, worked for the government to explain the provisions of the Wheeler-Howard bill in meetings with the various tribes in South Dakota in the early 1930s; he "was impressed with the opportunities" it outlined. Reifel, who had a long career in the BIA before winning a seat in Congress in 1960, believed much of the opposition to the IRA among Lakota people stemmed from the nature of the relationship between the government and the Indian tribes. The government held Indian lands in trust and made "every honest effort . . . to protect the Indians in the use of their property," but the same rules and regulations that were established to protect or exercise that trust meant that the secretary of the interior retained ultimate control, creating the feeling "that the tribal council did not get enough authority to really do the things they wanted to do on behalf of the people they represented." Looking back after fifty years, Reifel insisted "there is nothing in the Indian Reorganization Act that harms any Indian tribe or any Indian individual who has property." The IRA created the tribal constitutions; it was "up to the people to amend those constitutions and make them useful."[56]

But Robert Burnette, a Brulé of another generation, writing in the wake of violent confrontations between Indian militants and the tribal government on the Pine Ridge Reservation, offers a very different view of the IRA. Burnette was born in Rosebud, South Dakota, in 1926. He served in the marines during World War II and returned home to face continued racism and the threat of termination. He blamed much of the poverty and the loss of land he saw in Lakota country on collusion between corrupt tribal officials and the BIA. In 1952 he was elected to the Rosebud Tribal Council; two years later he was elected tribal president. From the 1950s until his death in 1984, he was known as a combative champion of Indian civil rights, tribal self-determination, and sovereignty. He became executive director of the National Congress of American Indians in 1961 and served as a mediator and advocate of nonviolent resistance during AIM's takeover of the BIA building in Washington in 1972 and at the siege at Wounded Knee in 1973 (see Chapter 9, pages 504–5 and 505–7). His book *The Tortured Americans* was published in 1971, and in 1974 he coauthored *The Road to Wounded Knee,* which traced the root causes of the siege back to the kind of tribal governments established under the Indian New Deal. One of his earliest memories was of campaigning in school against his tribe's acceptance of the IRA. He was eight years old at the time. "I remember John Collier coming to the Rosebud Indian Boarding School and exactly what he said there," Burnette recalled half a century later. "I felt like we were being fooled."[57]

JOHN COLLIER
An "Indian Renaissance," from the Annual Report of the Commissioner of Indian Affairs (1935)

This annual report is burdened with overcondensed statements of things done and more things yet to do; with urgencies, programs, and life-and-death necessities, all under the compulsion of speed.

It is all true. But the foundations of Indian life rest in a quiet earth. Indian life is not tense, is not haunted with urgencies, and does not fully accept the view that programs must be achieved, lest otherwise ruin shall swiftly befall.

Indian life is happy. Even the most poverty-stricken and seemingly futureless Indians still are happy. Indians have known how to be happy amid hardships and dangers through many thousand years. They do not expect much, often they expect nothing at all; yet they are able to be happy. Possibly this is the most interesting and important fact about Indians.

THE ACCELERATED TASK

The Indians and the Indian Service have had a difficult and challenging year, due to drought and depression; on the other hand, many Indians,

SOURCE: An "Indian Renaissance," from the *Annual Report of the Commissioner of Indian Affairs* for 1935, reprinted in Wilcomb E. Washburn, comp., *The American Indian and the United States: A Documentary History,* 4 vols. (Westport, Conn.: Greenwood Press, 1973), 921–26. Copyright © 1973 by Greenwood Press, Inc. Reproduced with the permission of ABC-CLIO, LLC.

and Indian property, have benefited from the generous relief appropriations. The effort to spend these relief funds wisely has meant extra work for the Service staff, which already had assumed the additional burden of launching the Indian reorganization program without benefit of new funds or personnel.

REORGANIZING INDIAN LIFE

The Indian Reorganization (modified Wheeler-Howard) Act was approved June 18, 1934. Its passage made mandatory a complete change in the traditional Federal Indian policy of individual allotment of land — which resulted in the break-up of Indian reservations — and of destroying Indian organization, institutions, and racial heritage to the end that the Indian as an Indian might disappear from the American scene with the utmost speed.

The next result of this policy has been the loss of two-thirds of the 139,000,000 acres owned by Indian tribes in 1887, the year when the General Allotment Act was adopted; and the individualization policy has broken up the land remaining on allotted reservations, has disrupted tribal bonds, has destroyed old incentives to action, and has created a race of petty landlords who in the generous Indian manner have shared their constantly shrinking income with the ever-increasing number of their landless relatives and friends.

The Indian Reorganization Act prohibits future allotments, and the sale of Indian lands except to the tribes; it restores to the tribes the unentered remnants of the so-called surplus lands of the allotted reservations thrown open to white settlement; it authorizes annual appropriations for the purchase of land for landless Indians, provides for the consolidation of Indian lands, and sets up a process which enables Indians voluntarily to return their individual landholdings to the protection of tribal status, thus reversing the disintegration policy.

The act also authorizes a ten-million-dollar revolving loan fund, the use of which is restricted to those tribes which organize and incorporate so as to create community responsibility. It is expected that the organization of Indians in well-knit, functional groups and communities will help materially in the creation of new incentives for individual and collective action. The Indian is not a "rugged individualist"; he functions best as an integrated member of a group, clan, or tribe. Identification of his individuality with clan or tribe is with him a spiritual necessity. If the satisfaction of this compelling sentiment is denied him — as it was for half a century or more — the Indian does not, it has been clearly shown, merge into white group life. Through a modernized form of Indian organization, adapted to the needs of the various tribes (a form of organization now authorized by law), it is possible to make use of this powerful latent civic force.

The Indian Reorganization Act was passed a few days before the end of the Seventy-third Congress. None of the authorized appropriations, however, became available until May 1935. For land purchases the authorized appropriation was reduced to one-half, or $1,000,000; the revolving credit fund was limited to a quarter of the authorization, or $2,500,000; for organizing expenses the amount was reduced from $250,000 to $175,000.

THE INDIANS HOLD THEIR
FIRST ELECTIONS

Congress had ordained in section 18 that each tribe must be given the unusual privilege of deciding at a special election whether it wanted to accept these benefits or reject them. Beginning with August 1934 and ending June 17, 1935, a series of 263 elections resulted in the decision by 73 tribes, with a population of 63,467 persons, to exclude themselves from the benefits and protection of the act, and by 172 tribes, with the population of 132,426 persons, to accept the act.

The participation of the Indians in these referendum elections was astonishingly heavy. In national elections, when a President is chosen and the interest of the voters is aroused through a long, intensive campaign, the average number of ballots cast does not exceed 52 percent of the total number of eligible voters; in referendum elections deciding on such matters as constitutional ratifications, bond issues, etc., when no personalities are injected into the campaign, less than 35 percent of the eligible voters participate. The referendum election on the Indian Reorganization Act did not concern itself with candidates and personalities, yet 62 percent of all adult Indians came to the polls and cast their ballots. . . .

The rejection of the Reorganization Act on 73 reservations, most of them very small (but including the largest reservation, that of the Navajos), was due in the main to energetic campaigns of misrepresentation carried on by special interests which feared that they would lose positions of advantage through the applications of the act. Joining hands in this campaign of misrepresentation were stockmen who feared that the Indians would run their own stock on land hitherto leased to white interests; traders who were afraid of losing their business through the competition of Indian consumers' cooperatives; merchants and politicians in white communities on the edge of reservations; a few missionaries who resented the extension of the constitutional guarantee of religious liberty and freedom of conscience to Indians (not an element in the Reorganization Act, but enforced as a policy by the present administration); lumber interests which did not want to see Indian tribes exploit their own forest resources. These interests, working frequently by the historic method of defrauding Indian tribes with the connivance of certain of their own leaders, spread extreme and bizarre falsehoods concerning the effects of the act.

Among the myths spread by adverse interests on various reservations were such as these: Acceptance of the act would cause Indian owners of allotments to lose their land, which would then be distributed among those Indians who had disposed of their allotments; all farm crops would be impounded in warehouses and thereafter would be equally distributed among the population; the Indians would be segregated behind wire fences charged with electricity; all the livestock would be taken from certain tribes; unalloted reservations would be thrown open to white entry; Indian dances and other religious ceremonies would be suppressed; Indians would not be allowed to go to Christian churches; certain Southwestern reservations would be turned over to Mexico, etc.

THE NAVAJO VOTE

On the Navajo Reservation, certain interests disseminated the most fantastic fictions in their effort to induce the 43,500 Navajos to reject the help the Federal Government was offering them. With the aid of these fictions, and by falsely connecting the referendum on the Reorganization Act with the unpopular but necessary stock reduction program, the propagandists succeeded in bringing about the exclusion of the Navajo Reservation by a very narrow margin of votes: 7,608 for acceptance; 7,992 against acceptance. Immediately after the result became known, Navajo leaders started a movement to reverse it through a renewed referendum which will be possible only through a new enabling act of Congress.

THE INDIAN RENAISSANCE

Considering the long history of broken treaties, pledges, and promises, the fact that 172 tribes with an Indian population of 132,000 accepted the word of the Government that the fundamental reorganization of their lives would not harm them is evidence of a new, more satisfactory relationship between the Indians and the Indian Service. The referendum elections served a most valuable purpose. They were palpable proof to the Indians that the Government really was ready to give them a voice in the management of their own affairs, and that the period of arbitrary autocratic rule over the tribes by the Indian Service had come to an end.

This evidence of good faith was reinforced by the request that the tribes begin immediately to formulate the constitutions and charters authorized by the act. Reservation committees and groups set to work at the unaccustomed task of drafting constitutions and of making plans and programs for the economic rehabilitation of the tribes. Charters and constitutions under the Reorganization Act, when once adopted, cannot be revoked or changed by administrative action. Personal government of the tribes by the Secretary of the Interior and the Indian Commissioner is brought to an end.

INDIAN EMERGENCY WORK

In the revivifying of the Indian spirit, the wide-opened benefits of Indian emergency conservation and of other relief work played an important part. It must be remembered that on many reservations the kind of depression which struck the Nation in 1929 had been a chronic condition for a long time, becoming acute when land sales dropped off and the revenue from farm and grazing lands leased to whites dropped almost to the vanishing point. Opportunities for wage work had been all but nonexistent on most reservations, and the psychology of the chronically unemployed had prevailed for so long that it was feared that most of the Indians had become unemployable.

This fear proved to be groundless. Indians young and old not merely accepted emergency relief work, but almost fought for the chance to labor. And they labored effectively. Through their effort the physical plant, the land, the water, the forests, have had many millions of dollars added to their use value in the last 2 years. Incalculable benefits have been derived from the improvement of 20 million acres of range, through the development of springs and wells and the construction of thousands of stock-water dams, through roads and truck trails, through the construction of thousands of miles of fences and telephone lines. There is not one reservation which, as a result of the emergency and relief work, is not a better place to live on, an easier place in which to gain a living from the soil.

A clear gain to the Indians — and to many white communities in the Indian country — accrued out of the grants from Public Works funds for new Indian community-school buildings, hospitals, and sanatoria, many of them built entirely by Indian labor. Yet the pressing need for structures of this kind has not been half filled. Nor is the Indian irrigation program, financed from emergency grants, more than one-third completed.

AFTER THE DEPRESSION — WHAT?

The benefit derived by the Indians from the emergency and relief work has many aspects. Thousands of the Indian workers have, for perhaps the first time in their lives, learned what it means to have sufficient nourishment of the right kind regularly. Other thousands have been able to acquire minimal household goods, clothing, livestock, and farm implements. Thousands of savings accounts have been started at the various agencies out of earnings of $2.10 per day for 20 days in the month during part of the year.

There have been entries on the debit side also. The number of bootleggers on the fringe of many reservations has multiplied; law enforcement has become more and more difficult. Automobile dealers with second-hand wrecks for sale have encouraged the younger Indians to obligate their potential earnings for years ahead; some traders have encouraged credit buying on far too lavish a scale.

But more important than these shortcomings due to the innate generosity of a race unfamiliar with wise consumption habits is the problem that arises from the introduction of a wage economy on reservations which will supply almost no permanent opportunity for wage work. After the depression is over and the emergency grants cease, what will happen to the now-working Indians?

REHABILITATION EMPHASIZED

To prepare for this inevitable crisis additional funds must be obtained for rehabilitation projects, such as land purchase, housing, the construction of barns and root cellars, the development of domestic water and sanitary facilities, the subjugation of land, the financing of purchases of seeds, implements, and livestock, the stimulation and development of Indian arts and crafts, and the organization and financing of sawmills, fisheries, and other industrial enterprises. This amended program would mean a playing down of the wage motive, a playing up of production for use.

If the necessary grants for this program be made, the Indians on many reservations should be able to pass gradually from relief work to subsistence farming, craft, and other supplemental industrial work of their own.

ROBERT BURNETTE AND JOHN KOSTER
A Blueprint for Elected Tyranny (1974)

Under the IRA, the once all-powerful agent was pushed from his dictatorial position in favor, usually, of a chairman-council form of elective government. For the first time in fifty years the Indians were allowed to pick their own leaders. This was a radical change from the traditional tribal government which had total democracy in council, advised by a smaller council of wise elders who had to agree unanimously on every decision and even then could not force their decisions on any adult male. Built into the BIA's chairman-council system were all the weaknesses, but none of the strengths, of local government in middle America. The white agent was retained in the form of the *superintendent,* a white BIA appointee who holds veto power over tribal finances. Through the superintendent, the BIA could still tell the Indian people how many cows they could buy or sell, how much timber they could cut, and what their school curricula should be. There was no system of checks and balances, no procedure through which inequities could be righted. It was a blueprint for elected tyranny. . . .

Before the IRA, there were almost as many tribal governing bodies as there were tribes. Owing

to restrictive federal policies, some tribes were actually without a government. The actual power on the reservations, as far as the government was concerned, was the Indian agent, acting on behalf of the secretary of the interior. The tribes themselves sometimes managed to maintain a link with their past in the form of traditional governing bodies. The form differed tribe by tribe. The Red Lake Chippewas of Minnesota maintained their traditional chief system, in which chieftainship was hereditary. The Sioux across South Dakota were operating under the three-quarters-majority council system that stemmed from the Sioux Treaty of 1868. This required that three-fourths of all adult males sign any legislation affecting the tribe. The Pueblo tribes of the Southwest operated their traditional Kiva system, which was strongly linked to their religion. The Crow tribe of Montana kept their general council system, a forum of one hundred people empowered to represent the rest of the tribe.

On their own, the Indian peoples had developed the checks and balances that were needed to keep a brake on ambition. Most plains tribes originally had at least two governing bodies that kept the power decentralized. Among the Cheyenne, for example, four old man chiefs served as advisers and executives, and a council of forty chiefs made up the legislative body. The police duties were assumed by three or more warrior societies, which were rotated to prevent any group from gaining power. Each warrior society was headed by a big war chief, assisted by nine little war chiefs.

SOURCE: Excerpts from Robert Burnette, *The Road to Wounded Knee* (New York: Bantam Books, 1974), 15–16, 180–87. Copyright © 1974 by Robert Burnette. Used by permission of Bantam Books, an imprint of Random House, a division of Penguin Random House LLC. All rights reserved. Any third party use of this material, outside of this publication, is prohibited. Interested parties must apply directly to Penguin Random House LLC for permission.

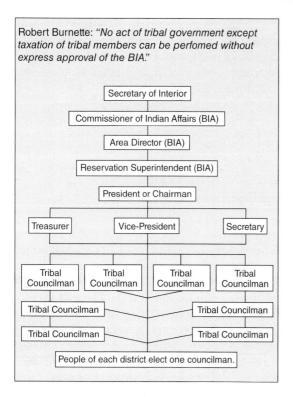

Robert Burnette: *"No act of tribal government except taxation of tribal members can be perfomed without express approval of the BIA."*

- Secretary of Interior
- Commissioner of Indian Affairs (BIA)
- Area Director (BIA)
- Reservation Superintendent (BIA)
- President or Chairman
- Treasurer — Vice-President — Secretary
- Tribal Councilman — Tribal Councilman — Tribal Councilman — Tribal Councilman
- Tribal Councilman — Tribal Councilman
- Tribal Councilman — Tribal Councilman

People of each district elect one councilman.

◆ **Chart 8.1 IRA-Style Tribal Government, according to Robert Burnette**

SOURCE: Robert Burnette, *The Road to Wounded Knee* (New York: Bantam Books, 1974), 295. Copyright © 1974 by Robert Burnette. Used by permission of Bantam Books, an imprint of Random House, a division of Penguin Random House LLC. All rights reserved. Any third party use of this material, outside of this publication, is prohibited. Interested parties must apply directly to Penguin Random House LLC for permission.

The various council chiefs expressed the will of the people, and the government had no right to compel anyone to take any action unless to do otherwise would threaten the whole tribe. . . .

The New Deal's Indian Reorganization Act of 1934 carried the promise of constitutional guarantees of liberty; finances for economic growth; an end to the steady loss of Indian lands; legal counsel needed by the tribes in order to cope with modern society; and lastly, the right to self-government to those who chose to adopt it.

Despite the golden promises, many traditional leaders were wary of anything that would disrupt the forms of government the Indians had created for themselves. The bitterly fought battle of the traditionals against the Indian Reorganization Act raged from 1934 until 1940. In the end, the Indian opposition was the victim of a provision of the act that allowed it to be adopted by 30 percent of the voting-age population of the reservation. This was a deviation both from Indian tradition and American democracy, since it allowed less than a majority to rule. The same provision that sets 30 percent as a quorum supposedly allows the Indians to petition for a referendum to recall the tribal constitution by securing at least 30 percent of the voting-age population's signatures. Yet the secretary of the interior has invariably ignored this and has categorically refused to hold referendums to repeal the tribal government system set up by the IRA. Thus the government has twisted its own rules for its own convenience.

In actual practice, a tribal council is a strange vintage of constitutional government: the federal government is divided into the executive, legislative, and judicial branches; the tribal constitutions created by the federal government provide for one single governing body, which tends to operate under constant conflicts of interest.

Under the IRA, the tribal president, chairman, or chief is generally empowered only to carry out the resolutions, ordinances, or directives of the tribal council. Thus, Indians have an executive who can only function whenever the tribal council orders him to act. Likewise, the vice-president, vice-chairman, or vice-chief can only act in the absence of the president, chairman, or chief.

The tribal secretary, although he may be a constitutional officer, is the keeper of the tribal records and as such is subject to the powers of the tribal council. The tribal treasurer is the custodian of all tribal funds and can disburse such funds only by orders of the tribal council.

The size of the tribal council depends on the size of the tribe. Many have as few as six members; the Navajo tribe has seventy-two. The average number is around sixteen.

These councilmen are elected by various methods. On the Sioux reservations of Rosebud and Pine Ridge, among others, the tribe has an open nonpartisan primary, in which anyone with the required number of signatures on his nominating petition can get on the ballot. The primary narrows the field down to two candidates for each office. These two vie for office in the final election, usually about two months after the primary.

On other reservations, like the Crow reservation of Montana, there is no primary. The general election is open, with as many as a dozen candidates running as spoilers to take votes away from their friend's political opponents. Anyone who thinks that Indian people lack political sophistication would find some of the elections held by the north plains tribes, the Sioux in particular, to be very instructive. Not the least compelling reason for seeking office is that tribal chairmen receive a five-figure income — not easy to come by on a reservation — and can control a great deal of patronage, such as jobs for relatives.

Tribal constitutions specifically grant tribal councils the power to act for and in behalf of the entire tribe, without consulting the wishes of the people.

The tribal council has the power to negotiate with the federal, state, and local governments; to legislate the economic, social, educational, and domestic affairs of the tribe; to establish a tribal court, maintain a law-and-order code; to control domestic relations; to charter subordinate tribal enterprises; and to regulate the appointment of guardians for minors and mental incompetents.

In the area of land, the tribal council was empowered with restricting undesirable persons from the reservation; making assignments of tribal land to members; employing legal counsel for the advancement and protection of the tribe; purchasing lands through condemnation in courts of competent jurisdiction; governing the inheritance of real and personal property; and executing leases on tribal land. In addition, the council had the power to veto any action that would destroy tribal property.

The council also had the power to expend tribal funds; to levy taxes on tribal members or require the performance of labor in lieu of taxes; to regulate tribal elections; to advise the secretary of the interior on budget estimates prior to submission to Congress or the Bureau of the Budget; and to regulate their own procedure.

Despite this impressive list of powers, tribal self-government was a charade. The tribal constitution provides that the secretary of the interior approve the tribal council's actions, which means that the conflict of interest inherent in Interior's control over the Indian tribes is written right into their constitutions.

To add to the confusion, the Department of the Interior holds that the charters issued to the tribes are separate and distinct documents with no application or control over the tribal constitutions. This is an extremely contradictory position for the Department of the Interior to take, since the tribal constitutions, *Powers of the Tribal Council,* say bluntly:

"To manage economic affairs and enterprises of the tribe in accordance with the terms of the charter which may be issued to the tribe by the Secretary of the Interior . . ."

Thus the government set up for the Indians by Congress violates the Congress's own form of government. Indians hate this second-class form of government because their original, traditional tribal governments were invariably far superior.

Time and again, the Department of the Interior has interfered in tribal affairs against the Indians' best interests. For instance, a tribe may have a tremendous reserve of oil and gas on their reservation and have no desire to have some oil company exploit their wealth. They would prefer to form a tribally owned oil company employing their own people and profiting the tribe. But government officials will be bribed and the BIA will begin applying pressure to force the tribal council members to enact a resolution to advertise the oil and gas leases in their reservation for public bids. . . . The BIA has habitually meddled in tribal business, usually to the tribe's detriment.

After the BIA had established blocks of land known as range units, they began making loans to the tribes to establish Indian credit corporations, under the tribal council's authority to charter subordinate organizations. The tribal credit corporation was totally controlled by the BIA's required secretarial-approval clause. This credit corporation was intended to advance money for Indians who desired to enter business. The funds were supposed to provide capital for opening filling stations and grocery stores, or buying livestock or farm machinery to be used in working the Indians' land. In actual practice, the BIA would only approve loans that led to Indian indebtedness.

Nearly every loan client was limited to a loan of five thousand dollars or less, when twelve thousand dollars would have ensured success. But despite the fact that the loans were failure-bound, the Indian Loan System had a national loss rate of less than 1 percent. The Indian—unlike the government—paid his debts.

This Indian's relations with the federal government began and usually ended with the BIA superintendent, and it was the superintendent, not the tribal council, who held the real power on most reservations. Except in rare cases, the balance of power has not changed since the days of the 1880s when the Indian agent ran his reservation like an army camp. Tribal government, as provided for by the Indian Reorganization Act and administered by the BIA, is now and always has been such a mess that those few tribes who escaped from the IRA government, like the Onondagas of upstate New York, feel that they are much better off under their traditional form of government.

In battles between the all-powerful superintendents and the Indian people, all too many elected officials washed their hands of the whole affair and let their constituents do their own fighting. Those elected officials who chose to try to defend their people were drawn into constant battles with the superintendents, but because of the pervasive apathy of reservation living and because of their lack of knowledge of how to appeal a decision, most individual Indians seemed to think that attempts to protect their people were hopeless. One could hardly expect the Indians to be informed on Indian law when 99.44 percent of the nation's lawyers know nothing of the matter either.

Another very special fact is that Indians or anyone else affected have the right to an administrative appeals system. This is a tiresome and almost endless process because the government on any level is not subject to time limitations. Most Indian appeals taken in this manner die a natural death for lack of persistence on the part of those who seek such adjudication.

Unlike the Indians, who felt strangled and frustrated by this morass of white tape, BIA officials seemed to thrive on it. But they took pains to stifle any challenge to their powers.

QUESTIONS FOR CONSIDERATION

1. What does Collier's discussion of the Indian Reorganization Act in his 1935 annual report illustrate about his vision of the IRA and his hopes for its impact on Indian America? What does the extract reveal about his attitudes toward Indian people and toward those who did not share his vision?

2. What is the tone of Collier's message, who is he addressing, and for what purpose?

3. How might Burnette's statements about the workings of the IRA refute Collier's claims that the act marked a decisive shift in the direction of Indian policy and initiated a new era in relations between Indians and the U.S. government? Compare Burnette's chart of tribal government with the chart of reservation government on page 382 in Chapter 7.

4. Despite its shortcomings, its paternalism, and its continuing colonialism, did the Indian New Deal break with past government policies? What was new about the Indian New Deal after all?

Indians in the Cities

WHEN GLENN EMMONS, a banker from New Mexico, became commissioner of Indian affairs under President Eisenhower in 1953, he devoted considerable energy toward improving the relocation program established by his predecessor, Dillon S. Myer. Emmons moved the Bureau of Relocation headquarters from Washington, D.C., to Denver to bring it closer to Indian populations and opened new field offices, secured additional funding, and stepped up publicity for the program. He placed great faith in relocation's ability to weaken tribalism and promote assimilation. In his annual report for 1954 he described the program in optimistic terms. Interest in relocating from the reservations was growing, stimulated by letters home from friends and relatives who had already moved to the cities; the numbers of relocatees were up, and relocation agencies were proving successful in finding jobs for Indians when they arrived in the cities. In addition, the Chicago Field Relocation Office assisted in the establishment of an All-Tribes American Indian Center in Chicago. This center, reported Emmons, "raised its own funds, and under the directorship of a board composed almost entirely of Indians, began providing opportunities for Indian relocatees to meet, engage in social and recreational programs, exchange experiences, and assist each other. Its operations were completely independent of the Bureau."[58]

Indian individuals and families looked for jobs and new lives in urban America long before the BIA program provided additional incentives; they continued to do so long after the program was phased out. Those who made the move often saw things quite differently from Emmons. Like other federal programs, urban relocation had mixed results. Indian people interviewed in Chicago around 1970 gave varied reasons for moving and their views of city life often depended on their age, gender, personality, and personal lives, as well as their experiences living and working in an urban environment. One middle-aged man who had moved to Chicago because he heard there were jobs there said: "I like it here. I raised my kids here. Sometimes they got in with the wrong crowd and there was some trouble, but they're all grown now, and everything worked out OK. My children are real city kids. . . . Chicago is their home." Others never came to terms with city life. "I wish I had never left home," said one woman. "This will never be home to me. It's dirty and noisy, and people all around, crowded." A thirty-year-old man recalled thinking the city was "wonderful" when he was a teenager, but he moved back and forth between the city and the reservation and felt he didn't fit in anywhere.[59] Whether they liked the city or not, Indian people who moved there were not just responding "to the prodding of federal bureaucrats who favored termination." In the words of one historian, they took "a stride toward freedom from Indian Bureau paternalism, economic insecurity, racial injustice, segregation, and second-class citizenship."[60] They did not always escape these old challenges in the city but they usually encountered new opportunities, as Ignatia Broker, an Ojibway or Anishinaabe elder and storyteller, found when she moved from the White Earth Reservation to Minneapolis during World War II.

IGNATIA BROKER
Brought to a Brotherhood (1983)

I got off the city bus and walked the short one-and-a-half blocks home as I have been doing for years around five o'clock each evening. Because this evening was warm, I walked slower than usual, enjoying the look and feel of the early spring. The earth that had been white was now brown, left uncovered by the melting snow. This brown was turning to green and the air was fragrant with the opening of spring.

Daylight still lingered and as I walked I looked at my neighborhood and thought about it. When I first moved here in the mid-1950s this was a mixed neighborhood of Spanish-speaking people and Catholic whites, and there were many children. Now the Spanish-speaking people are all gone. They left when the parochial school closed its doors, although the church is still here. Now the neighborhood is only four blocks long and two blocks wide, whittled down by urban renewal and the freeways which reach their tentacles all around us.

I reached my doorstep and sat enjoying the good day and remembering the past. It was funny, really, when I think about it. That day thirty years ago when we moved here, me and my children, we were the aliens looking for a place to fit in, looking for a chance of a new life, moving in among these people, some of whose "forefathers" had displaced my ancestors for the same reason: looking for a new life. Their fathers were the aliens then, and now they, the children, are in possession of this land.

SOURCE: Ignatia Broker, *Night Flying Woman: An Ojibway Narrative* (St. Paul: Minnesota Historical Society Press, 1983), 1–7. Copyright © 1983 by the Minnesota Historical Society. Reprinted with the permission of the publishers.

For a long time I was that Indian person with the two children. But it is good that children have a natural gift of accepting people, and so my children became a part of the neighborhood.

Thirty years in this neighborhood. My children went to school from here, they went to church from here, they were married from here and even though they are in faraway places they seem to have their roots here, for they had lived no other place while growing up.

I talked to my children, even when they were very small, about the ways of the Ojibway people. They were good children and they listened, but I had a feeling that they listened the same as when I read a story about the Bobbsey twins or Marco Polo. I was speaking of another people, removed from them by rock and roll, juvenile singers, and the bobbing movement of the new American dance.

My two, born and raised in Minneapolis, are of that generation of Ojibway who do not know what the reservation means, or the Bureau of Indian Affairs, or the tangled treaties and federal — so called — Indian laws which have spun their webs for a full century around the Native People, the First People of this land.

Now my children are urging me to recall all the stories and bits of information that I ever heard my grandparents or any of the older Ojibway tell. It is important, they say, because now their children are asking them. Others are saying the same thing. It is well that they are asking, for the Ojibway young must learn their cycle.

I have been abroad in this society, the dominating society, for two-thirds of my life, and yet I am a link in a chain to the past. Because of this, I shall do as they ask. I can close my eyes and I am back in the past.

I came to the Twin Cities from the reservation in 1941, the year Pearl Harbor was attacked. I went to work in a defense plant and took night classes in order to catch up on the schooling I had missed. I was twenty-two years old and aching for a permanent, settling-down kind of life, but the war years were unstable years for everyone, and more so for the Indian people.

Although employment was good because of the labor demand of the huge defense plants, Indian people faced discrimination in restaurants, night clubs, retail and department stores, in service organizations, public offices, and worst of all, in housing. I can remember hearing, "This room has been rented already, but I got a basement that has a room. I'll show you." I looked at the room. It had the usual rectangular window, and pipes ran overhead. The walls and floors were brown cement, but the man with a gift-giving tone in his voice said, "I'll put linoleum on the floor for you and you'll have a toilet all to yourself. You could wash at the laundry tubs."

There was of course, nothing listed with the War Price and Rationing Board, but the man said it would cost seven dollars a week. I know that he would have made the illegal offer only to an Indian because he knew of the desperate housing conditions we, the first Americans, faced.

I remember living in a room with six others. It was a housekeeping room, nine by twelve feet in size, and meant for one person. It was listed with the price agency at five dollars a week, but the good landlady collected five dollars from each of us each week. However, she did put in a bunk bed and a rollaway which I suppose was all right because we were on different shifts and slept different times anyway. It was cramped and crowded but we had a mutual respect. We sometimes shared our one room with others who had no place, so that there might be nine or ten of us. We could not let friends be out on the street without bed or board. As long as our landlady did not mind, we helped and gave a place of rest to other Ojibway people.

Our paydays were on different days and so whoever had money lent carfare and bought meat and vegetables. Stew was our daily fare because we had only a hot plate and one large kettle.

I mention this practice because I know other Indian people did the same thing, and sometimes whole families evolved from it. This was how we got a toehold in the urban areas — by helping each other. Perhaps this is the way nonmaterialistic people do. We were a sharing people and our tribal traits are still within us.

I think now that maybe it was a good thing, the migration of our people to the urban areas during the war years, because there, amongst the millions of people, we were brought to a brotherhood. We Indian people who worked in the war plants started a social group not only for the Ojibway but for the Dakota, the Arikara, the Menominee, the Gros Ventres, the Cree, the Oneida, and all those from other tribes and other states who had made the trek to something new. And because we, all, were isolated in this dominant society, we became an island from which a revival of spirit began.

It was not easy for any of us during the war years and it became more difficult after the war had ceased. Many Native People returned to the reservations after our soldiers came home from the foreign lands, but others like me stayed and took the buffeting and the difficulties shown us by an alien society.

The war plants closed and people were without jobs. The labor market tightened up and we, the Native People — even skilled workers — faced bias, prejudice, and active discrimination in employment. I know because when I was released from my defense job I answered many advertisements and always I was met with the words, "I'm sorry but we don't hire Indians because they only last the two weeks till payday. Then they quit."

It was around this time that I met and married a veteran who was passing through to the reservation. He got a job with the railroad. To be close to that job and because of the bias in housing, we moved to the capitol side of the river, to an area of St. Paul called the river flats. It was a poor area. Many of the houses had outdoor toilets; many were but tar-paper shacks. Surprising, but it was so in this very large city. It was here our two children were born and I, like a lot of other Indian women, went out and did

day work — cleaning and scrubbing the homes of the middle-income people.

Many Indian families lived on the river flats, which became vibrant with their sharing. People gave to each other because times were bad. No Indian family dared approach the relief and welfare agencies of the Twin Cities. They knew that they would only be given a bus ticket and be told to go back to the reservation where the government would take care of them as usual. This was the policy of the public service agencies, and we put up with it by not asking for the help to which we had a legal right. We also suffered in other ways of their making. My husband was recalled to service and died in Korea. After this I moved from the river flats. I took the clerical training and got my first job at a health clinic.

Because my husband died fighting for a nation designed for freedom for all, I felt that I must help extend that freedom to our people. I joined a group of Indians who had banded together to form an Indian help agency. We built a welfare case to challenge the policy of sending our people back to the reservation, and we were successful. After that, the tide of Indians moving to Minnesota's urban areas increased, and today there are ten thousand of us. As the number grew, new-fangled types of Indian people came into being: those demanding what is in our treaties, those demanding service to our people, those working to provide these services — and all reaching back for identity.

When I see my people every day and know how they are doing, I do not feel so lost in the modern times. The children of our people who come to our agency have a questioning look, a dubious but seeking-to-learn look, and I truly believe that they are reaching back to learn those things of which they can be proud. Many of these children were born and raised in the urban areas and they do not make any distinctions as to their tribes. They do not say, "I am Ojibway," or "I am Dakota," or "I am Arapaho," but they say, "I am an Indian." Now they, too, are looking to their tribal identity.

QUESTIONS FOR CONSIDERATION

1. What reasons does Ignatia Broker give for making the move to the city? Does her account provide evidence to support the view that relocation was a "stride toward freedom"?

2. What difficulties did she encounter? What does she tell us about how people managed to adjust to their new urban environment, rebuild communities, and maintain their identities?

3. The government's policy of urban relocation operated on the assumption that Indian people would be swallowed up in city life and cease being Indians. In what ways did Ignatia Broker's account confound these bureaucratic expectations?

Documents of Indian Militancy

T HE DRAMATIC TAKEOVER IN 1969 of Alcatraz Island by Indian students often serves as a starting point for discussing the Red Power movement, and confrontations around the country involving the American Indian Movement (AIM) increasingly attracted the media spotlight in the 1970s. But the dramatic events and charismatic personalities that capture public attention usually emerge from, and often obscure, deeper movements, longer lasting developments, and the contributions of other individuals. The militant spirit that flared into open confrontation after 1969 had been gathering momentum throughout the decade. The arguments for Indian self-determination, the fundamental goal of AIM, had been articulated by young Indians even before AIM was founded in 1968. One was Clyde Warrior, a young Ponca activist from eastern Oklahoma, whose story "qualifies as the top story the press missed in the years leading up to Alcatraz."[61]

After its founding in 1961, the National Indian Youth Council (NIYC) began to carry out acts of protest and civil disobedience. Young Indian speakers began to appear on college campuses, at meetings of national organizations, and at hearings of government agencies that affected Indian life but that usually operated without input from Indian people. The young activists distrusted non-Indian politicians and denounced some older tribal leaders as "Uncle Tomahawks" who held on to their positions by cozying up to those non-Indian politicians. They raised the level of debate on Indian affairs to new levels and introduced it in areas where it had never been discussed before. Historian Alvin Josephy, who served as a consultant on Indian affairs to Secretary of the Interior Stewart Udall, knew many of the young Indian activists. "They were a new generation," he wrote, "proud of their Indian heritage, unwilling to share their fathers' acceptance of white paternalism, and contemptuous of the society of the white man, which everywhere around them seemed to be falling into disarray."[62]

Clyde Warrior was the most charismatic and important leader of this emerging youth movement.[63] Born near Ponca City, Oklahoma, in 1939, he was raised by his grandparents and as a teenager traveled Indian country as a powwow dancer. He became increasingly vocal about the need for Indians to reject white images of them, to take pride in their Indian heritage, and to hold on to traditional values in modern times. He became a founding member and president of the NIYC and advocated taking direct action to effect change. Indians, said Warrior, were "getting fed up" and it was only a question of time before they did something about it.[64] Like Malcolm X in the Black Power movement, Warrior was eloquent and militant in his prophecies and prescription for revolution, and like Malcolm X he alarmed white America and discomfited many of his own people. But he became "almost a legendary hero to young Indians throughout the country."[65]

In speeches and in writings, Warrior repeatedly articulated the demands and desires of Indian people for freedom. President Lyndon Johnson's administration was pledged to the War on Poverty, with programs like Head Start and other initiatives administered through the Office of Economic Opportunity (OEO). But Warrior insisted that Indians would never escape poverty so long as white men continued to run their affairs and make decisions for them. He delivered the speech reprinted here at a hearing of the President's National Advisory Commission on Rural Poverty in Memphis, Tennessee, in 1967.

Even as he worked to free Indian people from dependency on white America and its government, Warrior succumbed to dependency of another sort. Known as a hard drinker, he battled alcoholism. In the summer of 1968, as events began to spin out of control in Southeast Asia and the United States, his liver failed, and he was dead within a few days. He was twenty-eight. In the next five years, Indian activists seized Alcatraz, marched on the nation's capital, and battled U.S. armed forces on the plains of South Dakota. The world's media was there to record it all, but "the prophet of Red Power wasn't around to see what would become of his prophecies."[66]

In November 1969, eighty-nine young Indians took over Alcatraz Island, "the Rock," a former maximum-security federal penitentiary in San Francisco Bay that had been abandoned six years earlier. Mostly urban Indians and college students from the Bay Area, the occupiers identified themselves as "Indians of All Tribes," and proclaimed the island Indian land. They also called for an American Indian university, museum, and cultural center to be established there. The occupiers received support from hippies and other members of the 1960s "counterculture" who saw Indians as more spiritual, more ecologically attuned, and more communal in their relations than capitalist America and identified with their struggle against American conformity. Celebrities like Jane Fonda put in an appearance.[67] The government cut off water and electricity supplies in the spring of 1970 and eventually the seizure of Alcatraz fizzled out. Media attention was diverted elsewhere. In June 1971, nineteen months after the takeover began, federal marshals quietly removed the fifteen remaining protesters. But Alcatraz made a lasting impact that carried over into the escalating activism of the 1970s. The protests there brought Indians and their grievances to the attention of the world. Alcatraz served as a warning for the United States that Indian rights could no longer be ignored and became a symbol of hope for Indian people who realized that they need no longer suffer in silence. Wilma Mankiller (see Chapter 9, "Indian Leadership at the End of the Twentieth Century," pages 549–51), who visited the island many times during the takeover, recalled: "I'd never heard anyone actually tell the world that we needed someone to pay attention to our treaty rights, that people had given up an entire continent, and many lives, in return for basic services like health care and education, but nobody was honoring those agreements. For the first time, people were saying things I felt but hadn't known how to articulate. It was very liberating."[68]

CLYDE WARRIOR
"We Are Not Free":
From Testimony before the President's National Advisory Commission on Rural Poverty (1967)

Most members of the National Indian Youth Council can remember when we were children and spent many hours at the feet of our grandfathers listening to stories of the time when the Indians were a great people, when we were free, when we were rich, when we lived the good life. At the same time we heard stories of droughts, famines and pestilence. It was only recently that we realized that there was surely great material deprivation in those days, but that our old people felt rich because they were free. They were rich in things of the spirit, but if there is one thing that characterizes Indian life today it is poverty of the spirit. We still have human passions and depth of feeling (which may be something rare in these days), but we are poor in spirit because we are not free—free in the most basic sense of the word. We are not allowed to make those basic human choices and decisions about our personal life and about the destiny of our communities which is the mark of free mature

people. We sit on our front porches or in our yards, and the world and our lives in it pass us by without our desires or aspirations having any effect.

We are not free. We do not make choices. Our choices are made for us; we are the poor. For those of us who live on reservations these choices and decisions are made by federal administrators, bureaucrats, and their "yes men," euphemistically called tribal governments. Those of us who live in non-reservation areas have our lives controlled by local white power elites. We have many rulers. They are called social workers, "cops," school teachers, churches, etc., and now OEO employees. They call us into meetings to tell us what is good for us and how they've programmed us, or they come into our homes to instruct us and their manners are not always what one would call polite by Indian standards or perhaps by any standards. We are rarely accorded respect as fellow human beings. Our children come home from school to us with shame in their hearts and a sneer on their lips for their home and parents. We are the "poverty problem" and that is true; and perhaps it is also true that our lack of reasonable choices, our lack of freedoms, our poverty of spirit is not unconnected with our material poverty.

SOURCE: Testimony of Clyde Warrior before the President's National Advisory Commission on Rural Poverty, February 2, 1967, in *Red Power: The American Indians' Fight for Freedom,* ed. Alvin M. Josephy Jr. (New York: McGraw-Hill, 1971), 72–77.

The National Indian Youth Council realizes there is a great struggle going on in America now between those who want more "local" control of programs and those who would keep the power and the purse strings in the hands of the federal government. We are unconcerned with that struggle because we know that no one is arguing that the dispossessed, the poor, be given any control over their own destiny. The local white power elites who protest the loudest against federal control are the very ones who would keep us poor in spirit and worldly goods in order to enhance their own personal and economic station in the world.

Nor have those of us on reservations fared any better under the paternalistic control of federal administrations. In fact, we shudder at the specter of what seems to be the forming alliances in Indian areas between federal administrators and local elites. Some of us fear that this is the shape of things to come in the War on Poverty effort. Certainly, it is in those areas where such an alliance is taking place that the poverty program seems to be "working well." That is to say, it is in those areas of the country where the federal government is getting the least "static" and where federal money is being used to bolster the local power structure and local institutions. By "everybody being satisfied," I mean the people who count and the Indian or poor does not count. . . .

Fifty years ago the federal government came into our communities and by force carried most of our children away to distant boarding schools. My father and many of my generation lived their childhoods in an almost prison-like atmosphere. Many returned unable even to speak their own language. Some returned to become drunks. Most of them had become white haters or that most pathetic of all modern Indians — Indian haters. Very few ever became more than very confused, ambivalent and immobilized individuals — never able to reconcile the tensions and contradictions built inside themselves by outside institutions. As you can imagine, we have little faith in such kinds of federal programs devised

for our betterment nor do we see education as a panacea for all ills. In recent days, however, some of us have been thinking that perhaps the damage done to our communities by forced assimilation and directed acculturative programs was minor compared to the situation in which our children now find themselves. There is a whole generation of Indian children who are growing up in the American school system. They still look to their relatives, my generation, and my father's to see if they are worthy people. But their judgment and definition of what is worthy is now the judgment most Americans make. They judge worthiness as competence and competence as worthiness. And I am afraid me and my fathers do not fare well in the light of this situation and judgment. Our children are learning that their people are not worthy and thus that they individually are not worthy. Even if by some stroke of good fortune, prosperity was handed to us "on a platter" that still would not soften the negative judgment our youngsters have of their people and themselves. As you know, people who feel themselves to be unworthy and feel they cannot escape this unworthiness turn to drink and crime and self-destructive acts. Unless there is some way that we as Indian individuals and communities can prove ourselves competent and worthy in the eyes of our youngsters there will be a generation of Indians [who] grow to adulthood whose reaction to their situation will make previous social ills seem like a Sunday School picnic.

For the sake of our children, for the sake of the spiritual and material well-being of our total community we must be able to demonstrate competence to ourselves. For the sake of our psychic stability as well as our physical well-being we must be free men and exercise free choices. We must make decisions about our own destinies. We must be able to learn and profit by our own mistakes. Only then can we become competent and prosperous communities. We must be free in the most literal sense of the word — not sold or coerced into accepting programs for our own good, not of our own making or choice.

Too much of what passes for "grassroots democracy" on the American scene is really a slick job of salesmanship. It is not hard for sophisticated administrators to sell tinsel and glitter programs to simple people — programs which are not theirs, which they do not understand and which cannot but ultimately fail and contribute to already strong feelings of inadequacy. Community development must be just what the word implies, Community Development. It cannot be packaged programs wheeled into Indian communities by outsiders which Indians can "buy" or once again brand themselves as unprogressive if they do not "cooperate." Even the best of outside programs suffer from one very large defect — if the program falters helpful outsiders too often step in to smooth over the rough spots. At that point any program ceases to belong to the people involved and ceases to be a learning experience for them. Programs must be Indian creations, Indian choices, Indian experiences. Even the failures must be Indian experiences because only then will Indians understand why a program failed and not blame themselves for some personal inadequacy. A better program built upon the failure of an old program is the path of progress. But to achieve this experience, competence, worthiness, sense of achievement and the resultant material prosperity Indians must have the responsibility in the ultimate sense of the word. Indians must be free in the sense that other more prosperous Americans are free. Freedom and prosperity are different sides of the same coin and there can be no freedom without complete responsibility. And I do not mean the fictional responsibility and democracy of passive consumers of programs; programs which emanate from and whose responsibility for success rests in the hands of outsiders — be they federal administrators or local white elitist groups.

Many of our young people are captivated by the lure of the American city with its excitement and promise of unlimited opportunity. But even if educated they come from powerless and inexperienced communities and many times carry with them a strong sense of unworthiness. For many of them the promise of opportunity ends in the gutter on the skid rows of Los Angeles and Chicago. They should and must be given a better chance to take advantage of the opportunities they have. They must grow up in a decent community with a strong sense of personal adequacy and competence.

America cannot afford to have whole areas and communities of people in such dire social and economic circumstances. Not only for her economic well-being but for her moral well-being as well. America has given a great social and moral message to the world and demonstrated (perhaps not forcefully enough) that freedom and responsibility as an ethic is inseparable from and, in fact, the "cause" of the fabulous American standard of living. America has not however been diligent enough in promulgating this philosophy within her own borders. American Indians need to be given this freedom and responsibility which most Americans assume as their birth right. Only then will poverty and powerlessness cease to hang like the sword of Damocles over our heads stifling us. Only then can we enjoy the fruits of the American system and become participating citizens — Indian Americans rather than American Indians.

Perhaps, the National Indian Youth Council's real criticism is against a structure created by bureaucratic administrators who are caught in this American myth that all people assimilate into American society, that economics dictates assimilation and integration. From the experience of the National Indian Youth Council, and in reality, we cannot emphasize and recommend strongly enough the fact that no one integrates and disappears into American society. What ethnic groups do is not integrate into American society and economy individually, but enter into the mainstream of American society as a people, and in particular as communities of people. The solution to Indian poverty is not "government programs" but in the competence of the person and his people. The real solution to poverty is encouraging the competence of the community as a whole.

[The] National Indian Youth Council recommends for "openers" that to really give these people "the poor, the dispossessed, the Indians," complete freedom and responsibility is to let it become a reality not a much-heard-about dream and let the poor decide for once, what is best for themselves. . . .

INDIANS OF ALL TRIBES
Proclamation to the Great White Father and to All His People (1969)

We, the native Americans, re-claim the land known as Alcatraz Island in the name of all American Indians by right of discovery.

We wish to be fair and honorable in our dealings with the Caucasian inhabitants of this land, and hereby offer the following treaty:

We will purchase said Alcatraz Island for twenty-four dollars (24) in glass beads and red cloth, a precedent set by the white man's purchase of a similar island about 300 years ago. We know that $24 in trade goods for these 16 acres is more than was paid when Manhattan Island was sold, but we know that land values have risen over the years. Our offer of $1.24 per acre is greater than the 47¢ per acre the white men are now paying the California Indians for their land.°

We will give to the inhabitants of this island a portion of the land for their own to be held in trust by the American Indian Affairs and by the bureau of Caucasian Affairs to hold in perpetuity — for as long as the sun shall rise and the rivers go down to the sea. We will further guide the inhabitants in the proper way of living. We will offer them our religion, our education, our lifeways, in order to help them achieve our level of civilization and thus raise them and all their white brothers up from their savage and unhappy state. We offer this treaty in good faith and wish to be fair and honorable in our dealings with all white men.

We feel that this so-called Alcatraz Island is more than suitable for an Indian Reservation, as determined by the white man's own standards. By this we mean that this place resembles most Indian reservations in that:

1. It is isolated from modern facilities, and without adequate means of transportation.

2. It has no fresh running water.

3. It has inadequate sanitation facilities.

4. There are no oil or mineral rights.

5. There is no industry and so unemployment is very great.

6. There are no health care facilities.

7. The soil is rocky and non-productive; and the land does not support game.

8. There are no educational facilities.

9. The population has always exceeded the land base.

10. The population has always been held as prisoners and kept dependent upon others.

Further, it would be fitting and symbolic that ships from all over the world, entering the Golden Gate, would first see Indian land, and thus be reminded of the true history of this nation. This tiny island would be a symbol of the great lands once ruled by free and noble Indians.

American Indian Center

° A reference to the money offered to the Pit River Indians of northern California by the Indian Claims Commission as compensation for the loss of their lands.

SOURCE: Reprinted in Virgil J. Vogel, ed., *This Country Was Ours: A Documentary History of the American Indian* (New York: Harper and Row, 1972), 228–29. Courtesy, Adam Fortunate Eagle Nordwall.

QUESTIONS FOR CONSIDERATION

1. To what extent do Clyde Warrior's views of the system parallel those of Robert Burnette (see "Two Views of the Indian Reorganization Act," pages 476–79)?

2. Non-Indians, bewildered by the new wave of militancy, would sometimes ask, "What do Indians want?" What answers do the documents provide?

3. How do these documents seem to define tribal sovereignty, and why is sovereignty so important for Indian peoples?

4. Do the goals these documents describe seem achievable in modern America?

Indians and World War II

I N EVERY WAR THE UNITED STATES HAS FOUGHT, Native Americans have con-tributed a disproportionately high number of soldiers relative to their popula-tion and have suffered a disproportionately high rate of casualties relative to total losses. Their reputation as "natural warriors" frequently earned them dangerous assignments, and their courage in battle often enhanced that reputation. Indian communities value military service and honor their veterans, and, as in World War I, many young Indian men took the opportunity to be part of a warrior tradition during the Second World War. Nevertheless, like other men who en-listed, Indians had multiple reasons for serving in World War II: a sense of duty, patriotism, belief in the cause, hatred of Nazism as a threat to their freedom, peer pressure, a break from the dull routine of life to take part in historic events,

◆ Figure 8.1 **Banning the Swastika**
© Bettmann/CORBIS.

escape from the hardships of the Depression, and more. Indian people served all across the globe during World War II and encountered new experiences both in and out of combat.

Many Indians considered themselves full citizens of the United States, at one with the nation in its war against Germany, Japan, and Italy. Their actions reflected that allegiance. Navajos and other southwestern tribes who had formerly used the swastika motif in blanket weaving, basketry, and sand painting signed a multitribal resolution in 1940 outlawing the symbol's use because Nazi Germany had adopted it (Figure 8.1). "A symbol of friendship among our forefathers for many centuries has been desecrated," the resolution stated.

◆ Figure 8.2 **Iroquois Declare War on the Axis Powers on the Steps of the U.S. Capitol, June 1942**
© Bettmann/CORBIS.

◆ Figure 8.3 **Indian Women in the Marine Corps Reserve**
© CORBIS.

In other instances, tribes insisted on retaining and emphasizing their autonomy, even as they supported the same goals as the United States. In July 1942, delegates from the Six Nations of the Iroquois met in conference and drafted a formal declaration of war against the Axis powers. The next day, a spokesman for the confederacy read the declaration in a thirty-minute national radio broadcast and then, in a ceremony on the steps of the U.S. Capitol, the Iroquois presented the declaration to Vice President Henry A. Wallace (Figure 8.2). As "the oldest, though smallest, democracy in the world today," the Iroquois cited the need to stop the atrocities of the Axis nations and declared that a state of war existed between the Six Nations and Germany, Japan, and Italy. In this carefully orchestrated ceremony, the Iroquois Confederacy made clear to the United States and the world that it entered the war as an independent sovereign state pursuing its own foreign policy.[69]

◆ Figure 8.4 **Navajo Code Talkers, December 1943**
USMC via National Archives/AP Photo.

During the war, Indian men and women served in every branch of the armed forces. The women in Figure 8.3 — from left to right, Minnie Spotted Wolf (Blackfeet), Celia Mix (Potawatomi), and Viola Eastman (Chippewa/Sioux) — were in the marine corps reserve. They were photographed together at Camp Lejeune in North Carolina.

The Navajo code talkers contributed to American victory in the Pacific by conveying coded messages in Navajo that the Japanese were never able to crack. In Figure 8.4, Navajo code talkers Corporal Henry Bake Jr. and Private George Kirk convey radio messages in the jungle of Bougainville Island, Papua New Guinea, in December 1943.

◆ Figure 8.5 **Flag Raising at Iwo Jima**
Joe Rosenthal/AP Photo.

◆ **Figure 8.6 Quincy Tahoma, *First Furlough* (1943)**
National Museum of the American Indian, Smithsonian Institution (catalog number P13149).

In a photograph that defined the war for many Americans (Figure 8.5), marine private Ira Hayes (arms stretched at far left) was recorded participating in the historic flag raising on Mount Suribachi during the Battle of Iwo Jima. The presence of a Native American in this iconic moment had great symbolic appeal, and the government and the media focused on Hayes as a representative of national unity to promote fundraising efforts for the war.

As Indian soldiers' actions contributed to the events of the war, the war had immediate and lasting effects on them and their families and communities. Once reunited with their families (Figure 8.6), returning veterans faced old problems and new, postwar challenges.

QUESTIONS FOR CONSIDERATION

1. What do these images tell us about how and why Native Americans made the war their own?

2. The Iroquois maintained that, having declared war against Germany in World War I and never having officially made peace, they did not need to declare war again. Why then did they make another formal declaration of war?

3. What do these images suggest about wartime experiences that would have been similar for Indians and non-Indians and about experiences that would have been unique to Native Americans?

REFERENCES

1. John Collier Jr., foreword to *The Assault on Assimilation: John Collier and the Origins of Indian Policy Reform*, by Lawrence C. Kelly (Albuquerque: University of New Mexico Press, 1983), xiii.

2. John Collier, *From Every Zenith* (Denver: Sage Books, 1963), 126.

3. Frederick E. Hoxie, *This Indian Country: American Indian Activists and the Place They Made* (New York: Penguin, 2013), 282.

4. D'Arcy McNickle, *Native American Tribalism: Indian Survivals and Renewals* (New York: Oxford University Press, 1973), 93.

5. Alvin M. Josephy Jr., *Now That the Buffalo's Gone: A Study of Today's American Indians* (Norman: University of Oklahoma Press, 1982), 218.

6. Vine Deloria Jr., "This Country Was a Lot Better Off When the Indians Were Running It," *New York Times Magazine*, March 8, 1970, reprinted in *Red Power: The American Indians' Fight for Freedom*, ed. Alvin M. Josephy Jr. (New York: McGraw-Hill, 1971), quote at 239.

7. Brenda J. Child, *Boarding School Seasons* (Lincoln: University of Nebraska Press, 1998), 14–15.

8. Margaret Connell Szasz, *Education and the American Indian: The Road to Self-Determination since 1928*, 3rd ed. (Albuquerque: University of New Mexico Press, 1999), chaps. 4–8.

9. Jennifer McLerran, *A New Deal for Native Art: Indian Arts and Federal Policy, 1933–1943* (Tucson: University of Arizona Press, 2009).

10. Reprinted in Wilcomb E. Washburn, comp., *The American Indian and the United States: A Documentary History* (Westport, Conn.: Greenwood Press, 1973), 2:910.

11. Elmer R. Rusco, *A Fateful Time: The Background and Legislative History of the Indian Reorganization Act* (Reno: University of Nevada Press, 2000).

12. David E. Wilkins, *American Indian Politics and the American Political System* (Lanham, Md.: Rowman and Littlefield, 2002), 134.

13. Paul C. Rosier, *Rebirth of the Blackfeet Nation, 1912–1954* (Lincoln: University of Nebraska Press, 2001), quote at 3–4.

14. Klara B. Kelley and Peter M. Whiteley, *Navajoland: Family Settlement and Land Use* (Tsaile, Ariz.: Navajo Community College Press, 1989), 11.

15. Richard White, *The Roots of Dependency: Subsistence, Environment, and Social Change among the Choctaws, Pawnees, and Navajos* (Lincoln: University of Nebraska Press, 1983); chap. 10 discusses the environmental factors.

16. Edward T. Hall, *West of the Thirties: Discoveries among the Navajo and Hopi* (New York: Doubleday, 1994), 136. For fuller treatment of these issues, see Peter Iverson, *Diné: A History of the Navajos* (Albuquerque: University of New Mexico Press, 2002), and Peter Iverson, ed., *"For Our Navajo People": Diné Letters, Speeches, and Petitions, 1900–1960* (Albuquerque: University of New Mexico Press, 2002).

17. Harvard Project on American Indian Economic Development, *The State of the Native Nations: Conditions under U.S. Policies of Self-Determination* (New York: Oxford University Press, 2008), 4.

18. Kenneth William Townshend, *World War II and the American Indian* (Albuquerque: University of New Mexico Press, 2000), chap. 2; Colin G. Calloway, Gerd Gemünden, and Susanne Zantop, eds., *Germans and Indians: Fantasies, Encounters, Projections* (Lincoln: University of Nebraska Press, 2002); Glen Penny, *Kindred by Choice: Germans and American Indians Since 1800* (Chapel Hill: University of North Carolina Press, 2013).

19. Dean Kohlhoff, *When the Wind Was a River: Aleut Evacuation in World War II* (Seattle: University of Washington Press, 1995).

20. Bunny McBride, *Molly Spotted Elk: A Penobscot in Paris* (Norman: University of Oklahoma Press, 1995), quote at 223.

21. David E. Wilkins, *Hollow Justice: A History of Indigenous Land Claims in the United States* (New Haven: Yale University Press, 2013), chaps. 3–5, quote at 125.

22. Quoted in Robert M. Kvasnicka, *The Commissioners of Indian Affairs, 1824–1977* (Lincoln: University of Nebraska Press, 1979), 294–95.

23. Francis Paul Prucha, ed., *Documents of United States Indian Policy* (Lincoln: University of Nebraska Press, 1975), 233.

24. Deborah Shames, ed., *Freedom with Reservation: The Menominee Struggle to Save Their Land and People* (Madison: University of Wisconsin Press, 1972), 7–8.

25. On Menominee termination see Roberta Ulrich, *American Indian Nations from Termination to Restoration, 1953–2006* (Lincoln: University of Nebraska Press, 2010), chap. 2; for the Menominees' longer battle, see David R. M. Beck, *The Struggle for Self-Determination: History of the Menominee Indians since 1854* (Lincoln: University of Nebraska Press, 2005).

26. Donald L. Fixico, *Termination and Relocation: Federal Indian Policy, 1945–1960* (Albuquerque: University of New Mexico Press, 1986), 116–17; Ulrich, *American Indian Nations from Termination to Restoration*, chap. 3.

27. Fixico, *Termination and Relocation*, 185.

28. For example, see Edward Charles Valandra, *Not without Our Consent: Lakota Resistance to Termination, 1950–59* (Urbana: University of Illinois Press, 2006).

29. Quoted in Wilcomb E. Washburn, ed., *Handbook of North American Indians*, vol. 4, *History of Indian-White Relations* (Washington, D.C.: Smithsonian Institution Press, 1988), 315; Paul C. Rosier, "'They Are Ancestral Homelands': Race, Place, and Politics in Cold War Native America, 1945–1961," *Journal of American History* 92 (March 2006), 1300–1326; Thomas W. Cowger, *The National Congress of American Indians: The Founding Years* (Lincoln: University of Nebraska Press, 1999).

30. Ulrich, *American Indian Nations from Termination to Restoration*, chaps. 9 and 13; Nancy Oestreich Lurie, "Ada Deer: Champion of Tribal Sovereignty," in *Sifters: Native American Women's Lives*, ed. Theda Perdue (New York: Oxford University Press, 2001), 223–40.

31. R. Warren Metcalf, *Termination's Legacy: The Discarded Indians of Utah* (Lincoln: University of Nebraska Press, 2002).

32. Malinda Maynor Lowery, *Lumbee Indians in the Jim Crow South: Race, Identity, and the Making of a Nation* (Chapel Hill: University of North Carolina Press, 2010); Christopher Arris Oakley, "'When Carolina Indians Went on the Warpath': The Media, the Klan, and the Lumbees of North Carolina," *Southern Cultures* (Winter 2008), 55–84.

33. George P. Castile, *To Show Heart: Native American Self-Determination and Federal Indian Policy, 1960–1975* (Tucson: University of Arizona Press, 1998), 13.

34. Nancy Shoemaker, "Urban Indians and Ethnic Choices: American Indian Organizations in Minneapolis, 1920–1950," *Western Historical Quarterly* 19 (November 1988), 434.

35. James B. LaGrand, *Indian Metropolis: Native Americans in Chicago, 1945–75* (Urbana: University of Illinois Press, 2002).

36. Joan Weibel-Orlando, *Indian Country, L.A.: Maintaining Ethnic Community in Complex Society* (Urbana: University of Illinois Press, 1991), 22.

37. Donald L. Fixico, *The Urban Indian Experience in America* (Albuquerque: University of New Mexico Press, 2000), 7.

38. Morris W. Foster, *Being Comanche: A Social History of an American Indian Community* (Tucson: University of Arizona Press, 1991), 131.

39. Weibel-Orlando, *Indian Country, L.A.*, 1.

40. Nicholas G. Rosenthal, *Reimagining Indian Country: Native American Migration and Identity in Twentieth-Century Los Angeles* (Chapel Hill: University of North Carolina Press, 2012).

41. J. Matthew Shumway and Richard H. Jackson, "Native American Population Patterns," *Geographical Review* 85 (April 1995), 185–201, figures at 187, 193; Fixico, *Urban Indian Experience*; Matthew C. Snipp, *American Indians: The First of This Land* (New York: Russell Sage Foundation, 1989), 83.

42. Fixico, *Urban Indian Experience*.

43. *Federal Power Commission v. Tuscarora Indian Nation*, 362 U.S. 99 (1960); Joy Ann Bilharz, *The Allegany Senecas and Kinzua Dam: Forced Relocation through Two Generations* (Lincoln: University of Nebraska Press, 1998); Laurence M. Hauptman, *In the Shadow of Kinzua: The Seneca Nation of Indians since World War II* (Syracuse, N.Y.: Syracuse University Press, 2013).

44. Laurence M. Hauptman, *The Iroquois Struggle for Survival: World War II to Red Power* (Syracuse, N.Y.: Syracuse University Press, 1985).

45. Daniel M. Cobb and Loretta Fowler, eds., *Beyond Red Power: American Indian Political Activism since 1900* (Santa Fe, N. Mex.: School for Advanced Research, 2007); Daniel M. Cobb, *Native Activism in Cold War America: The Struggle for Sovereignty* (Lawrence: University Press of Kansas, 2008).

46. Paul C. Rosier, *Serving Their Country: American Indian Politics and Patriotism in the Twentieth Century* (Cambridge, Mass.: Harvard University Press, 2009); Cobb, *Native Activism*.

47. Quoted in Castile, *To Show Heart*, 41.

48. Josephy, *Red Power*, 71–77.

49. Trova Hefferan, *Where the Salmon Run: The Life and Legacy of Billy Frank Jr.* (Olympia: Washington State Heritage Center, and Seattle: University of Washington Press, 2012).

50. Bradley G. Shreve, *Red Power Rising: The National Indian Youth Council and the Origins of Native Activism* (Norman: University of Oklahoma Press, 2011).

51. Stephen Cornell, *The Return of the Native: American Indian Political Resurgence* (New York: Oxford University Press, 1988), 94–95.

52. Thomas Biolsi, *Organizing the Lakota: The Political Economy of the New Deal on the Pine Ridge and Rosebud Reservations* (Tucson: University of Arizona Press, 1992), xx.

53. Josephy, *Now That the Buffalo's Gone*, 219.

54. Kenneth R. Philp, ed., *Indian Self-Rule: First-Hand Accounts of Indian-White Relations from Roosevelt to Reagan* (Salt Lake City, Utah: Howe Brothers, 1986), 28–29, 47–48, 101.

55. Quotes from Biolsi, *Organizing the Lakota*, 126–27.

56. Reifel's views are expressed in Joseph H. Cash and Herbert T. Hoover, eds., *To Be an Indian: An Oral History* (St. Paul: Minnesota Historical Society Press, 1995), 124–25, and Philp, *Indian Self-Rule*, 76–78.

57. *Encyclopedia of North American Indians*, ed. Frederick E. Hoxie (Boston: Houghton Mifflin, 1996), s.v. "Burnette, Bob," by Alvin M. Josephy Jr.; Burnette quote in Philp, *Indian Self-Rule*, 104.

58. Glenn L. Emmons, *Annual Report of the Commissioner of Indian Affairs for 1954*, reprinted in Prucha, *Documents*, 237–38.

59. Merwyn S. Garbarino, "Life in the City: Chicago," in *The American Indian in Urban Society*, ed. Jack O. Waddell and O. Michael Watson (Boston: Little, Brown, 1971), 171, 179–82.

60. Kenneth R. Philp, "Stride toward Freedom: The Relocation of Indians to Cities, 1952–1960," *Western Historical Quarterly* 16 (April 1985), 175–90, quote at 176–77; LaGrand, *Indian Metropolis*.

61. Paul Chaat Smith and Robert Allen Warrior, *Like a Hurricane: The Indian Movement from Alcatraz to Wounded Knee* (New York: New Press, 1996), 38.

62. Josephy, *Red Power*, 71.

63. Smith and Warrior, *Like a Hurricane*, 38; Paul R. McKenzie-Jones, *Clyde Warrior: Tradition, Community, and Red Power* (Norman: University of Oklahoma Press, 2015).

64. Quoted in Smith and Warrior, *Like a Hurricane*, 37.

65. Josephy, *Red Power*, 71.

66. Smith and Warrior, *Like a Hurricane*, 58.

67. Sherry L. Smith, *Hippies, Indians, and the Fight for Red Power* (New York: Oxford University Press, 2012), chap. 3.

68. Quoted in Troy R. Johnson, *The Occupation of Alcatraz Island: Indian Self-Determination and the Rise of Indian Activism* (Urbana: University of Illinois Press, 1996), 128.

69. Townshend, *World War II*, 123.

SUGGESTED READINGS

Bernstein, Alison. *American Indians and World War II: Toward a New Era in Indian Affairs*. Norman: University of Oklahoma Press, 1991.

Biolsi, Thomas. *Organizing the Lakota: The Political Economy of the New Deal on the Pine Ridge and Rosebud Reservations*. Tucson: University of Arizona Press, 1992.

Burnette, Robert, and John Koster. *The Road to Wounded Knee*. New York: Bantam Books, 1974.

Castile, George P. *To Show Heart: Native American Self-Determination and Federal Indian Policy, 1960–1975*. Tucson: University of Arizona Press, 1998.

Chamberlain, Kathleen P. *Under Sacred Ground: A History of Navajo Oil, 1922–1982*. Albuquerque: University of New Mexico Press, 2000.

Cobb, Daniel M. *Native Activism in Cold War America: The Struggle for Sovereignty*. Lawrence: University Press of Kansas, 2008.

Cobb, Daniel M., and Loretta Fowler, eds. *Beyond Red Power: American Indian Political Activism since 1900*. Santa Fe, N. Mex.: School for Advanced Research, 2007.

Cohen, Fay G. *Treaties on Trial: The Continuing Controversy over Northwest Indian Fishing Rights*. Seattle: University of Washington Press, 1986.

Cornell, Stephen. *The Return of the Native: American Indian Political Resurgence.* New York: Oxford University Press, 1988.

Cowger, Thomas W. *The National Congress of American Indians: The Founding Years.* Lincoln: University of Nebraska Press, 1999.

Deloria, Vine, Jr. *Custer Died for Your Sins: An Indian Manifesto.* New York: Macmillan, 1969.

Deloria, Vine, Jr., and Clifford Lytle. *The Nations Within: The Past and Future of American Indian Sovereignty.* New York: Pantheon, 1984.

Edmunds, R. David, ed. *The New Warriors: Native American Leaders since 1900.* Lincoln: University of Nebraska Press, 2001.

Fixico, Donald L. *Termination and Relocation: Federal Indian Policy, 1945–1960.* Albuquerque: University of New Mexico Press, 1986.

——. *The Urban Indian Experience in America.* Albuquerque: University of New Mexico Press, 2000.

Fortunate Eagle, Adam. *Heart of the Rock: The Indian Invasion of Alcatraz.* Norman: University of Oklahoma Press, 2002.

Hosmer, Brian, and Colleen O'Neill, eds. *Native Pathways: American Indian Culture and Economic Development in the Twentieth Century.* Boulder: University Press of Colorado, 2004.

Hoxie, Frederick E. *This Indian Country: American Indian Activists and the Place They Made.* New York: Penguin, 2013.

Iverson, Peter. *Diné: A History of the Navajos.* Albuquerque: University of New Mexico Press, 2002.

——, ed. *"For Our Navajo People": Diné Letters, Speeches, and Petitions, 1900–1960.* Albuquerque: University of New Mexico Press, 2002.

——. *"We Are Still Here": American Indians in the Twentieth Century.* Wheeling, Ill.: Harlan Davidson, 1998.

Jaimes, M. Annette, ed. *The State of Native America: Genocide, Colonization, and Resistance.* Boston: South End Press, 1992.

Johnson, Troy R. *The Occupation of Alcatraz Island: Indian Self-Determination and the Rise of Indian Activism.* Urbana: University of Illinois Press, 1996.

Johnson, Troy R., Joanne Nagel, and Duane Champagne, eds. *American Indian Activism: Alcatraz to the Longest Walk.* Urbana: University of Illinois Press, 1997.

Josephy, Alvin M., Jr. *Now That the Buffalo's Gone: A Study of Today's American Indians.* Norman: University of Oklahoma Press, 1982.

——, ed. *Red Power: The American Indians' Fight for Freedom.* New York: McGraw-Hill, 1971.

Kelly, Lawrence C. *The Assault on Assimilation: John Collier and the Origins of Indian Policy Reform.* Albuquerque: University of New Mexico Press, 1983.

LaGrand, James B. *Indian Metropolis: Native Americans in Chicago, 1945–75.* Urbana: University of Illinois Press, 2002.

Lobo, Susan, and Kurt Peters, eds. *American Indians and the Urban Experience.* Walnut Creek, Calif.: AltaMira Press, 2001.

Lowery, Malinda Maynor. *Lumbee Indians in the Jim Crow South: Race, Identity, and the Making of a Nation.* Chapel Hill: University of North Carolina Press, 2010.

McLerran, Jennifer. *A New Deal for Native Art: Indian Arts and Federal Policy, 1933–1943.* Tucson: University of Arizona Press, 2009.

Nagel, Joanne. *American Indian Ethnic Renewal: Red Power and the Resurgence of Identity and Culture.* New York: Oxford University Press, 1996.

Nesper, Larry. *The Walleye War: The Struggle for Ojibwe Spearfishing and Treaty Rights.* Lincoln: University of Nebraska Press, 2002.

Olson, James S., and Raymond Wilson. *Native Americans in the Twentieth Century.* Urbana: University of Illinois Press, 1984.

O'Neill, Colleen M. *Working the Navajo Way: Labor and Culture in the Twentieth Century.* Lawrence: University Press of Kansas, 2005.

Parman, Donald L. *Indians and the American West in the Twentieth Century.* Bloomington: Indiana University Press, 1994.

Philp, Kenneth R., ed. *Indian Self-Rule: First-Hand Accounts of Indian-White Relations from Roosevelt to Reagan.* Salt Lake City, Utah: Howe Brothers, 1986.

——. *John Collier's Crusade for Indian Reform, 1920–1954.* Tucson: University of Arizona Press, 1977.

——. *Termination Revisited: American Indians on the Trail to Self-Determination, 1933–1953.* Lincoln: University of Nebraska Press, 1999.

Rawls, James J. *Chief Red Fox Is Dead: A History of Native Americans since 1945.* Fort Worth: Harcourt Brace, 1996.

Rosenthal, Nicholas G. *Reimagining Indian Country: Native American Migration and Identity in Twentieth-Century Los Angeles.* Chapel Hill: University of North Carolina Press, 2012.

Rosier, Paul C. *Rebirth of the Blackfeet Nation, 1912–1954.* Lincoln: University of Nebraska Press, 2001.

——. *Serving Their Country: American Indian Politics and Patriotism in the Twentieth Century.* Cambridge: Harvard University Press, 2009.

Shreve, Bradley G. *Red Power Rising: The National Indian Youth Council and the Origins of Native Activism.* Norman: University of Oklahoma Press, 2011.

Smith, Paul Chaat, and Robert Allen Warrior. *Like a Hurricane: The Indian Movement from Alcatraz to Wounded Knee.* New York: New Press, 1996.

Smith, Sherry L. *Hippies, Indians, and the Fight for Red Power.* New York: Oxford University Press, 2012.

Taylor, Graham D. *The New Deal and American Indian Tribalism: The Administration of the Indian Reorganization Act, 1934–45.* Lincoln: University of Nebraska Press, 1980.

Townshend, Kenneth William. *World War II and the American Indian.* Albuquerque: University of New Mexico Press, 2000.

Ulrich, Roberta. *American Indian Nations from Termination to Restoration, 1953–2006.* Lincoln: University of Nebraska Press, 2010.

Viola, Herman. *Warriors in Uniform: The Legacy of American Indian Heroism.* Washington, D.C.: National Geographic, 2005.

Weibel-Orlando, Joan. *Indian Country, L.A.: Maintaining Ethnic Community in Complex Society.* Urbana: University of Illinois Press, 1991.

Wilkins, David E. *Hollow Justice: A History of Indigenous Land Claims in the Unites States.* New Haven: Yale University Press, 2013.

Wilkinson, Charles F. *Blood Struggle: The Rise of Modern Indian Nations.* New York: W. W. Norton, 2005.

9

Self-Determination and Sovereignty

1970–2010

FOCUS QUESTIONS

1. What do self-determination and sovereignty mean for Indian tribes in modern America?

2. What were the aims and achievements of the American Indian Movement?

3. How have federal Indian policies changed over the past forty years or so?

4. What are the bases of Indian legal rights in the United States, and what role has the modern Supreme Court played in defending or compromising those rights?

5. What values, resources, and tactics have Indian people utilized in rebuilding their nations in the modern era?

NEW POLICIES, NEW MILITANCY

IN 1968 PRESIDENT JOHNSON HAD CALLED FOR a new Indian policy "expressed in programs of self-help, self-development, self-determination." In 1970 President Richard Nixon delivered a "Special Message on Indian Affairs" to Congress. The president began by acknowledging that on virtually every scale of measurement—health, employment, income, education—Indians ranked at the bottom. This condition was the heritage of centuries of injustice and of government policies that had oscillated between two extremes: federal paternalism that worked to produce excessive dependence on the government, and the more recent termination that sought to end the trustee relationship between the federal government and Indian people. What was needed, declared Nixon, was a new policy that would "strengthen the Indian's sense of autonomy without threatening his sense of community" — one that would enable Indians to become independent of federal control without being cut off from federal concern and support. "We must assure the Indian that he can assume control of his own life without being separated involuntarily from the tribal group." Rejecting past policies, Nixon called for a new relationship in which the federal government and Indian communities played complementary roles:

> It is long past time that the Indian policies of the federal government began to recognize and build upon the capacities and insights of the Indian people. Both as a matter of justice and as a matter of enlightened social policy, we must begin to act on the basis of what the Indians themselves have long been telling us. The time has come to break decisively with the past and to create the conditions for a new era in which the Indian future is determined by Indian acts and Indian decisions.[1]

Nixon selected a Mohawk, Louis R. Bruce, to head the Bureau of Indian Affairs (BIA). Bruce saw that a new generation of Indians was pushing for self-determination as they, not Washington, understood it. "Not in this century has there been such a volume of creative turbulence in Indian country," he said. "The will for self-determination has become a vital component of the thinking of Indian leadership. . . . It is an irreversible trend, a tide in the destiny of American Indians that will eventually compel all of America once and for all to recognize the dignity and human rights of Indian people."[2] The government was formally committed to a policy of self-determination, but what that actually meant was often, and sometimes bitterly, contested.

Tribal leaders sought to address the need for self-determination from within their communities as well. Elected Navajo tribal chairman in 1970, Peter MacDonald outlined the goals of his administration in his inaugural address in January 1971: "First, what is rightfully ours, we must protect; what is rightfully due us we must claim. Second, what we depend on from others, we must replace with the labor of our own hands, and the skills of our own people. Third, what we do not have, we must bring into being. We must create for ourselves."[3] Self-determination within Indian communities meant Indian people making their own decisions, running their own affairs, and charting their own futures in ways that were consistent with their own cultures and values.

Even as the president charted a new course in Washington and tribal leaders called for greater self-government, developments elsewhere were reshaping Indian relations with American society. Pivotal books like *Custer Died for Your Sins: An Indian Manifesto* (1969), by Vine Deloria Jr. and Dee Brown's best-selling indictment of the Indian wars, *Bury My Heart at Wounded Knee* (1970) affected the way many Americans viewed the nation's past and its present dealings with Native peoples. Native and non-Native students alike began to demand classes that addressed these issues, and the first Native American studies programs were established in the early 1970s. Concurrently, the American Indian Movement intensified the pressure on the government and society, culminating in a violent standoff at Wounded Knee, South Dakota, that brought the struggles of Indian people to the attention of the world.

The American Indian Movement

Since its founding in 1968 to protect Native people from police harassment in Minneapolis, the American Indian Movement (AIM) had grown in size and expanded its agenda. On Thanksgiving Day 1970, declared a national day of mourning by AIM leader Russell Means, protesters staged demonstrations at Plymouth Rock and the *Mayflower II* (a replica of the ship that brought the first English settlers to New England in 1620). AIM members protested again in 1971 on Mount Rushmore (where the sculpted heads of "enemy" presidents look out over Lakota land). AIM leaders were active in efforts to secure and protect fishing rights in the Great Lakes region in 1972–73. AIM demonstrators denounced the beating, unlawful imprisonment, and killing of Indians such as Raymond Yellow Thunder, an Oglala from Pine Ridge who was beaten to death in February 1972 in Gordon, Nebraska, a reservation border town, and Leroy Shenandoah, an Onondaga Green Beret veteran and a member of the honor guard at President Kennedy's funeral who was beaten and shot to death in March 1972 by Philadelphia police, who called the killing "justifiable homicide." The new sense of political aggressiveness gained national attention with the "Trail of Broken Treaties," in which a caravan of Indians traveled across the United States from the West Coast, via Minneapolis, to Washington, D.C., arriving there in November 1972 with more than five hundred protesters. The organizers brought a twenty-point document proposing that the federal government reestablish a treaty-making relationship with Indians. The Twenty Points document also demanded that the government review treaty violations, abolish the BIA and establish an Office of Federal Indian Relations and Community Reconstruction; provide protection for Indian religious freedom and cultural integrity; and provide funding and support for health, housing, education, employment, and economic development.

◆ **The "Native American Embassy"**
Members of the American Indian Movement stand ready to defend their occupation of the BIA building — here renamed the Native American Embassy — in November 1972. © *Bettmann/CORBIS.*

The protest almost resulted in violence when Indian militants occupied the BIA building for six days, but with a national election looming, the government did not want open conflict with the first Americans in the streets of the nation's capital. They agreed to review the protesters' twenty demands and fund their transportation home. The Twenty Points did not make their way into the policies of the Nixon administration.

Siege at Wounded Knee

The new strategies of direct confrontation on the part of the militant pan-Indian leaders also produced strains and divisions within Indian society. Young AIM radicals questioned the legitimacy of tribal governments set up under the Indian Reorganization Act and criticized many tribal leaders as self-serving BIA pawns. On the other hand, many tribal chairmen had worked hard within the system to obtain services for their communities. They, and other older, more conservative Indians, sometimes disliked AIM; they regarded the new tactics and political aggression as inappropriate and not in their people's best interests, fearing the militants would create a backlash. When young militants returned to the Wind River Reservation in Wyoming and called on the Arapahos to embrace the new activism, their ignorance of tribal protocol and their own language alienated Arapaho elders.[4]

The differences between militants and tribal chairmen came to a head on the Pine Ridge Reservation in South Dakota in 1973. In January, a young Lakota named Wesley Bad Heart Bull was stabbed to death; his accused white killer was charged with only second-degree manslaughter and allowed to go free after one day in jail.

Angry Lakotas demanded the charge be changed to one of murder, and AIM protesters clashed with police in Custer, South Dakota. Wesley Bad Heart Bull's mother
was arrested, charged with assaulting a police officer, and sentenced to three to
five years in jail. The tribal chair, Richard Wilson, condemned AIM and banned it
from Pine Ridge. As tensions and violence mounted, the BIA requested federal marshals at Pine Ridge. Confronted with this display of federal force, AIM leaders Dennis
Banks, Russell Means, and about two hundred activists, with the support of Oglala traditional leaders, took over the village of Wounded Knee in February 1973. Wounded
Knee had been the site of the massacre of Big Foot's band in 1890 (see page 334)
and was well known to the American public from the title of Dee Brown's book. Banks
and Means chose the place as a symbolic location to dramatize their opposition to
the BIA and their demands for self-determination and a return of tribal sovereignty.

From Wounded Knee, the AIM leaders announced the creation of the Oglala
Sioux Nation, declared independence from the United States, and defined their
national boundaries as those established by the Treaty of Fort Laramie in 1868.
(See "The Sioux, the Treaty of Fort Laramie, and the Black Hills," pages 341–55.)
Federal marshals, FBI agents, troops, and armored vehicles surrounded the village,
and the world's media flocked to Wounded Knee.

◆ **Wounded Knee Settlement**
Russell Means (foreground) and Assistant U.S. Attorney General Kent Frizzell sign an agreement. Frizzell smoked a sacred pipe with AIM leaders, but the peace settlement failed. Means
said "the government broke it before the ink was dry."[5] *AP Photo.*

The Wounded Knee siege lasted seventy-one days against a background of violence, murder, and suspicion. Two Indians were killed and several others wounded as the military fired more than half a million rounds of ammunition into the AIM compound. At one point, the government considered launching an open assault on the village, but after protracted negotiations between AIM and the FBI, the Indians finally agreed to end their occupation on the condition that the government hold a full investigation into their grievances and demands. "Once again, we Indians had accepted the white man's promises — just as our ancestors had," reflected Russell Means. "Once again, the government of the United States had lied."[6]

Means subsequently ran for tribal chairman, but the election was accompanied by arson, violence, intimidation, and murder attributed to tribal chair Richard Wilson's men. Wilson won by a narrow margin, but conditions on Pine Ridge remained tense. In 1975, two FBI agents were murdered, a crime for which AIM activist Leonard Peltier was arrested, tried, convicted, and sentenced to double life imprisonment on what many regarded as the shakiest of evidence. The election of Al Trimble as tribal chairman in 1976 restored a measure of calm to the reservation. But Peltier, imprisoned in 1977, remained in jail; he was denied parole in 2009 and is not eligible for another hearing until 2024, by which time he will be 79. His case remains a source of heated controversy; many people see him as a political prisoner and a symbol of America's continuing oppression of its Native peoples.[7]

Legacies of Wounded Knee

The standoff at Wounded Knee garnered considerable international attention. With the United States bogged down in a war in Vietnam, its violent confrontation with Native people at home stood as a test of the country's proclaimed ideals.[8] American media coverage of the events at Wounded Knee tended to take a "war correspondent" approach, focusing on exchanges of gunfire and resurrecting images from movie Westerns of "hostile Indians" rather than examining the root issues of the conflict.[9] Those roots stretched back to the Treaty of Fort Laramie in 1868 (see "The Sioux, the Treaty of Fort Laramie, and the Black Hills," pages 341–55), the annexation of the Black Hills in 1877, and the establishment of a new style of tribal government under the IRA in 1934, which had imposed minority government on Pine Ridge. In June 1973, after the siege ended, Senator James Abourezk of South Dakota, the chairman of the United States Senate Subcommittee on Indian Affairs, held hearings at Pine Ridge to investigate the causes of the confrontation. Ramon Roubidoux, Russell Means's Sioux attorney, pinned much of the blame on the IRA, which was supposed to restore self-government. "But as you know," Roubidoux told the committee, "self-government by permission is not self-government at all. . . . I think this committee should realize that we have got a very serious situation throughout the country."[10]

The confrontation at Wounded Knee, then, was more than a media event or even an attempt to overthrow a corrupt tribal government. Its goal was to free Pine Ridge from the shackles imposed by the federal government and to inspire other tribes to follow suit. By restoring responsible governments of their own, Indian peoples would regain their sovereignty, take care of their own affairs, and be able to determine their own futures. But in the opinion of Lakota writer and activist Vine Deloria Jr., Wounded Knee gave AIM only temporary visibility in the media and failed to resolve deeper problems between Indians and the United States. AIM became "stalled in its own rhetoric" and the movement lost momentum. "Wounded Knee," concluded Native authors Paul Chaat Smith and Robert Allen Warrior, "proved to be the final performance of AIM's daring brand of political theater."[11]

Other less dramatic demonstrations and developments followed. In 1974 the International Indian Treaty Council was organized, with the goal of bringing the struggles of indigenous peoples around the globe to the attention of the world community. In 1978, recalling the Cherokees' Trail of Tears and the Navajos' Long Walk, Clyde Bellecourt led the "Longest Walk" of Indian protesters from Alcatraz to Washington, D.C. Gradually, though, legal assault and FBI persecution drove many AIM leaders into hiding.[12]

Some observers, Native and non-Native, criticized the AIM leaders as publicity hounds — "the media's chiefs" — and asserted that the real work of reforming Indian policy went on outside the spotlight. Northern Cheyenne elder and tribal leader Ted Rising Sun said AIM "excited people for the moment" but produced no lasting positive results: "AIM was a big disturbance, but no real substance." Anishinaabe writer Gerald Vizenor disparaged the AIM leaders as "mouth warriors."[13] Some Indian women believed that AIM did not adequately represent their concerns, and in the mid-1970s they established the activist group WARN (Women of All Red Nations). WARN tackled issues such as domestic violence and the involuntary sterilization of Native women by the Indian Health Service (see page 511) and tried to reassert Native rights and protect Native cultures.

Others, Native and non-Native, saw AIM and the broader Red Power movement as a galvanizing and transformative force that generated an Indian demographic and cultural renaissance. AIM helped to increase the number of Indian organizations, newspapers, tribal colleges, and American Indian studies programs; it dramatically raised the level of awareness and political action; and it served as a catalyst for an American Indian ethnic renewal whose impact was reflected in growing Indian population figures recorded in U.S. censuses in the last decades of the twentieth century (see Chart 10.1, "American Indian Population Growth Rate, 1900–2010," page 574).[14] Russell Means said AIM lit a fire that brought renewed hope and pride across Indian country and struck a powerful blow for Native sovereignty.[15] The AIM activists had effectively focused public concern on the plight and protests of Native Americans. AIM gave many young Indian people a reason to mobilize and get involved in their own political and personal battles, and it fought for self-determination and social justice through local activism as well as national political protest. In Minneapolis/St. Paul, for example, AIM worked with local Native parents to start two community survival schools that taught Native languages and traditional values and helped repair some of the cultural damage done by American educational policies.[16] AIM today continues to work for Indian rights and Indian communities, but with less militant confrontation and much less media visibility.

Whatever else it achieved, AIM demonstrated dramatically that the "Indian wars" did not end in 1890, that Indian people had not disappeared, and that Indian–U.S. relations would continue to be marked by conflict as long as American society encroached on Indian resources and denied Indian rights. Mounting Indian activism and growing public awareness of the continuing injustices in the government's dealings with the first Americans did ultimately prompt changes in policy.

FROM PATERNALISM TO PARTNERSHIP

While frustrated Indian militants were taking to the streets in the 1970s, Congress responded to President Nixon's recommendations and passed a series of laws on Native American land claims, political status, education, social services, and religious freedom, measures that promised to protect Indian rights and increase the participation of Indian people in running their own affairs. In 1970 Nixon signed a bill returning Blue Lake to Taos Pueblo, ending a sixty-four-year fight by the people of Taos to regain the lands that President Theodore Roosevelt had proclaimed part of what is now Carson National Forest. (Roosevelt had initiated the national parks movement in the United States; the majority of the parks were established in the West and many of them were on Indian land.) Lands were also returned to the Yakama Nation in Washington State and to Warm Springs in Oregon.

In 1965 Alaska Natives had created the Alaska Federation of Natives (AFN), a statewide organization designed to pursue the land claims of Alaska's Native peoples. Oil discoveries on Alaska's North Slope in the 1950s and 1960s brought Native land issues to national attention, and the AFN pushed for a comprehensive settlement of Native land claims. The Alaska Native Claims Settlement Act (ANCSA) of 1971 was intended to resolve those land claims and open the area to pipeline construction. It extinguished Native subsistence hunting rights and aboriginal claims in almost all of Alaska in return for $962.5 million placed in an Alaska Native Fund and fee simple (full ownership) title to 44 million acres, or about one-ninth of the state. The act created a dozen regional for-profit corporations, which owned the 44 million acres and administered the fund, and more than two hundred village corporations (Map 9.1). A thirteenth regional corporation was later established for Alaska Natives who no longer resided in Alaska. Each Alaska Native received one hundred shares of stock in both a village and a regional corporation. Some Native people saw ANCSA as just another land steal by the United States and a raw deal for Alaska Natives, and discontent with some of ANCSA's provisions led to later amendments to the legislation. There remain ongoing concerns that, although the corporations can pursue economic development and allocate dividends to their members, they are not suited to conduct the full range of governmental responsibilities needed in Native Alaska.

Congress passed many other acts in the early 1970s. The Indian Education Act of 1972 provided funding for Indian children who attended public schools. In 1973, responding to tireless lobbying by Ada Deer and other Menominee leaders, Congress passed the Menominee Restoration Act, returning the Menominees' tribal

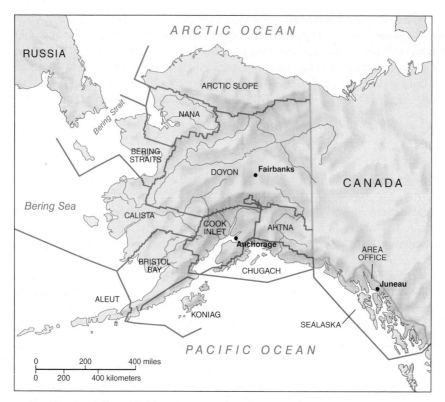

◆ **Map 9.1 Alaska's Native Regional Corporations**
The Alaska Native Claims Settlement Act in 1971 created a dozen regional corporations and more than two hundred village corporations.

status and restoring their access to federal programs. The Indian Finance Act in 1974 authorized federal grants and loans to federally recognized tribes to promote economic development and led to the creation of the Indian Business Development Program. The Indian Self-Determination and Educational Assistance Act of 1975 gave tribes instead of government officials the right to administer federal assistance programs. Tribal governments could now contract to provide services previously carried out by the Department of the Interior and the Department of Health, Education, and Welfare. However, the programs were still affected by federal spending priorities. Under the Tribal Self Governance Act of 1994, tribes "compacted" with the federal government to receive a lump sum for all the services they provided and decided for themselves how those funds should be allocated.[17]

Protecting Women's Reproductive Rights

One product of increased activism by Native people and increased responsiveness on the part of the federal government was greater protection for Indian families and for the personal sovereignty of Native women. From the days of the early republic, American government and society regarded the extended family structures and the relative personal and sexual freedom of women in many Native societies as evidence of instability. As the breakdown of traditional economies, the assault on cultural values and gender relations, increasing poverty and alcoholism, and other forces of colonialism took their toll, American attitudes toward Indian families and parenting hardened: Indian families were increasingly labeled "dysfunctional," and Indian mothers and fathers were deemed "unfit" parents. Such attitudes justified assaults on Indian families, Indian women, and Indian children for many years.

In 1974 Dr. Connie Pinkerton-Uri, a Choctaw physician working at the Indian Health Service (IHS) facility in Claremore, Oklahoma, uncovered evidence that Indian women were being sterilized there, apparently without their informed consent. The story broke in the Native newspaper *Akwesasne News* and generated outrage and national investigation. In 1976 Senator James Abourezk of South Dakota, chairman of the Senate Subcommittee on Indian Affairs, asked the General Accounting Office to conduct an investigation. The GAO investigators visited four of the twelve Indian Health Service area offices (in Aberdeen, South Dakota; Albuquerque, New Mexico; Phoenix, Arizona; and Oklahoma City). They found that 3,406 Native women between the ages of fifteen and forty-four were sterilized between 1973 and 1976. They also reported violations of the regulations for sterilizations that had been established by the Department of Health, Education, and Welfare. The GAO did not find evidence of forced sterilization or genocide, but Native Americans conducted their own investigations and reported incidents of women being coerced into sterilization with threats of losing their medical benefits or of having their children taken away, and of women signing consent forms while under sedation or without complete information. The sterilization numbers were clearly much higher than those reported by the GAO. Several reports indicated that IHS doctors sterilized at least 25 percent and perhaps as much as 50 percent of Native American women in the health service areas between 1970 and 1976, with devastating effects on families and communities, as well as adverse physical and psychological effects on the women themselves. Dr. Pinkerton-Uri denounced "the warped thinking of doctors who think the solution to poverty is not to allow people to be born" and dismissed the argument that a poor woman with children was "better off" sterilized: "She's still going to be poor. She just won't be able to have children."[18]

The national exposure of what appeared to many people to be a systematic attempt to limit Indian population growth generated new regulations for federally funded sterilizations that prohibited the sterilization of minors, allowed patients to be accompanied by witnesses (and interpreters if necessary) during their discussions with a doctor, and assured patients that their medical benefits would not be affected by their decisions. In 1976 Congress passed the Indian Health Care Improvement Act, granting tribes the right to manage or control IHS programs. Many tribes took over IHS facilities and began operating their own health services. However, although sterilization abuse was curbed, it was not eliminated, and assaults on Native women's reproductive rights continue today.[19]

Regaining Rights: Child Welfare and Religious Freedom

For most of the twentieth century, similar attitudes about Indian families, parents, and poverty led judges, social workers, and adoption agencies to assume that Indian children would be better off with white families. Growing numbers of Indian children disappeared into state child welfare systems until, by the 1970s, between one-fourth and one-third of all Indian children were in non-Indian homes or institutions, "a staggering loss of kids and culture." In 1978 Congress, in what longtime Native American Rights Fund (NARF) staff attorney Walter Echo-Hawk termed "one of its finest hours," passed legislation to address the crisis. The Indian Child Welfare Act of 1978 renounced the practice of transferring care of Indian children to non-Indians, required state courts to apply Native cultural values when placing Indian children, and placed responsibility for the welfare of Indian children squarely with their tribe. Children could no longer be removed from a family without the tribe or extended family members being duly notified; children were to be placed with extended family, tribal members, or other Indian families in preference to non-Indian families; and tribal courts were to have ultimate jurisdiction in matters relating to child welfare services whenever possible. "This sweeping statute," wrote Echo-Hawk more than thirty years after its passage, "remains one of the most impressive human rights and tribal sovereignty laws ever passed by Congress."[20]

That same year, in the American Indian Religious Freedom Act, Congress declared its intention "to protect and preserve for American Indians their inherent right of freedom to believe, express, and exercise" their traditional religions, "including but not limited to access to sites, use and possession of sacred objects, and the freedom to worship through ceremonials and traditional rights."[21] Despite its promise, the joint resolution by Congress was a policy statement, lacking legal teeth for enforcement. The Supreme Court continued to allow the federal government and state governments to intrude upon the religious life of Native peoples, and Congress later had to amend the act to provide greater protection as Native people continued the struggle for their religious rights (see page 526).

TAKING BACK EDUCATION

As Indian communities regained responsibility for their children's welfare, so too did they take back responsibility for their children's education. Important new initiatives in Indian education and cultural patrimony stemmed from the growing movement toward self-determination. Traditionally, Native American parents and elders taught their children in a community setting. But well into the twentieth century, government-sponsored schools made every effort to separate Indian students from their communities and rid them of their tribal heritage, language, and understandings, so that they could act, speak, and think like non-Indian Americans. The schools and colleges that Indian students attended operated to meet the goals of American society. They failed to meet many of the needs of their Indian students, and, not surprisingly, Indian students frequently failed at those institutions (see "The Educational Assault on Indian Children," pages 391–402). Indian people established their own schools early on — the Cherokee Nation established its own educational system in the nineteenth century and opened the nondenominational Cherokee Female Seminary in eastern Oklahoma in 1851 — but not until the 1960s and 1970s were Indian people and communities able to have a significant voice in planning and running some of their institutions of higher education.[22] "It was not until Indians themselves became participants in determining their future," stated a report on Tribal Colleges by the Carnegie Foundation, "that true advancement and productive interaction began."[23]

Indian Education for Indian Students

In 1969 a Senate subcommittee published a report on Indian education that was subtitled "A National Tragedy — A National Challenge." The committee declared, "We are shocked at what we discovered."[24] The report marked an end to the government's educational assault on Indian cultures and languages, but the legacy of that assault left Indian peoples and communities with a formidable task as they began to repair what had been broken in the past, to prepare for future challenges, and to educate Indian children to succeed in modern American society while at the same time cultivating traditional values and ways of knowledge.

In some places, Indian parents and communities took steps to ensure that young people had access to the kind of culturally grounded education that generations of federal educational policy had tried to erode. Amid ongoing struggles for sovereignty against the United States and Canada, New York State, and the provinces of Ontario and Quebec, parents of the Akwesasne Mohawk Nation established the Akwesasne Freedom School in 1979. Reclaiming the right to determine the education of their own children as a fundamental attribute of nationhood and a means of reversing the assimilation process, Mohawk parents and teachers, traditional chiefs, and clan mothers immerse students in Mohawk ways of thinking, learning, and speaking. For more than thirty years, the Akwesasne Freedom School has endeavored to ensure that "the next generation of Mohawk Nation leaders has the necessary teachings and that Mohawk sovereignty will continue."[25]

Prior to the 1960s, there were no institutions of higher education in Indian country. Tribal colleges filled the void.[26] In 1966 the Navajos established the Rough Rock Demonstration School near Chinle, Arizona. Two years later, they founded the first tribal college on the Navajo Reservation: Navajo Community College — now Diné College — in Tsaile, Arizona. Students who previously had to leave the reservation for higher education in an alien environment now had the option of attending college closer to home in an institution that tried to incorporate Navajo values in its administration and classes. In the words of a former dean of instruction, the college's mission has always been "to perpetuate Navajo-ness": to find ways to synthesize Navajo and Western knowledge "and instill this knowledge into young Navajo men and women so they will survive in the dominant society while maintaining their heritage."[27] Indian tribes founded fifteen more two-year

◆ **Navajo Women Graduating from Dartmouth College**
Young Navajo women celebrate their college graduation. Sheina Yellowhair, Jonathea D. Tso, Poonam Aspaas, Sophina Manheimer, and Marla Yazzie graduated from Dartmouth in 2004. *Photo by Linda M. Welch. Courtesy of the photographer and the graduates.*

institutions in the next decade. Tribal colleges, created and administered by Indian people and generally located on or near Indian reservations, grew out of a widespread conviction that most institutions of higher education had failed abysmally to provide a learning environment for Indian people of traditional background. In 1972 tribes formed the American Indian Higher Education Consortium to help Indian students gain access to higher education. The consortium's lobbying in Congress resulted in passage of the Tribally Controlled Community Colleges Act in 1978, which provided funding for the colleges.

Severe budget cuts during the Ronald Reagan presidency (1981–89) threatened to eradicate many of the gains made. A task force commissioned to evaluate education among American Indians and Alaska Native people issued a report entitled "Indian Nations at Risk" in 1991. The report established goals to guide federal, tribal, private, and public schools serving Native students to better meet the educational, social, cultural, and spiritual needs of those students and their communities. Indian educators lobbied hard to hold the government to its treaty commitments and trust responsibility to provide an education for Indian children. In 1992 President Bill Clinton held a White House Conference on Indian Education. In 1995 a "National American Indian/Alaska Native Education Summit" was held in Washington, D.C. From that summit, Indian educators produced a draft that was circulated among Indian educational organizations and, after revisions, was eventually submitted to the White House. In 1998 President Clinton signed the Executive Order on American Indian and Alaska Native Education, which affirmed "the unique political and legal relationship" between the federal and tribal governments and recognized "the unique educationally and culturally related academic needs" of Native students. Many Indian educators regarded it as a landmark event, though they recognized how much work remained to be done and knew too well that the Indian education budget was vulnerable to political mood swings and economy-minded lawmakers.[28]

Title VII of the No Child Left Behind Act, signed into law by President George W. Bush in 2002, reaffirmed the federal government's trust responsibility to Indian people for the education of Indian children and recommitted the government to work with the tribes to meet not only basic elementary and secondary educational needs "but also the unique educational and culturally related academic needs of these children." The legislation's promises sounded similar to those of Clinton's executive order, but the Bush administration did not provide adequate resources to meet No Child Left Behind goals that applied to Indian country. Many Indian people were confirmed in their belief that if they wanted quality education they would have to provide it themselves.[29] At the beginning of the twenty-first century, Indian tribes ran more than one hundred tribal elementary and secondary schools, and tribal colleges continue to provide Indian people with an Indian education in their own communities and in keeping with their own values.[30]

Tribal Colleges

Today the American Indian Higher Education Consortium (AIHEC) contains thirty-eight tribally controlled colleges and universities in the United States and more are being developed. Some tribal colleges have been operating for more than forty years. The Rosebud Sioux chartered Sinte Gleska College in 1971 (named after the chief known to whites as Spotted Tail, who pulled his grandchildren from Richard Henry Pratt's boarding school at Carlisle, Pennsylvania, in the 1880s). It began as a two-year college; today it is a four-year undergraduate college with one thousand students, a master's degree program in education, and a Lakota studies department.[31] Others are quite new: for example, Comanche Nation College in Lawton, Oklahoma, was established in 2002; the Cheyenne and Arapaho Tribal College, located on the campus of Southwestern Oklahoma State University, started in 2006.

Lakota scholar and activist Vine Deloria Jr. (see pages 547–49) criticized American colleges and universities for training professionals but not producing people. "Education," he wrote, "is more than the process of imparting and receiving information, . . . it is the very purpose of human society and . . . human societies cannot really flower until they understand the parameters of possibilities that the human personality contains."[32] Many non-Indian educators share Deloria's sentiments, but the sense that Western education does not address the whole person has permeated Indian responses to non-Indian teachers and schools from colonial times to the present. Tribal colleges offer a more holistic approach to learning and the kind of education that young Indian people can rarely find in mainstream American colleges. They integrate Native American traditions into their curriculum, providing classes in tribal language, art, philosophy, and history at the same time they offer students access to the skills needed in the modern world. "While we want to give our graduates the ability to go anywhere they want," said Janine Pease-Pretty on Top, former president of Little Big Horn College on the Crow Reservation, "we need them all desperately here on the reservation. Our first goal is to train young people to serve their own community: we need engineers, data processors, dental technicians, specialists in animal husbandry, premed, everything." Students study the Crow language and "come out of here knowing what it is to be Crow," she said, but they "must also pass college algebra."[33] In some ways, tribal colleges may be realizing Luther Standing Bear's dream of an education built on the exchange of knowledge between Indian America and Anglo-America (see "What a School Could Have Been Established," pages 424–28).

Tribal colleges have impressive rates of success where federal education policies and mainstream colleges have failed. Most colleges have relatively small enrollments and minuscule budgets. Inadequate facilities and low salaries are typical, and college administrators sometimes struggle just to keep the doors open. One reporter called tribal colleges "underfunded miracles."[34] Henrietta Mann, a Cheyenne elder who taught at the University of Montana and Montana State University, calls them "miracles of persistence" that "have had to build their institutional foundations dollar-by-dollar, grant-by-grant, program-by-program, and literally brick by brick."[35] Despite President George W. Bush's vowed commitment to tribal colleges, Bush-era funding cuts hampered the colleges' efforts. The colleges are community institutions and they share their communities' problems. As James Shanley, president of Fort Peck Community College in Montana, pointed out, the most serious problem facing Indian education today is poverty. Poverty and its attendant socioeconomic problems affect students from first graders to college, causing dropouts, which add to the cycle of community poverty, and tribal colleges struggle to break such cycles.[36] Nevertheless, enrollment of American Indian students at tribal colleges and universities has grown at almost twice the rate of enrollment in higher education in general. By 2005, 30,000 students were enrolled in tribal colleges and were working toward two-year, four-year, and advanced degrees. The colleges provide support services for students, many of whom are older and must overcome financial obstacles and competing family commitments to attend school and complete their degrees. They train people for work on and off the reservation and also prepare students for transfer to mainstream colleges, where their rate of success is far higher than that of Indian students who go directly from reservation communities.

In the words of one study, more was accomplished in the years "since the founding of the first tribal college to meet the higher education needs of the tribes and their members than in the two hundred years since the first Indian graduated from Harvard University."[37] The number of Indian people enrolled in college in the 1950s was about 2,000. By the 1970s it had risen to 10,000. In 2000, it had reached 147,000 and by 2010 it was close to 200,000.[38] The Carnegie Foundation's 1989 report concluded that the network of tribal colleges "providing education and community service in a climate of self-determination" lay "at the heart of the spirit of renewal" in Indian country.[39] In the 1990s Vine Deloria said that "tribal colleges may be the most important movement we have in Indian country today."[40]

THE STRUGGLE FOR NATURAL RESOURCES

As Indian communities worked to cultivate their human resources through education, many also faced challenges and opportunities in exploiting the natural resources of their homelands. In the nineteenth century, the United States wanted Indian land; in the twentieth and twenty-first centuries, it wanted Indian resources. Coal, gas, oil, uranium, timber, and water were vital to the nation's economy and, some said, to national security. For Indian communities whose reservation lands contained such resources, the sale of those resources offered the potential for significant economic development. But access to natural and energy resources on Native American lands has also been debated as an issue of sovereign rights. As Native Americans embraced self-determination and realized educational goals, they struggled to protect their rights regarding resources that were vital to their traditional and spiritual ways of life, and to exercise their own decisions about utilizing such resources.

Coal, Uranium, and Oil

When the United States assigned Indians to reservations in the nineteenth century, it generally placed them on barren lands other Americans did not want. Ironically, many western reservations lay on one of the world's richest mineral belts. It is estimated that reservations contain one-third of all low-sulphur coal in the western United States, one-fifth of the country's reserves of oil and natural gas, and more than half of the nation's uranium deposits. With the onset of the Cold War and the escalating energy demands of modern America following the end of World War II, Indian tribes came under intense pressure from energy companies and the U.S. government to develop and market these resources. With few economic alternatives, tribal leaders found themselves negotiating — or, at that time, found the BIA negotiating for them — with outsiders eager to get at their resources, just as their ancestors had. In some cases, Indian reservations were transformed into energy colonies, exporting their valuable resources to the outside world and getting little in return.[41]

Entrenched in an economic crisis decades in the making, the Navajo Reservation, comprising 16 million acres straddling Arizona, New Mexico, and Utah, became the scene of extensive exploitation of energy resources and enduring conflict. The livestock reduction program of the 1930s and 1940s had eroded the traditional Navajo economy, and the war-related industries of World War II hadn't fully offset the widespread poverty. Attractive offers to develop their energy resources seemed to offer Navajos the promise of prosperity. Peabody Coal Company signed leases with the Hopis and Navajos in 1966 to begin coal strip-mining operations on the Black Mesa plateau, an area of the Four Corners region that overlaps the Navajo and Hopi reservations. And some Navajos did reap the rewards of the profitable exports; royalties from mining operations injected much-needed income into the reservation's economy and provided funds for Navajo Community College and scholarships for Navajo students. Some Navajos, notably tribal chairman Peter MacDonald (who worked closely with energy companies in the 1970s and 1980s), grew rich. But most Navajos benefited little from the power they were producing for other people. Like the people of a third world country, most Navajos remained poor, as the benefits and profits from exploitation of their rich resources left the reservation. Navajo energy resources provided power for Albuquerque, Phoenix, Los Angeles, and other cities, but many Navajo homes lacked running water or electricity. Smoke from the huge power plant at Four Corners blackened the sky. Navajo lambs were stunted, spat blood, and died. In July 1979, the nation's

◆ **Coal Mine on the Navajo Indian Reservation near Shiprock, New Mexico**
Open pit coal mines brought much needed revenue to the Navajo Nation but degraded the environment. © *Buddy Mays/Alamy.*

worst release of radioactivity occurred when United Nuclear Corporation's uranium tailings dam failed at Church Rock, just outside the Navajo Reservation: 100 million gallons of radioactive water flooded into the Rio Puerco River, and 10,000 sheep died.

Many Navajos bitterly opposed the ensuing despoiling of the area. Uranium mining scarred the land and injured the people. The dangers of exposure to excessive levels of radiation were not so well understood at the time, and companies sometimes cut corners on what regulations did exist. Navajo miners pulled uranium out of the ground by hand, and many contracted lung cancer and other respiratory ailments later in life. Nearly 1.4 million tons of uranium ore were extracted from Monument Valley, and Navajo country today contains more than one thousand abandoned uranium mines and four former uranium mills (Map 9.2). Navajos were "the forgotten victims of America's Cold War." In 1990 the United States issued a formal apology and promised to compensate the families of Navajo men injured or killed by radiation in the government mines, but for victims' families such compensation was too little, too late.[42]

At Laguna Pueblo in New Mexico, Anaconda Corporation operated the world's largest uranium strip mine from 1952 to 1981. At its peak of operations, the mine employed 650 workers. The Laguna tribe became relatively wealthy, but the local economy changed completely from agriculture to wage-based mining. When the

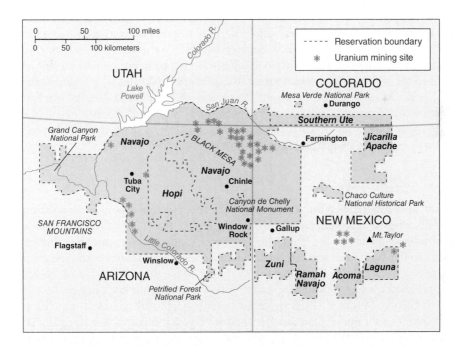

◆ **Map 9.2 Uranium Ore Mining Areas**
The Four Corners area of the United States, regarded by many people as a special and sacred place, became pockmarked with uranium mining sites in the twentieth century.
SOURCE: Adapted from a map by Deborah W. Reade for Peter Eichstaedt, *If You Poison Us: Uranium and Native Americans* (Santa Fe, N. Mex.: Red Crane Books, 1994). © Peter Eichstaedt.

extractable ore reserve was exhausted, Anaconda pulled out, and the Lagunas were left with a huge crater and piles of radioactive slag. (Anaconda later agreed to pay the tribe $34.6 million for cleanup and reclamation projects.) Lagunas who had become accustomed to earning regular wages were now unemployed. In addition, residents suffered from mining-related ailments; many of the new homes built with the mine profits were found to be radioactive, and local water sources were all contaminated.

Black Mesa and Laguna served as warnings to other tribes of the long-term damage that could be incurred in return for short-term gain. By the 1970s, Indian tribes with valuable mineral resources were becoming more organized and less vulnerable to exploitation by energy companies. In 1975 leaders from twenty-five tribes formed CERT, the Council of Energy Resource Tribes, whose goal was to secure better terms from corporations and to exert political influence through collective action. In 1982 Congress passed the Indian Mineral Development Act to encourage tribes to mine their lands as a way to become economically self-sufficient. But, after seeing the impact of America's energy demands, many tribes took a cautious approach. The Jicarilla Apaches of New Mexico and the Assiniboines and Sioux of Fort Peck in Montana drilled their own oil wells. The Northern Cheyennes in Montana sit on between 5 and 10 million tons of strippable coal, but in the 1970s they took the unprecedented step of canceling their coal mining leases and having the U.S. Environmental Protection Agency designate the air above their reservation as Class I, a standard that tolerates almost no degradation of air quality and that usually applies only to national parks and wilderness areas. The government's attempt in the late 1980s to settle conflicts between Navajos and Hopis who inhabited a "joint use area" by removing Navajo families was seen by many people as an effort to open the region's rich coal resources to exploitation. Navajos who regarded the area as sacred land refused to move.[43] The Navajo Nation established its own Environmental Protection Agency, and in 1987 the Navajos and Hopis renegotiated their leases with Peabody Coal. In 1996 approximately 75 percent of the Navajo Nation's operating budget still depended on royalties from coal sales.[44]

Fighting For and Against Water

In the arid American West, water is a scarce and precious resource. Population growth, irrigation, power plants, and desert cities like Phoenix and Las Vegas place enormous demands on the West's limited water supply. At the same time, Indian tribes in the West need water to sustain and develop their reservations, and even to survive. "Water is the life blood, the key to the whole thing," declared Madonna Thunderhawk, a Lakota water-rights activist on the Standing Rock Reservation in North Dakota, in 1985.[45] The struggle for water brought Indians into competition and conflict with non-Indian ranchers and state governments and into court. To the chagrin of many of their neighbors, Indians prevailed in some of these cases. But, in keeping with other rulings since 1970, the Supreme Court has decided against tribes in 90 percent of the water-related cases it has ruled on.[46]

The basis for water-rights cases was laid in the first decade of the twentieth century when the Supreme Court decided the case of *Winters v. United States*.

The suit was brought to prevent a white settler from damming the Milk River and diverting water from the Fort Belknap Reservation in Montana. Although the Court at that time was generally unsympathetic to Indians, it found in favor of the tribe. The *Winters* doctrine, as the Court's decision became known, declared that when Congress established reservations it did so with the implicit intention that the Indians should have sufficient water to live. Indian reservations, said the Court, had "reserved water rights" that the federal government was bound to protect. For much of the century, the *Winters* doctrine remained a paper victory, and non-Indians continued to divert water from Indian lands. Nevertheless, the courts have upheld *Winters,* and the doctrine is the foundation on which western tribes have won important water-rights cases. The *Winters* doctrine has been a source of tension, as non-Indian ranchers had their water supply terminated during droughts while flows to neighboring Indian reservations continued uninterrupted. American society has had a hard time adjusting to the realization that, in the words of one legal scholar of water rights, "the debt has come due" and one way or another "it must be paid."[47] Competition for water in the West continues with numerous lawsuits over how much water tribes are entitled to, how they can use it, whether they can lease it, and so on. The tribes, the states, and the federal government continue to wrestle with finding equitable ways to allocate an ever-diminishing resource in an area of the country where control of water means power and prosperity.

The assault on Native resources and communities has not been restricted to the United States, nor have Native peoples within U.S. borders been the only ones to feel the impact of American energy consumption. The struggle of Cree Indians in northern Quebec attracted attention in both the United States and Canada in the late twentieth century as a test case of modern society's exploitation and disregard of Native peoples and the environment—and in this case, the Indians were fighting *against* water.

In 1970 the premier of Quebec announced plans for Hydro-Quebec, the largest hydroelectric project in the world, to dam major rivers that drained into James Bay, which is at the southern end of Hudson Bay and is the largest bay and estuary system on the continent. The project subsequently expanded to include dams on the La Grande River, the third-largest river in Quebec. Construction began two years later. Five major rivers were dammed or diverted and more than 4,000 square miles of forest were flooded to generate electric power for eastern Canada and the northeastern United States. "One day, after we had lived in our land for thousands of years," said Grand Chief Matthew Coon-Come, "a decision was made to block our rivers, cut down our forests, and flood our lands. No one came to talk to us. We were not told of these plans. All of this just happened."[48]

By 1985, Phase I of the Hydro-Quebec project had been completed at a cost of $20 billion, but the costs to the Crees were also considerable. People were relocated to make way for dams that flooded ancient hunting territories and sacred places. Migrating birds could find nowhere to land. In 1984 a sudden release of water from one reservoir drowned 10,000 migrating caribou. As Anishinaabe activist Winona LaDuke explained: "There are many things Cree people have taken for granted over countless generations: that the rivers will always flow, the sun and moon will alternate, and there will be six seasons of the year. . . . That is how the time is counted here in the North, in seasons based on the migrations of caribou, geese, sturgeons, and other relations and on the ebb and flow of ice and water." But, since Hydro-Quebec went into effect, "the rivers do not always flow, the animals are not always there, and strange as it may seem, there are no longer six seasons in some parts of this land."[49]

Having failed to stop Phase I in the courts, the Crees widened their campaign against Phase II. They lobbied for non-Native support in Canada and the United States, pointing out to audiences in New York and New England that *they* bore a share of responsibility for the devastation of the Cree homeland and that what was going on to the north was environmental racism and just as threatening as the destruction of the Amazonian rain forests. "This is what I want you to understand," said Coon-Come. "It is not a dam. It is a terrible and vast reduction of our entire world. It is the assignment of vast territories to a permanent and final flood."[50]

Contracts for selling the power in the United States began to be delayed and canceled. In 1994 the new premier of Quebec shelved Phase II of the James Bay project. Coon-Come was awarded the Goldman Environmental Prize for his fifteen-year fight against the project, but Hydro-Quebec continued to propose plans for diverting and damming the Great Whale and Rupert rivers, which run through the heart of Cree territory. In 2002, in a move that surprised and alarmed many environmentalists, the James Bay Cree High Council endorsed a new agreement with Hydro-Quebec that cleared the way for completion of the final phase of the project. In return for a share of the profits from a huge new hydroelectric plant, the Crees agreed to support the diversion of much of the Rupert River to the plant. By 2007 construction on the giant project was under way, but the Cree Nation was divided on the issue. In 2009 construction work began on a new hydroelectric plant on the Romaine River, which runs along Quebec's Lower North Shore. The La Romaine plant was designed to include four dams and was expected to take eleven years to build at an estimated cost of $6.5 billion. In 2010 the Innu Native people of northeastern Quebec filed a motion for injunction; they opposed the construction as illegal, undertaken without their consent, and as a threat to the region's wildlife and the Innu way of life.

SOVEREIGNTY GOES TO COURT

Like the Innu, Native peoples in the United States often found that protecting their homelands and future required defending and reasserting their rights in court, working within the system as well as against the system. In the past, Indian warriors had fought battles to defend their lands and their way of life and had lost. In the late twentieth century, Indians took their fights to the courtroom — and frequently they won. Indians and their attorneys, often with the support of the Native American Rights Fund that was founded in 1970, reached back into history and uncovered laws and treaties that were supposed to guarantee and protect their rights but that were often ignored in days when Indians had no voice in the courts. In the new social and political climate of reform created by the upheavals of the 1960s and 1970s, judicial opinion was more sympathetic to the notion that the nation should live up to its treaty commitments. The courtroom replaced the battlefield as the arena where Indians could best promote and protect their people's interests. They went to court to bring land claims, to defend treaty rights, to assert their sovereign rights to manage their reservation resources and protect their environments, and to clarify their right to define tribal membership.

Victories for Tribal Rights

Examples of these courtroom conflicts occurred all across the country. In Nevada, Northern Paiutes watched for decades as a dam across the Truckee River lowered water levels at Pyramid Lake, nearly destroying the rare cui-ui, the Lahontan trout on which the Paiutes had subsisted from time immemorial, and threatening to destroy the lake itself. In 1970 the Paiutes filed suit to have the water level restored and won their case. In Maine, the Penobscot and Passamaquoddy Indians brought suit for the return of about two-thirds of the state's land to the tribes (Map 9.3). The Indian Trade and Intercourse Act of 1790 declared that no transfers of Indian land were valid unless they had the approval of Congress, but none of the land sales that occurred in Maine after that date had been submitted for approval. If the United States was to respect its own laws, the Indians believed they had a watertight case. In 1980 President Jimmy Carter signed the Maine Indian Claims Settlement Act, paying the Indians $81.5 million in compensation for lands taken in contravention of the 1790 law. Also in 1980, the Supreme Court found in favor of the Sioux in the Black Hills case (see "The Sioux, the Treaty of Fort Laramie, and the Black Hills," pages 341–55). In both cases, however, Anglo-American justice was limited by its own remedies: Indian people who insisted that the land be returned saw the settlements as "selling out" ancestral lands.

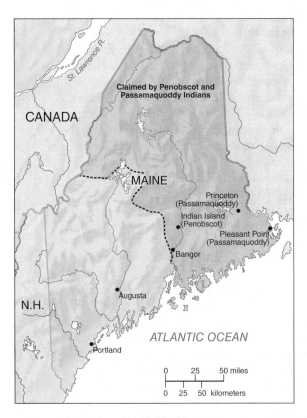

◆ **Map 9.3 Indian Land Claims in Maine**
The Penobscot and Passamaquoddy tribes claimed that about two-thirds of the state (roughly the area north and east of the line) had been taken from them illegally. In 1980 the tribes were paid $81.5 million in compensation.

The Indian Civil Rights Act of 1968 guaranteed tribal citizens many of the protections in the Bill of Rights. Some people feared that the Indian Civil Rights Act would erode the autonomy of tribal governments, but the Supreme Court declared in *Santa Clara Pueblo v. Martinez* (1978) that the act was enforceable in tribal courts; only persons detained by tribal law could seek relief in federal court. Santa Clara Pueblo was traditionally a matrilineal society but had adopted European patrilineal patterns of descent. In 1939 the tribal council passed an ordinance denying membership to the children of women who married outside the tribe, but granting it to the children of Santa Clara men who married outside. Julia Martinez, a Santa Clara woman, married a Navajo. Their children were subsequently denied membership in Santa Clara Pueblo. Martinez sued the tribe. The tribal council argued that the tribe had the right to establish its own membership criteria. The Supreme Court agreed, noting that Indian tribes were "distinct, independent political communities retaining their original natural rights in matters of local self-government" and that tribal governments "have the power to make their own substantive law in internal matters."[51] A tribe's right to determine its own membership is a crucial attribute of sovereignty. In 2012, Santa Clara took its own measures to redress the state of affairs when tribal members voted to change the membership rules.

The struggle for fishing rights that began with "fish-ins" in the 1960s produced some significant legal victories in the 1970s and 1980s. In 1973 the United States, representing fourteen tribes, sued the state of Washington over the issue of fishing rights. The next year, U.S. District Judge George Boldt ruled that Indians were entitled to catch up to 50 percent of the fish returning to "the usual and accustomed places" designated by the treaties of the 1850s. Non-Indian fishermen reacted to the *Boldt* decision, as it became known, in anger and disbelief: Judge Boldt was burned in effigy, and there were outbreaks of violence. A federal task force was appointed to try to avert a "fishing war" in Washington, but the struggle over fishing rights continued, even as most people came to realize that environmental destruction reduced the stakes. What good was the right to 50 percent of the harvest if there were no salmon to harvest, or if the fish that were caught were unfit to eat? The ripples from the *Boldt* decision went beyond Washington State and beyond fishing rights. "It changed the empty concept of 'tribal sovereignty' into something that needed to be taken seriously," wrote one journalist. "And it transformed the way state and tribal governments interact."[52]

To many Americans, it seemed that Indians were claiming and receiving special rights and privileges; non-Indians thought that Indians should be treated "just like everyone else." In 1983, for instance, the U.S. Court of Appeals for the Seventh Circuit upheld the claims of Wisconsin Anishinaabeg that the treaties they had signed guaranteed their right to continue hunting, fishing, and gathering in the areas ceded by those treaties. The *Voigt* decision generated a backlash among local fishermen, and there was racial violence every spring spearfishing season during the 1980s as Indians attempted to exercise their rights.[53] After the Penobscot and Passamaquoddy in Maine won a land settlement in 1980, several Iroquois tribes brought successful land claims cases in upstate New York. In 1985 the Oneida Nation won a significant victory when the courts declared that claims brought under the Trade and Intercourse Act were not barred by the passage of time, leaving the way open for the Oneidas to file suit. Land claims often put a cloud over property titles and generated a backlash among non-Indian property owners, most of whom bought their lands in good faith long after the Indians lost them and felt they were being punished for the sins of past generations. A common response was "the Indians sold the land, didn't they?"[54]

Tired of complaints that Indians enjoyed unfair privileges, Marge Anderson, chief executive of the Mille Lacs Band of Ojibwe in Minnesota, responded:

> When Indian incomes are level with yours, when our schools are as good as yours, our houses as warm, our kids as safe and our woods and streams as clean as yours, when our babies first open their eyes to a future as bright as yours, then we'll talk about level playing fields. Whether out of greed or out of racism or out of ignorance, there are always some who will go after Indian self-determination and economic development in ways as old as Columbus, as bold as Custer and as devious as any federal land grabber.[55]

Unfortunately for Indian people, one of the key figures "going after" Indian self-determination was Justice William Rehnquist of the U.S. Supreme Court. As chief justice, Rehnquist led the Court in a sustained assault on tribal sovereignty.

Chipping Away at Tribal Sovereignty

Reaching back to *Worcester v. Georgia* in 1832, the Supreme Court often "served as the conscience of federal Indian law, protecting tribal powers and rights against state action, unless and until Congress clearly states a contrary intention." After Congress and the executive branch embraced the policy of Indian self-determination, however, the Supreme Court emerged as the major threat to tribal sovereignty. Following in the wake of Indian court victories of the 1970s and early 1980s, and with conservative Republican appointees William Rehnquist, Anthony Kennedy, Sandra Day O'Connor, and Antonin G. Scalia on the bench, the Court tended to favor state sovereignty over tribal sovereignty and weakened the body of laws protecting Indian rights and liberties. Under Chief Justice Warren Burger (1969–85), the Supreme Court ruled in favor of Indians in 58 percent of the cases that came before it; under Chief Justice Rehnquist (1986 until his retirement in 2005), the Court ruled *against* Indians in 88 percent of cases. Rehnquist's record on the Court has been described as a systematic assault on Indian rights, based on a nineteenth-century discourse of Indian savagery and diminished rights.[56]

In *Oliphant v. Suquamish* (1978), with Judge Rehnquist writing for the majority, the Supreme Court struck down tribal jurisdiction over crimes committed by non-Indians on reservations (see "The Supreme Court and Tribal Sovereignty: The *Oliphant* Decision and Its Impact in Indian Country," pages 539–46). Subsequently, in *Duro v. Reina* (1990), the Court further limited the scope of tribal criminal jurisdiction, holding that a tribe's right to govern its own affairs does not include criminal jurisdiction over an Indian who is not a tribal member. Congress moved quickly to override the *Duro* decision in 1991 by passing legislation that affirmed the authority of tribes to exercise criminal jurisdiction over all Indians within their reservation. In 1981, in *Montana v. United States,* the

Supreme Court reversed a lower court ruling and declared that the Crow tribe did not have authority to regulate hunting and fishing by non-Indians on non-Indian-owned land within their reservation.

Congress passes laws, but the effect of those laws often depends on how the Supreme Court interprets them. The American Indian Religious Freedom Act of 1978 contained no enforcement provisions, and the declaration of policy did not translate into immediate and actual protection of Indian religious freedoms. Indians had to fight in court for the right to take eagle parts (federal law protects eagles as an endangered species) for religious ceremonies, to wear long hair or hold sweat lodges when in prison, and to protect sacred sites. In 1988, in *Lyng v. Northwest Indian Cemetery Protective Association,* the Supreme Court overturned a lower court injunction on the building of a logging road in the Six Rivers National Forest in California that the Yurok Indians argued would cause irreparable damage to sacred sites. In April 1990, in *Oregon v. Smith,* the case of two members of the Native American Church (NAC) who had been dismissed from their jobs by the Oregon Department of Education for using peyote, the U.S. Supreme Court ruled that state governments could prosecute people who used controlled substances as part of a religious ritual without violating their constitutional rights of religious freedom. The decision meant that hundreds of thousands of members of the Native American Church in twenty-two states became subject to arrest and imprisonment because of their form of worship; as NAC members pointed out, they now prayed in fear. Many Americans, Indian and non-Indian, saw the Court's decision as a major threat to Native American religion and to religious freedom in general. Ho-Chunk leader Reuben Snake Jr. organized a coalition and spent the last years of his life fighting to overturn the *Smith* decision. He died in 1993, just a year before Congress, responding to overwhelming public sentiment, passed the Native American Free Exercise of Religion Act in 1994, which protected Native American rights to use peyote in traditional religious ceremonies in all fifty states and strengthened the American Indian Religious Freedom Act.[57]

The Alaska Native Claims Settlement Act granted lands to Native villages in fee simple, but in 1998, in *Alaska v. Native Village of Venetie Tribal Government,* the Supreme Court ruled that Venetie's 1.8 million acres of fee simple land and the lands held by Native corporations were not "Indian country" and consequently the tribal government lacked authority to tax a non-Native contractor who was building a school in the village. The Rehnquist Court took such a consistently "anti-Indian" stance that some legal scholars feared it was pursuing a policy of "judicial termination."[58]

By the turn of the millennium, many Indian people and scholars of Indian law were convinced that the U.S. Supreme Court had abandoned its historic role and the foundations on which it had traditionally based its decisions in favor of an assault on the sovereignty of Indian tribes.[59] In 2001 the Supreme Court ruled in *Nevada v. Hicks* that tribes do not have civil jurisdiction over the conduct of state officials operating on the reservation, and, in *Atkinson Trading Company v. Shirley,* that the Navajo Nation had no right to tax non-Indian businesses operating on fee land within the reservation. President George W. Bush's nomination in 2005 of John Roberts Jr. to replace William Rehnquist as chief justice indicated that the conservative trend of Supreme Court decisions affecting Indian country would continue. Yet there were exceptions to the trend: in 2004, in what many tribes viewed as a major victory given the recent slate of Supreme Court decisions, the Court ruled that Congress has authority to recognize the inherent power of Indian tribes to prosecute nonmember Indians for certain crimes committed on reservations. *United States v. Lara,* a case involving an Indian from another reservation who punched a tribal police officer, could have removed tribes' jurisdiction over other Indians who came onto their reservations. Instead, the ruling overturned the 1990 *Duro v. Reina* decision, which held that tribes no longer had such power, and affirmed Congress's authority to enact the amendment known as the "Duro fix."[60]

In the middle of the twentieth century, legal scholar Felix S. Cohen wrote that "like the miner's canary, the Indian marks the shift from fresh air to poison gas in our political atmosphere, and our treatment of Indians, even more than our treatment of other minorities, reflects the rise and fall in our democratic faith."[61] At the end of the century, Frank Pommersheim, a law professor and appellate justice on the Rosebud Sioux and Cheyenne River Sioux reservations, reported that "the present ratio of fresh air to gas is not necessarily encouraging" and worried that there seemed to be "no national moral commitment to ensure that the fresh air will not dissipate further."[62] By 2010, with a new administration declaring its commitment to effect real change for Indian peoples, things were much improved, but the challenge implicit in Cohen's comment remained.

A NEW ERA IN WASHINGTON?

"New eras" in U.S.–Indian affairs are nothing new. Throughout the twentieth century, various presidents promised great changes during their administrations. Sometimes things improved; sometimes they got worse; Indian communities often noticed little difference. But in the first decade of the twenty-first century there were indications, in Washington, D.C., and in Indian country, that things were different this time, and that the United States and its first peoples had indeed entered a new era.

Changes at the BIA

On September 8, 2000, at a ceremony acknowledging the 175th anniversary of the Bureau of Indian Affairs, Assistant Secretary for Indian Affairs Kevin Gover delivered a historic speech. This was no time for celebration, said Gover, a Pawnee; "Rather it is a time for reflection and contemplation, a time for sorrowful truths to be spoken, a time for contrition." In an emotional review of U.S. Indian policy and the abuses visited upon Indian peoples, Gover announced, "We must first reconcile ourselves to the fact that the works of this agency have at various times profoundly harmed the communities it was meant to serve." These things occurred "despite the efforts of many good people with good hearts who sought to prevent them," and they continued to haunt Indian communities even when the BIA at long last began to serve as an advocate for Indian people. On behalf of the

BIA and its 10,000 employees, Gover extended a formal apology "for the historical conduct of this agency" and made a pledge to Indian people:

> Never again will this agency stand silent when hate and violence are committed against Indians. Never again will we allow policy to proceed from the assumption that Indians possess less human genius than the other races. Never again will we be complicit in the theft of Indian property. Never again will we appoint false leaders who serve purposes other than those of the tribes. Never again will we allow unflattering and stereotypical images of Indian people to deface the halls of government or lead the American people to shallow and ignorant beliefs about Indians. Never again will we attack your religions, your languages, your rituals, or any of your tribal ways. Never again will we seize your children, nor teach them to be ashamed of who they are. Never again.

Gover asked for healing and looked to a new era in which Indian people and the BIA would work together to meet the challenges of the modern world. Relatives from the Pawnee tribe sang songs of healing after the speech.[63]

Many people were moved by Gover's speech. Many Indian people were encouraged to think that the dark days finally were over and that real progress could now be made. But Gover could speak only for the BIA, not for the whole government, and he recognized the irony "that it took an American Indian to officially apologize to American Indians" for what non-Indians had done to them.[64] Tex Hall, then president of the National Congress of American Indians, cautioned that the apology would be meaningless unless it was accompanied by actions to correct past wrongs and continuing injustices. Just two years earlier, the U.S. Commission on Civil Rights had issued a report entitled "A Quiet Crisis: Federal Funding and Unmet Needs in Indian Country" that concluded: "Native Americans continue to rank at or near the bottom of nearly every social, health, and economic indicator."[65] If the federal government was going to make amends, it needed to undertake large-scale change and reparations in its support of Native people and communities. "Would Gover's pledge be yet another broken promise?" Or did his speech "signal a new era for the BIA and for Indian Country generally, coincident with the new millennium?"[66]

The BIA today is indeed a very different agency from that which carried out programs of cultural genocide in the nineteenth century. For one thing, it has the largest number of Native employees in its history, with American Indian or Alaska Native people constituting 90 percent of its staff. And the agency has endeavored to reform itself. In an effort to eradicate "excessive bureaucracy" and streamline the process by which tribes administer BIA and Indian Health Service funds, Congress passed the Indian Self-Determination Act Amendments of 1994, specifying the terms of contracts entered into by the federal government and tribal organizations. That same year, President Bill Clinton pledged to honor tribal sovereignty based on the government's "unique legal relationship with Native American tribal governments." The BIA role was becoming increasingly advisory, as Indian tribes assumed greater responsibility over their own affairs, developed their own businesses, and planned for their futures; the bureau itself experienced dramatic downsizing in the 1990s. "The role of the federal government should be to support and to implement tribally inspired solutions to tribally defined problems," said Ada Deer, whom Clinton appointed as the first woman assistant secretary for Indian affairs. "The days of federal paternalism are over."[67]

Nevertheless, in 1996 John Echohawk, executive director of the Native American Rights Fund, filed a class action suit against the secretary of the interior on behalf of half a million beneficiaries for the misuse of billions of dollars held in trust by the BIA. It became the largest class action suit ever certified against the U.S. government. The Indian Trust Fund was established in the late nineteenth century after the Allotment Act placed Indian lands in trust of the federal government (see "The Dawes Allotment Act [1887]," pages 385–89), and the disbursement of oil and gas royalties and other income from resources on Indian trust lands was assigned to the BIA. But the United States had no accurate accounting of the hundreds of thousands of Indian beneficiaries nor of the billions of dollars owed them. "The BIA has spent more than 100 years mismanaging, diverting and losing money that belongs to Indians," said Echohawk.

The plaintiff class (the lead plaintiff was Elouise Cobell, a member of the Blackfeet Indian Nation) demanded that the government account for deposits to and withdrawals from about 500,000 Individual Indian Money (IIM) accounts that it had set up over more than a century. These IIM accounts received (and continue to receive) revenue from the lease of land, oil, water, and timber assets that the government holds in trust for individual Indians. In many cases, the amounts paid to Indian beneficiaries had become miniscule because the assets had become fractioned among multiple holders through inheritance. Clearly, the government had been abusing its management of the accounts, and Indians weren't seeing the full profits of their leased assets. In 2001 the U.S. District Court of the District of Columbia ruled in the Indians' favor. The judge said the government was guilty of "fiscal and government irresponsibility in its purest form" and gave the Departments of the Interior and the Treasury five years to correct the situation.[68]

The Department of the Interior's failure to address the problems in a timely fashion, and charges of contempt of court leveled against several secretaries of the Interior and the Treasury, left many people feeling that it was "business as usual" at the BIA. Senator Ben Nighthorse Campbell, a Cheyenne from Colorado, commented, "There seems to be an institutional rot that does not seem to go away."[69]

The case of *Cobell v. Salazar* dragged on for fourteen years, spanned the tenure of three presidents, and involved four secretaries of the interior as defendants (it was formerly *Cobell v. Babbitt, Cobell v. Norton,* and *Cobell v. Kempthorne*). The original claim was for $137 billion.[70] Finally, in December 2009 the Department of the Interior negotiated a settlement by which the government agreed to pay $3.4 billion ($1.4 billion, minus attorney's fees, in payments to plaintiffs through an Accounting/Trust Administration Fund and $2 billion to establish a Trust Land Consolidation Fund for the repurchase of lands from willing sellers) and to create an Indian Education Scholarship fund of up to $60 million. Cobell pointed out that the settlement was significantly less than what Indians were owed and would not solve the underlying problems, but she acknowledged that it was the best solution likely. She called on the Obama administration to honor its promises to improve education, law enforcement, and economic conditions in Indian country. "We have spent too much time looking backward, trying to address the terrible wrongs of the past," she said. "Now it is my hope we can move forward."[71] The House and Senate approved the settlement in November 2010, and the following month President Obama signed the Claims Resolution Act that appropriated the funds for the settlement. Elouise Cobell died in 2011.

Repatriation and a New Museum

For generations, soldiers, tourists, scientists, and collectors had looted Indian country of material culture and human remains. Museums had put Indian artifacts and even Indian bones on display without regard to Indian peoples' feelings about the significance of the objects or the offensiveness of the displays. The 1906 Antiquities Act and the 1979 Archaeological Resources Protection Act declared Indian bones and objects found on federal land the property of the United States, and between 600,000 and 2 million skeletal remains were housed in museums, laboratories, historical societies, and universities across the country. The Smithsonian Institution alone held the remains of about 18,500 Native American people. Archaeologists and anthropologists studied Indian bones to learn about diet, mortuary customs, levels of health, and causes of death, but most Indian people regarded this as continuing exploitation and a denial of their status as human beings.

In the 1970s, Indian activists began to challenge the right of non-Indian museums to hold religious and other artifacts and skeletal remains of Indian people, and they actively sought the repatriation of those items. In the 1980s, the Pawnees waged a bitter fight to recover ancestral remains from the Nebraska State Historical Society and other repositories. Pawnee people believed that many of their social problems stemmed from the disturbance of graves and demanded ceremonial reburial of the bones to free the spirits of their ancestors by returning them to the earth. Some scholars argued that this would be a terrible loss to science, but public opinion favored the Indians' position that it was a question of basic human decency — their grandparents should be left to rest in peace — and the state returned the bones for reburial.

The Zunis of New Mexico demanded the return of carved wooden war gods from museums and private collections. They pointed out that since the war gods are communally owned and cannot be sold or given away, any war gods that have been removed from their proper shrines must be stolen property. "They are the spiritual guardians of the Zuni People. When they are removed from their shrines Zuni religious leaders cannot pray to them, and their vast powers cause fires, earthquakes, wars, storms, and wanton destruction in our world."[72] Once recovered, the gods could be placed in the desert and continue the cycle of decay back to the earth. The Iroquois demanded the return of twelve wampum belts from the New York State Museum, arguing that these were the tribal archives and belonged in Onondaga (where the records of the Iroquois Confederacy were kept), not on display in Albany. The twelve belts were restored to Onondaga chiefs in a ceremony in Albany in 1989.

In 1989 Congress passed a law requiring the Smithsonian Institution to return most of its skeletal remains and grave goods to Indian communities. In 1990 President George H. W. Bush signed into law the Native American Grave Protection and Repatriation Act (NAGPRA), requiring all institutions receiving federal funds to inventory their collections of Indian artifacts and human remains, share the lists with Indian tribes, and return, when appropriate, the items the tribes requested.

Some individuals and institutions complied reluctantly with the legislation. Contentious issues remain, as illustrated by the continuing controversy over the disposition of the skeletal remains of Kennewick Man (see page 20) — in 2010 the Department of the Interior added new regulations to NAGPRA that allowed tribes to claim "even those remains whose affiliation cannot be established scientifically, as long as they were found on or near the tribe's aboriginal lands."[73] In 2006 it was reported that Geronimo's skull was among those that had been disinterred and taken to the secret Skull and Bones society at Yale University. In 2009, the centennial of Geronimo's death, his descendants sued Skull and Bones as part of a lawsuit seeking to recover all of Geronimo's remains, wherever they may be, and have them returned to New Mexico for reburial at the headwaters of the Gila River, Geronimo's birthplace.[74] In general, however, public opinion and national law have come to agree that human remains and religious objects should be returned to their original communities and not be pored over by anthropologists or displayed for tourists.

Museums and Indians have had a troubled history. As repositories of the art and artifacts of the Native peoples of this continent, museums were colonial institutions that put Native people and their cultures on display. They usually depicted Indians as frozen in time and as a vanished or vanishing race, and they sometimes housed human remains and sacred objects. Until relatively recently, most museums collected, managed, and displayed objects with little or no concern for how those objects should be treated or for the communities from which they came. NAGPRA initiated a new era of more collaborative relations with Native peoples and greater sensitivity to Native concerns about what should and should not be displayed. But museums have remained, essentially, white institutions displaying Native objects for non-Native audiences.[75]

The National Museum of the American Indian (NMAI) was conceived to be different. In 1989 Congressman Ben Nighthorse Campbell (Northern Cheyenne) of Colorado and Senator Daniel Inouye of Hawaii introduced a bill and Congress established the NMAI, a tribute to the Native peoples of the Americas, to be built on the last available site on the National Mall in Washington, D.C. W. Richard West Jr., a Southern Cheyenne from Oklahoma and a Washington lawyer with a law degree from Stanford, was appointed the museum's founding director. Douglas Cardinal, a Métis/Blackfeet architect whose previous works included the Canadian Museum of Civilization in Ottawa, was hired to design the building. The project required raising $219 million in private funding, with $30 million donated by "gaming tribes" (see pages 594–99) — the Mashantucket Pequots and Mohegans in Connecticut and the Oneidas in New York. It was, to say the least, an ambitious undertaking.

◆ **National Museum of the American Indian**
Built from earth-colored textured limestone, the NMAI
stands out against the other imposing buildings on the
Mall. It is five stories high and covers 250,000 square
feet. Facing east, set in its own landscape that includes
four habitats — forest, wetland, meadow, and croplands
where the "sacred three sisters" (corn, beans, and squash)
are grown using traditional agricultural techniques — the
museum is designed to reflect both the ancient and contemporary presence of Native peoples. *J. Scott Applewhite/
AP Photo.*

The NMAI opened on September
21, 2004. More than 25,000 people from
more than 500 Native nations attended
the opening ceremony and walked in
a huge procession down the Mall to
the new museum. It was the largest
gathering ever of American Indians
in the nation's capital. In his speech
at the museum's opening, W. Richard
West Jr. noted that "once in a great
while, something so important and so
powerful occurs that, just for a moment, history seems to stand still — and
silent — in honor." For centuries, Native peoples had struggled to survive
"the cruel and destructive edge of colonialism." Now the NMAI stood as
a symbol of hope "that the hearts and
minds of all Americans, beyond this
museum and throughout the Americas,
will open and welcome the presence
of the first peoples in their history and
in their contemporary lives," and that,
at long last, the "different histories,
cultures, and peoples of the Americas
can come together in new mutual understanding and respect."[76] Part of the
agenda of the NMAI was to counter
the effects of the past agendas of other
museums. It would be international
in scope. It would recognize the deep
history of the Native peoples of this
continent yet at the same time provide a
forum for celebrating and sharing living
Native cultures. It would acknowledge
the catastrophic consequences of contact and colonization, but its emphasis
would be on survival and achievement
rather than tragedy and demise. Museum curators would work with Native communities in setting up exhibits. It would house more than 800,000 objects, but it would
also be a gathering place for Native people and a stage for dances, demonstrations,
film screenings, lectures, and other live performances. It would give voice to Native
peoples in a place where they had seldom been heard. It was to be a Native space, "a
museum that is more than a museum . . . a living place bearing witness."[77] The challenge was to create the landscape, the buildings, and the exhibits to match the vision.

The museum and its opening received mixed reviews in the press. Some reporters did not know what to make of Indian people wearing traditional regalia while chatting on cell phones.[78] Critics complained that the exhibits were flat; not sufficiently scientific, challenging, or educational; and too uniformly positive. They believed that the NMAI ran the risk of replacing old stereotypes with new ones. James Lujan, a writer and filmmaker from Taos Pueblo, asked whom the museum was for, really. Its main message is "we're still here," but since Lujan and other Native people know that already, "it logically follows that the museum was built for those who don't know." While he hoped the non-Native public would learn something, "All I know is that I didn't."[79] Other people felt there was not enough attention to conquest, colonization, and catastrophe. If the theme was the survival of Native peoples and cultures, wasn't the NMAI missing an opportunity to educate the public about what Native peoples have survived?[80]

Richard West envisioned the NMAI as a meeting ground where the public would see the connection between the cultural origins of this hemisphere and what happened in the past five hundred years "in a way where some kind of real understanding can occur that sets the stage for cultural reconciliation over a long haul."[81] As Amy Lonetree points out, the NMAI confronts "centuries of unresolved trauma" as it tells the stories of Native peoples. Within the limits of its exhibition spaces, it must honor indigenous worldviews, challenge stereotypes, and convey the brutal histories of the past five hundred years.[82] To what extent the museum can foster understanding and reconciliation remains to be seen.

A New Embassy and a New "White Father"

In the first week of November 2009, two historic events with great potential significance for Native America took place in Washington, D.C.: the opening of the Tribal Nations Embassy and a Tribal Nations conference with a new president who vowed to work with the tribes "to bring about meaningful change." Some tribes already had offices and ambassadors in the nation's capital, but the National Congress of American Indians had worked for years to establish an embassy for all the tribes it represents. In early 2009 the NCAI was able to purchase a building in Washington, and on November 3, 2009, tribal representatives, administration officials, members of Congress, and international dignitaries gathered for the ceremonial opening of the Embassy of Tribal Nations. "For the first time since settlement," NCAI president Jefferson Keel, a Chickasaw, explained, "tribal nations will have a permanent home in Washington, D.C., where they can more effectively assert their sovereign status and facilitate a much stronger nation-to-nation relationship with the federal government."[83]

Two days later President Barack Obama hosted a Tribal Nations conference with almost four hundred tribal leaders. He described it as a "unique and historic event, the largest and most widely attended gathering of tribal leaders in our history." During the 2008 election, Obama had campaigned in Indian country more than any other presidential candidate. Many Indian people worked for his campaign. Obama was adopted into the Crow Nation, and he joked about whether, as an African American, he would fit the role of the "Great White Father." His victory at the polls in November signaled a renewal of hope for Native Americans after eight years of Republican government in Washington.

A year after the election, in his address to the conference delegates, Obama acknowledged the sorry record of U.S.–Indian relations: "it's a history marked by violence and disease and deprivation. Treaties were violated. Promises were broken. You were told your lands, your religion, your cultures, your languages were not yours to keep." He acknowledged the appalling conditions in many areas of Indian country: "some of your reservations face unemployment rates of up to 80 percent. Roughly a quarter of all Native Americans live in poverty. More than 14 percent of all reservation homes don't have electricity. And 12 percent don't have access to a safe water supply." To ensure that Native Americans would have a seat at the table when important decisions that affected their lives were made, Obama announced several new appointments: Kimberley Teehee, a Cherokee, would serve as his Native American policy advisor; Jodi Archambault Gillette, a Standing Rock Sioux as well as an Ivy League graduate (and an accomplished powwow dancer), was appointed deputy associate director of the Office of Intergovernmental Affairs, the first Native American to serve as White House liaison with the more than 560 Indian tribes in the United States (she later moved to the Department of the Interior as deputy assistant secretary for policy and economic development); and Larry Echo Hawk, a Pawnee, was named assistant secretary for Indian affairs. President Obama directed relevant federal agencies to hold "listening sessions" on American Indian and Alaska Native issues around the country and to submit detailed plans within ninety days of how they intended to improve tribal consultation and collaboration. He committed $3 billion of the Recovery Act to help address some of the most pressing needs in Indian country: $100 million to spur job creation in tribal economies; $500 million to modernize the Indian Health Service; $170 million for Indian education; and $277 million for Indian school construction, along with budget increases for the BIA, the IHS, and tribal colleges. He looked forward to enacting health insurance reform, developing clean energy sources such as wind and solar power on reservations, and working with tribes to increase safety and reduce violent crime on reservations. "The shocking and contemptible fact that one in three Native American women will be raped in their lifetimes," declared the president, "is an assault on our national conscience that we can no longer ignore."

Obama ended by saying: "I know you've heard this song from Washington before. I know you've often heard grand promises that sound good but rarely materialize. And each time you're told, 'this time will be different.'" But this time, he assured them, it would be different: "you will not be forgotten so long as I'm in this White House."[84]

DOCUMENTS

A Woman's View from Wounded Knee

·•·✕✕✕✕✕✕✕◆✕✕✕✕✕✕✕·•·

B ORN MARY BRAVE BIRD ON THE ROSEBUD RESERVATION in South Dakota, Mary Crow Dog grew up with no father and did not get along with her mother. Home was a one-room cabin without electricity or running water. Mary described herself as "a natural-born rebel," and so she had a hard time at the St. Francis Boarding School, where the Catholic nuns beat the children for disobedience. "At age ten," she said, "I could drink and hold a pint of whiskey." At age twelve the nuns beat her for holding hands with a boy. At age fifteen she was raped. The reservation communities "were places without hope where bodies and souls were being destroyed bit by bit." Schools left many of the students illiterate; there were few jobs. Poverty and hopelessness seemed to be everywhere. Looking back, it seemed that her early life "was just one endless, vicious circle of drinking and fighting, drinking and fighting."[85] Then she met Leonard Crow Dog and went to Wounded Knee.

"The American Indian Movement hit our reservation like a tornado," Mary said, "like a new wind blowing out of nowhere, a drumbeat from far off getting louder and louder."[86] As militant young Indians from the cities joined forces with older traditional leaders on the reservations, the movement grew in scope and gathered momentum. The tribal chairman at Pine Ridge, Richard Wilson (see page 506), and his heavily armed henchmen or GOONs (Guardians of the Oglala Nation) braced for a confrontation. Federal marshals and FBI agents arrived on the scene. Without really knowing why, Mary joined a caravan of cars headed for Pine Ridge. The events that followed changed her life. Her account, written years later, gives a sense of what the movement meant to young people like her. It also proves a unique perspective from within the compound during the siege at Wounded Knee from a woman who took a stand there and gave birth there.

MARY CROW DOG
I Would Have My Baby at Wounded Knee (1991)

. . . It began to dawn upon me that what was about to happen, and what I personally would

SOURCE: Mary Crow Dog and Richard Erdoes, *Lakota Woman* (New York: Harper Perennial, 1991), 123–26, 130–32, 137–38. Copyright © 1990 by Mary Crow Dog and Richard Erdoes. Used by permission of Grove/Atlantic, Inc. Any third-party use of this material outside of this publication is prohibited.

be involved in, would be unlike anything I had witnessed before. I think everybody who was there felt the same way—an excitement that was choking our throats. But there was still no definite plan for what to do. We had all assumed that we would go to Pine Ridge town, the administrative center of the reservation, the seat of Wilson's and the government's power. We had always thought that the fate of the Oglalas would be settled there. But as the talks progressed it became clear that nobody wanted us to storm Pine Ridge, garrisoned as it was by the goons, the marshals, and the FBI. We did not want to be slaughtered. There had been too many massacred Indians already in our history. But if not Pine Ridge, then what? As I remember, it was the older women like Ellen Moves Camp and Gladys Bissonette who first pronounced the magic words "Wounded Knee," who said, "Go ahead and make your stand at Wounded Knee. If you men won't do it, you can stay here and talk for all eternity and we women will do it."

When I heard the words "Wounded Knee" I became very, very serious. Wounded Knee — Cankpe Opi in our language — has a special meaning for our people. There is the long ditch into which the frozen bodies of almost three hundred of our people, mostly women and children, were thrown like so much cordwood. And the bodies are still there in their mass grave, unmarked except for a cement border. Next to the ditch, on a hill, stands the white-painted Catholic church, gleaming in the sunlight, the monument of an alien faith imposed upon the landscape. And below it flows Cankpe Opi Wakpala, the creek along which the women and children were hunted down like animals by Custer's old Seventh, out to avenge themselves for their defeat by butchering the helpless ones. That happened long ago, but no Sioux ever forgot it.

Wounded Knee is part of our family's history. Leonard's great-grandfather, the first Crow Dog, had been one of the leaders of the Ghost Dancers. He and his group had held out in the icy ravines of the Badlands all winter, but when the soldiers came in force to kill all the Ghost Dancers he surrendered his band to avoid having his people killed. Old accounts describe how Crow Dog simply sat down between the rows of soldiers on one side, and the Indians on the other, all ready and eager to start shooting. He had covered himself with a blanket and was just sitting there. Nobody knew what to make of it. The leaders on both sides were so puzzled that they just did not get around

to opening fire. They went to Crow Dog, lifted the blanket, and asked him what he meant to do. He told them that sitting there with the blanket over him was the only thing he could think of to make all the hotheads, white and red, curious enough to forget fighting. Then he persuaded his people to lay down their arms. Thus he saved his people just a few miles away from where Big Foot and his band were massacred. And old Uncle Dick Fool Bull, a relative of both the Crow Dogs and my own family, often described to me how he himself heard the rifle and cannon shots that mowed our people down when he was a little boy camping only two miles away. He had seen the bodies, too, and described to me how he had found the body of a dead baby girl with an American flag beaded on her tiny bonnet.°

Before we set out for Wounded Knee, Leonard and Wallace Black Elk prayed for all of us with their pipe. I counted some fifty cars full of people. We went right through Pine Ridge. The half-bloods and goons, the marshals and the government snipers on their rooftop, were watching us, expecting us to stop and start a confrontation, but our caravan drove right by them, leaving them wondering. From Pine Ridge it was only eighteen miles more to our destination. Leonard was in the first car and I was way in the back.

Finally, on February 27, 1973, we stood on the hill where the fate of the old Sioux Nation, Sitting Bull's and Crazy Horse's nation, had been decided, and where we, ourselves, came face to face with our fate. We stood silently, some of us wrapped in our blankets, separated by our personal thoughts and feelings, and yet united, shivering a little with excitement and the chill of a fading winter. You could almost hear our heartbeats.

It was not cold on this next-to-last day of February — not for a South Dakota February anyway. Most of us had not even bothered to wear gloves. I could feel a light wind stirring my hair, blowing it gently about my face. There were a few snowflakes in the air. We all felt the presence of

---

° See the flag bonnet pictured on page 335.

the spirits of those lying close by in the long ditch, wondering whether we were about to join them, wondering when the marshals would arrive. We knew that we would not have to wait long for them to make their appearance.

The young men tied eagle feathers to their braids, no longer unemployed kids, juvenile delinquents, or winos, but warriors. I thought of our old warrior societies — the Kit Foxes, the Strong Hearts, the Badgers, the Dog Soldiers. The Kit Foxes — the Tokalas — used to wear long sashes. In the midst of battle, a Tokala would sometimes dismount and pin the end of his sash to the earth. By this he signified his determination to stay and fight on his chosen spot until he was dead, or until a friend rode up and unpinned him, or until victory. Young or old, men or women, we had all become Kit Foxes, and Wounded Knee had become the spot upon which we had pinned ourselves. Soon we would be encircled and there could be no retreat. I could not think of anybody or anything that would "unpin" us. Somewhere out on the prairie surrounding us, the forces of the government were gathering, the forces of the greatest power on earth. Then and there I decided that I would have my baby at Wounded Knee, no matter what. . . .

Wounded Knee lasted seventy-one long days. These days were not all passed performing heroic deeds or putting up media shows for the reporters. Most of the time was spent in boredom, just trying to keep warm and finding something to eat. Wounded Knee was a place one got scared in occasionally, a place in which people made love, got married Indian style, gave birth, and died. The oldest occupants were over eighty, the youngest under eight. It was a heyoka place, a place of sacred clowns who laughed while they wept. A young warrior standing up in the middle of a firefight to pose for the press; Russell Means telling the photographers, "Be sure to get my good side."

We organized ourselves. The biggest room in the store became the community hall. A white man's home, the only house with heat and tap water, became the hospital, and women were running it. The museum became the security office. We all took turns doing the cooking, sewing shirts, and making sleeping bags for the men in bunkers. We embroidered the words "Wounded Knee" on rainbow-colored strips of cloth. Everybody got one of those as a badge of honor, "to show your grandchildren sometime," as Dennis [Banks] said. We shared. We did things for each other. At one time a white volunteer nurse berated us for doing the slave work while the men got all the glory. We were betraying the cause of womankind, was the way she put it. We told her that her kind of women's lib was a white, middle-class thing, and that at this critical stage we had other priorities. Once our men had gotten their rights and their balls back, we might start arguing with them about who should do the dishes. But not before.

Actually, our women played a major part at Wounded Knee. We had two or three pistol-packing mamas swaggering around with six-shooters dangling at their hips, taking their turns on the firing line, swapping lead with the feds. The Indian nurses bringing in the wounded under a hail of fire were braver than many warriors. The men also did their share of the dirty work. . . .

For a while I stayed at the trading post. But it was too much for me. Too many people and too little privacy. I figured that I would have my baby within two weeks. I moved into a trailer house at the edge of Wounded Knee. By then daily exchanges of fire had become commonplace. The bullets were flying as I got bigger and bigger. One day the government declared a cease-fire so that the women and children could leave. One of the AIM leaders came up to me: "You're leaving. You're pregnant, so you've got to go." I told him, "No, I won't. If I'm going to die, I'm going to die here. All that means anything to me is right here. I have nothing to live for out there." . . .

Again I come back to the old Cheyenne saying: "A nation is not lost as long as the hearts of its women are not on the ground." As the siege went on our women became stronger. One bunker was held by a married couple. When the husband was hit by several bullets, the wife insisted on holding the position alone. Women "manning" a bunker got into a two-way radio argument with some marshals. The girls finally took up a megaphone, shouting across no-man's-land so that everybody could hear: "If you SOBs don't shut up, we'll call in the men!" One girl got hit in the white church. A bullet ricocheted and grazed her hand. It was just a flesh wound. She went on as if nothing had happened. During a firefight there was one young woman in particular who held off seven marshals while some of the men got behind shelter. All she had was an old pistol. She used that to scare them off. That was Gray Fox's wife. She was really good with a gun. I guess some of the men did not like her because of that. Especially, I think, those who scrambled to safety while she covered them.

One of the good things that happened to me at Wounded Knee was getting to know Annie Mae Aquash, a Mi'kmaq Indian from Nova Scotia who became my close friend.[87] She was a remarkable woman, strong-hearted and strong-minded, who had a great influence upon my thinking and outlook on life. I first noticed her when an argument arose among some of the women. One group, as I remember, called themselves the "Pie Patrol." Why, I do not know. There were no pies and they did not do much patrolling as far as I could see. They were loud-mouth city women, very media conscious, hugging the limelight. They were bossy, too, trying to order us around. They were always posing for photographers and TV crews, getting all the credit and glory while we did the shit work, scrubbing dishes or making sleeping bags out of old jackets.

Annie Mae gave these women a piece of her mind and I took her side. So we hit it off right away and became instant buddies. Annie Mae taught me a lot. She could make something out of nothing. She made nice meals with seemingly no provisions except dried beans and yellow peas. After I gave birth she made a tiny Wounded Knee patch for little Pedro. She was older than I and already a mother, divorced from a husband whose heart was not big enough for her. Annie Mae found among us Sioux an Indian culture her own tribe had lost. She was always saying, "If I'm going to die, I'm going to die. I have to die sometime. It might as well be here where I'd die for a reason." She had a premonition that her militancy would bring her a violent death, and in this she was right. She had heard the call of the owl. . . .

. . . It is not always wise for an Indian woman to come on too strong. Annie Mae was found dead in the snow at the bottom of a ravine on the Pine Ridge Reservation. The police said that she had died of exposure, but there was a .38-caliber slug in her head. The FBI cut off her hands and sent them to Washington for fingerprint identification, hands that had helped my baby come into the world. . . .°

° In 2003 two former members of AIM were indicted for Anna Mae Aquash's murder. Fritz Arlo Looking Cloud was sentenced to life in prison; John Graham, living in Vancouver, was extradited to the United States, stood trial in 2010, and was sentenced to life in prison. In 2008 a federal grand jury indicted Vine Richard Marshall, Russell Means's bodyguard at the time, with aiding and abetting the murder. Marshall was found not guilty.

QUESTIONS FOR CONSIDERATION

1. What does Mary Crow Dog's account reveal about relations between men and women in Sioux society and in the community at Wounded Knee?

2. Why did AIM appeal to people of Mary's generation and background?

3. What role does history play in the occupation at Wounded Knee?

The Supreme Court and Tribal Sovereignty: The *Oliphant* Decision and Its Impact in Indian Country

P RESIDENT NIXON'S MESSAGE TO CONGRESS in 1970 seemed to mark a new era of optimism for Indian peoples. Nixon clearly rejected past federal policies of paternalism and termination and espoused a policy of self-determination as beneficial to Indian peoples and to the nation as a whole. In the years between Nixon's address and the Supreme Court decision in *Oliphant v. Suquamish* in 1978, some of the promise contained in Nixon's message was realized. Important new legislation passed through Congress, and Indian communities took significant steps in managing programs, running their own schools, and exerting political influence, both within Congress and through the media. They even won some landmark victories in American courts.

But tribal sovereignty — the rights of Indian nations to govern themselves — remained vulnerable. A nation's self-government includes the right to make and impose one's own laws, both on one's own citizens and on outsiders who enter the nation. In Indian country, this became a complicated and contentious issue as more and more non-Indians took up residence within reservation boundaries. On many reservations, allotment had created a checkerboard pattern of land holding, with non-Indians living alongside Indians. Further sales and leases, migrations of Indians to the cities, and intermarriage brought more non-Indians on to reservations, with the result that by the late twentieth century some reservations contained more non-Indian than Indian residents. What was their legal status? Were they subject to tribal law, even though they were not tribal citizens? Did someone fall under tribal law the moment they stepped on to the reservation? If not, how could tribes regulate and police their own communities? More and more cases challenging Indian sovereignty in this respect reached the Supreme Court.

Mark Oliphant, a non-Indian who assaulted a tribal police officer on the Port Madison Reservation of the Suquamish tribe near Seattle, was arrested by the tribal authorities. The reservation was small, and non-Indian residents heavily outnumbered Indian residents. Oliphant challenged the tribe's authority to prosecute him, arguing in federal court that, as a non-Indian, he was immune from tribal law and subject only to state or federal law. The Marshall cases in the 1830s seemed to have made clear that Indian tribes are "distinct political communities, having territorial boundaries, within which their authority is exclusive," but the Supreme Court now found new limits on tribal sovereignty. Overturning the rulings of lower courts, the Supreme Court decided that tribal courts do *not* have criminal jurisdiction over non-Indians. The ruling applied not only to small reservations such as that of the Suquamish, where Indian residents were in a minority, but to all Indian country.

The *Oliphant* decision has been strongly criticized by both Native and non-Native legal scholars as a calculated assault on Indian tribes' inherent powers of self-government. Many see it as "result oriented"; that is, the Court intended from the outset to limit tribal sovereignty and used shaky evidence and faulty legal reasoning to do so. In the assessment of attorney and professor Bruce Duthu, the *Oliphant* case took a local level conflict between a private citizen and an Indian tribe, turned it into "a collision of framework interests between two sovereigns, and in the process revived the most negative and destructive aspects of colonialism as it relates to Indian rights." It transformed the nature of litigation in Indian country "by elevating challenges to the exercise of tribal power into challenges about the very *existence* of tribal power." Peter Maxfield, a non-Indian law professor at the University of Wyoming, not accustomed to making extreme statements, concluded: "The justification that the Court used to reach its result can only be characterized as reprehensible." Robert Williams Jr. goes further: "*Oliphant,* as written by Rehnquist, cites, quotes, and relies upon racist nineteenth-century beliefs and stereotypes to justify an expansive, rights-destroying, present-day interpretation of the Marshall model." Indians could not possibly have been imagined to possess the power to police non-Indians because they were viewed as lawless and uncivilized. It was, Williams concludes, "one of the worst Supreme Court Indian rights decisions of the twentieth century, or any century for that matter."[88] As Bruce Duthu argued in a *New York Times* editorial (reprinted in this section), by stripping away the tribes' powers to prosecute non-Indians who commit crimes on reservations, the Supreme Court seriously compromised the ability of Indian nations to protect their own citizens and rendered Native women increasingly vulnerable to sexual violence.

Supreme Court of the United States
Oliphant v. Suquamish Indian Tribe (1978)

Mr. Justice Rehnquist delivered the opinion of the Court.

. . . Located on Puget Sound across from the city of Seattle, the Port Madison Reservation [of the Suquamish tribe] is a checkerboard of tribal community land, allotted Indian lands, property held in fee-simple by non-Indians, and various roads and public highways maintained by Kitsap County.[1]

The Suquamish Indians are governed by a tribal government which in 1973 adopted a Law and Order Code. The Code, which covers a variety of offenses from theft to rape, purports to extend the Tribe's criminal jurisdiction over both Indians and non-Indians. Proceedings are held in the

which no persons reside. Residing on the reservation is an estimated population of approximately 2,928 non-Indians living in 976 dwelling units. There live on the reservation approximately 50 members of the Suquamish Indian Tribe. Within the reservation are numerous public highways of the State of Washington, public schools, public utilities and other facilities in which neither the Suquamish Indian Tribe nor the United States has any ownership or interest."

---

1. According to the District Court's findings of fact, "[T]he Port Madison Indian Reservation consists of approximately 7,276 acres of which approximately 63% thereof is owned in fee-simple absolute by non-Indians and the remainder 37% is Indian-owned lands subject to the trust status of the United States, consisting mostly of unimproved acreage upon

---

Source: 425 U.S. 191, 98 S.Ct. 1011, 55 L. Ed. 2d. 209. Reprinted from David H. Getches, Charles F. Wilkinson, and Robert A. Williams Jr., *Cases and Materials on Federal Indian Law,* 4th ed. (St. Paul, Minn.: West Group, 1998), 532–39. Used with permission of Thomson Reuters.

Suquamish Indian Provisional Court. Pursuant to the Indian Civil Rights Act of 1968, 25 U.S.C. § 1302, defendants are entitled to many of the due process protections accorded to defendants in federal or state criminal proceedings. However, the guarantees are not identical. Non-Indians, for example, are excluded from Suquamish tribal court juries.

Both petitioners are non-Indian residents of the Port Madison Reservation. Petitioner Mark David Oliphant was arrested by tribal authorities during the Suquamish's annual Chief Seattle Days celebration and charged with assaulting a tribal officer and resisting arrest. After arraignment before the tribal court, Oliphant was released on his own recognizance. Petitioner Daniel B. Belegarde was arrested by tribal authorities after an alleged high-speed race along the reservation highways that only ended when Belegarde collided with a tribal police vehicle. Belegarde posted bail and was released. Six days later he was arraigned and charged under the tribal code with "recklessly endangering another person" and injuring tribal property. Tribal court proceedings against both petitioners have been stayed pending a decision in this case. . . .

I

Respondents do not contend that their exercise of criminal jurisdiction over non-Indians stems from affirmative congressional authorization or treaty provision. Instead, respondents urge that such jurisdiction flows automatically from the "Tribe's retained inherent powers of government over the Port Madison Indian Reservation." . . .

The Suquamish Indian Tribe does not stand alone today in its assumption of criminal jurisdiction over non-Indians. Of the 127 reservation court systems that currently exercise criminal jurisdiction in the United States, 33 purport to extend that jurisdiction to non-Indians. . . .

The effort by Indian tribal courts to exercise criminal jurisdiction over non-Indians, however, is a relatively new phenomenon. And where the effort has been made in the past, it has been held that the jurisdiction did not exist. Until the middle of this century, few Indian tribes maintained any

semblance of a formal court system. Offenses by one Indian against another were usually handled by social and religious pressure and not by formal judicial processes; emphasis was on restitution rather than on punishment. In 1834 the Commissioner of Indian Affairs described the then status of Indian criminal systems: "With the exception of two or three tribes, who have within a few years past attempted to establish some few laws and regulations amongst themselves, the Indian tribes are without laws, and the chiefs without much authority to exercise any restraint." H.R.Rep. No. 474, 23d Cong., 1st Sess., at 91 (1834).

It is therefore not surprising to find no specific discussion of the problem before us in the volumes of United States Reports. But the problem did not lie entirely dormant for two centuries. A few tribes during the 19th century did have formal criminal systems. From the earliest treaties with these tribes, it was apparently assumed that the tribes did not have criminal jurisdiction over non-Indians absent a congressional statute or treaty provision to that effect. For example, the 1830 Treaty with the Choctaw Indian Tribe, which had one of the most sophisticated of tribal structures, guaranteed to the Tribe "the jurisdiction and government of all the persons and property that may be within their limits." Despite the broad terms of this governmental guarantee, however, the Choctaws at the conclusion of this treaty provision "express a *wish* that Congress *may grant* to the Choctaws the right of punishing by their own laws any white man who shall come into their nation, and infringe any of their national regulations." Such a request for affirmative congressional authority is inconsistent with respondents' belief that criminal jurisdiction over non-Indians is inherent in tribal sovereignty. Faced by attempts of the Choctaw Tribe to try non-Indian offenders in the early 1800s the United States Attorneys General also concluded that the Choctaws did not have criminal jurisdiction over non-Indians absent congressional authority. See 2 Opinions of the Attorney General 693 (1834); 7 Opinions of the Attorney General 174 (1855). . . .

At least one court has previously considered the power of Indian courts to try non-Indians and it also held against jurisdiction. . . . *Ex parte Kenyon,* 14 Fed. Cases 353 (WD Ark. 1878). . . .

The conclusion of Judge Parker was reaffirmed only recently in a 1970 Opinion of the Solicitor of the Department of the Interior. See 77 I.D. 113 (1970).

While Congress was concerned almost from its beginning with the special problems of law enforcement on the Indian reservations, it did not initially address itself to the problem of tribal jurisdiction over non-Indians. For the reasons previously stated, there was little reason to be concerned with assertions of tribal court jurisdiction over non-Indians because of the absence of formal tribal judicial systems. . . .

It was in 1834 that Congress was first directly faced with the prospect of Indians trying non-Indians. In the Western Territory Bill, Congress proposed to create an Indian territory beyond the western-directed destination of the settlers; the territory was to be governed by a confederation of Indian tribes and was expected ultimately to become a State of the Union. While the bill would have created a political territory with broad governing powers, Congress was careful not to give the tribes of the territory criminal jurisdiction over United States officials and citizens traveling through the area. The reasons were quite practical:

> Officers, and persons in the service of the United States, and persons required to reside in the Indian country by treaty stipulation, must necessarily be placed under the protection, and subject to the laws of the United States. To persons merely travelling in the Indian country the same protection is extended. The want of fixed laws, of competent tribunals of justice, which must for some time continue in the Indian country, absolutely requires for the peace of both sides that this protection be extended.

H.R.Rep. No. 474, 23d Cong., 1st Sess., at 18 (1834). Congress' concern over criminal jurisdiction in this proposed Indian Territory contrasts markedly with its total failure to address criminal jurisdiction over non-Indians on other reservations, which frequently bordered non-Indian settlements. The contrast suggests that Congress shared the view of the Executive Branch and lower federal courts that Indian tribal courts were without jurisdiction to try non-Indians.

This unspoken assumption was also evident in other congressional actions during the 19th century. [The opinion discusses amendments to the Nonintercourse Act in 1854 and the Major Crimes Act of 1885.]

. . . While Congress never expressly forbade Indian tribes to impose criminal penalties on non-Indians, we now make express our implicit conclusion of nearly a century ago that Congress consistently believed this to be the necessary result of its repeated legislative actions.

In a 1960 Senate Report, that body expressly confirmed its assumption that Indian tribal courts are without inherent jurisdiction to try non-Indians, and must depend on the Federal Government for protection from intruders. In considering a statute that would prohibit unauthorized entry upon Indian land for the purpose of hunting or fishing, the Senate Report noted:

> . . . One who comes on such lands without permission may be prosecuted under State law but a non-Indian trespasser on an Indian reservation enjoys immunity. *This is by reason of the fact that Indian tribal law is enforcible against Indians only; not against non-Indians.*
>
> *Non-Indians are not subject to the jurisdiction of Indian courts and cannot be tried in Indian courts on trespass charges.* Further, there are no Federal laws which can be invoked against trespassers. . . .

S.Rep. No. 1686, 86th Cong., 2d Sess., 2–3 (1960) (emphasis added).

II

While not conclusive on the issue before us, the commonly shared presumption of Congress, the Executive Branch, and lower federal courts that tribal courts do not have the power to try non-Indians carries considerable weight. "Indian law" draws principally upon the treaties drawn and executed by the Executive Branch and legislation passed by Congress. These instruments, which beyond their actual text form the backdrop for the intricate web of judicially made Indian law, cannot be interpreted in isolation but must be read in light of the common notions of the day and the assumptions of those who drafted them.

While in isolation the Treaty of Point Elliott, 12 Stat. 927 (1855), would appear to be silent as to tribal criminal jurisdiction over non-Indians, the addition of historical perspective casts substantial doubt upon the existence of such jurisdiction. In the Ninth Article, for example, the Suquamish "acknowledge their dependence on the Government of the United States." As Chief Justice Marshall explained in *Worcester v. Georgia,* 6 Pet. 515, 551–552, 554 (1832), such an acknowledgement is not a mere abstract recognition of the United States' sovereignty. "The Indian nations were, from their situation, necessarily dependent on [the United States] for their protection from lawless and injurious intrusions into their country." *Id.,* at 555. By acknowledging their dependence on the United States, in the Treaty of Point Elliott, the Suquamish were in all probability recognizing that the United States would arrest and try non-Indian intruders who came within their Reservation. Other provisions of the Treaty also point to the absence of tribal jurisdiction. Thus the Tribe "agree[s] not to shelter or conceal offenders against the laws of the United States, but to deliver them up to the authorities for trial." Read in conjunction with 18 U.S.C. §1152, which extends federal enclave law to non-Indian offenses on Indian reservations, this provision implies that the Suquamish are to promptly deliver up any non-Indian offender, rather than try and punish him themselves.

By themselves, these treaty provisions would probably not be sufficient to remove criminal jurisdiction over non-Indians if the Tribe otherwise retained such jurisdiction. But an examination of our earlier precedents satisfies us that, even ignoring treaty provisions and congressional policy, Indians do not have criminal jurisdiction over non-Indians absent affirmative delegation of such power by Congress. Indian tribes do retain elements of "quasi-sovereign" authority after ceding their lands to the United States and announcing their dependence on the Federal Government. See *Cherokee Nation v. Georgia,* 5 Peters 1, 15 (1831). But the tribes' retained powers are not such that they are limited only by specific restrictions in treaties or congressional enactments. As the Court of Appeals recognized, Indian tribes are proscribed from exercising both those powers of autonomous states that are expressly terminated by Congress *and* those powers *"inconsistent with their status."*

Indian reservations are "a part of the territory of the United States." *United States v. Rogers,* 4 How. 567, 571 (1846). Indian tribes "hold and occupy [the reservations] with the assent of the United States, and under their authority." *Id.,* at 572. Upon incorporation into the territory of the United States, the Indian tribes thereby come under the territorial sovereignty of the United States and their exercise of separate power is constrained so as not to conflict with the interests of this overriding sovereignty. "[T]heir rights to complete sovereignty, as independent nations [are] necessarily diminished." *Johnson v. McIntosh,* 8 Wheat. 543, 574 (1823).

We have already described some of the inherent limitations on tribal powers that stem from their incorporation into the United States. In *Johnson v. McIntosh,* supra, we noted that the Indian tribes' "power to dispose of the soil at their own will, to whomsoever they pleased," was inherently lost to the overriding sovereignty of the United States. And in *Cherokee Nation v. Georgia,* supra, the Chief Justice observed that since Indian tribes are "completely under the sovereignty and dominion of the United States, . . . any attempt [by foreign nations] to acquire their lands, or to form a political connexion with them, would be considered by all as an invasion of our territory, and an act of hostility."

. . . Protection of territory within its external political boundaries is, of course, as central to the sovereign interest of the United States as it is to any other sovereign nation. But from the formation of the Union and the adoption of the Bill of Rights, the United States has manifested an equally great solicitude that its citizens be protected by the United States from unwarranted intrusions on their personal liberty. The power of the United States to try and criminally punish is an important manifestation of the power to restrict personal liberty. By submitting to the overriding sovereignty of the United States, Indian tribes therefore necessarily give up their power to try non-Indian citizens of the United States except in a manner acceptable to Congress. This principle would have been obvious a century ago when most Indian tribes were characterized by a "want of fixed laws [and] of competent tribunals of justice." H.R.Rep. No. 474, 23d Cong., 1st Sess., at 18 (1834). It should be no less obvious today, even though present-day Indian tribal courts embody dramatic advances over their historical antecedents.

In *Ex parte Crow Dog*, 109 U.S. 556 (1883), the Court was faced with almost the inverse of the issue before us here — whether, prior to the passage of the Major Crimes Act, federal courts had jurisdiction to try Indians who had offended against fellow Indians on reservation land. In concluding that criminal jurisdiction was exclusively in the tribe, it found particular guidance in the "nature and circumstances of the case." The United States was seeking to extend United States

> law, by argument and inference only, . . . over aliens and strangers; over the members of a community separated by race [and] tradition, . . . from the authority and power which seeks to impose upon them the restraints of an external and unknown code . . . ; which judges them by a standard made by others and not for them. . . . It tries them, not by their peers, nor by the customs of their people, nor the law of their land, but by . . . a different race, according to the law of a social state of which they have an imperfect conception. . . .

Id. at 571. These considerations, applied here to the non-Indian rather than Indian offender, speak equally strongly against the validity of respondents' contention that Indian tribes, although fully subordinated to the sovereignty of the United States, retain the power to try non-Indians according to their own customs and procedure. . . .

. . . We recognize that some Indian tribal court systems have become increasingly sophisticated and resemble in many respects their state counterparts. We also acknowledge that with the passage of the Indian Civil Rights Act of 1968, which extends certain basic procedural rights to *anyone* tried in Indian tribal court, many of the dangers that might have accompanied the exercise by tribal courts of criminal jurisdiction over non-Indians only a few decades ago have disappeared. Finally, we are not unaware of the prevalence of non-Indian crime on today's reservations which the tribes forcefully argue requires the ability to try non-Indians. But these are considerations for Congress to weigh in deciding whether Indian tribes should finally be authorized to try non-Indians. They have little relevance to the principles which lead us to conclude that Indian tribes do not have inherent jurisdiction to try and punish non-Indians. The judgments below are therefore

Reversed.

MR. JUSTICE BRENNAN took no part in the consideration or decision of this case.

MR. JUSTICE MARSHALL, with whom The Chief Justice [Burger] joins, dissenting.

I agree with the court below that the "power to preserve order on the reservation . . . is a sine qua non of the sovereignty that the Suquamish originally possessed." In the absence of affirmative withdrawal by treaty or statute, I am of the view that Indian tribes enjoy as a necessary aspect of their retained sovereignty the right to try and punish all persons who commit offenses against tribal law within the reservation. Accordingly, I dissent.

N. BRUCE DUTHU
Broken Justice in Indian Country (2008)

One in three American Indian women will be raped in their lifetimes, statistics gathered by the United States Department of Justice show. But the odds of the crimes against them ever being prosecuted are low, largely because of the complex jurisdictional rules that operate on Indian lands. Approximately 275 Indian tribes have their own court systems, but federal law forbids them to prosecute non-Indians. Cases involving non-Indian offenders must be referred to federal or state prosecutors, who often lack the time and resources to pursue them.

The situation is unfair to Indian victims of all crimes — burglary, arson, assault, etc. But the problem is greatest in the realm of sexual violence because rapes and other sexual assaults on American Indian women are overwhelmingly interracial. More than 80 percent of Indian victims identify their attacker as non-Indian. (Sexual violence against white and African-American women, in contrast, is primarily intraracial.) And American Indian women who live on tribal lands are more than twice as likely to be raped or sexually assaulted as other women in the United States, Justice Department statistics show.

Rapes against American Indian women are also exceedingly violent; weapons are used at rates three times that for all other reported rapes.

Congress should step in and clearly establish the authority of Indian tribes to investigate and prosecute all crimes occurring on Indian lands — no matter whether tribal members or nonmembers are involved.

Historically, Indian tribes have exercised full authority over everyone within Indian lands. A number of the early federal treaties expressly noted a tribe's power to punish non-Indians. Toward the latter part of the nineteenth century, however, federal policy shifted away from tribal self-government in favor of an effort to dismantle tribal government systems. Criminal law enforcement, especially in cases involving non-Indians, increasingly came to be viewed as a federal or state matter.

Thirty years ago, the Supreme Court formalized the prohibition against tribes prosecuting non-Indians with its decision in *Oliphant v. Suquamish Indian Tribe*. In this case, a Pacific Northwest tribe was attempting to try two non-Indian residents of the Port Madison Reservation for causing trouble during the annual Chief Seattle Days celebration — one for assaulting an officer and resisting arrest and the other for recklessly endangering another person and harming tribal property. The court held that the tribe, as a "domestic dependent nation," did not possess the full measure of sovereignty enjoyed by states and the national government, especially when it came to the affairs of non-Indian citizens.

Then in 1990, the court extended its *Oliphant* ruling to cases involving tribal prosecution of Indian offenders who are not members of that tribe. Congress subsequently passed new legislation to reaffirm the power of tribes to prosecute non-member Indian offenders, but it left the *Oliphant* ruling intact.

This means that when non-Indian men commit acts of sexual violence against Indian women, federal or state prosecutors must fill the jurisdictional void. But law enforcement in sexual violence cases in Indian country is haphazard at best, recent studies show, and it rarely leads to prosecution and conviction of non-Indian offenders. The Department of Justice's own records show that in 2006, prosecutors filed only 606 criminal cases in all of Indian country. With more than 560 federally recognized tribes, that works out to a little more than one criminal prosecution for each tribe.

Even if outside prosecutors had the time and resources to handle crimes on Indian land more efficiently, it would make better sense for tribal governments to have jurisdiction over all reservation-based crimes. Given their familiarity with the community, cultural norms and, in many cases, understanding of distinct tribal languages, tribal governments are in the best position to create appropriate law enforcement and health care responses — and to assure crime victims, especially victims of sexual violence, that a reported crime will be taken seriously and handled expeditiously.

Congress should enact legislation to overrule the *Oliphant* decision and reaffirm the tribes' full criminal and civil authority over all activities on tribal lands. This law should also lift the sentencing constraints imposed in 1968 that restrict the criminal sentences that tribal courts can impose to one year in jail and a $5,000 fine. In cases of rape, state court sentences typically exceed 8 years, while federal sentences are more than 12 years. Tribes should have the latitude to impose comparable sanctions. (A bill pending in Congress would extend tribal sentencing authority to three years, with more latitude in cases of domestic violence, but its prospects of passage are uncertain.)

Congress recently allocated $750 million for enhancing public safety in Indian country. This money will help tribes hire and train more police, build detention facilities and augment federal investigative and prosecutorial capacity for Indian country crimes. Ideally, the grant process will be efficient enough to make sure that this money reaches the places most in need.

But financial aid will not be enough to stop sexual violence against Indian women. Tribal courts have grown in sophistication over the past 30 years, and they take seriously the work of administering justice. Congress must support their efforts by closing the legal gaps that allow violent criminals to roam Indian country unchecked.

QUESTIONS FOR CONSIDERATION

1. Mescalero Apache chief Wendell Chino once described tribal sovereignty as "a bundle of rights." What effect did the *Oliphant* ruling have on that bundle? How does the ruling support or contradict the assertion in President Nixon's message to Congress that "we must assure the Indian that he can assume control of his own life"?

2. What arguments and evidence does the Court present to support its decision? What is the relevance of the demographic information provided in the Court's note 1 (page 540) to the outcome of the case?

3. What does the dissenting opinion identify as the only basis for removing an aspect of tribal sovereignty?

4. Do Professor Duthu's recommendations offer a reasonable remedy for the situation that the *Oliphant* decision aggravated? Would they impinge on non-Indian rights? Would they go far enough?

Indian Leadership at the End of the Twentieth Century

THROUGHOUT THEIR HISTORY, Indian people and communities have struggled to adapt to new conditions. Some tribes, like the Navajos and Cherokees, have done so successfully time and time again in the face of recurrent setbacks and severe adversity. Successful adjustment has usually entailed balancing old and new, holding on to the past as well as embracing the future. As historian Frederick Hoxie noted from his study of Crow leadership during the difficult era around the beginning of the twentieth century, "political cultures respond to new environments and new pressures with a 'modern' version of their traditional culture."[89] Many tribal leaders still try to cope with a changing world in a manner consistent with tribal values and practices. The following autobiographical passages show the importance of two prominent Indian leaders: Vine Deloria Jr. (1933–2005); and Wilma Mankiller (1945–2010), who served as principal chief of the Cherokee Nation of Oklahoma from 1985 to 1995. Both drew upon traditional values and tribal history as guides to personal and political behavior in the modern world. Mankiller interspersed passages of Cherokee history in her autobiography; Deloria urged leaders to ground their leadership in the traditional values of their tribes and communities. Even after their passings, Mankiller and Deloria remain influential figures in Indian country.

Vine Deloria Jr. was "without question the foremost Native American intellectual of our time," and arguably "one of the most important voices of the twentieth century." He shaped the legal and political environment Native Americans occupied by the end of the twentieth century and inspired countless young Native scholars and activists who carried his ideas into the twenty-first century.[90] A Standing Rock Sioux, Deloria was born in Martin, a border town on the Pine Ridge Reservation in South Dakota, in the depth of the Great Depression. Strangely, he said, the Depression was actually good for the people on Pine Ridge because federal programs devised to deal with the national economic crisis "were also made available to Indian people, and there was work available for the first time in the history of the reservations."[91] World War II changed things. Reservation programs were cut and the U.S. government turned its attention and its finances to winning the war. Many young Sioux men went off to fight; many Sioux families left the reservation to work in defense plants on the West Coast. Returning veterans found it difficult to resume a life of poverty on the reservation after seeing the comparative affluence of the outside world.

Deloria left the reservation in 1951 when his family moved to Iowa. He attended Iowa State University (earning a BS degree in 1958), served a stint in the marines, and entered seminary at the Lutheran School of Theology in Moline, Illinois. In 1964 he was elected executive director of the National Congress of

◆ **Vine Deloria Jr. (2005)**
Author and activist Vine Deloria Jr. (1933–2005), a
Standing Rock Sioux, was one of the foremost Native
American intellectuals of the twentieth century. © *Chris
Richards.*

American Indians, a position he held for three years. In 1967 he entered law school
at the University of Colorado, earning his doctorate in 1970. As a writer, professor
(at the University of Arizona, then at the University of Colorado), and an outspoken advocate of Indian rights, Deloria brought attention to Native American concerns and to important issues in Indian country that mainstream society ignored,
preferred to forget, or misunderstood.

Eloquent, irreverent, and prolific, Deloria articulated the anger and frustrations of many Native Americans, and he wrote with a lethal wit that exposed many
of the stereotypes and hypocrisies that governed Indian policies, affected Indians'
lives, and even infiltrated Indian societies. In 1969 he published a groundbreaking
collection of essays entitled *Custer Died for Your Sins: An Indian Manifesto.* The
book took on race relations in the United States, the federal bureaucracies that
hampered Indian life and stifled Indian efforts, Christian churches, and white
academics who made their careers as so-called experts on Indians, a subject to
which Deloria regularly returned.[92] In a way that no American Indian author had
done before, Deloria put non-Indians on the defensive. His portrayal of anthropologists in one of the more famous passages of the book resonated with many
Native people and has stood as an indictment of non-Indian academics working
in Indian country. Every summer, he wrote, white anthropologists invaded Indian
reservations. They were easy to spot: "Go into any crowd of people. Pick out a tall
gaunt white man wearing Bermuda shorts, a World War II Army Air Force flying
jacket, an Australian bush hat, tennis shoes, and packing a large knapsack incorrectly strapped on his back. He will invariably have a thin sexy wife with stringy
hair, an IQ of 191, and a vocabulary in which even the prepositions have eleven
syllables." He was there to "observe" but rarely wrote anything down because he
already knew everything. "An anthropologist comes out to Indian reservations to
make OBSERVATIONS. During the winter these observations will become books
by which future anthropologists will be trained, so that they can come out to reservations years from now and verify the observations they have studied."[93]

Deloria did more than poke fun and point out absurdities. He articulated the
concept of tribal sovereignty and conceptualized "the essential doctrine of tribal
self-determination." *Custer Died for Your Sins* "inspired a generation of American

Indian activism" and brought Deloria wide recognition as "the intellectual voice and legal mind behind the Indian civil rights movement."[94] Deloria followed that book with *We Talk, You Listen: New Tribes, New Turf* (1970), *God Is Red: A Native View of Religion* (1973), and *Behind the Trail of Broken Treaties: An American Declaration of Independence* (1974). Subsequent publications ranged across federal Indian policy, Indian treaties, Indian religion, scientific racism, stereotypes, "New Age" appropriations of Indian rituals, the absurdities of American foreign policy, environmental plundering, and the continued abuses of human rights. As he wrote in the *New York Times Magazine* in 1970, "It just seems to a lot of Indians that this continent was a lot better off when we were running it."[95]

Deloria wrote the following essay in response to a huge jump in Indian population reported in the 1980 U.S. census. The demographic trends he discussed then have become even more pronounced in subsequent census reports. Likewise, many of Deloria's comments about the ramifications of the new popularity of being Indian and the fundamental requirements for leadership have enduring relevance in Indian country today.

Traditionally, the name *Mankiller* was a title conferred on Cherokee war leaders. Cherokee women who distinguished themselves, sometimes in battle, earned the title of *Ghigau* or "Beloved Woman." Perhaps the most famous Mankiller of the eighteenth century, Outacite, visited London as part of a Cherokee delegation to the king, but he has been surpassed in history by a namesake and beloved woman of the twentieth century. Wilma Mankiller is the first woman ever elected to the office of principal chief of the Cherokee Nation. Mankiller was born in 1945 to a Cherokee father and a Dutch-Irish mother. One of eleven children, she grew up in rural poverty in Adair County, Oklahoma, in a house with no electricity or running water. The house was located on Mankiller Flats, a 160-acre allotment granted to her grandfather in 1907 when the federal government dismantled the Cherokee government, divided up the land, and created the state of Oklahoma. In 1956 the family moved to San Francisco under the BIA relocation program. Like many other young Indians of her generation, Mankiller found that mixing with other Indians in a new urban environment generated increased political consciousness and commitment to her Indian heritage, exactly the opposite of what the government hoped to achieve by its relocation program. She became active in the Indian rights movement in San Francisco, visiting Alcatraz during its occupation by Indian students (see pages 485–86).

In 1977, after divorcing her husband of eleven years, Mankiller returned to Oklahoma. She had two daughters, Felicia and Gina, no job, and no car. She began working for the Cherokee Nation as a volunteer, started new programs, and obtained grants to run them. In 1981 she became director of the Cherokee Nation Community Development Department and in 1983 was elected deputy chief of the Cherokee Nation. Two years later, when President Reagan appointed Cherokee chief Ross Swimmer head of the BIA, Mankiller stepped into the office he vacated. Critics gave her little chance of being elected in her own right, and she fought gender prejudice. The next year she married Charlie Soap, a Cherokee traditionalist and community worker.[96]

◆ Wilma Mankiller

Wilma Mankiller (1945–2010), the first woman to be elected chief of a major Indian tribe, was the principal chief of the Cherokee Nation for ten years. In January 1998, Mankiller received the Presidental Medal of Freedom from President Bill Clinton in recognition of her strong and creative leadership of the Cherokee Nation. *Dennis Cook/AP Photo.*

Reelected to a four-year term in 1987, and then reelected yet again with more than 80 percent of the vote in 1991, Mankiller served as principal chief of the Cherokee Nation for ten years. During her tenure, she initiated a revitalization in Cherokee country. Tribal membership increased from 55,000 to 156,000, the number of tribal employees almost doubled to 1,271, and the tribal budget doubled to $86 million. The tribe built three health centers and added nine children's programs. Mankiller testified before Congress on issues ranging from health care to Indian sovereignty, and she met with three U.S. presidents.[97] She compared her job as Cherokee chief to that of a chief executive officer running a small country.[98] "We are more of a republic than a reservation and exist in a complex set of laws in relationship to the U.S. government," she explained. "We view it as a dual citizenship."[99] Mankiller brought to politics a strong belief in the importance of maintaining traditional values and applying them to the solution of contemporary problems. She also brought a belief in leadership roles for women in politics. "Women can help turn the world right side up," she told an audience in Denver in 1994. "We bring a more collaborative approach to government. And if we do not participate, then decisions will be made for us."[100] *Ms.* magazine named her Woman of the Year in 1987, and she was inducted into the National Women's Hall of Fame in 1993. In 1998 President Clinton awarded her the Medal of Freedom — the highest civilian award given by the U.S. government — in recognition of her extraordinary efforts on behalf of Indian peoples.

In her book, *Mankiller: A Chief and Her People,* written with journalist Michael Wallis, she relates her personal odyssey from childhood in rural Oklahoma, to life as an unhappy housewife in the San Francisco area, through the civil rights struggles of the 1960s, back to the Cherokee Nation in the late 1970s, and into national and international prominence in the 1980s and 1990s. She weaves her own story with the history of the Cherokee people. It was, she said, inconceivable to do it any other way.[101] Her own life story of struggle, courage, and triumph in the face of adversity parallel a larger struggle by Indian peoples to overcome the legacies of the past. "We will," said Mankiller, "enter the twenty-first century more on our own terms than we have entered any other century."[102] Chad Smith, elected chief in 1999, led the Cherokees into the new century committed to building a Cherokee future on Cherokee terms and using Cherokee talent.[103]

In 1979 Wilma Mankiller was involved in a freak head-on collision with a car driven by her best friend, Sherry Morris. Morris died; Mankiller almost died. Surgeons operated seventeen times and at one point considered amputating her right leg. A year after the accident, she was diagnosed with myasthenia gravis, a debilitating disease of the nervous system. In 1989 she was hospitalized with a severe kidney infection and the next year underwent a kidney transplant. In the winter of 1996, while a fellow at Dartmouth College, she was diagnosed with lymphoma, a form of cancer. She battled her health problems for the rest of her life. Her death in 2010 deprived Indian country and America of a woman who showed how to lead with grace, courage, and generosity.

The extracts from her autobiography reprinted here focus on her term as deputy chief and her election as principal chief in her own right. In the words of historian Theda Perdue, Mankiller's courage in the face of adversity and her service to her community embodied the values of past generations of Cherokee women, values that had survived recurrent assault. Mankiller herself believed she could not have achieved what she did had it not been for the ordeals she suffered and survived: "After that, I realized I could survive anything," she said. "I had faced adversity and turned it into a positive experience—a better path. I had found the way to be of good mind."[104]

VINE DELORIA JR.
The Popularity of Being Indian: A New Trend in Contemporary American Society (1984)

Unless the increase in the Indian population during the 1970s was due to a remarkable increase in the Indian birthrate, the 1980 census is badly out of kilter and suggests a new social phenomenon of which few people have been aware: the establishment of Indian ancestry as proof of respectability and acceptance in American life has replaced the older concept of American respectability defined by Anglo-Saxon heritage.

In 1980 the federal census allowed people to identify their racial background themselves for the first time. In previous census reports ethnicity was determined by other means. The result of the new method was an increase in the American Indian population beyond anyone's wildest estimate. In 1960 the census reported 523,591 Indians in the United States. That figure jumped to 792,730 in 1970, and the last census showed a count of 1,418,195 Indians in the United States.

SOURCE: "The Popularity of Being Indian: A New Trend in Contemporary American Society," from *Spirit and Reason: The Vine Deloria, Jr., Reader* (Golden, Colo.: Fulcrum, 1999), 230–40. Reprinted by permission of Fulcrum Publishing.

Obviously this latter figure bears some examination. Let us look first at why there has been such a dramatic increase in the number of people identifying themselves as Indians and then address the more important issue — what are the implications of the significant increase of would-be Indians for the Indian community and its culture?

Traditionally Indians were seen as the ultimate underclass. Original residents of this continent, Indians stood in the way of the advances of Western civilization and consequently had to be extinguished or neutralized in some fashion if settlement were to proceed at its anticipated pace. Many tribes were pushed to remote and barren lands away from the major centers of population where they were expected to become sedentary agriculturalists, existing as best they could on fragments of their ancestral lands. The annual reports of the Commissioner of Indian Affairs testify that the experiment in farming was not successful in many areas of the West and the Indian population declined precipitiously, reaching an all-time low of 237,196 in 1900. Indians did not prosper under the ministrations of civilization.

The unpopularity of being identified as an American Indian affected early census reports. Whenever possible, if a person could pass as a white, the chances were that he or she did. Unquestionably, early census reports failed to identify many mixed-blood Indians as Indians.

It was probably not until the reforms of the New Deal in 1934, and following, that people began once again to identify themselves as Indians. With the passage of the Indian Reorganization Act and the Oklahoma Indian Welfare Act in 1934 and 1936, it became profitable to be an Indian. Certain federal services were made available to tribal members which had not been part of the Indian's lot in previous decades.

However, while the New Deal probably emphasized Indian ancestry for the people who already identified as Indians, there is little evidence that people crossed over from white to Indian identification simply to take advantage of these services or to seek special favors from the government because of their racial identification. In general the number of programs available to non-Indians was considerably greater and more beneficial than that available to Indians.

The Indian population remained at reasonably predictable levels until 1970, so that while the 1940, 1950, and 1960 census reports may be slightly undercounted, there is no reason to suppose that they dreadfully underrepresented the number of Indians. Even the many programs made available to tribes in the War on Poverty did not produce much of an increase in the number of Indians in the United States. One would have expected a large increase between 1960 and 1970 if the sole reason for claiming Indian blood was to acquire eligibility for services provided for Indians by the federal government. The halcyon days of the Office of Economic Opportunity were 1964 to 1968, and with the onset of the Nixon administration the tenor of federal policy was to reduce or eliminate social programs. Although people might have considered themselves Indians in 1964, with the reduction of social programs at the end of the sixties there was no reason to continue the masquerade because the economic benefits inherent in the Indian status were definitely on the decline.

Public opinion was significantly tilted in favor of Indians at the beginning of the seventies. Alcatraz and succeeding activist events may have galvanized the Indian image and made it seem romantic, perhaps even mysteriously exciting, to claim to be an Indian. But the Indian occupation of the Bureau of Indian Affairs in fall 1972 and the occupation and siege of Wounded Knee brought retaliation against Indians by the federal government so that adopting a prominent position as an Indian was not the best way to make one's mark in the world. Continuing cutbacks of federal Indian funds and the withering of reservation and community programs in the late seventies foretold a desperate situation in Indian country for most people, and at the end of the seventies there was no merit — except perhaps some personal emotional stability — that accrued from claiming Indian blood or ancestry.

We must, then, still account for an increase in the Indian population by an astounding 78 percent between the 1970 and 1980 census reports on the basis of nonbiological factors. Never in human history have so many members of the majority undertaken to identify themselves as members of one of the most historically despised minorities of their society. The general tendency of societies traditionally has been to assimilate burdensome minorities quietly and above all to shun identification with them. A glance at Mexico and other nations south of the border will show that, while there is a majority of Indian blood present in the gene pool of those nations, there is hardly an eagerness to identify with that large racial stock of Indianness. On the contrary, people go out of their way to separate themselves from Indian ancestry, denying sometimes even the heritage that is patently obvious on their faces and in their behavior.

In spite of historical animosity toward Indians, Americans apparently consider Indian identity an important factor in maintaining a sense of personal worth. The old verities that once undergirded American social status seem to have eroded substantially, to the point where identification as an Indian is more prestigious and more comforting than continued identification as a member of the majority. The Anglo-Saxon culture — particularly that of the North Atlantic region — which once defined mainstream American values, heritage, and ancestry, has apparently given way to a new conception of respectability in which a trace of Indian blood adds a sense of stability. This new conception is extremely curious. The conditions of Indian life have not materially improved in recent decades, not so much because Indians have lacked opportunity but more as a result of the increased opportunities for the accumulation of wealth available to members of the majority. Identifying with a group that continues to lag significantly behind the rest of society economically would seem to be a foolish endeavor. Certainly identifying as an Indian also brings with it the assumed but rarely articulated accusation that the individual has not been able to function adequately in this society. So economics alone cannot explain the increased Indian population.

There is some merit in suggesting that identification as an Indian brings with it certain institutional rewards. Colleges and universities today give preference in admission to minorities, and it may well be that non-Indians, eager to obtain admission to law schools or colleges of medicine, are claiming an Indian ancestry in order to leapfrog their fellow applicants who seek admission on the basis of merit alone. The American Indian Law Center in New Mexico reports that it continues to be astounded at the number of alleged Indians attending law schools in various parts of the country. In checking on the applicants, the American Indian Law Center is unable to identify very many as Indians. But a few individuals changing races in order to gain admission to professional schools can hardly have swelled the ranks of American Indians by some 625,000 people, unless law schools are being less than candid about the number of people applying for admission.

Another reason frequently given for the startling increase in the Indian population is the application of Title IV of the Indian Education Act to public schools. Under that law, funds are made available to public school systems that have a certain number of Indians attending them. Though school districts may have greatly inflated the figures in order to receive federal funds, identification under these conditions is a function of the school administrators and not a matter of individual preference or belief when filling out census forms. A school official may certify a certain number of Indians in his school for purposes of receiving federal funds. However, this number remains pretty much a creature of the Department of Education; it generally does not spill over into other statistics. There is no good reason to suppose that temporary identification of a student as an Indian during one school year would carry over into a permanent self-image several years later when the census taker arrived at the door.

Closely related to Indian identification for the purpose of qualifying for federal education funds is identification for the purpose of avoiding forced busing to achieve racial balance. In the late sixties in Denver, a busing plan was put forward which allowed minority children then attending a neighborhood school to escape busing to other parts of town. In a matter of hours the number of Indians in Denver showed a dramatic increase, and there were speculations that Denver might be the world's only wholly American Indian city. Yet forced busing for purposes of integration has not been an imminent peril in people's minds for several years. Claiming an Indian ancestor for the purpose of exempting one's children from busing would again be only a temporary expedient, not a permanent shift from one racial group to another.

Having eliminated biology, economics, admission policies to schools, Title IV funding, and busing as reasons for the increase in Indian identification in the seventies, we now come to the evaluation of personal motives to explain this phenomenon. In American life, the perceived status of the Indian considerably transcends any other status and makes it a desirable complement to one's other personal attributes and accomplishments. The increase in the number of Indians seems to be directly related to the rising interest in religious experience. In the middle sixties, Indians were already acclaimed as the world's first and best ecologists by members of the counterculture. Pop posters proclaimed the Indian reverence for the land, and the protests and occupations almost always featured an Indian activist orating vigorously before the television cameras on some topic advanced as an important religious belief. The demand for restoration of lands, first at Blue Lake in New Mexico and later at Yakima, Warm Springs, and other reservations, laid heavy emphasis on the religious aspect of the land. Since reverence for lands, sacred places, and environment were sadly lacking in Western religions, people began to see their interest in ecology as encompassing important, new religious dimensions.

By 1972, when the Indians occupied the Bureau of Indian Affairs headquarters in Washington, D.C., citing religion as a valid reason for conducting protests was a popular pastime among Indians. The later marches on Washington always featured a number of medicine men who conducted ceremonies and admonished the crowds to follow the old tribal traditions. Since few people had been raised in traditional culture, almost anything that seemed right at the time became a form of traditionalism, and popular ceremonies such as the sweat lodge quickly spread across the country. Indeed, the sweat lodge, conducted under an amazing variety of auspices, became the ritual that united the national Indian movement and provided it with a degree of homogeneity.

In the middle and late seventies the number of medicine men and ceremonies proliferated rapidly. Southern California and the Dakotas in particular experienced an explosion of medicine men, so that it was a rare Indian who did not have access to some form of traditional Indian religious experience. That the medicine man and the ceremonies might have little to do with the actual traditions of any particular tribe seemed not to bother anyone participating in these activities. Few Indians questioned the activities of the contemporary medicine men, and as a result, the divergence from the Indian norm became almost an industry in itself. To be welcomed and sometimes revered by Indians in the neighborhood, an individual needed only bluster to claim a spiritual office in a tribe — generally the more distant the tribe, the more exaggerated were the alleged credentials.

The increased interest in tribal religions did not, unfortunately, influence the ethical behavior of those who professed to have special traditional religious experiences. Both Indians and whites were callously exploited by alleged medicine men who were busy peddling a new form of Indian religion that centered primarily on recycled slogans concerning "Mother Earth." This new statement of the ancient Indian relationship to the Earth asked little in the way of personal commitment and generated a great deal of excitement in the practitioners and participants. People began to feel that they had reestablished the old linkage to the rhythms and revelations of the planet. Heavy emphasis was given to the recitation of pious phrases that people believed would invoke ancient earth spirits and exempt an individual from the guilt that involvement with contemporary industrial society inevitably created.

Books and newspaper articles reinforced the movement of people toward Indian religious experiences. The writings of John Neihardt and Frank Waters on Indian life became immensely popular, and every summer caravans of young whites made their pilgrimages to Third Mesa and Pine Ridge in search of the ultimate reality. People who had little in the way of an Indian heritage found themselves having dreams wherein their past lives, always as Indians, were revealed to them. Upon awakening they adopted Indian names and proudly proclaimed their solidarity with Indians. Once accepted by a circle of Indians, there seemed to be no returning to the life of the ordinary American citizen. The Black Elk phraseology and the Hopi history thereafter seemed to bind together diverse groups of Indians and whites-newly-arrived-as-Indians in a contemporary religious experience that transcended all other considerations. In short, Indian culture became a national culture, not because whites adopted the culture as their own, but because they became Indian and helped to define its contemporary expressions and loyalties.

It is interesting to note what was happening to Indians during this same period. The onset of the War on Poverty saw a strengthening of tribal governments on a scale never imagined by John Collier in the thirties.° Prior to 1960 most tribes had what might charitably be called "shadow" governments; they had little income and few programs and did very little business as corporate entities. Beginning with the Area Redevelopment Administration and continuing until the present time, tribal governments have had to take on a great many new responsibilities, almost all of them in the program area. The old Community Action Programs of the poverty war led to more sophisticated institutions

that included industrial parks, school systems, and housing authorities. Many tribal governments, in the past twenty years, have become larger than the governments of western towns and counties with a similar population base.

Traditionally Indians conducted their affairs in a highly informal atmosphere. That is to say, formal institutional life was minimized in favor of adherence to customs and kinship responsibilities. With a strong sense of tribal identity, a confirmed isolation from daily intercourse with other groups, and a legend of origin that informed the people that they were specifically chosen from among the peoples of the world to be possessors of a specific religious revelation, tribes did not need to juxtapose the institutions of society against the individual. Social and community disapproval and the shame that misbehavior might bring to families were sufficient to maintain law and order in all but the most pressing circumstances. Today most of the functions that Indians performed spontaneously according to the customs of their tribe are the subject of an agency or institution, tribally operated to be certain, yet imbued with the impersonality that we see in the modern world with its transpersonal activities.

The primary experience of Indians since they went onto the reservations has been one of confronting and resolving their relationship with the non-Indian educational system. From allotment, which was supposed to be a practical experience in the handling of property, to relocation, which was to provide Indian families with firsthand knowledge of the urban areas, almost all federal efforts to assist Indians have been premised on the belief that Indians could and would adopt the educational values of the larger society. In our time, the postwar era, Indians have become considerably more familiar with education of all kinds. Vocational education has expanded significantly in training programs conducted both on the reservations and in the urban areas. Indians have been admitted to college and graduate professional schools in increasingly greater numbers than at any time in the past. Although still

---

° For more on Collier, see pages 445–51.

statistically underrepresented, Indians are rapidly becoming accustomed to undertaking difficult educational programs and succeeding in them.

Like other Americans, with the expansion of educational opportunities Indian communities have become subject to the ministrations of the professional specialist and consultant. The division of labor and functions in traditional society was an important part of Indian life, but it was not linked to any set of institutional objectives that sought social stability as an end product. Specialist functions were performed for individuals, and it was in the informal setting that specialties were recognized and approved. The expansion of the functions and tasks of the tribal governments today has meant the inclusion of the specialist in the activities of the Indian community. As in other American communities, however, the specialist/professional follows a personal code of ethics and is responsible to the institutional employer. Usually, the specialist/professional is more likely to serve the community on the basis of his or her own skills and activities than on the basis of the needs of the community. Indian communities have accordingly changed significantly in the manner in which they view themselves and their access to the knowledge that enables them to succeed and survive in the contemporary world.

If we take the movement of non-Indians toward the Indian way of life — at least toward identification with a set of behaviors and attitudes that they see as Indian — and the movement of Indians, their tribes, and communities toward the American institutional mainstream, we have a strange phenomenon. Indians seem determined to shed a substantial portion of their heritage even while non-Indians are frantically adopting whatever part of the heritage they can discern and feel comfortable performing. The result of this confusion has been the blurring, almost beyond redemption, of the traditions of the individual tribal groups. It is now enough for a person to be fairly prominent in Indian affairs and have sufficient political clout to turn aside any determined inquiries regarding the extent of his Indian heritage. Leadership in

Indian communities has consequently become a matter of media exposure rather than community endorsement or approval. Often it is the individual's connection with non-Indian institutions that verifies his or her Indian identity: if accepted by a well-known non-Indian institution as an Indian, the individual is regarded as an Indian — even by many Indians.

The current ambiguity associated with the Indian community cannot continue indefinitely. The banks of the Indian mainstream have long since overflowed, and as the energies of the Indian movement reach out and include people who have not previously considered themselves Indians or as more people decide to become Indians and willingly leap into the fray, a decided lack of community cohesion results. Loyalties to family, clan, and tribe become faint, and allegiance to political networks and institutional connections become considerably stronger. The Indian landscape takes on the aspect of a charade played out before a bewildered audience that is unable to spot the players or their numbers and has not the slightest idea how one obtains a program for this ritual drama.

A scrutiny of the past may provide clues to the solution of the current problems in the Indian community. The Indian relationship to the United States was originally a political relationship, even though the conflict between Indians and members of the majority was primarily racial in character. In the last two decades the political relationship has matured into a rather precisely defined legal relationship in which rights and responsibilities are determined either by Congress or by the courts. The racial conflict has evolved and for a while appeared to be cultural conflict, but more recently it has become the great counterlifestyle for many people. The specifics of culture have given way to the generalities of fashion, and as the precision of personal behavior becomes less meaningful, a great many things that are simply alternatives to the activities of the majority are considered to be within the sphere of Indian behavior.

Much of what has happened to Indians in the contemporary world was probably predictable once the isolation of the Indian communities was disturbed by the developments of the postwar world. Interstate highways, airplanes, rural electrification, and the entrance of radios, televisions, and telephones in reservations have made a significant difference in the way Indians live their lives and in the manner in which they understand the world. Like other rural people, Indians are presently in a state of deep and profound culture shock, and this trauma cannot easily be overcome. The electric universe continues to transmit more information to Indian communities than they can possibly absorb and understand. And as with other Americans, about all Indians can do is try to fend off the most depressing aspects of contemporary life and hope for better days.

The present situation in Indian country calls for the most intelligent and determined leadership to express itself in an unqualified endorsement of traditions and values that have always been associated with the respective tribes and communities. Today Indians need to speak up but not in the same sense as the sixties and seventies required them to speak. The Indian community needs to address its problems, and it can best perform this task by addressing itself and engaging in new kinds of dialogue within tribes and between tribes. Standards of conduct ought to be reestablished, and individuals should be willing to subscribe to them and follow them. A careful accounting of the tribal cultural heritage is important for every Indian group, and impostors must be driven out. Each Indian tribe has the right, and the responsibility, to determine the criteria for establishing tribal membership. Elected tribal leaders need to develop a new sense of corporate responsibility that can break the present networking with larger institutions and reestablish the old codes of proper conduct and concern that once characterized Indians as a distinct group.

There is every indication that at the grass roots of different tribes this new sense of identity and meaning is emerging. The recent election of Peterson Zah to the chairmanship of the Navajo tribe is a good sign that at the local level the Navajos have chosen to bring their government closer to themselves and force it to perform useful functions for the community as a whole. A new group of Indian leaders seems to be emerging in other places that would demonstrate that the old cohesion that once marked tribes as a people set apart is stirring and making itself felt. Whatever values and beliefs Indians might contribute to American society as a whole cannot be made as long as there is such confusion regarding the real strengths of Indian life. It will be only when Indians begin to speak with a coherent point of view that they will be in a position to assist in the continuing task of improving American society. One cannot hazard exactly what that contribution might be, but it should be of lasting value.

As the attention of the federal government was directed toward Indian communities in the postwar years, a pattern for relationships developed in which Indians recited their problems and a bewildering multitude of bureaucrats, experts, and politicians stepped forward with promises of assistance and assurances of understanding. Considering the situation today, no one standing outside the Indian community is exactly certain what the best approach is for handling the problems of the Indian community. Few people want to dwell primarily on problems, and fewer people still can suggest solutions without identifying the areas where energies must be directed.

Nevertheless, it seems incumbent on us today to discard the mere recitation of wrongs and problems and call people back to a confidence in themselves that can begin to address the areas that demand attention. In the old days — customs, traditions, and whatever institutions were in vogue had a mission to serve the people. If they did not prove useful, they were discarded. That critical sense of utility now seems to be surfacing again. Let us not view it as disruptive but as an opportunity to move forward again toward new horizons and accomplishments. By counting the people who respond to the opportunities of the contemporary world, we will be able to determine how many Indians there really are.

WILMA MANKILLER
Returning the Balance (1993)

"I, Wilma P. Mankiller, do solemnly swear, or affirm, that I will faithfully execute the duties of Principal Chief of the Cherokee Nation. And will, to the best of my abilities, preserve, protect, and defend the Constitutions of the Cherokee Nation and the United States of America. I swear, or affirm, further that I will do everything within my power to promote the culture, heritage, and tradition of the Cherokee Nation." . . .

By the time I took the oath of office, my eldest daughter, Felicia, had married, and I had my first grandchild, Aaron Swake. I was a forty-year-old grandmother, as well as the first woman to serve as chief of a major tribe. I told the reporters, who seemed to materialize from out of nowhere, that the only people who were really worried about my serving as chief were members of my family. That was because all of them knew very well how much time I tended to devote to my job. My daughters were, of course, concerned about my health. But my little grandson thought it was great that his grandma was the chief. . . .

One thing that I never tried to become as chief was "one of the boys," nor am I a "good ol' girl." I never will be. That goes against my grain. I do know how to be political and to get the job done, but I do not believe that one must sacrifice one's principles. Gradually, I noticed changes within the tribe and especially within the council.

Rural development was, and still remains, a high priority on my list of goals. For me, the rewards came from attempting to break the circle of poverty. My feeling is that the Cherokee people, by and large, are incredibly tenacious. We have survived so many major political and social up-

heavals, yet we have kept the Cherokee government alive. I feel confident that we will march into the twenty-first century on our own terms.

We are staffed with professionals — educators, physicians, attorneys, business leaders. Already, in the 1800s, we fought many of our wars with lawsuits, and it was in the courts where many of our battles were won. Today, we are helping to erase the stereotypes created by media and by western films of the drunken Indian on a horse, chasing wagon trains across the prairie. I suppose some people still think that all native people live in tepees and wear tribal garb every day. They do not realize that many of us wear business suits and drive station wagons. The beauty of society today is that young Cherokee men and women can pursue any professional fields they want and remain true to traditional values. It all comes back to our heritage and our roots. It is so vital that we retain that sense of culture, history, and tribal identity.

We also are returning the balance to the role of women in our tribe. Prior to my becoming chief, young Cherokee girls never thought they might be able to grow up and become chief themselves. That has definitely changed. From the start of my administration, the impact on the younger women of the Cherokee Nation was noticeable. I feel certain that more women will assume leadership roles in tribal communities. . . .

In 1987, after I had fulfilled the balance of Ross Swimmer's term as chief, I made the decision to run on my own and to win a four-year term of office. It was not an easy decision. I knew the campaign would be most difficult. I talked to my family and to my people. I spent long hours discussing the issues with Charlie Soap, whom I had married in 1986. Charlie had contracted with private foundations to continue development work with low-income native community projects. His counsel to me was excellent. He encouraged me to run. So did many other people.

But there were others who were opposed to my continuing as chief. Even some of my friends and advisers told me they believed the Cherokee people would accept me only as deputy, not as an elected principal chief. Some of those people came to our home at Mankiller Flats. I would look out the window and see them coming down the dirt road to tell me that I should give up any idea of running for chief. Finally, I told Charlie that if one more family came down that road and told me not to run, I was going to run for sure. That is just what happened.

I made my official announcement in early 1987, calling for a "positive, forward-thinking campaign." I chose John A. Ketcher, a member of the tribal council since 1983, as my running mate for the June 20 election. In 1985, John had been elected by the council to succeed me as deputy chief when I became principal chief. An eleven-sixteenths bilingual Cherokee, John was born in southern Mayes County in 1922. A veteran of World War II and a graduate of Northeastern State University in Tahlequah, Ketcher, as I do, considered unity and economic development to be the two priorities for the Cherokee Nation. . . .

I drew three opponents in the race for principal chief. I had to face Dave Whitekiller, a postal assistant from the small community of Cookson and a former councilman; William McKee, deputy administrator at W. W. Hastings Indian Hospital, in Tahlequah; and Perry Wheeler, a former deputy chief and a funeral home director from Sallisaw, in Sequoyah County.

From the beginning, the best description of the campaign came from someone on the council, who said there was an "undercurrent of viciousness." I ignored things that were going on around me. I did the same thing I had always done — went out to the communities and talked to as many of the Cherokee people as possible about the issues. I tried to answer all their questions. My critics claimed that I had failed to properly manage and direct the Cherokee Nation, which was obviously false. Our revenue for 1986 was up $6 million, higher than it had ever been

to that point. I was not about to lose focus by warring with my opponents.

The election eliminated all the candidates except for Perry Wheeler and me. None of us had received more than 50 percent of the votes. I had polled 45 percent to Wheeler's 29 percent. We had to face each other in a July runoff. My supporters worked very hard during those last few weeks. Charlie was one of my main champions. On my behalf, Charlie visited many rural homes where English is a second language to remind the people that prior to the intrusion of white men, women had played key roles in our government. He asked our people to not turn their backs on their past or their future.

Charlie's help was especially important because I was stricken with my old nemesis, kidney problems, during the final weeks of the campaign. Finally, just before the election, I had to be hospitalized in Tulsa, but the physicians never determined the exact location of the infection and could not bring it under control. The lengthy infection and hospitalization would nearly cost me not only the election but also my life, since it brought on extensive and irreversible kidney damage. From that point forward, I was repeatedly hospitalized for kidney and urinary-tract infections, until I underwent surgery and had a kidney transplant in 1990.

Wheeler, an unsuccessful candidate for the chief's job against Ross Swimmer in 1983, tried to make my hospitalization a major issue. He waged a vigorous and negative runoff campaign. He publicly stated that I had never been truthful about my health. It all reminded me of the way Swimmer had been attacked when he was battling cancer. Wheeler, whom I can best describe as an old-style politician, also made claims that I had not hired enough Cherokee people for what he called the higher-paying tribal posts. . . .

When all the ballots from thirty-four precincts plus the absentee votes were tallied, the woman who supposedly knew nothing about politics was declared the winner. The night of the runoff election, we went to the Tulsa Powwow, where my daughter Gina was being honored. In a photograph taken that evening, Charlie, Gina, Felicia, and I look very tired and worn, as if we had just been through a battle. Later that night, we returned to Tahlequah to check on the election results. When the votes of the local precincts were counted, it appeared that I had won easily. Everyone around me was celebrating, but I was concerned about the absentee votes. Once that vote was included, I allowed myself to celebrate.

At last, the Cherokee Nation had elected its first woman as principal chief — the first woman chief of a major Native American tribe. I had outpolled Wheeler, and John Ketcher had retained his post as deputy chief. Wheeler conceded victory to me shortly before midnight.

At long last, I had the mandate I had wanted. I had been chosen as principal chief of the Cherokee Nation by my own people. It was a sweet victory. Finally, I felt the question of gender had been put to rest. Today, if anyone asks members of our tribe if it really matters if the chief is male or female, the majority will reply that gender has no bearing on leadership. . . .

If I am to be remembered, I want it to be because I am fortunate enough to have become my tribe's first female chief. But I also want to be remembered for emphasizing the fact that we have indigenous solutions to our problems. Cherokee values, especially those of helping one another and of our interconnections with the land, can be used to address contemporary issues.

QUESTIONS FOR CONSIDERATION

1. What do Deloria and Mankiller regard as the major challenges confronting Indian people at the end of the twentieth century?

2. Both writers, in different ways, deal with issues of identity. What concerns does Deloria express about the growing trend to identify with and as Indians? What identity issues does Mankiller confront?

3. In what ways do Deloria and Mankiller find traditional solutions to modern-day problems? What qualities do they suggest are required for Indian leaders to succeed in a fast-paced and complex modern world?

PICTURE ESSAY

Indian Artists Depict Modern Indian Life

FOR A LONG TIME NON-INDIANS DOMINATED representations of Indian life, but they have never monopolized it. Indian people have always interpreted their past and present in their own ways and they continue to do so in literature, art, and film. Modern-day Native artists provide commentary on Indian experiences and depict aspects of Indian life that non-Indian artists have often missed or ignored. They have dismantled old notions among some non-Indians that "Indian art" comprises only baskets, blankets, and pottery, and they employ new forms of expression while responding to traditional inspirations and values.[105] They often offer non-Indian audiences fresh, and sometimes troubling, perspectives on American history and contemporary American society.

In 1958 Sioux artist Oscar Howe was rejected by the Philbrook Museum's *Annual* because his work was considered too modern and abstract to be "Indian." Howe was furious. "There is much more to Indian art than pretty, stylized pictures," he said. "Are we to be held back forever with one phase of Indian painting?"[106] In the decades since that incident, Native artists have answered Howe's question with a resounding "No!" They have developed other styles, creating works of art that are abstract, humorous, ironic, and discomfiting, as well as those that are visually beautiful. Many works combine traditional and new elements in their subject matter, composition, and style. In depicting Indian life today and the challenges and opportunities Indian people face, artists confront ugliness as well as beauty, draw on tradition as well as display innovation, and celebrate survival in the midst of disruption. They work against attitudes and assumptions that continue to inflict damage on Indian communities. Some make explicit social and political statements.

As Chippewa artist David Bradley conveys, Indian country by the end of the twentieth century was a complex mix of old and new, of continuity and change (Figure 9.1). Many artists offer comments and insights on the challenges Indian people face living in modern America and on the persistence of traditional ways and values in contemporary society. As in many other societies, humor often functions as a coping mechanism for dealing with hardship and hard times, and Native artists employ humor and irony, poking fun at enduring stereotypes and sometimes at themselves.

Harry Fonseca, an artist of Maidu/Portuguese/Hawaiian descent, has painted a series of pictures featuring the trickster figure Coyote. "I believe my Coyote paintings to be the most contemporary statements I have painted in regard to traditional beliefs and contemporary reality," said Fonseca. "I have taken a universal Indian image, Coyote, and have placed him in a contemporary setting."[107] In *Coyote Woman in the City* (Figure 9.2), Coyote is a woman walking the city streets.

561

◆ Figure 9.1 **David P. Bradley,** *Indian Country Today* **(1997)**
Photo © David P. Bradley and Peabody Essex Museum, Salem, Massachusetts, USA/Bridgeman Images.

◆ **Figure 9.2 Harry Fonseca, *Coyote Woman in the City* (1979)**
Hood Museum of Art, Dartmouth College, Hanover, New Hampshire; gift of the Class
of 1962. By permission of Harry Fonseca Trust, Santa Fe, N. Mex.

Indian tribes enjoy unique political status as sovereign nations within the United States. But, as this sculpture by Onondaga Peter Jones suggests (Figure 9.3), their efforts to control their own lives and lands are often severely curtailed. Historic loss of lands, depletion of resources, lack of economic bases, limited educational opportunities, erosion of languages and traditions, pressing health and social problems — all hamper Indian political aspirations, even as they motivate them. Racist attitudes and stereotypes, intrusions by the federal and state governments, and the sometimes stifling hand of the BIA also present obstacles to self-government. How might one interpret the bound arms on Peter Jones's sculpture — what does tribal sovereignty amount to when it is subject to the plenary power of Congress, limitations imposed by the courts, and other constraints on tribal self-government?

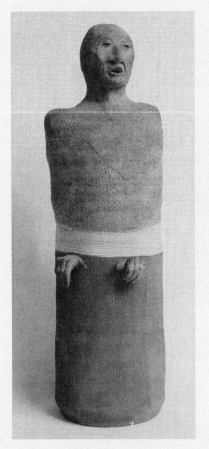

◆ Figure 9.3 **Peter Jones, *Sovereign Indian***
Courtesy of the Iroquois Indian Museum,
www.iroquoismuseum.org.

◆ **Figure 9.4** **Jack Malotte,** *It's Hard to Be Traditional When You're All Plugged In*
Used by permission of Jack Malotte.

In "It's Hard to Be Traditional When You're All Plugged In," Jack Malotte (Western Shoshone, b. 1953) shows an Indian in sunglasses in front of ceremonial symbols and electronic entertainment systems (Figure 9.4). This mixed media work was featured in an exhibit on Indian Humor at the National Museum of the American Indian–New York in 1998. Malotte said at the time:

> Prize-winning traditional dancers make me laugh. White Indian experts make me laugh. Christian Indians make me laugh. White artists who paint Indian things better than Indians make me laugh. Indian tacos being called a traditional food makes me laugh. Indians who call themselves cowboys make me laugh. Mixing Indian culture with the dominant society makes me laugh.[108]

In "Before Here Was Here," Pawnee/Yakama artist and poet Bunky Echo-Hawk (b. 1973) foregrounds an iconic grouping in which a Native elder relates a story and imparts traditional wisdom to the young, against the backdrop of the world's largest retail company and a symbol of American global capitalism and consumerism (Figure 9.5).

◆ Figure 9.5 **Bunky Echo-Hawk, *Before Here Was Here***
Bunky Echo-Hawk (Pawnee/Yakama).

QUESTIONS FOR CONSIDERATION

1. In what ways do the works of art shown here challenge popular notions of what constitutes "Indian art"?

2. What suggestions do these paintings and the Jones sculpture make about Indian peoples' adjustments to new ways and their presence and participation in modern America?

3. What do the works of art say about Indian identity in modern America?

REFERENCES

1. Francis Paul Prucha, ed., *Documents of United States Indian Policy* (Lincoln: University of Nebraska Press, 1975), 256–58.

2. Quoted in Mark N. Trahant, "The 1970s: New Leaders for Indian Country," in *Indians in American History*, eds. Frederick E. Hoxie and Peter Iverson, 2nd ed. (Wheeling, Ill.: Harlan Davidson, 1998), 238.

3. Quoted in Peter Iverson, *The Navajo Nation* (Albuquerque: University of New Mexico Press, 1981), 130–31.

4. Loretta Fowler, *Arapahoe Politics, 1851–1978* (Lincoln: University of Nebraska Press, 1982), 282–84.

5. Quoted in Robert Burnette and John Koster, *The Road to Wounded Knee* (New York: Bantam Books, 1974), 245.

6. Russell Means, with Marvin J. Wolf, *Where White Men Fear to Tread: The Autobiography of Russell Means* (New York: St. Martin's Press, 1995), 293.

7. Leonard Peltier, *Prison Writings: My Life Is My Sun Dance*, ed. Harvey Arden (New York: St. Martin's Press, 1999).

8. Paul C. Rosier, *Serving Their Country: American Indian Politics and Patriotism in the Twentieth Century* (Cambridge, Mass.: Harvard University Press, 2009), 260–70.

9. Mary Ann Weston, *Native Americans in the News: Images of Indians in the Twentieth Century Press* (Westport, Conn.: Greenwood Press, 1996), 142–45.

10. Quoted in Alvin M. Josephy Jr., *Now That the Buffalo's Gone: A Study of Today's American Indians* (Norman: University of Oklahoma Press, 1982), 217–18.

11. Robert Allen Warrior, "'Temporary Visibility': Deloria on Sovereignty and AIM," in *Native American Perspectives on Literature and History*, ed. Alan R. Velie (Norman: University of Oklahoma Press, 1994), 51–61, quote at 58; Paul Chaat Smith and Robert Allen Warrior, *Like a Hurricane: The Indian Movement from Alcatraz to Wounded Knee* (New York: New Press, 1996), 269.

12. Rex Weyler, *Blood of the Land: The Government and Corporate War against the American Indian Movement* (New York: Random House, 1982); Ward Churchill and Jim Vander Wall, *Agents of Repression: The FBI's Secret Wars against the Black Panther Party and the American Indian Movement* (Boston: South End Press, 1988); Ward Churchill, "The Bloody Wake of Alcatraz: Political Repression of the American Indian Movement during the 1970s," *American Indian Culture and Research Journal* 18 (Fall 1994), 253–300.

13. Ted Rising Sun quoted in Joanne Nagel, *American Indian Ethnic Renewal: Red Power and the Resurgence of Identity and Culture* (New York: Oxford University Press, 1996), 136, 169; Gerald Vizenor, "Dennis of Wounded Knee," *American Indian Quarterly* 7 (Spring 1983), 51–65, quote at 64; George Pierre Castile, *To Show Heart: Native American Self-Determination and Federal Indian Policy, 1960–1975* (Tucson: University of Arizona Press, 1998), chap. 5.

14. Nagel, *American Indian Ethnic Renewal*.

15. Means, *Where White Men*.

16. Julie L. Davis, *Survival Schools: The American Indian Movement and Community Education in the Twin Cities* (Minneapolis: University of Minnesota Press, 2013).

17. Harvard Project on American Indian Economic Development, *The State of the Native Nations: Conditions under U.S. Policies of Self-Determination* (New York: Oxford University Press, 2008), 21.

18. Jane Lawrence, "The Indian Health Service and the Sterilization of Native American Women," *American Indian Quarterly* 24 (Summer 2000), 400–419; Pinkerton-Uri quote at 412.

19. Lawrence, "The Indian Health Service and the Sterilization of Native American Women"; Andrea Smith, *Conquest: Sexual Violence and American Indian Genocide* (Cambridge, Mass.: South End Press, 2005), chap. 4.

20. Walter R. Echo-Hawk, *In the Courts of the Conqueror: The 10 Worst Indian Law Cases Ever Decided* (Golden, Colo.: Fulcrum, 2010), 218–19, 222–23. Matthew L. M. Fletcher, Wenona T. Singel, and Kathryn E. Fort, eds., *Facing the Future: The Indian Child Welfare Act at 30* (Lansing: Michigan State University Press, 2009), contains a dozen essays on the "well-intentioned but problematic federal legislation."

21. Prucha, *Documents*, 288–89.

22. Devon Abbott Mihesuah, *Cultivating the Rosebuds: The Education of Women at the Cherokee Female Seminary, 1851–1909* (Urbana: University of Illinois Press, 1993), 61; U.S. Senate Committee on Labor and Public Welfare, "Indian Education: A National Tragedy and Challenge," in *Red Power: The American Indians' Fight for Freedom*, ed. Alvin M. Josephy Jr. (New York: McGraw-Hill, 1971), 155–62.

23. The Carnegie Foundation for the Advancement of Teaching, *Tribal Colleges: Shaping the Future of Native America* (Princeton, N.J.: Carnegie Foundation for the Advancement of Teaching, 1989).

24. "Indian Education," 156.

25. Harvard Project on American Indian Economic Development, *Honoring Nations: Celebrating Excellence in Tribal Governance*, 2005 ed., 8–13.

26. Charles F. Wilkinson, *Blood Struggle: The Rise of Modern Indian Nations* (New York: W. W. Norton, 2005), 284.

27. Paul Willeto, "Diné College Struggles to Synthesize Navajo and Western Knowledge," *Tribal College Journal* 9 (Fall 1997), 11.

28. Margaret Connell Szasz, *Education and the American Indian: The Road to Self-Determination since 1928*, 3rd ed. (Albuquerque: University of New Mexico Press, 1999), chap. 8. Clinton's Executive Order 13096 is reprinted as Appendix 3 in *Education and the American Indian*.

29. Jon Reyhner and Jeanne Eder, *American Indian Education: A History* (Norman: University of Oklahoma Press, 2004), 321–22; Civil Rights Commission report cited in *American Indian Politics and the American Political System*, by David E. Wilkins, 2nd ed. (Lanham, Md.: Rowman and Littlefield, 2007), 89.

30. Wilkinson, *Blood Struggle*, 287.

31. Wilkinson, *Blood Struggle*, 282–83.

32. Vine Deloria Jr., *Indian Education in America* (Boulder, Colo.: AISES, 1991), 20–21. See also Vine Deloria Jr., and Daniel R. Wildcat, *Power and Place: Indian Education in America* (Golden, Colo.: Fulcrum, 2001).

33. Quoted in Fergus M. Bordewich, *Killing the White Man's Indian: Reinventing Native Americans at the End of the*

Twentieth Century (New York: Doubleday, 1996), 275–78. (At the time of the interview, her name was Pease-Windy Boy.)

34. "Tribal Colleges: Gains for 'Underfunded Miracles,'" *Christian Science Monitor*, May 21, 1997, 12.

35. Maenette Kape'ahiokalani Padeken Ah Nee-Benham and Wayne J. Stein, eds., *The Renaissance of American Indian Higher Education: Capturing the Dream* (Mahwah, N.J.: Lawrence Erlbaum Associates, 2003), xviii–xix.

36. James Shanley, "Educating a Closed Population Pool," in Harvard Project, *State of the Native Nations*, 213–15.

37. Norman T. Oppelt, *The Tribally Controlled Indian College: The Beginnings of Self-Determination in American Indian Education* (Tsaile, Ariz.: Navajo Community College Press, 1990), x.

38. Wilkinson, *Blood Struggle*, 288.

39. Carnegie Foundation, *Tribal Colleges*.

40. Quoted in Szasz, *Education*, 239.

41. Donald L. Fixico, *The Invasion of Indian Country in the Twentieth Century: American Capitalism and Tribal Natural Resources* (Niwot: University Press of Colorado, 1998).

42. Doug Brugge, Timothy Benally, and Esther Yazzie-Lewis, eds., *The Navajo People and Uranium Mining* (Albuquerque: University of New Mexico Press, 2006); Barbara Rose Johnston, Susan Dawson, and Gary Madsen, "Uranium Mining and Milling: Navajo Experiences in the American Southwest," in *Indians and Energy: Exploitation and Opportunity in the American Southwest*, eds. Sherry L. Smith and Brian Frehner (Santa Fe, N. Mex.: SAR Press, 2010), chap. 6; Judy Pasternak, *Yellow Dirt: An American Story of a Poisoned Land and a People Betrayed* (New York: Free Press, 2010), 1.4 million figure at 114.

43. Emily Benedek, *The Wind Won't Know Me: A History of the Navajo-Hopi Land Dispute* (Norman: University of Oklahoma Press, 1999).

44. *News from Indian Country* 10, no. 17 (mid-September 1996), 8A.

45. Quoted in Marianna Guerrero, "American Indian Water Rights: The Blood of Life in Native North America," in *The State of Native America: Genocide, Colonization, and Resistance*, ed. M. Annette Jaimes (Boston: South End Press, 1992), 207–8.

46. Wilkins, *American Indian Politics*, 76.

47. Lloyd Burton, *American Indian Water Rights and the Limits of the Law* (Lawrence: University Press of Kansas, 1991), 140–41; David H. Getches, Charles F. Wilkinson, et al., *Cases and Materials on Federal Indian Law*, 4th ed. (St. Paul, Minn.: West Group, 1998; 5th ed., 2004; 6th ed., 2011), chap. 11. Page and chapter references in this and subsequent notes are to the fourth edition unless otherwise noted.

48. Matthew Coon-Come, "A Reduction of Our World," in *Our People . . . Our Land: Reflections on Common Ground—500 Years*, ed. Kurt Russo (Bellingham, Wash.: Florence R. Kluckhohn Center, 1992), 82; Hans M. Carlson, *Home Is the Hunter: The James Bay Cree and Their Land* (Vancouver: University of British Columbia Press, 2008).

49. Winona LaDuke, foreword to *Strangers Devour the Land*, by Boyce Richardson (1976; repr., Post Mills, Vt.: Chelsea Green Publishing, 1991), ix.

50. Coon-Come, "Reduction," 82.

51. Getches, Wilkinson et al., *Federal Indian Law*, 509–20; John R. Wunder, *"Retained by the People": A History of American Indians and the Bill of Rights* (New York: Oxford University Press, 1994), 153–56.

52. Rob Carson/Associated Press, "*Boldt* Decision Has Rippling Effects 40 Years Later," *The Washington Times*, February 9, 2014, http://www.washingtontimes.com/news/2014/feb/9/boldt-decision-has-rippling-effects-40-years-later/#ixzz3CAQNPb6c.

53. Larry Nesper, *The Walleye War: The Struggle for Ojibwe Spearfishing and Treaty Rights* (Lincoln: University of Nebraska Press, 2002).

54. Christopher Vecsey and William A. Starna, eds., *Iroquois Land Claims* (Syracuse, N.Y.: Syracuse University Press, 1988).

55. Quoted in Wilkins, *American Indian Politics*, 157.

56. Ben Welch, "A Slippery Slope," *American Indian Report* 17 (October 2001), 12–17; Robert A. Williams Jr., *Like a Loaded Weapon: The Rehnquist Court, Indian Rights, and the Legal History of Racism in America* (Minneapolis: University of Minnesota Press, 2005); Echo-Hawk, *Courts of the Conqueror*, 423.

57. Getches, Wilkinson et al., *Federal Indian Law*, chap. 10; Carolyn N. Long, *Religious Freedom and Indian Rights: The Case of* Oregon v. Smith (Lawrence: University Press of Kansas, 2000); Echo-Hawk, *Courts of the Conqueror*, chap. 11.

58. For detailed discussions, see Getches, Wilkinson et al., *Federal Indian Law*, 253–55; N. Bruce Duthu, "Implicit Divestiture of Tribal Powers: Locating Legitimate Sources of Authority in Indian Country," *American Indian Law Review* 19, no. 2 (1994), 353–402; David H. Getches, "Conquering the Cultural Frontier: The New Subjectivism of the Supreme Court in Indian Law," *California Law Review* 84 (December 1996), 1573–1655; David E. Wilkins, *American Indian Sovereignty and the U.S. Supreme Court: The Masking of Justice* (Austin: University of Texas Press, 1997), chaps. 5–6; Philip P. Frickey, "A Common Law for Our Age of Colonialism: The Judicial Divestiture of Indian Tribal Authority over Nonmembers," *Yale Law Review* 109 (October 1999), 1–85.

59. See, for example, "Indians in Court: A Look at the Rise and Decline of Indian Law," special issue, *American Indian Report* 17 (October 2001).

60. *American Indian Report* (July 2004), 10.

61. Quoted in David H. Getches and Charles F. Wilkinson, *Cases and Materials on Federal Indian Law*, 2nd ed. (St. Paul, Minn.: West Publishing, 1986), xxx.

62. Frank Pommersheim, *Braid of Feathers: American Indian Law and Contemporary Tribal Life* (Berkeley: University of California Press, 1995), 51.

63. "Gover Issues Historic Apology," *American Indian Report* 16 (October 2000), 10.

64. *Indian Country Today*, September 20, 2000.

65. Wilkins, *American Indian Politics*, 164–68.

66. Christopher Buck, "'Never Again': Kevin Gover's Apology for the Bureau of Indian Affairs," *Wicazo Sa Review* 21 (Spring 2006), 97–126; quotes at 99, 107.

67. Quoted in Bordewich, *Killing*, 313.

68. Wilkins, *American Indian Politics*, 3–7.

69. Quoted in *American Indian Report* 15 (April 1999), 3.

70. David Wilkins, *Hollow Justice: A History of Indigenous Claims in the United States* (New Haven: Yale Univer-

sity Press, 2013), chap. 7, traces the tortuous history of the case.

71. "Obama Admin Strikes $3.4B Deal in Indian Trust Lawsuit," *New York Times*, December 8, 2009; "Congress Shortchanges the Indians," *New York Times*, March 15, 2010.

72. Roger Anyon, "Zuni Repatriation of War Gods," reprinted in *Native American Voices: A Reader*, eds. Susan Lobo and Steve Talbot, 2nd ed. (Upper Saddle River, N.J.: Prentice Hall, 2001), 329.

73. Quoted in Robert S. McPherson, *Viewing the Ancestors: Perceptions of the Anaasázi, Mokwič, and Hisatsinom* (Norman: University of Oklahoma Press, 2014), 9.

74. James C. McKinley Jr., "Geronimo's Heirs Sue Secret Yale Society over His Skull," *New York Times*, February 19, 2009, http://www.nytimes.com/2009/02/20/us/20geronimo.html.

75. Karen Coody Cooper, *Spirited Encounters: American Indians Protest Museum Policies and Practices* (Lanham, Md.: AltaMira Press, 2008); Susan Sleeper-Smith, ed., *Contesting Knowledge: Museums and Indigenous Perspectives* (Lincoln: University of Nebraska Press, 2009).

76. W. Richard West Jr., "Remarks on the Occasion of the Grand Opening Ceremony" (speech, National Museum of the American Indian, Washington, D.C., September 21, 2004).

77. Amanda J. Cobb, ed., "The National Museum of the American Indian," special issue, *American Indian Quarterly* 29 (Summer/Fall 2005), quotes at 368, 380. See also Amy Lonetree and Amanda J. Cobb, eds., *The National Museum of the American Indian: Critical Conversations* (Lincoln: University of Nebraska Press, 2008).

78. Akim D. Reinhardt, "Defining the Native: Local Print Media Coverage of the NMAI," in Cobb, "National Museum," 450–65.

79. James Lujan, "A Museum of the Indian, Not for the Indian," in Cobb, "National Museum," 510–16.

80. Amy Lonetree, ed., "Critical Engagements with the National Museum of the American Indian," special issue, *American Indian Quarterly* 30 (Summer/Fall 2006), esp. 597–618, 632–45.

81. Amanda J. Cobb, "Interview with W. Richard West," in Cobb, "National Museum," 517–37, quotes at 520, 532.

82. Amy Lonetree, *Decolonizing Museums: Representing Native America in National and Tribal Museums* (Chapel Hill: University of North Carolina Press, 2012).

83. Quoted in *USA Today*, November 3, 2009.

84. "President Obama Delivers Remarks at White House, Tribal Nations Conference," *Washington Post*, November 5, 2009.

85. Mary Crow Dog, with Richard Erdoes, *Lakota Woman* (New York: Harper Perennial, 1991), 4, 15, 54.

86. Crow Dog, *Lakota Woman*, 73.

87. On Annie Mae Aquash, see Devon Abbott Mihesuah, "Anna Mae Pictou-Aquash: An American Indian Activist," in *Sifters: Native American Women's Lives*, ed. Theda Perdue (New York: Oxford University Press, 2001), 204–22; also Devon Abbott Mihesuah, *Indigenous American Women: Decolonization, Empowerment, Activism* (Lincoln: University of Nebraska Press, 2003), 115–27.

88. N. Bruce Duthu, *American Indians and the Law* (New York: Viking Penguin, 2008), 20; Duthu, *Shadow Nations: Tribal Sovereignty and the Limits of Legal Pluralism* (New York:

Oxford University Press, 2013), 7; Duthu, "Implicit Divestiture," 353–402; Peter C. Maxfield, *"Oliphant v. Suquamish Tribe:* The Whole Is Greater than the Sum of the Parts," *Journal of Contemporary Law* 19 (Fall 1993), 391, quoted in Getches, Wilkinson, and Williams, *Federal Indian Law*, 542; Robert A. Williams Jr., *Like a Loaded Weapon: The Rehnquist Court, Indian Rights, and the Legal History of Racism in America* (Minneapolis: University of Minnesota Press, 2005), chap. 7.

89. Frederick E. Hoxie, "Building a Future on the Past: Crow Indian Leadership in an Era of Division and Reunion," in *Indian Leadership*, ed. Walter Williams (Manhattan, Kans.: Sunflower University Press, 1984), quote at 84.

90. Steve Pavlik and Daniel R. Wildcat, eds., *Destroying Dogma: Vine Deloria Jr. and His Influence on American Society* (Golden, Colo.: Fulcrum, 2006), quotations at viii, xi; Frederick E. Hoxie, *This Indian Country: American Indian Activists and The Place They Made* (New York: Penguin, 2012), 337.

91. "This Country Was a Lot Better Off When the Indians Were Running It," *New York Times Magazine*, March 8, 1970, reprinted in Josephy, *Red Power*, quote at 239.

92. For example, Vine Deloria Jr., "Marginal and Submarginal," in *Indigenizing the Academy: Transforming Scholarship and Empowering Communities*, ed. Devon Abbott Mihesuah and Angela Cavender Wilson (Lincoln: University of Nebraska Press, 2004), 16–30.

93. Vine Deloria Jr., *Custer Died for Your Sins: An Indian Manifesto* (New York: Macmillan, 1969), 84.

94. Pavlik and Wildcat, *Destroying Dogma*, quotes at xi, 157–58.

95. "This Country Was a Lot Better Off," quote at 247.

96. Wilma Mankiller and Michael Wallis, *Mankiller: A Chief and Her People* (New York: St. Martin's Press, 1993), ix.

97. *New York Times*, April 6, 1994.

98. *The Dartmouth*, April 19, 1994.

99. *Los Angeles Times*, November 1, 1993.

100. Mankiller and Wallis, *Mankiller*, 242.

101. Comments at Native American Studies Colloquium, Dartmouth College, winter 1996.

102. *The Dartmouth*, January 24, 1996.

103. Chad Smith, "Rebuilding a Nation" (public talk at Dartmouth College, November 1999).

104. Theda Perdue, *Cherokee Women: Gender and Culture Change, 1700–1835* (Lincoln: University of Nebraska Press, 1998), 195; Mankiller and Wallis, *Mankiller*, 229.

105. See, for example, the fine art of the Santa Fe Indian School directed by Dorothy Dunn beginning in 1932. Bruce Bernstein and W. Jackson Rushing, *Modern by Tradition: American Indian Painting in the Studio Style* (Santa Fe: Museum of New Mexico Press, 1995).

106. Marjorie Devon, ed., *Migrations: New Directions in Native American Art* (Albuquerque: University of New Mexico Press, 2006), quote at 2.

107. Qutoted in Margaret Archuleta and Rennard Strickland, *Shared Visions: Native American Painters and Sculptors in the Twentieth Century*, 2nd ed. (New York: Free Press, 1993), 95.

108. Quoted in Suzan Harjo, "Without Reservation," *Native Peoples Magazine*, Spring 1998, http://www.nativepeoples.com/Native-Peoples/Spring-1998/Without-Reservation/.

SUGGESTED READINGS

Ah Nee-Benham, Maenette Kape'ahiokalani Padeken, and Wayne J. Stein, eds. *The Renaissance of American Indian Higher Education: Capturing the Dream*. Mahwah, N.J.: Lawrence Erlbaum Associates, 2003.

Ambler, Marjane. *Breaking the Iron Bonds: Indian Control of Energy Development*. Lawrence: University Press of Kansas, 1990.

American Indian Report: Indian Country's News Magazine. Fairfax, Va.

Bailey, Garrick A., ed. *Indians in Contemporary Society*. Washington, D.C.: Smithsonian Institution, 2008. Vol. 2 of *Handbook of North American Indians*, edited by William C. Sturtevant.

Bordewich, Fergus M. *Killing the White Man's Indian: Reinventing Native Americans at the End of the Twentieth Century*. New York: Doubleday, 1996.

Brugge, Doug, Timothy Benally, and Esther Yazzie-Lewis, eds. *The Navajo People and Uranium Mining*. Albuquerque: University of New Mexico Press, 2006.

The Carnegie Foundation for the Advancement of Teaching. *Tribal Colleges: Shaping the Future of Native America*. Princeton, N.J.: Carnegie Foundation for the Advancement of Teaching, 1989.

Cornell, Stephen. *The Return of the Native: American Indian Political Resurgence*. New York: Oxford University Press, 1988.

Crow Dog, Mary. *Lakota Woman*. With Richard Erdoes. New York: Harper Perennial, 1991.

Davis, Julie L. *Survival Schools: The American Indian Movement and Community Education in the Twin Cities*. Minneapolis: University of Minnesota Press, 2013.

Davis, Mary B., ed. *Native America in the Twentieth Century: An Encyclopedia*. New York: Garland, 1994.

Deloria, Philip J. *Playing Indian*. New Haven: Yale University Press, 1998.

Deloria, Vine, Jr., and Clifford Lytle. *The Nations Within: The Past and Future of American Indian Sovereignty*. New York: Pantheon, 1984.

Deloria, Vine, Jr., and Daniel R. Wildcat. *Power and Place: Indian Education in America*. Golden, Colo.: Fulcrum, 2001.

Devon, Marjorie, ed. *Migrations: New Directions in Native American Art*. Albuquerque: University of New Mexico Press, 2006.

Duthu, N. Bruce. *American Indians and the Law*. New York: Viking Penguin, 2008.

———. *Shadow Nations: Tribal Sovereignty and the Limits of Legal Pluralism*. New York: Oxford University Press, 2013.

Echo-Hawk, Walter R. *In the Courts of the Conqueror: The 10 Worst Indian Law Cases Ever Decided*. Golden, Colo.: Fulcrum, 2010.

Edmunds, R. David, ed. *The New Warriors: Native American Leaders since 1900*. Lincoln: University of Nebraska Press, 2001.

Eichstaedt, Peter H. *If You Poison Us: Uranium and Native Americans*. Santa Fe, N. Mex.: Red Crane Books, 1994.

Fine-Dare, Kathleen S. *Grave Injustice: The American Indian Repatriation Movement and NAGPRA*. Lincoln: University of Nebraska Press, 2002.

Fixico, Donald L. *American Indians in a Modern World*. Lanham, Md.: Rowman AltaMira Press, 2008.

———. *Indian Resilience and Rebuilding: Indigenous Nations in the Modern American West*. Tucson: University of Arizona Press, 2013.

———. *The Invasion of Indian Country in the Twentieth Century: American Capitalism and Tribal Natural Resources*. Niwot: University Press of Colorado, 1998.

Getches, David H., Charles F. Wilkinson, et al. *Cases and Materials on Federal Indian Law*. 4th ed. St. Paul, Minn.: West Group, 1998. 5th ed., 2004; 6th ed., 2011.

Grinde, Donald A., and Bruce E. Johansen. *Ecocide of Native America: Environmental Destruction of Indian Lands and Peoples*. Santa Fe, N. Mex.: Clear Light Publishers, 1995.

Grounds, Richard A., George E. Tinker, and David E. Wilkins, eds. *Native Voices: American Indian Identity and Resistance*. Lawrence: University Press of Kansas, 2003.

Harvard Project on American Indian Economic Development. *The State of the Native Nations: Conditions under U.S. Policies of Self-Determination*. New York: Oxford University Press, 2008.

Hosmer, Brian, and Colleen O'Neill, eds. *Native Pathways: American Indian Culture and Economic Development in the Twentieth Century*. Boulder: University Press of Colorado, 2004.

Hoxie, Frederick E. *This Indian Country: American Indian Activists and the Place They Made*. New York: Penguin, 2012.

Indian Country Today (newspaper). Available online.

Iverson, Peter. *Diné: A History of the Navajos*. Albuquerque: University of New Mexico Press, 2002.

———. *"We Are Still Here": American Indians in the Twentieth Century*. Wheeling, Ill.: Harlan Davidson, 1998.

Jaimes, M. Annette, ed. *The State of Native America: Genocide, Colonization, and Resistance*. Boston: South End Press, 1992.

Janda, Sarah Epple. *Beloved Women: The Political Lives of LaDonna Harris and Wilma Mankiller*. Dekalb: Northern Illinois University Press, 2007.

LaDuke, Winona. *All Our Relations: Native Struggles for Land and Life*. Boston: South End Press, 1999.

Lonetree, Amy. *Decolonizing Museums: Representing Native America in National and Tribal Museums*. Chapel Hill: University of North Carolina Press, 2012.

Lonetree, Amy, and Amanda J. Cobb, eds. *The National Museum of the American Indian: Critical Conversations*. Lincoln: University of Nebraska Press, 2008.

Mankiller, Wilma, and Michael Wallis. *Mankiller: A Chief and Her People*. New York: St. Martin's Press, 1993.

Means, Russell. *Where White Men Fear to Tread: The Autobiography of Russell Means*. With Marvin J. Wolf. New York: St. Martin's Press, 1995.

Pasternak, Judy. *Yellow Dirt: An American Story of a Poisoned Land and a People Betrayed.* New York: Free Press, 2010.

Pavlik, Steve, and Daniel R. Wildcat, eds. *Destroying Dogma: Vine Deloria Jr. and His Influence on American Society.* Golden, Colo.: Fulcrum, 2006.

Pevar, Stephen L. *The Rights of Indian Tribes.* 4th ed. New York: Oxford University Press, 2012.

Rawls, James J. *Chief Red Fox Is Dead: A History of Native Americans since 1945.* Fort Worth, Tex.: Harcourt Brace, 1996.

Rosier, Paul C. *Serving Their Country: American Indian Politics and Patriotism in the Twentieth Century.* Cambridge, Mass.: Harvard University Press, 2009.

Smith, Dean Howard. *Modern Tribal Development: Paths to Self-Sufficiency and Cultural Integrity in Indian Country.* Walnut Creek, Calif.: AltaMira Press, 2000.

Smith, Paul Chaat, and Robert Allen Warrior. *Like a Hurricane: The Indian Movement from Alcatraz to Wounded Knee.* New York: New Press, 1996.

Smith, Sherry L., and Brian Frehner, eds. *Indians and Energy: Exploitation and Opportunity in the American Southwest.* Santa Fe, N. Mex.: SAR Press, 2010.

Tiller, Veronica E. Velarde, ed. and comp. *Tiller's Guide to Indian Country: Economic Profiles of American Indian Reservations.* Albuquerque: BowArrow, 2005.

Ulrich, Roberta. *American Indian Nations from Termination to Restoration, 1953–2006.* Lincoln: University of Nebraska Press, 2010.

Utter, Jack. *American Indians: Answers to Today's Questions.* 2nd ed. Norman: University of Oklahoma Press, 2001.

Wilkins, David E. *American Indian Politics and the American Political System.* 2nd ed., Lanham, Md.: Rowman and Littlefield, 2007. 3rd ed. (with Heidi Kiiwetinepinesiik Stark), 2010.

———. *American Indian Sovereignty and the U.S. Supreme Court: The Masking of Justice.* Austin: University of Texas Press, 1997.

———. *Hollow Justice: A History of Indigenous Claims in the United States.* New Haven: Yale University Press, 2013.

Wilkins, David E., and K. Tsianina Lomawaima. *Uneven Ground: American Indian Sovereignty and Federal Law.* Norman: University of Oklahoma Press, 2001.

Wilkinson, Charles F. *Blood Struggle: The Rise of Modern Indian Nations.* New York: W. W. Norton, 2005.

Williams, Robert A., Jr. *Like a Loaded Weapon: The Rehnquist Court, Indian Rights, and the Legal History of Racism in America.* Minneapolis: University of Minnesota Press, 2005.

10

•••×××××××◆×××××××•••

Nations within a Nation: Indian Country Today

FOCUS QUESTIONS

1. What factors determine Indian identity in modern America?

2. In what ways is the federal government attempting to forge new relationships with Indian peoples, and how have Native Americans responded?

3. How do Indian nations distinguish themselves from other U.S. governing bodies?

4. How has gaming affected Native communities, both positively and negatively?

5. What measures are Indian nations taking to improve conditions in Indian country?

6. What is tribal sovereignty and why is it so important?

A TWENTY-FIRST-CENTURY RENAISSANCE

LAKOTA AUTHOR JOSEPH MARSHALL III WROTE that the turn of the new century meant that "the Lakota have made it through another winter" — a very long winter.[1] For Indian people throughout the country, the turn of the millennium was an occasion to remember the hardships they had survived, assess challenges they continued to face, and embrace new opportunities to ensure that Indian country at the end of the twenty-first century would be stronger than it was at the beginning of the century.

American Indians have now entered their sixth century since Europeans first arrived on the continent. Indian America continues to defy easy and narrow descriptions. The legacies of conquest, colonization, cultural assault, and failed government policies of dependency are still evident in harrowing statistics, broken lives, and stifled hopes. As a group, Native Americans are still among the most impoverished people in the United States. Some reservations remain notorious for poverty, alcoholism, and unemployment. Indian nations have been pushed to the brink, but they have survived and are now rebuilding and in some cases prospering. Wrapping up his survey of the struggles waged by Indian nations in modern America, legal scholar Charles Wilkinson concludes: "Never has this land seen such staying power."[2]

Throughout Indian country tribes are reasserting their rights to self-governance, providing services formerly administered by the federal government, pursuing new economic endeavors, taking over education, running language programs, improving health and living conditions, challenging and confounding old stereotypes about identity and culture, and preserving and applying tribal values in the modern world. With changes in Washington, D.C., and with the Native American population on the rise, Indian country today is forging a renaissance.[3] New sources of prosperity, tribal sovereignty, political influence, and cultural revitalization are creating new conditions, new rules, and new relations with American society. Native American nations, communities, and individuals still struggle, and sometimes fail, to overcome the legacies of colonialism, oppression, and dependency. But in all kinds of ways, they are beginning to "transcend the half millennium of culture shock brought about by the confrontation with Western civilization." In the first year of the new millennium, just a few years before his death, Vine Deloria Jr. predicted: "When we leave the culture shock behind, we will be masters of our own fate again and able to determine for ourselves what kind of lives we will lead."[4]

The Census: An Evolving Profile of Indian America

American Indians were first counted as a separate group in the U.S. census in 1860, but that census did not include Indian people living on reservations and in Indian

2007	Cherokees amend tribal constitution to grant citizenship "by blood" only
2009	President Obama begins holding annual Tribal Nations conferences in Washington, D.C.
2009	Department of the Interior reaches $3.4 billion settlement in the *Cobell* case
2010	President Obama signs *Cobell* settlement into law as part of the Claims Resolution Act
2010	Congress passes the Tribal Law and Order Act
2010	U.S. census records a population of 2.9 million American Indians, with another 2.3 million people claiming partial Indian ancestry
2010	United States endorses the United Nations Declaration on the Rights of Indigenous Peoples
2013	Congress passes Violence Against Women Reauthorization Act
2013	U.S. Supreme Court decides the "Baby Veronica" case
2014	President Obama makes first visit to Indian country as president
2014	President Obama establishes the White House Council on Native American Affairs
2014	First gathering of the National Congress of Black American Indians
2014	Native Language Immersion Student Achievement Act introduced into Congress
2015	Federal judge orders cancellation of Washington Redskins' federal trademark registrations, stating the logo might denigrate Native Americans

Territory. Not until 1890 were Indians counted throughout the country. In 1900 the Indian population of the United States was recorded at 237,196, or only .3 percent of the nation's total recorded population. It was clear evidence, many people believed, that Indians were on the brink of extinction. But the 1900 census was off the mark. In those days, census enumerators classified race on the basis of observation — in other words, you were counted as an Indian if you "looked" like one. Census counters failed to identify many Indian people, and many Indians chose not to be identified. Instead of continuing decline and disappearance in the twentieth century, Indian population rebounded, at first slowly and then dramatically (see Chart 10.1). In a changing social climate marked by increased Indian activism, increased interest in Indian cultures, and increased prestige and opportunities associated with Indian heritage, many people who had not done so before literally stood up to be counted as Indians.

In 2000 the Census Bureau used self-identification as its criterion and allowed respondents to check more than one box for the first time ever; the results of that census showed that the Indian population had risen to 2.5 million, with an additional 1.6 million people identifying themselves as part Indian — American Indian and white, American Indian and black, and so on — in the "American Indian in combination" category. Improved health conditions, higher birth rates, and lower death rates accounted for some of the increases — more Indians were being born and living longer — but the huge rise in American Indian population in the second half of the twentieth century was due to changing patterns in ethnic identity rather than natural increase: far more people were calling themselves Indians (see pages 551–55).[5] In the 2010 census, those numbers again increased considerably, with 2.9 million residents identifying as Indian and another 2.3 million identifying as part Indian (Chart 10.1). According to the 2010 census, self-identified Indians now account for 1.7 percent of America's total population.

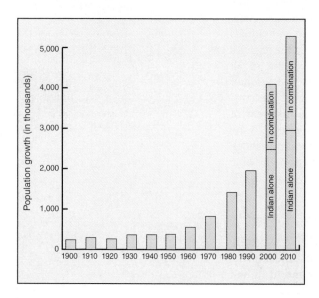

◆ Chart 10.1 **American Indian Population Growth Rate, 1900–2010**
Source: U.S. Census Bureau.

The 2000 and 2010 censuses also calculated tribal populations, again including an "in combination" category. In both years, the Cherokees and Navajos were reported as the largest tribes. Alaska Natives have been counted since 1880 but were generally reported in the "American Indian" category until 1940, when they began to be enumerated separately as Eskimo and Aleut. The census now uses a combined "American Indian or Alaska Native" response category to gather data on both population groups. The state with the highest proportion of Native population is Alaska, where 14.8 percent identified as American Indian and Alaska Native alone, and 19.6 percent of the population identified itself as full or part American Indian or Alaska Native in 2010 (Map 10.1).

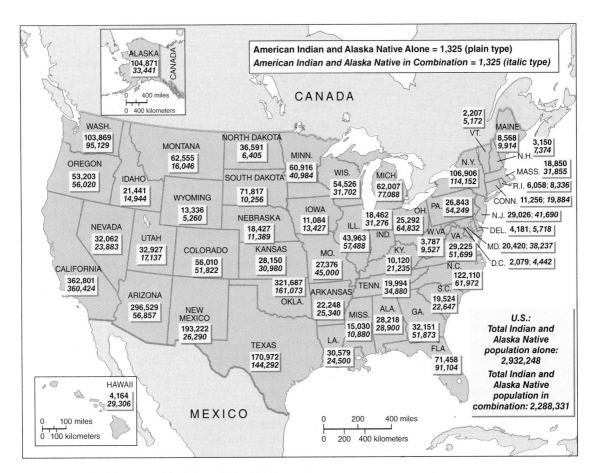

◆ Map 10.1 **Indian Populations, 2010**

In the first decade of the twenty-first century, Indian populations continued to grow steadily in every state, rebounding dramatically after the massive declines of previous centuries.
SOURCE: U.S. Census Bureau, Table 2. American Indian and Alaska Native Population for the United States, Regions, and States, and for Puerto Rico: 2000 and 2010. *The American Indian and Alaska Native Population: 2010 Census Briefs*. Issued January 2012.

In addition to huge increases in the numbers of people reporting as American Indians and Alaska Natives, the 2000 and 2010 censuses confirmed patterns of population distribution that earlier censuses had already identified: most American Indians are located in the West and Midwest, with more than 50 percent of America's Indian population living in just ten states. Almost one in four Indian people reside in either Oklahoma or California, and the Indian population of California is now as high as it was before European contact. In 2010, 78 percent of American Indians and Alaska Natives in both census categories (alone or in combination) lived outside of "American Indian and Alaska Native areas" (federal or state reservations, off-reservation trust lands, etc.). Well over half of all American Indians live in urban areas, although often in cities close to reservations, where they can move with ease between both communities. New York City and Los Angeles have the largest populations (112,000 and 54,000 respectively in 2010), followed by Phoenix, Oklahoma City, and Anchorage, Alaska, although Anchorage, with 36,000, has the greatest proportion of American Indian and Alaska Natives (12 percent of the total population).

Who Is an Indian?

There is no simple answer. The question is a contentious one that goes beyond mere numbers to the issue and nature of tribal and cultural survival in the twenty-first century. Neither Indian tribes nor the federal government applies a single criterion for identifying who is an Indian. Different Indian nations have different rules for membership. Urban Indians may have different criteria for identifying as Indians than do reservation Indians.[6] The BIA defines Indians as people who are members of federally recognized tribes, but some Indian people do not belong to recognized tribes. The government counts as Indian those people who have (depending on the purpose) one-half or one-quarter ancestry, but degree of ancestry, or "blood," in itself might not be sufficient for membership in some tribes, and in some cases may not be required at all for membership. Residence, status in the community, and many other factors can play into whether one is regarded as Indian. The same person might be regarded as an Indian by some people and as non-Indian by others. Individuals may think of themselves as ethnically, culturally, or politically Indian. As ethnic identities become increasingly complex and flexible, the same person might consider him- or herself Indian for some purposes and in some situations but not in others.

Indian nations historically determined membership with little or no regard to "blood." Members of other tribes and even Europeans could become tribal members through marriage, adoption, or even choice. In many areas of the country, intermarriage between Indians and non-Indians was more common than armed conflict. Around Puget Sound, for example, Native people and their offspring had extensive and intimate relations with immigrants and their offspring, with the result that the descendants of the Indians who were there when Europeans first arrived are now "inextricably tangled in the cultural, economic, and racial threads of a social fabric designed by non-Indians."[7]

◆ **Dwayne Wilcox, *Wow, Full-Blooded White People* (2008)**
Drawing on the stylistic traditions of ledger art (see "The Fort Marion Artists," pages 433–38), Oglala Lakota artist Dwayne Wilcox, born in 1957, pokes fun at ideas of blood quotas by turning the tables on Anglo-American tourists, or "reversing the gaze." His ledger art conveys some of the absurdity of having outsiders determine who is or is not an "authentic" Indian. *Hood Museum of Art, Dartmouth College, Hanover, New Hampshire; purchased through the Guernsey Center Moore 1904 Fund. Used by permission of the artist.*

In many areas, Indian people and African Americans have had long histories of intermarriage, with the result that some people identify themselves as black Indians. The first gathering of the National Congress of Black American Indians was held in Washington, D.C., in July 2014. Ethnic groups change as human relations change, and many Indian peoples define themselves on their own terms, perhaps distinguishing themselves from outsiders on the basis of clan and kinship or involvement in community and ceremony, rather than a measured tribal and ethnic identity.[8] "Blood" often has little to do with it.

But the U.S. government has attempted to institutionalize definitions of Indianness. The terms *Indian* and *tribe,* introduced by non-Indians, became crucial terms for classifying a huge array of people. Federal bureaucrats tried to reduce multiple ways of being Indian to simple and static categories. Government criteria for identifying Indians in the wake of extensive intermarriage with non-Indians introduced concepts of blood quotas, which remain to this day, though they are often inconsistently applied and with damaging results. Generally the federal government applies a 25 percent "blood quantum" (that is, one must be at least one-quarter Indian to qualify). As Indian people continue to marry non-Indians, this level of "Indian blood" will inevitably become less common, or "diluted," with the result that Indians will eventually "disappear" or be defined out of existence if they continue to be identified according to this measure. As activist and writer Ward Churchill sees it, "North America's Native peoples have been bound ever more tightly into the carefully crafted mechanisms of oppression and eventual negation."[9]

Today, even though census figures show a growing number of Native Americans, and despite a willingness to let Natives define themselves (at least statistically), identity is still a crucial issue. More than 50 percent of all Indians are married to non-Indians. If current trends continue, it has been projected that only about 8 percent of Indian people will have one-half or more Indian ancestry by the year 2080. As Cherokee demographer Russell Thornton predicts, "a point will be reached — perhaps not too far in the future — when it will no longer make sense to define American Indians in genetic terms, only as tribal members or as people of Indian ancestry or ethnicity."[10] One journalist asks, "How much blending can occur before Indians finally cease to be Indians?"[11]

Census figures based on self-identification are not always good enough for skeptics, Native and non-Native, who point out that an Indian identity might provide access to land claim settlements, casino wealth, scholarships, health benefits, mineral and resource royalties, or other rights. Are some of the "new Indians" really just "wannabes"? Are people who self-identify as Indian but who lack tribal affiliation really Indian? Should urban Indians who have never lived on the reservation qualify as tribal members, especially when membership means access to tribal services or per capita payments from oil and gas leases? Should blood quota play any role in measuring Indianness? If not, what criteria should be applied? Should the federal government or other outside agencies have any say regarding how Indian communities determine their own membership?

Some Indian communities have attempted to tighten up the tribal rolls by excluding people who marry non-Indians or the children of people who have married outsiders, but it is uncertain what the long-term effects of such policies will be. Other communities reject the idea of measuring "Indian blood": on Pine Ridge Reservation in South Dakota, the Oglalas abandoned blood quantum as a criterion of tribal enrollment, basing membership instead on factors such as residency and commitment to the Oglala people.[12]

For many years the Cherokee Nation of Oklahoma determined membership by tracing descent from a person on the 1906 tribal roll rather than on the degree of blood. The tribal roll was compiled to divide land among tribal members under the allotment process and contained three categories: "Cherokees by Blood," "Intermarried Whites," and "Freedmen." But in 2007 the Cherokees voted for an amendment to the tribal constitution that limited citizenship to descendants of "by blood" tribal members listed on the rolls, thereby revoking the tribal citizenship of an estimated 2,800 people descended from freedmen, people the Cherokees once held as slaves but who received citizenship in the Cherokee Nation after the Civil War (as mandated by the Treaty of 1866 with the federal government). The 2007 Cherokee freedmen vote sparked anger and controversy and divided Cherokees. Principal Chief Chad Smith and others defended the Cherokees' right to define their own membership as a fundamental attribute of sovereignty. Critics saw it as an act of racial discrimination, although most other Indian nations have a blood requirement for citizenship. The Congressional Black Caucus threatened to block the $300 million the Cherokees received annually in federal funds unless the tribe reinstated the people who had been disenfranchised, but it relented when the Cherokee Nation agreed to allow the issue to be resolved in the courts.[13] In 2011 the Cherokee District Court declared the freedmen amendment void as a matter of law since it violated the Treaty of 1866, but it was overturned later that year by the Cherokee Supreme Court. Both sides subsequently filed complaints in federal court.

What it means to be Indian continues to be a complex and sometimes divisive issue. Some companies now advertise DNA testing services as a "fast, simple and noninvasive" method of producing "irrefutable results" for "determining Native

◆ **Cherokee Freedmen**
A group of Cherokee Freedmen and their supporters demonstrate at the State Capitol in Oklahoma City in 2007. *AP Photo.*

American lineage for tribal enrollment."[14] Like blood quotas, DNA testing offers one measure of determining identity, but biological proof of Native American ancestry does not in itself guarantee membership in tribes that might place higher value on sustained family ties, cultural knowledge, and community involvement. DNA testing may seem foolproof, but it raises the specter of the kind of racial science that whites applied to Indians in the nineteenth century and it may pose a new threat to tribal sovereignty.[15]

"Recognized" and "Nonrecognized" Tribes

The question "Who is really an Indian?" is posed to tribes as well as to individuals.[16] The BIA acts not only as trustee for Indian resources, but it also decides which groups are formally recognized as Indian tribes. Tribes with whom the United States made treaties or otherwise established a governmental relationship are recognized. There are currently 567 federally recognized tribes, including more than 220 Alaska Native villages (Map 10.2). Many other Indian groups are not formally recognized as Indian "tribes" by the U.S. government; some are recognized by the state in which they live but not by the federal government. Many unrecognized groups are quite small, but the Lumbees of Robeson County in North Carolina, with more than 50,000 members, are the largest tribe east of the Mississippi. The state of North Carolina recognizes the Lumbees as an Indian tribe, but the U.S. government has not yet found them eligible for federal recognition. Indian groups who lack federal recognition do not qualify for federal assistance programs for Indians administered through agencies like the BIA and the Indian Health Service, nor do they benefit from the status of being identified as Indian nations. For example, they are not recognized as Indians for the purposes of the Indian Gaming Regulatory Act of 1988, which allows tribes to engage in gaming activities as a form of economic development on tribal land (see pages 594–99). The growth of tribal gaming has raised the stakes in federal recognition, making it a bitterly contested issue and "a major preoccupation" in Indian country in the twenty-first century.[17]

In 1901, in *Montoya v. United States,* the U.S. Supreme Court adopted a working definition of tribe as "a body of Indians of the same or similar race, united in community under one leadership or government, and inhabiting a particular though sometimes ill-defined territory." But the concept of tribe has always essentially been an externally imposed category that poorly reflects the complexity and diversity of Indian societies and political structures, and deciding which groups "fit" the definition and why they do or do not fit it has always been a problem. In 1978 Congress created the Federal Acknowledgment Project in the BIA to evaluate the claims of nonrecognized tribes and established seven criteria that a petitioning tribe must meet in order to secure federal recognition, including evidence of its historic and continuous identification as an Indian group, evidence of the Indian identity of its members, and evidence of its governing procedures. Later known as the Branch of Acknowledgment and Research

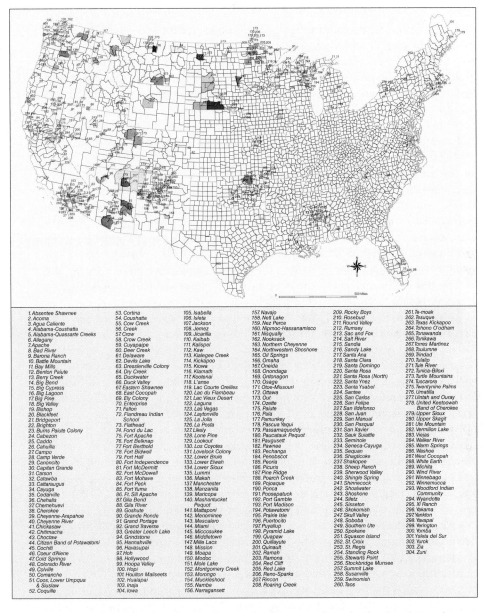

1. Absentee Shawnee
2. Acoma
3. Agua Caliente
4. Alabama-Coushatta
5. Alabama-Quassarte Creeks
6. Allegany
7. Apache
8. Bad River
9. Barona Ranch
10. Battle Mountain
11. Bay Mills
12. Benton Paiute
13. Berry Creek
14. Big Bend
15. Big Cypress
16. Big Lagoon
17. Big Pine
18. Big Valley
19. Bishop
20. Blackfeet
21. Bridgeport
22. Brighton
23. Burns Paiute Colony
24. Cabezon
25. Caddo
26. Cahuilla
27. Campo
28. Camp Verde
29. Canoncito
30. Capitan Grande
31. Carson
32. Catawba
33. Cattaraugus
34. Cayuga
35. Cedarville
36. Chehalis
37. Chemehuevi
38. Cherokee
39. Cheyenne-Arapahoe
40. Cheyenne River
41. Chickasaw
42. Chitimacha
43. Choctaw
44. Citizen Band of Potawatomi
45. Cochiti
46. Coeur d'Alene
47. Cold Springs
48. Colorado River
49. Colville
50. Comanche
51. Coos, Lower Umpqua & Siuslaw
52. Coquille
53. Cortina
54. Coushatta
55. Cow Creek
56. Creek
57. Crow
58. Crow Creek
59. Cuyapaipe
60. Deer Creek
61. Delaware
62. Devils Lake
63. Dresslerville Colony
64. Dry Creek
65. Duckwater
66. Duck Valley
67. Eastern Shawnee
68. East Cocopah
69. Ely Colony
70. Enterprise
71. Fallon
72. Flandreau Indian School
73. Flathead
74. Fond du Lac
75. Fort Apache
76. Fort Belknap
77. Fort Berthold
78. Fort Bidwell
79. Fort Hall
80. Fort Independence
81. Fort McDermitt
82. Fort McDowell
83. Fort Mohave
84. Fort Peck
85. Fort Yuma
86. Ft. Sill Apache
87. Gila Bend
88. Gila River
89. Goshute
90. Grande Ronde
91. Grand Portage
92. Grand Traverse
93. Greater Leech Lake
94. Grindstone
95. Hannahville
96. Havasupai
97. Hoh
98. Hollywood
99. Hoopa Valley
100. Hopi
101. Houlton Maliseets
102. Hualapai
103. Inaja
104. Iowa
105. Isabella
106. Isleta
107. Jackson
108. Jemez
109. Jicarilla
110. Kaibab
111. Kalispel
112. Kaw
113. Kialegee Creek
114. Kickapoo
115. Kiowa
116. Klamath
117. Kootenai
118. L'anse
119. Lac Courte Oreilles
120. Lac du Flambeau
121. Lac Vieux Desert
122. Laguna
123. Las Vegas
124. Laytonville
125. La Jolla
126. La Posta
127. Likely
128. Lone Pine
129. Lookout
130. Los Coyotes
131. Lovelock Colony
132. Lower Brule
133. Lower Elwah
134. Lower Sioux
135. Lummi
136. Makah
137. Manchester
138. Manzanita
139. Maricopa
140. Mashantucket Pequot
141. Mattaponi
142. Menominee
143. Mescalero
144. Miami
145. Miccosukee
146. Middletown
147. Mille Lacs
148. Mission
149. Moapa
150. Modoc
151. Mole Lake
152. Montgomery Creek
153. Morongo
154. Muckleshoot
155. Nambe
156. Narragansett
157. Navajo
158. Nett Lake
159. Nez Perce
160. Nipmoc-Hassanamisco
161. Nisqually
162. Nooksack
163. Northern Cheyenne
164. Northwestern Shoshone
165. Oil Springs
166. Omaha
167. Oneida
168. Onondaga
169. Ontonagon
170. Osage
171. Otoe-Missouri
172. Ottawa
173. Out
174. Ozette
175. Paiute
176. Pala
177. Pamunkey
178. Pascua Yaqui
179. Passamaquoddy
180. Paucatauk Pequot
181. Paugusett
182. Pawnee
183. Pechanga
184. Penobscot
185. Peoria
186. Picuris
187. Pine Ridge
188. Poarch Creek
189. Pojoaque
190. Ponca
191. Poospatuck
192. Port Gamble
193. Port Madison
194. Potawatomi
195. Prairie Isle
196. Puertocito
197. Puyallup
198. Pyramid Lake
199. Quapaw
200. Quillayute
201. Quinault
202. Ramah
203. Ramona
204. Red Cliff
205. Red Lake
206. Reno-Sparks
207. Rincon
208. Roaring Creek
209. Rocky Boys
210. Rosebud
211. Round Valley
212. Rumsey
213. Sac and Fox
214. Salt River
215. Sandia
216. Sandy Lake
217. Santa Ana
218. Santa Clara
219. Santa Domingo
220. Santa Rosa
221. Santa Rosa (North)
222. Santa Ynez
223. Santa Ysabel
224. Santee
225. San Carlos
226. San Felipe
227. San Ildefonso
228. San Juan
229. San Manual
230. San Pasqual
231. San Xavier
232. Sauk Suiattle
233. Seminole
234. Seneca-Cayuga
235. Sequan
236. Shagticoke
237. Shakopee
238. Sheep Ranch
239. Sherwood Valley
240. Shingle Spring
241. Shinnecock
242. Shoalwater
243. Shoshone
244. Siletz
245. Sisseton
246. Skokomish
247. Skull Valley
248. Soboba
249. Southern Ute
250. Spokane
251. Squaxon Island
252. St. Croix
253. St. Regis
254. Standing Rock
255. Stewarts Point
256. Stockbridge Munsee
257. Summit Lake
258. Susanville
259. Swinomish
260. Taos
261. Te-moak
262. Tesuque
263. Texas Kickapoo
264. Tohono O'odham
265. Tonawanda
266. Tonkawa
267. Torres Martinez
268. Toulumne
269. Trinidad
270. Tulalip
271. Tule River
272. Tunica-Biloxi
273. Turtle Mountains
274. Tuscarora
275. Twentynine Palms
276. Umatilla
277. Uintah and Ouray
278. United Keetoowah Band of Cherokee
279. Upper Sioux
280. Upper Skagit
281. Ute Mountain
282. Vermilion Lake
283. Viejas
284. Walker River
285. Warm Springs
286. Washoe
287. West Cocopah
288. White Earth
289. Wichita
290. Wind River
291. Winnebago
292. Winnemucca
293. Woodford Indian Community
294. Wyandotte
295. XI Ranch
296. Yakama
297. Yankton
298. Yavapai
299. Yerington
300. Yomba
301. Ysleta del Sur
302. Yurok
303. Zia
304. Zuni

◆ **Map 10.2 Federal and State Recognized Reservations in the Continental United States**

Indian country today comprises 567 different Indian tribes, bands, and Alaskan village corporations. The majority of Indian people today live in urban areas, and there are also many nonrecognized groups and groups without reservation land.

SOURCE: National NAGPRA, National Park Service, U.S. Department of the Interior, www.nps.gov/nagpra/documents/resMAP.HTM.

and now known as the Office of Federal Acknowledgment, this office is typically staffed by a small team of anthropologists, ethnohistorians, and genealogists. The government expects petitioning groups to provide a paper trail documenting such things as common Indian ancestry, continuous community and political leadership, and historical association with a particular territory. The BIA modified its acknowledgment procedures in the 1990s and is doing so again, but the process remains expensive and time consuming and is often demeaning and potentially divisive. Petitioning groups expend a tremendous amount of money and energy in compiling the necessary documentation, with no guarantee that their claim will be successful.

More than two hundred groups have petitioned for federal recognition since 1978; most have been turned down. Tribes who have secured recognition through the BIA include the Grand Traverse Band of Ottawa and Chippewa (1980), the Narragansetts (1983), the Gay Head (Aquinnah) Wampanoags (1987), the San Juan Southern Paiutes (1990), and the Mohegans (1994). Some groups have turned to Congress to try to circumvent the long bureaucratic process. Congress has acknowledged some tribes, including the Pascua Yaqui near Tucson (1978), the Mashantucket Pequots (1983), the Aroostook Mi'kmaqs of Maine (1991), and the Match-E-Be-Nash-She-Wish Band of Potawatomis in Michigan (1999).

Members of President Bill Clinton's administration (1993–2001) extended eleventh-hour recognition to several tribes (including the Nipmucks in Massachusetts and the Duwamish outside Seattle), only to have the citations revoked by appointees of President George W. Bush (2001–2009). The Chinooks in Washington State first applied for federal recognition in the 1970s. Assistant Secretary for Indian Affairs Kevin Gover granted them recognition in the last weeks of the Clinton administration, but the neighboring Quinault tribe (on whose reservation the Chinooks were placed in the nineteenth century) filed a lawsuit, and in 2002 the new assistant secretary reversed Gover's decision. For Chinooks it was difficult not to see the outcome as politically driven, and they continued to fight for recognition legislation. The BIA extended recognition to the Eastern Pequot Tribal Nation in 2002 and to the Schaghticoke Tribal Nation in 2004, but after the bureau's Interior Board of Indian Appeals sent the cases back for reconsideration, the BIA reversed its earlier decision and revoked recognition in 2005. Also in 2005, the BIA turned down the Vermont Abenakis, who had first applied for recognition in the 1980s. In Massachusetts the Wampanoags of Mashpee, who had been found not to be an Indian tribe in a court case in 1977, finally won federal recognition as an Indian tribe in 2007. In 2009 the Delaware tribe of Oklahoma (formerly considered part of the Cherokee Nation) was restored to federal recognition, as was the Wilton Rancheria in northern California (after tribal members settled a lawsuit against the federal government for being wrongfully terminated fifty years earlier). In 2010 the Obama administration approved the petition of the Shinnecock Indians on Long Island, ending the tribe's thirty-two-year struggle to obtain federal recognition.[18] The Little Shell Tribe of Chippewa Indians of Montana was preliminarily approved for recognition under the Clinton administration, recognition was delayed for eight years under the George W. Bush administration, and then it was denied in 2009 by the

Obama administration, but its case may be reconsidered. In 2014, the 200-member Pamunkey tribe in Virginia won federal recognition, a decision that drew protests over the tribe's long-standing policy of trying to preserve its collective Indian identity by banning marriage to African Americans.

Whether pursued through the BIA or through Congress, acknowledgment is fundamentally about identity: who or what constitutes an Indian tribe, and who gets to decide? Since the government makes the determination, petitioning groups must try and fit their histories into the criteria the government has established. But the government has no single definition of Indianness, and acknowledgment decisions often seem inconsistent, even arbitrary. Concerns that tribes, once recognized, would immediately open casinos have often politicized the acknowledgment process. Even positive decisions generate criticisms, and sometimes lawsuits. Groups who are denied recognition lack access to many legal and financial benefits. Many groups who lack federal recognition do not conform to standard notions of Indianness; for example, many nonrecognized groups are heavily intermarried with non-Indian neighbors, and the recognition process becomes mired in issues of racial identity. Some nonrecognized groups are small. Others, like the Lumbees and the United Houma Nation of Louisiana, with 17,000 members, are huge but do not easily fit the federal regulations' model of tribalism. They often resent the fact that they have to comply with criteria laid down by someone else to be recognized for who they say and know they are. Members of unacknowledged California tribes have pointed out that no one questioned their ancestors' identities when they were being murdered during the Gold Rush. "Nobody asked me to prove I was an Indian when I was kidnapped from my home at age five and taken across state lines to the Stewart Indian Boarding School in Carson City, Nevada—and now I have to prove it?" said Clara LeCompte, a Mountain Maidu elder. "That's disgusting to me."[19]

Critics complain the decisions are based on politics, stereotypes, and legal fictions. Tribes may know their own histories well but they have to meet definitions of Indianness and tribalism imposed by government officials. The standardized recognition process and criteria take little account of the diversity of Indian peoples and cultures produced by centuries of interaction with non-Indians, and the bureaucratic scrutiny and legal regulations "work to preserve colonial patterns of domination and to establish new strategies of state control."[20]

The federal government currently recognizes 567 tribes but many states recognize tribes that are not federally recognized (twenty-one states recognize a total of seventy-three tribes, by one count). Although Indian people have lived in what is now Virginia for more than 12,000 years and their histories have been documented since colonial times, racial ideology and racist legislation denied their existence: as in many areas of the South in the early twentieth century, people were either "white" or "colored" and census records assigned Indian people to the "colored" category. Virginia Indians did not satisfy Pocahontas-driven stereotypes. Although the state of Virginia recognizes eleven tribes, the federal government recognized none until the Pamunkeys won recognition in 2014.[21] In Vermont, the attorney general's office had warned that federal recognition would open the way for the

Abenakis to open a casino; once their petition for federal recognition was denied, that fear was removed and the Vermont legislature voted to approve limited state recognition as a minority group, which enables them to market their crafts as Abenakis and apply for housing and education grants allocated for minorities.

Tribes that are already federally recognized sometimes are reluctant to see others recognized. Some fear that if "fraudulent" groups obtain state or federal recognition it will diminish the standing of "authentic" tribes. In 2009 the Inter-Tribal Council of the Five Civilized Tribes in Oklahoma passed a resolution objecting to state recognition of "Indian heritage groups and cultural clubs" and calling on Congress to limit federal funding to federally recognized tribes.[22] Tribes who seek recognition sometimes exclude from membership individuals whose identity they fear may weaken the case for recognition. In 2014 the Department of the Interior initiated reforms in the federal acknowledgment process, a system that had been described as "broken, long, expensive, burdensome, intrusive, unfair, arbitrary and capricious, less than transparent, unpredictable, and subject to undue political influence and manipulation."[23] Whatever reforms are made, many people point out that tribal existence is independent of U.S. government recognition.

Old Stereotypes and New Images

Native Americans today express their Indianness in multiple ways and frequently lead lives that do not square with popular assumptions about what "real" Indians do. In 2002 astronaut John Herrington, a member of the Chickasaw Nation of Oklahoma, became the first Native American to walk in space. In 2003 Private Lori Piestewa, a Hopi single mother, died in the war in Iraq; she is believed to be the first Native American servicewoman killed in combat. In 2006 pairs figure skater Naomi Lang, a member of the Karuk tribe of California, became the first Native American to participate in the Winter Olympics (with Russian-born partner Peter Tchernyshev); Notah Begay III, whose parents are Navajo and Pueblo, is the first Native American to join a PGA tour; Navajo race-car driver Cory Witherill is the first Native American to compete in the Indy 500; Jacoby Ellsbury, Navajo, was a star rookie on the 2007 Boston Red Sox World Championship baseball team and now plays for the New York Yankees. Iroquois lacrosse player Lyle Thompson — one of three remarkable lacrosse-playing brothers — was nominated for the best male college athlete award in 2014. Indian people today are found in virtually all walks of life. Many achieve success in modern society — as soldiers, doctors, attorneys, artists, musicians, writers, reporters, scientists, teachers and professors, businessmen and businesswomen, movie stars, athletes, and federal, state, and tribal officials — while continuing to be Indian in their identity, retaining their tribal membership and maintaining their adherence to tribal traditions. As they always have, Indians display tremendous diversity in culture, behavior, and opinion. Yet one thing they have in common is that they can expect to deal with non-Indians' stereotypes and misconceptions, whether in the form of media images, innocent questions from new friends at college, insensitive behavior by sports fans, or openly racist hostility from anti-Indian groups.[24]

◆ **A Native American Soldier in Afghanistan**
Four days before Christmas 2009, during the war in Afghanistan, a U.S. marine sergeant of Hopi descent prays in Helmand Province. © *Bryan Denton/CORBIS.*

From their first contacts with a few Native peoples, Europeans tended to generalize about all Indians. Many modern Americans likewise expect all Indians to look, dress, speak, and live like the horseback-riding, buffalo-hunting Indians they have seen depicted on television or in the movies; Indian people who do not fit these images are often regarded as somehow "less Indian." The public, the media, and even the courts subscribe to the notion that Indians who change with the times "lose" their culture. All cultures change — indeed they must if they are to survive, and change is constant in broader American culture. But some people feel that Indians cannot be Indians if they drive pickup trucks rather than ride horses, live in condominiums in town instead of in tipis on reservations, wear business suits instead of buckskins, or communicate through social media rather than with smoke signals. Such ideas freeze Indian people in an unchanging past that, for many Indians, was never part of their culture in the first place. Public attitudes often harden as Indian tribes assert their tribal sovereignty or start making money through gaming and other businesses — many Americans want to see evidence that tribal members are culturally Indian as they exercise their political and economic rights. "Contemporary Native American people face a fascinating dilemma," wrote Native scholar and novelist Louis Owens. "In order to be seen and to have their voices heard, indigenous Americans must pose as 'Indians.'"[25]

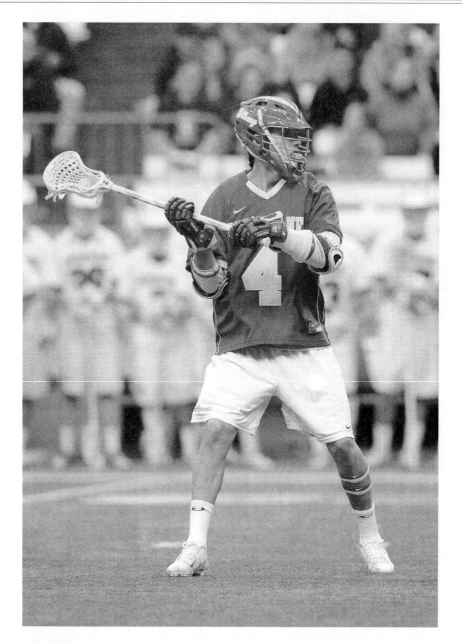

◆ **Lyle Thompson**
Albany Great Danes midfielder Lyle Thompson prepares to pass during an NCAA lacrosse
game against the Syracuse Orange at the Carrier Dome in Syracuse, New York, in 2013.
Rich Barnes/CSM/Landov.

A glance at the names of automobiles, such as the Jeep Cherokee, or at the logos on grocery store products such as Land O'Lakes butter reveals that using stereotypical Indian images is common in American popular culture. Professional and high school sports teams use Indian logos or "mascots," a practice that has become increasingly controversial as more people take offense at distorted images and cultural appropriations; for example, the Washington Redskins insist on retaining their team name (see "Playing Indian and Fighting Mascots," pages 618–24). Indians themselves sometimes employ the same clichés that other people find offensive as a marketing strategy: visitors to the Mashantucket Pequots' Foxwoods casino in southeastern Connecticut, for instance, see Plains Indian–style statues and décor, with generic "Indian" symbols such as tomahawks, arrows, feathers, and buffalo.

Many negative stereotypes stem from generations of contact and colonialism: loss of land, loss of hope, and economic and social disruption produced alcoholism, poverty, and unemployment in many communities; but these stereotypes are often regarded as characteristic of all Indians. At the same time, as more people question the values of modern American society and worry about the environmentally destructive path we are on, new and often more positive stereotypes have emerged: Indians are spiritual people who live in harmony with nature and possess virtues our own society seems to have lost. Stressing the positive aspects of Indian society as an implicit criticism of non-Indian society is not new — Jean-Jacques Rousseau and other eighteenth-century writers did it with their depictions of "the noble savage." Yet any stereotyping, whether negative or positive, holds people to different standards and tends to dehumanize them.

To counter such stereotypes, increasing numbers of Native people insist on greater intellectual and cultural sovereignty, the right to define their own identities and tell their own stories. History is contested ground. Who tells it — who "owns the past" — matters. Until recently, non-Indians have monopolized the writing of Indian history. Colonial writers often dehumanized Indian people, early historians regularly dismissed them, and modern scholars rarely incorporate Native American knowledge and voices in their work. Filmmakers have been equally insensitive and uninformed, offering negative and stereotypical portrayals of Indian people and the Indian past. Many Indian people argue that knowledge from Indian communities should stay in the communities and that Indian people should write their own histories using Native sources of knowledge, speak their own languages, and make their own films and videos.[26] At the very least, they demand that non-Indian scholars should exercise greater responsibility and be held to greater accountability than in the past.[27]

The continued development of Native American studies programs at universities and colleges; increasing numbers of Native faculty; the recent organization and growth of the Native American and Indigenous Studies Association, which brings together Native and non-Native scholars from the United States and around the world; and a florescence of work by Native filmmakers, writers, and artists are all changing how Native Americans' past and present are portrayed and understood.

SELF-RULE AND SELF-HELP

Beginning in 2009 President Obama hosted annual White House Tribal Nations conferences with Native leaders in Washington, D.C. In 2014 he visited Indian country for the first time as president. By executive order he established the White House Council on Indian Affairs to strengthen the federal government's partnership with tribal governments to build and sustain "prosperous and resilient tribal communities" by promoting economic development, improving health care, enhancing tribal justice systems and law enforcement, increasing educational quality and education, and protecting Native lands and environment. Some Indian people say that Obama did more for Indian country in a few years than had all his predecessors, but many point out that what they do themselves is far more important than what the president or the BIA does and President Obama himself acknowledged that tribal nations do better when they make their own decisions. To survive in the modern world, and to ensure their survival in the future, Indian

◆ **President Obama Visits Indian Country**
President Barack Obama and First Lady Michelle Obama display a star quilt given to them by David Archambault II (left), Chairman of the Standing Rock Sioux Tribe, during their visit to the Standing Rock Reservation in North Dakota in June 2014. *Charles Rex Arbogast/AP Photo.*

nations must do more than operate their own governments; they must exercise their tribal sovereignty to protect their lands and their sacred spaces, manage their own resources, preserve their traditions, build their economies, and educate their young people.

Nations, Not Minorities

To achieve these goals, tribes have to defend their unique status as nations within a nation. Tribal leaders constantly remind the United States that "Indian people are nations, not minorities," with inherent sovereign rights of self-government that existed before conquest and that can be eroded but not erased. The right of tribes to govern their members and territories, legal scholars agree, "flows from a preexisting sovereignty limited, but not abolished, by their inclusion within the territorial bounds of the United States."[28] European nations recognized these rights when they made treaties with Indians. The United States recognized them when it made its treaty with the Delawares in 1778, the first of nearly four hundred ratified U.S–Indian treaties. Although the United States officially stopped making treaties with Indian tribes in 1871, those treaties remain the law of the land. The pledges they contain form the basis for many Indian rights in modern America, shape the tribes' dealings with the federal and state governments, and continue to define the status of tribes as sovereign nations.[29] The U.S. Constitution recognizes these sovereign rights as well. In *Worcester v. Georgia* (1832), the Supreme Court acknowledged that before invasion, Indians were distinct, separate, and independent nations, governed by their own laws and with their own institutions. Indian tribes are still nations with their own laws and institutions, and they have reclaimed many sovereign rights: for instance, the power to define tribal membership, to determine their own forms of government, and to control the use of tribal lands, including regulations for hunting, fishing, and environmental protection.

But tribes struggle constantly to preserve their sovereignty. States often try to interfere — although they can extend political jurisdiction over Indian tribes only if they have congressional approval to do so — and the federal government sometimes exercises its trust responsibility to Indian tribes in ways that undermine tribal self-determination. The tribal sovereignty that many people regard as crucial to the survival of Indian nations in the twenty-first century is repeatedly challenged and threatened, sometimes negotiated and compromised, and often simply not understood.[30] People who don't understand tribal sovereignty often feel threatened by it and by tribes that exercise it, said the late Marge Anderson, former chief executive for the Mille Lacs Band of Ojibwe; it is necessary to educate people so they understand that "we exercise sovereignty when we actively assume governance over our own communities." W. Ron Allen, chair of the Jamestown S'Klallam tribe in Washington State and a past president, secretary, and treasurer of the National Congress of American Indians, recommends: "A chapter in all [American] civics textbooks should explain that the American political system is made up of multiple political structures, within which tribes are a unique set of communities."[31]

Third Sovereigns, Triple Citizens, and Tribal Justice

The United States and the states constitute sovereign governments. So do Indian tribes. "Today," writes legal scholar Charles Wilkinson, "the tribes, not the BIA, govern Indian Country," and the tribes "are full-service governments." Many tribes have their own legislatures, courts, police forces, businesses, schools, colleges, health facilities, social service agencies, environmental agencies, cultural centers, and language programs. Tribal governments interact regularly and routinely with federal, state, and local governments and with non-Indian citizens, and they conduct tribal business in Washington, D.C., and state capitals as well as on the reservation.[32] As Dakota attorney Susan M. Williams explains, tribal governments differ from state governments in that they do not represent and serve a "coincidental collection of citizens who happen to live in the same geographic area." Tribal governments are responsible for the well-being and safety of communities "defined by generations upon generations of cultural, political, and religious traditions and social relations." In addition to carrying out the usual governmental functions — providing utilities and social services, building and maintaining infrastructure, and promoting economic development — they must also protect tribes' cultural and environmental resources for generations to come.[33]

Working out relations between the United States and hundreds of tribal governments on a multitude of issues remains a formidable task. Indians reside within the United States and within the borders of individual states, and the situation produces much complexity and ambiguity. Tribal members are in fact "triple citizens." In 1924 the Indian Citizenship Act conferred U.S. citizenship on all Indians who had not already been made citizens by special legislation. Like other U.S. citizens, Indian people are also citizens of their states. Indian people who are enrolled members of their tribe are also citizens of that tribe.[34] At the same time, many non-Indian people live on reservations and therefore fall under the jurisdiction of tribal governments in some respects, even though they are not tribal citizens.

There are three main bodies of law in the United States: federal law, state law, and Indian law. Indian people generally, and non-Indians in certain cases, are subject to all three. Indians not on reservations are generally subject to federal, state, and local laws. Only federal and tribal laws apply on reservations, however, unless Congress has provided otherwise. Consequently, when Indians step off the reservation they become subject to local or state jurisdiction; a non-Indian who enters a reservation is subject to tribal jurisdiction in civil matters. In states where Public Law 280 applies, the state has some form of civil and criminal jurisdiction over the reservations.

The relationship of federal/state/Indian law is a tangle of overlapping and sometimes conflicting jurisdictions. What, for instance, are the rights of non-Indian residents of Indian reservations, who are subject to tribal laws, courts, and taxes but have no say in tribal government? What are the rights of non-Indians who are visiting or working on reservations or the rights of Indians visiting from another reservation? And how should the federal government reconcile its obligations to protect both Native religious practices and endangered species when, as sometimes happens, those obligations are in conflict? In 2005 a Northern Arapaho on the Wind River Reservation shot a bald eagle to obtain feathers, a plume, and a wing for his participation in the Sun Dance. He was arrested and charged with violating the Bald and Golden Eagle Protection Act.[35] In 2006 a U.S. district judge dismissed the charges, ruling that although the government had a duty to protect eagles it also had a compelling interest in protecting tribal religions and tribal cultures. That decision was overturned by the Tenth Circuit Court of Appeals in 2008, however, and in February 2009 the Supreme Court denied review of the case.

As such issues continue to come before the courts, the U.S. Supreme Court will continue to define the extents and limits of tribal sovereignty. Over the past thirty years, the Court has taken a very narrow interpretation of tribal sovereignty, and its rulings have more often hindered than helped Indian nations as they endeavor to rebuild their communities. The election of President Obama and the possibility of new appointees to the Supreme Court offered hope for change, but many Native Americans felt the changes needed to go deeper than new faces on the bench. According to Walter Echo-Hawk, "the greatest challenge facing advocates and others concerned about the well-being of Native people is to root out . . . vestiges of racism and colonialism in the law and replace them with legal principles more in keeping with the postcolonial world."[36]

"Indian law" usually refers to the laws enacted by Congress and court cases relating to Indian tribes, but there has always been another kind of Indian law—the laws by which tribes live and settle their own disputes. Although traditionally not written down and cited like Anglo-American laws, these indigenous philosophies and principles often guided individual behavior, governed relationships, and ensured justice among tribal members, and in some places they continue to do so. In the late nineteenth century, Congress displaced the traditional dispute resolution systems of many tribes by imposing the Courts of Indian Offenses, but today more than 175 Indian nations have developed their own tribal criminal justice systems. While most tribal courts are based on a Western model of justice, some tribes incorporate traditional methods of dispute resolution into their legal systems.

Navajo courts employ Navajo values and traditions in adjudicating civil disputes that often involve non-Navajos as well as Navajos. In 1982 the Navajo Nation established the Peacemaking Division of its judicial system. It is not intended to replace the Navajos' formal court system but provides an alternative forum for resolving certain types of disputes. Whereas Anglo-American legal practices tend to be adversarial, with courts finding for one or the other party and sometimes imposing heavy penalties or fines or awarding sizable damages, Navajo courts aim to achieve reconciliation, and Navajo judges draw upon and apply key Navajo concepts such as *Hózhó* (harmony), *K'é* (peacefulness and solidarity), and *K'éí* (kinship) in their rulings. "To the Navajo way of thinking, justice is related to healing because many of the concepts are the same," former Navajo Supreme Court Justice Robert Yazzie explained. There is no precise term for "guilty" in the Navajo language. Yazzie called it "a nonsense word in Navajo law" because "guilt" implies a moral fault that demands punishment; Navajo court decisions are more concerned with helping a victim than finding fault, with reintegrating the individual with the group, and with sustaining relationships with relatives and community. In a peacemaking system there is no need for force, coercion, or control. There are no plaintiffs or defendants; no "good guys" or "bad guys." "Distributive justice abandons fault and adequate compensation (a fetish of personal injury lawyers) in favor of assuring well-being for everyone. Restoration is more important than punishment." In the words of former Navajo Supreme Court justice Raymond D. Austin, the Navajo dispute resolution or "peacemaking" system "brings parties and communities together on amicable terms, costs a fraction of adversarial court litigation, does not cast blame on wrongdoers, and identifies and treats the underlying cause of the problem."[37] Other tribes also have "peacemaker courts" that aim to provide restorative justice. The mainstream American justice system, meanwhile, has repeatedly failed Native Americans.

BUILDING PROSPERITY IN INDIAN COUNTRY

In 2012 the median household income for the nation as a whole was $51,371; for American Indian and Alaska Native households it was $35,310. The poverty rate for the nation as a whole was 15.9 percent; for American Indians and Alaska Natives it was 29.1 percent, the highest rate of any group.[38] Despite the well-publicized wealth generated by some tribal casinos, poverty and economic underdevelopment remain chronic problems and major challenges in large areas of Indian country.

The Indian Self-Determination and Education Assistance Act of 1975 transferred responsibility for planning, implementing, and administering many programs to the tribes, but the severe cuts in the Indian budget following the election of Ronald Reagan as president in 1980 meant that many of those programs could not be funded. Maintaining tribal sovereignty and tribal services required increasing tribal economic independence.

In the past, the laws, policies, and projects of the federal government were seen as the key factors in economic development on Indian reservations, but federal projects all too often petered out without any lasting improvement in reservation economies. Today many Indian tribes have taken charge of their own economic affairs and are demonstrating that Indian sovereignty rather than federal policy seems to be the crucial factor in determining prosperity in Indian country. "The clear trend is for Indian governments to eschew their long-imposed role as extension agents of federal antipoverty programs and to engage in the task of genuine self-rule by building institutions and creating favorable conditions for investments." When the tribes, rather than the BIA or other outsiders, take the responsibility for their own economic futures — deciding, implementing, and being accountable for their own economic strategies — and pursue projects compatible with their cultures and values, they can achieve sustainable economic development and rebuild their nations.[39] But what projects meet these requirements, and have they seen success in practice?

Economic Success through Sovereignty

A 2004 report by the Harvard Project on American Indian Economic Development concluded that "tribal self-rule — *sovereignty* — has proven to be the only policy that has shown concrete success in breaking debilitating economic dependence on federal spending programs and replenishing the social and cultural fabric that can support vibrant and healthy communities and families." From this perspective, tribal sovereignty becomes a valuable economic resource — and assaults on tribal sovereignty pose an even greater threat to tribal survival.[40] With each successful tribal business model put into operation, sovereignty, so long sought as an inalienable right, proves necessary for the economic survival of Native communities.

Many tribes are competing, and thriving, in the world of modern capitalism, yet some people question whether Native communities can survive incorporation into the global capitalist market system. Can they still be Indians if they are successful capitalists? Many nations have developed successful models of tribal capitalism, following "Native pathways" of economic development and redistributing business profits for community benefit.[41] The Mississippi Band of Choctaws provides a clear example of economic success achieved by a tribe on its own terms. In 1979 unemployment on the Choctaw reservation was about 80 percent. That year the Choctaws elected Phillip Martin chief, and he led the tribe until 2007, when he was eighty years old. Under his leadership, the tribe achieved a remarkable economic turnaround. They ran several manufacturing plants in addition to promoting gaming and tourism and used the income generated on the reservation to supplement federal contracts in providing educational, health, and other services to Choctaw people. The tribe opened the Silver Star Hotel and Casino in 1994 and a second casino, the Golden Moon, eight years later. The Pearl River Resort now includes the casinos, a theme park, and a golf club.

The Mississippi Band of Choctaw Indians rapidly became one of the ten largest employers in Mississippi, providing more than eight thousand jobs for tribal members and others (more than 65 percent of its workforce is non-Indian). The unemployment rate on the reservation plunged to about 4 percent, and life expectancy rose significantly. There were new scholarships for Choctaw students. Tribal revenues helped the Choctaws to invest more than $210 million in economic development projects in Mississippi. As the tribe became a business center and major employer, it expanded its court system to accommodate the increase in cases.[42] Like other communities in the Gulf region, the Mississippi Choctaw reservation was hard hit by Hurricane Katrina in 2005. (Gulf Coast communities such as the Houmas had barely recovered from Katrina when their shrimp-fishing economy was devastated by the British Petroleum oil leak in 2010.)

Culturally appropriate projects sometimes have goals and values that go beyond their economic success. Tribal efforts to reinstitute buffalo herds have been "a truly holistic restoration project" that helped to restore ecological, social, cultural, and spiritual health to Plains Indian communities even when such projects, as in the case of the Cheyenne River Sioux tribe's community-based bison operation, proved economically unsuccessful.[43] Other, more successful economic enterprises, critics say, are not nearly so culturally grounded.

Gaming: A Devil's Bargain?

Tribes with few untapped natural resources and limited economic opportunities turned to gaming in the late twentieth century as a way of generating income and employment. In this they are not alone. As one scholar of Indian gaming notes, state and local governments have also turned to games of chance to fund services in an age of federal cutbacks: "Government-sponsored gambling has become the revenue-raising activity of choice among governments in the United States."[44] The unique status of Indian tribes and their lands makes gambling extremely lucrative in Indian country — generally, income generated on reservation land is exempt from federal and state taxes, and tribal gaming operations (like state lotteries) are not subject to taxation by federal or neighboring state governments. Some tribes have staged "economic miracles." But gaming is a contentious issue in many parts of the country.[45]

After the Third Seminole War of 1855–58, a few hundred Seminoles remained in Florida, hiding in the Everglades to avoid forced removal to Oklahoma. For 130 years they lived in poverty. Then in 1979 they opened a bingo hall and offered prizes up to $10,000, ignoring a state law that prohibited jackpots of more than $100. The state of Florida tried to close down the bingo hall, but the Seminoles sued in federal court and the U.S. Supreme Court upheld the right of the Seminoles and other tribes to operate bingo games free from state regulation. In 1987 the Supreme Court ruled in *California v. Cabazon* that, despite Public Law 280, a state that permitted any form of gambling could not prohibit Indians from operating gambling facilities. The next year, Congress passed the Indian Gaming Regulatory Act (IGRA). Under the act, a tribe that wants to operate Class III or "casino-type" gambling must request that the state in which its lands are located enter into negotiations for a "compact" in which the tribe and state work out issues of jurisdiction, revenue sharing, and other questions relating directly to the operation of casinos. IGRA initially gave tribes the right to sue states in federal court if they failed to negotiate in good faith but the Supreme Court ultimately struck down this remedy as a violation of the state's sovereign immunity under the Eleventh Amendment. Some tribes have complained that the compacts violate their sovereignty, but regardless, gaming has become a common if controversial form of economic development in Indian country.

The development of gaming operations on Indian reservations has opened unprecedented opportunities for economic growth for some tribes. With millions of dollars in annual revenues from gaming facilities on their south Florida reservations, in 2006 the Florida Seminoles purchased Hard Rock International for $965 million. Known for their cultural conservatism, Seminoles successfully adopted gaming as a new economic venture, just as they had previously done with tourism and commercial craft production. Seminole gaming provides jobs for thousands of people, most of them non-Indians, thereby giving a significant boost

◆ **Florida Seminoles Purchase Hard Rock International**
Seminoles in ceremonial dress wave from the Hard Rock
Cafe marquee in Times Square, New York City, in 2006
after purchasing Hard Rock International for $965 million.
Kathy Willens/AP Photo.

to the local economy.[46] In addition to making monthly payments to tribal members, the Florida Seminoles are able to fund community services and scholarships for their members.

Two states, California and Connecticut, grant a monopoly to Indian tribes to operate gambling facilities in exchange for a higher percentage of the revenues. The Cabazon Band, with a small reservation 130 miles east of Los Angeles, has improved its community support systems since opening the Fantasy Springs Casino Resort in 2000. In 2002 all tribal members had guaranteed employment; the tribe was providing social services and building housing for members returning to the reservation, and the multimillion-dollar Cabazon Cultural Museum was opened. Unsurprisingly, the financial success of such businesses has attracted attention from those in government who wish to benefit from the prosperity: "Once ignored or thrust aside by policy makers, the Cabazon began getting visits from members of Congress, senators, and state officials, who came seeking campaign contributions and espousing pro-Indian positions on a variety of issues." By 2002 eighteen tribes in southern California had opened Class III casinos, many with multimillion-dollar entertainment complexes. The Agua Caliente Band of Cahuilla Indians spent more than $230 million on its casino and used casino revenues to begin work on a new tribal museum. The Viejas Band of Kumeyaay Indians wiped out unemployment on the reservation and used casino revenues for housing, social services, and environmental projects.[47] When Arnold Schwarzenegger was elected governor of California in 2003, he said the tribes should pay a "fair share" of their earnings to the state because Indian gaming in California had a substantial effect on the local and state economies as well as within the Native communities that adopted it.

Perhaps more than any other tribe, the Mashantucket Pequots of Connecticut have demonstrated the transformative power of gaming, but recent developments point to the dangers of overextending and suggest that gains can be short-lived. The Pequots were a major economic and political power in southern New England at the beginning of the seventeenth century. But the English destroyed their main village in 1637 and declared the tribe extinct (see pages 98–99), and for almost 350 years the Pequots seemed to be on the verge of disappearing. But the Pequots held on to their tiny land base and their identity. Under the leadership of Richard "Skip" Hayward, tribal chair from 1975 to 1998, the Mashantucket Pequots won federal recognition as an Indian tribe in 1983. After experimenting with a number of ventures for economic development, they turned first to bingo and then to high-stakes gambling. Within easy driving distance of several major cities, the Mashantucket Pequots' Foxwoods casino was widely believed to be the most profitable casino in the world. Profits provided the tribe with housing, health care, education, care for the elderly, and cultural programs. The casino employed 10,000 workers, a boost to the economy of southern Connecticut, and sent more than $3.7 billion annually to the state. The Pequots were once again a major economic and political power in the region. In an ironic twist of history, some local residents saw the Pequot tribe as an expanding business entity threatening to engulf their small towns in a flood of tourists and traffic. The income from Foxwoods provided funds for the construction of the $193 million Mashantucket Pequot Museum and Research Center, opened in 1998. The museum features exhibits of Pequot history and culture, houses an extensive library, and also undertakes archaeological research. However, by 2014, the museum and other gains looked to be in jeopardy as the weight of debt incurred in building a huge new hotel and other shifts in the financial climate took their toll.

Competition also made an impact as other tribes hoped to emulate the Pequots' success or at least win a measure of economic independence by going into bingo and gaming. The Pequots' neighbors in Connecticut, the Mohegans, opened their casino in the fall of 1996. Closer to the interstate than Foxwoods, the Mohegan Sun in its first six months of operation earned a profit of $55.3 million, of which the tribe got 60 percent. The Mohegans used the money for college scholarships, a new home for the elderly, and a campaign to retrieve tribal artifacts.[48]

Some states and individuals who stand to lose money to Indian gaming have been vocal in protesting against it. Donald Trump even brought a lawsuit against the federal government, claiming that Indian gaming operations had an "unfair advantage" over his own Atlantic City casinos because they did not have to comply with state regulations as he did. But with an economic downturn at the beginning of the new century, many states showed a new willingness to cooperate with Indian gaming to secure a piece of the pie, most notably in New York State, where the negative economic effects of 9/11 were most severe.[49]

In 1988 Indian gaming in a few bingo halls earned about $121 million. In 2001 Indian casinos brought in $12.8 billion, and that figure almost doubled by 2006, far outpacing the gambling revenues in Las Vegas. Despite a downturn in gaming revenues during the recession that began in 2008 and that put both Foxwoods

♦ The Foxwoods Casino

The gargantuan Foxwoods casino, owned and operated by the Mashantucket Pequot tribe of southern Connecticut, brings in millions of dollars every year. Foxwoods features six casinos with more than 7,200 slots, 380 table games, the largest poker room in New England, high-stakes bingo, and a high-tech race book. In addition, there are four hotels, shops and restaurants, spas, golf courses, state-of-the-art theaters, and meeting facilities. Attracting about 50,000 visitors a day, Foxwoods offers entertainment by world-famous stars, elegant dining, and specialty shopping. Some critics claim the Pequots and other tribes who go into the gaming business are "selling out," capitalizing on their Indian heritage but sacrificing traditional values for easy money. Others respond that the criticism stems from the fact that casino tribes are shattering stereotypes of Indian poverty and that the new wealth serves to preserve and revive their culture, not to undermine it. © *World Photo Collection/Alamy.*

and Mohegan Sun deeply in debt, the industry has stabilized and recovered. According to the National Indian Gaming Commission, 246 tribes operating a total of 449 tribal gaming facilities in 28 states (figures vary as facilities open and close) netted $28 billion in 2013, a figure that exceeds national spending on other entertainment options (e.g., movies, sports games, concerts) combined. Most of the gaming operations are small to mid-size facilities: 78 reported gaming revenue between $100 million and $250 million; 214 reported gaming revenues between $10 million and $100 million; 79 reported gaming revenue between $3 million and $10 million; and 78 operations reported gaming revenue less than $3 million. Additional revenue comes in from hotels, restaurants, entertainment, and shopping at Indian gaming facilities. Indian gaming facilities and related nongaming operations create hundreds of thousands of jobs, pay employees billions of dollars in wages, and add billions of dollars to state coffers.[50]

Contrary to some popular notions that all Indians eagerly pursue the get-rich-quick opportunities it offers, gaming has generated tensions and differences of opinion within Indian country and can have a polarizing effect in Indian communities. Disputes between pro- and anti-gaming factions escalated to intimidation, violence, and arson in some Iroquois communities. In 1994 and again in 1997, Navajos in a tribal referendum voted against gaming on their reservation, but they later voted to allow slot-machine gaming, and in 2008 the Navajo Nation opened its first casino, the Fire Rock Casino near Gallup, New Mexico, in the hope of generating income and jobs to combat reservation poverty and unemployment.[51] In 2013 the Navajo Nation opened its fourth casino, a $180 million resort at Twin Arrows near Flagstaff, Arizona.

The National Indian Gaming Association says that "gaming has replaced the buffalo as the mechanism used by American Indian people for survival. . . . [It is] the first — and only — economic development tool that has ever worked on reservations."[52] But not all Indian people hunted buffalo, and not all Indian people agree on the benefits of gaming. Supporters of gaming point out that the income generated goes back into the community, providing jobs, social service programs, utility services, clinics, housing, schools, scholarships, and hope for the future. "Every cent of Indian gaming revenue goes right back into services for tribal people," said Marge Anderson in 1993. "Two years ago, unemployment for my 2,400 member tribe in Minnesota was 45 percent and is now zero."[53] Profits from gaming also improve the community infrastructure and fuel the development and growth of other businesses. With prosperity comes self-sufficiency, opportunities for economic diversification, and the ability to exercise true self-determination. Gaming tribes can afford the costly legal battles necessary to protect tribal rights and resources and can exert political influence in the form of lobbying and campaign contributions that, it could be argued, effect improvements for all Indian people.

But the relationship between gaming profits and political engagement also produced scandal in 2006 in the case of Washington lobbyist Jack Abramoff, who bilked half a dozen casino tribes of millions of dollars. Many Indian people denounce gambling as a social vice and an affront to their tribal values. They worry about the impact of gaming and the sudden influx of money and people into communities unaccustomed to dealing with either in large quantities. They fear it will undermine tribal community, culture, and values, and they caution that a new stereotype of Indians as wealthy casino operators distorts reality and may prove harmful to all Indians. Casino revenues disproportionately benefit a relatively small number of tribes, and in some cases non-Indian financial backers seem to take the lion's share of the profits. Some fear that Congress may respond to growing fears about Indian gaming by returning to termination tactics, arguing that the government need no longer maintain its trust relationship with tribes who are independently wealthy. They note that tribal sovereignty is rarely challenged so long as Indians remain economically dependent but that sovereignty comes under attack when tribes exercise it to become financially successful.

The success of tribes like the Mohegans, the Pequots, and the Shakopee Mdewakanton Sioux in Minnesota—all of whom operate casinos near large cities—has generated a backlash among some non-Indians and has renewed concern in some circles about the powers and the unique status of Indian nations within the United States. Federal recognition in 2010 opened the way for the Shinnecocks of Southampton on Long Island to open a casino just twenty miles from Manhattan, a prospect that caused divisions within the community and provoked alarm among their Long Island neighbors.[54] Casinos have also brought heightened attention to questions of Indian identity. Some residents resent their Indian neighbors' new financial and political influence; others attack the gaming Indians as being "too white" or "too black" to be "real Indians." New racist stereotypes that depict all Indians as rolling in money also imply that wealthy Indians cannot be "real" Indians. Despite multiple examples throughout history of Indians responding to new economic conditions, participating in and shaping the American economy, and enjoying wealth and prosperity, a common perception remains that real Indians are poor Indians.[55]

Some people ask why Native Americans need federal assistance when so much money is flowing into Indian pockets and argue that "casino tribes" should share their wealth with poorer tribes to alleviate the problems in Indian country. But as the Native American Rights Funds points out in its pamphlet, "Dispelling the Myths about Indian Gaming," only a few tribes have struck it rich and "the notion that the federal government should make rich tribes share their wealth with poorer ones is absurd and, more importantly, illegal. If the state of Michigan generates extra money from its lottery, the federal government doesn't take money away from Michigan and give it to Mississippi. Remember, each of these tribes is a sovereign nation with their rights guaranteed by treaties and the Constitution of the United States." Tribes must use their gaming revenues to create and maintain tribal police, firefighting stations, and ambulance services; health and child-care services, educational assistance programs, cultural enhancement, and numerous other human service programs.[56] "I would shudder to think what Indian country would look like without the revenues that come in from Indian gaming," said the Assistant Secretary for Indian Affairs Kevin Washburn in 2014.[57]

Opening a casino represents an exercise of tribal sovereignty, yet many leaders question the wisdom of entering into compacts with state governments, as required under the Indian Gaming Regulatory Act, to operate high-stakes gaming: does not such action compromise a tribe's sovereignty in pursuit of quick money? The Indian Gaming Regulatory Act prohibits state taxation of tribal casinos, but some tribes pay a large share of their casino revenues to the states.[58] Now well-established in many areas of Indian country, gaming confronts shifting economic climates and remains a mixed blessing, bringing new problems and challenges along with new wealth, new benefits, and new opportunities.

HOMELANDS OR WASTELANDS

Other economic opportunities also bring mixed blessings. The Three Affiliated Tribes of North Dakota—the Mandans, Hidatsas, and Arikaras, who were devastated by smallpox in 1837 and who lost the best part of their Fort Berthold Reservation to flooding when the Garrison Dam was built in the 1950s—now sit on top of a fortune. The Bakken Shale deposit in North Dakota and Montana is estimated to hold 4.3 billion barrels of oil, making it the biggest oil field in U.S. history, and improved drilling techniques have turned it into one of the fastest growing oil-production areas in the country. After generations of poverty, tribal members and the tribal treasury are now receiving millions in yearly oil production income. The oil boom has also created jobs, generated income for tribal casinos and other businesses, and brought people back to the reservation. Oil companies have drilled dozens of wells and are even drilling below Lake Sakakawea, the 180-mile-long reservoir that flooded 10 percent of the reservation when the dam was built. The oil boom is expected to continue, with predictions that North Dakota could pass Alaska in oil production by the end of the decade. Once wealthy farmers and traders (see pages 263–64), the Three Affiliated Tribes are now dealing with wealth again—and with the environmental problems produced by hydraulic fracturing or fracking.

The days are over when the BIA and energy companies could decide between them how to exploit reservation resources. Now Indian tribes themselves call the shots. Some tribes have ceased being energy colonies and have become energy developers. In 2005 Congress passed the Indian Tribal Energy Development and Self-Determination Act, which gives tribes the option of entering into "tribal energy resource agreements" with the secretary of the interior; these agreements provide tribes with a kind of preapproval for energy development and thereby cut down bureaucratic red tape and delays.[59] But tribes with energy resources still come under intense pressure to exploit them, face formidable political and economic realities in making choices, and sometimes find that achieving economic prosperity may not be compatible with traditional values.

Many people argue that unless the tribes can make economic progress they stand to lose their traditional culture in the face of poverty and dependence. Others maintain that the land is sacred and should not be scarred by mining and drilling operations. They question the wisdom of pursuing quick wealth by extracting mineral resources from their reservations or from storing radioactive waste in and on their land. "Where will we all be 20 or 25 years from now when the coal is all consumed and the companies operating these gasification plants have cleaned up all the resources and moved away?" one Navajo asked. "There will be nothing; they will be working elsewhere and we will be sitting on top of a bunch of ashes with nothing to live on."[60] The question of how to pursue economic development without damaging their homelands remains a challenge for many tribes.

Nuclear Waste in Indian Country

The pressure to generate economic development on the reservations has led tribal governments to consider housing toxic wastes. The U.S. Department of

Energy (DOE) offered $100,000 study grants to encourage tribes and rural communities to explore storing nuclear waste in monitored retrievable storage (MRS) facilities until a planned permanent DOE site at Yucca Mountain, Nevada, could be licensed. The Skull Valley Goshute, Mescalero Apache, Northern Arapaho, Fort McDermitt Paiute-Shoshone, Lower Brulé Sioux, Chickasaw, Sauk & Fox, Alabama-Coushatta, Ponca, Eastern Shawnee, Caddo, Yakima, and other Native groups applied for the study grants. Some of these tribes have since reconsidered, but others continue to explore the projects, and several have accepted MRS facilities on their reservations (Map 10.3).[61] The economic incentives offered are attractive in communities where unemployment and poverty are commonplace, but critics of MRS facilities point out that the long-term environmental problems outweigh any short-term economic benefits. They denounce the dumping of nuclear waste on Indian reservations as "environmental racism": American society wants the benefits of nuclear power, but no one wants the waste in their backyard, so it is sent to Indian country.

In February 1994 the Mescalero Apache tribal council signed an agreement with Minnesota's Northern States Power Company, representing thirty-three nuclear energy companies, to establish a private storage site for 40,000 metric tons of spent nuclear fuel from commercial power plants. Tribal chair Wendell Chino explained the move as a step toward achieving tribal economic independence and self-sufficiency by providing jobs and income for the tribe. Other Mescaleros opposed the decision as violating sacred land and jeopardizing their children's futures. The Skull Valley Goshutes in Nevada also leased land for an MRS facility. Although tribes are subject to federal environmental laws, they are exempt from state acts that often are stricter than federal legislation, and tribal advocates of MRS sometimes dismiss state opposition by invoking their sovereignty. Other Indian peoples are demanding federal enforcement of environmental laws and are creating their own regulations to protect their people and resources.

The threat of contamination from leakage of nuclear waste became acute at Prairie Island, Minnesota, where the Mdewakanton Dakota community lives literally next door to a nuclear power plant and a nuclear waste storage plant. When Northern States Power Company (now a subsidiary of Xcel Energy) planned to store waste from its Prairie Island reactors outside, on a historic site and burial ground in the Mississippi floodplain, an alliance of Indians, environmental groups, and other concerned citizens formed the Prairie Island Coalition to oppose the plan. In 1994 the Minnesota state legislature passed a law limiting the number of storage casks at the site to seventeen and requiring the power company to find a new site. The Prairie Island Indian community and their allies refuse to accept official assurances that the plant and storage facility are safe and continue to lobby for removal of the nuclear waste. In 2011 the U.S. Nuclear Regulatory Commission extended the plant's license for another twenty years, although the catastrophe at the Fukushima Daiichi nuclear plant in Japan following the earthquake and tsunami in 2011 heightened anxieties about such plants everywhere. Xcel Energy is carrying out a major overhaul of the plant.

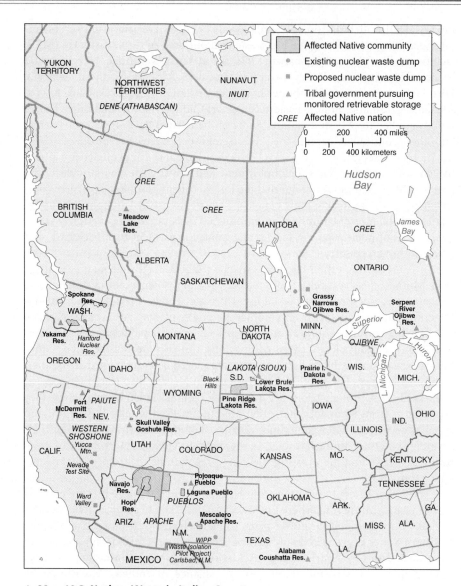

◆ Map 10.3 **Nuclear Waste in Indian Country**

The construction of nuclear waste storage facilities on some reservations may offer short-term economic opportunities to the tribes, but many Indians and non-Indians regard the dumping of nuclear waste as a prime example of "environmental racism" that poses long-term threats to neighboring communities.

SOURCE: Map by Zoltán Grossman of the Midwest Treaty Network. Adapted from Winona LaDuke, *All Our Relations* (Cambridge, Mass.: South End Press, 1999). Reprinted by permission.

The Department of Energy planned to open an underground repository at Yucca Mountain by 2017, but the Western Shoshones fought the project, arguing that the site is on land guaranteed to them by treaty in 1863. Many more Americans worried about the dangers involved in transporting nuclear waste to the new site. In 2009 the Obama administration announced that the Yucca Mountain site was no longer an option, and Congress reduced its funding.

The Earth Hurts

Pollution of the air, land, and water, destruction of animal and plant life, and relentless exploitation of natural resources all run counter to traditional Native ideals of living with the earth. The Arctic tundra is being used as a dumping ground for nuclear waste, and toxic PCBs have been found in Eskimo mothers' milk. At the Mohawk community of Akwesasne on the banks of the St. Lawrence River in upstate New York, where the people used to hunt, farm, and fish, so many chemicals were dumped into the water by nearby industrial plants that it became unsafe to eat fish or game, cultivate the soil, or raise cattle. Scientists caught snapping turtles with so many PCBs in their bodies that they constitute toxic waste, an event with ominous significance for a people whose creation stories tell that the world was formed on the back of a huge sea turtle. The pollution that threatens Navajos in Arizona and Mohawks at Akwesasne threatens everyone, as does the human-induced climate change that threatens Native people who depend on the ice of the circumpolar arctic regions or whose coastal villages face submergence under rising sea levels. "The earth hurts," said the late Navajo elder Roberta Blackgoat, a long-time opponent of the desecration of Navajo land. "The planet is in danger. . . . It is everybody's future."[62]

Many tribes are fighting back. Northern Cheyennes continue to fend off proposals to turn their Montana homeland into the largest coal strip mine in the United States. "I feel like I have lived a lifetime fighting coal strip mining," said Gail Small of Native Action, a grassroots organization committed to fighting coal development and ensuring the survival of the Northern Cheyenne community.[63] In 2005 the Navajo government passed a law banning uranium mining in Navajo country, but Navajo people have also clashed with their tribal government as they continue to fight the environmental costs of developing energy resources in their homeland. A grassroots Navajo environmental group effectively protested the proposed building of a new power plant in northwestern New Mexico by Sithe Global Power and the Diné Power Authority, which was established by the Navajo Nation Council.[64] In *Navajo Nation, et al. v. United States Forest Service, et al.,* a Ninth Circuit Court of Appeals panel of judges ruled that operators of the Arizona Snowbowl, a ski resort located north of Flagstaff, could not extend its season by making artificial snow from wastewater. Overturning a lower court decision in favor of the project, the appeals court accepted the arguments of the Hopi, Navajo, Yavapai, and other tribes that making snow with contaminated water on the sacred San Francisco Peaks (see Map 1.5, page 42) constituted a violation of their religious rights and of the Religious Freedom Restoration Act of 1993.[65] Then, upon rehearing the case in 2008, the court *en banc*° reversed the decision, and in 2009 the Supreme Court declined to review the Navajos' case. Navajo president Joe Shirley Jr. issued a statement on the sanctity of the San Francisco Peaks and called for help in preserving them; Native Americans, environmental groups, and others formed a "Save the Peaks" coalition, and Navajos requested that the United Nations intervene to protect the mountain as a sacred site. In 2012 a federal appeals court ruled in favor of the ski resort's plans to upgrade, clearing the way for the Arizona Snowbowl to become "the first ski resort in the world to use 100 percent sewage effluent to make artificial snow."[66] In spite of this setback, the tribes continue their fight.

Some tribes provide models, and high standards, for the rest of America to emulate in areas of environmental protection, water quality management, and fish restoration. Some federal environmental statutes accord tribes "TAS" (Treatment as States) status, which allows them to serve as the principal governmental steward of their natural resources. Qualifying tribes can, for example, set their own standards for air emissions and discharges into tribal waterways at levels that must meet — and may even exceed — national standards. The Isleta Pueblo in New Mexico, the first tribe accorded TAS status in 1992, set water quality standards for the Rio Grande flowing through the pueblo higher than those of the federal government, in part to protect tribal members' use of the waters for religious and ceremonial purposes. The federal government approved Isleta's water quality standard and a federal court upheld the EPA's authority to make it binding on the city of Albuquerque. Albuquerque subsequently spent more than $60 million to upgrade its water treatment facilities so that its discharges into the Rio Grande complied with the tribe's stringent water quality standards.[67] Many tribes are beginning to provide clean renewable energy by harnessing the massive wind resources of their homelands; tribes in the Dakotas and Nebraska are collaborating through the Intertribal Council on Utility Policy on plans to develop the first large-scale Native owned and operated wind farms in the country. On the other hand, Wampanoags at Mashpee and Aquinnah oppose construction of a wind farm in Nantucket Sound that would infringe on sacred rituals by obstructing their view of the sunrise. As always, Native communities are negotiating paths to progress while respecting their homelands and rituals and have many (sometimes conflicting) opinions about how best to do so.

There are also ongoing efforts to reverse the effects of past desecrations. In 2007 Judge Ricardo Martinez ruled that the treaty fishing right imposed an obligation on Washington State to refrain from reducing fish runs with culverts that blocked salmon from reaching spawning grounds. In 2010 agreements were signed by which Klamath River dams would be removed to protect endangered Indian treaty fisheries. The Klamath River, straddling the border of Oregon and California, once contained the Pacific Coast's third most productive salmon

---

° *en banc:* A majority of the circuit judges reviewing "a question of exceptional importance."

fishery and was the economic and cultural mainstay of the Yurok, Hoopa, and Karuk Indians. Between 1908 and 1962 half a dozen dams were built along the Klamath, blocking salmon runs and degrading water quality. Farmers and ranchers benefited from hydropower and pumped irrigation water, but salmon populations plummeted. Despite growing protests from Indians and commercial fishermen, the George W. Bush administration continued diverting water for irrigation. Low river flows, high water temperatures, and congested conditions produced a proliferation of parasites, and in 2002 more than 34,000 (some estimates say 60,000) Chinook and Coho salmon died in the Klamath, "the largest adult salmon die-off in the history of the American West." Tribes who relied on the salmon harvest and sports and commercial fishermen were hit immediately, but the full impact of the disaster was not felt until four years later, when the offspring of the salmon who died in 2002 would have made their spawning run. By then the Klamath stock was so depleted that the federal government placed 700 miles of Pacific coastline, from San Francisco to central Oregon, off-limits to commercial salmon fishing for most of the 2006 season. Many commercial fishermen went bankrupt. The government cancelled the entire Pacific salmon fishing season in both 2008 and 2009. Experts warned that the Klamath basin was "in a permanent crisis." After years of conflict, Indians, commercial fishermen, ranchers, farmers, and environmentalists came together to try and save the river. The government made fish passage a condition of relicensing the dams. PacifiCorp, the owner of the dams, considered building fish ladders, but ladders are of limited effectiveness, and building them would have cost more than removing the dams. In 2010 the various parties and state and federal governments made an agreement to remove four of the dams, with California, Oregon, and the U.S. Congress pledging $1 billion for river restoration. If the agreement is carried out, it will be the world's biggest dam removal project.[68]

Global Warming and New Partnerships

In 1977 Iroquois delegates to the Non-Governmental Organizations of the United Nations in Geneva, Switzerland, issued a "call to consciousness" to the Western world. "The way of life known as Western Civilization is on a death path on which their own culture has no viable answers," they warned. "When faced with the reality of their own destructiveness, they can only go forward into areas of more efficient destruction." The delegates saw the air becoming foul, water being poisoned, trees dying, animals disappearing, and the weather changing. They felt it was time to break away from Western concepts of exploiting and subjugating the natural world and embrace Native ways of living with the natural world. "The traditional Native peoples hold the key to the reversal of the processes in Western Civilization which hold the promise of unimaginable future suffering and destruction."[69] Decades later, Western civilization at large has not varied from its "death path." Anishinaabe author and activist Winona LaDuke, who ran as vice-presidential candidate of the Green Party in the 1996 and 2000 elections, articulated a growing awareness that "at some point, there will be no more 'frontiers' to conquer."[70] Kiowa author N. Scott Momaday called on Western society to live with a "moral comprehension" of the Earth; the alternative, he noted, "is that we shall not live at all."[71]

Increasing evidence and recurrent scientific reports about the accelerating rate and likely repercussions of global warming have convinced many people — Native and non-Native — of the urgent need for change everywhere, including Indian country. Warning that the amount of carbon dioxide in the atmosphere now exceeds what many scientists believe constitutes a temperature tipping point (350 parts per million), LaDuke calls for a moratorium on fossil fuels extraction and calls on tribes to "stop doing stupid stuff." Targeting proposed Crow and Navajo mining projects that would add billions of metric tons of carbon to the atmosphere, she writes: "Combusting coal is, well, so last millennium, and Navajo and Crow tribal leadership are intent on resurrecting and staying wedded to a dysfunctional and archaic fossil fuels economy . . . it doesn't matter if that coal is burned in the U.S., or if it's burned in China. We all live in the same world."[72]

Some people believe that a return to traditional indigenous ways is the only chance for humanity to survive in the twenty-first century. Indigenous communities struggling to protect their homelands have found increasing numbers of allies among concerned non-Indian organizations and have formed new action groups of their own. Organizations like Honor the Earth, founded in 1993, promote cooperation between Native Americans and environmentalists. Part of President Obama's Third U.S. National Climate Assessment, released in 2014, dealt exclusively with the effects of climate change on Native communities. Rising sea levels and coastal erosion in the Pacific Northwest and Gulf Coast; melting permafrost in the Arctic, and recurrent and longer droughts in the Southwest and California threaten subsistence practices, village locations, food and water supplies. "The consequences of observed and projected climate change have and will undermine indigenous ways of life that have persisted for thousands of years," said the report. The government allocated $10 million to help tribes cope with the effects of climate change, a step in the right direction but a puny sum given the scope of the crisis.[73]

In recent years Native American elders, tribal leaders, scholars, and tribal colleges have collaborated with scientists and researchers from NASA, the National Oceanic and Atmospheric Administration (NOAA), and other organizations to address issues of climate change.[74] Scientists using satellite imagery and indigenous peoples witnessing encroaching shorelines and declining subsistence resources reaffirm each other's findings about the effects of climate change. The American Indian and Alaska Native Climate Change Working Group has been active for more than fifteen years. Daniel Wildcat, a Yuchi member of the Muscogee Nation of Oklahoma and the director of the Haskell Environmental Research Studies Center at Haskell Indian Nations University in Lawrence, Kansas, calls for Western scientists to embrace Earth-based indigenous knowledge in facing the planet's pressing problems and prescribes some heavy doses of "indigenous realism" for Western society's ailing relationship to the natural world.[75]

Because indigenous peoples are at the forefront in feeling the impacts of global warming, many Indian tribes and organizations are on the frontlines in the fight to turn from fossil fuels to clean energy. Tribal liaisons from the National Wildlife Federation, which partners with tribes to protect wildlife and habitat from climate change, report that, while our elected officials fail to act on the greatest threat we have ever seen, "Every day, tribal citizens are drawing the line and saying no. No more coal mining. No more oil drilling. No more digging up the earth so that corporations can profit off of exploiting our land, our water and our climate. We are stopping them one project at a time and collectively, we are making a difference."[76] For example, a grassroots organization called EcoCheyenne, which promotes renewable and sustainable energy, is fighting to stop the development of a huge coal mine on the eastern edge of Northern Cheyenne country. Thousands of people have joined the Cowboys and Indians Alliance, a coalition of farmers, ranchers, and Native Americans committed to stopping construction of the Keystone XL pipeline. If completed, the pipeline would transport diluted bitumen from the tar sands of Alberta, where production has already damaged Native lands and water, 2,000 miles to refineries on the Gulf Coast of Texas. In April 2014 the Alliance staged a five-day "Reject and Protect" protest in Washington, D.C., and pitched tipis on the National Mall (See the Picture Essay, "Tribal Sovereignty in Action," on pages 633–38). The protestors presented a hand-painted tipi to the National Museum of the American Indian as a gift to President Obama and a symbol of their hopes for protected land and clean water. "Keystone XL is a death warrant for our people," said Oglala Sioux Tribal President Bryan Brewer. "President Obama must reject this pipeline and protect our sacred land and water. The United States needs to respect our treaty rights and say no to Keystone XL."[77] Obama vetoed the pipeline bill in 2015.

In 2014 the Environmental Protection Agency finalized a new Environmental Justice Policy, in the works since 2011, for working with indigenous peoples to meet the growing challenges they face. In addition, the EPA has committed to incorporating Traditional Ecological Knowledge (TEK) into its environmental science, policy and decision-making processes, and to take into account concerns regarding information on sacred sites, cultural resources, and other traditional knowledge.[78]

BUILDING WELL NATIONS

The legacies of colonialism and oppression endure in Indian country and have, at times, resulted in self-destructive acts and sickness among Indian people. Rebuilding Indian nations requires more than restoring self-government and developing reservation economies. It also requires restoring the physical and spiritual health of Indian communities after generations of dispossession, dependency, cultural assault, and racism. In some areas, building well nations° involves restoring the health of land that has been scarred by the extraction of uranium, coal, and other energy resources and contaminated by cancer-causing pollutants, and restoring the flow and health of the water. It also involves Indian people taking greater control of their health services, education, and cultural property; protecting the health, safety, and well-being of women and children; and balancing new and traditional ways. As the evidence from the Mississippi Band of Choctaws shows, tribes that run their own affairs and control their own health care facilities can achieve a dramatic improvement in the health of their members as well as in the economic development of the community.[79]

Although standards of health have improved, Indian communities confront major challenges in HIV and AIDS, diabetes, teen suicides, and other problems common to modern American society. At the end of the twentieth century, tuberculosis rates among Indian people were more than seven times the national average; alcohol-related deaths were ten times higher; fetal alcohol syndrome was thirty-three times more common; and suicide rates were four times greater among Indian teenagers than among non-Indians. The rate of Type 2 diabetes (also known as adult-onset diabetes) among Indian adults is three times that for the rest of the population and, as in the rest of the population, it is skyrocketing among young people as well. It is approaching epidemic proportions in some Indian communities.[80]

Confronting Drugs and Alcohol

Injected into Indian country from colonial times onward as a means of stimulating trade and undermining Indian independence, alcohol continues to disrupt Indian communities, break up Indian families, shatter Indian lives, and threaten Indian futures. Many tribal leaders regard alcoholism as their primary enemy. In 1977 the American Indian Policy Review Commission declared alcohol abuse "the most severe and widespread health problem among Indians," and things are little better today. Estimates of the rate of alcoholism on some Indian reservations range from 50 percent to 80 percent. Growing up on a reservation in South Dakota, Mary Crow Dog recalled, "I started drinking because it was the natural way of life. My father drank, my stepfather drank, my mother drank. . . . I think I grew up with the idea that everybody was doing it." She said, "The men had nothing to live for so they got drunk and drove off at ninety miles an hour in a car without lights, without brakes, and without destination, to die a warrior's death."[81] Seventy percent of all treatment services provided by the Indian Health Service in the early 1990s were alcohol-related. So many Indian babies are affected by fetal alcohol syndrome that some Indian people insist that if it is not halted, "we will cease to exist as Indians."[82]

° The concept of well nations is taken from *Well Nations Magazine,* a publication designed to provide Indians and other people with helpful information regarding physical, emotional, mental, and spiritual health.

◆ **Diego Romero,** *The Drinker* **(1993)**
Cochiti Pueblo artist Diego Romero (b. 1964) uses traditional Pueblo pottery techniques, but he gives them a new and often disturbing twist by adding social commentary. Romero says, "My dialogue centers around industrialization of Indian land, cars, automobiles, broken hearts, bars, Indian gaming." He uses "a language of symbols and metaphors" so that his art speaks to everyone: "I've always felt that a person from Japan or Germany can come and look at one of my pots and see exactly what's going on."[83] *Denver Art Museum: Funds Provided by the Laura Musser Fund, 1993.102. Photograph © Denver Art Museum.*

Myths and stereotypes about Indian drinking are common and damaging.[84] In fact, Indian people have resisted and protested against the use of alcohol since colonial times.[85] Many Indian people fight alcoholism by returning to Indian ways and values. "I haven't touched a drop of liquor for years," wrote Mary Crow Dog, "ever since I felt there was a purpose to my life, learned to accept myself for what I was. I have to thank the Indian movement for that, and Grandfather Peyote, and the pipe."°[86] In 1987 the tribal council of the Cheyenne River Sioux declared

° Pipes play a sacred role in Lakota culture and in peyote ceremonialism.

war on alcohol abuse with the goal of eliminating it from the reservation, and its Healthy Nations Program continues the fight against that and other problems.[87]

As in other places in America, drug trafficking and methamphetamine addiction have become severe problems in some Indian communities. Methamphetamine produces a euphoric high but with devastating side effects that include anorexia, convulsions, high blood pressure, heart failure, strokes, suicidal tendencies, child abuse and neglect, violence, and even murder. Meth-addicted mothers give birth to meth-addicted babies. The methamphetamine-use rate among Native Americans is three times that among the general population. Some fear "it just may be the most formidable enemy the tribes have had to battle yet." The San Carlos Apache tribe reported that 25 percent of patients admitted into their emergency room in 2005 tested meth-positive. "The use, production and trafficking of meth is destroying my community," said San Carlos chairwoman Kathleen Kitcheyan in testimony before the Senate Committee on Indian Affairs, "shattering families, endangering our children, and threatening our cultural and spiritual lives." Darrel Rides at the Door, a drug and alcohol counselor at Blackfeet Nation in Browning, Montana, said the same thing: "It's destroying our culture, our way of life, killing our people," he told the *New York Times*. Rides at the Door uses traditional healing therapies to help combat addiction and the inroads of drugs in peoples' lives. Many communities are treating methamphetamine as a new enemy, declaring war on it, and implementing community watch and awareness programs to fight against it. On the Navajo Reservation, the Navajo Methamphetamine Task Forces involve elders, young people, recovering addicts, current users, and health and law enforcement to combat this "tidal wave of destruction." The U.S. government has increased funding for law enforcement in Indian country but tribal police resources are stretched thin in the fight against drug gangs.[88]

Balancing Ways of Healing

As U.S. citizens, Indians and Alaska Natives are eligible for Medicare, Medicaid, veterans, and other public health benefits. Members of federally recognized tribes who live on or near a reservation or an Alaska Native village are eligible to receive health care from the Indian Health Service, which is located in the Department of Health and Human Services and funded by annual appropriations from Congress. Like other Americans, many Native people are covered by private health insurance through their jobs.[89] It is too early to tell how the Affordable Care Act will play out in Indian country.

Taking responsibility for the health and well-being of tribal citizens is a key component of tribal sovereignty. In 2006, with South Dakota proposing a ban on abortions, Cecilia Fire Thunder, the first female president of the Oglala Sioux, announced that she planned to open an abortion clinic on the reservation. The clinic—called Sacred Choices—would be open to all women, Native and non-Native. While some people viewed the matter as a moral issue, Fire Thunder pointed out that it was also an issue of tribal sovereignty: the Oglalas had the right to establish the clinic on their reservation even if the state banned abortions elsewhere.[90]

Although Fire Thunder was subsequently impeached—one of the charges being that she exceeded her authority as tribal president in organizing the clinic without consulting the tribal council—and South Dakota voters defeated the abortion ban in the November 2006 elections anyway, her stand against state legislation highlighted the link between tribal sovereignty and health care for tribal members.

Many tribes are taking over Indian Health Service hospitals and clinics and running them themselves. Some Indian communities supplement the Western-style medicine provided by the IHS with more holistic, community-based, and culturally connected forms of healing. The Navajos have moved "closer to true self-determination in medical care" not only by playing a greater role in the delivery of IHS services and producing their own physicians but also by preserving traditional herbal, ceremonial, and cultural ways of healing. Some Western medical procedures can conflict with traditional understandings of health and well-being, and Navajo people sometimes have to accommodate biomedical technologies and Western understandings of health and illness to promote healing. At the same time, many non-Indian physicians have begun to take more note of Native healing practices. They increasingly recognize that both Native and non-Native traditions have a role to play, an approach that Dr. Lori Arviso Alvord, the first Navajo woman to become a surgeon, has consistently advocated. Some people may visit a doctor to obtain medication that will help relieve the *symptoms* of an illness while still relying on traditional healing rituals to provide a cure. The benefit of combining Native and Western approaches and healing practices was demonstrated in 1993 when a "mystery illness" struck the Southwest. Navajo healers helped the Centers for Disease Control identify the cause of the disease—the hantavirus carried by deer mice and other rodents—and Western medical practitioners were able to bring it under control.[91]

Combining Western and traditional knowledge in holistic and culturally centered approaches to healing has been shown to work—even to be necessary—in restoring the health of communities.[92] Whether it can work to restore the health of the planet remains to be seen.

Restoring Safety to Native Women

Native Americans today are more than twice as likely to be victims of violence than other Americans. Poverty, drug and alcohol abuse, domestic abuse, frustration, and despair all contribute to Indian-on-Indian violence, but Congress and the Supreme Court are also partly responsible for the escalation of interracial violence on reservations. The Major Crimes Act of 1885 authorized the federal government to exercise jurisdiction over major crimes committed in Indian country; Public Law 280 in 1953 delegated jurisdiction over crimes on Indian lands to state courts in certain states; and the Indian Civil Rights Act of 1968 imposed most of the requirements of the Constitution's Bill of Rights on Indian tribes and limited the penalties tribal courts could impose to one year in prison and $5,000 in fines for each offense. The Supreme Court in *Oliphant v. Suquamish* (see pages 539–46) stripped tribes of the power to prosecute crimes committed by non-Indians on the reservations.[93] In addition, tribal police forces struggle to provide adequate coverage for their citizens. In 2006 the Standing Rock Reservation in North Dakota and South Dakota had a total of nine police officers (with generally only two or three on duty at any one time) to patrol 2.3 million acres; the violent crime rate on the reservation was more than eight times the national average.[94] Although the size of tribal police departments is growing significantly, in 2011 there were fewer than 3,000 tribal and BIA law enforcement officers within Indian country, or less than two officers per 1,000 residents. The average tribal police department had fewer than three police officers to serve up to 10,000 residents and patrol up to 500,000 acres. On some reservations, it could take a responding officer hours to get to a victim or crime scene in a remote area.[95]

Indian women are particularly vulnerable. As in other areas of the world, European and American soldiers employed sexual violence as a tool of conquest and a weapon of war against Native peoples. Colonial attitudes depicted Native women as lacking in morals and as prime targets for sexual predation and reformation. The legacies of racial, sexual, and class oppression, and of stereotypes about "squaws," continue to haunt the lives of Indian women today.[96] A report issued by the Indian Law Resources Center in 2013, echoing a 2006 report by Amnesty International entitled *Maze of Injustice*, states:

> Native women and girls are not safe now. Violence against Native women and girls has reached epidemic levels in Indian country and Alaska Native villages — rates that are 2½ times higher than violence against any other group of women in the United States. Native women are more than twice as likely to be stalked than other women. One in three Native women will be raped in her lifetime, and six in ten will be physically assaulted. The murder rate for Native women is ten times the national average on some reservations. Alaska Native women are subjected to the highest rate of forcible sexual assault in the country. One in two Alaska Native women will experience sexual or physical violence, and "an Alaska Native woman is sexually assaulted every 18 hours."[97]

As Bruce Duthu shows in "Broken Justice in Indian Country" (see pages 545–46), Native women and girls have had less protection from such violence and less access to justice because the vast majority of perpetrators were non-Indian and therefore immune from prosecution by tribal courts. A 2009 report on sexual violence against Indian women in Minnesota found that rapes on upstate reservations increased during hunting season: a non-Indian could drive up from the Twin Cities and be home in five hours and the tribal police could not arrest him.[98] A Native woman, abused and battered in her own home in front of her children by a non-Indian spouse, or an Indian teenager date-raped by a non-Indian visiting the reservation, had no recourse in tribal court. Indian and Alaska Native nations are the only governments in the United States that lack the legal authority to protect their citizens from violence by any persons. The statistics underrepresent the crisis: many, perhaps most, rape victims do not report the crime; they fear retribution, do not expect justice, and experience discrimination from non-Indian agencies. When Indian victims do turn to federal and state authorities, those authorities often fail to prosecute. According to a U.S. Government Accountability Office report in 2010, federal authorities declined to prosecute 67 percent of Indian country matters referred to them that involved sexual abuse and related matters.[99]

Criminal jurisdiction on Indian lands is divided among federal, tribal, and state governments; complicated jurisdictional issues delay, prolong, and sometimes preclude the investigation and prosecution of sex crimes in Indian country. Whether or not the victim is a member of a federally recognized Indian tribe, whether or not the perpetrator is a member of a federally recognized Indian tribe, and whether or not the alleged crime took place on tribal land determine if the crime should be investigated by tribal, federal, or state police; if it should be prosecuted by a tribal prosecutor, state prosecutor (district attorney), or federal prosecutor (U.S. attorney); and if it should be tried in tribal, state, or federal court.[100]

Congress has taken steps to address the crisis. In 2005 it expanded and reauthorized the Violence Against Women Act, first passed in 1994, with specific provisions and funding for tribal law enforcement agencies and services. In 2010, Congress passed, and President Obama signed, the Tribal Law and Order Act. The new law required the Department of Justice to track and deal with declining prosecutions in Indian country, gives tribal police more authority (they can now arrest non-Indian suspects and can be deputized to enforce federal laws), and allows tribal courts to impose sentences of up to three years instead of just one year and fines of up to $15,000. It also increased funding for federal and tribal police officers.

In 2013, President Obama signed into law the Violence Against Women Reauthorization Act, which contains provisions allowing tribal courts to prosecute certain non-Indian sex offenders in certain categories of crimes. As author Louise Erdrich pointed out in a *New York Times* op. ed. urging passage of VAWA through the House of Representatives, where some Republicans were balking, "What seems like dry legislation can leave Native women at the mercy of their predators or provide a slim margin of hope for justice."[101] The new law effectively meant that *Oliphant v. Suquamish* was partially repealed. But the law generally did not take effect until March 2015 and gaps and procedural obstacles remain. The crimes must meet certain criteria and the tribes must guarantee the defendants certain rights. Many tribes still lack the funding and resources to provide the lawyers, judges, public defenders, police forces, record keeping services, detention facilities, and other requirements under the new law. A tribe can only prosecute non-Indian offenders who have ties to the tribe. Tribes do not have jurisdiction over crimes between non-Indians or over crimes committed by strangers. So, VAWA 2013 "is restricted to crimes of domestic or dating violence, thus leaving crimes of rape, sexual assault, and sex trafficking largely unprosecuted if committed by a stranger in Indian country."[102] Because the Supreme Court (in *Alaska v. Native Village of Venetie Tribal Government*) ruled that Alaska Native Claims Settlement Act lands were "not Indian country," VAWA does not apply to the vast majority of Alaska Native villages. VAWA 2013 therefore "is a limited *Oliphant*-fix, restoring only limited tribal criminal jurisdiction for certain crimes by non-Indians in Indian country."[103]

Native women and girls continue to be victims of a tangled maze of jurisdictions. Restoring their safety, according to the Indian Law Resource Center Report, requires restoring full criminal jurisdiction to Indian nations and ensuring that the tribes have the institutional capacity and resources to exercise that jurisdiction. Many tribes and organizations are working to combat, prevent, and punish violence against women, and federal, state, and tribal authorities sometimes collaborate effectively, with cross-deputation agreements and data-sharing, for example. Their efforts need to be supported by further reforms in federal law to allow more robust criminal authority and funding to support law enforcement and tribal courts in their efforts to keep their citizens safe.[104] Although VAWA generally did not go into effect until 2015, the Pascua Yaqui Tribe of Arizona, the Tulalip Tribes of Washington, and the Umatilla Tribes of Oregon took advantage of a pilot program and are the first in the country to exercise special criminal jurisdiction for certain crimes against women, under the 2013 VAWA. Their efforts are sure to be challenged on the grounds that Congress lacks the power to subject non-Indian U.S. citizens to criminal trials in the courts of tribal nations that provide them no avenues for political representation or participation.

The Welfare of Indian Children

The Indian Child Welfare Act (ICWA) of 1978 represented a major step in stemming the removal of children from Indian country into non-Indian families, but adoption rates remain high in Indian country and ICWA does not provide iron-clad guarantees for the rights of Indian parents, families, and children. In 2009 a non-Indian mother gave up her baby for adoption at birth by a white couple. The child's father, Dusten Brown, who had been briefly engaged to the mother, was a citizen of the Cherokee Nation and invoked ICWA to prevent the adoption. The South Carolina courts agreed and Brown was given custody. In 2011, after the child had lived with the adoptive parents for two years, she was given to her father, whom she had never met. What became widely known as "the Baby Veronica case" attracted extensive media coverage and many people expressed outrage that a family was being torn apart. Brown, they said, had abandoned the child before she was born and was not really an Indian, having minimal "blood." The adoptive parents appealed the decision to the U.S. Supreme Court. In a 5–4 decision in 2013 the Supreme Court overturned the lower court's ruling. The majority opinion held that the procedures required by ICWA to end parental rights did not apply because Brown never had physical custody of his biological daughter, having given up his rights before her birth; ICWA's requirement to make extra efforts to preserve the Indian family did not apply because no other Cherokee relatives stepped forward to assert custody and no Indian families sought to adopt the child. The case was sent back to the South Carolina courts, and the South Carolina Supreme Court finalized the adoption. After one and a half years with her biological father, and despite an attempt by the Oklahoma State Court to stay the transfer, the child was handed back to her adoptive parents. The case involved many legal motions and heated emotions and Indian tribes worried that the Supreme Court's decision might presage another round of assaults on tribal sovereignty.

Revitalizing Nations: Preserving Language and Culture

All indigenous peoples confront the challenge of preserving traditional culture and tribal heritage in the modern world. Preserving and revitalizing tribal cultures and traditions is not just a way for Native Americans to demonstrate their continuing Indianness to outsiders. For many tribes, it is key to individual and communal health and well-being. Traditional ways and tribal values offer guides for good living and a path back to harmony after generations of disruption. Providing young people with an education that grounds them in tribal ways is crucial to community health and well-being and to the future of their Indian nations. Protecting cultural artifacts preserves vital connections to those who went before. In 1992 Congress adopted amendments to the National Historic Preservation Act that permit federally recognized tribes to assume greater responsibility for the preservation of significant historic properties on tribal lands. Tribes who wish to do so may assume any or all of the functions of a state historic preservation officer with respect to tribal land. Some tribes have their own archaeologists. Repatriation (see pages 530–31) is also, for many Indian people, a question of health. Human remains and sacred objects that have been wrenched from their proper place may jeopardize the spiritual well-being and the physical health of a community, even of a universe. Recovering ancestors' bones or important sacred objects can be a healing experience that begins to restore harmony to the world.

Along with the repatriation of physical belongings, the issue of language survival is critical to Native American communities, and the evidence of a worldwide language crisis is well documented. It has been predicted that in the course of the twenty-first century, 3,000 of the world's existing 6,000 languages will die out and another 2,400 will come close to extinction. In other words, 90 percent of the world's languages are on the endangered languages list. As the late MIT linguist Ken Hale explained, language loss has far-reaching repercussions for scholars and scientists as well as for the community, and amounts to a "catastrophe for human intellectual and cultural diversity, a disaster comparable in its extent to losses in other aspects of our environment."[105] Loss of traditional languages that encompass deeper knowledge about the natural world may reduce people's capacity to understand and live in that world in an era of escalating change. In many Native American communities, the popular culture peddled by the media threatens to complete the work of linguicide that the boarding schools began.

Just as the U.S. government in the late nineteenth century saw the destruction of Indian languages as an effective means of erasing tribal culture and identity, so Indian people today see language revival as a means of restoring them. Many Native communities have developed or are developing language immersion programs for children. In 1990 Congress passed the Native American Languages Act. The law recognized that "the traditional languages of Native Americans are an integral part of their cultures and identities and form the basic medium for the transmission, and thus survival, of Native American cultures, literature, histories, religions, political institutions, and values." The act states that it is the policy of the United States to "encourage and support the use of Native American languages as a medium of instruction."[106] Additional legislation provided grants for recording oral histories and teaching languages in classrooms, but Indian people realize that language preservation and revitalization lie in their own hands: if they don't use it, they will lose it.[107]

Immersion programs such as that at the Nizipuhwahsin Center on the Blackfeet Reservation in Montana or the Mohawk Akwesasne Freedom School (see page 513) demonstrate the potential for such efforts to pull languages back from the brink and turn things around. The late Darryl Robes Kipp, an army veteran with a master's in education from Harvard, and two other tribal members founded the Piegan Institute in 1987, with a commitment to preserving Blackfeet and other Native languages. Like others dedicated to the struggle to preserve languages, Kipp pointed out that language is more than just a means of communication; it is a cultural prism through which to see the world and a storehouse of knowledge. "Our language is our library," he said. "And Blackfeet is totally unlike English, so it gives the child another thinking blueprint." Some Native college students are also actively involved in preserving their languages, acutely aware that the threat of language extinction increases as each Native-speaking elder passes on. In December 2006 Congress passed the Esther Martinez Native American Languages Preservation Act, establishing grants for programs designed to preserve Indian languages and reverse language loss. Speaking and thinking in one's Native language and knowing one's traditional ways does not render Indian people backward, said Kipp; it empowers them to participate in modern tribal and American society. Education in the boarding schools and other institutions where Native languages were suppressed or ignored "was a journey to lead us away from who we really are. . . . Language relearning is a journey home."[108]

At the beginning of the twentieth century, Congress was funding schools where Native students were beaten for speaking their languages. In the twenty-first century, Congress acted in support of Native language preservation. In 2014, two bills were introduced into the U.S. Senate: the Native Languages Reauthorization Act, to ensure the survival and continuing vitality of Native American languages, and the Native Language Immersion Student Achievement Act, to authorize the secretary of education to award grants to schools and private or tribal nonprofit organizations to develop and maintain programs that support the use by schools of Native American languages as their primary language of instruction.

Native philosophy and teachings often stress the need for people to consider the impact of their actions on those yet unborn, and to look ahead to the seventh generation as a guide for living. In the rapidly changing and tumultuous twenty-first century, the responsibility of handing on a good world across the generations is truly formidable. Tribal communities are working hard to ensure that lands and resources, languages, traditions, values, education, community health, and tribal sovereignty are handed down intact.

Through centuries of struggle and generations of political activism, and contrary to the United States' expectations and predictions, Native Americans not only survived as a people but also ensured the existence of Indian country within the United States. The terms of the continuing relationship between the United States and the Indian nations within its borders are still being considered, contested, and constructed.[109]

"When all has been said and done," wrote former Navajo Supreme Court Justice Raymond D. Austin, "all American Indian peoples want is the right to live as Indians in their own country."[110] As they continue to strive for that goal in the twenty-first century, will the values embedded in traditional teachings continue to serve Indian people as they have in the past? Indian America will survive, but what will be the terms of that survival? What will Indian country look like? Philip Deloria writes that Indian people were "thoroughly creative in crafting an Indian life in the twentieth-century United States."[111] If the history of the past five hundred years is any guide, they will be equally creative in crafting an Indian life in the twenty-first century United States.

◆ **Powwow Dancer**
An Indian dancer competes at a northern Plains powwow at the Buffalo Bill Historical Center in Cody, Wyoming, 1995. The word *powwow* derives from an Algonquian term for medicine men, and early European colonists often applied it to any gatherings in which medicine men participated. Today the term refers to Indian social events that revolve around dancing, drumming, and singing. Always a crucial part of Native American religious and communal life, dancing persisted even while missionaries and government agents tried to suppress what they regarded as "heathenish practices." In the late twentieth and early twenty-first centuries, powwows have flourished as Indian people across the United States and Canada seek ways to come together to celebrate their heritage, preserve traditional dances, and demonstrate new forms of cultural expression.

For many Indian people in modern America, powwows are an important way to reaffirm their identity and participate in their culture in a dramatic and public way. © *Kevin R. Morris/CORBIS.*

DOCUMENTS

Playing Indian and Fighting Mascots

⋯⋅◆⋅⋯

AFTER MORE THAN FIVE HUNDRED YEARS of contact with Europeans, after surviving the traumas of colonialism and policies of detribalization, and after sustaining a remarkable comeback in the last one hundred years, and while battling multiple challenges on many fronts, Indian people in the United States today still confront major problems in the images that other people have created of them. Non-Indians have "played Indian" since colonists donned Indian attire and dumped British tea in Boston Harbor, and possibly even before that. In modern days, troubled by environmental degradation, postindustrial society, and a host of other ills in the world, many people continue to "turn" to Indians. Emulating what they believe to be Indian ways, they hope they will somehow acquire greater wisdom, live at one with the Earth, reconnect with their better inner selves, find freedom, or give themselves new identities. Some Indians cater to this desire to "play Indian" by staging ceremonies, conducting sweatbaths for ritual purification, and bestowing Native wisdom for a price. Many more are bemused by it, while others are enraged by what they regard as continuing colonial exploitation and cultural appropriation. Whatever the motivations and meanings of "playing Indian," it generates images and ideas about Indianness that can be damaging and troubling for Indian people themselves.[112] "Playing Indian" takes many forms and ranges from role-playing by children, through cultural appropriation, to outright racism. The most contested involves using Indian mascots and dressing up in paint and feathers for a sports event.

Dartmouth College, the University of Oklahoma, and Stanford University retired their Indian mascots in the 1970s (although, at least at Dartmouth, pockets of resistance to the change remain and individual displays of the old Indian symbol sometimes recur). But some universities and colleges continue to use Indian names, symbols, and logos, while fans wear "war paint," perform "war dances" and chants, and, literally, "drum up" support. In face of protests and complaints from Indian people, many high schools have changed the names of their sports teams from "Chiefs," "Warriors," and "Braves" and have dropped the use of Indian symbols; others refuse to change. Sports fans and the general public regularly see derogatory depictions of Indian people and culture whenever the Washington Redskins, Kansas City Chiefs, Chicago Blackhawks, Cleveland Indians, and Atlanta Braves play.

Many non-Indians find it difficult to understand why Indian people get so upset about these representations. With so many problems to confront, they say, don't Indians have anything better to do? Other people tell Indians, and themselves, that the caricatures and grotesque performances they use are intended to "honor" the country's first peoples. Some Indian people are not bothered by these images, and some Indian teams use Indian logos themselves. Many, however, find them offensive and demeaning, believing that their use points to deep issues of power and racism that still pervade American society and popular culture. Stereotypical images dehumanize Indian people by reducing them to props and invoking them for their association with "wildness," violence, or supposed physical attributes. For many non-Indians, some of whom have never met a real Indian person, these clichés come to represent all that it means to be Indian. Like the racist stereotypes that have been served up to the general public by movies and television, these images adversely affect daily human relationships and individual self-esteem and feed into "more tangible" problems such as alcohol abuse, college and high school dropout rates, unemployment, poverty, and, some would argue, the treatment of Native people by state and local governments and of Native issues by the courts.[113]

In 2005 the American Psychological Association called for the immediate retirement of all American Indian mascots, images, and symbols by schools, colleges, sports teams, and organizations, citing a growing body of literature that demonstrates the harmful effects of racial stereotyping, especially on the self-esteem of young Native Americans.[114] Also in 2005, the National Collegiate Athletic Association (NCAA), the governing body of college sports, banned the use of American Indian nicknames and mascots by sports teams during its postseason tournaments. The decision affected eighteen colleges, whose nicknames and mascots the NCAA deemed "hostile and abusive." Florida State University (FSU) appealed the decision, protesting that the Seminole tribe of Florida sanctions the use of the tribal name and the Chief Osceola mascot. (At FSU football games, a white student wears a Plains headdress and war paint, rides a horse, and brandishes a lance — none of which Osceola would have done.) The NCAA allowed FSU to continue using the nickname "Seminoles" but rejected appeals from some other universities. The Seminole Nation of Oklahoma joined other tribes in signing a statement condemning the use of Indian names and mascots by colleges. In 2007 the University of Illinois ended its use of "Chief Illiniwek" as a mascot and logo in compliance with the NCAA restrictions. The University of North Dakota (UND) refused to abide by the NCAA requirement, and in 2006 a state judge granted an injunction allowing the university to continue using its "Fighting Sioux" nickname and logo, pending the outcome of a trial. In 2007 UND and the NCAA settled their lawsuit, giving the school three years to gain support from the state's Sioux tribes. In 2009 UND's University Senate, which includes faculty, staff, students, and representatives of the administration, passed a resolution opposing the nickname despite unanimous opposition to the resolution from student senators. In 2010, despite the Spirit Lake Sioux tribe's support for the nickname and logo, the North Dakota Board of Higher Education ordered UND to drop its "Fighting Sioux" nickname at the end of the 2010–11 athletic season. Opposition continued in some quarters, but in a state referendum in 2012 more than two-thirds of North Dakota voters decided to retire the name and logo, and the state Board of Higher Education concurred. The school was allowed to choose a new name in 2015.

The issue of Native mascots and team names has come into sharpest focus with the name of the football team in the nation's capital and in a case that is the most publicized of an ongoing series of attempts by Indian people to get professional, college, and high school sports teams, and other groups and organizations, to stop using Indian names, mascots, and logos to rally support for or market their products. In 1992 a group of Native Americans that included Vine Deloria Jr. and Suzan Shown Harjo (Muscogee/Cheyenne) petitioned the U.S. Patent and Trademark Office to void the trademark rights of the Washington Redskins on the basis that the team's name and logo were disparaging to Native Americans and therefore violated the law. In 1999 the federal Trademark Trial and Appeal Board found in favor of the Native American plaintiffs. The Washington Redskins appealed the decision, and a federal district court judge overturned it in 2003. The plaintiffs then appealed the 2003 ruling. In 2009 the Supreme Court let stand the court of appeals ruling that the plaintiffs had moved too slowly: the first Redskins trademark was issued in 1967, and the lawsuit was not filed until 1992, during which time the team had lost access to valuable evidence and made investments "in reliance on the apparent validity of the trademarks."[115] A second case, with younger plaintiffs, *Blackhorse et al. v. Pro Football, Inc.*, was filed in 2014. The U.S. Patent and Trademark Office again cancelled some of the Washington Redskins' trademarks because they were disparaging to Native people. The team's owners filed an appeal; in July 2015 a federal judge reaffirmed the earlier ruling and ordered cancellation of the team's federal trademark registrations. The team planned to appeal the ruling. Several media outlets stopped printing and using the name. Fifty U.S. senators signed a letter urging the NFL to stand "on the right side of history" and change the team's name. Comedian Chris Rock and ex-boxer Mike Tyson described it as a racial slur. Hillary Clinton, and many others, called on the Washington Redskins to give up a name and logo that Native people find offensive. A report from the Center for American Progress in 2014, citing the harmful effects of Native mascots and team names on young people, echoed a growing feeling that "the need to eliminate these derogatory representations and stereotypes is urgent and long past due."[116] The controversy continues.

In January 2013 Suzan Shown Harjo published the following article restating some of her core objections to the use of the name. In October 2013 Dan Snyder, the owner of the Washington Redskins, sent an open letter to fans laying out his position on the team's name (pages 622–24). In March 2014 he sent another letter to "Redskins Nation," announcing the foundation of his new charity organization, "The Washington Redskins Original American Foundation." Snyder had toured Indian country, listened to Indian people, and found "heart-wrenching" conditions. Indian people "have genuine issues they truly are worried about," he said, "and our team's name is not one of them." With the new foundation, the Washington Redskins would go beyond simply honoring Native Americans and "provide meaningful and measurable resources that provide genuine opportunities for Tribal communities. With open arms and determined minds, we will work as partners to begin to tackle the troubling realities facing so many tribes across our country." Critics denounced it as an effort to "buy votes"; Suzan Harjo called it a stunt.

SUZAN SHOWN HARJO
Washington "Redskins" Is a Racist Name: U.S. Pro Football Must Disavow It (January 2013)

Can the Washington team not see that its name celebrates a vile history of bounty hunting and mutilation of Native Americans? All major Native American organizations have called for the Washington pro football franchise to end its team's despicable name. Why? Because it's a racial slur and—no matter how many millions it spends trying to sanitize it and silence Native peoples—the epithet is not, was not, and will not be an honorific.

Many Native people cannot bear to say or hear the r-word, while some use it, or "'skins", in the same way that some African American people use the n-word, but are not OK with those of other races using it. Lawyers for the team's owners cite any use of the r-word by Native persons to support their contention that we are fine with it; they've even spied around Facebook for use of the term by the native young people who filed suit in 2006 in the ongoing *Blackhorse et al. v Pro Football case.*

Edward Bennett Williams was the franchise's only owner to meet with Native people who oppose the name, and that was in 1972. Owners have maintained in court since 1992 that the name "honors Indians." But in overlapping litigation of 21 years and counting, no Native representatives have testified that they are honored, while Native friends of the court have stood up against the name and the "honoring" myth.

At the same time, the franchise's owners have said that the name means only the football team and has nothing to do with Native peoples. What then, pray tell, do they mean to suggest by that "Indian" profile and feathers (and by that stereotype-laden fight song, which didn't stop being offensive just because "scalp 'em" was removed)?

The Washington "Indian" head was pasted on the sides of garbage bins on most D.C. street corners from the 1970s to 1990s. Then, the complexion of the "Indian" matched the team's burgundy color. Gradually, but not so subtly, the color changed to the brown-black of the "Indian" skin on today's helmets, which poses the questions: is someone considering a commensurate name change to target the supposed skin color of other people? And how fast would that repugnant idea be shot down by the fans, who don't notice, don't mind, or look the other way now?

As loathsome as it is for the franchise to impose this false identity, its name is even more vile, because it is rooted in the commodification of Native skin and body parts as bounties and trophies. Some Europeans arrived here with millennial history of chopping off enemies' heads and mounting them on stakes, and of scalping, skinning, dismembering, and other tortures and trophy-hunting. Some Native peoples engaged in ritual versions of some of these practices, while many did not, but beheadings and grave robbing were so unusual that they remain prominent in Native oral histories.

Many Native peoples became prey of European countries, companies, and colonies, and of Americans, whose bounty proclamations set targets, proof of "Indian kill" and prices. Some bounties were paid for any person of a stated Native nation, in which case a captive, dead body, or scalp with hair or ears or other cultural identifier would suffice. Others were paid on a sliding scale for men, women, and children, in which case at least the front skin or scalped private parts would have to be produced in order to establish the rate of pay.

SOURCE: Suzan Shown Harjo, "Washington 'Redskins' Is a Racist Name: U.S. Pro Football Must Disavow It." *The Guardian*, January 17, 2013. http://www.theguardian.com/commentisfree/2013/jan/17/washington-redskins-racism-pro-football. Copyright Guardian News & Media Ltd 2013.

The British bounty on the Mi'kmaq Nation (Halifax, 1749), for example, was a straightforward "ten Guineas for every Indian Micmac taken or killed, to be paid upon producing such Savage taken or his scalp."

More complex were the Massachusetts Bay bounties against the Penobscot Nation in 1755 (prices in pounds)—male prisoners (above age 12), 50 each, or for scalps "as Evidence of their being killed," 40 each; and female prisoners or males (under 12), 25 each, or their scalps, 20 each—and Pennsylvania bounties against the Lenni Lenape Nation in 1756 (prices in pieces of eight): 130 for the "Scalp of Every Male Indian Enemy" and 50 for the "Scalp of Every Indian Woman, produced as evidence of their being killed."

There are some who claim that the "scalp evidence" has nothing to do with Indian or bloody skin, because they cannot find the words *skin* or *red* in bounty documents. They do not allow that scalp *is* skin, and that the skin of the head, with or without hair, is insufficient evidence of gender or age. (They also claim that Native people introduced themselves as "Red Skin," because that's how Europeans translated to English what Native men said in their tribal languages, when they likely said they were a Red, Blood, or Related Person or Man.)

Cheyenne Scholar Dr. Leo Killsback did not obscure meaning in his November 2012 ICTMN° column: "The bodies of the 39 Dakota men" (who were federally hanged at Mankato, Minnesota in 1862) "were skinned and preserved by the Mayo Clinic for further 'scientific' study."

Records of military and congressional investigations into the 1864 Sand Creek Massacre illustrate that "scalping" and other terms were euphemisms for Colorado Volunteers mutilating Cheyenne people and wearing and displaying genitalia, fetuses, and other "battle trophies."

Native peoples from ocean to ocean have long experience with twisted words, meanings and thinking, and we recognize echoes of a past that we do not want to repeat. This issue is part of cultural reclamation and protection of sovereign identity and good name that are ongoing in Native nations today.

———————————

° ICTMN: Indian Country Today Media Network.

DAN SNYDER
Letter to Washington Redskins Fans (October 2013)

To Everyone in our Washington Redskins Nation:

As loyal fans, you deserve to know that everyone in the Washington Redskins organization—our players, coaches and staff—are truly privileged to represent this team and everything it stands for. We are relentlessly committed to our fans and to the sustained long-term success of this franchise.

That's why I want to reach out to you—our fans—about a topic I wish to address directly: the team name, "Washington Redskins." While our focus is firmly on the playing field, it is important that you hear straight from me on this issue. As the owner of the Redskins and a lifelong fan of the team, here is what I believe and why I believe it.

Like so many of you, I was born a fan of the Washington Redskins. I still remember my first Redskins game.

Most people do. I was only six, but I remember coming through the tunnel into the stands at RFK with my father, and immediately being struck by the enormity of the stadium and the passion of the fans all around me.

———————————

SOURCE: "Letter from Washington Redskins owner Dan Snyder to fans." *The Washington Post*, October 9, 2013. Online at http://www.washingtonpost.com/local/letter-from-washington-redskins-owner-dan-snyder-to-fans/2013/10/09/e7670ba0-30fe-11e3-8627-c5d7de0a046b_story.html. Accessed November 14, 2014. Used by permission.

I remember how quiet it got when the Redskins had the ball, and then how deafening it was when we scored. The ground beneath me seemed to move and shake, and I reached up to grab my father's hand. The smile on his face as he sang that song . . . he's been gone for 10 years now, but that smile, and his pride, are still with me every day.

That tradition—the song, the cheer—it mattered so much to me as a child, and I know it matters to every other Redskins fan in the D.C. area and across the nation.

Our past isn't just where we came from—it's who we are.

As some of you may know, our team began 81 years ago—in 1932—with the name "Boston Braves." The following year, the franchise name was changed to the "Boston Redskins." On that inaugural Redskins team, four players and our Head Coach were Native Americans. The name was never a label. It was, and continues to be, a badge of honor.

In 1971, our legendary coach, the late George Allen, consulted with the Red Cloud Athletic Fund located on the Pine Ridge Indian Reservation in South Dakota and designed our emblem on the Redskins helmets. Several years later, Coach Allen was honored by the Red Cloud Athletic Fund. On the wall at our Ashburn, Virginia, offices is the plaque given to Coach Allen—a source of pride for all of us. "Washington Redskins" is more than a name we have called our football team for over eight decades. It is a symbol of everything we stand for: strength, courage, pride, and respect—the same values we know guide Native Americans and which are embedded throughout their rich history as the original Americans.

I've listened carefully to the commentary and perspectives on all sides, and I respect the feelings of those who are offended by the team name. But I hope such individuals also try to respect what the name means, not only for all of us in the extended Washington Redskins family, but among Native Americans too.

Consider the following facts concerning the "Washington Redskins" name:

(1) The highly respected Annenberg Public Policy Center polled nearly 1,000 self-identified Native Americans from across the continental U.S. and found that 90 percent of Native Americans did not find the team name "Washington Redskins" to be "offensive."

(2) In an April 2013 Associated Press survey, 79 percent of the respondents stated the Washington Redskins should not change their name, while only 11 percent believed the team's name should change.

Paul Woody, a columnist for the *Richmond Times Dispatch*, interviewed three leaders of Virginia Native American tribes this May. They were all quoted by Mr. Woody as stating that the team name doesn't offend them—and their comments strongly supported the name "Washington Redskins." Also in May, SiriusXM NFL Radio hosted Robert Green, the longtime and recently retired Chief of the Fredericksburg-area Patawomeck Tribe, who said, among other things:

> Frankly, the members of my tribe—the vast majority—don't find it offensive. I've been a Redskins fan for years. And to be honest with you, I would be offended if they did change [the name, Redskins . . . This is] an attempt by somebody . . . to completely remove the Indian identity from anything and pretty soon . . . you have a wipeout in society of any reference to Indian people. . . . You can't rewrite history—yes there were some awful bad things done to our people over time, but naming the Washington football team the Redskins, we don't consider to be one of those bad things.

Our franchise has a great history, tradition and legacy representing our proud alumni and literally tens of millions of loyal fans worldwide. We have participated in some of the greatest games in NFL history, and have won five World Championships. We are proud of our team and the passion of our loyal fans. Our fans sing "Hail to the Redskins" in celebration at every Redskins game. They speak proudly of "Redskins Nation" in honor of a sports team they love.

So when I consider the Washington Redskins name, I think of what it stands for. I think of the Washington Redskins traditions and pride I want to share with my three children, just as my father shared with me—and just as you have shared with your family and friends.

I respect the opinions of those who disagree. I want them to know that I do hear them, and I will continue to listen and learn. But we cannot ignore our 81-year history, or the strong feelings of most of our fans as well as Native Americans throughout the country. After 81 years, the team name "Redskins" continues to hold the memories and meaning of where we came from, who we are, and who we want to be in the years to come.

We are Redskins Nation and we owe it to our fans and coaches and players, past and present, to preserve that heritage.

With Respect and Appreciation,
Dan Snyder

P.S. Wherever I go, I see Redskins bumper stickers, Redskins decals, Redskins t-shirts, Redskins everything. I know how much this team means to you, and it means everything to me as well. Always has. I salute your passion and your pride for the Burgundy & Gold.

QUESTIONS FOR CONSIDERATION

1. What arguments and tactics does Suzan Shown Harjo employ in her article, and how effective are they?

2. What counterarguments and tactics does Snyder employ in his letter? Are they effective? Are they likely to convince people who are not fans of the team?

3. Why do these issues appear to have such staying power in American society? Why might non-Indian people feel such strong attachment to so-called Indian symbols?

U.S.–Indian Relations on a World Stage

AMERICAN INDIANS ARE OFTEN CONSIDERED as little more than a subplot in the history of the United States. But long before the United States existed as a nation—fewer than 240 years ago—the Native peoples of the continent lived in an international context. Indian nations established diplomatic relations with other Indian nations, and after European invasion, they had political relationships with the Spanish, French, Dutch, and English and with individual English colonies as well. As the young United States began to establish its dominance, some tribes continued to maintain alliances with the British in the North and with the Spanish in the South, and Indian nations in different areas and eras forged multitribal coalitions to resist American expansion. Some Indians traveled to Europe on diplomatic missions in colonial times (see "Atlantic Travelers: Indians in Eighteenth-Century London," pages 188–93), and they continued to do so in the nineteenth and twentieth centuries: Ojibwa George Copway addressed the third World Peace Congress in Frankfurt am Main, Germany, in 1850; Deskaheh traveled on an Iroquois passport to Britain and then to Geneva to speak at the League of Nations in 1923.

Today, indigenous peoples worldwide have positioned themselves in international rather than subnational contexts, reaching beyond their own territories and beyond the confines of national law into the international arena and developing increasing connections with Native indigenous peoples in other countries based on similar experiences and shared challenges.[117] Iroquois and Hopi have taken causes to the United Nations in Geneva rather than to Washington. As evidenced by the name of their professional organization, Native American and Indigenous Studies, many scholars working in the field of Native studies now adopt comparative approaches and global perspectives in their work. Indian peoples have a long history of viewing themselves and their relations with the United States in an international context. The United States has rather less experience viewing its treatment of Native Americans in an international context, but in the twenty-first century it finds that it must.

On September 13, 2007, the General Assembly of the United Nations voted to adopt the Declaration on the Rights of Indigenous Peoples, a nonbinding document that sets out the individual and collective rights of the estimated 370 million indigenous peoples of the world in matters of self-determination, culture, identity, language, employment, health, education, and other issues. The document took more than twenty-two years to produce. In 1985 the U.N. Working Group on Indigenous Populations began developing a set of human rights standards that would protect the world's indigenous peoples. It completed its draft of the Declaration on the Rights of Indigenous Peoples in 1993; the draft was then referred to the Commission on Human Rights, which established another working group to examine its terms and to fine-tune the wording and provisions. Some nations expressed concerns about some key provisions of the declaration, such as indigenous peoples' right to self-determination and control over natural resources existing on their traditional lands. The final version of the declaration was adopted in 2006 by the Human Rights Council (the successor body to the Commission on Human Rights) and was referred to the General Assembly for voting in September 2007: 143 countries voted in favor of the declaration, 4 voted against it, and 11 abstained. Australia, Canada, New Zealand, and the United States—all countries with small indigenous populations—voted against it.

U.N. Secretary-General Ban Ki-moon described the declaration's adoption as "a historic moment when UN Member States and indigenous peoples have reconciled with their painful histories and are resolved to move forward together on the path of human rights, justice and development for all." But not all member states agreed. The Bush administration refused to approve the declaration, leaving the United States open to charges of hypocrisy when it claimed to support human rights in other areas. Ambassador John McNee of Canada said his country had "significant concerns" about the language in the document. The provisions on lands, territories, and resources "are overly broad, unclear and capable of a wide variety of interpretations," he noted, and could put into question matters that have been settled by treaty.

Australia changed its vote in favor of the declaration in 2009; New Zealand and then Canada followed suit in 2010. Native Americans pushed the Obama administration to honor its campaign promises and align with the rest of the world in its commitment to indigenous rights, and in December 2010 the president announced that the United States endorsed the U.N. declaration—the last country to do so.

Resolution 61/295 establishing the Declaration on the Rights of Indigenous Peoples begins with a lengthy preamble in which the U.N. General Assembly acknowledges that indigenous peoples "have suffered from historic injustices as a result of . . . their colonization and dispossession of their lands, territories and resources" that had prevented them from exercising "their right to development in accordance with their own needs and interests." Denouncing racism and discrimination, the resolution affirms the inherent rights of indigenous peoples the world over, including their right to equality and justice, their right to be different, their right to their own lands and resources, their rights affirmed in treaties and other agreements with nation-states, their right to determine their own futures in accordance with their own cultural values and traditions, and their right to share responsibility for the upbringing and education of their children. It welcomes "the fact that indigenous peoples are organizing themselves for political, economic, social and cultural enhancement" and recognizes "that respect for indigenous knowledge, cultures and traditional practices contributes to sustainable and equitable development and proper management of the environment." Seeing the declaration as the basis for improved relations and future partnerships between indigenous peoples and nation-states, the General Assembly presented the following forty-six articles "as a standard of achievement to be pursued in a spirit of partnership and mutual respect." The states that endorse the U.N. Declaration do not "give" Native people rights; they recognize their inherent rights.

GENERAL ASSEMBLY OF THE UNITED NATIONS
United Nations Declaration on the Rights of Indigenous Peoples (September 13, 2007)

ARTICLE 1

Indigenous peoples have the right to the full enjoyment, as a collective or as individuals, of all human rights and fundamental freedoms as recognized in the Charter of the United Nations, the Universal Declaration of Human Rights and international human rights law.

ARTICLE 2

Indigenous peoples and individuals are free and equal to all other peoples and individuals and have the right to be free from any kind of discrimination, in the exercise of their rights, in particular that based on their indigenous origin or identity.

ARTICLE 3

Indigenous peoples have the right to self-determination. By virtue of that right they freely determine their political status and freely pursue their economic, social and cultural development.

SOURCE: U.N. General Assembly, 61st Session. Resolution 61/295, United Nations Declaration on the Rights of Indigenous Peoples. © 2007 United Nations. Reprinted by permission of the United Nations.

ARTICLE 4

Indigenous peoples, in exercising their right to self-determination, have the right to autonomy or self-government in matters relating to their internal and local affairs, as well as ways and means for financing their autonomous functions.

ARTICLE 5

Indigenous peoples have the right to maintain and strengthen their distinct political, legal, economic, social and cultural institutions, while retaining their right to participate fully, if they so choose, in the political, economic, social and cultural life of the State.

ARTICLE 6

Every indigenous individual has the right to a nationality.

ARTICLE 7

1. Indigenous individuals have the rights to life, physical and mental integrity, liberty and security of person.

2. Indigenous peoples have the collective right to live in freedom, peace and security as distinct peoples and shall not be subjected to any act of genocide or any other act of violence, including forcibly removing children of the group to another group.

ARTICLE 8

1. Indigenous peoples and individuals have the right not to be subjected to forced assimilation or destruction of their culture.

2. States shall provide effective mechanisms for prevention of, and redress for: (a) Any action which has the aim or effect of depriving them of their integrity as distinct peoples, or of their cultural values or ethnic identities; (b) Any action which has the aim or effect of dispossessing them of their lands, territories or resources; (c) Any form of forced population transfer which has the aim or effect of violating or undermining any of their rights; (d) Any form of forced assimilation or integration; (e) Any form of propaganda designed to promote or incite racial or ethnic discrimination directed against them.

ARTICLE 9

Indigenous peoples and individuals have the right to belong to an indigenous community or nation, in accordance with the traditions and customs of the community or nation concerned. No discrimination of any kind may arise from the exercise of such a right.

ARTICLE 10

Indigenous peoples shall not be forcibly removed from their lands or territories. No relocation shall take place without the free, prior and informed consent of the indigenous peoples concerned and after agreement on just and fair compensation and, where possible, with the option of return.

ARTICLE 11

1. Indigenous peoples have the right to practise and revitalize their cultural traditions and customs. This includes the right to maintain, protect and develop the past, present and future manifestations of their cultures, such as archaeological and historical sites, artefacts, designs, ceremonies, technologies and visual and performing arts and literature.

2. States shall provide redress through effective mechanisms, which may include restitution, developed in conjunction with indigenous peoples, with respect to their cultural, intellectual, religious and spiritual property taken without their free, prior and informed consent or in violation of their laws, traditions and customs.

ARTICLE 12

1. Indigenous peoples have the right to manifest, practise, develop and teach their spiritual and religious traditions, customs and ceremonies; the right to maintain, protect, and have access in privacy to their religious and cultural sites; the right to the use and control of their ceremonial objects; and the right to the repatriation of their human remains.

2. States shall seek to enable the access and/or repatriation of ceremonial objects and human remains in their possession through fair, transparent and effective mechanisms developed in conjunction with indigenous peoples concerned.

ARTICLE 13

1. Indigenous peoples have the right to revitalize, use, develop and transmit to future generations their histories, languages, oral traditions, philosophies, writing systems and literatures, and to designate and retain their own names for communities, places and persons.
2. States shall take effective measures to ensure that this right is protected and also to ensure that indigenous peoples can understand and be understood in political, legal and administrative proceedings, where necessary through the provision of interpretation or by other appropriate means.

ARTICLE 14

1. Indigenous peoples have the right to establish and control their educational systems and institutions providing education in their own languages, in a manner appropriate to their cultural methods of teaching and learning.
2. Indigenous individuals, particularly children, have the right to all levels and forms of education of the State without discrimination.
3. States shall, in conjunction with indigenous peoples, take effective measures, in order for indigenous individuals, particularly children, including those living outside their communities, to have access, when possible, to an education in their own culture and provided in their own language.

ARTICLE 15

1. Indigenous peoples have the right to the dignity and diversity of their cultures, traditions, histories and aspirations which shall be appropriately reflected in education and public information.
2. States shall take effective measures, in consultation and cooperation with the indigenous peoples concerned, to combat prejudice and eliminate discrimination and to promote tolerance, understanding and good relations among indigenous peoples and all other segments of society.

ARTICLE 16

1. Indigenous peoples have the right to establish their own media in their own languages and to have access to all forms of non-indigenous media without discrimination.
2. States shall take effective measures to ensure that State-owned media duly reflect indigenous cultural diversity. States, without prejudice to ensuring full freedom of expression, should encourage privately owned media to adequately reflect indigenous cultural diversity.

ARTICLE 17

1. Indigenous individuals and peoples have the right to enjoy fully all rights established under applicable international and domestic labour law.
2. States shall in consultation and cooperation with indigenous peoples take specific measures to protect indigenous children from economic exploitation and from performing any work that is likely to be hazardous or to interfere with the child's education, or to be harmful to the child's health or physical, mental, spiritual, moral or social development, taking into account their special vulnerability and the importance of education for their empowerment.
3. Indigenous individuals have the right not to be subjected to any discriminatory conditions of labour and, inter alia, employment or salary.

ARTICLE 18

Indigenous peoples have the right to participate in decision-making in matters which would affect their rights, through representatives chosen by themselves in accordance with their own procedures, as well as to maintain and develop their own indigenous decision-making institutions.

ARTICLE 19

States shall consult and cooperate in good faith with the indigenous peoples concerned through their own representative institutions in order to obtain their free, prior and informed consent before adopting and implementing legislative or administrative measures that may affect them.

ARTICLE 20

1. Indigenous peoples have the right to maintain and develop their political, economic and social

systems or institutions, to be secure in the enjoyment of their own means of subsistence and development, and to engage freely in all their traditional and other economic activities.

2. Indigenous peoples deprived of their means of subsistence and development are entitled to just and fair redress.

ARTICLE 21

1. Indigenous peoples have the right, without discrimination, to the improvement of their economic and social conditions, including, inter alia, in the areas of education, employment, vocational training and retraining, housing, sanitation, health and social security.

2. States shall take effective measures and, where appropriate, special measures to ensure continuing improvement of their economic and social conditions. Particular attention shall be paid to the rights and special needs of indigenous elders, women, youth, children and persons with disabilities.

ARTICLE 22

1. Particular attention shall be paid to the rights and special needs of indigenous elders, women, youth, children and persons with disabilities in the implementation of this Declaration.

2. States shall take measures, in conjunction with indigenous peoples, to ensure that indigenous women and children enjoy the full protection and guarantees against all forms of violence and discrimination.

ARTICLE 23

Indigenous peoples have the right to determine and develop priorities and strategies for exercising their right to development. In particular, indigenous peoples have the right to be actively involved in developing and determining health, housing and other economic and social programmes affecting them and, as far as possible, to administer such programmes through their own institutions.

ARTICLE 24

1. Indigenous peoples have the right to their traditional medicines and to maintain their health practices, including the conservation of their vital medicinal plants, animals and minerals. Indigenous individuals also have the right to access, without any discrimination, to all social and health services.

2. Indigenous individuals have an equal right to the enjoyment of the highest attainable standard of physical and mental health. States shall take the necessary steps with a view to achieving progressively the full realization of this right.

ARTICLE 25

Indigenous peoples have the right to maintain and strengthen their distinctive spiritual relationship with their traditionally owned or otherwise occupied and used lands, territories, waters and coastal seas and other resources and to uphold their responsibilities to future generations in this regard.

ARTICLE 26

1. Indigenous peoples have the right to the lands, territories and resources which they have traditionally owned, occupied or otherwise used or acquired.

2. Indigenous peoples have the right to own, use, develop and control the lands, territories and resources that they possess by reason of traditional ownership or other traditional occupation or use, as well as those which they have otherwise acquired.

3. States shall give legal recognition and protection to these lands, territories and resources. Such recognition shall be conducted with due respect to the customs, traditions and land tenure systems of the indigenous peoples concerned.

ARTICLE 27

States shall establish and implement, in conjunction with indigenous peoples concerned, a fair, independent, impartial, open and transparent process, giving due recognition to indigenous peoples' laws, traditions, customs and land tenure systems, to recognize and adjudicate the rights of indigenous peoples pertaining to their lands, territories and resources, including those which were traditionally owned or otherwise occupied or used. Indigenous peoples shall have the right to participate in this process.

ARTICLE 28

1. Indigenous peoples have the right to redress, by means that can include restitution or, when this is not possible, just, fair and equitable compensation, for the lands, territories and resources which they have traditionally owned or otherwise occupied or used, and which have been confiscated, taken, occupied, used or damaged without their free, prior and informed consent.

2. Unless otherwise freely agreed upon by the peoples concerned, compensation shall take the form of lands, territories and resources equal in quality, size and legal status or of monetary compensation or other appropriate redress.

ARTICLE 29

1. Indigenous peoples have the right to the conservation and protection of the environment and the productive capacity of their lands or territories and resources. States shall establish and implement assistance programmes for indigenous peoples for such conservation and protection, without discrimination.

2. States shall take effective measures to ensure that no storage or disposal of hazardous materials shall take place in the lands or territories of indigenous peoples without their free, prior and informed consent.

3. States shall also take effective measures to ensure, as needed, that programmes for monitoring, maintaining and restoring the health of indigenous peoples, as developed and implemented by the peoples affected by such materials, are duly implemented.

ARTICLE 30

1. Military activities shall not take place in the lands or territories of indigenous peoples, unless justified by a relevant public interest or otherwise freely agreed with or requested by the indigenous peoples concerned.

2. States shall undertake effective consultations with the indigenous peoples concerned, through appropriate procedures and in particular through their representative institutions, prior to using their lands or territories for military activities.

ARTICLE 31

1. Indigenous peoples have the right to maintain, control, protect and develop their cultural heritage, traditional knowledge and traditional cultural expressions, as well as the manifestations of their sciences, technologies and cultures, including human and genetic resources, seeds, medicines, knowledge of the properties of fauna and flora, oral traditions, literatures, designs, sports and traditional games and visual and performing arts. They also have the right to maintain, control, protect and develop their intellectual property over such cultural heritage, traditional knowledge, and traditional cultural expressions.

2. In conjunction with indigenous peoples, States shall take effective measures to recognize and protect the exercise of these rights.

ARTICLE 32

1. Indigenous peoples have the right to determine and develop priorities and strategies for the development or use of their lands or territories and other resources.

2. States shall consult and cooperate in good faith with the indigenous peoples concerned through their own representative institutions in order to obtain their free and informed consent prior to the approval of any project affecting their lands or territories and other resources, particularly in connection with the development, utilization or exploitation of mineral, water or other resources.

3. States shall provide effective mechanisms for just and fair redress for any such activities, and appropriate measures shall be taken to mitigate adverse environmental, economic, social, cultural or spiritual impact.

ARTICLE 33

1. Indigenous peoples have the right to determine their own identity or membership in accordance with their customs and traditions. This does not impair the right of indigenous individuals to obtain citizenship of the States in which they live.

2. Indigenous peoples have the right to determine the structures and to select the membership of their institutions in accordance with their own procedures.

ARTICLE 34

Indigenous peoples have the right to promote, develop and maintain their institutional structures and their distinctive customs, spirituality, traditions, procedures, practices and, in the cases where they exist, juridical systems or customs, in accordance with international human rights standards.

ARTICLE 35

Indigenous peoples have the right to determine the responsibilities of individuals to their communities.

ARTICLE 36

1. Indigenous peoples, in particular those divided by international borders, have the right to maintain and develop contacts, relations and cooperation, including activities for spiritual, cultural, political, economic and social purposes, with their own members as well as other peoples across borders.

2. States, in consultation and cooperation with indigenous peoples, shall take effective measures to facilitate the exercise and ensure the implementation of this right.

ARTICLE 37

1. Indigenous peoples have the right to the recognition, observance and enforcement of treaties, agreements and other constructive arrangements concluded with States or their successors and to have States honour and respect such treaties, agreements and other constructive arrangements.

2. Nothing in this Declaration may be interpreted as diminishing or eliminating the rights of indigenous peoples contained in treaties, agreements and other constructive arrangements.

ARTICLE 38

States in consultation and cooperation with indigenous peoples, shall take the appropriate measures, including legislative measures, to achieve the ends of this Declaration.

ARTICLE 39

Indigenous peoples have the right to have access to financial and technical assistance from States and through international cooperation, for the enjoyment of the rights contained in this Declaration.

ARTICLE 40

Indigenous peoples have the right to access to and prompt decision through just and fair procedures for the resolution of conflicts and disputes with States or other parties, as well as to effective remedies for all infringements of their individual and collective rights. Such a decision shall give due consideration to the customs, traditions, rules and legal systems of the indigenous peoples concerned and international human rights.

ARTICLE 41

The organs and specialized agencies of the United Nations system and other intergovernmental organizations shall contribute to the full realization of the provisions of this Declaration through the mobilization, inter alia, of financial cooperation and technical assistance. Ways and means of ensuring participation of indigenous peoples on issues affecting them shall be established.

ARTICLE 42

The United Nations, its bodies, including the Permanent Forum on Indigenous Issues, and specialized agencies, including at the country level, and States shall promote respect for and full application of the provisions of this Declaration and follow up the effectiveness of this Declaration.

ARTICLE 43

The rights recognized herein constitute the minimum standards for the survival, dignity and well-being of the indigenous peoples of the world.

ARTICLE 44

All the rights and freedoms recognized herein are equally guaranteed to male and female indigenous individuals.

ARTICLE 45

Nothing in this Declaration may be construed as diminishing or extinguishing the rights indigenous peoples have now or may acquire in the future.

ARTICLE 46

1. Nothing in this Declaration may be interpreted as implying for any State, people, group or person any right to engage in any activity or to perform any act contrary to the Charter of the United Nations or construed as authorizing or encouraging any action which would dismember or impair, totally or in part, the territorial integrity or political unity of sovereign and independent States.

2. In the exercise of the rights enunciated in the present Declaration, human rights and fundamental freedoms of all shall be respected. The exercise of the rights set forth in this Declaration shall be subject only to such limitations as are determined by law and in accordance with international human rights obligations. Any such limitations shall be non-discriminatory and strictly necessary solely for the purpose of securing due recognition and respect for the rights and freedoms of others and for meeting the just and most compelling requirements of a democratic society.

3. The provisions set forth in this Declaration shall be interpreted in accordance with the principles of justice, democracy, respect for human rights, equality, non-discrimination, good governance and good faith.

QUESTIONS FOR CONSIDERATION

1. In what areas has the United States historically denied indigenous people their rights as defined by the U.N. declaration?

2. In what areas is the United States already in compliance with the declaration?

3. In what areas does the United States still have work to do to come into compliance with the declaration? Which provisions seem especially challenging for the United States?

4. What does Article 46.1 suggest about how far reaching the changes resulting from the declaration will be?

PICTURE ESSAY

Tribal Sovereignty in Action

INDIAN NATIONS IN MODERN AMERICA FACE recurrent challenges to their sovereignty and constraints on their exercise of self-government (see the Peter Jones sculpture on page 564). Sometimes they have to make compromises in order to work effectively with federal, state, and local authorities and with non-Indian businesses and residents. Nevertheless, Indian tribes steadfastly defend their sovereign rights as nations within a nation and routinely exercise powers of self-government. As the images in this picture essay suggest, tribal sovereignty manifests itself in many forms, from enforcing tribal law to maintaining the health of the community and the environment.

Tribes publicly exercise their sovereignty in a number of ways. At the international level, the Iroquois asserted their status as a sovereign nation when they issued their own declaration of war against Germany and Japan (see page 493) and they continue to do so when the Iroquois Nationals lacrosse team travels abroad on Iroquois passports. (In 1987 the International Lacrosse Federation recognized the Iroquois as an independent nation, meaning they could compete as a national team, just like the United States or Canada.) At the local level, many tribes issue their own license plates for reservation residents, both as a source of revenue and as an affirmation of tribal sovereignty.

Most Indian tribes in the United States now have flags. Like the flags of other nations, these flags are symbols of sovereignty and display images that express national identity and recall national history.[118] The flag of the Pawnee Nation of Oklahoma (Figure 10.1) reflects the tribe's long relationship with the United States. The red wolf's head, set against a blue field, represents the Pawnees (Plains tribes referred to the Pawnees as "wolves"); the stylized flag at upper left represents the United States, and the crossed pipe and tomahawk represent peace and war respectively. The eight arrowheads stand for the wars in which the Pawnees have fought in the service of the United States: the Plains Indian wars, the Spanish American War, World War I, World War II, the Korean War, the Vietnam War, Operation Desert Storm, and the Iraq War. "Like the flag of the United States, the Pawnee Indian Flag should never be desecrated and it should never touch the ground."[119]

Tribal governments come in many shapes and sizes. Since the Indian Reorganization Act in 1934, at least 160 Indian nations have adopted a constitutional form of government under the IRA and more than 75 have developed constitutions outside of the IRA framework. Many others do not have written constitutions. No federal law requires tribes to adopt any particular kind of constitution and it is up to the tribes themselves to decide if they want one — "a matter of

◆ **Figure 10.1 Pawnee Nation Flag**
Courtesy of the Pawnee Nation of Oklahoma.

tribal sovereignty and tribal initiative." For example, the Navajo Nation rejected the IRA and continued to govern by an extensive set of governmental codes, customs, and traditions.[120] The Tlingit and Haida tribes founded the Central Council of Tlingit and Haida Indian Tribes of Alaska (CCTHA) in 1935 and adopted a constitution in 1973. The governing body of CCTHA consists of a Tribal Assembly and an Executive Council. Delegates to the Tribal Assembly are elected from the Haida and Tlingit communities and the Assembly elects from its delegates the president and other officers who make up the Executive Council. The delegates assemble each year in Juneau beginning the third Thursday in April.[121] A sovereign entity with a government-to-government relationship to the United States, CCTHA describes its mission as "preserving our sovereignty, enhancing our economic and cultural resources, and promoting self-sufficiency and self-governance for our citizens through collaboration, service, and advocacy." In this photograph, delegates stand for the swearing ceremony of new delegates at the start of the 78th Annual Tribal Assembly in the Elizabeth Peratrovich Hall in Juneau, Alaska, in April 2013 (Figure 10.2).

Even small reservations have their own tribal police. Swift Sanchez, a sergeant with the Suquamish Tribal Police, logs a call on a computer in her vehicle while on patrol on the Suquamish Reservation in Washington State in 2010 (Figure 10.3). After *Oliphant v. Suquamish* (see pages 539–46) tribal police officers like Sergeant Swift had jurisdiction over Indians on the reservation but only in civil cases over non-Indians, which created major problems for law enforcement in crimes such as sexual violence by outsiders against Indian

◆ **Figure 10.2 Tlingit Tribal Assembly**
The Juneau Empire, Michael Penn/AP Photo.

◆ **Figure 10.3 Tribal Police**
Ted S. Warren/AP Photo.

women. The Tribal Law and Order Act (2010) and the Violence Against Women Act (2013) went some way toward remedying those problems, enhancing the powers of tribal police and tribal courts in some situations.

Most Indian tribes operate their own court systems. Indians and non-Indians who come before tribal courts often encounter a different philosophy of justice than they would experience in state or federal court. The Navajo Nation court system is the largest and most established tribal legal system in the world. The Judicial Branch of the Navajo Nation consists of a system of seven district courts, seven family courts, seven peacemaker courts, and a supreme court. In this photograph, Associate Justice Lorene Ferguson of the Navajo Supreme Court, right, with Associate Justice Marcella King-Ben, left, questions counsel during oral arguments in a case about whether tribal courts have jurisdiction in a lawsuit against a pharmaceutical company (Figure 10.4). Frank Pommersheim, a scholar of federal Indian law and Supreme Court judge for two Lakota tribes, regards tribal courts as "crucibles of sovereignty" and believes that "the wisdom and integrity of tribal law and tribal courts, properly and consistently informed by tradition and evolving contemporary tribal standards," are "the best bulwark against federal encroachment."[122]

Tribes also protect the health of the community, the environment, and the culture. Many manage forestry, fishing, and water quality; provide welfare services

◆ **Figure 10.4 Navajo Supreme Court**
Greg Wahl-Stephens, Pool/AP Photo.

◆ Figure 10.5 **Language Immersion Program**
The Bismarck Tribune, Lauren Donovan/AP Photo.

and social programs that include housing and care centers for children, the elderly, and the sick; and maintain programs of cultural preservation and language revitalization.

For many Native people, speaking their indigenous language and conducting affairs in their own language constitutes an important act of sovereignty. Preserving the language for future generations is a key attribute of cultural sovereignty. In this 2012 photo, Tom Red Bird, a fluent Lakota speaker, spends his day helping in an experimental program that provides Lakota immersion classes for children at Sitting Bull Community College at Fort Yates, North Dakota (Figure 10.5).

Protecting the environment for future generations is an act of sovereignty as well as stewardship. When the Cowboy and Indian Alliance staged a five-day protest in Washington, D.C., in 2014 against construction of the Keystone Pipeline, the protestors pitched tipis on the National Mall. In clear sight of the Capitol Building, the tipis represented a powerful reminder to Congress of continuing treaty rights that the United States stood to breach if it allowed construction of the pipeline to proceed across tribal lands. The image reflects the ongoing participation of sovereign Indian nations within the political system of the United States (Figure 10.6).

◆ **Figure 10.6 Tipis on the Mall**
Saul Loeb/AFP/Getty Images.

QUESTIONS FOR CONSIDERATION

1. What do these images convey about what it means to be a nation within a nation in twenty-first-century America?

2. Indian tribes are sometimes described as "third sovereigns" in the United States. What does this mean, and what can that sovereignty look like?

REFERENCES

1. Joseph M. Marshall III, *The Day the World Ended at Little Bighorn: A Lakota History* (New York: Penguin, 2007), 217.
2. Charles F. Wilkinson, *Blood Struggle: The Rise of Modern Indian Nations* (New York: W. W. Norton, 2005), 383.
3. Harvard Project on American Indian Economic Development, *The State of the Native Nations: Conditions under U.S. Policies of Self-Determination* (New York: Oxford University Press, 2008).
4. Vine Deloria Jr. and Daniel R. Wildcat, *Power and Place: Indian Education in America* (Golden, Colo.: Fulcrum, 2001), 133.
5. Joanne Nagel, *American Indian Ethnic Renewal: Red Power and the Resurgence of Identity and Culture* (New York: Oxford University Press, 1996), chap. 4; Nancy Shoemaker, *American Indian Population Recovery in the Twentieth Century* (Albuquerque: University of New Mexico Press, 1999).
6. Susan Lobo, "Is Urban a Person or a Place? Characteristics of Urban Indian Country," in *Native American Voices: A Reader,* ed. Susan Lobo and Steve Talbot, 2nd ed. (Upper Saddle River, N.J.: Prentice Hall, 2001), 56–66.
7. Alexandra Harmon, *Indians in the Making: Ethnic Relations and Indian Identities around Puget Sound* (Berkeley: University of California Press, 1998), 2.
8. See, for example, Harmon, *Indians in the Making*; Morris W. Foster, *Being Comanche: A Social History of an American Indian Community* (Tucson: University of Arizona Press, 1991).
9. Ward Churchill, "The Crucible of American Indian Identity: Native Tradition versus Colonial Imposition in Postconquest North America," in *Contemporary Native American Cultural Issues*, ed. Duane Champagne (Walnut Creek, Calif.: AltaMira Press, 1999), 40.
10. Russell Thornton, *American Indian Holocaust and Survival: A Population History since 1492* (Norman: University of Oklahoma Press, 1987), 236–37.
11. Fergus M. Bordewich, *Killing the White Man's Indian: Reinventing Native Americans at the End of the Twentieth Century* (New York: Doubleday, 1996), 300, 333.
12. M. Annette Jaimes, "Federal Indian Identification Policy: A Usurpation of Indigenous Sovereignty in North America," in *The State of Native America: Genocide, Colonization, and Resistance,* ed. M. Annette Jaimes (Boston: South End Press, 1992), 134.
13. Gabrielle Tayac, ed., *IndiVisible: African–Native American Lives in the Americas* (Washington, D.C.: National Museum of the American Indian, Smithsonian Institution, 2009), 117–31.
14. For example, *American Indian Report* (September 2005), 25; *American Indian Report* (January 2007), 27; Nagel, *American Indian Ethnic Renewal,* chap. 9.
15. Kim Tallbear, *Native American DNA: Tribal Belonging and the False Promise of Genetic Science* (Minneapolis: University of Minnesota Press, 2013).
16. Nagel, *American Indian Ethnic Renewal,* 237.
17. Amy E. den Ouden and Jean M. O'Brien, eds., *Recognition, Sovereignty Struggles, and Indigenous Rights in the United States: A Sourcebook* (Chapel Hill: University of North Carolina Press, 2013), 5.
18. "U.S. Recognizes an Indian Tribe on Long Island, Clearing the Way for a Casino," *New York Times,* June 15, 2010.
19. Mark Edwin Miller, *Forgotten Tribes: Unrecognized Indians and the Federal Acknowledgment Process* (Lincoln: University of Nebraska Press, 2004), quote at 266; Bruce Granville Miller, *Invisible Indigenes: The Politics of Nonrecognition* (Lincoln: University of Nebraska Press, 2003), chap. 4; Renée Ann Cramer, *Cash, Color, and Colonialism: The Politics of Tribal Acknowledgment* (Norman: University of Oklahoma Press, 2005); George Roth, "Recognition," in Garrick A. Bailey, ed. *Indians in Contemporary Society* (Washington, D.C.: Smithsonian Institution, 2008), 113–28. Brian Klopotek, *Recognition Odysseys: Indigeneity, Race, and Federal Recognition in Three Louisiana Communities* (Durham, N.C.: Duke University Press, 2011) compares the recognition process experiences of the Tunica-Biloxi (recognized in 1981), the Jena Band of Choctaws (recognized in 1995), and the Clifton Choctaws who are currently seeking recognition.
20. Den Ouden and O'Brien, eds., *Recognition, Sovereignty Struggles, and Indigenous Rights,* 9, 17.
21. Den Ouden and O'Brien, eds., *Recognition, Sovereignty Struggles, and Indigenous Rights,* 116–17.
22. Den Ouden and O'Brien, eds., *Recognition, Sovereignty Struggles, and Indigenous Rights,* 121; Mark Edwin Miller, *Claiming Tribal Identity: The Five Tribes and the Politics of Federal Acknowledgment* (Norman: University of Oklahoma Press, 2013).
23. Gale Courey Toensing, "Washburn's Bold Plan to Fix Interior's Federal Recognition Process," *Indian Country Today,* June 28, 2014, http://indiancountrytodaymedianetwork.com/2013/06/28/washburns-bold-plan-fix-interiors-federal-recognition-process-150151.
24. Paul Chaat Smith, *Everything You Know about Indians Is Wrong* (Minneapolis: University of Minnesota Press, 2009).
25. Louis Owens, *Mixedblood Messages: Literature, Film, Family, Place* (Norman: University of Oklahoma Press, 1998), 128.
26. For discussion of such issues, see Devon Abbott Mihesuah, *Natives and Academics: Researching and Writing about American Indians* (Lincoln: University of Nebraska Press, 1998); Susan A. Miller and James Riding In, eds., *Native Historians Write Back: Decolonizing American Indian History* (Lubbock: Texas Tech University Press, 2011); Beverly R. Singer, *Wiping the War Paint off the Lens: Native American Film and Video* (Minneapolis: University of Minnesota Press, 2001).
27. Linda Tuhiwai Smith, *Decolonizing Methodologies: Research and Indigenous Peoples* (New York: Zed Books, 1999).
28. *Cohen's Handbook of Federal Indian Law,* ed. Nell Jessup Newton (LexisNexis, 2012), 207.
29. Susan Shown Harjo, ed., *Nation to Nation: Treaties between the United States and American Indian Nations* (Washington, D.C.: Smithsonian Books, 2014).
30. David E. Wilkins, *American Indian Politics and the American Political System*, 2nd ed. (Lanham, Md.: Rowman and Littlefield, 2007), chap. 2.

31. Marge Anderson, "Educate, Educate, Educate"; W. Ron Allen, "We Are a Sovereign Government," both in Harvard Project, *State of the Native Nations*, quotes at 30, 77.

32. Charles F. Wilkinson, afterword to Walter R. Echo-Hawk, *In the Courts of the Conqueror: The 10 Worst Indian Law Cases Ever Decided* (Golden, Colo.: Fulcrum, 2010), 465–66.

33. Susan M. Williams and Sarah Works, "Preservation of Life: Guiding Principles of Indian Tribal Governments," in Harvard Project, *State of the Native Nations*, 188–92.

34. Wilkins, *American Indian Politics*.

35. "Case Pits Bald Eagle against Sacred Rites," *Chicago Tribune*, January 29, 2007.

36. Echo-Hawk, *Courts of the Conqueror*, 5.

37. Chief Justice Robert Yazzie, "Life Comes from It: Navajo Justice," in "The Ecology of Justice," special issue, *In Context* 38 (Spring 1994), 29; Raymond D. Austin, *Navajo Courts and Navajo Common Law: A Tradition of Self-Governance* (Minneapolis: University of Minnesota Press, 2009), quote at 202.

38. From the U.S. Census Bureau, "American Indians by the Numbers," *Information Please Database*, © 2007 Pearson Education, Inc., http://www.infoplease.com/spot/aihmcensus1 .html.

39. Stephen Cornell and Joseph P. Kalt, *What Can Tribes Do? Strategies and Institutions in American Economic Development* (Los Angeles: UCLA American Indian Studies Center, 1992); Harvard Project, *State of the Native Nations*, 113 (quote), 121.

40. Joseph P. Kalt and Joseph William Singer, *Myths and Realities of Tribal Sovereignty: The Law and Economics of Indian Self-Rule* (Cambridge, Mass.: Harvard Project on American Indian Economic Development, 2004), 1. See also Harvard Project, *State of the Native Nations*.

41. Duane Champagne, "Tribal Capitalism and Native Capitalists: Multiple Pathways of Native Economy," in *Native Pathways: American Indian Culture and Economic Development in the Twentieth Century*, ed. Brian Hosmer and Colleen O'Neill (Boulder: University Press of Colorado, 2004), chap. 14.

42. See http://www.choctaw.org; Robert H. White, *Tribal Assets: The Rebirth of Native America* (New York: Henry Holt, 1990), chap. 2.

43. Sebastian Felix Braun, *Buffalo Inc.: American Indians and Economic Development* (Norman: University of Oklahoma Press, 2008); Ken Zontek, *Buffalo Nation: American Indian Efforts to Restore the Bison* (Lincoln: University of Nebraska Press, 2007).

44. W. Dale Mason, *Indian Gaming: Tribal Sovereignty and American Politics* (Norman: University of Oklahoma Press, 2000), 43.

45. For studies of Indian gaming and its associated issues, see Mason, *Indian Gaming*; Steven Andrew Light and Kathryn R. L. Rand, *Indian Gaming and Tribal Sovereignty: The Casino Compromise* (Lawrence: University of Kansas Press, 2005); Jessica R. Cattelino, *High Stakes: Florida Seminole Gaming and Sovereignty* (Durham, N.C.: Duke University Press, 2008).

46. Jessica R. Cattelino, "Casino Roots: The Cultural Production of Twentieth-Century Seminole Economic Development," in Hosmer and O'Neill, *Native Pathways*, chap. 4; Cattelino, *High Stakes*.

47. Nicolas G. Rosenthal, "The Dawn of a New Day? Notes on Indian Gaming in Southern California," in Hosmer and O'Neill, *Native Pathways*, chap. 5, quote at 92.

48. *New York Times*, June 4, 1997, A27.

49. Jeff Hinkle, "Deal: State Lawmakers Willing to Play for a Piece of the Gaming Pie," *American Indian Report* 18 (January 2002), 12–15.

50. Alan P. Meister, Kathryn R. L. Rand, and Steven Andrew Light, "Indian Gaming and Beyond: Tribal Economic Development and Diversification," *South Dakota Law Review* 54 (Fall 2009), 375–97; http://www.nigc.gov/Gaming_Revenue_Reports.aspx; http://www.indiangaming.org/info/2013_Annual_Report .PDF. The NIGC provides a list of gaming tribes and their facilities at http://www.nigc.gov/Portals/0/NIGC%20Uploads /readingroom/listandlocationoftribalgamingops/abc.pdf. Thanks to Bruce Duthu for the comparison with spending on other forms of entertainment.

51. Meister, Rand, and Light, "Indian Gaming," 386–87.

52. Quoted in Nicholas C. Peroff, "Indian Gaming, Tribal Sovereignty, and American Indian Tribes as Complex Adaptive Systems," *American Indian Culture and Research Journal* 25, no. 3 (2001), 144.

53. *Indian Country Today*, August 25, 1993.

54. Ariel Levy, "Reservations: A Tribe Stakes Its Identity on a Casino—in the Hamptons," *New Yorker*, December 13, 2010, 40–49.

55. Donald L. Bartlett and James B. Steele, "Special Report: Indian Casinos: Wheel of Misfortune," *Time*, December 16, 2002, 44–56; Jeff Benedict, *Without Reservation* (New York: HarperCollins, 2001); Kim Isaac Eisler, *Revenge of the Pequots* (New York: Simon and Schuster, 2001); Cattelino, *High Stakes*, 7–8; and Alexandra Harmon, *Rich Indians: Native People and the Problem of Wealth in American History* (Chapel Hill: University of North Carolina Press, 2010); Alexandra Harmon, Colleen O'Neill, and Paul C. Rosier, "Interwoven Economic Histories: American Indians in a Capitalist America," *Journal of American History* 98 (2011), 698–722.

56. "Dispelling the Myths about Indian Gaming," *Native Americans Rights Fund*, http://www.narf.org/pubs/misc/gaming.html.

57. Rob Capriccioso, "Indian Gaming Reform: What Is Congress Plotting, and How Will SCIA Chair Jon Tester Respond?" *Indian Country Today*, July 28, 2014, http:// indiancountrytodaymedianetwork.com/2014/07/28/indian -gaming-reform-what-congress-plotting-and-how-will-scia -chair-jon-tester-respond.

58. Light and Rand, *Indian Gaming*.

59. Harvard Project, *State of the Native Nations*, 165.

60. Quoted in Donald A. Grinde and Bruce E. Johansen, *Ecocide of Native America: Environmental Destruction of Indian Lands and Peoples* (Santa Fe, N. Mex.: Clear Light Publishers, 1995), 138.

61. On the controversies surrounding MRS facilities, see David R. Lewis, "Native Americans and the Environment: A Survey of Twentieth-Century Issues," *American Indian Quarterly* 19 (Summer 1995), 423–50; and Winona LaDuke, *All Our Relations: Native Struggles for Land and Life* (Boston: South End Press, 1999), chap. 5.

62. Quoted on back cover of Grinde and Johansen, *Ecocide*.

63. Quoted in LaDuke, *All Our Relations,* 85.

64. "Navajos and Environmentalists Split on Power Plant," *New York Times,* July 7, 2007; Dana E. Powell and Dáilan J. Long, "Landscapes of Power: Renewable Energy Activism in Diné Bikéyah," in *Indians and Energy: Exploitation and Opportunity in the American Southwest,* ed. Sherry L. Smith and Brian Frehner (Santa Fe, N. Mex.: SAR Press, 2010), chap. 10.

65. *American Indian Report* (May 2007), 5.

66. Leslie Macmillan, "Resort's Snow Won't Be Pure This Year; It'll Be Sewage," *The New York Times,* September 26, 2012, http://www.nytimes.com/2012/09/27/us/arizona-ski-resorts-sewage-plan-creates-uproar.html.

67. N. Bruce Duthu, *American Indians and the Law* (New York: Viking Penguin, 2008), 97–98.

68. Echo-Hawk, *Courts of the Conqueror,* 391–92, 456; Jacques Leslie, "Rough Water," *Earth Island Journal,* Spring 2010, 41–45. My thanks to Blythe George for her assistance on this topic.

69. Akwesasne Notes, ed., *Basic Call to Consciousness* (1st ed., 1978; rev. ed., Summertown, Tenn.: Book Publishing Co., 1991), 71–79.

70. Winona LaDuke, foreword to *Strangers Devour the Land,* by Boyce Richardson (1976; repr., Post Mills, Vt.: Chelsea Green Publishing, 1991), xvi; LaDuke, *All Our Relations,* 197.

71. N. Scott Momaday, *The Man Made of Words: Essays, Stories, Passages* (New York: St. Martin's Press, 1997), 49.

72. Winona LaDuke, "Climate Change: What Will It Take to Get Back to 350 (ppm)?" *Indian Country Today,* April 25, 2014, http://indiancountrytodaymedianetwork.com/2014/04/25/climate-change-what-will-it-take-get-back-350-ppm-154596.

73. "Obama's Climate Change Report Lays Out Dire Scenario, Highlights Effects on Natives," *Indian Country Today,* May 6, 2014, http://indiancountrytodaymedianetwork.com/2014/05/06/obamas-climate-change-report-lays-out-dire-scenario-highlights-effects-natives-154763.

74. See, for example, "Protecting Our Home: Native Leaders, Western Scientists Collaborate," *Tribal College Journal of American Indian Higher Education* 22 (Fall 2010), supplement.

75. Daniel R. Wildcat, *Red Alert! Saving the Planet with Indigenous Knowledge* (Golden, Colo.: Fulcrum, 2009).

76. Garrit Voggesser and Alexis Bonogofsky, "Back to 350, Part 2: Confronting Climate Change in Indian Country," *Indian Country Today,* April 30, 2014, http://indiancountrytodaymedianetwork.com/2014/04/30/back-350-part-2-confronting-climate-change-indian-country-154673.

77. "Thousands March with Cowboy and Indian Alliance at 'Reject and Protect' to Protest Keystone XL Pipeline," 350.org, April 26, 2014, http://350.org/thousands-march-with-cowboy-and-indian-alliance-at-reject-and-protect-to-protest-keystone-xl-pipeline/.

78. Read more at "EPA Finalizes Environmental Justice Policy Supporting Indigenous Peoples," *Indian Country Today,* July 24, 2014, http://indiancountrytodaymedianetwork.com/2014/07/24/epa-finalizes-environmental-justice-policy-supporting-indigenous-peoples-156045.

79. Harvard Project, *State of the Native Nations,* 225–27.

80. Shelley Swift, "Diabetes: Native America Wrestles with a Dangerous Epidemic," *American Indian Report* 16 (November 2000), 12–15.

81. Mary Crow Dog, with Richard Erdoes, *Lakota Woman* (New York: Harper Perennial, 1991), 15, 45.

82. Roberta Ferron, a Rosebud Sioux, quoted in *Chief Red Fox Is Dead: A History of Native Americans since 1945,* by James Rawls (Fort Worth, Tex.: Harcourt Brace, 1996), 86.

83. Roger Matuz, ed., *St. James Guide to Native North American Artists* (Detroit: St. James Press, 1997), 493.

84. Philip A. May, "The Epidemiology of Alcohol Abuse among American Indians: The Mythical and Real Properties," in Champagne, *Contemporary Native American Cultural Issues,* 227–44.

85. See, for example, the speech by Hagler, a Catawba chief in 1754, in *The World Turned Upside Down: Indian Voices from Early America,* ed. Colin G. Calloway (Boston: Bedford Books, 1994), 108. Peter C. Mancall, *Deadly Medicine: Indians and Alcohol in Early America* (Ithaca, N.Y.: Cornell University Press, 1995), examines the introduction of alcohol and its impact on Indians in colonial times; William E. Unrau, *White Man's Wicked Water: The Alcohol Trade and Prohibition in Indian Country, 1802–1892* (Lawrence: University Press of Kansas, 1996), shows how the United States introduced alcohol to Indians and then implemented futile policies to try and control its flow.

86. Crow Dog, *Lakota Woman,* 45.

87. Statistics on alcoholism are in Bordewich, *Killing,* 247–48.

88. *American Indian Report* (January 2007), 10; Michelle Tirado, "Deadly Addiction: Methamphetamine in Indian Country," *American Indian Report* (June 2006), 10–13; Sarah Kershaw, "Through Indian Lands, Drugs Travel a Shadowy Trail," *New York Times,* February 19, 2006, 20–21.

89. Jennie R. Joe, "Health and Health Issues in the United States," in Bailey, ed., *Indians in Contemporary Society,* 97–105.

90. *American Indian Report* (May 2006), 18–19.

91. Wade Davies, *Healing Ways: Navajo Health Care in the Twentieth Century* (Norman: University of Oklahoma Press, 2001); Maureen Trudelle Schwarz, *Navajo Lifeways: Contemporary Issues, Ancient Knowledge* (Norman: University of Oklahoma Press, 2001); Maureen Trudelle Schwarz, *"I Choose Life": Contemporary Medical and Religious Practices in the Navajo World* (Norman: University of Oklahoma Press, 2008); Lori Arviso Alvord and Elizabeth Cohen Van Pelt, *The Scalpel and the Silver Bear* (New York: Bantam Books, 1999).

92. Harvard Project, *State of the Native Nations,* 226.

93. Echo-Hawk, *Courts of the Conqueror,* 441–42.

94. *Maze of Injustice: The Failure to Protect Indigenous Women from Sexual Violence* (New York: Amnesty International Publications, 2006), 43.

95. Figures cited in *Restoring Safety to Native Women and Girls and Strengthening Native Nations* (Washington, D.C.: Indian Law Resource Center, 2013), 37.

96. Andrea Smith, *Conquest: Sexual Violence and American Indian Genocide* (Cambridge, Mass.: South End Press, 2005); Kathryn W. Shanley, "Blood Ties and Blasphemy: American Indian Women and the Problem of History," in *Native Women's History in Eastern North America before 1900: A Guide to Research and Writing,* ed. Rebecca Kugel and Lucy Eldersveld Murphy (Lincoln: University of Nebraska Press, 2007), 107–30; *Maze of Injustice.*

97. *Restoring Safety,* 1.

98. Cited in Louise Erdrich, "Rape on the Reservation," *New York Times*, February 26, 2013, http://www.nytimes .com/2013/02/27/opinion/native-americans-and-the-violence -against-women-act.html?hp&_r=2&.

99. *Restoring Safety*, page 43.

100. *Maze of Injustice*, 27.

101. Louise Erdrich, "Rape on the Reservation," *New York Times*, Feb. 26, 2013.

102. *Restoring Safety*, 21.

103. *Restoring Safety*, 18.

104. *Restoring Safety*, 87.

105. Ken Hale, "On Endangered Languages and the Importance of Linguistic Diversity," in *Endangered Languages: Language Loss and Community Response*, ed. Lenore A. Grenoble and Lindsay J. Whaley (Cambridge: Cambridge University Press, 1998), 192.

106. "Native American Languages Act," *United States Code Annotated* (St. Paul, Minn.: West Publishing, 1995), chap. 31 in Title 25.

107. *Tribal College: The Journal of American Indian Higher Education* 11 (Spring 2000) is dedicated to Native languages and contains a resource guide.

108. Kipp "library" quote in Wilkinson, *Blood Struggle*, 363; Darrell Robes Kipp, "A Blackfeet Educator Discusses the Importance of Learning the Blackfeet Language" and "Why Teach an Ancient Language?" both in *Lewis and Clark and the Indian Country: The Native American Perspective*, ed. Frederick E. Hoxie and Jay T. Nelson (Urbana: University of Illinois Press, 2007), 255–57, 295–307; "journey" quote at 299.

109. Frederick E. Hoxie, *This Indian Country: American Indian Activists and the Place They Made* (New York: Penguin, 2012); N. Bruce Duthu, *Shadow Nations: Tribal Sovereignty and the Limits of Legal Pluralism* (New York: Oxford University Press, 2013).

110. Austin, *Navajo Courts*, xxiv.

111. Philip J. Deloria, *Indians in Unexpected Places* (Lawrence: University Press of Kansas, 2004), 135.

112. Philip J. Deloria, *Playing Indian* (New Haven, Conn.: Yale University Press, 1998); Colin G. Calloway, Gerd Gemünden, and Susanne Zantop, eds., *Germans and Indians: Encounters, Fantasies, and Projections* (Lincoln: University of Nebraska Press, 2002).

113. Carol Spindel, *Dancing at Halftime: Sports and the Controversy over American Indian Mascots* (New York: New York University Press, 2000); C. Richard King and Charles Fruehling Springwood, eds., *Team Spirits: The Native American Mascots Controversy* (Lincoln: University of Nebraska Press, 2001); C. Richard King, *The Native American Mascot Controversy: A Handbook* (New York: Scarecrow Press, 2010).

114. The full text of the APA resolution is at http://www.apa .org/releases/ResAmIndianMascots.pdf. See also "'Redskins' May Have Psychological Impact beyond Native Americans," *Indian Country Today*, May 19, 2010.

115. Adam Liptak, "Redskins' Challengers Rebuffed," *New York Times*, November 17, 2009.

116. Erik Stegman and Victoria Phillips, *Missing the Point: The Real Impact of Native Mascots and Team Names on American Indian and Alaska Native Youth* (Center for American Progress, July 2014), 2.

117. Harvard Project, *State of the Native Nations*, 83–89.

118. Donald T. Healy and Peter J. Orenski, *Native American Flags* (Norman: University of Oklahoma Press, 2003).

119. http://www.pawneenation.org/government.

120. *Cohen's Handbook of Federal Indian Law*, 271; Austin, *Navajo Courts*.

121. http://www.ccthita.org/government/legislative/GoverningDocs /Constitution-Amended-4.20.13.pdf.

122. Frank Pommersheim, *Braid of Feathers: American Indian Law and Contemporary Tribal Life* (Berkeley: University of California Press, 1995), 57, quoted in Duthu, *Shadow Nations*, 72.

SUGGESTED READINGS

Ambler, Marjane. *Breaking the Iron Bonds: Indian Control of Energy Development*. Lawrence: University Press of Kansas, 1990.

American Indian Report: Indian Country's News Magazine. Fairfax, Va.

Austin, Raymond D. *Navajo Courts and Navajo Common Law: A Tradition of Tribal Self-Governance*. Minneapolis: University of Minnesota Press, 2009.

Bailey, Garrick A., ed. *Indians in Contemporary Society*. Washington, D.C.: Smithsonian Institution, 2008. Vol. 2 of *Handbook of North American Indians*, edited by William C. Sturtevant.

Braun, Sebastian Felix. *Buffalo Inc.: American Indians and Economic Development*. Norman: University of Oklahoma Press, 2008.

Brugge, Doug, Timothy Benally, and Esther Yazzie-Lewis, eds. *The Navajo People and Uranium Mining*. Albuquerque: University of New Mexico Press, 2006.

Bruyneel, Kevin. *The Third Space of Sovereignty: The Postcolonial Politics of U.S.–Indigenous Relations*. Minneapolis: University of Minnesota Press, 2007.

Cattelino, Jessica R. *High Stakes: Florida Seminole Gaming and Sovereignty*. Durham, N.C.: Duke University Press, 2008.

Cohen, Felix. *Cohen's Handbook of Federal Indian Law*, ed. Nell Jessup Newton. LexisNexis, 2012.

Deloria, Philip J. *Playing Indian*. New Haven: Yale University Press, 1998.

Deloria, Vine, Jr., and Clifford Lytle. *The Nations Within: The Past and Future of American Indian Sovereignty*. New York: Pantheon, 1984.

Den Ouden, Amy E., and Jean M. O'Brien, eds. *Recognition, Sovereignty Struggles, and Indigenous Rights in the United States: A Sourcebook*. Chapel Hill: University of North Carolina Press, 2013.

Devon, Marjorie, ed. *Migrations: New Directions in Native American Art*. Albuquerque: University of New Mexico Press, 2006.

Duthu, N. Bruce. *American Indians and the Law*. New York: Viking Penguin, 2008.

———. *Shadow Nations: Tribal Sovereignty and the Limits of Legal Pluralism*. New York: Oxford University Press, 2013.

Echo-Hawk, Walter R. *In the Courts of the Conqueror: The 10 Worst Indian Law Cases Ever Decided*. Golden, Colo.: Fulcrum, 2010.

Fixico, Donald L. *American Indians in a Modern World*. Lanham, Md.: AltaMira Press, 2008.

————. *Indian Resilience and Rebuilding: Indigenous Nations in the Modern American West*. Tucson: University of Arizona Press, 2013.

Grinde, Donald A., and Bruce E. Johansen. *Ecocide of Native America: Environmental Destruction of Indian Lands and Peoples*. Santa Fe, N. Mex.: Clear Light Publishers, 1995.

Grounds, Richard A., George E. Tinker, and David E. Wilkins, eds. *Native Voices: American Indian Identity and Resistance*. Lawrence: University Press of Kansas, 2003.

Harjo, Susan Shown, ed. *Nation to Nation: Treaties between the United States and American Indian Nations*. Washington, D.C.: Smithsonian Books, 2014.

Harmon, Alexandra. *Rich Indians: Native People and the Problem of Wealth in American History*. Chapel Hill: University of North Carolina Press, 2010.

Harvard Project on American Indian Economic Development. *The State of the Native Nations: Conditions under U.S. Policies of Self-Determination*. New York: Oxford University Press, 2008.

Hosmer, Brian, and Colleen O'Neill, eds. *Native Pathways: American Indian Culture and Economic Development in the Twentieth Century*. Boulder: University Press of Colorado, 2004.

Hoxie, Frederick E. *This Indian Country: American Indian Activists and the Place They Made*. New York: Penguin, 2012.

Indian Country Today (newspaper). Available online.

Jaimes, M. Annette, ed. *The State of Native America: Genocide, Colonization, and Resistance*. Boston: South End Press, 1992.

King, C. Richard. *The Native American Mascot Controversy: A Handbook*. New York: Scarecrow Press, 2010.

King, C. Richard, and Charles Fruehling Springwood, eds. *Team Spirits: The Native American Mascots Controversy*. Lincoln: University of Nebraska Press, 2001.

Klopotek, Brian. *Recognition Odysseys: Indigeneity, Race, and Federal Recognition in Three Louisiana Communities*. Durham, N.C.: Duke University Press, 2011.

LaDuke, Winona. *All Our Relations: Native Struggles for Land and Life*. Boston: South End Press, 1999.

Light, Steven Andrew, and Kathryn R. L. Rand. *Indian Gaming and Tribal Sovereignty: The Casino Compromise*. Lawrence: University Press of Kansas, 2005.

Mason, W. Dale. *Indian Gaming: Tribal Sovereignty and American Politics*. Norman: University of Oklahoma Press, 2000.

Maze of Injustice: The Failure to Protect Indigenous Women from Sexual Violence. New York: Amnesty International Publications, 2006.

Meister, Alan P., Kathryn R. L. Rand, and Steven Andrew Light. "Indian Gaming and Beyond: Tribal Economic Development and Diversification." *South Dakota Law Review* 54 (Fall 2009), 375–97.

Miller, Mark Edwin. *Claiming Tribal Identity: The Five Tribes and the Politics of Federal Acknowledgment*. Norman: University of Oklahoma Press, 2013.

————. *Forgotten Tribes: Unrecognized Indians and the Federal Acknowledgment Process*. Lincoln: University of Nebraska Press, 2004.

Pevar, Stephen L. *The Rights of Indian Tribes*. 4th ed. New York: Oxford University Press, 2012.

Restoring Safety to Native Women and Girls and Strengthening Native Nations. Washington, D.C.: Indian Law Resource Center, 2013.

Schwarz, Maureen Trudelle. *"I Choose Life": Contemporary Medical and Religious Practices in the Navajo World*. Norman: University of Oklahoma Press, 2008.

Shanley, Kathryn W. "Blood Ties and Blasphemy: American Indian Women and the Problem of History." In *Native Women's History in Eastern North America before 1900: A Guide to Research and Writing*, edited by Rebecca Kugel and Lucy Eldersveld Murphy, 107–30. Lincoln: University of Nebraska Press, 2007.

Smith, Andrea. *Conquest: Sexual Violence and American Indian Genocide*. Cambridge, Mass.: South End Press, 2005.

Smith, Dean Howard. *Modern Tribal Development: Paths to Self-Sufficiency and Cultural Integrity in Indian Country*. Walnut Creek, Calif.: AltaMira Press, 2000.

Smith, Paul Chaat. *Everything You Know about Indians Is Wrong*. Minneapolis: University of Minnesota Press, 2009.

Smith, Sherry L., and Brian Frehner, eds. *Indians and Energy: Exploitation and Opportunity in the American Southwest*. Santa Fe, N. Mex.: SAR Press, 2010.

Stegman, Erik, and Victoria Phillips. *Missing the Point: The Real Impact of Native Mascots and Team Names on American Indian and Alaska Native Youth*. Washington, D.C.: Center for American Progress, 2014.

Tallbear, Kim. *Native American DNA: Tribal Belonging and the False Promise of Genetic Science*. Minneapolis: University of Minnesota Press, 2013.

Tayac, Gabrielle, ed. *IndiVisible: African–Native American Lives in the Americas*. Washington, D.C.: National Museum of the American Indian, Smithsonian Institution, 2009.

Tiller, Veronica E. Velarde, ed. and comp. *Tiller's Guide to Indian Country: Economic Profiles of American Indian Reservations*. Albuquerque, N. Mex.: BowArrow, 2005.

Treuer, Anton. *Everything You Wanted to Know about Indians but Were Afraid to Ask*. Minneapolis: Minnesota Historical Society Press, 2012.

Truer, David. *Rez Life*. New York: Atlantic Monthly Press, 2012.

Utter, Jack. *American Indians: Answers to Today's Questions*. 2nd ed. Norman: University of Oklahoma Press, 2001.

Warrior, Robert, ed. *The World of Indigenous North America*. New York: Routledge, 2015.

Wildcat, Daniel R. *Red Alert! Saving the Planet with Indigenous Knowledge*. Golden, Colo.: Fulcrum, 2009.

Wilkins, David E. *American Indian Politics and the American Political System*. 2nd ed., Lanham, Md.: Rowman and Littlefield, 2007; 3rd ed. (with Heidi Kiiwetinepinesiik Stark), 2010.

Wilkins, David E., and K. Tsianina Lomawaima. *Uneven Ground: American Indian Sovereignty and Federal Law*. Norman: University of Oklahoma Press, 2001.

Wilkinson, Charles F. *Blood Struggle: The Rise of Modern Indian Nations*. New York: W. W. Norton, 2005.

INDEX

Note: Letters in parentheses following pages refer to:

- *(c)* for charts
- *(d)* for documents
- *(e)* for picture essays
- *(i)* for illustrations
- *(m)* for maps
- *(t)* for tables

Abalone Shell Mountain, 41, 46
Abeel, John. *See* Cornplanter (Ki-on-twog-ky)
Abenaki Indians, 16, 38, 93, 98, 102, 104, 155–56, 156(t), 157, 157(i), 160, 163–64, 173(d), 174–75(d), 178(d), 179–80(d), 183(d), 277, 582, 583–84
Abourezk, James, 507, 511
Abramoff, Jack, 598
"Account of His Fight with the Blackfeet, An" (Lewis; 1806), 283–86(d)
"Account of Negotiations Leading to the Casco Bay Treaty, An" (Sauguaarum; 1727), 176–77(d)
Ácoma Pueblo, 86
Activism. *See* Militancy
Adams, John, 279
Adena culture, 32–33
Afghanistan, war in, 585(i)
Africa, American contact with, 76, 104
African Americans, 147, 257, 279, 280, 357, 394, 467, 534, 577, 583
African slaves, 74(m), 104, 126, 140, 142, 145–46, 147, 256–57, 317
Agents
    of British Indian Department, 154–55
    reservations and, 379, 381–84, 382(c), 406, 407, 421(d)
    school attendance enforced by, 393–94
    Standing Bear's opposition of, 423(d), 424–28(d)
    tribal religion and, 410
Agriculture. *See also* Corn
    after European contact, 77
    Algonquian village and, 64–65(e), 66(i)
    allotment of lands to Indians for, 391
    Aztec, 81
    California and, 317, 319
    in Chaco Canyon, 29
    Cherokee Indians and, 37, 161, 234(d), 288(d)
    Columbian exchanges and, 76–77
    dam construction and, 464, 604–5
    in Eastern Woodlands, 31–37, 34(m), 35(i), 255, 256(i)

before European contact, 62(e)
    Great Basin foragers and, 24–25
    Great Plains and, 26, 26(i), 37, 166, 170
    Iroquois Indians and, 163, 207, 234
    in Mesoamerica, 27, 29, 33
    in Mississippian cultures, 37
    in Native America (1450), 34(m)
    pollution and, 603–5
    in precontact societies, 21
    slavery and, 104
    in southwestern United States, 27–31
    Southwest farmers and, 27–31
    transition to, 27–31
    warfare and, 157, 161, 207, 234(d)
    women, early agriculture and, 21, 37
Ah-jon-jon (the Light), 300–302(e), 303(i)
Ahkeah, Sam, 43
AIDS, 608
AIM. *See* American Indian Movement (AIM)
Akwesasne Freedom School, 513
Akwesasne Mohawk Nation, 513
Alabama-Coushatta Indians, 601
Alaska, 17, 19, 22, 73, 143, 226, 228, 229, 232, 245(e), 246(e), 404, 409, 448, 453, 575, 600
Alaska Federation of Natives (ANF), 509
Alaska Native Brotherhood, 409
Alaska Native Claims Settlement Act (ANCSA; 1971), 509, 510(m), 526, 613
Alaska Natives
    census and, 575–76, 575(m), 592
    education and, 513–15
    employed by Bureau of Indian Affairs, 528
    land claims and, 509, 526
    native regional corporations in, 410(m), 509–10
    Obama's "listening sessions" and, 534
    poverty and, 592
    public health benefits available to, 610
    recognition of tribes and, 580, 581(m)
    relocation of, 461
    violence against women and, 612–13
    World War II and, 453
Alaska v. Native Village of Venetie Tribal Government (1998), 526, 613
Albany Congress (1754), 154
Alcatraz Island, takeover of (1965), 399, 465–66, 470, 485(d), 486–87(d), 486(i), 490(d), 549, 552(d)
Alcohol, traders and, 145
Alcoholism, 608–10
    causes and nature of, 145
    confronting, 333, 334, 608–10, 609(i)

fetal alcohol syndrome and, 608
    Healthy Nations Program and, 610
    impact of, 511, 573
    individual experiences of alcoholism, 279, 333, 408, 486(d)
    myths and stereotypes about, 587, 609–10
Aleut. *See* Alaska Natives
Algonquian Indians, 12, 14, 38–39, 64–65(e), 90–91, 92, 93, 100, 110(d), 144, 155, 157, 617
Allen, Elsie, 397
Allen, George, 623(d)
Allen, W. Ron, 589
Allotment Act, Dawes (1887), 385–89, 386(m), 388(i)
All-Pueblo Council, 446
All-Tribes American Indian Center, 481(e)
Alvord, Lori Arviso, 611
America, invasions of, 72–131
    Columbian exchanges, 76–79
    cooperation, contagion, and conflict, 105–9(d)
    by English, 95–104
    first contacts and mutual appraisals, 72–76
    by French, 90–95
    Hurons and, 110–19(d), 111(m)
    images of, 127–31(e), 127(i), 128(i), 129(i), 130(i), 131(i)
    Mi'kmaqs and, 113–14(d), 119–20(d)
    by Spanish, 79–90
    wars of independence and, 121–26(d)
American history, before Columbus, 4, 14–67. *See also* Precontact societies
    belief in Indians being a truly indigenous people and, 19–20
    Bering Strait crossing in, 14, 16–17, 19–20
    creation stories and, 16–19, 40–51(d)
    determining, 14–20
    early American cities, settlements, and centers, 62–67
    migration theories and, 16–19, 18(m)
    native origins and, debates over, 19–20
    precontact societies and, 20–39
    seaborne strangers and, 39
American Horse, 221, 232
American Indian and Alaska Native Climate Change Working Group, 606
American Indian Chicago Conference, 467

644

A B O U T   T H E   A U T H O R

Colin G. Calloway is John Kimball Jr. 1943 Professor of History and Professor of Native American Studies at Dartmouth College. He served for two years as associate director and editor at the D'Arcy McNickle Center for the History of the American Indian at the Newberry Library in Chicago and taught for seven years at the University of Wyoming. His publications include *Victory with No Name: The Native American Defeat of the First American Army* (2015); *Pen and Ink Witchcraft: Treaties and Treaty Making in America Indian History* (2013); *White People, Indians, and Highlanders: Tribal Peoples and Colonial Encounters in Scotland and America* (2008); *The Shawnees and the War for America* (2007); *The Scratch of a Pen: 1763 and the Transformation of North America* (2006); *One Vast Winter Count: The Native American West Before Lewis and Clark* (2003); *The American Revolution in Indian Country* (1995); and two books for the Bedford Series in History and Culture: *Our Hearts Fell to the Ground: Plains Indians Views of How the West Was Lost* (1996) and *The World Turned Upside Down: Indian Voices from Early America* (2016; 1994).

ABOUT THE COVER ART

O-o-be, a Kiowa Woman, Fort Sill, Oklahoma, 1895. At the end of the nineteenth century, most Americans assumed that Indians were a tragic and vanishing race and that Native cultures were dying out. O-o-be, a young Kiowa woman wearing a smile and a hide dress decorated with elk teeth, clearly had other ideas. *National Museum of the American Indian, Smithsonian Institution (catalog number P13149).*